OXFORD MEDICAL PUBLICATIONS

Brain Function and Psychotropic Drugs

Brain Function
and
Psychotropic Drugs

HEATHER ASHTON
University of Newcastle upon Tyne

Oxford New York Tokyo
OXFORD UNIVERSITY PRESS
1992

RM
315
.A748
1992

Oxford University Press, Walton Street, Oxford OX2 6DP
Oxford   New York   Toronto
Delhi   Bombay   Calcutta   Madras   Karachi
Petaling Jaya   Singapore   Hong Kong   Tokyo
Nairobi   Dar es Salaam   Cape Town
Melbourne Auckland
and associated companies in
Berlin   Ibadan

Oxford is a trade mark of Oxford University Press

Published in the United States
by Oxford University Press, New York

©Heather Ashton, 1987, 1992

Based on Brain systems, disorders, and psychotropic drugs, published by OUP in 1987.

A catalogue record for this book is available from the British Library

Library of Congress Cataloging in Publication Data
Ashton, Heather.
Brain function and psychotropic drugs / Heather Ashton.
p.   cm. — (Oxford medical publications)
Rev., updated, and shortened ed. of: Brain systems, disorders, and
psychotropic drugs. 1987.
Includes bibliographical references and index.
1. Psychotropic drugs — Physiological effect.   2. Brain.   3. Brain-Effect of drugs on.
4. Mental illness — Chemotherapy.   5. Neuropsychopharmacology.
I. Ashton, Heather. Brain systems, disorders, and psychotropic drugs.
II. Title.   III. Series.
[DNLM: 1. Brain — drug effects.   2. Brain — physiology.
3. Mental Disorders — physiopathology.   4. Psychotropic Drugs — pharmacology.
WL 300 A828b   RM315.A748   1992
615'.788 — dc20   91–46177
ISBN 0–19–262243–9 (h/b)
ISBN 0–19–262242-0 (p/b)

Typeset by
Colset Pte Ltd, Singapore
Printed in Great Britain by
Dotesios Ltd., Trowbridge, Wilts.

Preface

This book is based on a previous volume, *Brain systems, disorders, and psychotropic drugs*, published five years ago. The original aim, which remains the same, was to suggest how various functional systems in the brain normally operate together to influence human behaviour; how these systems may dysfunction in neuropsychiatric disorders; and how the systems may be affected, either therapeutically or adversely, by psychotropic drugs.

The initial impetus to attempt such a book stemmed from the requirements of teaching the principles of psychopharmacology to second year medical students. It was clear that the actions of psychotropic drugs could not be discussed without first giving some idea of the mechanisms of the disorders for which they are used. In turn, disorders of mood, thought, and behaviour are not comprehensible without a basic knowledge of the brain systems which normally control these variables. And so one is led full circle, for it is also necessary to know how psychotropic drugs affect normal brain function in order to interpret their effects on malfunctioning systems. How is it that many psychotropic drugs produce dysphoria in normal subjects yet improve symptoms in disturbed subjects, while others exert sought-after euphoric effects in certain individuals but aggravate mental disorders in others? A single book which covered all these aspects of psychopharmacology was not, to my knowledge, available.

From the viewpoint of research, a similar lack seemed to exist. In this case, a somewhat different order applies: knowledge of pharmacodynamics can shed light on the mechanisms of brain disorders, and also on normal brain function. The partial illumination of anxiety disorders and of the GABA-receptor complex by benzodiazepines, of pain mechanisms and opioid receptors by opiate analgesics, and of schizophrenia and dopaminergic systems by antipsychotic drugs are examples of this 'reverse' process. However, workers in different aspects of neuropharmacology sometimes appear limited by their specialities, although a broad understanding is needed to answer important questions raised by laboratory studies. What relation, for instance, does the behaviour of an infant monkey separated from its mother bear to human depression, or that of an electrically punished rat to human anxiety neurosis or to pain control mechanisms? How far can laboratory models used for testing psychotropic drug effects be applied to their clinical use in man?

There also seemed to be a gap in the literature for those concerned with clinical treatment. Psychiatrists, clinical psychologists, physicians, and general practitioners have not always displayed an understanding of normal brain systems, and have sometimes appeared ignorant of the pharmacodynamics of drugs prescribed with such profligacy. For example, the enormous prescribing of benzodiazepines and the ensuing problem of benzodiazepine dependence need not have occurred if more attention had been paid to basic knowledge of the reward systems of the brain and the part they play in drug dependence (especially after previous experience with barbiturates and amphetamines). Similarly, deaths from some food and drug interactions with monoamine oxidase inhibitors could have been prevented if contemporary knowledge about their mode of action had been applied.

It seemed to me that many of those concerned with the workings of the brain, whether for teaching, research, clinical practice, or for pure interest, might find a use for a book which bridged several disciplines in the neurosciences. I therefore attempted – with feelings both of humility and temerity – to supply this need. The fact that the original book is now sold out suggests that it did indeed fill a certain gap in the literature and prompted the present volume.

Meanwhile important recent advances in fields as diverse as receptor identification and classification, brain imaging techniques, neuronal plasticity, the biochemistry of memory, the genetics and neuropathology of psychiatric disease (to name but a few), and the introduction of whole new classes of centrally acting drugs, have if anything increased the need for an integrated approach to normal and abnormal brain functions and the effects of psychotropic drugs.

In this book, strenuous efforts have been made to achieve two almost incompatible goals: to bring the information as far as possible up to date, and at the same time to shorten the text substantially. Such constraints almost inevitably lead to a certain oversimplification and to omission in some areas. For example, there is no space for a detailed description of cognitive processes and neural networks (which might have been considered under Learning and Memory), nor for some clinically important subjects such as aggressive and sexual disorders and disorders of appetite (which might have been included under Reward and Punishment). It is of course impossible to cover the full range of human brain function in one book. A further difficulty is that, in spite of major advances in many areas, we are still only dimly beginning to see how the brain achieves feeling, thinking, and behaving. Thus it is not always possible to link brain systems to clinical disorders.

Nevertheless, I hope that the book may provide a general background for students of the neurosciences and may also serve as a starting point for others interested in particular areas of psychiatry, psychology, neurophysiology, psychopharmacology, and related fields.

Newcastle upon Tyne   H.A.
January 1992

Contents

1. Overview

Functional systems of the brain

The behaviour of man is governed by the integrated activity of three main functional systems in the brain: the systems for arousal, for reward, and for cognition, learning, and memory. Each of these systems encompasses a spectrum of active states. Mechanisms for waking interact with those for sleeping; reward mechanisms interact with those for punishment; learning and memory include forgetting and unlearning. The combined operation of these mechanisms determines an individual's responsiveness at any moment, his or her state of consciousness, motivation, and the effect of previous experiences. Together they define the individual's perception and interpretation of external and internal stimuli, determine his or her emotional state, recruit the appropriate somatic accompaniments, and shape the degree and direction of behavioural reactions. Interplay between these systems allows for an almost infinite variety of responses and mental states.

In determining behaviour, these systems are inextricably interconnected and operationally indivisible. They are simultaneously active, utilize the same neurotransmitters and neuromodulators, and share overlapping anatomical pathways. Yet, paradoxically, it is necessary to separate the systems in order to describe them, and in the following chapters arousal and sleep, reward and punishment, and learning and memory are considered sequentially. This forced distinction is artificial, since activity in each system is influenced by, and itself influences, activity in others. Some constantly recurring themes which apply to all the systems are mentioned in general terms here; more detailed examples are given later in relation to particular topics.

Patterns of neural activity

Stimulation of each system can be envisaged to generate a complex three-dimensional pattern of neural activity extending through many levels of the nervous system. The shape of the pattern is characteristic of the system or subsystem activated and is initially constrained by the anatomy of its neural connections. However, the pattern of one system may merge and intermingle with patterns simultaneously generated by other systems.

As the neural pathways cross and recross, the resultant activity is modulated, facilitated or inhibited here and there, with the formation of further intricate patterns coalescing at some points, separating at others, to produce continuously shifting complexes, ebbing, flowing, and reforming moment by moment. A particular emotion, memory or thought exists as a transitory shape; it has a form and structure composed of the temporal and spatial firing patterns of multisynaptic neuronal complexes, but it is evanescent. When not actually occurring, it is represented only by a network of potential pathways. The pathways are constitutionally 'hardwired' as a result of evolution, but are functionally adaptable and changeable through the process of learning and memory. The pathways themselves and the intensity of neural traffic within them differ subtly between individuals, and influence personality characteristics, vulnerability to psychiatric disease, and response to psychotropic drugs.

In many instances these patterns of brain activity comprise a series of representations of the external and internal environment. Stimulation of retinal cells, for example, can conjure up multiple 'maps', specialized for different features of the environment, in the visual cortex, its relay stations, and its association areas. There is evidence for a space/time representation in the hippocampus, and for a sensory neuromatrix (probably overlapping with a motor representation) involving large parts of the cortex. Such representations contribute to an awareness of self and provide a body image which is not only internal but also related to the environment. Similar representations no doubt underlie many other functions including thought processes and emotional states. Some of these representations may be evoked by external stimuli, but some are generated and maintained by internal self-perpetuating neuronal oscillators (impulse generators) operating through pairs of ion channels (Changeux 1985; Llinas 1987). The combined output of such multiple representations are important in computing and selecting appropriate behaviours. Distortion or fragmentation of the representations by disease, injury or drugs can give rise to disorders such as amnesic syndromes, phantom limb phenomena and body image alterations.

A feature of the patterns generated by different types of neural activity appears to be a considerable degree of hemispheric asymmetry both at cortical and subcortical levels. Such asymmetry may reflect an evolution towards the more efficient use of neural space by specialization of functions in each hemisphere. Thus, in most individuals the processes of language, logical analysis, and symbolic reasoning occur largely in the left hemisphere while those of selective attention, visuospatial discrimination, and certain sensory experiences occur mainly in the right hemisphere. Normally the functions of the two hemispheres are closely integrated, but certain disorders, such as the syndrome of hemineglect and perhaps some symptoms of schizophrenia, may reflect asymmetric disturbances of hemisphere function or defective transfer of information between the hemispheres.

Multiple neurotransmitter systems

Combinations of the same neurotransmitters and neuromodulators are utilized by all the main functional systems in complex multisynaptic circuits connected in series and in parallel, and containing many regulatory feedback loops. The behavioural effect produced by a transmitter released at a synapse depends on the system in which it is operating. For example, serotonergic activity may promote sleep in one system, but generate anxiety, activate punishment mechanisms, inhibit reward mechanisms, or suppress pain in other systems. The effect of a neurotransmitter may also depend on the degree of activity in a particular circuit. Thus, certain levels of noradrenergic activity can be rewarding in some brain areas, but excessive activity in the same areas becomes aversive. Different receptors for the same transmitter may mediate different (excitatory or inhibitory) actions, so that the effect of the same transmitter also depends on the population of its receptors activated at any site. The effect of a transmitter which in isolation initiates a rapid, phasic, synaptic response, may in integrated systems be influenced by the action of other neurotransmitters and neuromodulators producing long-lasting changes in neuronal excitability, thus tonically altering the background on which the transmitter acts (Bloom 1985). In some cases a single neurotransmitter can mediate both fast and slow responses, depending on the receptor activated. Furthermore, many neurones in the brain liberate two or more neurotransmitters simultaneously, each of which modulates the others' action.

Redundant back-up systems

Many systems employ a redundancy of multiple back-up circuits, each performing similar functions via different anatomical and chemical pathways. For example, feeding behaviour in animals can be increased through specific dopaminergic, α-noradrenergic, or opioid pathways in the hypothalamus. The same behaviour can be decreased through serotonergic or β-noradrenergic pathways and by the polypeptide calcitonin. Activity in separate, but connected, GABA-ergic pathways can produce either effect by inhibition of dopaminergic neurones that promote feeding or of serotonergic neurones which suppress feeding. Similarly, pain sensation can be suppressed through discrete noradrenergic, serotonergic, dopaminergic, or opioid and perhaps cholinergic pathways. The particular pain suppression system activated may depend partly on the type of stress to which the animal is exposed. This elaborate organization of redundant back-up systems appears to be a feature of many, if not all, vital, life-sustaining processes.

Diversity of neuronal receptors

Neurotransmitters and neuromodulators exert their various effects in the central nervous system by interacting with specific neuronal receptors. This interaction may result in the opening of an ion channel or the activation of a second messenger system. The immediate result may be an initiation, an inhibition, or an alteration in the rate of firing of a neurone. At the same time, a cascade of intracellular biochemical and biophysical events may be triggered, such as activation of protein kinases, changes in the cell nucleus, and activation or expression of genes. The type of cascade triggered by the transmitter/receptor interaction and the direction and degree of the final effect on the firing of the neurone depend on the properties and distribution of the receptors (as well as on the 'conditioning' effects of other transmitters and modulators acting upon the receptor at the same time).

Of great importance in the operation of the functional systems which determine behaviour is the fact that receptors for transmitters are diverse. There are several subtypes of receptor for each neurotransmitter, and the different subtypes mediate different effects. In addition, pre-synaptic autoreceptors appear to control transmitter release and to be sensitive to different concentrations of transmitter. Details of the biochemistry of individual neurotransmitters, the molecular conformation of the various receptors, or the biochemical cascade produced by their interactions are beyond the scope of this book, but various receptor subtypes are described where relevant in the ensuing chapters.

Receptor plasticity

In addition to their diversity, receptors for neurotransmitters exhibit plasticity. They are dynamic structures whose density and sensitivity undergo adaptive changes in response to alterations in agonist supply. A chronic decrease in the supply of a neurotransmitter to its receptors, for example by a drug which inhibits its release, leads to the emergence of new or previously inactive receptors so that the functional activity of the synapse is restored. Conversely, a chronic increase in receptor activation is followed by a reduction in receptor density. In some cases receptors appear to be engulfed into the cell membrane; in others there is a decrease in affinity for the agonist. By these and other mechanisms the balance of synaptic activity is reinstated.

The phenomenon of receptor plasticity is of particular importance in relation to the chronic administration of drugs, since many drugs affect the synaptic release of neurotransmitters, or act as agonists and antagonists at specific neurotransmitter receptors. For example, the sedating effect of many central nervous system depressants declines after chronic administration, so that a larger dose is required to produce the original effect. This decline in efficacy largely results from homeostatic receptor adaptations within the central nervous system. Such changes occur with many different types of drugs; they form the basis of pharmacodynamic tolerance and contribute to the development of drug dependence. On the other hand, receptor adaptations may possibly be necessary for the therapeutic efficacy of some chronically administered drugs, such as antidepressant and antipsychotic agents.

Plasticity in the central nervous system

The whole central nervous system exhibits a remarkable degree of plasticity. Axonal growth, collateral sprouting, formation of new synapses and changes in cortical 'maps' can all occur after central or peripheral nerve lesions. Growth of new synapses, activation of previously 'silent' synapses, and changes in the efficiency of existing synapses (particularly in dendritic spines) probably occur continually and are fundamental processes underlying learning and memory. Plastic changes are most marked in young animals and at certain critical periods of growth, but can also occur throughout life at all levels in the central nervous system. Thus, the patterns of neuronal activity evoked by various stimuli and the responses they elicit tend to change over time. Such changes allow for great flexibility and individual variation in behavioural responses.

Disorders of functional systems

In such an intricate and dynamic organization, it is not surprising that occasional dysfunction or maladaptation occurs. It is emphasized here that certain behavioural and psychiatric disorders can be viewed as dysfunctions of the brain systems controlling behaviours. Thus, in later chapters, anxiety states and sleep disorders are considered as dysfunctions mainly affecting arousal systems; drug dependence and chronic pain syndromes are discussed as dysfunctions of reward and punishment systems; the various amnesic syndromes clearly constitute disorders of learning and memory systems. Depression and mania appear to involve primarily reward and punishment systems, while some forms of schizophrenia may reflect abnormalities of integration between the various systems. Since no system operates in isolation, there is considerable overlap between many of these conditions.

This classification may seem obvious, but in medical practice such disorders are usually described and classified in terms of their symptoms, with little consideration of the underlying systems or processes producing the symptoms. Depressive disorders, for example, are defined in clinical psychiatry as consisting of a cluster of symptoms (a syndrome) in which depression of mood is a central feature. The clinical syndrome is carefully separated from the symptom of depression which may occur in various organic disorders, or as a result of certain infections, drugs, or environmental events in normal subjects. Similarly, the diagnosis of schizophrenia depends on the presence of certain alterations of thought and affect, after the exclusion of known organic causes (such as drugs, brain tumours, and epilepsy) which can cause the same psychotic symptoms.

Consideration of psychological symptoms in terms of functional systems of the brain may give a greater insight into the mechanisms of the syndromes, and provide a more rational basis for pharmacological and other treatments. This view takes into account the extensive overlap between different psychiatric states, as exemplified by the clinical terms anxiety/depression and schizoaffective psychosis, since the functional systems themselves overlap. It accommodates the fact that the same symptoms may be found in a variety of disorders and can be experienced by normal subjects. The patterns of neuronal firing described above could be similarly perturbed or distorted by an endogenous biochemical abnormality, a physical lesion, a virus, a drug, an outside event, and many other agents, to produce the same mental state. In fact, it is becoming clear that many psychiatric disorders, including schizophrenia and depression, are not clinical entities, but heterogeneous illnesses often accompanied by structural changes in the brain. In addition, the systems view draws no sharp distinction between normality, and psychiatric or behavioural disease. Instead, it allows for a continuum of individuals who, depending on the details of their structural and functional brain organization, are more or less likely to develop insomnia, anxiety, depression, schizophrenia, drug dependence, or chronic pain (or any combination of these) when exposed to greater or lesser 'doses' of precipitating or aggravating agents. The particular symptoms developed would depend on the site and degree of the perturbation, and the neurological background on which it was acting.

Psychotropic drugs

Psychotropic drugs exert their effects on mental state and behaviour by interacting directly or indirectly with neurotransmitter and neuromodulator systems in the brain. Many of them act as agonists or antagonists at specific receptor sites; others affect the synthesis, storage, release, reuptake, or metabolism of one or more neurotransmitters, while some disrupt neurotransmission by altering the properties of neuronal membranes. Particular attention is paid in following chapters to pharmacodynamics, the mechanisms of drug action, since these are of great importance for providing a rational basis of drug treatment of psychiatric disorders and for understanding the factors which produce them.

For several reasons the effects of psychotropic drugs on the functional systems of the brain are relatively unspecific. First, as already mentioned, the same neurotransmitters and neuromodulators are utilized by all systems. Thus, even drugs which affect only one transmitter or receptor can alter the function of several systems. Secondly, because of the integration between and within the systems, alteration of function of one neurotransmitter affects the balance of activity in antagonistic or synergistic transmitter systems.

Thirdly, drug actions are rarely confined to one transmitter system, to one receptor type or subtype, or to one part of the brain. In the case of the antipsychotic drugs, a stereospecific interaction with certain dopamine receptor subtypes in particular limbic structures may be responsible for the therapeutic effects in some types of schizophrenia. However, the simultaneous action of the drugs on the similar receptor subtypes in a different part of the brain (basal ganglia) can give rise to serious adverse effects. Similarly, with narcotic analgesics, interactions with specific opioid receptor subtypes may produce analgesia, but interactions with other opioid receptors cause sedation, dysphoria, or hedonic effects which may lead to drug dependence. There is a clear need for drugs which act not only on specific receptor subtypes, but which also confine their effects to localized brain regions. Such drugs are gradually emerging and are mentioned where relevant.

This relative non-specificity of action of psychotropic drugs leads to difficulties of classification. For example, drugs usually classed as sedatives, hypnotics, or anxiolytics are here described in relation to their effects on arousal and sleep systems. Many of them, however, are also drugs of dependence, examples of which are discussed under reward and punishment systems. Similar difficulties occur with many of the other drug groups. In fact, the properties of psychotropic drugs overlap as much as the symptoms of psychiatric disease and for the same reasons.

Another recurring theme which emerges from consideration of psychotropic drugs is that none of them are curative in any psychiatric disease. They may provide long-lasting symptomatic relief and allow time for natural remission to occur, but often only by introducing a further abnormality into an already disturbed system. A hypnotic may produce sleep in an insomniac, but the sleep is not normal sleep and may become yet more abnormal when the drug is stopped. An antidepressant may lighten mood in a depressive illness, but in some subjects it may precipitate mania. It is questionable whether further development of present-day psychotropic drugs will ever achieve cures in such conditions. In degenerative states, such as Alzheimer's dementia and perhaps schizophrenia, present drugs cannot be expected to replace lost neurones. The new generation of psychotropic agents may perhaps include nerve growth factors or neural implants which encourage the innate capacity of surviving neurones to grow, make new connections, and re-establish the integrity of functional systems of the brain. These possibilities are just appearing on the horizon.

Part I
Arousal and sleep

2. Arousal and sleep systems

All the general principles described in Chapter 1 apply to arousal and sleep systems. They interact with other functional systems and generate patterns of neural activity which may at times have an asymmetric hemispherical distribution. They utilize many transmitters and employ multiple redundant back-up systems. They are subject to malfunction, as manifested in anxiety states and sleep disorders, and they are exquisitely sensitive to centrally-acting drugs. The neurological organization of these systems is described in this chapter; functional disorders and the effects of psychotropic drugs are discussed in Chapters 3 and 4.

Arousal systems

The ability to support consciousness is a fundamental attribute of the human brain. However, the degree of consciousness can vary from full alertness and vigilance, through a series of different levels and types of awareness, to deep sleep. These variable states of arousal, reactivity, or responsiveness, along with their somatic accompaniments, are largely controlled by the arousal systems of the brain.

There has been much discussion concerning the definition and measurement of arousal. Is it a behaviour or a psychological state? Can it be measured by its somatic accompaniments, such as motor activity or heart rate, or by its electrical correlates, such as the frequency and degree of synchronization of electroencephalographic activity? There are many instances in which these variables do not match (Vanderwolf and Robinson 1981). For example, low voltage fast activity on the electro-encephalogram (EEG) is usually associated with behavioural arousal, but such EEG activity can also occur during behavioural sleep, as in paradoxical sleep, after some drugs, and in human subjects in coma.

Even when behavioural and EEG arousal apparently match, the quality of arousal may vary widely: it may consist of generalized vigilance, concentrated selective attention, motor readiness or activity, and each of these conditions may be accompanied by variable emotional states. Arousal occurs during laughing, but also during crying, and in fear or anger. Arousal, though a convenient term, is clearly not a unitary phenomenon operating along a single dimension. It is a complex of different states of neural activity produced through a variety of combinations of several anatomical and functional subsystems, resulting in changeable patterns of brain and behavioural response to internal or external stimuli. Thus, it is not surprising that arousal cannot be measured in terms of any one variable, any more than 'emotionality' could be defined in terms of any one emotion. In referring to different states of arousal, it is necessary to specify which manifestations and which types of response are involved.

Arousal systems in the brain appear to include at least two closely integrated components (Routtenberg 1968): a general arousal system (Arousal System I), which exerts a tonic background control over central nervous system excitability, and a goal-directed or emotional arousal system (Arousal System II), which contributes phasic and affective components of arousal and is also concerned in selective attention. Both subsystems influence the somatic responses to external and internal stimuli. These systems allow for both very rapid (phasic) and for sustained (tonic) responses of the whole organism to the environment. The selection of the appropriate response to a stimulus is greatly influenced by activity in reward and punishment systems (Chapter 5), and by learning and memory (Chapter 8), but the state of readiness to respond, and the speed and degree of the response, is mainly determined by activity in arousal systems.

General arousal

The general arousal system is a non-specific system which exerts a tonic control on the degree of responsiveness of the cerebral cortex and many subcortical structures (Mountcastle 1974; Webster 1978). A major neurological substrate is the brainstem reticular formation, a system of nerve cells and fibre tracts which links sensory information from the internal and external environment with the cortex and with effector-motor systems (Fig. 2.1). The reticular formation receives an input, in afferent collaterals from the sensory pathways and via the spinothalamic tracts, from virtually all the sensory systems of the body. Its connections include fibres from pathways subserving pain, temperature, touch, pressure, from visceral sensory endings, from vestibular, auditory, olfactory and retinal pathways, and from brain areas concerned with thoughts and emotions. These connections are not specific for sensory modality since impulses from different sense organs impinge on the same reticular neurones. The output from the reticular formation is transmitted by long ascending fibres which are diffusely distributed to all cortical areas and also to other parts of the brain, and by descending motor fibres in the reticulospinal tracts.

The anterior part of the reticular formation, and also a central core of ascending fibres, carry mainly facilitatory influences to the cortex. This

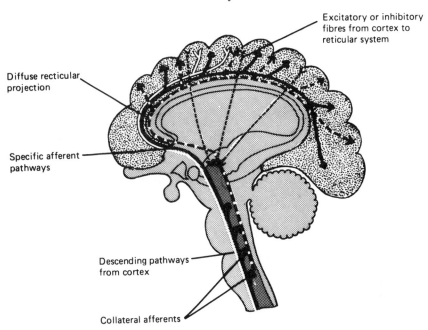

Excitatory or inhibitory
fibres from cortex to
reticular system

Diffuse recticular
projection

Specific afferent
pathways

Descending pathways
from cortex

Collateral afferents

Fig. 2.1 Diagram of brainstem reticular formation and some connections
involved in the general arousal system. Specific afferent pathways, ascending
to localized cortical areas, also send inputs via afferent collaterals to the
reticular formation. The output from the reticular formation is diffusely
distributed to all cortical areas. Other outputs (not shown) are distributed to
other parts of the brain and to the spinal cord. By this mechanism, a specific
sensory stimulus not only excites a localized area of cortex but also, through the
reticular formation, causes diffuse cortical excitation, allowing evaluation of the
stimulus. Feedback systems, which may be either excitatory or inhibitory, also
pass from cortex to reticular system. The appropriate behavioural response is
then transmitted via descending pathways from the cortex.

portion comprises the reticular activating system, which has long been
thought to be of primary importance in maintaining consciousness.
Electrical stimulation of this area in animals evokes immediate and
marked cortical EEG activation, and will cause a sleeping animal to
awake instantaneously (Moruzzi and Magoun 1949). Furthermore, the
neuronal activity provoked by reticular activating system stimulation is
very widespread, including the whole cortex, thalamic nuclei, basal
ganglia, hypothalamus, other portions of the brainstem, and the spinal
cord. This diffuse activation continues for up to a minute after the initial
stimulation.

The reticular activating system appears to provide a background level
of stimulation which lowers the cortical threshold to excitation from

other pathways, including the specific sensory tracts. Thus, for example, a visual stimulus excites not only the visual cortex through its specific afferent pathways, but also the whole cortex through non-specific pathways from the reticular activating system. The discrete, specific projections allow the cortex to discriminate the origin and type of stimulus, while the diffuse non-specific projections, along with intracortical connections, presumably allow other parts of the cortex to evaluate the significance of each specific sensory stimulus in relation to the present situation, memories of past events, associated sensory input, and other relevant factors. The effect of sensory information entering the cortex via the specific sensory pathways, and therefore the behavioural response to it, is in this way modulated by the non-specific input from the reticular activating system.

However, reticular cells possess an intrinsic tone maintained by neuronal oscillators which confer an inherent rhythmicity independent of sensory input (Changeux 1985; Llinas 1987). In surgical preparations in which afferent input to the reticular activating system is sectioned (encéphàle isolé; Bremer 1935; Fig. 2.2), some cortical activity is maintained, as shown by the fact that such preparations show alternating patterns of sleep and wakefulness on the EEG. On the other hand, if the brain is sectioned rostral to the reticular activating system (Bremer's cerveau isolé preparation) consciousness is lost and a state of perpetual sleep supervenes. Similar data is sometimes provided by disease. Thus, when the reticular activating system is damaged by haemorrhage, tumour, or infection, the patient loses consciousness even if the cortex is still intact. Pharmacological evidence also attests to the importance of the reticular activating system in maintaining consciousness. Drugs

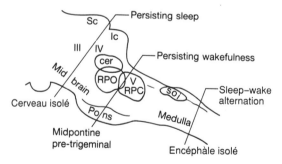

Fig. 2.2 Diagram of section through cat brain indicating location and effects of cerveau isolé, encéphàle isolé, and midpontine pre-trigeminal preparations. cer, nucleus coeruleus; RPC, nucleus reticularis pontis caudalis; RPO, nucleus reticularis pontis oralis; sol, nucleus parasolitarius; Ic, inferior colliculus; Sc, superior colliculus; III, oculomotor nucleus; IV, trochlear nucleus; V, trigeminal nucleus. (From Salamy 1976, by kind permission of John Wiley & Sons Inc., New York.)

which directly depress neuronal activity in the reticular activating system (low doses of barbiturates) decrease the level of consciousness, while drugs which directly stimulate activity at this site (amphetamines) have an alerting effect (Fig. 2.3).

The effect of reticular activating system activity on the cortex is modified by interacting feedback systems from cortex to reticular formation (Fig. 2.1). Descending cortico-reticular fibres may be either

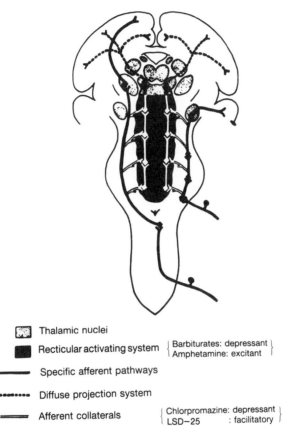

Thalamic nuclei

Recticular activating system { Barbiturates: depressant }
                              { Amphetamine: excitant   }

—————— Specific afferent pathways

•••••••• Diffuse projection system

══════ Afferent collaterals { Chlorpromazine: depressant }
                              { LSD–25   : facilitatory }

Fig. 2.3 Diagram showing sites of action of drugs affecting activity in the reticular activating system and its afferent collaterals. Drugs which directly affect activity in the reticular activating system (barbiturates, depressant; amphetamine, stimulant) alter the level of consciousness by effects on the diffuse cortical projection system. Drugs which depress activity in the afferent collaterals (chlorpromazine) do not impair consciousness because they do not affect the intrinsic tone of the reticular activating system. LSD-25 appears to facilitate transmission through the afferent collaterals, enhancing the diffuse cortical effects of sensory stimulation. (From Bradley 1961, by kind permission of Oxford University Press.)

excitatory or inhibitory. Activity in excitatory pathways further stimulates the reticular activating system so that the arousing effect of the
original stimulus is magnified. Conversely, when descending inhibitory
pathways are activated, the effect of the original stimulus is damped
down and limited. Thus, the brain exerts a selective control over its own
sensory input so that the arousing effect of relevant stimuli is greater than
that of irrelevant stimuli.

Goal-directed and emotional arousal

Closely connected with the general arousal system is a second arousal
system which appears to supply cortical responses with emotional qualities such as fear and anxiety, anger, pleasure, and aversion. To a large
extent, this system determines the quality and strength of the response
to any stimulus, and its activity adds a selective, goal-directed aspect to
arousal behaviour.

The main anatomical basis for this aspect of arousal is the limbic system, a heterogeneous group of functionally-related structures surrounding the midbrain (Papez 1937; MacLean 1949, 1969; Isaacson 1974, 1982;
Fig. 2.4). It includes tissues derived from the limbic lobe of the paleo-
cortex (cingulate, parahippocampal, hippocampal and dentate gyri,
induseum griseum, olfactory lobe and bulb), related subcortical nuclei
(amygdaloid nucleus, anterior thalamic, septal and hippocampal nuclei),

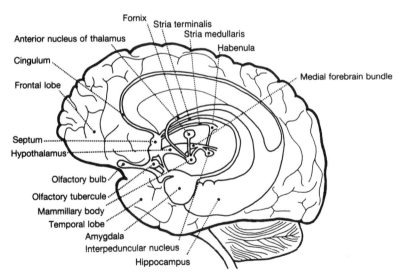

Fig. 2.4 Some structures and connections of the limbic system. Schematic
diagram of the classic limbic system proposed by Papez (1937) and MacLean
(1949). (From Stinus et al. 1984)

and fibre tracts (fornix, mammillothalamic tract, stria terminalis, and olfactory tract). These structures are closely interconnected with each other and also with the thalamus, hypothalamus, striatum, reticular activating system and median forebrain bundle.

Certain of the limbic nuclei appear to be directly involved in controlling emotional tone. For example, electrical stimulation of some parts of the amygdala in many animal species produces rage, aggression, and attacking behaviour, while stimulation of other parts of the amygdala inhibits this behaviour. There also seems to be a separation between fear and flight behaviour on the one hand and aggressive attacking behaviour on the other, depending upon which part of the amygdala is stimulated or sectioned. Stimulation of the septal region has a taming effect on various animals, and decreases most emotional responses, while destruction increases emotional and social responses. Interconnected with these limbic nuclei are nuclei in the lateral, ventromedial, and posterior hypothalamus, which appear to generate basic drives such as hunger, thirst, and sex.

All these nuclei also form part of the reward systems, described in Chapter 5. Electrical stimulation in many limbic areas appears to be highly rewarding in all animals species studied and it is thought that their activity contributes an element of incentive or motivation that leads to reward-seeking behaviour in arousal. Also of importance are 'punishment' areas where electrical stimulation is aversive. These appear to be involved in avoidance behaviour. At present, it is not possible to define exactly the neurophysiological substrates for separate emotions: presumably each emotion involves activation of a unique pattern of limbic and neocortical structures. The question is discussed further in relation to anxiety in Chapter 3 and to other emotions related to reward and punishment in Chapter 5. There is evidence of some right hemispherical specialization for the experience of emotions (Ross 1984; Geschwind 1983).

These emotional components of arousal mediated by the limbic system are integrated with the mechanisms for learning and memory, in which the hippocampus plays a vital role (Chapter 8). Through learning and memory, the arousing effects of repeated stimuli can be either enhanced or extinguished.

The reticular and limbic arousal systems interact closely with each other. In many ways, they can be thought of as complementary, the general arousal system providing a tonic background of cortical responsiveness while the goal-directed system focuses attention onto factors relevant at the moment. However, Routtenberg (1968) proposes that in certain respects the systems are mutually inhibitory, activity in one tending to suppress activity in the other. He suggests that there is a dynamic equilibrium between the two systems, and it seems likely that maximally efficient behaviour under different circumstances requires a shifting optimal balance of activity between general and limbic arousal and their interactions with other cortical and subcortical systems.

Selective attention

As already mentioned, the brain exerts a selective control over its own sensory input. It is not a passive recipient of the multitude of environmental stimuli which impinge on it, but contains mechanisms which allow it to avoid distraction by irrelevant stimuli and to direct attention towards behaviourally relevant stimuli. Such selective attention is a complex process which includes several components such as vigilance, concentration, focusing, scanning, and exploration. The process involves co-operative activity within the reticular and limbic arousal systems, and in connected cortical and subcortical sensory and motor structures.

Observations, reviewed by Mesulam (1983), on patients with the syndrome of unilateral neglect and related experiments with laboratory primates have shed some light on the brain structures involved in selective attention. The posterior parietal cortex appears to be of particular importance. Patients with lesions in this area tend to ignore sensory events occurring within the contralateral half of the sensory field. Effects are most pronounced if the damage is on the right side of the brain: such patients may neglect to dress the left side of the body, ignore objects on the left, and fail to read or write on the left half of a page. They may deny that the left side of the body belongs to them: 'Even when a hand, for example, is pinched so hard that the patient winces or cries out, they still deny that the hand is theirs' (Melzack 1990, p. 90).

In the monkey, electrophysiological recordings have shown that individual neurones in the inferior parietal cortex increase their firing rate when the animal looks at or approaches motivationally relevant objects, such as food when the animal is hungry or water when it is thirsty. Detection of similar stimuli which have no motivational relevance does not increase the firing rate of the cells. It appears that these neurones are able to associate sensory information with internal drives and that increased firing corresponds to a state of heightened selective attention. In man, recordings from electrodes implanted deep in various brain areas show that cortical evoked responses associated with attention are also generated from the inferior parietal cortex with associated inputs from the hippocampus and frontal cortex (Smith *et al.* 1990). Mesulam (1983) suggests that these connections enable the brain to make a series of overlapping representations (sensory, motor, motivational) of the outside world and to take the appropriate action. These processes are relatively specialized in the right hemisphere which, unlike the left hemisphere, has a good understanding of bilateral corporal and extracorporal space (Cook 1986). In man, selective attention related to semantic information probably involves Wernicke's area (Chapter 8), and the dorsolateral prefrontal cortex appears to control higher levels of visuospatial and linguistic attention (Posner and Presti 1987).

Somatic arousal

Both arousal systems give off efferent connections which activate body responses to arousal (Fig. 2.5). Descending fibres from the reticular formation in the reticulospinal tracts play a major role in regulating muscle tone and are also involved in posture and movement. Thus, part of the response to excitation of the general arousal system is increased muscle tone, increased reflexes, an alert posture and readiness for movement, while inhibition of this system produces muscular relaxation. Centres for autonomic control of cardiovascular, respiratory, and other responses are also situated in the reticular formation. The limbic system, through its hypothalamic connections, is a major determinant of both autonomic and endocrine responses to arousal. Increased activity in the limbic arousal system results in increased sympathetic activity and increased output of anterior and posterior pituitary hormones, while decreased activity leads to a predominance of vegetative parasympathetic activity. There are also close interconnections between limbic and striatal

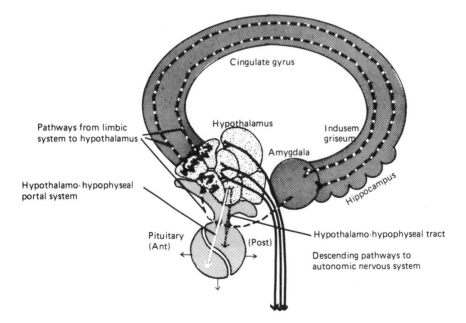

Fig. 2.5 Diagram of some central connections involved in peripheral arousal responses.

structures (Mogenson 1984) and alterations in muscle tone normally accompany emotional responses. Different emotions may trigger different somatic responses: the pallor of fear, the purple of rage, the blush of shame. Different patterns of cardiovascular and electrodermal activity are evoked by rewarding, as compared with frustrating, conditions (Tranel 1983). However, reports from subjects with spinal cord injuries show that such peripheral responses are not essential for the subjective experience of emotion (Lang *et al.* 1972). Somatic changes occurring in states of arousal are described in Chapter 3.

Neurotransmitters and arousal

In view of the multiplicity of synaptic connections required for the integrated control of arousal, it is not surprising that several neurotransmitters are utilized. Cell bodies containing noradrenaline, dopamine, and serotonin are all present in the reticular formation, and cell groups containing cholinesterase, indicating cholinergic transmission, have also been demonstrated. Many of these neurones have overlapping projections to cortical and limbic areas, and it has therefore proved difficult to assign particular functions to individual cell groups.

Cholinergic systems

The distribution of cholinergic pathways in the brain is described by Cuello and Sofroniew (1984; Fig. 2.6) and Reavill (1990). One pathway from the reticular activating system to the cortex appears to be choli-

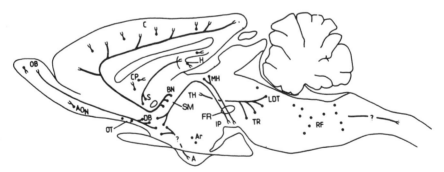

Fig. 2.6 Diagram of cholinergic cell groups and major cholinergic pathways in the rat brain. OB, olfactory bulb; AON, anterior olfactory nucleus; DB, nucleus of the diagonal band; S, septum; CP, caudate putamen; H, hippocampus; BN, nucleus basalis; A, amygdala; TH, thalamus; Ar, arcuate nucleus; TR, tegmental reticular system; LDT, lateral dorsal tegmental nucleus; RF, hindbrain reticular formation; C, cortex; IP, nucleus interpeduncularis; SM, stria medullaris; MH, medial habenula; OT, olfactory tubercle; FR, fasiculus retroflexus. Classical motor and autonomic preganglionic neurones are not represented. (From Cuello and Sofroniew 1984.)

nergic. Thus, stimulation of the reticular activating system produces both EEG and behavioural arousal, accompanied by increased release of acetylcholine from the cerebral cortex. There is an increase in acetylcholine turnover in the cortex during arousal and a decrease in slow wave sleep. Mason and Fibiger (1979) demonstrated a functional interaction between cholinergic and noradrenergic systems in the brain, and suggest that cholinergic activity modulates activity in noradrenergic systems to influence the degree of behavioural arousal.

A system of cholinergic neurons with their cell bodies in various forebrain nuclei (nucleus of diagonal band, medial and lateral preoptic nuclei, nucleus basalis, and the extrapeduncular nucleus) project to all parts of the cerebral cortex. One of the functions of this system may be in learning and memory (Chapter 8). Cholinergic neurones in the periventricular system are involved in reward and punishment systems (Chapter 5). Both nicotinic and muscarinic cholinergic receptors are present in the brain but their functions are not clear. Nicotinic receptors control ion channels and mediate rapid excitatory responses; muscarinic receptors affect intracellular events and exert slower modulatory actions (Strange 1988).

Noradrenergic systems

Monoamine-containing cell groups in the reticular formation have been localized by histofluorescence techniques (Table 2.1). Cell groups containing noradrenaline are designated A_{1-7}. Groups A_{1-5} project to the spinal cord and hypothalamus, and may be involved in autonomic

Table 2.1 Monoamine-containing cell groups in the reticular formation

Cell group	Transmitter	Nuclei	Projections
$A_{1,2}$	noradrenaline	various	spinal cord
$A_{3,4,5}$	noradrenaline	various	hypothalamus, preoptic area
$A_{6,7}$	noradrenaline	locus coeruleus and subcoeruleus	thalamus, neocortex, limbic system, cerebellum, spinal cord
$A_{8,9}$	dopamine	substantia nigra	corpus striatum
A_{10}	dopamine	ventral tegmentum	limbic system, frontal cortex
$A_{11,12,13}$	dopamine	various	hypothalamus, thalamus, median eminence
B_{1-9}	serotonin	raphe nuclei and several other nuclei	wide distribution in diencephalon and spinal cord

function. Groups $A_{6,7}$ constitute the locus coeruleus, a collection of only a few thousand neurones with extremely diffuse projections to many areas including the cerebral cortex, limbic system and spinal cord (Fig. 2.7a). Individual neurones in the locus coeruleus innervate huge territories; for example a single cell may project both to the cortex and to the cerebellum (Saper 1987). Such connections suggest widely distributed functions and the locus coeruleus is thought to be involved in general and limbic arousal (Jouvet 1972, 1977; Webster 1978; Jacobs 1984), selective attention (Mason 1979; Clark *et al.* 1984), vigilance (Saper 1987), anxiety and fear reactions (Gray 1982; Chapter 3), affective and pain responses (Redmond 1987; Chapter 5), and cortical plasticity (Pettigrew 1978; Chapter 8). The extensive afferent and efferent connections of the locus coeruleus suggest that it may function (among other things) as an alarm relay or 'enabling' system associated with attention and anticipation (Redmond 1987; Karli 1984), and that it provides an important link between the general and limbic arousal systems.

Electrical stimulation of the locus coeruleus produces increased EEG arousal with behavioural signs of fear and anxiety, while bilateral destruction in animals produces loss of forebrain noradrenaline and continuous slow wave sleep. Direct recording from single noradrenergic neurones in the locus coeruleus in freely-moving cats, rats, and monkeys (Jacobs 1984) show that the firing of these cells is strongly state-dependent, the highest firing rates occurring during behavioural arousal and attention, and the lowest during sleep.

Adrenergic pathways in the median forebrain bundle are also involved in reward and reinforcement (Chapter 5) which contributes part of the goal-directed limbic arousal system. Noradrenergic pathways in general are thought to play a role in the mechanism of drive and aggression.

A role of catecholamines in arousal is further indicated by the observations that behavioural and EEG arousal is produced both in animals and humans by the injection of noradrenaline into the cerebral ventricles or directly into the substance of the brain and that L-dopa and sympathomimetic drugs produce increased arousal, while depletion of brain monoamines with reserpine causes EEG and behavioural de-arousal (Candy and Key 1977; Vanderwolf and Robinson 1981).

The effects of noradrenaline released by noradrenergic neurones in the reticular formation depend on the type of noradrenergic receptor activated. Adrenergic receptor subtypes are described in more detail in Chapter 11. They include post-synaptic α_1-receptors, which in general mediate excitatory effects, and post-synaptic β-receptors, which generally mediate depressant effects in the central nervous system (Bevan *et al.* 1977; Aghajanian and Rogawski 1983). Adrenergic α_2 autoreceptors exert an inhibitory modulatory control over noradrenaline release. The distribution of these receptors differs in different parts of the brain. The

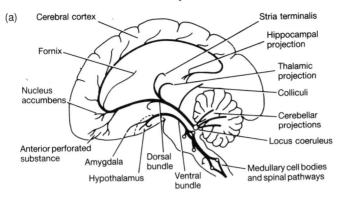

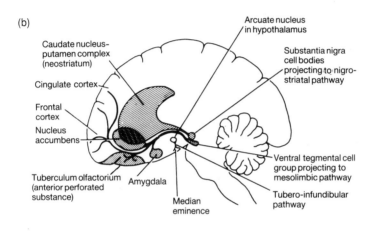

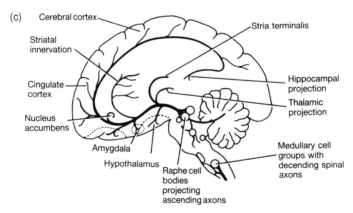

Fig. 2.7 Monoaminergic pathways in the brain. (a) Noradrenergic pathways. (b) Dopaminergic pathways. (c) Serotonergic pathways. Note wide distribution of noradrenergic and serotonergic pathways and more discrete dopaminergic projections. Diagrams are based on animal data. (From Kruk and Pycock 1979.)

neocortex contains both α_1 and β-receptors, and may show either excitatory or depressant responses to noradrenaline. The locus coeruleus contains mainly α_2-receptors and the iontophoretic application of noradrenaline depresses the firing of neurones in this nucleus. The dorsal raphe nuclei contain mainly α_1-receptors and are almost universally activated by the iontophoretic application of noradrenaline (Aghajanian and Rogawski 1983).

Dopaminergic systems

Cells of groups A_{8-13} in the reticular formation contain dopamine (Table 2.1 Fig. 2.7b). Groups $A_{8,9}$ constitute the substantia nigra, project to the corpus striatum, and affect muscle tone. Group A_{10}, situated in the ventral tegmental area, consists of the cell bodies of the dopaminergic mesolimbic pathway. These cells project along the median forebrain bundle to limbic areas and to the frontal cortex. This pathway is involved in limbic-mediated arousal; its stimulation by application of dopamine to the nucleus accumbens produces intense arousal, hypervigilance, hyperactivity and exploratory behaviour in several animal species (Stevens 1979). Furthermore, the cell bodies of Group A_{10} lie within the reward area found from self-stimulation experiments (Chapter 5). Single unit recording of the activity of dopaminergic cells in the substantia nigra and ventral tegmental area (Jacobs 1984) show a stable rate of discharge with little variation between quiet waking and sleep. However, the discharge rate increases during movement and appears to be particularly related to purposive movements. Groups A_{11-13} project to parts of the hypothalamus, thalamus, and median eminence; their functions are not clear, but they are involved in the release of hypothalamic and pituitary hormones. Dopaminergic systems involved in schizophrenia and in Parkinsonism, and dopamine receptor subtypes are described in Chapter 13.

Serotonergic systems

Cell groups B_{1-9} in the reticular formation all contain serotonin (Table 2.1, Fig. 2.7c). Groups B_{1-3} project to the spinal cord; the others have diffuse connections, passing along the median forebrain bundle, the whole cerebral cortex and also limbic and hypothalamic structures. The functions of these systems are not clear, but the upper and lower raphe nuclei which contain the cells of $B_{7,8}$ and B_{1-3} are involved in arousal and sleep in animals. Single unit recordings from the dorsal raphe nuclei in freely moving cats (Jacobs 1984) shows that the discharge rate of these serotonergic cells is closely related to the level of behavioural arousal: the highest rates of discharge occur during arousal, lower rates during slow wave sleep, and the cells become completely quiescent during paradoxical sleep. Their activity appears to be modulated, but not controlled, by noradrenergic activity. It is thought that serotonergic pathways from the raphe nuclei play a part in general perception (Andorn *et al.* 1989) and, by controlling ascending traffic through afferent collaterals into the reticular formation, may normally protect the brain from being overwhelmed by sensory information. Serotonergic pathways in the median forebrain bundle may interact with adrenergic and dopaminergic pathways in reward functions (Chapter 5). Serotonin receptor subtypes are described in Chapter 3.

Jacobs (1984) suggests that the various monoaminergic systems subserve different but related functions in arousal: noradrenergic and serotonergic systems, with their widespread projections, may transmit information to the rest of the central nervous system concerning the animal's general behavioural state, while the more discretely projecting dopaminergic systems may be related to purposive movements and changes of muscle tone related to focused attention. The cell bodies of noradrenergic, serotonergic, and dopaminergic neurones in the reticular formation all appear to be autoactive, showing regular spontaneous activity during quiet waking; this property may largely account for the intrinsic tone of the reticular activating system.

Histaminergic systems

Histaminergic neurones have been identified in several magnocellular nuclei of the hypothalamic mammillary region in the rat. They project diffusely to large areas of the cortex with a distribution resembling that of monoaminergic pathways (Pollard and Schwartz 1987; Nicholson 1987). It seems likely that histamine is a central neurotransmitter, and three types of histamine receptors have been demonstrated in the brain (Schwartz *et al.* 1986). These include H_1 and H_2 receptors, similar to those in peripheral tissues, and H_3 receptors which are probably autoreceptors modulating histamine release and synthesis. Stimulation of H_1 and H_2 receptors profoundly potentiates a variety of excitatory signals including depolarization induced by excitatory amino acids and synaptically-evoked spikes, and Schwartz *et al.* (1986) suggest that histamine acts as a 'waking amine', an action probably involving both H_1 and H_2 receptors. Pollard and Schwartz (1987) quote evidence that some histaminergic neurones in the caudal hypothalamus of cats discharge tonically during waking and paradoxical sleep, while others are selectively activated during waking. In addition, histamine antagonists (especially H_1-receptor antagonists) which enter the brain have sedative actions in man.

Present knowledge thus suggests that several transmitter systems, cholinergic, noradrenergic, dopaminergic, serotonergic and histaminergic, are involved in various aspects of arousal. This list is unlikely to be exhaustive; for example, the dopaminergic pathway from the ventral

tegmental area to the nucleus accumbens is subject to feed-back control
in which the neurotransmitter is GABA (Stevens 1979), and there is growing evidence that various polypeptides are involved in arousal and sleep
and that these may be co-secreted with monoamines. Neurotransmitter
systems involved in sleep are described later in this chapter. The locus
coeruleus contains dopamine and opioids as well as noradrenaline and
has receptors for GABA (Redmond 1987) and acetylcholine (Mason and
Fibiger 1979). In addition, excitatory amino acids, such as glutamate
(Chapter 8) are almost certainly involved in most excitatory processes in
the brain.

Performance and arousal

The relationship between the level of arousal and performance is complex. If, for example, performance is measured as reaction time and this
is plotted against an index of arousal such as subjective alertness, heart
rate, or electrodermal activity, it is found that the speed of response
becomes faster as the subject becomes more alert, but at a certain point,
when the subject becomes over-aroused, the speed of response begins to
decline. Such considerations led to the formation of the 'Yerkes-Dodson

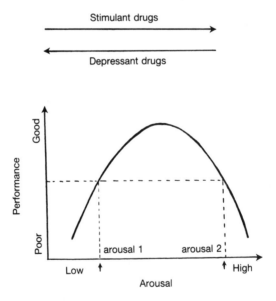

Fig. 2.8 Relationships between level of arousal and performance. Performance
is maximal when the level of arousal is optimal for a given task, but declines
when the level of arousal is below (arousal 1) or above (arousal 2) the optimal
level. Central stimulant drugs may improve performance in relatively under-
aroused subjects, but impair it in highly aroused subjects; central depressant
drugs may have the opposite effects. (From Ashton and Stepney 1982.)

law' (Corcoran 1965), which holds that the quality of performance is related in an inverted U-shaped function to arousal level. Thus, performance is poor when subjects are under-aroused, and also when they are over-aroused, with the optimal level of arousal lying somewhere in the middle (Fig. 2.8). The situation is further complicated by the fact that the particular level of arousal which is optimal for performance depends on the nature of the task. In general, complex tasks, especially those requiring fine motor co-ordination, are performed better at relatively low levels of arousal, while less demanding tasks are performed better at higher levels of arousal. Peak performance on a particular task presumably reflects an optimal balance of activity between the general and limbic arousal systems.

These relationships are important in determining the effects of drugs on performance. Central nervous system stimulant drugs may improve performance in relatively under-aroused subjects. However, in moderately or highly aroused subjects, such drugs may impair performance by making them over-aroused. A similar dual effect on performance may occur with central nervous system depressants; the performance of highly aroused subjects may be enhanced when the arousal level is reduced, while that of relaxed subjects may be reduced in efficiency. Arousal levels of different subjects vary according to personality (Eysenck 1967, 1981), circumstances and pathological states such as anxiety neuroses, and the effects of drugs on performance vary with individuals and cannot always be predicted.

Electroencephalographic measures of arousal

Some aspects of arousal can be measured by behavioural testing, subjective report, and recording of peripheral autonomic activity (Chapter 3). However, the most direct and sensitive non-invasive method of measuring cortical activity is by means of the EEG. Surface recorded brain potentials are thought to reflect local currents flowing in the dendrites of the superficial cortex and may be paced from the thalamus. Characteristic patterns are generated in different states and both the amplitude and the frequency of surface waves are determined to a great extent by activity in the reticular activating system.

EEG wave bands and power-frequency spectrum

EEG wave bands are conventionally divided into four frequency bands (Table 2.2). Although the exact designation of each frequency band is arbitrary, the different frequencies (although they may overlap) do not occur as a continuum from 1 to 40 Hz, but seem to reflect different types of brain activity. These activities may be localized in different cortical

Table 2.2 Electroencephalographic wave bands

Wave band	Frequency (Hz)	Approximate amplitude (μV)	Characteristic associated activity
delta	1–3	100	deep sleep depressant drugs
theta	4–7	100	some pathological states
alpha	8–13	50	awake relaxation
beta	14–40+	20	increased arousal,
beta$_1$	14–26		mental activity
beta$_2$	27–40		stimulant and
beta$_3$	over 40		depressant drugs

References: Cooper *et al*. 1980; Stein (1982); Saletu (1980).

areas during different mental activities and psychological states (Lorig and Schwartz 1989).

The amplitude of waves at each frequency can be measured as the power-frequency spectrum which allows analysis of shifts of frequency and/or amplitude under different conditions and electrode positions (Fink 1978). Hemispheric differences in frequency are associated with various mental tasks in normal subjects: linguistic tasks tend to induce greater fast activity in the left hemisphere, while visuospatial tasks induce greater fast activity in the right hemisphere. EEG frequency is also extremely sensitive to the effects of centrally acting drugs and a wide range of psychotropic drugs give distinctive profiles on spectral analysis (Itil and Soldatos 1980; Saletu 1989).

Cortical evoked potentials

Signal averaging techniques have made it possible to record cortical evoked responses to stimuli such as light, sound, and somatic sensory stimuli. The early, small amplitude, components of these potentials (up to 50 ms after the stimulus) reflect the passage of impulses through the brainstem to the primary and secondary cortical sensory areas. The later components reflect more generalized cortical activation, and are thought to be associated with cognitive events. Various well-defined positive and negative waves occurring up to about 500 ms post-stimulus have been identified and changes in amplitude and latency have been associated with different states of arousal, attention, decision making, linguistic processing, and with centrally acting drug effects (Shagass and Straumenis 1978; Shagass 1977; Dongier *et al*. 1977; Fenton 1984; Neville 1985; Hillyard 1985; Kutas and Hillyard 1984; Roth 1987). Slow event-related cortical potentials such as the contingent negative variation (Walter *et al*. 1964) also show changes in different emotional and cognitive states and are altered by psychoactive drugs (Tecce *et al*. 1978; Ashton *et al*. 1974, 1976, 1980, 1981).

Brain mapping tehniques

Recent developments in computer technology have allowed spatial and temporal mapping and multivariate analysis of EEG data including both power spectra and evoked potentials. Such techniques are helping to provide a picture of abnormalities in local and hemispheric cortical activity in neurological and psychiatric disorders (Roth 1987; Maurier *et al*. 1989) and to show topographical differences in the actions of various psychotropic drugs (Itil *et al*. 1985; Saletu 1989). Complementary techniques for measuring brain electrical activity, such as magnetoencephalography (Hoke *et al*. 1989; Lancet 1990b) are under development.

Sleep systems

Towards the lower extreme of the arousal spectrum lies the phenomenon of sleep, itself an expression of two distinct levels of arousal. The two types of sleep, orthodox and paradoxical, are conventionally described in terms of their EEG accompaniments (Oswald 1980; Hartmann 1976; Salamy 1976; Koella 1981).

Orthodox sleep

Orthodox sleep is somewhat arbitrarily divided into four stages which merge into one another, and represent a continuum of decreasing cortical and behavioural arousal (Fig. 2.9). Stage 1 is a transient phase, occurring at the onset of sleep, in which the EEG shows a tendency towards synchronization, predominant alpha activity (8–13 Hz) and a general flattening of the trace. Stage 2 consists of low amplitude waves, punctuated by sleep spindles which are bursts of synchronized electrical activity at 12–15 Hz. Stages 3 and 4 are associated with increasing amounts of high voltage synchronized delta waves at 1–3 Hz. These latter stages represent the deepest level of sleep and are also termed slow wave sleep (SWS). Neuronal firing rates are decreased in the majority of brain cells, and delta activity is most intense in frontal and cortical regions (Buchsbaum *et al*. 1982).

Somatic accompaniments of orthodox sleep include decreased peripheral sympathetic activity, and a reduction in brain blood flow with a shift from frontal to temporal regions (Ingvar 1979). The eyes show slow rolling movements and the pupils are constricted. Some degree of tone

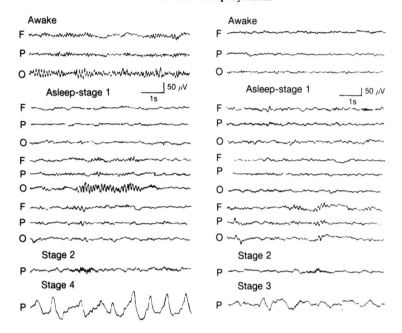

Fig. 2.9 EEG characteristics of orthodox sleep stages in two subjects. Locations of leads: F, frontal; P, parietal; O, occipital. (From Dement and Kleitman 1957.)

is preserved in the skeletal muscles and the tendon reflexes are usually present although they may be depressed in Stage 4. However, co-ordinated movements such as turning over in bed, occur in Stage 2. Considerable endocrine activity occurs during SWS and in man there is a surge in output of growth hormone which peaks early in the night during the first SWS episode (Adam and Oswald 1977; Horne 1988). Prolactin and, in early puberty, luteinizing hormone and testosterone also show sleep dependent secretion (Oswald 1976).

Paradoxical sleep

Paradoxical sleep or rapid eye movement sleep (REMS) has quite different characteristics. The EEG shows low voltage, unsynchronized fast activity similar to that found in the alert conscious state. The eyes show rapid jerky movements which can be recorded on the electro-oculogram. The jaw muscles relax at the onset of REMS and the tone of the skeletal muscles is completely lost, with absence of tendon reflexes. However, this state is periodically interrupted by spasmodic jerky movements of the limbs with hypertonus and momentarily increased tendon reflexes. Peripheral autonomic activity is increased: the heart rate becomes

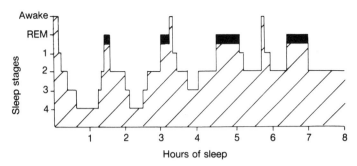

Fig. 2.10   Distribution of sleep stages during a night in normal young adults. (From Horne 1976.)

irregular with bursts of tachycardia, the blood pressure fluctuates, respiration becomes irregular, sweating and penile erection occurs, and there is an increased output of adrenaline and free fatty acids. There is an increase in blood flow to the brain which may reach levels above those of wakefulness (Oswald 1976); maximal rates of flow occur in the frontal and parietal regions (Ingvar 1979; Heiss *et al.* 1985), and the firing rate of most neurons is increased.

Dreaming has been closely associated with REMS (Aserinsky and Kleitman 1953), but also occurs in orthodox sleep (Freemon 1972). The mental experiences during REMS are often more vivid, but dramatic and often frightening dreams are not uncommon at the onset of orthodox sleep (Vogel 1975, 1978). Such hypnagogic hallucinations (Ashworth 1989; Pearce 1988) occur in normal subjects but may also be associated with anxiety, alcohol, benzodiazepines and narcolepsy. It seems clear that some form of mentation and therefore cortical activity occurs in all sleep stages.

The distribution of orthodox and REMS during a night's sleep in normal young adult subjects is shown in Fig. 2.10. Orthodox sleep makes up about 75 per cent of total sleeping time. Early in the night there is a predominance of SWS (Stages 3 and 4) while Stage 2 sleep predominates later. The first REM episode occurs about 90 min after the onset of sleep, lasting only a few minutes. REM episodes recur approximately every 90 min and last longer as the night progresses. There are normally between four and six episodes of REMS per night. One or two brief awakenings also commonly occur during the night. The sleep pattern is influenced by age, the amount and proportion of both SWS and REMS being greater in infants and smaller in the aged. Changes in sleep patterns produced by disease and drugs are mentioned in later sections.

Neural mechanisms of sleep

Both types of sleep are largely the result of active processes promoted and maintained by neural mechanisms in the lower brainstem, basal fore-brain, pons, and vestibular nuclei and parts of the limbic system. Electrical stimulation of the lower brainstem and areas in the basal forebrain produces EEG synchronization and behavioural sleep in intact animals, and records from single neurones in these areas show that they begin to discharge 1–2 min before the onset of natural sleep (Bloch and Bonvallet 1960; Bremer 1970). Conversely, complete transection of the brain-stem rostral to the bulbar portion, isolating the brain from the lower portion of the reticular formation, causes marked insomnia in cats with desynchronization of the EEG and ocular signs of increased wakefulness (Batini *et al.* 1959; Fig. 2.2). Thus, the lower portion of the reticular formation contains mechanisms for activating orthodox sleep by means of inhibitory fibres to the reticular activiting system and, probably, via relays in the thalamic nuclei, to the cortex.

The neural mechanisms for REMS appear to originate in the pons, brain-stem, and vestibular nuclei. Stimulation and section experiments have demonstrated separate centres in these areas which control EEG desynchronization and flaccid paralysis on the one hand and the super-imposed phasic events of clonic limb and eye movements on the other (Jouvet 1967, 1973; Chase and Morales 1984). REMS appears to be a sub-cortical phenomenon since it can occur after decortication; SWS on the other hand depends on the integrity of the cortex (Jouvet 1973).

The mechanisms which promote both orthodox and REMS are thought also to have reciprocal inhibitory connections with the active waking systems, so that activation of the sleep mechanisms at the same time inhibits awakening, and vice versa. Thus, both awakening and sleep result from the combination of active waking or sleeping mechanisms and passive de-waking or de-sleeping mechanisms (Koella 1981).

Neurotransmitters and sleep

Several neurotransmitters, neuromodulators, and hormones appear to interact in a highly complex manner in the sleep-wakefulness cycle. These include serotonin (and possibly melatonin), noradrenaline, dopamine, acetylcholine, GABA, and probably various polypeptides and hormones.

Serotonergic systems

There is considerable evidence that serotonergic mechanisms are of prime importance in sleep in animals. Depletion of brain serotonin by chloro-phenylalanine (*p*-CPA), which inhibits serotonin synthesis, is followed in cats by marked insomnia, the degree of which is proportional to the decrease in cerebral serotonin. This insomnia is reversed by small doses of the serotonin precursor 5-hydroxytryptophan (5-HTP). Similarly, surgical destruction of the mesencephalic and pontine raphe system produces severe insomnia proportional to the decrease in serotonin in the nerve terminals. In intact animals, parenteral injection of 5-HTP or the injection of small doses of serotonin into the carotid artery or fourth ventricle induce behavioural sleep with EEG synchronization, while the administration of serotonin antagonists decreases sleep.

While it seems clear that serotonin promotes SWS in animals, its role in REMS is less clear. Monnier and Gaillard (1981) suggest that there is some specialization in the raphe system, the anterior part being concerned with SWS and the posterior part with the priming of REMS. In addition, different subtypes of serotonin receptors (Chapter 3) may mediate different aspects of sleep and wakefulness. Antagonists at 5-HT$_2$ receptors increase SWS and wakefulness (Dugovic et al. 1989). However, the raphe nuclei also contain 5-HT$_{1A}$ receptors in high density and Idzikowski et al. (1986) suggest that these may mediate SWS.

Serotonin also seems to be involved in sleep in man, although the role of the various 5-HT receptor sub-types is not clear. As in rats, SWS is increased by the 5-HT$_2$ antagonist ritanserin, both in normal subjects (Adam and Oswald 1987; Idzikowski et al. 1986) and in patients with dysthymic disorders (Paiva et al. 1988) but there is no effect on REMS. L-tryptophan has been found to increase SWS in several studies reviewed by Hartmann (1979), although the effects on REMS are variable.

Melatonin

Melatonin is synthesized from serotonin in the pineal gland but may also occur in other parts of the brain, notably the hypothalamus (Koslow 1974). The output of pineal melatonin increases during darkness and is suppressed by daylight. A role for this substance in sleep is suggested by observations that it induces sleep in chicks, cats, rats (Holmes and Sugden 1982), and man (Waldhauser et al. 1990). Its physiological role is not known but it has been suggested that it acts as a synchronizer for various diurnal rhythms (Krause and Dubovich 1990). Subhypnotic doses administered at appropriate local times are reported to hasten sleep readjustment and alleviate jet-lag in travellers across time zones (Petrie et al. 1989).

Noradrenergic and dopaminergic systems

Serotonergic neurones in the raphe nuclei are connected anatomically with noradrenergic cells in the locus coeruleus and dopaminergic cells in the ventral tegmentum. The functional relationship between these systems is probably important in the sleep-waking cycle through mutually inhibitory feedback loops (Kostowski 1975). While serotonergic activity promotes SWS, catecholamine systems inhibit SWS and promote waking (Koella 1981). Enhancement of central catecholaminergic activity produces behavioural and EEG arousal, while reduction of such activity induces behavioural and/or EEG sedation.

The role of catecholamines in REMS is not clear. In man, REMS is decreased by the α_2 adrenergic agonist clonidine (which reduces noradrenaline release) and increased by the α_2 antagonist yohimbine (Kanno and Clarenbach 1985). However chronic administration of drugs which deplete central monoamine systems or block adrenergic receptors (reserpine, methyldopa) increase REMS, while drugs which increase central monoamine activity (L-dopa, amphetamine, monoamine reuptake blockers, monoamine oxidase inhibitors) decrease REMS (Hartmann 1976; Kay et al. 1976; Wyatt and Gillin 1976). In manic depressive and schizophrenic psychoses there are profound abnormalities in REMS which may be related to abnormal central monoamine function (Chapters 11 and 13).

Cholinergic systems

Present evidence suggests that cholinergic mechanisms, as well as producing arousal, induce or facilitate paradoxical sleep. The rate of liberation of acetylcholine from the cerebral cortex (Jasper and Tessier 1971) and corpus striatum (Gadea-Ciria et al. 1973) of the cat is increased during REMS compared with slow wave sleep. Injection of acetylcholine or carbachol in the region of the locus coeruleus induces REMS in animals (George et al. 1964), and atropine reduces REMS in cats (Jouvet 1969). In man, anticholinergic drugs such as atropine and scopolamine suppress REMS, while anticholinesterases appear to increase REMS. Thus, nightmares and excessive dreaming are common symptoms of anticholinesterase poisoning and industrial workers exposed to organophosphates have been found to have longer REM periods than normal or reduced latency of REMS (Wyatt and Gillin 1976).

GABA-ergic systems

The general inhibitory actions of GABA are likely to be involved in sleep. Jasper et al. (1965) showed that the release of GABA from the cat's cerebral cortex is increased during EEG synchrony, and infusion of GABA induces cortical synchronization and behavioural sleep (Godschalk et al. 1977). In man, benzodiazepines and barbiturates, which enhance GABA activity in the central nervous system (Chapter 3) promote Stage 2 orthodox sleep and inhibit REMS and SWS (Kay et al. 1976); (Chapter 4). In addition, GABA-ergic systems in several parts of the brain exert an inhibitory control over the release of neurotransmitters associated with arousal, including noradrenaline, dopamine and acetylcholine.

Polypeptides

The possibility that various polypeptides are involved in sleep has been investigated for many years. These studies are reviewed by Drucker-Colin (1981), Inque *et al.* (1982), and Koella (1983). For example, cross-circulation experiments in dogs showed that a blood-borne substance from a sleeping donor induced EEG synchrony in the recipient and a dialysate from the venous blood draining the brain in sleeping rabbits which would induce SWS in recipient rabbits. The sleep-inducing agent was subsequently isolated and identified as a polypeptide containing eleven amino acids, with a molecular weight of approximately 800; it was named delta sleep inducing peptide (DSIP). This substance was later found also to increase REMS in cats and to be present in the human brain. Pappenheimer *et al.* (1967) collected the cerebrospinal fluid of sleep-deprived goats and isolated a tetrapeptide that induced SWS on intra-ventricular injection in several animal species. This substance has since been isolated from human urine and found to be a muramyl peptide (Garcia-Arraras 1981; Krueger *et al.* 1985). Difficulties in the interpretation of such studies were discussed by Drucker-Colin (1981) who concluded that the existence of a specific sleep-inducing peptide in animals was not yet proved conclusively.

In man, circulating polypeptides do not appear to be critical for sleep since conjoined twins with shared circulations have independent cycles of sleep, waking, REMS and orthodox sleep (Lenard and Schulte 1972). However, peptide sleep-promoting factors produced in the brain may be part of a multitude of hypnogenic or de-awaking substances signalling sleepiness in states of sleep deprivation, and they may also be involved in the circadian rhythmicity so characteristic of sleep.

Certain polypeptide hormones may also play a part in the modulation of sleep. For example, it has been suggested that the release of growth hormone during SWS early in the night triggers the subsequent appearance of REMS (Stern and Morgane 1977). Growth hormone induces a dose-dependent increase of REMS in cats, rats, and humans (Drucker-Colin 1981). Other pituitary hormones and brain polypeptides including substance P, cholecystokinin, somatostatin, neurotensin, endogenous opioids, arginine vasopressin, vasoactive intestinal polypeptide, hypothalamic releasing factors, as well as steroid hormones including oestrogens have all been implicated as possible neuromodulators of sleep processes (Drucker-Colin 1981; Koella 1983).

Sleep deprivation

Although most adults normally sleep for 6–8 h each night, insomnia is a common complaint and is associated with feelings of ill-health.

However, major deleterious effects resulting from sleep deprivation have been difficult to demonstrate experimentally. The literature is reviewed by Horne (1988). Total sleep deprivation leads to impairment of performance in tasks requiring vigilance, since there is an increasing tendency for subjects to snatch 'microsleeps'. In continuous prolonged tasks, a marked deterioration in performance begins after about 18 h (Mullaney *et al.* 1983). However, performance in short tasks remains remarkably normal. After 60 h total sleep deprivation, performance in games of darts and table tennis remained at 97 per cent and 100 per cent of pre-deprivation values in one study reported by Wilkinson (1965). Neurological and psychological changes occur including visual disturbances, tremor, slowness of speech, nystagmus, misperceptions, visual hallucinations, and depersonalization, increased suggestibility, subjective lassitude, anxiety, and decreased pain tolerance. Total sleep deprivation combined with isolation has been used in 'brain washing' techniques.

Recovery from total sleep deprivation is characterized by a rebound of SWS and later of REMS, usually at the expense of Stages 1 and 2 sleep which appear to be more 'expendable'. Kales *et al.* (1970), in a study of 205 h of total sleep deprivation, found that in the first three recovery nights SWS increased 350, 250, and 200 per cent, respectively, from pre-deprivation levels. REMS showed a smaller and delayed rebound, increasing 30, 60, and 20 per cent over the same nights. Total sleeping time was increased during recovery nights, with an increase is 50 per cent on the first night, smaller increases on succeeding nights, and a return to normal on the fourth night.

Healthy young adults appear to adjust remarkably well to moderate total sleep limitation (e.g., from 8 to 6 h for 6 weeks). A greater percentage of time is devoted to SWS, at the expense of Stages 1 and 2 and REMS, and few adverse effects have been demonstrated (Horne and Wilkinson 1985). However, more severe partial sleep deprivation, combined with work stress, has been found to impair cognitive performance and vigilance and to have deleterious effects on mood in medical house officers (Orton and Gruzelier 1989; Deary and Tait 1987). Naturally occurring short sleepers have comparatively large amounts of SWS and small amounts of Stages 1 and 2 and REMS (Jones and Oswald 1968).

Early reports of severe psychological effects after selective deprivation of REMS have not been supported by later work and numerous studies have reported only mild disturbances after REMS deprivation for up to 14 consecutive nights. These include irritability, anxiety, increased appetite, difficulty in concentration, possibly some disturbance of memory function, but normally little impairment in psychometric tests (Vogel 1975; Horne 1988). On recovery nights, there is a rebound with an increase in REMS time and intensity, increased vividness of dreams and sometimes nightmares (Oswald 1980; Beersma *et al.* 1990).

More marked and longer-lasting changes occur after drugs which reduce both REMS and SWS (Oswald 1980; Chapter 4).

Selective deprivation of SWS has been less studied. However, Agnew *et al.* (1967) reported that deprived subjects became depressed and lethargic, physically inactive and less responsive to the environment. Johnson *et al.* (1974) found impairment in vigilance tasks similar to that after total sleep deprivation. Rebound in SWS occurs on recovery nights. Comparisons of selective sleep state deprivation in animals and man suggest that REMS deprivation leads to increased cortical excitability while SWS deprivation leads to decreased cortical excitability (Vogel 1975).

Function of sleep

Despite growing information on the mechanisms which generate and regulate sleep, its function remains enigmatic. The overwhelming desire to sleep when deprived, and the rapid restoration of SWS and REMS after deprivation suggest that both types of sleep are necessary in man. Horne (1988) proposed that only a proportion of sleep, 'core sleep' (Stages 3 and 4 SWS and the first three cycles of REMS), is essential for normal function in man: the remainder of sleep, 'optional sleep' (mainly Stage 2 sleep) is dispensable. This claim is based on the findings that only SWS and a portion of REMS are reclaimed after sleep deprivation and that normal subjects can adapt with little difficulty to reduced sleep periods composed of 'core sleep'. Horne suggests that optional sleep in mammals is a behavioural drive which conserves energy and occupies unproductive hours. Core sleep, however, includes both orthodox SWS and paradoxical sleep and, since these states are so different physiologically, most authors have assumed that their functions also differ.

Orthodox sleep

It is generally accepted that sleep is necessary for growth in the young and that it performs restorative functions in the adult, although the precise nature of these functions is not clear. Much evidence (quoted by Adam and Oswald 1977; Oswald 1976) supports the idea that SWS is connected with anabolic activity throughout the body. Anabolic hormones, including growth hormone, prolactin, luteinizing hormone, and testosterone are released during SWS. Growing animals and humans sleep more than adults, and sleep deprivation in the young stunts growth. SWS and growth hormone secretion appear to increase in adults after physical exercise and other factors which increase cerebral metabolic rate, including body heating and sustained, demanding attention (Horne 1988). SWS is correlated with changes in body weight: acute starvation and hyperthyroidism, in which there is increased protein catabolism during the day, are associated with increased SWS and growth hormone output during the night, while in hypothyroidism SWS is decreased. In addition, a wide range of body tissues in animals and man show increased rates of protein synthesis or mitoses during sleep. However, somatic restorative processes can be achieved during relaxed wakefulness and do not require sleep (Horne 1979, 1988).

SWS, in which the majority of cortical neurons have reduced firing rates and cortical responsiveness is at its lowest, may be of particular importance for anabolic processes in the brain. Increased concentrations of ATP and RNA and increased rates of protein synthesis have been found in the brains of rats, cats, and golden hamsters during sleep, and lower concentrations during sleep deprivation. Other workers have related SWS to memory consolidation (Broughton and Gestaut 1973; Stern and Morgane 1977; Ekstrand *et al.* 1977) and to cognitive processes related to daytime visual load (Horne 1988), both of which may require protein synthesis in the brain.

Paradoxical sleep

The function of REMS is even less clear than that of SWS; nor is it known whether the separate hypo- and hypertonic phases of REMS subserve different functions. It seems possible that one of the functions of REMS in some mammals is to conserve heat and energy (Horne 1988). During REMS, peripheral vasoconstriction occurs in the heat dissipating vascular organs of rabbits, cats, and other mammals, suggesting a thermoregulatory function. Furthermore, the amount of REMS is greater in small mammals, who can conserve relatively more energy during sleep than in larger mammals, and is more abundant in rodents that hibernate than in non-hibernating rodents of similar size. Sleep in general, including hibernation, appears to have originated as an adaptive process in response to environmental factors such as difficulty in finding food and low temperatures. It may also serve to protect some animals from predators.

However, these considerations do not appear to apply to primates, and it is quite possible that REMS, like other subcortical processes, has further evolved to perform different or more complex functions. Among apes, the amount of REMS is no longer negatively correlated with size, but is more abundant in larger species. These differences may be related to the length of time the infant remains immature. Horne (1988) suggests that in primates REMS, which is greatest in the human fetus, is basically a fetal state retained into adulthood which serves to keep the cortex stimulated. Such stimulation might conceivably enhance neuronal growth and the formation of synaptic contacts in the absence of external stimulation.

Many investigations have sought to establish a link between REMS and memory. Sleep in general seems to improve memory and learning in animals and man, while sleep deprivation, especially REMS deprivation, impairs these processes. Thus, it has been suggested that sleep, especially REMS, is necessary for some memory processes. Circumstantial evidence often adduced in support of a connection between REMS and memory includes the observations that memory defects in old age, Korsakoff's and Alzheimer's dementias, other brainstem lesions, and mental retardation are associated with decreased amounts of REMS, while infants and children have increased amounts of REMS. However, interpretation of the many conflicting results is difficult, and in critical reviews Vogel (1975) and Horne (1988) conclude that an effect of REMS deprivation on memory is not established.

REMS has also been closely connected with dreaming, although it now appears that dreams can occur in both sleep stages. The observations of increased cerebral blood flow and a rapid rate of firing of most cerebral neurons during REMS give evidence of a particularly high level of brain activity. Current thinking suggests that dreams may be a by-product of this activity, which is related as much to forgetting as to remembering. Thus, Moiseeva (1979) suggested that during REMS the brain is 'editing' information received during the day and maintaining or establishing some synaptic connections by rehearsal while inhibiting others. Crick and Mitchison (1983) made the similar suggestion that 'unlearning' occurs during REMS, in which unwanted memory traces are removed and strong ones reinforced. Dreams presumably appear as fragments of these processes which happen to each consciousness.

Further investigations of the tantalizing connections between REMS, dreaming, memory, and temporal lobe epilepsy are discussed in Chapter 9. Alterations of sleep in psychotic states are described in Chapters 11 and 13, and drug effects on SWS and REMS are mentioned in Chapters 4, 12 and 14.

3. Disorders of arousal and sleep systems

Since the organization of sleep and wakefulness is highly elaborate and their function much influenced by external events, it is not surprising that disorders of these systems are common. As discussed in Chapter 2, sleeping and waking mechanisms operate together as a homogeneous functional unit, the final output of which determines the level of arousal. Thus, disorders of one mechanism inevitably tend to affect others: anxiety is accompanied by insomnia; poor night-time sleep is associated with daytime sleepiness. However, for convenience the disorders are divided here into those which are mainly manifested in the waking state (for example anxiety syndromes) and those whose main characteristic is sleep disturbance (for example insomnia and hypersomnia). Sleep disturbances in chronic pain syndromes, depression, and schizophrenia are discussed in later chapters.

Anxiety states

Anxiety is a normal adaptive response to certain types of stress; it increases 'drive' and, at optimal levels, improves behavioural efficiency (Fig. 2.8). The manifestations of clinically described anxiety states are similar to those experienced by normal subjects exposed to anxiety-provoking situations and any psychophysiological differences appear to be quantitative rather than qualitative (Lader 1978, 1980). Thus clinical anxiety has been defined as 'anxiety which is more severe, more persistent or more pervasive than the individual is accustomed to or can bear' (Lader 1980, p. 226). Vulnerability to stress appears to be linked to certain genetic factors such as trait anxiety (Eysenck 1967; Roth 1984; Cloninger 1987) and to environmental influences. Anxiety may be induced, especially in susceptible subjects, by certain drugs, endocrine and metabolic disturbances, and temporal lobe lesions.

Anxiety as a recognized psychiatric disorder is common. The overall prevalence in the general population is more than 10 per cent, and it appears to be twice as common in females as males (Uhlenuth *et al.* 1983). Various types of anxiety disorder are distinguished clinically, including generalized anxiety, panic disorder, agoraphobia and other phobias, stress reactions and obsessive-compulsive disorders. Such distinctions may be somewhat artificial since there is a considerable overlap of symptoms, which also merge with normality and with other psychiatric disorders, particularly depression. Some studies indicate that up to 70 per cent of patients with panic disorders develop depression (Gorman *et al.* 1989). The difficulties of clinical classification are discussed by Tyrer (1985, 1989) who argues eloquently for a simple descriptive term, the general neurotic syndrome, to encompass most categories.

Clinical manifestations

Symptoms

Both psychological and somatic symptoms occur in anxiety states (Gelder *et al.* 1983). A major psychological symptom is a pervading sense of apprehension and fear, usually without apparent or sufficient cause. Somatic symptoms may be related to any body system and may include palpitations, shortness of breath, dizziness, gastrointestinal disturbances, loss of libido, headaches and tremor. Panic attacks are commonly experienced as storms of increased autonomic activity combined with a feeling of dread, fear of imminent death or loss of control, often occurring suddenly without obvious provocation. Anxiety symptoms may lead to changes in behaviour, particularly avoidance of perceived fear-provoking situations, such as occurs in agoraphobia.

Somatic changes

The symptoms of anxiety are accompanied by somatic alterations. Since the pioneering work of Cannon (1936) and Selye (1956) on the profound neuroendocrine changes induced by stress, much research has been devoted to identifying and quantitating somatic variables in anxiety. The results of many such studies have been reviewed by Lader (1978, 1980), Mason (1972) and Lang *et al.* (1972). In general, the somatic changes associated with anxiety are similar in normal subjects and anxious patients. Patients with anxiety syndromes are characterized not so much by abnormal resting levels of neuroendocrine activity, as by enhanced responsiveness to stressful stimuli and slower than normal rates of habituation to repeated stimuli.

Stress-induced changes include increases in heart rate, blood pressure, sweat gland activity, respiration rate, and muscle tension. The output of catecholamines, serotonin, corticosteroids and endogenous opioids are also increased. These changes may all be exaggerated in anxiety states. It is clear that the pituitary-adrenocortical and sympathetic nervous systems respond sensitively to psychological influences and to stress. Anticipation, novelty, uncertainty, and unpredictability seem to be particularly potent stimulating factors for both catecholamine and corticosteroid secretion (Mason 1972). There does not appear to be a clear differention for particular emotional states.

Central changes

Increased cortical arousal in anxiety is evidenced by EEG changes, which include decreased alpha activity, increased fast beta activity, especially in the right hemisphere (Tucker *et al.* 1977), and changes in cortical evoked potentials (Shagass *et al.* 1978). Positron emission tomography studies show increased neuronal activity (increased blood flow and oxygen utilization) bilaterally in the temporal lobe in normal subjects during anticipatory anxiety (Reiman *et al.* 1989*a*) and in patients during panic attacks induced by sodium lactate infusions (Reiman 1987; Reiman *et al.* 1989*b*). Prior to a panic attack, cortical activation appears to be increased in the right parahippocampal gyrus, an observation in line with studies showing that the right hemisphere is especially involved in emotional arousal, vigilance and selective attention (Chapter 2). Panic attacks also occur in association with tumours and other lesions of the right temporal lobe (Drubach and Kelly 1989).

Pharmacological provocation of anxiety

Variable degrees of anxiety can be induced in the laboratory by stressors such as mental arithmetic, electric shocks and hypoglycaemia, but perhaps surprisingly patients with spontaneously occurring panic attacks do not usually develop such reactions when exposed to laboratory stress. However, a variety of pharmacological agents can trigger panic attacks in a large proportion of these patients and sometimes cause anxiety in normal subjects. These agents include sympathomimetic drugs, sodium lactate, carbon dioxide, serotonin agonists, caffeine, beta-carbolines, as well as hyperventilation, and other agents reviewed by Lader and Bruce (1986), Gorman *et al.* (1987), and Uhde and Tancer (1989). These studies have implicated several neurotransmitter systems in anxiety, as discussed below.

Mechanisms of anxiety

The clinical syndromes of anxiety have been widely regarded as states of over-arousal, and indeed the symptoms and signs are compatible with increased activity in all arousal systems (Chapter 2). While the subjective emotion of anxiety is relatively specific in that it is readily distinguishable from other emotions, most of the somatic changes also occur in other states of increased arousal, both pleasant and unpleasant. Thus, while there is little doubt that anxiety states are attended by enhanced levels of arousal, hyperarousal by itself is too broad a concept to encapsulate anxiety. Accordingly, attempts have been made to define particular neurological systems in which hyperactivity or dysfunction is specific to anxiety.

In general terms, a number of interconnected brain structures are likely to be interdependently involved in anxiety (Kuhar 1986). These include cortical areas, which recognize and evaluate potential threats, and limbic areas, which generate affective components of arousal and activate the autonomic and endocrine concomitants. Within the limbic system, the amygdala (Davis 1989; Kapp and Gallagher 1979), the hippocampus (Gray 1982), the locus coeruleus (Redmond 1987), the raphe nuclei (Dourish *et al.* 1986) and their connections appear to be particularly important, and several neurotransmitters have been implicated.

Noradrenergic systems

The manifestations of anxiety are clearly associated with increased central and peripheral noradrenergic activity. The source of over 70 per cent of this neurotransmitter in the brain is the locus coeruleus (Chapter 2) which has projections to the cerebral cortex, limbic system, reticular formation and spinal cord. Many studies reviewed by Redmond (1987) strongly suggest that this nucleus and its associated noradrenergic system is a neural substrate both for normal anxiety and for pathological anxiety and panic, and that it also constitutes the site of action of many anxiolytic drugs. For example, in the monkey, lesions of the locus coeruleus reduce fear responses while electrical stimulation elicits fear and anxiety reactions. Agents which increase locus coeruleus activity (α_2-adrenoceptor antagonists, carbon dioxide, caffeine) induce anxiety in normal subjects and panic in susceptible patients, while drugs which decrease the firing rate of locus coeruleus neurones (α_2-receptor agonists, benzodiazepines) prevent these effects and also have clinical anxiolytic activity.

The behavioural effects mediated by locus coeruleus activity are envisaged by Redmond (1987) to depend on the level of stimulation: moderate levels result in arousal with increased vigilance and selective attention (Chapter 2); high intensity stimulation produces anxiety, fear and panic, while low levels of activity are associated with inattentiveness and fearlessness. It is suggested (Redmond 1987; Gorman *et al.* 1989) that people prone to anxiety are relatively hyperreactive to noradrenergic stimuli and that this sensitivity may be largely due to a genetic predisposition.

Serotonergic systems

Serotonergic neurones in the brain are localized in the brainstem raphe nuclei and other nuclei in the pontine reticular formation which are involved in arousal and sleep (Chapter 2). The dorsal raphe nuclei normally exhibit spontaneous rhythmic activity, which depends on the integrity of a noradrenergic input, probably from brainstem sites including the locus coeruleus (Aghajanian *et al.* 1987). Blockade of this input results in cessation of spontaneous raphe activity in the anaesthetized rat. It may be inferred that increased noradrenergic activity activates serotonergic systems, and there is much evidence to suggest that increased serotonergic activity is associated with arousal, anxiety, and fear reactions.

Interest in serotonergic systems as neural substrates of anxiety has increased since the discovery of new anxiolytic drugs which appear to act on serotonin receptors and the recent identification of multiple serotonin (5-HT) receptor subtypes which are widely distributed in the brain. At present at least three types of serotonin receptors can be differentiated (Table 3.1). The raphe nuclei contain 5-HT_{1A} receptors. These are autoreceptors located on the somatodendritic portion of the raphe cell bodies. They operate a negative feedback system and their stimulation by endogenously released serotonin results in decreased serotonergic activity within the raphe nuclei and decreased release of serotonin at serotonergic nerve terminals. Agents which stimulate 5-HT_{1A} receptors (buspirone, geparone, ipsapirone) exhibit anxiolytic activity in some animal models, and buspirone has been shown in clinical tests to have anxiolytic activity in man (Chapter 4). The hippocampus, a limbic structure strongly implicated in anxiety (Gray 1982), also contains 5-HT_{1A} autoreceptors and agonists of these receptors cause a dose-dependent decrease in the amplitude of firing of hippocampal pyramidal layer (CA_1) cells. Dourish *et al.* (1986) suggest that the anxiolytic effects of 5-HT_{1A} receptor agonists results from inhibition of neural firing in the raphe nuclei and decreased serotonin synthesis both locally and in various terminal regions including the cortical, amygdaloid and septo-hippocampal projections.

Receptors of the 5-HT_2 subtype are located postsynaptically and are found in high concentration throughout much of the cerebral cortex in man. These receptors mediate excitatory responses but interact with postsynaptically located 5-HT_{1A} receptors which may oppose their actions. Agonists at 5-HT_2 receptors include the hallucinogenic drugs (Chapter 14) while the non-selective serotonin receptor agonist *m*-chlorophenylpiperazine (MCPP) has anxiogenic properties in man and can provoke panic attacks (Kahn *et al.* 1990). Relatively selective 5-HT_2 receptor antagonists (ketanserin, ritanserin) have anxiolytic activity in some animal tests and ritanserin has anxiolytic effects in man (Fozard 1987). Ritanserin is also an antagonist at 5-HT_{1C} receptors which may be involved in anxiety. Receptors of the 5-HT_3 subtype are also present in the brain (Jones 1988) in the area postrema and also cortical and limbic structures. They are situated postsynaptically and mediate excitatory responses. Antagonists of these receptors have anxiolytic effects in several animal species.

Table 3.1 Serotonin receptor subtypes

	5-HT*₁ₐ	5-HT₂	5-HT₃
Agonists	8-OH-DPAT	α-methyl-5-HT	2-methyl-5-HT,
Antagonists	(−) pindolol spiperone	ritanserin ketanserin methysergide pizotifen cinanserin mianserin	ondansetron
Partial agonists/ antagonists	buspirone ipsapirone geparone ergotamine		
Radioligands	[³H] 8-OH-DPAT [³H] ipsapirone	[³H] spiperone [¹²⁵H] lysergide	[³H] quipazine [³H] zacopride
Localization	raphe nuclei hippocampus (pre- and post-synaptic) cerebral blood vessels	cortex (layer IV) nucleus accumbens (post-synaptic) blood vessels	limbic and cortical areas peripheral neurones (post-synaptic) blood vessels gut
Membrane effects	hyperpolarization increased K⁺ conductance	depolarization decreased K⁺ conductance	depolarization increased cation conductance
Effector pathways (?)	cAMP ↓	PI turnover	?

*Other 5-HT₁ receptor subtypes (5-HT₁ᵦ, 5-HT₁ᴄ, 5-HT₁ᴅ) exist in some animal species. 5-HT₁ᵦ do not appear to be present in humans; the physiological importance of other 5-HT₁ subtypes in man is not clear. PI = phosphoinositol
8-OH-DPAT = 8-hydroxy-2-(di-n-propylamino)-tetralin; PI = phosphoinisitol
References: Peroutka (1988); Chopin and Briley (1987); Bradley et al. (1986); Andorn et al. (1989); Fozard (1987); Dourish et al. (1986); Traber and Glaser (1987); Richardson and Engel (1986); Aghajanian et al. (1987); Bobker and Williams (1990); Trends in Pharmacological Sciences (1990, 1991); Henderson (1990).

Other anxiolytic drugs which do not act directly on serotonin receptors nevertheless affect serotonergic activity. For example benzodiazepines (Chapter 4) decrease both noradrenaline and serotonin release and turnover and decrease firing in both the locus coeruleus and the raphe nuclei, and much of the anxiolytic effect of benzodiazepines may be mediated through serotonergic systems (Gray 1982; Nutt and Cowen 1987). Thus, both serotonergic and noradrenergic systems appear to be crucially involved in the generation of anxiety. Possibly a particular combination of activity between various brainstem systems is required (Gorman *et al.* 1989) since these systems also participate in many other behaviours related to arousal and sleep, memory and motivation.

GABA-ergic and other neurotransmitter systems

The operation of monoaminergic systems is modulated by other neurotransmitters which may also be involved in anxiety. There is much evidence that GABA-ergic systems are important. GABA receptors are present in many parts of the brain including cerebral cortex, limbic system and brainstem nuclei, and activation of GABA systems causes a reduction in activity of most excitatory transmitters in the brain. Localized changes in GABA activity have been shown to occur in rats exposed to acute and chronic stress (Otero Losada 1988, 1989; Trullas *et al.* 1987) and enhanced GABA activity may be a normal protective response to stress, preventing overactivity of excitatory systems. It has been suggested that anxiety states in man represent a malfunction of GABA responses to stress (Leonard 1985). The GABA receptor is also the primary site of action for the anxiolytic effects of benzodiazepines and barbiturates. Some authors propose that the activity of GABA receptor is in turn modulated by an endogenous peptide (or peptides) with anxiogenic properties, which may themselves constitute an endogenous basis for anxiety (Cooper 1985; File and Baldwin 1989). These questions are discussed further in Chapter 4.

The role of endogenous opioids and other neuropeptides (Widerlov *et al.* 1989), including cholecystokinin (Ravard and Dourish 1990), and of dopaminergic systems in anxiety is at present less clear, although they are probably involved. The part played by excitatory amino acid neurotransmitters is just beginning to be explored with the discovery of multiple receptor subtypes including N-methyl-D-aspartate (NMDA) receptors (Chapter 8) and the possible emergence of new anxiolytic drugs which act at these sites (Klockgether *et al.* 1987; Stephens *et al.* 1986; Stutzmann *et al.* 1989).

Models of anxiety

Various models of ways in which these various systems might operate together to produce anxiety have been suggested. The most detailed hypothesis is that of Gray 1981a, 1982, 1985, 1987a) who proposes that noradrenergic and serotonergic connections via the septohippocampal pathway interact with several limbic structures (hippocampus, temporal and prefrontal cortex, and others) to function as a match/mismatch comparator which compares actual with expected stimuli. If a mismatch or an aversive stimulus occurs, the system is activated to enhance general arousal, increase attention to checking the environment, to inhibit ongoing motor activity, and presumably if sufficiently activated, to engender an anxious frame of mind. The postulated comparator function of the septo-hippocampal system, which is supported by other authors (O'Keefe and Nadel 1978; Norton 1981; Rawlins 1984), is also related to learning and memory (Chapter 8) and to punishment avoidance behaviour (Chapter 5), all of which are involved in anxiety.

Gray's model fits in with the proposal (Gorman *et al.* 1989) largely derived from clinical studies, that panic disorder in humans commonly progresses in stages. Initially panic attacks appear to involve hyper-activity mainly in brainstem nuclei, but repeated panic attacks encourage the development of more generalized anticipatory anxiety, involving memory systems in limbic structures. Finally, learned strategies, involving higher cognitive levels, lead to phobic avoidance behaviours such as agoraphobia. Thus increasingly higher levels of brain organization are recruited as the condition evolves.

Sleep disorders

Sleep disorders are reviewed by Hartmann (1980), Parkes (1981, 1986) and Scott (1981). Some appear to result from over-activity in arousal systems, others may represent specific disturbances of REM or orthodox sleep mechanisms, while many are mixed. A concise neurophysiological classification is difficult, and here they are discussed under the clinical categories of insomnia, hypersomnia, and episodic sleep disturbances.

Insomnia

Individuals show great variability in their sleep requirements. Although most people allowed to sleep *ad libitum* do so for 7–8 h a day, some normal subjects require less than 3 h, and others over 12 h. Hartmann (1980) estimates that up to 30 per cent of the population at some time complain of difficulty in sleeping. Insomnia can be caused by any factor which increases the activity of the general or limbic arousal system or which decreases the activity of the brainstem and forebrain sleep systems (Chapter 2); many causes act on both systems.

Increased sensory stimulation of any kind tends to activate reticular arousal systems, resulting in difficulty in falling asleep. Common causes include pain or discomfort and external stimuli such as noises, bright lights, or extremes of temperature. Anxiety from any cause may also delay sleep onset. Here, the arousal presumably results from increased activity in limbic arousal systems. Conditions associated with generalized hyperactivity such as manic states and hyperthyroidism may also hinder the onset of sleep.

Drugs are an important cause of insomnia. Difficulty in falling asleep may result directly from the action of central nervous system stimulants such as tea, coffee, sympathomimetic amines and some antidepressants, especially monoamine oxidase inhibitors. Drug withdrawal after chronic use of hypnotics, tranquillizers, narcotics, and alcohol commonly causes a rebound syndrome with hyperexcitability, anxiety, and insomnia (Chapter 6). Rapidly metabolized central depressants such as alcohol, short-acting benzodiazepines, and barbiturates after enzyme induction has occurred (Chapter 4) may, on the other hand, cause early waking.

Difficulty in staying asleep is characteristic of certain types of depression. Patients typically complain of early waking but sleep records show many awakenings during the night, reduced Stage 4 sleep, increased time spent in REMS, and an abnormal distribution of sleep stages (Schultz *et al.* 1978). Such changes have been ascribed in some cases to alterations of cortisol secretion, or to more general abnormalities in circadian rhythm. Some depressed patients, in contrast, have hypersomnia. Alteration of sleep stages, increased dreaming, and nightmares may also occur in schizophrenia. Interference with circadian rhythms in normal subjects may cause difficulty in falling asleep or early waking.

Frequent arousals from sleep are associated with nocturnal myoclonus, 'restless legs syndrome', muscle cramps, bruxism, and headbanging. The aetiology of these conditions is in most cases unknown. The EEG often shows a normal sleep pattern and the repetitive movements usually occur during orthodox sleep (Hartmann 1980). However, myoclonus resulting from cortical or diencephalic lesions may arise in any sleep stage, while myoclonus due to spinal lesions is usually more apparent in orthodox sleep than REMS (Parkes 1981). Nocturnal myoclonus is common in patients with sleep apnoea, narcolepsy, and chronic renal failure and it may also occur in patients taking L-dopa or clomipramine (Parkes 1981, 1986). Other conditions associated with insomnia but also giving rise to daytime sleepiness are described in the next section.

Hypersomnia

The term hypersomnia is usually taken to include not only excessive total sleep, but also attacks of unwanted sleep and excessive daytime sleepiness. The latter symptom may occur in any type of insomnia.

Narcoleptic syndrome

The narcoleptic syndrome is the commonest cause of excessive day-time sleep, with an incidence of perhaps 20 000 in the UK. The mean age of onset is 24 years, and the frequency and symptoms tend to increase with age. Both sexes are equally affected and there is a positive family history in 46 per cent of cases (Parkes 1981); a genetic basis for the disease is likely (Aldrich 1991) but the mode of transmission is not understood and is probably heterogeneous (Guilleminault *et al.* 1989; Singh *et al.* 1990).

The most prominent complaint is of *sleep attacks* (narcolepsy): periods of sudden, irresistible sleep which may occur at any time and are some-times emotionally triggered. The attacks occur several times a day and usually last for some minutes, but may continue for hours or even days. *Cataplexy* (attacks of muscle weakness during which the patient may fall, although he or she feels fully conscious) may occur in combination with sleep attacks or independently. It is often precipitated by emotions such as anger or laughter. Attacks of *sleep paralysis* may occur with or without narcolepsy and cataplexy. These are associated with the onset or end of sleep and consist of complete inability to perform voluntary movements despite full consciousness. Characteristically, they include loss of the sense of passage of time and can be very frightening. *Hypnagogic hallucinations*, auditory or visual, which are sometimes experienced by normal subjects on falling asleep, may be particularly frequent and vivid in the narcoleptic syndrome. *Daytime dreams* often occur during narcoleptic attacks. Over 90 per cent of narcoleptics have disordered night sleep with extreme restlessness and many awakenings; a few patients have frequent nightmares. About 25 per cent of narcoleptics display *automatic behaviour* during waking hours. During these episodes, which can occur several times daily and last for minutes to hours, the subject appears drowsy or only half-awake and displays inappropriate, repetitive, or nonsensical behaviour. Loss of the sense of the passage of time is again typical and there is a subsequent complete or partial amnesia covering the period of the episode. The automatic behaviour seen in the narcoleptic syndrome is similar to that which occurs in transient amnesic attacks which may be associated with epilepsy, migraine, and psycho-genic states (Chapter 9).

Polygraphic recordings show abnormalities in the timing of REMS (Hartmann 1980). During cataplexy there is an immediate or almost immediate onset of REMS; in sleep attacks a REMS period starts within a few minutes, and night-time sleep in most narcoleptics is characterized by unusually short REMS latency. The narcoleptic syndrome appears to be the only known condition in which REMS occurs immediately or within minutes from sleep onset, the usual latency of REMS in normal subjects being about 90 min (Hartmann 1980). Thus narcolepsy appears to be a disorder of REMS and it has been suggested that it results from an inability to inhibit REMS, or that it is akin to epilepsy, so that the symptoms are essentially fits of REMS. Some narcoleptics have attacks which are similar to those of temporal lobe epilepsy.

Narcolepsy is sometimes precipitated by high carbohydrate foods, an observation which suggests an inborn error of carbohydrate metabolism, possibly a deficiency of cerebral glucose-6-phosphate. Deficiencies of central monoamine (especially noradrenergic) activity have also been suggested although no specific abnormality has been found in humans (Hartmann 1980; Scott 1981; Aldrich 1991). However, narcolepsy partially responds to treatment with sympathomimetic amines and mono-amine reuptake blockers. The possibility that narcolepsy is an immune related disease is discussed by Parkes *et al.* (1986) and Schulz *et al.* (1986).

Idiopathic hypersomnolence

Narcolepsy may merge with the condition of idiopathic hypersomnolence and the two syndromes may co-exist. Idiopathic hypersomnolence is less common, with a prevalence of about 4000 patients in the UK (Parkes 1981). It has a similar age of onset, sex distribution, and familial incidence to the narcoleptic syndrome and may be lifelong and disabling. However, there are differences in many respects. In idiopathic hypersomnolence the onset of daytime sleep tends to be gradual rather than sudden and can be resisted. Sleep does not occur suddenly in unusual circumstances although it may be precipitated by travelling, monotonous circumstances, comfort, and food. The somnolence differs from normal drowsiness only in its frequency and persistence. Patients with idiopathic hypersomnolence complain of recurrent daytime sleepiness and regularly take lengthy naps. Automatic behaviour is even more frequent (45 per cent) than in the narcoleptic syndrome and, like all the symptoms, tends to be worst in the morning. It may persist for 30–120 min after waking (sleep drunkenness) and is associated with a high incidence of traffic, household, and occupational accidents.

Night time sleep in idiopathic hypersomnolence is characterized by rapid sleep onset (1–3 min), a normal sleep pattern, a low incidence of reported dreams, few awakenings, and prolonged orthodox sleep. Total sleep time is usually 8–12 h and morning arousal is excessively difficult, the patients sleeping through alarms loud enough to wake their neighbours (Parkes 1981).

Idiopathic hypersomnolence appears to result from the excessive occurrence of orthodox sleep and may be due to increased activity or decreased inhibition of orthodox sleep-promoting structures in the brain. The fact that narcolepsy and idiopathic hypersomnolence are sometimes seen in the same patient suggests that the two disorders may have a similar pathology. Serotonergic mechanisms may possibly be involved in idiopathic hypersomnolence since it sometimes responds strikingly to the serotonergic receptor blocker methysergide and other drugs acting on serotonergic mechanisms, which are of no value in narcolepsy. Clonazepam at night is occasionally effective in both idiopathic hypersomnolence and cataplexy, perhaps because of its anticonvulsant effect. Stimulants such as dextroamphetamine and other sympathomimetic drugs, even in high dosage, produce little improvement in idiopathic hypersomnolence although they are useful in the narcoleptic syndrome.

Kleine–Levin syndrome

In this rare syndrome, periods of hypersomnolence appear at intervals of days or weeks and last for a similar time. It occurs chiefly in adolescent males and tends to resolve in a decade or two. Attacks consist of cycles of hyperphagia with irritability, hallucinations, headaches, and signs of autonomic and sexual hyperactivity, followed by hypersomnia lasting several days with irritability on awakening. The aetiology is unknown, but in view of the disturbance of sleep, sexual behaviour, and appetite, a hypothalamic disturbance seems likely (Scott 1981). There is no established treatment, but lithium salts may prevent attacks in some patients (Hartmann 1980).

Sleep apnoea syndromes

These syndromes, defined by Guilleminault *et al.* (1973) and Guilleminault and Tilkian (1976), consist of frequent and prolonged apnoeic periods during nocturnal sleep. Apnoea lasting up to 10 s occurs normally during REMS, but in sleep apnoea airflow through the oropharynx ceases for 20–120 s, 30 to several hundred times a night. Waking usually terminates each period of apnoea, with the result that sleep is seriously disturbed and the most prominent symptom is usually of excessive daytime sleepiness. Most patients are chronically tired and have frequent short sleep episodes during the day, sometimes resembling narcolepsy (which may co-exist); others have prolonged daytime sleep periods, and some have difficulty in morning arousal with episodes of automatic behaviour, similar to idiopathic hypersomnolence.

Sleep apnoea occurs predominantly in subjects over 40 years of age (though it can occur in children and infants) and is much more common in men than women (Parkes 1981). Two types have been described, although some patients have both types. In *central sleep apnoea* the respiratory movements of the diaphragm cease during the apnoeic priods. This type probably results from damage to brainstem centres or other neurological structures controlling respiration and is seen in bulbar poliomyelitis, bilateral cordotomy, Ondine's curse, Shy-Drager syndrome, muscular dystrophy and several other disorders (*Lancet* 1979). In *obstructive sleep apnoea* inspiratory movements continue during the apnoeic periods, which are caused by occlusion of the upper airway. The causes include acromegaly, Down's syndrome, enlarged tonsils or adenoids, and obesity, and snoring itself which is inordinately loud in this condition. The syndrome of obesity with obstructive sleep apnoea and excessive daytime sleepiness has been termed the Pickwickian syndrome.

Sleep apnoea usually, though not exclusively, occurs in REMS. In normal REMS, the automatic control of breathing is depressed and the respiratory response to increasing hydrogen ion and CO_2 concentration is decreased. This lack of respiratory response may be exaggerated in sleep apnoea. Cessation of breathing without reawakening can occasionally result in coma and death. Substantial falls of arterial oxygen saturation can occur during each apnoeic episode, and such recurrent periods of hypoxaemia may cause chronic progressive illness with intellectual deterioration, polycythaemia, and respiratory and cardiovascular failure (Parkes 1981; Guilleminault *et al*. 1984).

Treatment of obstructive sleep apnoea involves removal of the obstruction where possible. There is no specific treatment for central apnoea but stimulant drugs are sometimes of value. Hypnotic drugs are contraindicated in both types of sleep apnoea, because of the respiratory depression they produce.

Other organic sleep disorders

Encephalitis lethargica and other forms of encephalitis may cause narcolepsy, sleep reversal with profound drowsiness or sleep by day and alertness at night, or prolonged sleep or stupor lasting several weeks. The sites involved appear to be the midbrain tegmentum or posterior hypothalamus. Hypersomnolence is a feature of fever due to bacterial infections. Some bacteria, including the pneumococcus, contain muramyl peptides. These have been shown to act as sleep-promoting agents, possibly by interfering with serotonergic systems since they bind to serotonin receptors. This mechanism could possibly explain the sleepiness that accompanies pneumococcal and related infections. Severe head injury, brain tumours, uraemia, hepatic encephalopathy, anorexia nervosa, chronic alcoholism, other drugs, cerebrovascular disease, and dementia can all cause sleep disorders including insomnia, sleep reversal, prolonged sleep stupor, or coma. Sleep reversal is particularly common in the elderly in whom it may be associated with cerebrovascular disease or Alzheimer-type dementia. However elderly subjects tend to require less sleep at night but take daytime naps: these normal changes may lead to complaints of insomnia. A special problem in the elderly is iatrogenic insomnia, often resulting from overprescription of hypnotic drugs, especially benzodiazepines, which may cause or aggravate nocturnal confusion and disorientation, and automatic behaviour during the day.

Episodic sleep disturbances

Some sleep disturbances are characterized by sudden episodes during the night. They may all occur occasionally in normal subjects, but may constitute a clinical problem if they appear in exaggerated forms.

Occasional sleepwalking occurs in 15 per cent of children and 1-6 per cent of adults, and is associated with Stage 4 orthodox sleep. There is usually complete amnesia for the event. Rarely somnambulists walk considerable distances and can injure themselves, for example by falling out of windows; occasionally they perform complex premeditated acts which may include violence (Roper 1989; Crisp *et al.* 1990). In most cases sleepwalking occurs in isolated episodes and no particular treatment is required. Sleep talking can occur at any stage of sleep but is most frequent during Stage 2.

Secondary nocturnal enuresis after a period of controlled micturition occurs in 2.6 per cent of girls and 3.6 per cent of boys, and may occasionally persist to adulthood. In a few cases an abnormality of the urinary tract, epilepsy, diabetes, or a large fluid intake may account for the symptom, but usually no organic cause can be found. The enuretic episode typically occurs about 1-3 h after the onset of sleep during Stage 3 or 4 orthodox sleep, often before the first episode of REMS; it can occur during REMS (*British Medical Journal* 1968). Enuresis may occur during a brief arousal from sleep but usually there is complete amnesia for the event on awakening. Drug treatment is not usually required although imipramine is useful in some cases.

Night terrors occur mainly in children and are common during the early school years. The child suddenly sits up in bed, screams and appears terrified but usually there is no detailed associated dream. Sympathetic activity is increased as evidenced by tachycardia and increased respiratory rate. Sometimes the child stares wildly and appears to be hallucinating; usually he or she is inaccessible and difficult to wake. There is total amnesia for the event the next day. Night terrors are usually said to occur during Stage 3 or 4 sleep (Hartmann 1980; *British Medical Journal* 1971), but Scott (1981) states that the EEG shows a marked REMS pattern during such episodes. Night terrors usually resolve spontaneously after a time and no specific treatment is required.

In contrast with night terrors, nightmares are vivid, unpleasant dreams, associated with strong emotions of fear, with evidence of increased sympathetic activity. Not uncommonly, a sense of muscle paralysis or suffocation is present. They usually occur towards the end of a long period of REMS, frequently cause awakening, and are remembered. Increased frequency of nightmares occurs in narcolepsy and in psychiatric states including anxiety syndromes, depression, and schizophrenia. Several groups of drugs cause nightmares including cholinomimetic drugs, psychotomimetic drugs, and propranolol. Nightmares are common during the withdrawal syndrome from central nervous system depressant drugs and after general anaesthetics. They may also occur in starvation, fevers, or after prolonged sleep loss. In short, any factor leading to increased REMS may cause nightmares, which appear to consist of particularly intense periods of REMS with increased limbic (emotional) and autonomic activity.

However, frightening dreams can occur in orthodox sleep. Stein claims that 'in fact, the terrifying experience of the worst nightmares — being crushed, burnt, suffocated or pushed over the edge of a precipice — probably occur in . . . SWS and not REMS' (Stein 1982, p. 305).

4. Drugs acting on arousal and sleep systems

Nearly all psychotropic drugs act at some point on arousal and sleep systems in the brain. Central nervous system stimulants and depressants are classified according to whether they increase or decrease cortical arousal; anxiolytics and tranquillizers are designated by their effects on emotional arousal; antipsychotic drugs and antidepressants have specialized effects on arousal and sleep systems, and these systems are also affected by a wide range of other drugs from antihistamines to antihypertensive agents. This section considers some drugs used therapeutically for their effects on arousal: central nervous system depressants, classed as hypnotics, sedatives, and anxiolytics; and certain stimulants, the sympathomimetic amines and xanthines. The effects of other psychotropic drugs on arousal and sleep are discussed in later chapters: narcotic analgesics, alcohol, and cocaine (Chapter 7), antidepressants (Chapter 12), antipsychotic and psychotomimetic drugs (Chapter 14).

Hypnotics, sedatives, anxiolytics

Benzodiazepines

The drug explosion in the 1950s, which gave rise to antidepressants and antipsychotic drugs, also produced minor tranquillizers, now chiefly represented by the benzodiazepines. These became by the 1970s the most commonly prescribed of all drugs in the western world. Levels of prescribing are discussed by Balter *et al.* (1984) and Taylor (1987). Recently there has been some decline in benzodiazepine prescriptions, but it is estimated that there are 1.2 million long-term benzodiazepine users in the UK and several millions world-wide (Ashton and Golding 1989*a*).

Pharmacokinetics

The pharmacokinetics of benzodiazepines are reviewed by Greenblatt *et al.* (1981, 1983). They are well absorbed when taken orally, and distributed to brain and adipose tissue. The rate of distribution is variable and depends on the lipid solubility of the different drugs. This phase is

Table 4.1 Pharmacokinetic properties and relative potency of some benzodiazepines

Drug	Beta half-life in fit young subjects (h)*	Dose (mg) approximately equivalent to 10 mg diazepam
Alprazolam	6–12	0.5
Chlordiazepoxide	5–30 [36–200]*	25
Clobazam	16–60 [36–200]*	20
Diazepam	20–100 [36–200]*	10
Loprazolam	6–12	1–2
Lorazepam	10–20	1
Lormetazepam	10–12	1–2
Nitrazepam	15–38	10
Oxazepam	4–15	20
Temazepam	8–22	20
Triazolam[1]	2–5	0.5

* Half-life of active metabolite.
[1] Withdrawn in UK 1991.

followed by a more gradual decline in plasma concentration due to drug elimination (beta half-life) which shows great variability between different benzodiazepines (Table 4.1). Benzodiazepines undergo hepatic metabolism via oxidation or conjugation, and some form pharmacologically active metabolites. Oxidation is decreased in the elderly (Cook 1979), in patients with hepatic impairment, and in the presence of enzyme-inhibiting drugs. Conjugation is less influenced by age and disease; benzodiazepines which are conjugated include oxazepam, lorazepam and temazepam.

Actions

The actions of all benzodiazepines are broadly similar. They exert four major therapeutic effects: sedative/hypnotic, anxiolytic, muscle relaxant, and anti-convulsant, as well as an amnesic action. Different benzodiazepines differ considerably in potency (Table 4.1), in the relative potency of their separate actions (Bond and Lader 1988) and in affinity for the benzodiazepine receptor (see below).

Sedative/hypnotic effects. The benzodiazepines are effective hypnotics. A major site of this action is probably the brainstem reticular formation which is of central importance in arousal and sleep (Chapter 2). The reticular formation is very sensitive to depression by benzodiazepines; small doses decrease both spontaneous activity and responses to afferent stimuli and block cortical EEG arousal evoked by electrical stimulation of the reticular formation (Harvey 1985,

Baldessarini 1985; Haefely *et al.* 1981). In small doses, the benzodiazepines produce mainly anxiolytic effects, but increasing dosage leads to sedation and, as dosage is increased, to hypnosis and stupor. The changes in the waking EEG are similar to those produced by other sedative/hypnotic drugs: there is a decrease and slowing of alpha activity and an increase in low voltage fast activity especially in the beta range.

(i) Effects on sleep. The effects on sleep are reviewed by Hartmann (1976), Kay *et al.* (1976), and Wheatley (1981). In general, benzodiazepines hasten sleep onset, decrease nocturnal awakenings, increase total sleeping time, and often impart a sense of deep or refreshing sleep. However, the sleep induced by benzodiazepines differs from normal sleep in the duration of the various sleep stages (Fig. 4.1). Stage 2 sleep is prolonged and mainly accounts for the increased sleeping time. By contrast, the duration of SWS (Stages 3 and 4) is usually decreased although the normal nocturnal peaks in plasma concentrations of growth hormone, prolactin, and luteinizing hormone, are little affected. The duration of REMS is also reduced and its onset delayed. This abnormal sleep pattern probably arises because the drugs unselectively depress both arousal systems and the pontine and brain-stem mechanisms which actively promote SWS and REMS (Chapter 3).

These changes may occur with most benzodiazepines in normal subjects but there are considerable variations in response, depending on dosage, duration of treatment, individual benzodiazepines, and clinical state. The increase in total sleeping time is greater in patients with insomnia than in normal subjects and greatest in patients with the shortest baseline sleep.

(ii) Tolerance. The general mechanisms and types of drug tolerance are described in Chapter 6, to which the reader is referred for a full discussion. Tolerance to the hypnotic effects of benzodiazepines develops with chronic use (Petursson and Lader 1984) and may lead to escalation of dosage. Sleep latency, Stage 2 sleep, SWS, REMS, and intrasleep awakenings all tend to return towards pretreatment levels after some weeks (Adam *et al.* 1976; Kales *et al.* 1978). However, Oswald *et al.* (1982) found that self-ratings of sleep quality and delay to sleep onset remained stable in 97 poor sleepers taking nightly doses of lormetazepam (2 mg) or nitrazepam (5 mg) for 24 weeks. The number of self-reported dreams may increase on continued use but the dreams are less bizarre than before medication.

(iii) Rebound insomnia. Rebound insomnia commonly occurs on withdrawal of benzodiazepines. This is seen most dramatically when the drugs have been taken in high doses or for long periods, but can probably occur after only a week of low dose administration (Kales *et al.* 1978; Nicholson 1980*a*, *b*). There is often a marked rebound in sleep latency, which becomes longer than the premedication level, and in intrasleep

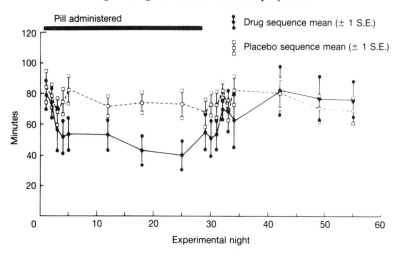

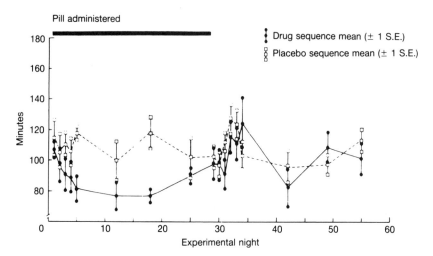

Fig. 4.1   Effect of chloridiazepoxide on slow wave sleep (SWS) and rapid eye movement sleep (REMS). Open symbols and dotted lines, placebo; filled symbols and solid line, chlordiazepoxide. Upper trace, effects on total SWS (n = 9) Lower trace, effects on total REM time (n = 9). (From Hartmann 1976, by kind permission of John Wiley & Sons Inc., New York.)

awakenings, which become more frequent than before medication. There may also be an increase in SWS. REMS also shows a rebound pattern with decrease in REMS latency, increase in total REMS time, eye movements, and intensity of dreaming. Nightmares may occur and add to the frequent awakenings. These symptoms, which occur both in normal subjects and in patients with insomnia, are most marked on cessation of benzodiazepines with short or moderately short half-lives and may last for many weeks. With triazolam, which has the shortest duration of action, some rebound effects may occur during the latter part of the night. With long acting benzodiazepines SWS and REMS may remain depressed for several weeks and then slowly return to baseline, sometimes without a rebound. These rebound effects are probably a reflection of pharmacodynamic tolerance (Chapter 6). They lead to continuation of usage and contribute to the development of dependence.

(iv) 'Hangover' effects. Residual effects of benzodiazepines are reviewed by Bond and Lader (1981), and Nicholson (1980a). Benzodiazepines with longer half-lives (Table 4.1), especially if used chronically, are more likely to cause prolonged sedation than those which are eliminated more rapidly. However, there are large individual variations in response to different benzodiazepines, and the results of single dose studies in normal subjects cannot necessarily be extrapolated to multiple dosing in anxious insomniacs. Metabolism of some benzodiazepines (for example nitrazepam) may be inefficient in the elderly, leading to cumulation and marked daytime residual effects.

Anxiolytic effects. Benzodiazepines are potent anxiolytic agents. In contrast to barbiturates, anxiolytic effects are exerted at low doses which produce minimal sedation. Many clinical trials have demonstrated clinical efficacy in patients with anxiety disorders, at least in the short term. Anxiolytic effects have been reported in normal subjects with high trait or state anxiety (Parrott and Kentridge 1982; Parrott and Davis 1983; O'Boyle *et al.* 1986). Benzodiazepines also alleviate experimentally induced anxiety behaviour in animals (File and Pellow 1983; Pellow and File 1986). The drugs suppress electrical activity in many limbic areas and other areas involved in anxiogenesis (Chapter 3), including the septal area, amygdala, hippocampus, hypothalamus, locus coeruleus and raphe nuclei (Tsuchiya and Kitagawa 1976; Robinson and Wang 1979), and decrease the turnover of acetylcholine, noradrenaline, serotonin and dopamine in these areas (Haefely *et al.* 1981).

Tolerance to the anxiolytic effects seems to develop less rapidly than to the hypnotic effects (Petursson and Lader 1981b). In clinical use, most patients reporting initial drowsiness find that it wears off in a few days, while the anxiolytic effect remains for weeks or months. However, it has been claimed that benzodiazepines are no longer effective in the treatment of anxiety after 1–4 months of continuous treatment (*Drug and Therapeutics Bulletin* 1980; Burrows and Davies 1984).

Muscular relaxant effects. Benzodiazepines induce skeletal muscle relaxation in doses which do not affect locomotion. They are useful for relieving spasticity due to upper motorneurone lesions, degenerative neurological disease, muscle pain and spasm, tetanus, and some neuromuscular disorders (Speth *et al.* 1980). The muscular relaxation adds to the therapeutic effects when benzodiazepines are used as hypnotics, anxiolytics, and for preoperative medication. The main site of this action is probably supraspinal: the effect of electrical stimulation of the medullary reticular formation on spinal neurones is suppressed by small doses and the tonic facilitatory influence of the reticular formation on spinal gamma neurones is attenuated (Harvey 1985). It is possible that polysynaptic inhibition in the spinal cord is also enhanced. Some degree of tolerance develops to the muscular relaxant effect.

Anticonvulsant effects.   Benzodiazepines exhibit anticonvulsant activity in man and animals. In animals they inhibit seizures induced by pentylenetetrazol or picrotoxin, but seizures induced by strychnine or electroshock are suppressed only in maximal doses which impair locomotor activity. They prevent seizures elicited by repeated electrical stimulation of the amygdala, and prevent photic seizures in baboons. The action appears to be due to suppression of the spread of electrical activity rather than to a local effect on the site of epileptic discharge. In both animals and man, tolerance to the anticonvulsant effect develops quickly (Haigh and Feely 1988). Nevertheless, benzodiazepines are the treatment of choice in status epilepticus, in fits induced by a variety of drugs and poisons, associated with withdrawal of alcohol and other depressants, and in pre-eclampsia. They are sometimes of value in psychomotor and myoclonic epilepsy.

Mechanisms of action

Benzodiazepine and GABA receptors.   The mechanism of action of benzodiazepines began to be elucidated with the discovery of specific benzodiazepine binding sites in the rat brain (Mohler and Okada 1977; Squires and Braestrup 1977). These sites have a high stereospecific and selective affinity for benzodiazepines, and are unevenly distributed, being concentrated in the cortex, limbic system, cerebellum, and certain other sites (Young and Kuhar 1980). They have since been found in the brain of many animal species including man (Nielsen *et al.* 1978; Mohler and Okada 1978; Buchsbaum *et al* 1987; Shinotoh *et al.* 1989).

     Later work, reviewed by Braestrup and Nielsen (1980), and Haefely (1990), showed that these sites are an integral part of the post-synaptic GABA$_A$ receptor, a multimolecular unit which controls a chloride channel and has receptor sites for GABA, benzodiazepines and other ligands, and probably barbiturates and some convulsants (Fig. 4.2). As indicated in Fig. 4.2, occupation of the GABA site by GABA causes configurational changes in the receptor complex which lead to the opening of chloride channels in the neuronal membrane. Chloride ions enter the cell, hyperpolarizing it and making it resistant to excitation. This is

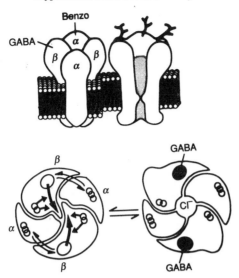

Fig. 4.2 Diagram of the GABA$_A$-benzodiazepine receptor-chloride channel complex. *Top*: Section perpendicular to neuronal membrane. *Bottom*: cross-section of receptor. The oval on the beta subunit represents the GABA binding site; the two overlapping circles on the same unit indicate the binding sites for barbiturates and convulsants. The three overlapping circles on the alpha subunit represent the binding sites for benzodiazepine agonists, antagonists, and inverse agonists. The closed conformation of the chloride channel is shown on the left, with GABA sites unoccupied. The open conformation of the channel, after occupation of the GABA sites by two molecules of GABA, is shown on the right. Large arrows indicate the gating functions of the GABA sites; smaller arrows show the allosteric influence of the other binding sites. (For full explanation see text.) (Modified with permission from Haefely 1990.)

the mechanism of GABA-mediated postsynaptic inhibition. Benzodiazepines potentiate this action by increasing the sensitivity of the GABA$_A$ receptor ion channel to GABA. The increase is about threefold with full agonists and only occurs if the concentration of GABA in the synaptic cleft is insufficient to saturate the GABA$_A$ receptors. However, benzodiazepines require the presence of GABA for their effects and their maximum action is limited by the availability of GABA. Benzodiazepines do not effect the synthesis, release or metabolism of GABA.

GABA is a universal inhibitory neurotransmitter and is present in over 30 per cent of brain synapses. Some GABA neurons (Purkinje cells in the cerebellum and neurones in the nigrostriatal pathway) have long axons and establish inhibitory contacts at distant sites. However, most GABA neurones have short axons and form local inhibitory circuits affecting cell bodies, axons and dendrites of excitatory (monoaminergic and cholinergic) neurones. Thus even small changes in GABA activity can have widespread inhibitory effects in other neurotransmitter pathways. The density of GABA/benzodiazepine receptors varies between individuals and shows alterations at specific brain sites in response to stress (Sepinwall and Cook 1979; Otero Losada 1988, 1989; Trullas *et al.* 1987). Such differences may account for individual differences in emotionality, vulnerability to stress and response to benzodiazepines.

The GABA-potentiating effect of benzodiazepines seems to explain many of their actions. Thus GABA-enhancement in the hippocampus and cortex would lead to anticonvulsant effects; in the reticular formation and striatum to muscular relaxation; in arousal systems to sedative/hypnotic effects, and in the limbic system to anxiolytic effects. There is some evidence that different subtypes of GABA$_A$ receptors mediate each of these different actions (Sieghart 1989; Cooper *et al.* 1987; Stephenson 1987*b*).

A second class of GABA receptor, the GABA$_B$ receptor, also exists (Table 4.2) but appears to play a less prominent role in mediating GABA effects and does not include a benzodiazepine binding site. Other lower affinity binding sites for benzodiazepines, in the brain and in the periphery, have been demonstrated (File and Pellow 1983; Pellow and File 1984) but their pharmacological importance is not yet clear.

Table 4.2 The main classes of GABA receptors

	GABA$_A$	GABA$_B$
Common agonist	GABA	GABA
Selective agonist	muscimol	baclofen
Selective antagonist	bicuculline	saclofen
Effector	Cl$^-$ channel (activates)	K$^+$ channel (activates)
		Ca^{2+} channel (inhibits)
		adenylate cyclase ↓
Allosteric modulation	benzodiazepines*	?
	barbiturates	
	some convulsants	

*Benzodiazepines and other ligands shown in Table 4.3
References: Haefely (1990); *Trends in Pharmacological Sciences* (1990).

Benzodiazepine receptor ligands.   The benzodiazepine receptor proved to be even more complex that at first supposed when it was discovered that it also responds to a range of synthetic ligands which are not benzodiazepines (Table 4.3). Some of these compounds are agonists and produce classical benzodiazepine-like effects. Others comprise a spectrum of partial agonists and competitive antagonists. They have some

Table 4.3 Some benzodiazepine receptor ligands

Receptor activity	Ligands	Effects
Agonists	benzodiazepines[1] cyclopyrrolones zopiclone suriclone triazopyridazines	anxiolytic; anticonvulsant; hypnotic; muscle relaxant
Partial agonists/ competitive antagonists	imidazodiazepines pyrazoloquinolines beta-carbolines	some benzodiazepine actions, but not others; antagonize one or more benzodiazepine effects; combine agonist and antagonist properties
Antagonists	imidazodiazepines flumazenil	reverse benzodiazepine effects; few intrinsic effects.
Inverse agonists	beta carbolines polypeptides (DBI)[2]	anxiogenic; convulsant; stimulant

[1] Benzodiazepines have varying affinities for the benzodiazepine receptor.
[2] DBI: diazepam binding inhibitor (Costa *et al.* 1983).

benzodiazepine-like actions but not others, antagonize one or more benzodiazepine effects, or combine agonist and antagonist properties. Some (for example flumazenil) are almost pure competitive antagonists with little intrinsic activity. Yet others are termed 'inverse agonists' (Braestrup *et al.* 1983); they bind to benzodiazepine receptors but produce opposite, anxiogenic, stimulant, and convulsant effects.

It is thought that the GABA receptor can exist in high or low affinity states for GABA. The action of benzodiazepine agonists favours the high affinity state, thereby enhancing the opening of Cl^- channels by GABA, while inverse agonists favour the low affinity state, opposing Cl^- channel opening and preventing GABA inhibition. Pure antagonists prevent the action of both agonists and antagonists. Thus the benzodiazepine receptor is capable of mediating opposite effects brought about by allosteric modulations of the receptor in response to different ligands (Haefely 1990). The spectrum of activity exerted by the series of benzodiazepine ligands suggests that the various actions of the benzodiazepines may be separable and that it may be possible to develop compounds with specific anxiolytic, anticonvulsant, sedative or muscular relaxant properties.

The existence of benzodiazepine receptors in the body implies that there is a natural substance (or substances) with which they normally interact. Hence there has been a search for endogenous benzodiazepine receptor ligands. Various substances including a polypeptide, diazepam binding inhibitor, DBI (Costa *et al*. 1983), a beta-carboline, tribulin (Sandler 1982), and a benzodiazepine metabolite, *N*-desmethyldiazepam (Stephenson 1987*a*), have been isolated from human and animal tissues but their physiological significance is not known. It is possible that there are two sets of endogenous ligands, one with anxiolytic and one with anxiogenic properties, and that some anxiety states are characterized by dysfunction of these GABA-regulating mechanisms, but at present these ideas are speculative.

Of the synthetic benzodiazepine ligands, the most studied is flumazenil. This substance reverses benzodiazepine effects in animals and man and has little intrinsic activity (Hunkeler *et al*. 1981; Darragh *et al*. 1982, 1983). Some clinical applications of flumezenil, for example in benzodiazepine overdose, are reviewed by Ashton (1985). In benzodiazepine-dependent animals, flumazenil can precipitate withdrawal reactions, but File and Hitchcott (1990) suggest that under certain circumstances it can also reverse the anxiety and decreased seizure threshold associated with benzodiazepine withdrawal.

Adverse effects

The acute toxicity of benzodiazepines is low, probably because their effects are limited by the availability of GABA, but chronic long-term use may be associated with a wide range of adverse effects (Ashton 1986).

Oversedation.   Oversedation may occur as a dose-related extension of the pharmacological effects of benzodiazepines, although a degree of tolerance develops. Psychomotor performance may be impaired and benzodiazepine use may contribute to traffic accidents (Skegg *et al*. 1979; Betts and Birtle 1982). Oversedation is most marked in the elderly (Castledon *et al*. 1977) in whom drowsiness, inco-ordination and ataxia leading to falls and confusional states may result even from small doses (Baldessarini 1985). Long-term benzodiazepine use may impair cognitive functioning (Lader 1987) and the learning of stress-coping strategies (Jenson *et al*. 1989; Gray 1987*b*). Amnesia can occur with single or multiple doses. It is debatable whether chronic benzodiazepine use may cause structural brain damage (Lader *et al*. 1984; Perera *et al*. 1987).

Disinhibition: paradoxical effects.   Occasionally benzodiazepines produce apparently stimulant effects, with aggressive, antisocial or hyperactive behaviour and exacerbation of seizures in epileptics (Rall and Schleifer 1980; Lader and Petursson 1981). Triazolam in high doses (0.5–1 mg) can produce a syndrome of severe anxiety, paranoia, hyperacusis, altered smell and taste, and paraesthesiae (*Drug and Therapeutics*

Bulletin 1979). These paradoxical effects, which are more common in anxious patients, have been attributed to disinhibition of behaviour previously suppressed by anxiogenic stimuli (Speth *et al.* 1980).

Affective reactions. Benzodiazepines can aggravate depression and provoke suicidal tendencies in depressed patients (Baldessarini 1985), and chronic benzodiazepine use can cause depression or 'emotional anaesthesia' in patients with no previous history of depressive disorder. On the other hand some patients experience euphoria, at least initially, and it is of interest that benzodiazepines have been found to have reinforcing properties in animals (Yanagita 1981; Chapter 5) and have abuse liability when used intravenously and orally in man (Griffiths *et al.* 1984).

Adverse effects in pregnancy. The teratogenic risks of benzodiazepines appear to be low (Beeley 1978), although congenital abnormalities mainly affecting the central nervous system have been reported in the infants of mothers who took high doses of benzodiazepines throughout pregnancy (Laegreid *et al.* 1987). The drugs readily traverse the placenta, are concentrated in fetal tissues since metabolism by the fetal liver is minimal, and can cause neonatal depression if given in late pregnancy (Stirrat and Beard 1973; Singh and Mirkin 1973). Infants exposed *in utero* may develop benzodiazepine withdrawal symptoms 2–3 weeks after birth. The drugs are also present in the mother's milk for some days after administration.

Metabolic, endocrine, and autonomic effects. Benzodiazepines may affect the central control of endocrine function. Decrease in plasma cortisol and increase in plasma prolactin and growth hormone concentrations have been reported following benzodiazepine administration (Beary *et al.* 1983; Petursson and Lader 1984).

Overdose and drug interactions. The effects of benzodiazepine overdose are reviewed by Ashton *et al.* (1989). Taken alone, benzodiazepines rarely produce serious effects. However, they depress the ventilatory response to carbon dioxide (Gilmartin *et al.* 1988) and in patients with obstructive pulmonary disease, benzodiazepines in moderate doses can cause carbon dioxide narcosis (Harvey 1985). Although depression of consciousness occurs after overdose, consciousness returns while blood concentrations are still very high, presumably because of the rapid development of tolerance, as in the case of alcohol (Chapter 6). Rebound insomnia and other benzodiazepine withdrawal effects occur during recovery from acute benzodiazepine overdose (Haider and Oswald 1970).

Benzodiazepines potentiate the depressant effects of other central nervous system depressants. These effects are mainly additive at the sites of action and can aggravate or precipitate respiratory failure, especially in the elderly or those with pulmonary disease. Benzodiazepines are involved in about 40 per cent of self-poisonings in the UK, usually in combination with other drugs (Proudfoot 1982).

Benzodiazepine dependence. Drug dependence in general is discussed in Chapter 6, and dependence on narcotic analgesics, alcohol, nicotine, and cocaine are described in Chapter 7. Benzodiazepine dependence is described here since it is closely related to the anxiolytic and hypnotic actions of the drugs.

Early experience with benzodiazepines suggested that dependence was rare (Marks 1978). It has since become clear, however, that dependence on benzodiazepines occurs readily and quickly in some patients and is not uncommon. Owen and Tyrer (1983) estimate that about one-third of patients taking benzodiazepines for six months become dependent, and some do so after only a few weeks of treatment (Murphy *et al.* 1984), while Kales *et al.* (1978) showed that withdrawal symptoms in the form of rebound insomnia can occur after administration of triazolam as a hypnotic for only 1 week. Some patients gradually escalate their dosage over time, but others become dependent while maintaining their original therapeutic dosage (Owen and Tyrer 1983). A few patients compulsively seek large doses of benzodiazepines in order to obtain euphoric effects and there is a growing tendency towards benzodiazepine abuse amongst multidrug abusers (Griffiths and Sannerud 1987). Present estimates suggest that perhaps half a million people in the UK are now dependent on benzodiazepines, and two or three million in the world (Owen and Tyrer 1983). Nearly 70 per cent of these are women. At present it is not possible to predict which patients are likely to become dependent, apart from those with a history of dependence on other drugs (Marks 1978). Tyrer *et al.* (1983) suggest that patients with a 'passive-dependent' personality type are vulnerable, and Ashton (1984) noted high scores for neuroticism in patients dependent on benzodiazepines.

(i) Benzodiazepine withdrawal syndrome. Drug withdrawal, or reduction in dosage, in patients who have become dependent on benzodiazepines gives rise to a definite abstinence syndrome, which can be of considerable severity and has similarities to the withdrawal reactions of other central nervous system depressant drugs which cause dependence (Chapter 6). The syndrome has been described by Petursson and Lader (1981*a, b,* 1984), Lader and Petursson (1981), Tyrer *et al.* (1983), Owen and Tyrer (1983), and Ashton (1984). Withdrawal symptoms may include all the psychological and somatic manifestations of anxiety mentioned in Chapter 3; these are often more severe than when benzodiazepines were first prescribed. In addition, new symptoms may emerge, including perceptual distortions, sensory hypersensitivity, muscle spasms, paraesthesiae and hallucinations. Rapid benzodiazepine withdrawal may precipitate convulsions and acute psychotic episodes. Withdrawal effects can occur in normal subjects as well as in patients with anxiety and insomnia.

The onset of the syndrome is related to the pharmacokinetic properties of the particular benzodiazepine involved. Withdrawal symptoms appear sooner on withdrawal from benzodiazepines with short elimination half-lives and are delayed after withdrawal from those with long half-lives. Increased anxiety between doses may occur with rapidly eliminated benzodiazepines such as triazolam (Oswald 1989) and alprazolam (Herman *et al.* 1987) and is probably a 'withdrawal' effect. The time course of the withdrawal syndrome is often characterized by the early appearance of acute anxiety and psychotic symptoms (1–2 weeks after withdrawal) (Murphy *et al.* 1984) followed by a prolonged period of gradually diminishing, but sometimes protracted, psychological and somatic symptoms (Ashton 1984, 1991*a*).

Possible mechanisms of the benzodiazepine withdrawal syndrome are discussed by Nutt (1990*b*). Animal work suggests that chronic benzodiazepine administration shifts the affinity of the $GABA_A$ receptor towards the inverse agonist state, with decreased affinity for GABA. This shift results in benzodiazepine tolerance, and cessation of benzodiazepines once the shift has occurred exposes a state of relative GABA underactivity. The consequent lack of GABA-inhibition allows a surge in output of other neurotransmitters normally controlled by GABA, including noradrenaline, serotonin, dopamine, acetylcholine, and others. Withdrawal symptoms probably result from excessive actions of various excitatory transmitters in specific brain areas.

In many patients regularly taking benzodiazepines, symptoms of withdrawal occur while they are still taking the drugs without reduction in dosage (Ashton 1984, 1987*c*; Cohen 1989). Thus, some patients complain simultaneously both of adverse effects attributable to benzodiazepine use and of benzodiazepine withdrawal phenomena. Such a merging of the symptomatology possibly reflects uneven development of tolerance to the various actions of benzodiazepines, with some types of benzodiazepine or GABA receptors undergoing adaptive changes more quickly than others.

Since dependence takes time to develop, it is best prevented by limiting the duration of benzodiazepine use and it is advisable to restrict regular benzodiazepine administration to periods of 7–14 days. The optimal method of withdrawing benzodiazepines in patients who have become dependent has not yet been determined; probably different regimes suit different patients and the management needs to be individually tailored. Various methods of slow dosage reduction combined with symptomatic treatment are described by Marks (1988). Nutt (1990*b*), File and Baldwin (1989), and Lader and Morton (1991) suggest that the judicious use of flumazenil, which is thought to reset the receptor shift induced by ben-zodiazepines and/or to antagonize endogenous anxiolytic ligands, may prove to be of therapeutic value.

Barbiturates

The barbiturates are used as anaesthetic agents (short acting bar-biturates), anticonvulsants (phenobarbitone and its derivatives), and rarely as hepatic enzyme inducers. They have a long history as sedative/hypnotics, but such a use is no longer recommended because of serious disadvantages including low therapeutic index, frequency of death from overdose, high incidence of drug dependence, and frequency of drug interactions. Nevertheless, a large population of patients, perhaps over half a million in the UK (Rogers *et al.* 1981), most of them elderly, still regularly take barbiturates as hypnotics.

Pharmacokinetics

The pharmacokinetics and actions of barbiturates are described by Harvey (1985) and by Rogers *et al.* (1981). The sodium salts are well absorbed and widely distributed in the body, being concentrated in fatty tissues from which they are only slowly eliminated (Table 4.4). Metabolism is mainly by hepatic microsomal enzymes; repeated administration of barbiturates rapidly causes enzyme induction which leads to pharmacokinetic tolerance (Chapter 6) and may also give rise to drug interactions.

Table 4.4   Some barbiturates and non-barbiturate hypnotics

Drug	Elimination half-life (h)	Hepatic enzyme induction
Barbiturate hypnotics		
amylobarbitone	17–34	+ +
pentobarbitone	21–46	+ +
phenobarbitone	48–144	+ +
Barbiturate intravenous anaesthetics		
sodium thiopentone	6	
methohexitone	70–125 min	
Non-barbiturate hypnotics		
chloral derivatives	8*	+
chlormethiazole	1–4	0
Antihistamines		
promethazine	12	0
Zopiclone	5–6	0

*Trichlorethanol: common metabolite of chloral derivatives.

Actions

Sedative/hypnotic effects.   Barbiturates are potentially depressants of all excitable tissues. However, the central nervous system is the most sensitive to this effect and the drugs can therefore produce central nervous system depression in doses which have little peripheral effect. Within the central nervous system, the reticular formation is most sensitive to barbiturates and small doses, which hardly affect transmission in primary sensory pathways, depress reticular formation responses to sensory stimuli and raise its threshold to direct electrical stimulation (Bradley and Key 1958; Sharpless 1970). Barbiturates also inhibit some reticulo-limbic pathways (Tsuchiya and Kitagawa 1976). These actions reduce activity in both general and limbic arousal systems. The barbiturates produce anxiolytic effects in animals (Gray 1981a, 1982), but their effects on anxiety in man are inseparable from their sedative actions and they are inferior to benzodiazepines as anxiolytic agents. In spite of the exquisite sensitivity of the reticular formation, barbiturate effects on the brain are fairly unselective and only slightly larger doses also depress medullary vital centres. For this reason, the barbiturates have a low therapeutic index. Pain sensation, however, is relatively spared until the moment of unconsciousness, and in small doses barbiturates are hyperalgesic; hence they are not reliable hypnotics in the presence of pain. In some circumstances low doses can induce paradoxical excitement, probably due to suppression of inhibitory pathways.

(i) Effects on sleep. Hypnotic doses of barbiturates invariably produce dose-dependent alterations in sleep stages (Kay *et al*. 1976; Evans *et al*. 1968; Oswald 1980). The changes are similar to those produced by benzodiazepines and consist of a decrease in sleep latency, decrease in number of awakenings, and prolonged sleeping time. The duration of Stages 3 and 4 (SWS) is usually reduced, REMS latency prolonged, and total EMS activity decreased. Tolerance to the hypnotic effects of barbiturates develops rapidly.

(ii) Rebound insomnia. Rebound insomnia, which may last for several weeks, occurs on discontinuation of barbiturates after regular use. The symptoms are similar to those described for benzodiazepines and include a decrease in total sleep time, increased number of wakenings, and nightmares or vivid dreams associated with increased REMS activity. As with benzodiazepines, these rebound effects lead to continuation of use and form part of the withdrawal syndrome in barbiturate-dependent subjects. With short acting barbiturates, a compensatory rebound occurs in the latter part of each night while the drug is still being taken.

(iii) Hangover effects. Since most of the barbiturates have long elimination half lives, hangover effects and residual psychomotor impairment are common, especially in the elderly.

Anaesthetic effects. The anaesthetic effects of barbiturates are an extension of the sedative/hypnotic effects. Barbiturates depress respiration in a dose-related manner: at hypnotic concentrations, respiration is depressed but probably little more than during normal sleep (Harvey 1985); at anaesthetic concentrations, the respiratory response to both carbon dioxide and to hypoxia are reduced (Marshall and Wollman 1980). Barbiturates also depress cardiovascular centres in the medulla and have ganglion blocking effects. In sufficient concentration, they depress myocardial tissue.

Anticonvulsant effects. Most barbiturates have anticonvulsant properties, but phenobarᴏitone and its congener primidone exert maximal anticonvulsant effects in subhypnotic doses and are therefore suitable for the treatment of epilepsy. They are effective in general tonic, clonic, and cortical focal seizures. Barbiturates limit the spread of seizure activity in the brain and also elevate seizure threshold.

Mechanisms of action

It now appears likely that many of the effects of barbiturates are explained by their interaction with specific binding sites on the $GABA_A$ post-synaptic receptor complex (Fig. 4.2; Braestrup and Nielson 1980). In low doses, barbiturates increase the affinity of this receptor for both benzodiazepines and GABA, and enhance the binding of these substances at their specific sites (Harvey 1985). Endogenous benzodiazepines are possibly involved in this action. In higher therapeutic (and toxic) doses, barbiturates bind to the $GABA_A$ receptor complex at specific sites which are directly linked to the chloride channel, prolonging the opening of this channel, causing a long-lasting post-synaptic neuronal hyperpolarization.

Adverse effects

Oversedation, paradoxical stimulant effects, affective reactions and effects in pregnancy are similar to those described for benzodiazepines.

Drug interactions. Drug interactions with barbiturates are common, largely because of hepatic enzyme induction. The activity of other drugs metabolized by these enzymes is reduced; conversely, the metabolism of barbiturates may be slowed by enzyme inhibition with monoamine oxidase inhibitors. Barbiturates also have additive effects with other central nervous system depressants.

Overdose. Barbiturate overdose still accounts for a number of deaths each year in the UK. Barbiturates have a low therapeutic index and the hypnotic dose is only about a tenth of that required to produce fatal respiratory depression. Furthermore, tolerance to the respiratory depressant effects develops to a lesser degree than to the sedative/hypnotic effects, so that as tolerance increases, the therapeutic index becomes even lower. Death usually occurs from respiratory failure, often with associated cardiovascular collapse and renal failure.

Tolerance, dependence, abuse. Pharmacokinetic tolerance to barbiturates, due to hepatic enzyme induction, has already been mentioned. Pharmacodynamic tolerance (Chapter 6) also occurs and is probably more important in relation to drug dependence. Tolerance to the sedative/hypnotic effects develops to a greater extent than to anticonvulsant and lethal effects. The development of tolerance leads to a tendency to escalate barbiturate dosage and to abstinence symptoms on drug withdrawal. In these circumstances barbiturate dependence rapidly develops.

In addition, barbiturates are frequently abused, although the incidence of this practice is hard to estimate. The number involved probably considerably exceeds that of opiate abusers. Barbiturate abuse often coexists with abuse of opiates, other sedatives, benzodiazepines, amphetamines, and cocaine. Like other drugs of abuse (Chapter 6), barbiturates have reinforcing properties in animals and can produce euphoria in man, especially when injected intravenously. Patterns of abuse are described by Jaffe (1980); they range from irregular short sprees of gross intoxication to the prolonged compulsive daily use of large doses. Chronic intoxication resembles alcohol intoxication, with general sluggishness, ataxia, dysarthria, irritability, and aggressiveness.

Withdrawal of barbiturates from dependent individuals produces an abstinence syndrome, the severity of which depends on previous dosage and degree of tolerance. Rebound insomnia, and psychological symptoms, such as anxiety and difficulty in concentration, are common and have been reported in many studies after only about 5 weeks of therapeutic doses (Oswald 1980; Evans *et al.* 1968; Ogunremi *et al.* 1973). These symptoms may persist for some weeks. More severe withdrawal symptoms include anxiety, restlessness, hallucinations, weakness, hypotension, gastrointestinal symptoms, delirium, and cardiovascular collapse or status epilepticus which may be fatal. The syndrome is similar to the alcohol withdrawal syndrome (Chapter 7) and is described more fully by Jaffe (1980).

Other drugs used in insomnia and anxiety

Hypnotics and sedatives

Chloral derivatives (chloral hydrate, triclofos, dichloralphenazone). In therapeutic doses, these are effective hypnotics, but cause respiratory and cardiovascular depression in overdose. Their hypnotic actions are similar to those of barbiturates and benzodiazepines and they probably interact with GABA$_A$ receptors (Cowen and Nutt 1982). They can produce dependence and an abstinence syndrome on withdrawal.

Chlormethiazole.   Chlormethiazole has hypnotic and anticonvulsant properties. Because of its short half-life (Table 4.4), it is relatively free of hangover effects and has been recommended for use in the elderly. It has also been used in the management of alcohol and narcotic withdrawal, but there appears to be a considerable danger of dependence, especially when large doses are used (Exton-Smith and McLean 1979; Wheatley 1981). An action on the GABA$_A$ receptor site, similar to that of barbiturates, has been demonstrated (Harrison and Simmonds 1983; Cross *et al.* 1989).

Zopiclone.   Zopiclone, a cyclopyrrolone (Table 4.3), is a non-benzodiazepine which binds to benzodiazepine receptors and has the full range of benzodiazepine agonist effects (*Lancet* 1990c). It is effective as a hypnotic, but like benzodiazepines can cause dependence, rebound insomnia (Dorian *et al.* 1983) and adverse psychiatric reactions (Committee on Safety of Medicines 1990). There have been few long-term studies and the drug is recommended for short-term use only.

Promethazine.   Promethazine is a phenothiazine derivative which is a histamine (H$_1$) receptor blocker and has antipruritic, anticholinergic, and sedative effects. It has a slow onset of action (1.5–3 h) and occasionally causes excitement rather than sedation. The hypnotic action probably results from central histamine (H$_1$) receptor antagonism (Chapter 2) combined with a mild neuroleptic effect (Chapter 14). Some phenothiazines with antipsychotic actions also have hypnotic effects (for example chlorpromazine); these drugs do not alter normal sleep stages and do not appear to cause rebound on withdrawal, but their general use as hypnotics is limited by adverse effects.

Other drugs used in anxiety

β-adrenoceptor antagonists.   Many of the somatic manifestations of anxiety, such as palpitations and tremor, are due to increased sympathetic activity with excessive activation of peripheral β-adrenoceptors. These symptoms can be reduced by β-adrenoceptor antagonists in normal subjects under stress (James *et al.* 1977; Taggart *et al.* 1973; *Lancet* 1985) and in patients with anxiety syndromes (Tyrer and Lader 1974; Turner 1976). By controlling peripheral sympathetic overactivity, these drugs may interrupt the vicious circle by which somatic symptoms reinforce psychic symptoms, but they have little effect on the subjective emotion of anxiety.

Clonidine.   Redmond (1987) suggested that pathological anxiety can result from functional overactivity of the locus coeruleus. Clonidine, which decreases the firing rate and release of noradrenaline from locus coeruleus neurones by stimulation of α_2-noradrenergic receptors, has been used with some success in treating anxiety associated with opiate and alcohol withdrawal (Lal and Fielding 1983; *Lancet* 1980; Keshavan and Crammer 1985) but it has not proved successful in benzodiazepine withdrawal (Joyce *et al.* 1990).

Serotonin receptor agonist/antagonists. A number of drugs acting on serotonin receptors have anxiolytic properties. *Buspirone* is a mixed agonist/antagonist at 5-HT$_{1A}$ receptors (Fozard 1987; Chopin and Briley 1987; Traber and Glaser 1987) and also has antagonist actions at presynaptic dopamine and benzodiazepine receptors (Eison and Eison 1984; Eison *et al.* 1986; Davis *et al.* 1988). It depresses the firing rate of dorsal raphe neurones but increases activity in the locus coeruleus (Dourish *et al.* 1986). Clinically, it has anxiolytic effects comparable with those of benzodiazepines, but without sedative/hypnotic, anticonvulsant or muscle relaxant effects (Levine 1988; Beaumont 1988; Lader 1989). However, the onset of action is delayed for about 3 weeks (Murphy *et al.* 1989) and in some patients it produces dysphoria and anxiogenic effects. Buspirone does not appear to produce dependence or a withdrawal syndrome, although most clinical studies have been of limited duration. The drug shows no cross-tolerance with benzodiazepines and does not alleviate anxiety associated with benzodiazepine withdrawal (Lader and Olajide 1987; Ashton *et al.* 1990). Antagonists of 5-HT$_{1C}$; 5-HT$_2$ and 5-HT$_3$ receptors also appear to have anxiolytic effects and are under development.

Antidepressants. A number of tricyclic antidepressant drugs (Chapter 12) have anxiolytic effects. They appear to be as effective as benzodiazepines in generalized anxiety and superior to benzodiazepines in panic disorders and agoraphobia (Tyrer 1989), and are also of value in depressive states associated with anxiety. Monoamine oxidase inhibitors are also effective in phobic and panic disorders (Shader *et al.* 1982; Rifkin and Siris 1984). Antidepressants may initially exacerbate anxiety, followed by an improvement in 2–3 weeks. The later improvement may be due to down-regulation of postsynaptic monoamine receptors or to a stabilizing effect at monoaminergic synapses, as discussed in Chapter 12.

Antipsychotic drugs. Some antipsychotic drugs (Chapter 14), have sedative, anticholinergic, and anxiolytic effects and may on occasion be of short-term use in severe anxiety disorders associated with panic, anxiety provoked by psychotomimetic agents, and autonomic and anxiety symptoms associated with the abstinence syndromes of central nervous system depressants.

Drug treatment in insomnia and anxiety

As discussed in Chapter 3, insomnia has many causes, and hypnotic drugs are not always, perhaps rarely, indicated (Hartmann 1980). The Marks and Nicholson (1984) reported the results of a conference on drugs and insomnia held at the National Institutes of Health, Bethesda. It was suggested that, for purposes of practical management, insomnia can be considered as transient, short-term, or chronic. Transient insomnia is due to an alteration in sleep conditions. Only occasionally is a hypnotic required; a rapidly eliminated preparation, used on a couple of occasions only, is recommended. Short-term insomnia may be due to emotional or physical stress. A hypnotic may be given for preferably not more than a week or two and ideally taken intermittently rather than regularly. A rapidly eliminated drug is usually appropriate, although a longer acting drug, such as diazepam, may be better if there is marked daytime stress. Chronic insomnia is usually secondary to other conditions, but in selected cases with no apparent cause the use of a hypnotic may be considered, in combination with general measures for improving sleep hygiene. Longer-acting benzodiazepines are thought to be most useful, but dosage should be intermittent (one night in three) and temporary (not more than a month).

The same principles apply to the drug treatment of anxiety. In the short term, anxiolytic drugs can be useful (Tyrer 1989) but it is doubtful whether drugs can ever provide a long-term solution for the control of anxiety states. In the long term, non-drug treatments, such as behavioural and cognitive therapy and anxiety management training, are probably more effective for neurotic disorders (Tyrer 1989). Such measures encourage learning, a process involving changes in the strength of synaptic connections (Chapter 8), to produce behaviours which are better adapted to the environment than the taking of exogenous pharmacological agents. Furthermore, any drug which effectively alleviates the distress of anxiety or insomnia is likely to affect reward and punishment systems in the brain (Chapter 5) and thus to carry a potential for producing drug dependence (Chapter 6), without altering the fundamental causes of the anxiety reaction.

Central nervous system stimulants

It may be significant that, compared with depressants, central nervous system stimulants are little used clinically. Yet stimulants in the form of tea, coffee, and caffeinated drinks are taken regularly by almost the whole population from childhood onwards. Chronic use of some central nervous system stimulants can lead to drug dependence. This may occur with amphetamine and to some extent with caffeine. Cocaine and nicotine are described in Chapter 7; psychotomimetic drugs in Chapter 14.

Sympathomimetic amines

Directly acting sympathomimetic amines act as central nervous system stimulants by activating receptors in the widely distributed noradrenergic pathways concerned in arousal (Chapter 2). *Adrenaline, noradrenaline, and isoprenaline* do not readily enter the brain when administered systemically in therapeutic doses, but may nevertheless produce restlessness and apprehension. The potent peripheral cardiovascular and metabolic effects of these drugs may contribute to their subjective effects. Indirectly acting sympathomimetic drugs act largely by releasing endogenous catecholamines; their actions are similar to directly acting agents but they penetrate the brain more readily.

Amphetamine

Amphetamine is a powerful central nervous system stimulant; the D-isomer (*dexamphetamine*) is more potent in this respect than the L-isomer. *Methamphetamine* and *methyl phenidate* are structurally related to amphetamine and are pharmacologically similar. Other less potent congeners, including *ephedrine, pseudoephedrine, phenylpropanolamine, propylhexidrine*, and *phenylephrine*, are available in several 'over-the-counter' preparations sold as nasal decongestants, cough and cold remedies, and slimming aids.

Actions on the central nervous system. The psychological actions of amphetamine in man depend greatly on dosage, individual personality characteristics, and the prevailing mood and expectations at the time of administration. Typically, a single oral dose of 10–30 mg produces a feeling of increased alertness with heightened self-confidence, and increased motor and speech activity. There is often an elevation of mood which may proceed to elation and euphoria (high doses and especially intravenous administration produces a 'high' which may encourage drug abuse; Chapter 7). Feelings of fatigue are postponed and the desire for sleep reduced. Effects on performance are variable. In mental or psychomotor tasks, responses may be more rapid, concentration improved and errors reduced; sometimes, however, errors are increased in spite of more rapid performance; memory may be improved or impaired. Physical activity in sport may be improved and fatigue postponed. The enhancing effects on performance are more marked in the presence of fatigue or sleep deprivation.

The effects of amphetamine on the waking EEG consist of desynchronization and a shift towards faster frequencies. The effects on sleep consist of a considerable reduction in REMS, a reduction in SWS, and a decrease in total sleep time. On discontinuation, there is a marked rebound, especially in REMS, which may last for many weeks (Oswald 1980). Amphetamine depresses appetite and has been used as an anorectic in the treatment of obesity. However, tolerance occurs rapidly and the effect in short-lived.

Sites and mechanisms of action. Amphetamine has stimulant effects throughout the nervous system. It facilitates monosynaptic and poly-synaptic transmission in the spinal cord and stimulates the medullary respiratory centre and lateral hypothalamic areas concerned with the control of feeding behaviour. It also stimulates the reticular activating system, where it lowers the threshold for arousal by electrical stimulation and reverses the depressant effects of barbiturates (Fig. 2.3). These effects are thought to be largely due to release of catecholamines from nerve terminals since they can be attenuated by depletion of monoamine stores with reserpine or 6-hydroxydopamine and by drugs which prevent catecholamine synthesis (Candy and Key 1977; Langer and Arbilla 1984). Amphetamine may also have some direct stimulant action on noradrenergic receptors and some reuptake-blocking effect. In addition to releasing noradrenaline, amphetamine releases dopamine from dopaminergic nerve terminals. Some of its effects, including aggravation of schizophrenic symptoms (Chapter 14), may be due to increased dopaminergic activity. There is evidence in animals that the rewarding effects are mediated in the nucleus accumbens (Carr and White 1986). In high doses, serotonin is also released and this may account for perceptual disturbances and add to psychotic symptoms.

Adverse effects. Acute overdose with amphetamine produces a toxic psychosis with extreme restlessness, tremor, insomnia, panic, confusion, irritability, and delirium. Psychotic features such as paranoia, hallucinations, and aggressiveness with suicidal or homicidal tendencies may be prominent. Cardiovascular effects include headache, pallor or flushing, palpitations, cardiac arrhythmias, anginal pain, and hyper- or hypotension with cardiovascular collapse. Gastrointestinal symptoms include dry mouth, nausea, vomiting, diarrhoea, and abdominal cramps. Death may occur from coma, convulsions, or cerebral haemorrhage. Chronic intoxication may produce a schizophreniform psychosis similar to that produced by cocaine (Chapter 7).

Tolerance develops to the anorexic and euphoric effects of amphetamines and may lead to increasing dosage. Chronic abusers develop tolerance to the lethal effects and daily dosage of 1700 mg has been reported (Weiner 1980*b*). Nevertheless, tolerance to the psychic effects is much less and a toxic psychosis often appears after weeks or months of continued use. Cessation of amphetamine use produces a withdrawal syndrome characterized by depression, hypersomnia with increased REMS, hyperphagia, and debility. Amphetamine dependence is similar to cocaine dependence and is discussed further in Chapter 7.

Clinical use.   The main clinical use of amphetamines is for narcolepsy, in which they prevent narcoleptic attacks and often improve cataplexy. Hyperkinetic children, apparently paradoxically, may become calmer when given amphetamines. The drugs are occasionally useful for combating excessive sedation induced by barbiturates in epileptics. Methylphenidate and methamphetamine have similar uses. Concern has been expressed about the presence of sympathetic amines such as phenylpropranolamine in proprietary preparations (Whitehouse 1987; Miller 1989). Such substances are occasionally abused and can cause adverse effects similar to those of amphetamine, including hypertension, cardiac arrhythmias and neuropsychiatric effects.

Anorectic agents.   A number of congeners of amphetamine have anorectic effects and have been used in the management of obesity. These include *diethylpropion, phentermine, fenfluramine, and mazindol.* The actions of these drugs are similar to those of amphetamine and the anorectic effect is due to an action on hypothalamic centres where these drugs cause release of monoamines and also have a reuptake blocking effect. Fenfluramine releases mainly serotonin and on chronic use can cause central serotonin depletion. Mazindol appears to release mainly dopamine. The drugs also have general stimulant effects on the brain and cardiovascular system, although less than amphetamines. They all, to a greater or lesser extent, affect sleep and mood, and can give rise to tolerance, dependence, and a withdrawal syndrome, although this is much less likely than with amphetamine. Fenfluramine has been shown to reduce REMS and SWS, increase intrasleep restlessness, and to cause rebound effects on sleep and depression of mood on withdrawal (Lewis *et al.* 1971; Oswald *et al.* 1971). Nightmares appear with increasing dosage (Mullen and Wilson 1974).

Pemoline is a structurally unrelated drug which has a central stimulant action; it has been used for reversing the effects of central nervous system depressants, for minimal brain dysfunction in children, and for improving alertness in senile dementia.

Xanthines

Theophylline, caffeine.   Theophylline and caffeine are chemically related plant alkaloids which are well absorbed from the gut and metabolized by the liver. They are potent central nervous system stimulants and have in addition many peripheral actions. Caffeine has virtually no therapeutic uses, although it is widely taken in tea, cocoa, chocolate, coffee, and coca cola, and is incorporated into several 'over-the-counter' preparations. Theophylline preparations are mainly used in medicine for their effects on the respiratory system and effects on the nervous system are usually unwanted.

The central actions of caffeine include an increased feeling of alertness, increased capacity for sustained intellectual performance, decreased reaction time, and increased magnitude of EEG evoked potentials (Ashton *et al.* 1974). Typists are said to work faster with fewer errors, but some tasks requiring fine psychomotor skills may be adversely affected by doses equivalent to one to three cups of coffee or 85–250 mg caffeine (Rall 1980). With increasing doses and in sensitive subjects, xanthines cause more pronounced central nervous stimulation with anxiety, restlessness, insomnia, tremor, hyperaesthesia, and release of catecholamines (Robertson *et al.* 1978). Stimulant effects on the heart, decreased peripheral vascular resistance, diuresis, and relaxation of bronchial smooth muscle are among the peripheral actions, especially of theophylline.

Sites and mechanisms of action.   Sites of action in the brain include the reticular formation and the medullary respiratory centres, in which sensitivity to the stimulant effects of carbon dioxide is enhanced and the respiratory depressant effects of barbiturates and opioids reversed. The xanthines also produce emesis by a central effect. The stimulant effects may result from an increased turnover of monoamines in the brain and block of receptors for adenosine (Rall 1980; Snyder 1981). Williams (1984) suggests that adenosine, a nucleoside with hypnogenic actions, may be a physiological modulator of central arousal systems.

Adverse effects.   Acute toxic effects include signs of intense central nervous system stimulation with excitement, delirium, sensory distur-bances, and focal and general convulsions which may be refractory to anticonvulsant agents. Vomiting is prominent and cardiovascular effects, including cardiac arrhythmias may occur. Such toxicity is rare with caffeine but less so with theophylline. The chronic ingestion of moderate to large amounts of coffee may occasionally give rise to headaches and somatic and psychological reactions similar to anxiety neurosis (Greden 1974). Patients with panic disorders are particularly sensitive to the anxiogenic effects of caffeine (Boulenger *et al.* 1984; Lee *et al.* 1985), and it may also exacerbate schizophrenic and manic-depressive symptoms (De Freitas and Schwartz 1979; Greden *et al.* 1978; Mikkelson 1978).

In heavy chronic users (12–15 cups of coffee/day) caffeine displays all the characteristics of a drug of abuse (Chapter 7). Double blind studies in which the dosage was manipulated have shown that caffeine is reinforcing in man and can produce tolerance and physical dependence with an abstinence syndrome of dysphoria, headache, lethargy, irritability, poor concentration, and anxiety (Griffiths *et al*. 1986; Griffiths and Woodson 1988). Other health hazards (reviewed by Ashton 1987*b*) are mostly associated with chronic use of high doses.

Part II
Reward and punishment

5. Reward and punishment systems

The idea of a goal-directed arousal system in the brain (Chapter 2) implies the existence of some mechanism for selecting appropriate goals, for initiating the behaviours required to achieve them, and for signalling when they have been attained. If a goal proves favourable for survival in the prevailing circumstances, it is advantageous to reinforce behaviour leading to it; if the goal proves to be unfavourable, behaviour leading to it must be suppressed and avoidance action taken in future. Such a signalling system may be provided by certain 'reward' and 'punishment' pathways in the brain discovered by Olds and Milner (1954). These are closely integrated with arousal systems and with learning and memory, and appear to be fundamental for motivation, and for goal-seeking and avoidance behaviour. They are thought to form the basis for instinctive drives such as hunger, thirst, and sex, and are probably the substrate of more complex emotional/cognitive states such as hope and disappointment.

Reward systems

Intracranial self-stimulation

Olds and Milner (1954), and Olds (1956, 1977) reported a series of experiments showing that rats will work to obtain electrical stimulation through electrodes implanted at specific sites in the brain. When allowed to stimulate themselves by pressing a lever, they would sometimes do so at the rate of over 100 times a minute for hours on end. The animals appeared to like the stimulation and it seemed that activity in certain parts of the brain generated a pleasurable or rewarding sensation. Furthermore, motivation for self-stimulation was so strong that the rats would learn to perform various tasks such as traversing complex mazes in order to obtain it. When food reward and the opportunity for intracranial self-stimulation were both restricted, animals preferred the stimulation, even at the cost of starvation (Routtenberg 1978). Such findings suggested that the effects of intracranial self-stimulation and food reward were similar and that rewarding stimulation sites were located in neural pathways subserving reinforcement of goal-directed behaviour in the natural state (Redgrave and Dean 1981).

The above type of self-stimulation behaviour was elicited most strik-ingly when the electrodes were implanted in the lateral hypothalamus, an area known to be related to feeding mechanisms. However, with some electrode placements responses are only obtained if the rats are motivated by sexual arousal rather than by hunger. If multiple sites for stimulation are provided, there is a tendency to alternate the self-stimulation from electrode to electrode and preferred sites may change depending on whether the animals are hungry or thirsty (Olds 1977; Redgrave and Dean 1981; Routtenberg 1978).

Sites which support intracranial self-stimulation have been found in all vertebrate species studied, including man, and patients describe different sensations according to electrode locations (Heath 1964; Redgrave and Dean 1981). These results suggest that there may be a complex of rewar-ding pathways in the brain subserving different types of reinforcement behaviour.

Anatomical sites

Anatomical locations from which various types of self-stimulation behaviour can be obtained have been mapped in many investigations reviewed by Redgrave and Dean (1981) and Routtenberg (1978). Table

Table 5.1 Some sites which support intracranial self-stimulation in various animal species

Brain area	Sites which support self-stimulation	
Forebrain	frontal cortex; olfactory nucleus; nucleus accumbens; septal area; amygdaloid nucleus; hypothalamus	entorhinal cortex; caudate nucleus; entopeduncular nucleus; hippocampus; ventral and medial thalamus; median forebrain bundle; dorsal noradrenergic bundle
Midbrain and brainstem	ventral tegmental area; raphe nuclei; superior cerebellar peduncle; mesencephalic nucleus of trigeminal nerve	substantia nigra; nucleus coeruleus; periaqueductal grey matter
Cerebellum	deep cerebellar nuclei	other cerebellar areas
Medulla	motor nucleus of trigeminal nerve; nucleus of tractus solitarius	

5.1 and Fig. 5.1 show many of the large number of sites which have been implicated. It is clear that self-stimulation sites are distributed widely in the brain, from the frontal lobes to the medulla, and that they include areas of very different function, from sensory processing to motor activity. Self-stimulation is also supported from sites in the fibre tracts connecting many of these areas, notably the median forebrain bundle. This runs in the lateral hypothalamus and carries ascending projections from the brainstem nuclei, including the locus coeruleus and raphe nuclei, to the diencephalon and telencephalon, as well as descending projections from the median forebrain. Routtenberg and Santos-Anderson (1977) suggest that the prefrontal cortex is vital to the intracranial self-stimulation system, and point out that it is the origin of fibre tracts which run through many self-stimulation loci throughout the neuraxis and that these pathways intermingle with the median forebrain bundle at the level of the hypothalamus. At least five well-established areas for self-stimulation lie in the path of the frontal cortex descending fibre system (Fig. 5.1).

Most, if not all, of the sites which support self-stimulation have anatomical connections with limbic structures, where the emotional, autonomic, and motor responses appropriate to reward may be generated. Many of these same pathways are also involved in arousal and in learning and memory systems. The discovery of brain rewarding areas seems to hold the key for understanding the normal processes of motivation, reinforcement, and learning. Nevertheless, intracranial self-stimulation itself remains an enigma: the exact neural circuitry involved, and the relation of this strange activity to physiological behaviour is far from clear.

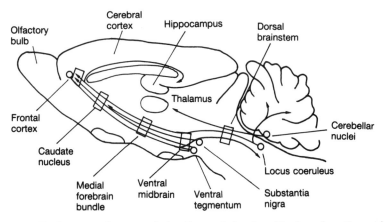

Fig. 5.1 Pathways of reward in the rat brain. Circles: location of cell bodies; rectangles: regions where reliable self-stimulation is obtained. (From Routtenberg 1978, by kind permission of W.H. Freeman and Co.)

Neurotransmitters

Noradrenaline

At first it seemed likely that noradrenaline was crucially involved in brain stimulation reward. Sites which elicit self-stimulation coincide with histological maps of noradrenergic nerve distribution (Stein *et al.* 1977; Stein 1978; Fig 2.7a). In particular, a dorsal noradrenergic pathway originates in the locus coeruleus and innervates the neocortex, cerebellum, hippocampus, and thalamus. A ventral pathway originates from noradrenaline-containing cells in the medulla and pons and innervates the hypothalamus and ventral parts of the limbic system. A periventricular pathway originates from various noradrenergic cell bodies and innervates the median regions of the thalamus and hypothalamus. All these pathways, and the locus coeruleus itself, support self-stimulation, and electrical stimulation of rewarding areas in the median forebrain bundle results in an increased liberation of noradrenaline and its metabolites from the lateral hypothalamus, while stimulation of neutral areas does not (Stein and Wise 1969). However, Routtenberg (1978) and Routtenberg and Santos-Anderson (1977) showed that complete destruction of the locus coeruleus had little effect on the rate of self-stimulation from an electrode in the dorsal brainstem in rats. At present the status of noradrenaline is uncertain: it seems to play a part in self-stimulation reward but it does not appear to be the only transmitter involved.

Dopamine

Although there are self-stimulation sites in the brain which are not near a dopaminergic system (Wise 1980), it seems likely that dopamine is an important transmitter in some reward pathways. There are dopaminergic fibres in the median forebrain bundle. These include the nigrostriatal pathway from substantia nigra to caudate nucleus and the mesolimbic pathway from the ventral tegmental area to the nucleus accumbens, olfactory tubercle, septal area, and frontal cortex (Redgrave and Dean 1981; Fig 2.7b). Neuronal mapping and stimulation studies of ventral tegmental and substantia nigra areas seem to indicate that self-stimulation is uniquely associated with dopamine containing cells (Wise 1980).

Pharmacological evidence supports the involvement of dopamine in reward systems. Drugs which inhibit dopamine synthesis or block dopamine receptors disrupt intracranial self-stimulation from a number of sites, even at the locus coeruleus, a predominantly noradrenergic structure. When dopamine blockade is limited to one hemisphere, self-stimulation responses are suppressed for that hemisphere but not for the other. Dopamine blockade also raises the electrical threshold for self-stimulation in a dose-dependent manner. Drugs which increase dopaminergic activity (amphetamines, cocaine) can increase rates of electrical self-stimulation, are avidly self-administered by animals, and are drugs of abuse in man (Chapters 6, 7). Stein and Belluzi (1987, 1988, 1989) demonstrated that the firing rate of individual neurones in the CA_1 area of isolated rat hippocampal brain slices could be modified by microinjection of dopamine or cocaine. The preparation was arranged so that increased rates of firing could trigger a self-microinjection of dopamine or cocaine into individual neurones. When delivered non-contingently these drugs had little effect on the firing rate of such cells, but after suitable priming, cells responded by increasing their firing rates contingently to trigger microinjections of cocaine or dopamine, but not placebo or opioid injections. Thus the firing of individual, isolated, cells could apparently be reinforced by dopaminergic drugs. It seems that even at the cellular level animals are programmed to seek reward. Other individual neurones in the CA_3 hippocampal fields responded similarly to the endogenous opioid dynorphin A (see below) but not to dopaminergic drugs. In parallel experiments in intact rats, dopamine and cocaine reinforced self-administration when injected into the same CA_1 hippocampal field but not into other hippocampal areas, while dynorphin A reinforced self-administration specifically by microinjection into the CA_3 hippocampal field.

These results led Stein (1989) to suggest that the functional unit of reward is a population of individual neurones ('hedonistic neurones') scattered around reward areas of the brain, which are responsive specifically to dopamine or opioids, and which are presumably connected to pathways controlling motivated behaviour. Phillips et al. (1989) and Phillips and Fibiger (1989) showed that there is an increase in dopamine metabolism, synthesis and release in the ventral tegmental area and nucleus accumbens during brain self-stimulation behaviour in rats, and that this increase is proportional to the stimulation rate and intensity. Dopaminergic pathways also appear to be involved in food rewards, both anticipation and ingestion (Blackburn et al. 1989; Royall and Klemm 1981) and to precopulatory and copulatory behaviour in male rats. Dopamine thus appears to be closely linked both with intracranial self-stimulation and with natural rewards, and dopamine release itself may be rewarding (Wise 1980). However, the increase in self-stimulation behaviour induced by dopaminergic drugs (amphetamine, cocaine) is blocked by naloxone (Schaefer and Michael 1990), suggesting that opioid mechanisms are also involved in dopaminergic reward functions.

Endogenous opioids

Both noradrenaline and dopamine have general effects in heightening arousal and increasing goal-seeking behaviour. However, reward can also be identified with reduction of arousal when the goal is achieved and satisfaction results. Stein (1978) suggested that the latter aspect of reward may be mediated by enkephalin or a related opioid peptide. In line with this suggestion is the observation that pharmacological agents which are apparently rewarding include not only stimulants such as amphetamine and cocaine, which release catecholamines, but also depressants such as morphine which act on endogenous opioid receptors.

In many brain areas the distribution of cell bodies containing endogenous opioids and of opioid binding sites overlaps very closely with that of catecholamine-containing cell areas, and rewarding sites (including the amygdala, locus coeruleus, pontine central grey, zona compacta of the substantia nigra, bed nucleus of the stria terminalis, and nucleus accumbens) contain beta-endorphin and other polypeptides as well as catecholamines (Elde *et al.* 1976; German and Bowden 1974). Thus, it seems likely that stimulation of the same rewarding areas releases both classes of neurotransmitters or modulators, and that both play an essential part in reward mechanisms. Stein (1978) reports experiments in which rats were found to work for injections of various opiates and opioids, including morphine and enkephalin, directly into the cerebral ventricles. The response was blocked by the specific opioid antagonist naloxone and also by noradrenaline depletion. Cooper (1984) notes that rats will also work to self-inject morphine specifically into the ventral tegmental area, and that this behaviour can be blocked by haloperidol, a dopamine receptor antagonist, or by 6-hydroxydopamine lesions of ascending dopaminergic pathways. Opioid-based reinforcement may therefore operate through catecholaminergic links, a possibility supported by Wise and Bozarth (1987). However, as described above, Stein (1989) found that the endogenous opioid dynorphin A (Table 5.2) could act directly as a reinforcer to isolated cells in the CA_3 hippocampal area, and it seems likely that opioid release may itself be reinforcing.

It seems reasonable to conclude that reward processes are regulated by the closely related joint actions of dopamine, possibly noradrenaline, and endogenous opioids, and Stein (1978) suggests that a normal action of endogenous opioids is to bring successful reward-seeking behaviour to a satisfying termination. A particular role for endogenous opioids in mediating social reward has been postulated by Panksepp (1981) and is discussed in Chapter 11.

Punishment systems

Anatomical pathways

Activity at certain sites in the brain appears to generate sensations that are strongly aversive; animals will work as avidly to avoid stimulation at these sites as they will to obtain stimulation at rewarding points (Olds and

Olds 1963; Delgado *et al*. 1954). A major anatomical pathway subserving aversive effects appears to be the periventricular system, a group of fibres running between the midbrain and thalamus with extensions into the hypothalamus, basal ganglia, limbic system, and cerebral cortex (Stein 1968). The median forebrain bundle and periventricular system probably interact, since they distribute fibres to various common sites along their paths (Criswell and Levitt 1975). A further pathway subserving aversion may originate in the dorsal raphe nuclei and distribute to periventricular regions of the brain, but some fibres run in the median forebrain bundle and terminate in various parts of the limbic system (Stein and Wise 1974). Destruction of either of these pathways results in a generalized defect in passive avoidance, so that an animal will no longer suppress behaviour that precipitates an aversive stimulus, such as an electric shock to the feet.

It has been suggested that these pathways act as a 'punishment' system favouring avoidance behaviour and also selecting the appropriate reward behaviour that will terminate a particular aversive state, for example, feeding in hunger, drinking in thirst, etc. (Stein 1971). The interaction between reward and punishment systems allows for many dimensions of reward and punishment. Activity in reward systems not only engenders active reward, but also inhibits activity in punishment systems. Conversely, activity in punishment pathways is positively aversive and also inhibits activity in reward pathways. Presumably, there can be innumerable degrees of partial inhibition or excitation in the different pathways, resulting in finely graded shades of reward/punishment activity. The arrangement appears to be similar to that described for the reciprocally connected arousal and sleep mechanisms in the brain (Chapter 2). Reward and punishment systems are also closely integrated with learning and memory systems (Chapter 8). Thus, lack of expected reward, as well as active punishment, is unpleasant; similarly, lack of expected punishment, as well as active pleasure, is rewarding. The hippocampal comparator system described in relation to anxiety neurosis (Chapter 3) is thought to be involved in forming the expectation of reward or punishment as a result of learning.

Neurotransmitters

Acetylcholine

The periventricular system appears to be at least partly cholinergic (Stein 1968). The deficit of passive avoidance resulting from destruction of this system can be reversed by local instillation of cholinergic drugs, such as carbachol or acetylcholine, while the local application of anticholinergic drugs, such as atropine, produces similar effects to surgical destruction.

Cholinergic systems are also closely involved in learning and memory (Chapter 8), and it is likely that certain aspects of these functions which

require suppression of behaviour are mediated through the periventricular system (Criswell and Levitt 1975). As already mentioned, the
periventricular system communicates with the limbic circuit, and many
limbic structures receive innervation from both the periventricular
system and the median forebrain bundle. Thus, together the two systems
can be envisaged to promote the seeking of reward and the suppression
of punished behaviour.

Other neurotransmitters may also mediate aversive effects in periventricular structures. From experiments involving the local injection of
various agonists and antagonists into the central grey and medial
hypothalamus, Schmitt *et al.* (1984) conclude that GABA, excitatory
amino acids, and opioids may all interact to modulate aversive reactions
in the rat.

Serotonin

The fibres from the raphe nuclei which run in the median forebrain
bundle are serotonergic (Fig 2.7c). Stein and Wise (1974) suggest that this
system acts antagonistically to the median forebrain bundle reward system and that goal-directed behaviour is reciprocally regulated through
noradrenergic and serotonergic pathways here. Thus, rewarding intracranial self-stimulation in the lateral hypothalamus is facilitated by the
intraventricular injection of noradrenaline, but suppressed by serotonin.
It is thought that the anxiolytic effects of benzodiazepines and other
anxiolytic drugs are exerted at least partly by decreasing activity in
serotonergic punishment pathways, and that activity in these pathways
is increased in anxiety.

Emotional components of reward and punishment

Reward and punishment systems are thought to be involved not only
with certain types of behaviour, but also with their subjective accompaniments or mood. Thus, rewarding events may presumably elicit a
range of pleasurable feelings (joy, contentment, hope, repletion), and
aversive events a range of unpleasant feelings (pain, fear, disgust, guilt,
depression). Omission of expected rewards or punishments may result in
other emotions (disappointment, relief) (Stein *et al.* 1977). The various
neurotransmitters presumably interact in complex ways and through
different pathways to involve particular emotions, and individuals may
differ in their sensitivity to reward and punishment (Gray 1981*b*).

Pain systems

A large component of the punishment mechanisms must be provided by
the systems responsible for signalling pain and nociception. Indeed, pain

and fear of pain are the strongest of punishing stimuli, and the same limbic structures involved in the reward and punishment systems described
above also provide the neural basis for the aversive drive and affect that
comprise the motivational dimensions of pain (Melzack 1986). Pain
systems are reviewed by Yaksh and Hammond (1982), Fields (1987), and
Melzack and Wall (1988).

Pain sensation

Pain is a complex experience resulting from variable interactions between
physical, emotional, and rational components. The physical component
(sensory-discriminative) is supplied by the nociceptive system described
below; the emotional component (motivational-affective) involves the
limbic system, including the punishment pathways; the rational component (cognitive-evaluative) is derived from the cerebral cortex. Excitatory
and inhibitory feedback systems link all components.

Two types of physical pain sensation are recognized: (a) *first pain* is
sharp or pricking, rapid in onset and brief in duration, well localized, and
can only be elicited from the skin, and (b) *second pain* is burning in
character, delayed in onset (up to 1 s after the stimulus) but prolonged,
poorly localized, and may be elicited from both skin and deep structures.
The reflex response to first pain is a phasic withdrawal reaction, whilst
that to second pain is a slowly developing tonic muscular contraction
(guarding or rigidity). First pain is responsible for withdrawal reflexes
and protects the body from injury; second pain probably only occurs in
the presence of tissue damage and may serve to splint or rest the affected
part. It is interesting that potent analgesic drugs such as morphine have
little effect on first pain in subanaesthetic doses.

In clinical and experimental settings, it is important to distinguish
between *pain threshold* and *pain tolerance*. The intensity of a stimulus
required to be perceived as painful (threshold) is variable, but the intensity of a painful stimulus that a subject will tolerate is even more variable
and depends on personality and on social, educational, cultural, and
environmental factors. Analgesic drugs and procedures have differing
effects on pain tolerance and pain threshold. A further important clinical
distinction is that between *acute pain* and *chronic pain* (Chapter 6).

Neuroanatomy of nociceptive pathways

The basic anatomical organization of pain pathways is shown diagrammatically in Fig. 5.2.

Nociceptors

Peripheral nociceptors are situated at the terminals of afferent neurones
whose cell bodies lie in the dorsal root ganglia. These nociceptors are of

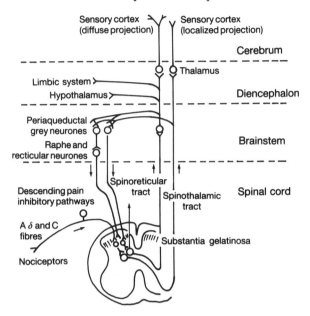

Fig. 5.2 Diagram of the organization of pain pathways. For explanation see text. (References: Thompson 1984a, b; Zimmerman 1981.)

two types: (a) high threshold mechanoreceptors connected to myelinated A delta axons which are relatively large diameter (6–30 μm) and fast-conducting (5–10 m/s), and (b) polymodal nociceptors, consisting of the bare terminals of C fibres which are unmyelinated, small diameter (0.25–1.5 μm) and slow conducting (1–2.5 m/s) (Melzack and Wall 1988). These different nociceptors largely underlie first and second pain respectively, but they are not specific for pain. They respond to other stimuli (pressure, chemicals, and heat) at stimulus intensities well below those that evoke pain, and central processes determine the threshold, intensity and time course of pain (Wall and McMahon 1986).

Substantia gelatinosa

The central axons of these sensory neurones enter the dorsal horns of the spinal cord where they give off branches which run up and down the cord for one or two segments. Many collaterals penetrate the substantia gelatinosa and terminate there on Golgi Type II cells. These cells also receive connections from adjacent spinal regions and from descending pathways from the brain. The interneurones of the substantia gelatinosa are probably important sites for the gating mechanism of pain described below.

Spinothalamic tract

The axons of the substantia gelatinosa interneurones terminate in the chief nucleus of the dorsal horn and synapse with the second order afferent neurones. These cross to the opposite side of the spinal cord and ascend in the lateral spinothalamic tract. In the brainstem, the spinothalamic tracts from each side merge and pass through the brainstem as the spinal lemniscus before terminating in the ventral posterior nucleus of the thalamus. From here, third order sensory axons pass to discrete localized projections on the sensory cerebral cortex. This system appears to be primarily responsible for well-localized, sharp first pain.

Spinoreticular pathways

Impulses in nociceptive fibres are also projected centrally through diffuse connections. Small spinal nerve root fibres connect, partly directly and partly through interneurones in the substantia gelatinosa, with cells in the dorsal horn of the spinal cord. These give rise to spinoreticular axons which ascend in crossed and uncrossed multisynaptic pathways, making numerous connections with the medullary reticular formation, to the intralaminar thalamic nuclei, the hypothalamus, and limbic areas including frontal cortex. From the thalamus, diffuse, non-specific projections pass to widespread areas of the cortex of both hemispheres, probably mediating the poorly localized second pain. Recent work suggests that the anterior cingulate cortex is critically involved in pain perception in man (Roland 1991). The intralaminar thalamic nuclei also give off more localized projections to the corpus striatum, which may be concerned with the reflex motor responses to painful stimuli. The hypothalamic projections connect with autonomic centres which supply the autonomic concomitants of pain, while the limbic connections are probably responsible for the emotional components. These spinoreticular pathways, with connections to reticular formation, limbic system and cortex, are also closely concerned in the arousal systems of the body (Chapter 2).

Descending inhibitory pathways

Inhibitory pathways descend from the periventricular and periaqueductal grey matter, and from the nucleus raphe magnus, the giant cell nucleus and other structures in the reticular formation, to the spinal cord. In the dorsal horn, these axons terminate on the endings of the first sensory neurones or on the connected interneurones in the substantia gelatinosa. These descending inhibitory pathways contribute to the spinal pain gate mechanisms.

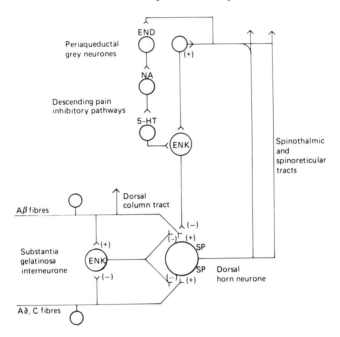

Fig. 5.3 Gate-control mechanisms in pain regulation. SP, substance P; ENK, enkephalin; END, endorphin; NA, noradrenaline; 5-HT, serotonin. For explanation see text. (Reference: Thompson 1984a.)

Spinal gate-control mechanisms in pain regulation

The original gate-control theory of Melzack and Wall (1965) has been modified in the light of later experimental findings (Melzack and Wall 1988). However, the basic concept that, due to local inhibitory control mechanisms, not all nociceptive impulses which reach the spinal cord are transmitted to the brain, remains unchallenged. It appears that the propagation of nociceptive impulses can be inhibited at spinal cord level by at least three systems, all of which probably interact with short interneurones in the substantia gelatinosa (Fig. 5.3).

Inhibition by afferent stimulation. The responses of dorsal horn neurones to peripheral nociceptive stimuli can be inhibited by simultaneous stimulation of large A fibre afferents. One mechanism for this inhibition is activation by the large A fibres of short substantia gelatinosa interneurones, which then presynaptically inhibit the dorsal horn spinothalamic cells. The effect of the presynaptic inhibition is to block the onward transmission of spinothalamic impulses resulting from nociceptor stimulation of dorsal horn cells, particularly those from small C fibre primary afferents. The degree to which potentially painful stimuli are propagated to higher centres thus depends on the relative proportions of small and large fibre activity. Stimulation of A fibres is thought to be an important mechanism of the analgesic action of transcutaneous electrical nerve stimulation, acupuncture, massage, and other counter-irritation procedures. As discussed below, substance P may be the excitatory transmitter from C fibre afferents to dorsal horn cells, and enkephalin may be the inhibitory transmitter liberated by the short interneurones in this system. There are in addition other mechanisms, including post-synaptic inhibition, for gating of pain by afferent stimuli, and for the excitatory and inhibitory effects of different spinal cord neurones (Melzack and Wall 1988).

Inhibition from periaqueductal grey and medullary raphe nuclei. Firing of dorsal horn cells in response to noxious stimuli can also be inhibited, and profound analgesia produced, by electrical stimulation of the periaqueductal grey matter in the brainstem or of the raphe nuclei in the medulla, to which it projects. Such stimulation is mediated by descending impulses from the medullary region impinging on dorsal horn cells or interneurones through pathways which are probably serotonergic but may involve an enkephalinergic link (Bowsher 1978*a*).

Inhibition from lateral reticular formation A further descending inhibitory system appears to originate from structures in the lateral reticular formation. Electrical stimulation of this area also produces deep analgesia and decreases the firing rate of dorsal horn cells in response to noxious stimuli. This system is believed to involve a catecholamine neurotransmitter, probably noradrenaline.

These pain gate control systems in the spinal cord provide another example of the way in which the nervous system controls its own sensory input, as discussed in relation to arousal (Chapter 2). In fact, the system is undoubtedly closely related to arousal systems, and pain sensation and responses are largely modulated by the degree and type of activity in arousal systems. For example, potentially painful stimuli may pass unnoticed during the excitement of sporting activities or may be greatly aggravated by fear of its consequences or by depression. Learning and memory are equally closely involved in pain, and fear of a previously experienced pain can generate similar responses to those evoked by the pain itself. Thus, limbic and cortical gate control mechanisms can add to those operating at spinal cord level.

Pain neurotransmitters and neuromodulators

Chemical mediators at sensory nerve endings

Nociceptors are stimulated by mechanical and thermal stimuli and are also sensitive to a number of chemical agents. Certain types of clinical pain, notably that of inflammation, probably derive from chemical activation by endogenous algesic agents. These include serotonin, histamine, bradykinin, adenophosphate, potassium, prostaglandins, leukotrienes, acetylcholine, and substance P. They are released peripherally after tissue injury and either activate or sensitize primary afferents. Many of these substances are also present in the central nervous system where they may act as transmitters or modulators, but their central functions are not understood. Chemical mediators of pain at sensory nerve endings are reviewed by Bond (1979), Zimmermann (1981), and Terenius(1981).

Substance P

Substance P is a undecapeptide which acts both as a neurotransmitter and a neuromodulator in various body systems; Oehme and Krivoy 1983; Otsuka and Yanagisawa 1987). Its major role in pain appears to be as an excitatory neurotransmitter at primary nociceptive nerve endings in the dorsal horn of the spinal cord. Substance P is present in small peripheral nerve fibres, their dorsal root ganglion cells, and in synaptic vesicles at their terminals in the substantia gelatinosa. It is released in a calcium-dependent manner in response to stimulation of nociceptive neurones but not after stimulation of large diameter afferents alone. When iontophoretically applied to the spinal cord or trigeminal nucleus caudalis, it excites only those neurones which respond to noxious stimuli. Intrathecal injection of substance P produces hyperalgesia, while depletion of spinal cord substance P (with capsaicin) or the application of substance P antagonists produces analgesia. Substance P produces slow excitatory postsynaptic potentials in dorsal horn neurones and it may be co-released from primary afferent nerve terminals with a fast-acting transmitter such as glutamate.

Under physiological conditions, the pre-or post-synaptic release of substance P may be controlled, at least partly, by the actions of short interneurones containing the endogenous opioid enkephalin. The distribution of enkephalin in the spinal cord and brain is similar to that of substance P, and enkephalinergic interneurones project onto the terminals of substance P-containing primary afferent fibres. Release of enkephalin from the interneurones is believed to reduce the release of substance P and the interaction between substance P-containing and enkephalinergic neurones is probably one of the mechanisms for the gate control of pain in the spinal cord.

In addition to substance P, other non-opioid polypeptides, including somatostatin, neurotensin, angiotensin II, vasoactive intestinal peptide and cholecystokinin, may be involved in pain modulation in the spinal cord and brain. The possible role of cholecystokinin is reviewed by Baber *et al.* (1989). This octapeptide is present in central areas associated with pain modulation, including cortex, periaqueductal grey, thalamus and spinal dorsal horn neurones. Small doses of cholecystokinin antagonize the analgesic effects of opioids while antagonists of cholecystokinin enhance opioid analgesia.

Monoamines

The supraspinal descending inhibitory systems which modulate nociceptive transmission in the spinal cord appear to be mediated by monoamine neurotransmitters. The analgesia produced by electrical stimulation of the periaqueductal grey and the medullary raphe nuclei is accompanied by release of serotonin in the spinal cord (Wilson and Yaksh 1980). This analgesia is blocked by agents which decrease serotonin synthesis and enhanced by agents which increase synaptic concentrations of serotonin.

A serotonergic link in the analgesia produced by opiates is suggested by the observation that the intrathecal administration of methysergide blocks the analgesic effect of morphine injected into the periaqueductal grey. The analgesia produced by periaqueductal stimulation is naloxone-reversible; tolerance and cross-tolerance to morphine develop after repeated stimulation (Lewis and Liebeskind 1983). Beta-endorphin may also contribute to this pain suppression system (Bolles and Fanselow 1982). Similar opioid and serotonergic pathways have been implicated in the anaesthesia produced by acupuncture (Han and Terenius 1982).

Electrical stimulation of the lateral reticular formation, on the other hand, produces an analgesic effect which appears to be mediated by noradrenaline. This analgesia is accompanied by release of noradrenaline in the spinal cord and is not affected by manipulation of serotonin concentrations (Zimmerman 1981). Direct application of noradrenaline and alpha-adrenergic stimulants to the spinal cord produces analgesia which is not affected by opioid or serotonin antagonists. Noradrenaline also appears to be involved in the analgesia produced by opiates (Yaksh 1982) and acupuncture (Han and Terenius 1982). Noradrenergic and serotonergic systems probably interact to produce optimum analgesia and may also control the activity of a third inhibitory pathway which is dopaminergic, descending from the substantia nigra to the spinal cord (Fitzgerald 1986).

Acetylcholine

There is increasing evidence (reviewed by Hartvig *et al.* 1989) that cholinergic (muscarinic) mechanisms are involved in pain pathways. Autoradiographic studies have revealed the existence of muscarinic receptors in the substantia gelatinosa of the spinal cord and of cholinergic interneurones on the dorsal horn. Cholinergic neurones are thought to interact with enkephalinergic, noradrenergic and serotonergic neurones, which all have terminals in the same areas. Muscarinic agonists have been shown to have antinociceptive effects when administered intrathecally in the rat. Nicotine receptor agonists have little antinociceptive activity.

Cholinergic antagonists attenuate the analgesic effects of intrathecally administered morphine, suggesting that in the spinal cord opioids act through a cholinergic link. In preliminary clinical studies, cholinomimetic drugs such as physostigmine and THA, administered parenterally or orally, appear to have analgesic effects and to potentiate morphine analgesia.

Amino acid transmitters

There appears to be a complex interaction between GABA and excitatory amino acids (and other transmitters) controlling nociceptive transmission in the spinal cord and brain. GABA activity in the dorsal horn of the spinal cord inhibits onward transmission of afferent nociceptive impulses (Duggan and Foong 1985) while in the medullary reticular formation and periaqueductal grey GABA modulates activity in descending monoaminergic pain suppressing pathways (Lovick 1987; Behdehami *et al* 1990). These effects appear to be mediated by $GABA_A$ receptors since they are blocked by bicuculline.

Glutamate and other excitatory amino acids are present in C fibres and their terminals in the dorsal horn and co-exist in most substance P-containing fibres. Stimulation of peripheral nociceptive afferents probably results in the co-release of both peptides and excitatory amino acids in the spinal cord. Glutamate appears to be involved in plastic neuronal changes following repetitive nociceptive stimulation (Dickenson 1990; Fitzgerald 1990). In particular, activation of NMDA receptors (Table 8.1) produces long-lasting increase in the firing rate of dorsal horn cells, amplifying, enhancing and prolonging the initial nociceptive discharge. This phenomenon is akin to hippocampal long-term potentiation (Chapter 8; Fig. 8.3) and may be important in prolonged nociceptive hypersensitivity states and in chronic pain syndromes (Chapter 6).

Endogenous opioid polypeptide systems

Endogenous opioids are reviewed in the *British Medical Bulletin* (1983), and much of the information is encapsulated briefly by Thompson (1984*b*). The term opioid refers to directly acting compounds whose actions are specifically antagonized by naloxone. *Opiates* are products derived from opium and the term is generally applied to morphine derivatives. *Narcotic analgesics* (Chapter 7) are agents which act on opioid receptors to produce naloxone-reversible analgesia.

Endogenous opioids. Of the endogenous opioid polypeptides, three classes appear to be of major physiological importance: *enkephalins* derived from the precursor pro-enkephalin; *dynorphins* derived from prodynorphin; and *endorphins*, derived from pro-opiomelanocortin

Table 5.2 Endogenous opioids and receptors

Endogenous opioids	Enkephalins	Dynorphins	Endorphins
Precursor	pro-enkephalin	pro-dynorphin	pro-opiomelanocortin
Peptides	(met) enkephalin (leu) enkephalin peptide E	beta-neoendorphin dynorphin A dynorphin B	beta-endorphin

Opioid receptors	mu	delta	kappa	?sigma
Endogenous agonists*	beta-endorphin dynorphin A enkephalins	enkephalins beta-endorphin dynorphin A	dynorphin A beta-endorphin enkephalins	?
Agonist drugs	narcotic analgesics	DPDPE	pentazocine ketacozine	phencyclidine cyclazocine
Antagonist	naloxone	naloxone (less potent than at mu receptors)	naloxone (less potent than at mu receptors)	naxolone (less potent than at mu receptors)
Effector pathways	cAMP ↓ K$^+$ channel activation	cAMP ↓ K$^+$ channel activation	Ca^{2+} channel inhibition	?
Some biological effects	analgesia, euphoria, respiratory depression, cough suppression, miosis, endocrine effects	analgesia, euphoria, motor functions, endocrine effects	analgesia (spinal), sedation, miosis	dysphoria, hallucinations, respiratory and motor stimulation, mydriasis

* listed in order of potency
DPDPE: D-Penicillamine, D-Penicillamine enkephalin (experimental drug)
References: Hughes and Kosterlitz (1983); Morley (1983); Atweh and Kuhar (1983); Jaffe and Martin (1980); Trends in Pharmacol. Sci. (1990).

(Table 5.2). These opioids are closely related structurally but differ in the length of their peptide chains. They function as short-acting neurotransmitters (shorter-length: enkephalins) or long-acting neuronal or hormonal modulators (longer-length: beta-endorphin, dynorphin) at their respective opioid receptors. Many of them interact with more than one receptor. There are several other endogenous opioids, including peptide E, alpha- and beta-neoendorphins, and others, whose function is less clearly understood.

Opioid receptors. There appear to be several distinct opioid receptor subtypes. These have different pharmacological profiles, tissue distributions, and binding properties, and probably mediate different though overlapping actions (Table 5.2). *Mu-receptors* are the main sites of action of the narcotic analgesics; naloxone and nalorphine are antagonists. *Delta-receptors* are activated by enkephalins, which have a greater affinity for them than for mu-receptors, and by beta-endorphin which has equal agonist activity at mu- and delta-receptors. Naloxone has less antagonist activity at delta than at mu-receptors. It is possible that mu- and delta-receptors represent high and low affinity states of a unitary receptor (Atweh and Kuhar 1983) and Pasternak (1987) suggests that there are at least two subtypes of mu receptors. *Kappa-receptors* respond to dynorphin and also to the synthetic analgesics ketazocine and pentazocine. These receptors appear to be involved in spinal analgesia. It has been suggested that mu-, delta- and kappa-receptors are interchangeable forms of a single opioid receptor complex (Barnard and Demoliou-Mason 1983). *Sigma-receptors* are probably not involved in analgesia, but may mediate some adverse effects of opioids. Agonists for these receptors include cyclazocine and phencyclidine (Chapter 7), and that activation of these receptors may account for the hallucinogenic properties of these drugs.

Like other receptors, the opioid receptors consist of a recognition site, to which drugs bind, and a translating mechanism which ultimately produces the biological response. The response is generally one of cellular inhibition which is achieved by membrane hyperpolarization due to opening of potassium channels, and by depression of transmitter release (Henderson 1983; North and Williams 1983). The endogenous opioid system as a whole appears to operate in the body as a widespread and complex inhibitory signalling mechanism in which selectivity is achieved by particular combinations of opioid peptides and receptors (Thompson 1984a,b).

Distribution and function. The distribution of opioid peptides and receptors in the brain is shown in Table 5.3. The distribution of the peptides differs somewhat from that of the receptors, and the distribution of each different opioid peptide is distinct. Within the central

Table 5.3 Distribution of opioid peptides and receptors

Distribution of opioid peptides (areas of highest concentration)

Methionine enkephalin	corpus striatum, caudate putamen, globus pallidus
	limbic system: olfactory bulb, tubercle, septum,
	  nucleus accumbens, hippocampus
	hypothalamus
	medulla, pons, spinal cord: periaqueductal grey,
	  substantia gelatinosa.

Beta-endorphin	hypothalamus, pituitary
Dynorphin	hypothalamus

Distribution of opioid receptors (mu, delta and kappa)

Location	? Effects mediated

Thalamic nuclei
Periaqueductal grey
Spinal cord-substantia gelatinosa,
  spinal nucleus trigeminal nerve,
  dorsal horns
	Analgesia
	  supraspinal
	  spinal

Cortex	Behavioural and mood effects

Limbic structures — hippocampus,
  thalamic nuclei, nucleus accumbens,
  amygdala
	Affective and cognitive
	  components of pain

Anterior and posterior pituitary
Hypothalamus
	Endocrine effects
	  stimulation (growth hormone,
	    ACTH, prolactin)
	  inhibition (leuteinising hormone
	    vasopressin, oxytocin)
	Thermoregulation

Brainstem nuclei	Autonomic effects
	  cough suppression, hypotension,
	  respiratory depression,
	  vomiting, miosis

Striatum	Locomotor behaviour
Ventral tegmentum	Appetite modulation, feeding behaviour

References: Cuello (1983); Atweh and Kuhar (1983); Khachaturian *et al*. (1985); Mansour *et al*. (1988)

nervous system, opioid peptides and their associated receptors are found most often in association with sensory, limbic and neuroendocrine systems. Enkephalinergic systems consist mainly of short neurones diffusely distributed; dynorphin systems have longer neurones, also widespread; endorphins are largely found in endocrine cells, but some neurones project as far down as the spinal cord. Enkephalins are co-stored with catecholamines in chromaffin tissue, while dynorphins are co-stored with vasopressin and endorphins are co-synthesized with corticotrophin in the hypothalamus and pituitary.

(i) Nociceptive systems. Opioid receptors and peptides are closely associated with systems subserving pain sensation at several levels and are of physiological importance in pain modulation. Enkephalins appear to control the responses of dorsal horn neurones; they may also modulate pain at higher sites in the central nervous system, but they are rapidly destroyed *in vivo* by enkephalinases and their analgesic effects are short-lived. Beta-endorphin is less rapidly degraded in the body and has more enduring analgesic effects. The role of dynorphin in pain modulation is still not clear.

While enkephalinergic systems in the spinal cord and elsewhere may be tonically active in pain modulation, the beta-endorphin system and further enkephalinergic activity appear to be triggered into action by noxious stimuli and other stresses. Thus, naloxone does not usually cause hyperalgesia unless the subject already has pain or has been subjected to prolonged pain (Buchsbaum *et al*. 1983). A variety of stresses appear to induce the release of endogenous opioids. These include electric foot-shock in rats (Bowsher 1978*a*), pregnancy (Sicuteri 1981), various types of severe pain (Sicuteri 1981), depressive disorders (Terenius 1982), and endotoxic, haemorrhagic, and spinal shock (Holaday and Faden 1982). In these conditions beta-endorphin may be co-released with ACTH, and enkephalins with adrenaline from the adrenal medulla and noradrenaline from peripheral nerves (Hughes 1983), as part of the general reaction to stress. Endorphins may also be involved in placebo analgesia (Fields and Levine 1984). The responsivity of an individual's endogenous opioid systems may affect his vulnerability or sensitivity to pain and stress.

(ii) Limbic system. Very high concentrations of opioid receptors are found in the amygdala and in the corpus striatum, especially the globus pallidus. Delta-receptors are located on presynaptic dopaminergic terminals in the corpus striatum and their action is to inhibit dopamine release. Mu-receptors are found in the same areas, but are not associated with dopaminergic terminals. Opioid receptors and peptides are also present in the hippocampus and cortex although in relatively low concentrations. In the cortex they tend to be distributed in polysensory association areas rather than in primary sensory cortex.

The opioid systems in limbic areas may play a role in mood and behaviour (Koob and Bloom 1983). Opioid receptors are found in rewarding areas (Chapter 5), and opioid agonists, such as morphine, are potent reinforcers in animals and support intracranial self-stimulation. The role of opioids in reward systems has been discussed above; their possible role in affective disorders is considered in Chapter 11. Limbic opioid systems are probably also involved in modulating the emotional components of pain, especially during arousal and stress, and they may also be involved in memory (Chapter 8). Thus, they appear to be intimately concerned in 'the whole pleasure-pain modality' (Bolles and Fanselow 1982, p. 26).

(iii) Endocrine and autonomic areas. Endogenous opioids also have important modulating actions in the endocrine system, especially on pituitary, hypothalamic, and associated autonomic functions. These actions are closely integrated with pain modulation and limbic activity, especially under stress, and may be involved in the endocrine abnormalities found in depression (Chapter 11).

It is clear that, like other complex functional systems, the nociceptive system utilizes a multitude of chemical mediators which together modulate nociceptive information at all levels from peripheral nociceptor to cerebral cortex to produce the final sensation of pain. The interactions of this apparent plethora of transmitters and modulators seem particularly intricate. However, of all the sensations pain is perhaps the one most immediately important for survival and is of fundamental importance in arousal, reward and punishment, and learning and memory. It is possible that several overlapping back-up systems have developed during the course of evolution. Of particular interest is the existence of multiple neurochemically and anatomically discrete pain suppressive systems. It appears that the physiological trigger for some of these systems is stress and that they represent an adaptation to certain emergency conditions in which pain suppression favours optimal coping behaviour. The particular pain suppression system activated appears to depend on the type of stress. (Lewis and Liebeskind 1983; Frenk *et al.* 1988).

Despite the elaborate organization of pain suppression systems, malfunction appears to occur in some chronic pain syndromes described in Chapter 6 and pain perception is altered in a number of psychiatric conditions, such as depression, anxiety, and schizophrenia.

6. Disorders of reward and punishment systems

Reward and punishment systems, described in Chapter 5, clearly serve adaptive functions in promoting behaviours which increase the chances of survival and preventing behaviours that lead in the opposite direction. In certain conditions, however, activity in these systems appears to be maladaptive, and these can be regarded as disorders of reward and punishment systems. Drug dependence and disorders of pain sensation are considered here in this category. Depressive syndromes, in which reward and punishment systems are also centrally involved, are discussed in Chapter 11. Reward and punishment systems are also involved in eating and psychosexual disorders and in aggressive behaviour which are not considered here.

Drug abuse and dependence

Reinforcing properties of drugs

Present evidence suggests that the biological basis for drug abuse lies in the reward systems of the brain. The same drugs which are abused by man act as reinforcers in animals: animals will learn to self-administer these drugs and will work either to continue self-administration or to avoid the administration of antagonists. A large number of drugs have been found by many authors (reviewed by Woods 1978) to have positive reinforcing properties in several animal species (Table 6.1). Negative reinforcement, the active avoidance of drug injection, occurs with opiate antagonists in opiate-dependent monkeys. Deneau *et al.,* (1969) observed that animals' patterns of drug-taking are often similar to those of human drug-takers. For example, ethanol-reinforced responding in monkeys, like that of human alcoholics, often takes the form of episodes of severe intoxication followed by abstinence-induced withdrawal states. Under certain conditions (including the use of large intravenous doses, schedules of continuous reinforcement, and continuous drug access) corresponding patterns are found between drug-reinforced responding in animals and human drug abuse (Woods 1978; Griffiths *et al.* 1983).

Woods (1978) noted that drug-seeking and drug-taking are, like intra-cranial self-stimulation, examples of operant behaviour, maintained

Table 6.1 Some drugs which act as reinforcers* in animal species

Alcohol	Marijuana
Amphetamines	Methadone
Apomorphine	Methyl phenidate
Barbiturates	Morphine
Benzodiazepines	Nicotine
Chlorphentermine	Nitrous oxide
Chloroform	Pentazocine
Clotermine	Phencyclidine
Cocaine	Phenmetrazine
Codeine	Pipadrol
Diethylpropion	Procaine
Ether	Propiram
Lacquer, thinners	Propoxyphene

* Animals will voluntarily self-administer these drugs after suitable priming, depending on dose, schedule, route of administration, and species. Routes of administration include: intravenous, intramuscular, inhalation, intracerebral, intragastric tube, and oral. Animal species include: rat, monkey, ape, baboon, dog, and others.
References: Woods 1978; Yanagita 1981; Deneau and Inoki 1967; Spealman and Goldberg 1982; Kaymakcalan 1979.

and influenced by the learned consequence of the behaviour and the current environmental conditions, in the same way as other reinforcement behaviours. It seems likely that all such behaviours are centrally mediated by the same neural pathways. In view of the compulsive nature of intracranial self-stimulation behaviour, it is not surprising to find it linked with the self-administration of drugs. Numerous observations show that drugs which are reinforcing can also enhance the rate of self-stimulation via electrodes implanted in reward pathways and lower the stimulus intensity at which electrical stimulation becomes rewarding. Enhanced self-stimulation behaviour, usually after an initial period of depression, has been shown after the administration of suitable doses of opiate, barbiturates, benzodiazepines, amphetamine, nicotine, and other drugs in the rat (Kornetsky *et al.* 1979; Olds and Travis 1960; Larson and Silvette 1975; Stein 1978; Haefely 1978). Drugs which do not affect, or which reduce self-stimulation, such as naloxone and chlorpromazine, have consistently been found not to be reinforcing in self-injection experiments. The precise localization of the intracranial electrodes appears to be important for drug effects on self-stimulation, suggesting that drugs act at very specific loci in the brain (Nelson *et al.* 1981).

Animal studies are in general validated in human work, and Jasinski *et al.* (1984) describe methods to assess abuse liability of drugs in drug abusers by quantitating their hedonic effects ('liking scores') and withdrawal symptoms. Their results support the hypothesis that the prime attribute of drugs liable to abuse is the ability to activate brain reward systems and/or to depress punishment systems. The exact mechanisms are not clear, but it is noteworthy that all reinforcing drugs can influence one or more of the putative transmitters involved (dopamine, noradrenaline, opioids, acetylcholine, serotonin; Chapter 5) or act upon the corresponding receptors. Some drugs appear to be directly rewarding, providing positive reinforcement in the form of a pronounced pleasurable 'kick'. This category includes cocaine, amphetamine and heroin which stimulate dopaminergic or opioid-mediated reward pathways (Chapter 5). With other drugs, the main effect appears to be a negative reinforcement resulting from decreased activity in punishment systems, probably by depressing serotonergic or cholinergic pathways. In this category are anxiolytic drugs, such as benzodiazepines and alcohol, which can be described as 'depunishing' drugs, providing different (but also hedonic) feelings associated with relief of punishment or protection from expected punishment.

Wise and Bozarth (1987) and Di Chiari and Imperato (1988) argue for a unitary theory of drug addiction and suggest that all addictive drugs have psychomotor stimulant effects exerted through a common action on dopaminergic pathways in the median forebrain bundle. However, as discussed in Chapter 5, Stein (1989) showed that self-administration behaviour could be reinforced selectively in rats by microinjection of either cocaine or opioids into different hippocampal cell areas. The evidence suggests that dopamine and opioid reward mechanisms are normally closely integrated. In man, the total phenomenon of drug dependence is undoubtedly complex and it is unlikely that only one neurotransmitter system is essentially involved. It is more likely that, in the pattern of neurological activity evoked by a particular drug, certain pathways are of greater or lesser importance in different individuals. Furthermore, a host of other factors discussed further below — pharmacological, constitutional, environmental, and social — all make variable contributions to the final goal-directed, drug-seeking behaviour. In its broadest sense, dependence or addiction has been defined as 'an emotional fixation . . . acquired through learning, which intermittently or continually expresses itself in a purposeful, stereotyped behaviour with the character and force of a natural drive, aiming at a specific pleasure or the avoidance of a specific discomfort' (Bejerot 1980, p. 254). This definition includes non-drug-orientated behaviours, such as compulsive sexual behaviour, gambling, overeating (Jonas and Gold 1986), excessive indulgence in athletic pursuits, and many others which may all depend upon activity in brain reward systems. Of the pharmacological factors, the development of drug tolerance and of drug withdrawal effects require special mention.

Drug tolerance

The responsiveness to a given blood or tissue concentration of a centrally acting drug (natural tolerance) varies widely between individuals and depends on many factors, including personality, environment, state at the time of administration, and expectations (Schachter 1971; Eysenck 1967; Ashton *et al.* 1981). Acquired drug tolerance in an individual is a state of diminished responsiveness of the body to a previously administered drug, so that a larger dose is required to elicit an effect of similar magnitude or duration. Tolerance develops to many drugs and, although it occurs with most drugs of abuse, it is not in itself a sufficient condition for drug dependence. For example, many people become tolerant to alcohol without apparently coming to crave its regular use (Madden 1979).

The degree of tolerance developed to a drug is not uniform throughout body systems. With the narcotics a high degree of tolerance develops to the respiratory depressant and analgesic effects, yet much of the hedonic effects appear to remain (Herz *et al.* 1980*b*). With barbiturates, tolerance to the respiratory depressant effects is less marked than that to the sedative effects, and with benzodiazepines, tolerance develops more rapidly to the sedative than to the anxiolytic effects. This heterogeneity is perhaps not surprising in view of the multiple mechanisms involved in tolerance and the fact that several operate simultaneously in various parts of the body.

Pharmacokinetic tolerance

The development of drug tolerance probably reflects a continuum of body adaptations from first exposure to long continued use, and involves pharmacokinetic and pharmacodynamic factors. Pharmacokinetic tolerance is usually the result of an increase in the rate of metabolism due to induction of hepatic drug metabolizing enzymes by the drug. It occurs with barbiturates, some other hypnotics, and nicotine, but is also seen with drugs which are not abused (Smith and Rawlins 1973). This type of tolerance develops over a period of several days and then reaches a plateau. On cessation of the drug, enzyme activity declines over a period of 6–8 weeks. Enzyme induction has little effect on the peak intensity of drug action, but decreases the duration of action. There is not usually more than a three-fold decrease in sensitivity (Jaffe 1980) and pharmacokinetic tolerance is of lesser importance in the development of drug dependence than pharmacodynamic tolerance.

Pharmocodynamic tolerance

Pharmacodynamic tolerance appears to result from a variety of tissue adaptations which decrease the response to a given concentration of a drug at its site of action. *Acute tolerance* can develop very rapidly: it can be demonstrated within minutes of a single administration of alcohol in the drug-naïve animal or non-alcoholic human. In man and animals the sedative/hypnotic effects of alcohol, barbiturates, and benzodiazepines are greater, at the same blood concentrations, immediately after drug administration when the blood concentration is rising than during recovery when the blood (and tissue) concentration is falling (Cicero 1978; Iverson and Iverson 1981). Acute tolerance tends to disappear within days if the drug is not repeated. The mechanisms involved are not clear. With some drugs, acute tolerance may be due to tachyphylaxis, caused by persistent occupation of receptors (nicotine) or by depletion of readily available transmitter stores (indirectly acting sympatho-mimetic amines; Bowman *et al.* 1968). However, it is possible that acute tolerance can also result from changes in receptor affinity for a drug, since receptor molecules may undergo conformational changes which allow alteration between active and inactive states (Triggle 1981).

Chronic tolerance occurs when drug administration is continued over a period of time. It has long been known that chronic exposure to central nervous system depressants results in a compensatory increase in the activity of excitatory systems which to some extent balances the depressant effects of the drug. Conversely, with central nervous system stimulants, a compensatory increase in inhibitory activity occurs. Within limits, these changes allow the animal to adapt to the continued presence of a drug in its body and to function relatively normally. These homeo-static changes may result from alterations in the output or turnover of excitatory or inhibitory neurotransmitters or neuromodulators, and/or to changes in the sensitivity and density of receptors. In some cases drug tolerance may arise from the actions of endogenous antagonists; for example, cholecystokinin antagonizes opiates (Chapter 7) and an endogenous benzodiazepine antagonist may partly mediate benzodia-zepine tolerance (Chapter 4). Such changes tend to occur over a time-course of the order of weeks rather than hours or days; they may last for months or even years after the cessation of some drugs such as alcohol (Cicero 1978).

Receptor modulation

Much recent work has shown that tissue receptors for neurotransmitters and neuromodulators exhibit plasticity: they are dynamic structures capable of making adaptive changes depending on the supply of agonist or antagonist. For example, decreasing the supply of an agonist at a synapse (either by cutting the presynaptic nerve or blocking the receptor with an antagonist) results after a time in an increase in receptor sensiti-vity, the so-called denervation supersensitivity. Conversely, a chronic increase in exposure to agonist results in a compensatory decrease of receptor sensitivity. Thus receptors are capable of tuning their receptivity up or down to compensate for changes in agonist supply. The result of such changes is a return towards normal function, or tolerance to the new conditions.

One mechanism by which receptor sensitivity can be altered is by changes in receptor density. Other mechanisms involve changes in receptor affinity or in the cascade of biochemical events within the cell initiated by the formation of the drug/receptor complex, and uncoupling of the receptor from its effector systems. Modulation of receptor sensitivity has been described by Sulser (1981), Berridge (1981), Triggle (1981), Perkins (1982), Costa (1981), Creese and Snyder (1980), Barnes (1981), and Hoffman and Lefkowitz (1980).

Since many drugs act as agonists or antagonists at receptor sites, it is not surprising that alterations of receptor sensitivity have been found to occur after chronic drug administration. A major effect appears to be on receptor density, and changes in the number of receptors have been demonstrated by a variety of methods following chronic dosing with many classes of drugs. These changes affect not only post-synaptic receptors, which mediate the effects of neurotransmitters, but also pre-synaptic receptors, which modulate neurotransmitter release (Langer 1980). The effects and clinical significance of receptor modulation resulting from antidepressant and antipsychotic drugs is discussed in Chapters 12 and 14, and it is clear that the phenomenon is not confined to dependence-producing drugs.

The action of central nervous system stimulants and depressants on their target receptors also affects the release and turnover of other neurotransmitters; this effect may indirectly cause changes in density in the receptors of such transmitters. Thus, β-adrenoceptor supersensitivity has been demonstrated after chronic administration of alcohol and opiates; increased density of muscarinic cholinergic receptors occurs after alcohol and barbiturates, and alcohol also appears to lead to down-regulation of dopamine receptors (Creese and Sibley 1981). In general, it would appear that the response of the brain to central nervous system depressants is down-regulation of receptors for inhibitory neurotransmitters and up-regulation of those for excitatory transmitters, while the response to stimulants is the opposite. However, the responses may be limited to certain sites and to certain types of receptors.

Because of this elaborate and dynamic arrangement, it is almost impossible for a chronically administered drug to exert actions limited to one neurotransmitter system or to one function of a system. Any drug which acts on the nervous system is likely also to affect transmitter release — which is in turn often linked by feedback mechanisms to transmitter synthesis and turnover. Thus barbiturates, opiates, benzodiazepines, and alcohol have been shown to affect the release and/or turnover of acetylcholine, noradrenaline, dopamine, serotonin, and

GABA (Okamoto 1978). Prolonged dosage with opiates decreases the synthesis and release of some endogenous opioids (Herz *et al*. 1980*a*; Herz 1981). Similar multiple changes in the release and turnover of neurotransmitters and modulators have been shown after long-term treatment with numerous other drugs. Such effects are by no means confined to drugs with dependence-producing potential and they may help to explain the rebound withdrawal effects which occur with many types of drugs.

Cross-tolerance

The development of tolerance to one drug may confer a degree of tolerance to other drugs to which an animal has not been exposed. Such cross-tolerance can result from pharmacokinetic or pharmacodynamic factors. Administration of an enzyme inducer will speed the metabolism of other drugs degraded by the same pathways. This type of *pharmacokinetic cross-tolerance* can give rise to drug interactions. Barbiturates, for example, increase the rate of metabolism of several other drugs including warfarin and phenytoin, and also of other barbiturates.

Pharmacodynamic cross-tolerance occurs between drugs which act similarly at the same receptor sites. Thus, tolerance to one barbiturate or benzodiazepine is associated with tolerance to all other barbiturates or benzodiazepines; tolerance to amphetamine confers tolerance to the effects of other sympathomimetic amines and to the anorectic effect of cocaine in animals (Jaffe 1980). Similar cross-tolerance occurs between opiates and opioids which act as agonists on the same opiate receptors. Sensitivity to antagonists acting on these receptors is however, greatly increased (Way and Glasgow 1978).

Reverse tolerance

Reverse tolerance, the development of increased sensitivity to the effects of a previously administered drug, has been reported in some cases. A course of a neuroleptic drug sometimes leads to increased susceptibility to extrapyramidal effects during a second course (Sovner and diMascio 1978) and some dopamine receptor agonists (amphetamine, cocaine) may increase the sensitivity to subsequent challenge with dopamine receptor agonists (Post 1978). These effects may be due to differential actions of the drugs on pre- and post-synaptic dopamine receptors.

Behavioural tolerance

Present evidence of synaptic changes resulting from chronic drug administration, as outlined above, does not appear to account for all the observed phenomena of tolerance, particularly for drugs of dependence. For example, rats learn to overcome the ataxic effects of alcohol if they receive the drug before performing tasks in which the absence of ataxia is rewarded or its presence punished, while rats given equal or greater doses of alcohol after the task, or who are not exposed to the task, do not overcome the ataxia to the same extent, although they become equally tolerant to other alcohol effects (Cicero 1978; Jaffe 1980). Similarly, tolerance to amphetamine anorexia is contingent, occuring only if the drug is given before and not after food (Carlton and Wolgin 1971). The concept of behavioural tolerance (critically reviewed by Demellweek and Goudie 1983 and Goudie and Griffiths 1986) suggests that an important component of drug tolerance is through adaptations of behavioural responses through learning and memory processes, including operant and classical conditioning (Siegel 1983, 1984, 1988; Bierness and Vogel-Sprott 1984; Chapter 8). No particular neurochemical mechanisms are assumed, but presumably they are the same as those which underlie learning and memory (Chapter 8). Thus, drugs may produce adaptative changes not only at their primary sites of action, but also in the pathways subserving the particular behaviours which they influence. It is possible that some cases of reverse tolerance are due to learning of a drug's rewarding effects, so that, after previous exposure, a smaller dose will trigger these effects in the manner of a conditional response.

Dosage escalation

The development of tolerance may lead to escalation of dosage in an attempt to obtain the original drug effect in the face of the counteracting body defences. Thus, narcotic addicts may exceed a dose that would produce fatal respiratory depression in a naïve subject, and alcoholics may retain their composure at blood alcohol concentrations that would fell a teetotaller. However, there appears to be a maximal limit to tolerance (Cicero 1978) and this varies considerably between different classes of drugs. Petursson et al. (1981) point out that tolerance does not necessarily lead to escalation of dosage of benzodiazepines, and gross escalation of nicotine dosage does not occur with smokers (Ashton and Stepney 1982). Whether or not dosage has increased, cessation of drug use in subjects who have become tolerant generally leads to withdrawal effects.

Withdrawal effects: abstinence syndrome

Relation to tolerance

When compensatory pharmacodynamic changes have taken place in the body in response to the presence of a drug, its sudden withdrawal can give rise to a number of adverse effects. These appear to represent rebound of activity in the systems affected by the drug and are largely the opposites of the original drug effects. In general, the abstinence syndrome of central nervous system depressant drugs is characterized by agitation and hyperexcitability, while that of stimulant drugs is characterized by fatigue, inertia, and general depression. Withdrawal effects occur not only with drugs which are abused, but also with other drugs which induce adaptive changes in the body. Thus, withdrawal of long-term neuroleptics is sometimes followed by exacerbation of tardive dyskinaesia, thought to be due to hypersensitivity of post-synaptic dopamine receptors in the corpus striatum (Chapter 14). Other examples are discussed by Grahame-Smith (1985). Withdrawal symptoms occurring on sudden cessation of chronically administered drugs are, in general, related to the development of tolerance and seem to be explicable in terms of the pharmacodynamic mechanisms described above, including those involved in behavioural tolerance. The distribution, duration, and severity of the symptoms depend on the particular body systems which have undergone adaptive modulations and the degree of adaptive changes induced. Withdrawal effects are reversed by an appropriate dose of the original drug, an effect which encourages continued use.

Clinical manifestations

The most dramatic abstinence syndromes occur on withdrawal, after tolerance has developed, of drugs which have potent reinforcing or rewarding effects. These drugs when used chronically cause widespread, though uneven, adaptive changes affecting the entire neuraxis and withdrawal effects can be demonstrated throughout the autonomic and central nervous system. The particular features of individual drug withdrawal syndromes are described in the sections on each drug.

A prominent withdrawal symptom from both depressants and stimulants which exert hedonic effects is a marked craving for the drug. This craving appears to be directly related to the degree to which the drug activates reward systems in the brain, and (in animals) supports self-administration and lowers the threshold for intracranial self-stimulation. Craving is a marked feature of opiate withdrawal, but it occurs to a lesser extent during withdrawal from drugs which have weaker intrinsic hedonic effects. Thus, it is not severe during withdrawal from benzodiazepines in spite of the presence of other widespread withdrawal symptoms (Ashton 1984) and is absent on withdrawal from drugs such as chlorpromazine which do not support self-stimulation in animals. Craving is usually drug-specific. However, if the drug is not available, withdrawal symptoms of some drugs may be partially alleviated by other drugs with similar actions (see cross-dependence, below). Substitution of other, more readily available, drugs for the original drug of dependence by addicts may lead to multiple drug abuse.

Craving is possibly the result of down-regulation of receptors in reward systems in the brain. It may lead to compulsive drug use and escalation of dosage as tolerance develops in these systems. On drug cessation, aversive symptoms may result from relative overactivity of punishment systems, leading to goal-directed, drug-seeking behaviour. In drug abusers, the initial motivation for reward may become gradually displaced to varying degrees by motivation to avoid the punishment of withdrawal.

Physical and psychological dependence

A distinction is often made between physical and psychological dependence. Physical dependence is said to have occurred when withdrawal of the drug produces physical effects. Such dependence can be so severe that sudden drug withdrawal is potentially lethal, as with barbiturates, but it can exist to a variable extent and can occur with drugs such as chlorpromazine which are not usually addictive. Psychological dependence is said to occur when withdrawal symptoms are limited to psychological effects such as anxiety or craving without life-threatening physical symptoms, and the term is often applied to amphetamine or cocaine dependence. However, there can be no true distinction between physical and psychological dependence since psychological symptoms clearly result from physicochemical events in the brain.

Cross-dependence

Withdrawal effects caused by abstinence from one drug may often be partially alleviated by other drugs, a phenomenon known as cross-dependence. Thus, the manifestations of withdrawal from heroin can be partially suppressed by other opioids such as methadone, and one barbiturate can substitute for another in reversing the barbiturate withdrawal syndrome. Partial cross-dependence also occurs between drug groups, and is seen between alcohol and barbiturates, and between sedative/hypnotics and anxiolytics. This phenomenon is probably similar to pharmacodynamic cross-tolerance described above. It has important clinical implications and forms the basis of substitution treatment of physical dependence.

Polydrug abuse

Many drug users take several types of drugs. In a study of Malaysian heroin addicts, Navaratnam and Foong (1990) found that the majority used at least four drugs — usually benzodiazepines, alcohol and cannabis in addition to heroin. The commonest reason given was that these drugs boosted the euphoria derived from heroin. In addition, some narcotic, barbiturate or benzodiazepine abusers also take stimulants such as cocaine and amphetamines to overcome central nervous system depressant effects or withdrawal effects (Kosten and Kosten 1989). Conversely, abusers of cocaine and amphetamines often use narcotics or barbiturates to relieve the 'crash' of withdrawal; the combination of cocaine and heroin use is particularly common. Some of these practices are influenced by availability and cost of drugs, but polydrug abuse now appears to be the norm among abusers of illicit drugs (Kreek 1987). The spectrum of individual drugs abused in different countries often changes over time and is subject to sociological influences (Mello and Griffiths 1987).

Time relationships

The time it takes for dependence to develop varies with drug, dosage, and dosage schedule and also with the criteria used for defining dependence. However, the process is initiated by the first dose and can develop very rapidly. Mild withdrawal effects in the form of REMS rebound can occur within a week after short-acting hypnotics given in therapeutic doses once nightly (Kales *et al.* 1978) and the opiate antagonist naloxone can precipitate withdrawal effects in subjects given therapeutic doses of opiates 8-hourly for 2 or 3 days. The degree of dependence increases over time and it is usually estimated that dependence to most central nervous system depressants develops within 2–4 months at therapeutic doses.

The time of appearance, severity, and duration of the withdrawal syndrome is influenced by pharmacokinetic factors. With rapidly eliminated drugs, withdrawal symptoms appear earlier and are more intense than with more slowly eliminated drugs. Abrupt displacement of opiates from their receptors by naloxone precipitates almost immediate symptoms, while discontinuation of long-acting opiates such as methadone produces withdrawal symptoms that are delayed, gradual in onset, and generally less severe. With rapidly eliminated drugs, withdrawal effects may develop between doses, increasing the motivation for continued drug use. The relief by the drug of the withdrawal effects acts as a further reinforcer of drug-using behaviour. This cycle of events is seen with cocaine, amphetamines, nicotine, and short-acting benzodiazepines. Many drug withdrawal regimes are based on the substitution of a long-acting preparation, for which there is cross-dependence.

The duration of withdrawal syndromes has probably been generally underestimated. Acute, severe physical symptoms do not usually last for more than a matter of weeks, but physical and psychological symptoms including sleep disorders, muscle pains, and anxiety can certainly continue for many months after benzodiazepine withdrawal (Ashton 1984) and craving can continue for a similar time after stopping cigarette smoking (Ashton and Stepney 1982). Prolonged withdrawal symptoms are also described for cocaine (Chapter 7). Prolonged withdrawal effects after other drugs would probably be found if they were specially investigated.

Interacting factors

The relationships between the reinforcing properties of drugs, tolerance, dependence, and compulsive drug use are complex. Patients receiving narcotics for pain relief, although developing tolerance, do not usually have problems in withdrawing these drugs when they no longer have pain and they rarely become compulsive drug users. The majority of people who drink alcohol regularly have become tolerant and may experience some withdrawal symptoms if deprived, yet do not become compulsive drinkers. Another often quoted example is that of American soldiers in Vietnam, many of whom became heroin dependent, but were able subsequently to stop drug-taking without serious difficulty or medical help (Alexander and Hadaway 1982). It appears that the interaction of many non-pharmacological factors including sociological and constitutional variables are important in drug abuse.

Sociological influences on drug-taking are discussed by Jaffe (1980) and Levison (1981) and the importance of learning and conditioning in drug dependence is discussed by Siegel (1988). Genetic factors in animals are discussed by George and Goldberg (1989) who point out that selective breeding can produce strains of rats and mice which differ markedly in their preference for reinforcing drugs such as alcohol and cocaine. Some strains will readily self-administer these drugs while others will actively avoid them. Such behaviours probably result from the interaction of several genes. In humans, twin and family studies have demonstrated a strong genetic element in some forms of drug abuse (Eysenck and Eaves 1980; Schuckit 1987). Genetically determined factors may include differences in drug metabolism (Sjoquist *et al.* 1982), tissue response, and personality make-up.

Personality variables have been investigated in relation to several drugs. No evidence has been found for an 'addictive personality', a trait or constellation of traits that describe all compulsive drug users (Jaffe 1980; Levison 1981). However, certain personality types may be more prone than others to abuse particular types of drugs. For example, compulsive users of directly rewarding drugs such as heroin, cocaine and amphetamines tend to exhibit personality characteristics largely encompassed within the dimension of psychoticism (Eysenck and Eysenck 1975), such as risk-taking, impulsivity, stimulus-seeking, rebelliousness, aggressiveness, and intolerance of frustration, and a high susceptibility to reward (Gray 1981*b*). Golding and Cornish (1987) showed a high correlation between scores for psychoticism and stimulus-seeking and illicit drug use among University students.

Conversely, individuals prone to take anxiolytics tend to have high scores for neuroticism and low scores for psychoticism and extraversion (Ashton 1984; Golding *et al.* 1983; Golding and Cornish 1987; Ashton and Golding 1989a). These individuals may be particularly sensitive to punishing stimuli and relatively insensitive to reward (Gray 1977, 1981b) and may therefore prefer 'depunishing' drugs. Ashton et al. (1981) noted that subjects with high scores for neuroticism experienced a lesser intoxication score ('high') from smoking the same dose of Δ^9-tetrahydrocannabinol than subjects with lower neuroticism scores. Thus, individuals who abuse rewarding drugs and those who become dependent on 'depunishing' drugs may represent two extremes of a population distribution whose motivation for taking different types of drug depends to some extent on their personality characteristics (Ashton 1989).

The basic pharmacological characteristics of drugs which are compulsively used appear to include: (1) an action on brain reward and punishment systems which either produces a pleasurable effect or allays discomfort, (2) the development of pharmacodynamic tolerance, and (3) the appearance of psychologically uncomfortable withdrawal effects on abstinence. These pharmacological factors, no combination of which is necessarily sufficient to produce drug dependence, interact with constitutional and environmental factors, influencing behaviour. With some drugs, the pharmacological influences may be extremely strong. For example, Villarreal and Salazar (1981) observe that all animals in experimental groups from seven different species will spontaneously self-administer amphetamine-like drugs when put in conditions in which they can, at first accidentally, operate a device that injects the drug. Allowed unlimited access to such drugs, monkeys will spontaneously continue self-administration to the point of death. With other drugs, such as cannabis and LSD, and possibly opiate narcotics (Alexander and Hadaway 1982), environmental factors may be more important, at least in humans; while with alcohol genetic influences may play a major part. Whatever the precipitating or aggravating factors, compulsive drug use is clearly a reward-seeking behaviour, mediated by reward and punishment systems in the brain, and directed towards obtaining repeated administrations of the drug.

Disorders of pain sensation

As described in Chapter 5, pain and fear of pain are major activators of punishment systems. Acute pain clearly subserves a useful function in protecting the body from injury, both by evoking an immediate withdrawal reaction and by providing an aversive stimulus which (via learning and memory) promotes future avoidance behaviour to noxious stimuli. The somatic reaction to acute pain is one of generalized arousal, with cortical, autonomic, motor, and endocrine activation. This response is well adapted to fight or flight behaviour. If circumstances require sustained physical activity, it may also be adaptive to inhibit pain sensation and powerful pain suppressive systems are temporarily activated by stress (Chapter 5). More persistent pain, resulting from tissue injury, excites the further response of skeletal muscle spasm around the site of injury which may help to rest and protect the affected tissue and so hasten recovery. Some forms of chronic pain, however, do not appear to be adaptive, while diminished sensitivity to pain exposes the body to damage. These conditions constitute disorders of pain sensation.

Decreased pain sensitivity

Insensitivity to pain may result from lesions in pain pathways at any site from the peripheral nerves to the brain (Bowsher 1978b). It also occurs rarely as a congenital condition sometimes associated with overactivity of opioid systems (Dehen et al. 1977; Yanagida 1978). States of lowered arousal due to drugs or disease, and some psychiatric abnormalities such as hysteria or schizophrenia may produce indifference to pain, and reactivity to noxious stimulation is reduced in profound metal deficiency (Bond 1979).

Chronic pain syndromes

Chronic pain can arise from structural or functional disease of most organs of the body and may be of varying duration. However, there are some heterogeneous disorders which have come to be grouped as chronic pain syndromes, partly because they are difficult to diagnose and treat and hence become longstanding, and partly because, whatever the underlying cause, they present a similar pattern of behaviour. The physiological accompaniments of chronic pain are quite different

Table 6.2 Some somatic and psychological features of clinical pain

Acute pain	Chronic pain
Tachycardia	Sleep disturbance
Increased cardiac output	Irritability; aggression
Increased blood pressure	Appetite disturbance
Pupillary dilation	Constipation
Palmar sweating	Psychomotor retardation
Hyperventilation	Lowered pain tolerance
Hypermotility	Social withdrawal
Escape behaviour	Abnormal illness behaviour
Anxiety state	(Masked) depression

Reference: Sternbach 1981.

from those of acute pain (Table 6.2.) In place of acute sympathetic responses, so-called vegetative signs emerge including sleep disturbances, irritability, and lowered pain tolerance. The psychological features of acute pain, which resemble anxiety, tend to be replaced in chronic pain by signs characteristic of depression. Conversely, many of the somatic symptoms of chronic pain also occur in depression, and there is a considerable overlap between the two conditions.

Chronic pain syndromes have been classified along a number of axes by the *International Association for the Study of Pain* (1986). The causes are diverse, and include pain resulting from organic causes and pain in which no organic cause can be found. Many of cases are intermediate in that an organic cause may be present but does not appear to be sufficient to account for the degree of pain complained of. Perhaps 50 per cent of patients have no adequate physical basis for pain, while many patients with apparently adequate lesions do not complain of pain. Hence it can be a difficult clinical problem to decide how much of a patient's pain is physical and how much is psychogenic in origin. Whatever the background, however, chronic pain can lead to a characteristic behaviour pattern in which the pain becomes the dominant feature of the patient's existence, vegetative symptoms are present, the patient becomes socially withdrawn and assumes the role of an invalid, and depression develops, either in the form of depressed mood or masked as somatic symptoms (Sternbach 1981).

Neurological disorders

Neurological disorders producing pain are reviewed by Bowsher (1978*b*), Bond (1979), and Lance and McLeod (1981). Central pain is discussed by Illis (1990) who stresses the point that peripheral mechanisms can induce central changes (see also Melzack and Wall 1988; Melzack 1990; Chapter 5).

Peripheral nerve lesions   Peripheral nerve lesions can produce neuropathic pain which is burning, shooting, or indescribably unpleasant. The pain probably results partly from interference with gate-control mechanisms due to damage to low-threshold mechanoreceptor fibres. If impulses from these large fibres do not reach the spinal cord, they cannot activate inhibitory interneurones which would normally suppress the input from small fibres; hence pain sensation is enhanced. In addition pain may result from altered neurophysiological properties of damaged peripheral nerves which may generate spontaneous impulses and show unusual sensitivity to mechanical disturbance (Lance and McLeod 1981). Thirdly, peripheral nerve injury can lead to long-lasting changes in the activity of spinal cord dorsal horn neurones, including enlargement of their receptive fields and alterations in output of various peptides

(Melzack and Wall 1988). Furthermore, the activity of pain suppressive systems in the brain, including affective components, may be altered in states of persistent pain. A combination of these effects may result in self-perpetuating activity leading to chronic, persistent pain long after the original injury has apparently healed. Activation of NMDA receptors by glutamate (Dickenson 1990, Chapter 5) is probably important in the mediation of these plastic neuronal changes.

(i) Causalgia. Partial damage to peripheral nerve trunks may give rise to causalgia, a particularly intense, but diffuse burning pain, accompanied by altered autonomic activity and trophic changes in the affected part. The local changes may result from a vicious circle in which the peripheral nerve lesion induces abnormal activity in primary afferent neurons, leading to alterations in synaptic information processing in the spinal cord. The thoraco-lumbar sympathetic outflow becomes involved in the process, disrupting the regulation of cutaneous blood flow and sweating. Abnormalities in sympathetic post-ganglionic activity in turn influence primary afferent activity in neurones from the lesioned nerve, thus completing the circuit (Janig 1985). However, as mentioned above, abnormal spinal cord activity almost inevitably affects ascending and descending pathways so that affective and cognitive factors also contribute to the pain of causalgia. Sympathetic blockade may abolish the pain and trophic changes.

(ii) Phantom limb pain. Amputation or deafferentation of a limb (or other parts of the body) is regularly associated with persistence of the body image or phantom of the affected part. The phantom may be painful or painless and tends to shrink and eventually to disappear over time. Phantom limb pain occurs in about 70 per cent of patients after amputation and persists in up to 50 per cent (Chapman and Bonica 1985; Melzack 1990). The pain may be perceived in definite parts of the phantom, which may seem to move or feel as if it is fixed in an uncomfortable position or as if it is distorted.

Several mechanisms probably contribute to phantom limb pain. Loss of gate-control, as in other peripheral nerve lesions, probably results from the deafferentation and may be combined with decreased activity in supraspinal pain suppression systems. Central mechanisms are discussed by Melzack (1990), who postulates that phantoms originate from abnormal activity in a widely distributed neural network or neuromatrix in the brain, containing a full sensory representation of the body. Such a neuromatrix would correspond to the patterns of neural activity envisaged in Chapter 1 which give rise to particular emotions (Chapter 2), thoughts and memories (Chapter 9) and other somatic or mental representations. The sensory neuromatrix is closely linked to the central representation of 'self': thus phantoms are always felt to be 'real' and are clearly identified with self, 'even when a phantom foot dangles in "mid-air" (without a connecting leg) a few inches above the stump' (Melzack 1990, p. 90). Such perception of self in a phantom is in marked contrast to the syndrome of unilateral neglect seen in lesions of the right parietal lobe, in which parts of the body are perceived as foreign and extraneous from the self (Chapter 2).

The phantom image is remarkably durable and persists after excision of large parts of the brain including somatosensory cortex and thalamus. Similar resistance to surgical ablation is shown by memory (Chapter 8) and in a sense a phantom *is* a memory, in which pain sensation can presumably be perpetuated by central changes similar to those which occur in other peripheral nerve lesions.

Dorsal root lesions.   Irreversible damage to the cell bodies of large afferent fibres in the dorsal root or trigeminal ganglia may occur as a result of herpes zoster and give rise to post-herpetic neuralgia. Stimulation of small fibres gives rise to intense, burning pain similar to causalgia, presumably because of loss of gate-control and other mechanisms as in peripheral nerve lesions (Bowsher 1978*b*). Damage to dorsal roots can be caused by compression in disease of the vertebral column and occurs in some neuropathies such as tabes dorsalis in which it may account for the typical 'lightning' pains.

Spinal cord and brainstem lesions.   Lesions involving the spinothalamic tracts, for example in multiple sclerosis, may initiate burning pain on the opposite side of the body below the lesion. Anaesthesia dolorosa after posterior inferior cerebellar artery thrombosis is probably due to interference with the descending inhibitory reticulospinal system. Trigeminal and glossopharyngeal neuralgia resemble 'lightning pains': the pain is repetitive, fleeting, severe, and occurs in paroxysms. These neuralgias have been ascribed to epileptiform discharges of the cranial nerve nuclei (Bowsher 1978*a*) or to demyelinization of the sensory neurones or mechanical irritation at the sensory root entry zone by tortuous cerebral arteries (*Lancet* 1984*b*). They may be triggered by afferent stimuli from peripheral areas supplied by the same nerve, for instance by speaking, chewing or swallowing. Some cases respond to anticonvulsant drugs, and to surgical destruction of the nerve roots (Hayward 1977).

Lesions in the thalamus and cerebral cortex.   Damage to the ventroposterior thalamic nuclei, usually as a result of a cerebrovascular accident, may produce the thalamic syndrome, in which partial sensory loss and hemiparesis is combined with a burning pain and autonomic changes similar to causalgia. The pain is continually present but aggravated by slight stimuli to the painful areas. The pain may be due to irritation of thalamic and autonomic pain pathways, loss of gating mechanisms at thalamic level, or both (Bowsher 1978b). Rarely, the sensory cortex may be the origin of pain which may accompany focal epileptic attacks arising in this area (Lance and McLeod 1981).

Migraine and other headaches.   The typical features of migraine are well known. The attack may be preceded by an aura (often visual) and, the ensuing headache is often unilateral, throbbing in quality, and accompanied by nausea, vomiting, photophobia, hyperaesthesia, irritability, and autonomic disturbances. Many clinical variants of greater or lesser severity are seen, including migrainous neuralgia (cluster headaches), headaches associated with anxiety or depression, and generalized psychogenic pain in other parts of the body — panalgesia (Sicuteri 1981). In certain individuals, headaches form part of the chronic pain syndrome.

The aura of the classical migraine attack probably results from a spreading depression (Leao's spreading depression), starting in the occipital cortex and proceeding anteriorly to the primary sensory and motor cortex, accompanied by a 20–30 per cent decrease in cerebral blood flow (Glover and Sandler 1989; Lauritzen 1987; Pearce 1984a, 1985). Spreading depression may be triggered by abnormal activity in the locus coeruleus and dorsal raphe nuclei, since electrical stimulation in these areas can evoke the response in monkeys. The spontaneous cause of such activity is unknown but may include stress and anxiety (which increase firing in these nuclei, Chapter 3) or paroxysmal epileptiform activity (there may be a genetic link between migraine and epilepsy). The headache itself probably results from secondary dilatation of extracerebral vessels, possibly mediated through vascular reflexes linked to the locus coeruleus and raphe nuclei (Goadsby et al. 1982).

Serotonergic influences are thought to be critically involved in both the cortical and vascular phenomena of migraine. Stimulation of the dorsal raphe nuclei, which can cause both cortical spreading depression and changes in extracerebral vessels (Glover and Sandler 1989), releases serotonin centrally. Migraine is also accompanied by a massive release of serotonin from platelets. Migraine can be provoked in migrainous subjects by serotonin receptor agonists and by agents which release serotonin; conversely it can be prevented or alleviated by serotonin antagonists (Fozard and Gray 1989). Receptors of the 5-HT$_1$ type (Table 3.1) may partly mediate the vascular changes; these are found in high density in the choroid plexus (Peroutka 1988). Activation of 5-HT$_2$ and 5-HT$_3$ receptors in vascular smooth muscle may cause vasodilatation, and release of serotonin from platelets (*Lancet* 1990a) may liberate other vasodilators such as prostaglandins, histamine and bradykinin. Liberation of such inflammatory mediators may also be involved in migraine associated with food allergies (Monro et al. 1984).

5-HT$_3$ receptor activation may mediate the associated vomiting (Fozard 1987).

The paroxysmal nature of migrainous headaches and their unilateral distribution remain unexplained. Patients with migraine and related headaches may also have abnormalities of endogenous opioid systems (Sicuteri 1981) and it has been suggested that fluctuations in pain intensity may result from variations in activity in pain-suppressing pathways (Fields 1988; Wall 1988b). Other causes of headache are reviewed by Hayward (1977) and Clough (1989).

Psychogenic factors

Petrie (1967) drew attention to the large variation between individuals in their perception of pain. Certain personality characteristics (reviewed by Bond 1979, 1980, and Merskey 1986) are associated with increased susceptibility to pain and may affect behavioural responses to pain. Pain may also be a prominent feature in several mental disorders, especially anxiety and depression, and most clinical pain syndromes are an inextricable mixture of psychological and somatic components. In a study of 97 patients attending a pain relief clinic, Tyrer et al. (1989) found that 32 per cent had sufficient symptoms to be classified as psychiatric cases on the Present State Examination; a further 22 per cent had minor neurotic systems and features of illness behaviour; 35 per cent had mainly organic pain, and 11 per cent were impossible to classify. Both organic and psychogenic pain can lead to 'learned pain behaviour' (Tyrer 1986) which is a characteristic of chronic pain syndromes. In terms of conscious experience, there is probably no difference between organic and psychogenic pain, although each may perpetuate and enhance the other. In clinical situations, affective components of pain are usually paramount; intellect plays a far less important role than emotion (Bond 1979). This is in marked contrast to experimentally-induced pain, in which cognitive strategies rather than personality variables determine pain tolerance (Lukin and Ray 1982).

Anxiety. Individuals prone to anxiety under stress have increased sensitivity to pain and complain of greater severity of pain when ill than more stable individuals. In anxiety disorders (Chapter 3), pain is a common complaint. Pains are often muscular and electrophysiological studies reveal increased muscle tension which may be the cause of the pain. In some patients, exquisitely tender nodules (possibly localized areas of muscle spasm) act as trigger spots for inducing widespread pain.

Hysteria. Hysterical personality traits are associated with exaggeration of symptoms, poor tolerance of pain, and demanding and manipulative behaviour. Such behaviour may be seen in some patients with chronic pain who appear to use their pain to dominate or tyrannize their families or to obtain secondary gains such as increased attention, liberation from responsibility, or financial gain.

Hypochondria.   Patients with hypochondriacal or obsessional personality traits commonly complain of pain. Such patients may become preoccupied with pain and fear of disease and demand constant explanation and reassurance.

Schizophrenia.   In some schizophrenic patients, pain is a prominent symptom: such pain is usually ill-defined and may be described in bizarre terms (Bond 1979). Other schizophrenic patients appear to be abnormally insensitive or tolerant to pain. They may maintain apparently uncomfortable positions for long periods of time and fail to react normally to painful external stimuli. It seems likely that altered pain responses are at least partly due to disturbances in the limbic control of affective components of pain (Chapter 13).

Depression.   Of all psychological states, depression is most closely linked to chronic pain. Pain accentuates depression of mood in individuals with depressive personality traits, and in turn such individuals experience more pain than those who are less prone to depression (Bond 1979). Significant depression occurs in a high proportion of chronic pain patients (Tyrer *et al.* 1989; Merskey 1986), while over half of patients hospitalized for depression complain of pain as a major symptom (Sternbach 1981). Thus, it appears that chronic pain can cause depression and that depression can cause the psychological experience of pain. The two conditions can become linked in a self-perpetuating circuit and may share common physiological pathways.

   In patients with pain secondary to depression and in those with depression secondary to pain, there is a tendency towards somatization, so that depression is masked and the major symptoms are physical (Sternbach 1981). Benedittis and Gonda (1985) found that patients with psychogenic pain tended to show greater right hemisphere EEG activation than those with somatogenic pain, and that psychogenic pain occurred more frequently on the left side of the body. These findings are interesting since emotional functions appear to involve predominantly the right hemisphere (Chapter 8) and there is some evidence of right hemisphere dysfunction in depression (Wexler 1980; Chapter 11).

Depressive facial pains.   Two types of chronic psychogenic facial pain appear to be particularly associated with masked depression (Hayward 1977; Bond 1979; Feinmann *et al.* 1984). In facial arthromyalgia (Costen's syndrome, temporomandibular joint dysfunction syndrome), the pain is localized to the region of the temporomandibular joint and its musculature. It is described as a dull ache, often with acute severe exacerbations. In atypical facial pain, the pain is felt deep in the soft tissues or bone and varies from a dull ache to severe throbbing. It may be localized to the teeth or involve the gums and tongue. A depressive aetiology is suggested by the observation that the syndromes often respond to treatment with tricyclic and related antidepressant drugs. However, pain relief may be independent of antidepressant effect, and not all patients fulfil diagnostic criteria for depressive disorder (Feinmann et al. 1984; Sharav et al. 1987).

Mechanisms of chronic pain syndromes

While most types of pain due to organic disease can be reasonably well explained in terms of increased nociceptive stimulation or disruption of gate control systems with secondary central changes, it is more difficult to pinpoint the mechanisms which lead to psychogenic pain and which produce the mixture of symptoms seen in chronic pain syndromes.

The close relationship between chronic pain and (possibly masked) depression has led to the suggestion (reviewed by Merskey 1986; Magni 1987) that the underlying basis for both conditions may be similar. Several observations indicate that a linking factor may be activity in certain central serotonergic systems. Thus, brain concentrations of serotonin are decreased in some types of depression (Asberg et al. 1976; Chapter 11) and depletion of brain serotonin in certain brain areas is associated with increased pain sensitivity and spontaneous pain (Moldofsky 1982; Johansson and von Knorring 1979). Conversely, increased brain serotonin activity is accompanied by decreased pain reactivity in animals (Moldofsky 1982), and treatment with antidepressants which increase central serotonergic activity can relieve both chronic pain and depression in man. It is possible that these drugs have analgesic actions which are independent of their antidepressant effects, and tricyclic antidepressants have been shown to potentiate the analgesic effects of morphine (Biegon and Samuel 1980). However, it has not yet been possible to find clinically potent analgesics amongst drugs which specifically interact with serotonin receptors.

Sternbach (1981) suggested that both chronic pain syndromes and depression result from central serotonin depletion, with underactivity in the serotonergic systems involved in pain suppression and mood control. The depletion may be a consequence of prolonged overactivity following the initial pain or stress. Alternatively, prolonged overactivity might lead to tolerance of serotonergic effects in the body. At present there is no evidence to support this hypothesis, despite undeniable evidence relating serotonin both to pain and to depression. However, the anatomical and physiological link between pain in depression and depression in chronic pain is likely to be found in limbic punishment systems, in which serotonergic mechanisms interact with a number of other transmitter systems.

There is strong evidence that serotonergic pain suppression systems are activated by opiates and endogenous opioids (Yaksh and Rudy 1978) and this observation has led to the suggestion that a primary causative factor in chronic pain syndromes might be an abnormally low concentration or activity of endogenous opioids, particularly of beta-endorphin. Accordingly, attempts have been made to ascertain whether concentrations of endogenous opioids are abnormal in chronic pain syndromes, and whether they are altered by measures which affect the pain. The answers to these questions are by no means clear-cut for many reasons. There have been major technological difficulties in identifying separate endogenous opioids; several endogenous opioids may be affected differentially in chronic pain; changes in opioid concentrations in blood or even cerebrospinal fluid may not reflect changes in activity in critical brain or spinal cord sites; and chronic pain syndromes are aetiologically heterogeneous.

However, several studies suggest that the cerebrospinal fluid concentration of beta-endorphin (or beta-endorphin-like peptides) is reduced in patients with a variety of chronic pain conditions compared with pain-free subjects (Akil *et al.* 1978*a,b*; Terenius 1982; Almay *et al.* 1980; Sicuteri 1981; Lipman *et al.* 1990). Concentrations of these peptides have been shown to increase during pain-free intervals (Sicuteri 1981) and when pain is relieved by electroacupuncture (Clement-Jones *et al.* 1979; Almay *et al.* 1980) or by intrathecal injection of saline placebo (Lipman *et al.* 1990). The ability of placebo to attenuate pain has been known for some time; the effect appears to be mediated through opioid mechanisms and is prevented by naloxone (Butler *et al.* 1983; Clement-Jones and Besser 1983; Levine *et al.* 1978) which also worsens clinical, but not experimental, pain (Fields 1987).

In chronic pain associated with depression the findings are confusing. Beta-endorphin-like activity has been found to be increased in patients with depression and psychogenic pain (Terenius 1982; Almay *et al.* 1980) and may fluctuate in manic-depressive patients (Knorring *et al.* 1978; Chapter 11). Opioid agonists and antagonists do not have therapeutic effects in depressive disorders. Although opioid agonists are potent analgesics in some conditions (Chapter 7), they have relatively little effect in experimental pain and are often ineffective in chronic pain syndromes.

The results of these and many other investigations indicate that (as with most clinical syndromes) it is unlikely that a single abnormality will be found to account for the manifestations of chronic pain syndromes. The role of other neurotransmitters or modulators of pain, such as acetylcholine (MacLennon *et al.* 1983), neurotensin (Luttinger *et al.*

1983), dopamine and noradrenaline (Sicuteri 1981), and Substance P (Almay *et al.* 1988) have yet to be elucidated. The greatest stimulus to the pain suppressive systems is stress (Chapter 5), which may be involved both as a cause and a result of chronic pain syndromes, but whether prolonged stress can produce exhaustion of, or tolerance to, intrinsic pain modulation systems has not yet been ascertained. It is clear, however, that seemingly peripheral symptoms can often result from primarily central processes.

From the practical point of view, it has become clear that conventional analgesic drugs do not represent the only pharmacological means for treating pain. A number of psychotropic drugs (reviewed by Melzack and Wall 1988) may, in some circumstances, have analgesic actions or add to the effects of analgesics, usually because of their actions on affective pain components. These include neuroleptics, antidepressants, anticonvulsants, and occasionally benzodiazepines. Non-drug procedures, such as acupuncture, transcutaneous nerve stimulation, and possibly hypnosis may also activate endogenous pain suppressive systems (Clement-Jones and Besser 1983). Of various surgical procedures (Bond 1979; Miles 1977), electrical stimulation of the periventricular and periaqueductal grey is of particular theoretical interest in view of the part these areas probably play in physiological pain modulation (Lewis and Liebeskind 1983).

7. Drugs acting on reward and punishment systems

The drugs described in this section exert major actions on reward and punishment systems (Chapter 5) and are all drugs of dependence (Chapter 6). Some have potent effects on pain systems and are of therapeutic importance (narcotic analgesics), but all are also used as recreational agents because of their rewarding properties. Other drugs which induce dependence, but are used therapeutically for their actions on arousal systems (central nervous systems depressants and stimulants) are described in Chapter 4. Antidepressant drugs and drugs which induce depression also affect reward and punishment systems, and these are discussed in Chapter 12. Psychotomimetic drugs are described in Chapter 14.

Narcotic analgesics, opiates, opioids

Narcotic analgesics, opiates, and opioids all act on endogenous opioid receptors (Chapter 5). The terminology relating to these drugs has been clarified by Hughes and Kosterlitz (1983). Narcotic analgesics are agents which act on opioid receptors to produce naloxone-reversible analgesia; opiates are drugs derived from opium; the term opioid describes any compound whose direct actions are specifically antagonized by naloxone.

Morphine

Morphine is the main active ingredient of opium and remains the standard agent against which other agents are measured. Other opioid agonists (Table 7.1) have generally similar actions.

Pharmacokinetics

Morphine is well absorbed after injection but absorption after oral administration is irregular and extensive first-pass metabolism occurs, so that higher doses are required for equivalent effect. The free base is rapidly distributed peripherally, but compared with other opioids (codeine, heroin) morphine crosses the blood/brain barrier rather slowly and reaches the brain in relatively small quantities, despite its potent

Table 7.1 Some opioid agonists, agonist/antagonists, and antagonists

Drugs	Oral potency* ratio	Duration of analgesic effect (h)	Main site of opioid receptor interaction
Opioid agonists			
morphine	1	4	mu
codeine	1/6	4	mu
dihydrocodeine	1/3	4	mu
dextropropoxyphene	1/6–1/9	10	mu
pethidine	1/8	2	mu
heroin	1.5	3–4	mu
dextromoramide	2	2	mu
methadone	3–4	8	mu
levorphanol	5	6	mu
Mixed agonist/antagonists			
nalorphine	2/3	1–4	mu, kappa, sigma
pentazocine	1/18	3	mu, kappa, sigma
buprenorphine	25[1]	8	mu
Antagonist		Antagonist effect	
naloxone	–	1–4	mu (delta, kappa, sigma)

*Oral potency ratio = oral dose of morphine/oral dose required for equivalent analgesic effect.
[1] Sublingual buprenorphine.
References: Rogers *et al.* 1981; Jaffe and Martin 1980; Houde 1979; Twycross and Lack 1983.

central effects. Detoxification is by hepatic metabolism and the products are mainly excreted in the urine. The elimination half-life is 18–60 h. Some enzyme induction occurs with chronic morphine administration, but tolerance is mainly due to pharmacodynamic factors.

Actions

Central nervous system. The main actions of morphine on the central nervous system are *analgesia, drowsiness, mood changes*, and *mental clouding*. Morphine is a powerful analgesic, affecting both the sensory and affective components of pain. Pain sensation is selectively depressed in doses which leave other sensations unaltered. Continuous dull pain and visceral pain are relieved at lower doses than sharp intermittent or cutaneous pain. Many patients report that pain is still present, but is less distressing after morphine. Experimental pain is less affected; morphine may produce little change in pain threshold although there is usually an increase in pain tolerance. Morphine can exert potent analgesic effects with little effect on the level of consciousness or motor reflex activity, but as the dose is increased subjects become drowsy, experience a feeling of pleasant indifference and warmth, and may sleep. The effect on the EEG is a shift towards low frequency, high voltage activity. Chronic doses reduce REMS and SWS and increase Stage 2 sleep.

Some patients experience a euphoria after morphine, and this is pronounced in morphine-dependent subjects. Rapid intravenous injection in addicts produces an intense 'thrill' lasting about 45 s, accompanied by warmth and flushing of the skin. This is followed by a period of sustained euphoria or 'high'. However, dysphoria may occur with difficulty in mentation and general lethargy.

Other central nervous system effects include nausea and vomiting, depression of cough reflexes, respiration and cardiovascular reflexes, and pupillary constriction. Tolerance develops to these effects, and also to the analgesic and euphoric actions. High doses of morphine can cause muscle rigidity, convulsions, and death from respiratory depression. Neuroendocrine effects include increased output of ACTH, prolactin, and growth hormone, and decreased output of thyrotropin and luteinizing hormone. Peripheral effects include arteriolar and venous dilatation and increased gastrointestinal smooth muscle tone.

Mechanisms of action

Morphine is a selective agonist of opioid mu-receptors, having only slight activity at delta- and kappa-receptors (Chapter 6). The analgesic action results from stimulation of mu-receptors at several levels in the central nervous system. In the spinal cord morphine has a direct depressant effect on cells in the substantia gelatinosa which respond to noxious peripheral stimuli (Duggan *et al*. 1977*a*, *b*). It also inhibits the release of substance P and other excitatory nociceptive neurotransmitters (Chapter 5). In man, single intrathecal doses of morphine and other opioids can produce pain relief lasting for 12–24 h (Behar *et al*. 1979; Cousins *et al*. 1979).

In the brain, morphine appears to increase activity in descending pain suppressive pathways originating in the periaqueductal grey matter and raphe nuclei, and affects the release of several neurotransmitters at various sites, including monoamines, acetylcholine, substance P and GABA (Jaffe and Martin 1980). A further locus of the analgesic action of morphine in the brain is in the limbic system. It is probably by an action here that it obtunds the affective components of pain. As already noted, the limbic system is richly endowed with mu as well as other opioid receptors, particularly in the amygdala and many other areas including the locus coeruleus. Opioids and opiates depress the firing rate of locus coeruleus cells in a sterospecific, naloxone-reversible manner, probably by a direct action on the neurones (Gold *et al*. 1979*a*; Henderson 1983). Release of noradrenaline from the widespread projections of the locus coeruleus is blocked and this effect may underlie the reduction of anxiety and the feeling of pleasant indifference evoked by morphine. Opiate actions on thalamic nuclei decrease the cortical release of acetylcholine (Jhamandas and Sutak 1976; Wood and Stotland 1980); this may diminish the arousing effects of painful stimuli and lead to drowsiness.

The hedonic effects of morphine presumably also result from actions on opioid receptors at limbic sites. Morphine is directly rewarding to animals who will work to receive injections of the drug into the cerebral ventricles or ventral tegmental area; it also enhances intracranial self-stimulation at several brain sites. These actions are reversed by naloxone, and sometimes by dopamine receptor antagonists, suggesting an opioid-dopamine link (Cooper 1984).

Adverse effects

Gastrointestinal effects.   Nausea and vomiting are common in ambulant patients, though less frequent in recumbent patients, and symptoms can largely be prevented by dopamine receptor antagonists. Addicts develop a high degree of tolerance to the emetic effects. Constipation is common in patients taking morphine therapeutically but can be controlled by purgatives. Little tolerance develops to this effect and morphine addicts are usually constipated.

Respiratory depression.   Morphine has a direct depressant effect on brainstem respiratory centres, discernible at doses which do not alter consciousness. The sensitivity of the respiratory centre to increases in carbon dioxide tension is decreased and the centres regulating respiratory rhythm are depressed, resulting in irregular or periodic breathing. Death from morphine overdose is nearly always due to respiratory arrest. Patients with reduced respiratory reserve or hepatic impairment are particularly vulnerable to these effects.

Effects in pregnancy.   Morphine crosses the placenta and is taken up by the fetus which is more sensitive than the adult to its depressant effects. Maternally administered morphine in late pregnancy and labour may depress respiration in the neonate. In addition, morphine dependence can develop *in utero* and a withdrawal syndrome develop after birth (Zelsen *et al.* 1973).

Drug interactions.   Phenothiazines, monoamine oxidase inhibitors, and tricyclic antidepressants may all exaggerate and prolong the central nervous system depressant effects of morphine. Some phenothiazines appear to enhance the analgesic effects of morphine; such a combination is sometimes valuable in the management of severe chronic pain (Thompson 1984*a*, *b*).

Hypersensitivity, idiosyncracy.   Allergic reactions occur occasionally in the form of skin rashes and asthma, probably related to histamine release. Anaphylaxis has been reported rarely following intravenous injections and it is possible that it occasionally accounts for sudden death in addicts.

Abuse, dependence, tolerance. Many of the opioids, particularly heroin, have a high dependence-producing potential since they readily induce hedonic effects, tolerance, and a withdrawal syndrome. The incidence of opiate abuse is probably about 100 000 in the UK and well over a million in the USA. It is of interest that long-term heavy opiate usage is not necessarily incompatible with apparently normal physical and mental health and long life (Brecher 1972) and, ex-heroin users have been maintained on high doses of methadone for over 10 years without ill-effects (Jaffe 1980). However, the annual death rate among young abusers is several times higher than that of matched control groups; causes of death include infections (including AIDS) resulting from unhygienic injection techniques, and overdoses and reactions to impurities in illicit supplies of fluctuating potency.

The hedonic effects of opioids in man, the reinforcing effects in animals, and the actions on opioid receptors in the limbic system have already been mentioned. These effects are probably due to activation of mu receptors; opioids which act on kappa receptors, appear to have less addictive potential and do not maintain reinforcement responses in animals. Kornetsky *et al.* (1979) showed a close relationship between the abuse potential in man of various drugs and their ability to lower the threshold for intracranial self-stimulation in rats. Of the drugs studied, morphine caused the maximum lowering of self-stimulation threshold; nalorphine, a partial agonist/antagonist, was intermediate, and the antagonist naloxone raised the threshold. Nelson *et al.* (1981) found maximal dose-dependent increases in self-stimulation with morphine if the stimulating electrodes were placed in the locus coeruleus or lateral hypothalamus and suggested that there are critical pathways for the reinforcing effects of morphine.

Pharmacodynamic tolerance develops rapidly to many of the effects of morphine and other opioids. Naloxone can precipitate a withdrawal reaction from therapeutic doses given for only a few days in man. Tolerance develops readily to the respiratory depressant, sedative, and emetic effects, but is less marked for the constipating effects. The question of how much tolerance develops to the hedonic effects is controversial. Many studies have shown little tolerance to the effects of intracranial self-stimulation in animals Kornetsky *et al.* 1979; Lorens 1976; Olds and Travis 1960). In man, it has been claimed that tolerance does develop to this effect and that the dose required to produce a 'rush' or 'high' must be continually escalated (Jaffe 1980). It is claimed that eventually many addicts continue to take opiates to avoid withdrawal effects rather than to receive rewarding effects. However,

Kornetsky *et al.* (1979) quote evidence that dependent subjects still experience both a 'rush' and a sustained 'high' and that these effects are continued over the entire course of addiction, with no evidence of tolerance.

A high degree of cross-tolerance develops between morphine, heroin and methadone, which act primarily on mu-receptors, but much less between these drugs and those such as ketazocine which act mainly on kappa-receptors. The degree of tolerance declines steadily after withdrawal and fatalities have occurred in addicts who have resumed their previous dosage after a period of abstinence.

Withdrawal syndrome. (i) Clinical features. The character of the opioid withdrawal syndrome varies with individuals, drugs, dosage, duration of use, and other factors. Time of onset and intensity depends mainly on pharmacokinetic factors. Symptoms are almost immediate and severe if withdrawal is precipitated by naloxone, rapid in onset with quickly eliminated drugs such as pethidine, and delayed or less intense with slowly eliminated drugs such as methadone. However, the general features of the abstinence syndrome are similar for all opiates.

Peak symptoms include those of widespread autonomic overactivity with increased glandular secretion, and cardiovascular and gastrointestinal symptoms. General central nervous system excitation is manifested by tremor, insomnia, restlessness, irritability, and dilated pupils. Psychological symptoms include intense anxiety, depression, and severe craving. Hallucinations are not a marked feature in comparison with alcohol, barbiturate, and benzodiazepine withdrawal, and convulsions are not usual. However, death can occur in debilitated subjects as a result of dehydration, acidosis, and cardiovascular collapse. Gross-symptoms recede in about 10 days, but are followed by a protracted abstinence syndrome with lethargy, inability to tolerate stress, hypochondriasis, depression, and continued craving – which may last several months. These effects contribute towards the high tendency to relapse in compulsive opiate users.

The neonatal withdrawal syndrome appears on the first day in the babies of heroin-dependent mothers, but may be delayed for several days in babies exposed to methadone *in utero*. It consists of irritability, high-pitched crying, hyperreflexia, increased sucking activity, and signs of autonomic overactivity. The signs are more severe after methadone than heroin (Zelsen *et al.* 1973).

(ii) Mechanisms. One of the mechanisms contributing to the withdrawal syndrome may be a deficiency of endogenous opioids resulting from chronic receptor activation by exogenous opiates. In rats, long-term morphine administration decreased the concentration of opioids in some brain areas and in plasma (Herz *et al.* 1980; Herz 1981; Herz and Hollt 1982). In human heroin addicts, Herz (1981) found reduced concentrations of beta-endorphin and methionine enkephalin in plasma and cerebrospinal fluid. In this context, it is interesting that acupuncture which stimulates endogenous opioid release, can alleviate acute symptoms in heroin withdrawal (Wen and Cheung 1973; Clement-Jones *et al.* 1979).

The rebound rise in noradrenergic activity which occurs on withdrawal from narcotics (and other central nervous system depressants) undoubtedly contributes to the anxiety and central nervous system hyperexcitability of the abstinence syndrome. Gold *et al.* (1978, 1979*a*) suggested that noradrenergic activity in the locus coeruleus is particularly implicated and that this could be controlled with the α_2-adrenoceptor stimulant clonidine, which inhibits release of noradrenaline at this site. Clonidine (5 μg/kg) was effective in the management of heroin withdrawal and also suppressed narcotic withdrawal signs in animals (Lal and Fielding 1983). The standard pharmacological treatment at present remains that of methadone substitution, although the success rate is not high (Menon *et al.* 1986). Other opioids such as the mixed agonist/ antagonist buprenorphine and the long-acting antagonist naltrexone are under trial, combined with behavioural and cognitive methods.

Other narcotic analgesics

A number of semisynthetic or synthetic opioids (Table 7.1) have actions similar to those of morphine due to effects mainly on mu-receptors.

Heroin

Heroin is diacetylmorphine. It is 1.5 times more potent than morphine as an analgesic. It is absorbed more rapidly from the gastrointestinal tract and enters the brain faster than morphine; hence it has a quicker onset of action.

Pethidine

Pethidine is a synthetic compound structurally different from morphine although its actions and adverse effects are similar at equianalgesic doses.

Methadone

Methadone is a synthetic substance which is structurally different from morphine but exerts similar effects. It reaches the brain in only small amounts, attaining a peak concentration within 1–2 h after oral administration, and causes less euphoria and drowsiness. It is bound to protein in various tissues, including the brain, and may gradually accumulate during chronic administration. On cessation of treatment, it is slowly released from these tissues. The elimination half-life after chronic administration is 22 h (Jaffe and Martin 1980). Methadone is mainly used in the management of withdrawal from other narcotics. Although it produces tolerance and dependence, management is easier and the abstinence syndrome is less intense.

Dextroprophoxyphene

Dextroprophoxyphene is similar in structure to methadone but has less potent analgesic effects. Overdose of this preparation can cause respiratory depression, convulsions, and hypotension as well as paracetamol toxicity. In high doses it has euphoric effects, and dependence and abuse may occur (Wall *et al.* 1980).

Fentanyl

Fentanyl is a synthetic opioid which has an analgesic potency 80–100 times that of morphine. It is short acting, the peak effect lasting only 20–30 min due to rapid redistribution. High doses produce marked muscular rigidity which is naloxone-reversible and may be due to an action on dopaminergic transmission in the corpus striatum.

Mixed opioid agonists/antagonists

A group of synthetic opioids have mixed agonist/antagonist actions at various opioid receptors (Rance 1983; Table 7.1). Many of these have been developed in an effort to find a potent analgesic that does not

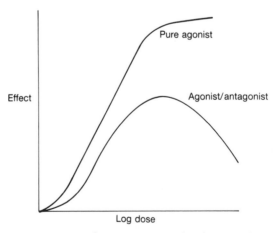

Fig. 7.1 Dose-response curve for a pure opioid agonist and a mixed agonist/ antagonist. For the agonist/antagonist, small doses produce agonist effects while reversal of the these effects occurs as dosage is increased and antagonistic actions develop. The maximum agonist effect is usually lower than that of a pure agonist.

produce respiratory depression or dependence and abuse. A singular property of some of these drugs is that small doses produce agonist effects (such as analgesia, respiratory depression or inhibition of gastro-intestinal motility) but reversal of these effects occurs as dosage is increased and antagonistic actions develop (Fig. 7.1). The maximum agonist effect (efficacy) of these drugs is usually lower than that of pure agonists. Many of them have greater effects on delta-, kappa-, and sigma-receptors than morphine and thus have rather different phar-macological profiles; some have agonist effects on some types of opioid receptors but antagonist effects on others. Suitable doses of mixed agonists/antagonists can reverse the toxic effects of agonists, but they can also precipitate withdrawal reactions and induce toxic effects of their own. Some produce pscyhotomimetic and dysphoric effects, thought to be mediated by sigma receptors.

Nalorphine

Nalorphine exerts mainly antagonistic effects on mu-receptors but agonist effects on kappa- and sigma-receptors. It antagonizes the effects of morphine and has some analgesic and respiratory depressant effects of its own. However, it produces bizarre and terrifying hallucinations which are naloxone-reversible and thought to be due to actions on sigma receptors. Because of its dysphoric effects, it has little abuse potential.

Pentazocine

Pentazocine has mainly antagonist actions at mu-receptors, but agonist effects at kappa- and sigma-receptors. It produces analgesia, sedation, respiratory depression, and constipation at low doses, but the intensity of these effects does not increase progressively with increased dosage. Its efficacy is less than that of morphine, and it is less likely to cause nausea and vomiting. Unlike morphine, it has stimulant effects on the cardiovascular system, and can cause systemic and pulmonary hyper-tension. High doses produce naloxone-reversible dysphoric and psycho-tomimetic effects, but at therapeutic doses these are less marked than with nalorphine. Pentazocine appears to have less dependence-producing potential than morphine-like drugs; nevertheless, dependence and com-pulsive use does occur.

Buprenorphine

Buprenorphine acts mainly on mu-receptors on which it has powerful agonist effects, but almost equivalent antagonist effects at higher doses. It has analgesic, sedative, respiratory depressant, emetic, and euphoric effects like morphine, but the actions are slower in onset and longer in duration, and do not continue to increase with increasing dosage. The respiratory depressant and other effects are not reversed by nalorphine and only partially by naloxone, probably because buprenor-phine is not easily displaced from receptors. Buprenorphine can precipi-tate withdrawal reactions in narcotic addicts and can also alleviate withdrawal symptoms after narcotic abstinence. Dependence and abuse occurs and its withdrawal after chronic use causes an abstinence syndrome after a delay of several days. However, its dependence poten-tial is much less than that of morphine. *Propiram* is a partial mu-receptor agonist similar to buprenorphine (Rance 1983).

Opioid antagonists

A few synthetic drugs have almost pure antagonist actions at opioid receptors. None of these are completely selective for one type of receptor.

Naloxone

Naloxone is a relatively selective antagonist at mu-receptors but has some antagonist activity at delta-, kappa- and sigma sites. It has almost no intrinsic agonist activity and in low doses produces little discernible effect on normal subjects apart from subtle effects on subjective mood ratings (File and Silverstone 1981). In very high doses (2–4 mg/kg) morphine-like euphoria or dysphoria occurs (Cohen *et al.* 1981). Small doses can cause hyperalgesia in subjects under stress, aggravate some types of clinical pain, and prevent or reverse placebo analgesia and analgesia caused by acupuncture (Levine *et al.* 1978; Frid and Singer 1979; Skjelbred and Lokken 1983). These actions are thought to be due to antagonist effects on endogenous opioid systems which have been activated by pain, stress, or treatment. Naloxone reverses the actions of narcotic analgesics and opioid agonists/antagonists, although the reversal of buprenorphine effects is only partial. It exerts some antagonistic action on the central nervous system depressant effects of nitrous oxide, barbiturates, benzo-diazepines and perhaps alcohol (Nuotto *et al.* 1983; Catley *et al.* 1981; Badawy and Evans 1981; Jeffcoate *et al.* 1979; Jeffreys *et al.* 1980). The effects of naloxone are very rapid in onset (within minutes), but the duration of effect is shorter than that of opiates. Thus, dosage must often be repeated in the treatment of narcotic overdose. Withdrawal reactions, which can be dangerous, are precipitated by naloxone in patients dependent on opiates or opioids.

Endogenous opioids

Purified preparations or synthetic analogues of various endogenous opioids have potent analgesic effects when administered intrathecally. Synthetic *beta-endorphin* can induce profound analgesia, sedation, and euphoria in patients with intractable pain. Intrathecal beta-endorphin used for obstetric anesthesia, provided complete relief of labour pains (Oyama *et al*. 1980, 1982). *Enkephalins* injected intrathecally or into the cerebral ventricles in animals have analgesic effects which are weaker and shorter-lasting than those of beta-endorphin. *Dynorphin* is a potent analgesic (Goldstein *et al*. 1981) and also produces behavioural effects (Katz 1980). Experience in the use of these substances in pain relief, narcotic withdrawal, or psychiatric states is still limited, but they all produce behavioural effects as well as analgesia, and Kosterlitz (1979) observes that all natural and synthetic opioids are liable to produce dependence.

Alcohol (ethanol)

Alcohol has few therapeutic uses, but in terms of social and medical consequences is probably the most important drug of dependence. Like other such drugs, it exerts hedonic effects, induces tolerance, and can produce an abstinence syndrome on withdrawal. The prevalence of alcohol dependence (alcoholism) is estimated to be about 5–10 per cent of the adult population in the USA and Western Europe (Rogers *et al*. 1981; Mello 1987), although this figure is imprecise because of the difficulty in defining alcoholism in countries where 90 per cent of adults drink alcohol. The prevalence of alcoholism in a population is closely related to the overall level of alcohol consumption, which is in turn related to the cost of alcohol relative to average income (Hore and Ritson 1982). In the UK, alcohol consumption doubled between 1950 and 1976, doubling again by 1990, and there are probably over a million alcoholics in Britain (Paton 1985) and many more with alcohol-related problems. The heavy social and medical consequences of alcohol use are discussed by Glatt (1977), Madden (1979) and Jaffe (1980), among others.

Pharmacokinetics

Alcohol is readily absorbed from the gut, mainly in the small intestine. Fats and carbohydrates delay absorption, and large amounts of alcohol are absorbed relatively slowly. Small single doses start to appear in the plasma within 5 min, reaching a peak after 30 min to 2 h. There is considerable individual variation in rate of absorption, which may be more rapid in chronic drinkers. Alcohol is widely distributed and penetrates the cerebrospinal fluid and placental barrier.

Alcohol is 95 per cent metabolized in the liver, the rest being excreted unchanged in the breath, urine, and sweat. In the liver it is oxidized to acetaldehyde. The major pathway is by cytoplasmic alcohol dehydrogenase using nicotinamide adenine dinucleotide (NAD) as coenzyme. Some of the toxic effects of alcohol may be due to accumulation of lactate, beta-hydroxybutyrate, glutamate, malate, and alpha-glycerophosphate which require NAD for their metabolism (Rogers *et al.* 1981). This accumulation results in impaired gluconeogenesis, hypoglycaemia, and fatty infiltration of the liver. Associated nutritional deficiencies in alcoholics may add to the tissue damage. Acetaldehyde is further converted in the liver mitochondria to acetyl coenzyme A which enters the tricarboxylic acid cycle to produce 7 kcal/g of alcohol. The rate of alcohol metabolism varies between individuals but is on average 10 ml/h. A modest increase in the rate of oxidation occurs in chronic alcoholics.

Chronic alcoholism is associated with reduced concentrations of cytosolic acetaldehyde dehydrogenase in the liver and erythrocytes (Thomas *et al.* 1982; Jenkins *et al.* 1982; Peters 1983; Agarwal *et al.* 1983). It is not clear whether a pre-existing deficiency of this enzyme predisposes to alcoholism or whether the deficiency is caused by heavy drinking. However, the observation that enzyme concentrations return to normal during abstinence suggests that excess consumption of alcohol impairs its own metabolism.

Other investigations have shown that acetaldehyde can condense *in vivo* with catecholamines to form tetrahydroisoquinolines, such as salsolinol, which have narcotic properties. Similarly, indole amines can condense with acetaldehyde to form tetrahydro- beta-carbolines (Blum *et al.* 1978). The importance of these metabolic conversions in the development of alcohol dependence is discussed below. It is possible that degradation products of these substances may contribute to neuronal degeneration in chronic alcoholism (Collins 1982).

Actions

Central nervous system

Acute effects.   Alcohol is a general central nervous system depressant, producing a dose-dependent decrease in the level of arousal in a manner similar to that of general anaesthetics. The most sensitive areas of the brain are polysynaptic structures such as the reticular activating system, so that impairment of consciousness occurs with small doses. This is manifested in deterioration of discrimination and judgement, concentration, attention, and psychomotor performance — a combination which may result in traffic accidents. The apparent stimulant effects of small doses are probably due to disinhibition. Effects on sleep are similar to those of other hypnotics and consist of a decrease in REMS and SWS, with rebound effects often occurring the same night as blood alcohol concentrations fall. Alcohol also impairs learning and memory.

The effect on mood is complex. Small doses produce mild euphoria and a pleasant sense of relaxation, similar to that seen with tranquillizing drugs. Increased aggression is common with slightly higher doses. Emotions may be generally dulled, but sometimes there may be an increased sense of poignancy. Depression with self-pity occurs in some subjects; gay hilarity and fatuousness in others. Intoxication can cause hallucinations or lapses of memory ('blackouts').

Alcohol has analgesic effects: the ingestion of 60 ml of 95 per cent alcohol raises the pain threshold by 35–40 per cent without alteration of other sensory perceptions; the emotional reaction to pain is also dulled (Ritchie 1980). This rather specific analgesic action combined with euphoria is reminiscent of the effects of morphine.

As dosage is increased, ataxia, slurred speech, and eventually stupor, deep anaesthesia, and coma ensue. The respiratory response to carbon dioxide is depressed; at blood concentrations of 400 mg/l or more, respiratory depression may be lethal. Vasomotor and cardiac centres are also depressed. Alcohol exerts anticonvulsant effects in doses that cause general depression, but a period of hyperexcitability with increased liability to convulsions occurs during recovery (Ritchie 1980).

Chronic effects.   Chronic alcoholism, with associated vitamin deficiencies, may lead to degenerative changes in brain cells. Wernicke's encephalopathy and Korsakoff's psychosis, which are associated with memory defects, are described in Chapter 9. They appear to be more common in individuals who have a genetic abnormality of the enzyme transketolase with reduced affinity for its coenzyme, thiamine (Rogers *et al.* 1981) and respond partially to thiamine. A significant loss of brain tissue, mainly from the white matter of the cerebral hemispheres, was shown in a necropsy study of 22 chronic alcoholics (10 with Wernicke's encephalopathy and 14 with liver disease; Harper *et al.* 1985). Peripheral neuropathy and retrobulbar neuritis are also associated with thiamine deficiency in alcoholics, and a pellagra-like state may occur due to nicotinic acid deficiency. Chronic alcoholism may also lead to chronic cerebral degeneration with dementia and demyelinization of the corpus callosum or central pontine areas. As already mentioned, toxic metabolites as well as thiamine deficiency may contribute.

Computed tomography (CT) techniques have shown that cerebral atrophy, as well as psychological impairment, is common in chronic alcoholics even in the absence of classical Wernicke-Korsakoff's syndrome. Lee *et al.* (1979) found evidence of cortical atrophy on CT scans in 49 per cent of a group of 37 young alcoholic males and 59 per cent had intellectual impairment on psychometric testing. Several other studies reported similar results (*British Medical Journal* 1981). While one in 10 patients seen in alcoholic units have clinically obvious organic brain damage, over half of the remaining 90 per cent have brain shrinkage and specific cognitive defects with particular impairment of memory, abstract thinking, problem-solving, and psychomotor speed. Psychological performance improves during a period of abstinence and even brain scan appearance can show slight slow improvement (*British Medical Journal* 1981). However, in a quantitative neuropathological necropsy study, Harper *et al*. (1987) found a highly significant (irreversible) loss of cortical neurones as well as neuronal shrinkage in the brains of chronic alcoholics compared with age-matched controls. The changes were most marked in the anterior part of the frontal lobes.

Effects on other systems

Alcohol also has acute and chronic cardiovascular, gastrointestinal, urinary and endocrine effects. In particular, it is a major cause of hepatic cirrhosis, the incidence of which is directly related to the level of alcohol consumption over time. The number of cases of alcoholic cirrhosis quadrupled in Britain between 1962 and 1982 (Saunders 1982) and continues to rise. It has adverse effects in pregnancy; fetal alcohol syndrome (Jones *et al*. 1974), consisting of maldevelopment particularly of the central nervous system, is common (up to 40 per cent incidence) in babies born to alcoholic mothers. Alcohol has additive effects with other central nervous system depressants and interacts with several other drugs. A general review of alcohol and disease is given by Sherlock (1982). Whether or not there are 'safe' levels for alcohol consumption is discussed by the Standing Medical Advisory Committee (1989).

Mechanisms of action in central nervous system

The mode of action of alcohol in the central nervous system is reviewed by Tabakoff and Hoffman (1987) and Gonzales and Hoffman (1991). The physical properties of alcohol, including its lipid solubility, are similar to those of general anaesthetics and it seems likely that they act in the same manner. All these compounds increase the fluidity of cell membranes and impair synaptic transmission: they probably act both pre-synaptically, decreasing neurotransmitter release, and post-synaptically, affecting neurotransmitter receptors. There is evidence that the presynaptic action is due to inhibition of calcium influx through voltage-dependent channels in nerve terminals, thus preventing the rise in intracellular calcium which normally acts as a trigger for neurotransmitter release (Harris and Hood 1980). This effect may be secondary to the increased membrane fluidity which uncouples the membrane receptor – intracellular effector mechanism (Franks and Lieb 1982, Anggard 1988). Carmichael and Israel (1975) showed that alcohol, in doses compatible with moderate to severe intoxication, reduces the release of at least six neurotransmitters from slices of rat cortex. These include, in order of their sensitivity to alcohol, acetylcholine, serotonin, dopamine, noradrenaline, glutamate, and GABA. *In vivo* experiments confirm that systemically administered alcohol causes a marked suppression of acetylcholine release from the cerebral cortex and reticular formation (Phillis and Jhamandas 1971; Erickson and Graham 1973), and this effect may partially explain its sedative actions. However, *in vivo* alcohol, in moderate doses given acutely, increases the output and turnover of monoamines both centrally and peripherally (Ritchie 1980; Mullin and Ferko 1983; Ellingboe 1978).

Alcohol, like benzodiazepines and barbiturates, may produce some of its depressant effects by enhancement of GABA activity. Nestoros (1980) found that alcohol potentiated the inhibition of firing of single cortical neurones produced by iontophoretically applied GABA in the cat. This effect appeared to be due to an action on the postsynaptic membrane and it seems likely that alcohol may interact at some site on the GABA receptor complex (Haefely 1989). This site is not the same as the benzodiazepine site, since alcohol does not bind to the benzodiazepine receptor. Acute administration of alcohol, however, increases the number of low affinity GABA binding sites and increases the binding of ^{3}H-diazepam (Ticku 1983). Alcohol may also interact with receptors for excitatory amino acids (Gonzales and Hoffman 1991) whose function is closely linked to that of GABA receptors (Chapter 8).

Central opioid mechanisms appear to be involved in the acute effects of alcohol. There is evidence that alcohol has a selective affinity for opioid delta, but not kappa, receptors (Tabakoff and Hoffman 1987), and it is possible that this effect may mediate its hedonic and analgesic effects. A further intriguing link between effects of alcohol and endogenous opioids is suggested by the possibility that acetaldehyde, the highly reactive metabolite of alcohol, may condense with catecholamines in the brain to form opioid-like alkaloids (Blum *et al*. 1978; Collins 1982). Endogenous formation of tetrahydroisoquinoline and salsolinol from dopamine has been demonstrated in normal humans, in alcoholics, and in patients with Parkinsonism treated with L-dopa. A similar isoquinoline alkaloid, tetrahydropapaveroline, is an intermediate in the biosynthesis of morphine in the opium poppy (papaver somniferum). Both tetrahydroisoquinoline and salsolinol have antinociceptive properties when injected intraventricularly in rats, with a potency similar to that of the enkephalins, and the effect is naloxone-reversible (Kemperman 1982). Isoquinoline alkaloids also potentiate morphine analgesia, increase ethanol-induced sleep time in mice, inhibit calcium binding to synaptic membranes, release endogenous stores of catecholamines, and some have hallucinogic properties (Kemperman 1982).

Furthermore, some studies have suggested that naloxone can reverse alcohol-induced coma in man (MacKenzie 1979; Jeffreys *et al.* 1980; Lyon and Anthony 1982; Jeffcoate *et al.* 1979) although these results were not confirmed by Bird *et al.* (1982). In animals, reversal of the acute effects of alcohol by opioid antagonists has been observed, but there is a significant genetically determined difference in the response (Kiianmaa *et al.* 1983; Prunell *et al.* 1987). Thus, the isoquinoline hypothesis in human alcoholism remains controversial, but if true it would appear that 'when one imbibes alcohol a central opiate-like substance is, in essence, produced' (Blum *et al.* 1978, p. 119).

In addition, acetaldehyde can condense with indoleamines, such as serotonin, to form tetrahydro-beta-carbolines. These substances have been demonstrated *in vivo* both in the rat and in man and their concentration increases after the parenteral administration of aceteldehyde (Kemperman 1983). These beta-carbolines are striking inhibitors of serotonin uptake and also bind weakly to serotonin receptors, resulting in decreased serotonergic activity in the brain. It is possible that this effect acutely contributes to the anxiolytic action of alcohol and chronically to the associated depression and sleep disturbances.

Tolerance and dependence

Behavioural and clinical aspects

Chronic alcohol consumption quickly leads to tolerance with profound adaptive changes in the body, especially in the central nervous system. The progression from tolerance, which occurs to some degree in regular drinkers, to dependence, with compulsive drinking behaviour and a severe withdrawal syndrome, is subtle and there is no clear dividing line. However, dependent subjects tend to consume larger amounts of alcohol within a given time, to drink faster and to report a stronger desire to continue drinking after a priming dose of alcohol than non-dependent drinkers (Wodak *et al.* 1983). Alcoholics tend to lose control over their drinking so that the behaviour becomes self-perpetuating. Some make repeated attempts at abstinence but then indulge in binge-drinking; others maintain a steady blood alcohol concentration by constant topping up. Eventually motivation becomes centred on alcohol and social disintegration occurs. In addition, periods of amnesia (alcoholic blackouts), disorders of affect (rage, depression, pathological jealousy), insomnia, hallucinations, and convulsions may occur in chronic alcoholics, probably as a combined result of alcohol intoxication and degenerative brain changes. A history of affective disorders (major depression, neurosis, and personality disorders) is more common in patients with alcoholic liver disease than in patients with non-alcoholic liver disease (Ewusi-Mensah *et al.* 1983), suggesting that some patients use alcohol, at least initially, as an antidepressant or tranquillizer.

There appears to be considerable individual variation in susceptibility to alcohol dependence and possibly also to alcohol-induced hepatic and neurological changes. The importance of genetic factors has been shown by family, twin and adoption studies which reveal a fourfold increased risk for alcoholism in children with alcoholic parents. The concordance rate for alcoholism in identical twins is higher than that for fraternal twins, whether raised by their parents or adopted separately or together. No clear explanation of the mechanism involved has yet emerged but some possibilities are discussed by Schuckit (1987). Blum *et al.* (1990) suggest, from molecular genetic studies, that there may be an association (in some cases) between alcoholism and a variation in a gene located on chromosome 11, which also codes for the dopamine D_2 receptor. These and other clinical aspects of human alcohol dependence are reviewed by Mello (1987).

Mechanisms of tolerance

Acute tolerance.   Some degree of pharmacokinetic tolerance occurs with repeated alcohol administration but pharmacodynamic tolerance is much more important. *Acute pharmacodynamic tolerance* occurs extremely rapidly and can be demonstrated in man and animals during the time course of absorption and elimination of a single dose.

Chronic tolerance.   Behavioural tolerance to alcohol in man may involve operant and classical conditioning and other forms of learning (Bierness and Vogel-Sprott 1984; Annear and Vogel-Sprott 1985; Shapiro and Nathan 1986; Newlin 1986). Pharmacodynamic tolerance after chronic administration appears to result from multiple complex adaptations involving both pre- and post-synaptic neurones and neuro-transmitter metabolism. Many of the changes occurring during tolerance are opposite to those of the acute response to alcohol. These changes may include increased sensitivity of the calcium-dependent pre-synaptic release of acetylcholine (Littleton *et al.* 1988); decreased post-synaptic GABA receptor density (Volicer and Biagioni 1982); decrease in central serotonergic activity (Kemperman 1983); complex changes in catechola-minergic activity (Mullin and Ferko 1983; Barbaccia *et al.* 1981); decrease of endogenous opioid concentrations (Schulz *et al.* 1980); and increased vasopressin release (Crabbe and Rigter 1980). In addition the formation of opioid-like alkaloids such as salsolinol may play a role in alcohol tolerance and dependence (Sjoquist *et al.* 1982).

Cross-tolerance

Some cross-tolerance to other central nervous system depressants develops in alcohol-tolerant subjects. Since the identification of opiate-like alkaloids in the central nervous system after alcohol ingestion, there has been much interest in the question of whether there is cross-tolerance between alcohol and opiates. If so, the dependence-producing effects of these classes of drugs might involve similar mechanisms. Some animal studies (Myers 1978) support an alcohol-opiate link. For example, morphine suppresses alcohol consumption in alcohol-dependent rodents, and naltrexone, a long-acting opioid antagonist, increases alcohol consumption in these animals. Morphine-dependent rats undergoing withdrawal prefer alcohol mixtures to water, suggesting that alcohol suppresses the morphine-withdrawal syndrome.

Alcohol withdrawal syndrome

Clinical features

Abrupt withdrawal from alcohol in subjects who have developed a high degree of tolerance causes an abstinence syndrome which is generally similar to that seen on withdrawal of hypnotics, and has some features in common with the narcotic withdrawal syndrome. The severity of the syndrome may correlate poorly with the amount and duration of previous alcohol consumption since it depends partly on individual drinking patterns (Jaffe 1980). Withdrawal symptoms usually appear within 12–72 h of total alcohol abstinence, but in subjects tolerant to high blood alcohol concentrations, even a relative drop can precipitate a withdrawal reaction. Chronic alcoholics who drink irregularly may experience withdrawal symptoms while continuing to drink.

In mild cases, the withdrawal syndrome consists of sleep disturbance, nausea, weakness, anxiety, and tremor lasting for less than a day. Such mild withdrawal symptoms may contribute to the hangover experienced after a drinking bout by individuals who are not chronic alcoholics. The classical syndrome in subjects with severe alcohol dependence starts similarly but proceeds to hyperreflexia, vomiting, abdominal cramps, and craving, followed by hallucinations. The intensity of this state increases to a peak within 24–48 h, and may culminate in major convulsions. Sleep disturbance is also prominent, with rebound of REMS.

If the syndrome progresses, a phase of delirium tremens is entered. The patient becomes disorientated, agitated, and a prey to terrifying hallucinations. This stage occurs about the third day of total abstinence and may be accompanied by exhaustion and fatal cardiovascular collapse. However, the syndrome appears to be self-limiting and recovery from the acute withdrawal reaction can begin within 5–7 days without treatment. A protracted abstinence syndrome, as with opiates, follows alcohol withdrawal, with weakness, depression and continued craving, and is likely to lead to relapse.

A neonatal withdrawal syndrome occurs in the babies of chronic alcoholic mothers. This occurs within 48 h of birth and includes sleep disturbances, tremor, hyperreflexia, and feeding difficulties.

Mechanisms of withdrawal syndrome

In view of the complex mechanisms involved in alcohol tolerance, it is not possible to explain particular features of the withdrawal syndrome in terms of any one neurotransmitter. Central degenerative changes and vitamin deficiencies associated with chronic alcoholism further confuse the picture. One mechanism, common to the narcotic withdrawal syndrome, may be a deficiency in central endogenous opioid concentrations (Schulz et al. 1980) and salsolinol (Collins et al. 1979). Such a deficiency might contribute to the craving and drug-seeking behaviour characteristic of early withdrawal.

The generalized central and autonomic overactivity probably results from increased release of and response to excitatory neurotransmitters including acetylcholine and catecholamines. As in the withdrawal syndromes of other central nervous system depressants, clonidine and propranolol partially relieve some of the symptoms due to noradrenergic overactivity (Wilkins et al. 1983). Benzodiazepines, other hypnotics and anticonvulsants which enhance central GABA activity are also effective. The management of alcohol withdrawal (including social and psycho-therapeutic measures) are discussed by Jaffe (1980). The relapse rate after withdrawal is unfortunately high, probably less than 20–30 per cent of patients remaining permanently abstinent (Hore and Ritson 1982).

Nicotine

Nicotine, a plant alkaloid structurally related to acetylcholine, has properties which make it perhaps the most subtly addictive of all drugs. Taken as tobacco, it vies with alcohol and caffeine for pride of place amongst recreationally used pharmacological agents. The prevalence of cigarette smoking in adults has declined to less than 35 per cent in Britain over the last decade, but tobacco use is rising in underdeveloped countries (Capell 1978; Taha and Ball 1980). The psychopharmacology of smoking is reviewed by Ashton and Stepney (1982) and Ashton and Golding (1989b).

Pharmacokinetics

When inhaled in cigarette smoke, nicotine is swiftly and efficiently absorbed from the lungs. It is also rapidly absorbed from the nasal mucosa when taken as snuff, but absorption from the buccal mucosa from chewing tobacco, nicotine-containing chewing gum, and the relatively alkaline smoke of cigars and pipe tobacco is slower. When swallowed, little nicotine reaches the bloodstream because it undergoes 'first pass' metabolism in the liver.

Once in the bloodstream, nicotine is quickly distributed throughout the body, reaching the brain in 7–8 s (Russell 1978a), where it is briefly concentrated (Larson and Silvette 1975; Schmiterlow et al. 1967). Inhaled puffs of cigarette smoke produce intermittent highly concentrated boli of nicotine in the blood. This factor appears to be important in determining the actions of nicotine, since similar doses given more slowly do not produce the same effects in animals (Armitage et al. 1969).

Nicotine is metabolized to cotinine, nicotine-N-oxide and other products, mainly in the liver, and its elimination half-life is approximately 2 h (Benowitz 1988). There is considerable interindividual variation in the rate of metabolism, and the rate is increased in chronic smokers. Due to hepatic enzyme induction, nicotine increases the rate of metabolism of several other drugs (Rogers et al. 1981). Nicotine and its metabolites are excreted by the kidney at a rate which depends on the pH of the urine and is greatest under acidic conditions (Feyerabend and Russell 1978).

Actions and mechanisms

Central nervous system

Biphasic effects.   The pharmacological actions of nicotine are mainly due to its ability to combine with nicotinic acetycholine receptors. Nicotine exerts a biphasic, dose-dependent stimulant/depressant action on these receptors at cholinergic synapses. The initial combination of nicotine with the receptor stimulates a response, but persistent occupation of the receptors and prolonged effects on the neuronal membrane may block further responses. The degree of stimulation versus block depends on the amount of nicotine present relative to the number of receptors available. In general, small doses of nicotine produce predominantly stimulant effects at synapses and larger doses produce mainly depressant effects. Lethal doses block synaptic transmission completely.

When puffs of cigarette smoke are intermittently inhaled, the time/dose relationship of nicotine reaching the brain can be such as to produce either stimulant or depressant effects. Thus, by varying factors such as size of puff and depth of inhalation, a smoker can obtain predominantly inhibitory or predominantly excitatory effects, or a mixture of both, from one cigarette. The ease with which nicotine can produce rapid, reversible, biphasic effects over a small dose range is probably a major factor determining the popularity of the smoking habit. These effects are exerted on many brain systems including those involved in arousal, reward, and learning and memory (Ashton and Golding 1989*b*; Pomerleau and Pomerleau 1989).

Effects on arousal. Small doses of intravenous nicotine or puffs of cigarette smoke introduced into the nostrils or lungs cause behavioural and EEG arousal in sleeping animals (Domino 1979; Hall 1970). These effects can be blocked by the centrally acting ganglion blocker, mecamylamine. Armitage *et al.* (1969) showed that electrocortical arousal produced by cigarette smoke or intravenous nicotine in anaesthetized cats was accompanied by increased output of acetylcholine from the cortex. Cigarette smoking in man also causes alerting effects on the EEG, producing low voltage, high frequency patterns and an increase in alpha wave frequency (Knott and Venables 1977; Murphree *et al.* 1967; Lambiase and Serra 1957; Mangan and Golding 1978; Church 1989). Cigarette smoking and intermittent intravenous shots of nicotine can also increase the magnitude of cortical evoked potentials (Ashton *et al.* 1974, 1980; Knott 1989). Smoking improves performance in tasks requiring vigilance and sustained attention in man (Wesnes and Warburton 1978; Warburton and Walters 1989).

Under certain conditions, however, smoking and nicotine may decrease the level of arousal. Armitage *et al.* (1969) showed that some doses could cause slowing of EEG activity and a fall in cortical acetylcholine output in the anaesthetized cat. Mangan and Golding (1978) demonstrated in human subjects that under conditions of mild stress, induced by white noise, smoking increased the amount of slow alpha-activity in the EEG. Ashton *et al.* (1980) found that the effect of nicotine on the slow cortical evoked potential (contingent negative variation) was dose-dependent, small doses causing a stimulant effect but larger doses producing a depressant effect.

These and other experiments show that nicotine and cigarette smoking can both increase and decrease arousal, at least partly through effects on cholinergic arousal systems. There appears to be an interaction between dose, personality, and environment which determines which effect predominates. Smokers can manipulate their nicotine dosage to obtain the desired effect in particular circumstances (Ashton and Watson 1970; Ashton *et al.* 1974, 1980; Armitage *et al.* 1968). Smokers themselves report that the subjective effects of smoking can be either in the direction of relaxation or of stimulation, and there is considerable evidence (reviewed by Ashton and Stepney 1982) that smokers self-regulate their nicotine intake when smoking cigarettes of different strength.

Effects on reward systems. Nicotine is reinforcing in animals: certain doses enhance intracranial self-stimulation and animals will self-administer nicotine (Deneau and Inoki 1967; Jarvik 1967; Ando and

Yanagita 1981; Spealman and Goldberg 1982). In humans, smoking is reported to be pleasurable by nearly 90 per cent of chronic smokers, although it clearly does not produce a 'high' comparable with that of many other drugs of dependence. In addition it reduces pain and anxiety in stressful situations (Pomerleau *et al*. 1984). Hall and Turner (1972) and Reavill (1990) demonstrated that nicotine increases the release of nor-adrenaline and dopamine from limbic areas and hypothalamus in ani-mals; this may be the basis for its rewarding effects. In addition, nicotine may interact with opioid reward systems (Karras and Kane 1980); smok-ing has been shown to increase plasma concentrations of beta-endorphin-beta-lipotrophin in man (Pomerleau *et al*. 1983).

Certain doses of nicotine may reduce activity in punishment systems, possibly by a depressant effect at cholinergic synapses. Such an effect would tend to allay unpleasant emotions such as anxiety, fear, frustra-tion, and anger. Situations which give rise to these emotions have been shown to be those which increase the intensity of smoking in smokers. Schachter *et al*. (1977) noted an increase in the number of cigarettes smoked under a high anxiety condition induced by electric shocks, and Mangan and Golding (1978) found an increase in the number and 'strength' of puffs when smokers were stressed by white noise. A similar relationship between stress and smoking intensity has been shown in questionnaire studies (Emery *et al*. 1968; Thomas 1973). Nicotine has been shown to attenuate the disruptive effects of stress on performance in several animal tests (Hutchison and Emley 1973; Nelsen 1978; Hall and Morrison 1973). Aggressive behaviour, in particular, appears to be modified by nicotine and smoking. Berntson *et al*. (1976), and Hutchison and Emley (1973) showed that nicotine decreased aggressive behaviour in animals, and in humans Heimstra (1973) found that subjects allowed to smoke during a 6 h vigilance task did not increase their ratings of aggression while smoking-deprived smokers and non-smokers did. Dunn (1978) reported that smoking prevented the disruption in performance caused by frustration in a complex perceptual motor task.

Effects on learning and memory.   Learning and memory are affected by the level of arousal and appear to involve particularly cholinergic pathways (Chapter 8). Nicotine and smoking have been shown to affect some learning and memory processes in animals and man. For example, Flood *et al*. (1978) reported that nicotine improved memory consolida-tion, and Alpern and Jackson (1978) observed complex dose-dependent biphasic effects of nicotine on various stages of the memory process in mice. Morrison and Armitage (1967) found that nicotine could increase the rate of learning of reward or avoidance tasks in rats, depending on the dose and time after injection. In man the effects of smoking on learning and memory are complex, dose-related and biphasic; in general smoking appears to improve selective attention and memory consolidation, while not affecting or slightly impairing initial learning (Andersson 1975; Mangan and Golding 1978, 1983; Andersson and Hockey 1977; Wesnes and Warburton 1978; Williams 1980; Ney *et al.* 1989).

Effects on other systems

Nicotine exerts its characteristic dose-dependent biphasic effects on both sympathetic and parasympathetic components of the autonomic nervous system. The typical effects of smoking a cigarette include tachycardia, peripheral vasoconstriction, and a rise in blood pressure from central and peripheral sympathetic stimulation, but bradycardia and a fall in blood pressure can result from parasympathetic stimulation or sympathetic depression. Low doses stimulate respiration by stimulation of medullary respiratory centres, chemoreceptors in the carotid and aortic bodies, and sensory receptors in the respiratory tract, but large doses produce respiratory paralysis. Nausea and vomiting may result from stimulation of the medullary chemoreceptor trigger zone, and peripheral vagal and spinal reflex pathways. The usual effect on the gastrointestinal tract is an increase in tone and motor activity. Metabolic and endocrine effects of smoking include a rise in plasma triglycerides, and of cortisol, antidiuretic hormone, and growth hormone.

Adverse effects

Acute nicotine poisoning, which may occur from exposure to nicotine-containing insecticide sprays, is marked by the rapid onset of salivation, nausea, vomiting, diarrhoea, tremor, sweating, and mental confusion. Cardiovascular and respiratory collapse ensue with paralysis of respiratory muscles, and this may be followed by terminal convulsions. The acutely fatal dose of nicotine for an adult is about 60 mg of the base; cigarettes deliver when smoked about 0.05–2.5 mg nicotine (Taylor 1980). Nicotine almost certainly contributes to some of the long-term health hazards of smoking, including neoplastic, cardiovascular and respiratory diseases and increased perinatal mortality (Hoffman *et al.* 1988; Bassenge 1988; Ashton 1991*b*).

Tolerance, dependence, withdrawal effects

Some pharmacokinetic tolerance to nicotine develops in smokers, but pharmacodynamic tolerance is more important in determining smoking behaviour.

Pharmacodynamic tolerance develops unevenly in smokers, who become tolerant to the emetic and irritant effects of nicotine but still exhibit tachycardia, rise in blood pressure, peripheral vasoconstriction, and endocrine and metabolic responses to smoking. Some aspects of tolerance appear to decrease rapidly: in chronic smokers the first cigarette of the day elicits greater cardiovascular responses than later cigarettes, and many smokers say that they get the greatest hedonic effects from the first daily cigarette.

Gross escalation of dosage of nicotine dosage does not occur in smokers. Since the rewarding effects of nicotine are probably derived from a combination of stimulant and inhibitory actions, and most smokers seek both these effects, they may be forced into maintaining a medium dosage. This fine balance between stimulant and inhibitory effects may constitute the root of the tobacco habit. Subjects can obtain mild hedonic effects from nicotine without the disruption of performance or after-effects that occur with other dependence-producing drugs. In fact, performance may be improved, as discussed above, and nicotine from cigarette smoke can be delivered in a controlled dosage to allow the subject to regulate his or her psychological comfort and performance in a way that is optimal in a range of environments (Ashton and Stepney 1982; Ashton and Golding 1989b).

Cessation of smoking can give rise to a definite abstinence syndrome (Jaffe 1980; Brecher 1972; Hatsukami et al. 1984). In keeping with the biphasic effects of nicotine, this syndrome shows characteristics of the withdrawal reaction from both stimulant and depressant drugs. Withdrawal effects include craving, nausea, headache, constipation, increased appetite and weight, lethargy, depression, irritability, anxiety, restlessness, decreased psychomotor performance, increased low frequency EEG activity, and fall in heart rate and blood pressure. The syndrome starts within 24 h of smoking cessation and some symptoms may persist for many months. However, the severity is variable and some smokers can give up without difficulty. The symptoms may be partially alleviated by nicotine chewing gum (Russell et al. 1980; Pomerleau and Pomerleau 1988) but the relapse rate of smokers advised to stop smoking for health reasons or attending anti-smoking clinics is high.

Cocaine

Cocaine, an alkaloid present in the leaves of the coca plant, is a potent local anaesthetic and also has central nervous stimulant properties similar to those of amphetamine (Chapter 4). It has marked hedonic effects and is subject to abuse, a practice which fluctuates in popularity but increased during the 1970s in the USA and Europe (Jaffe 1980) and escalated further, especially among young people, with the introduction of free base cocaine ('crack') in the 1980s (Fischman 1987).

Pharmacokinetics

Cocaine is lipid soluble; it is readily absorbed from the skin and mucous membranes and enters the central nervous system. It is mainly degraded by plasma and hepatic esterases, and about 10 per cent is excreted unchanged by the kidney. After oral or nasal application of the salt (cocaine hydrochloride), peak plasma concentrations are reached in 30–40 min and the plasma half-life is about 1 h. Psychological effects last for 30–40 min with no initial 'rush'. Used intravenously, subjective effects including a 'rush' occur within 1–2 min (Fischman 1987). Free base cocaine ('crack') can readily be prepared by heating the salt with ammonia and sodium bicarbonate. This preparation vaporizes when heated and can be smoked in a cigarette or free-base water pipe. Inhalation of 'crack' gives an effect similar to that of intravenous cocaine salt; peak plasma concentrations are reached almost immediately and the user experiences a powerful euphoric 'high'. However, the effect lasts only a matter of minutes and is followed by a 'crash' of severe dysphoria and craving. The rapid onset and brief duration of the extreme euphoria produced by certain forms of cocaine administration can lead to a compelling dependence (Fischman 1987; Strang and Edwards 1989; *Lancet* 1987*b*).

Actions

Local anaesthesia

Like other local anaesthetics, cocaine blocks nerve conduction when applied locally to nervous tissue. It prevents both the generation and conduction of nerve impulses by inhibiting the rapid influx of sodium ions through the neuronal membrane. The mechanism is thought to be displacement of calcium from sites on membrane phospholipids, causing configurational changes which constrict sodium channels (Rogers *et al.* 1981).

Central nervous system

Acute effects. Cocaine, and all related local anaesthetics, produce an initial central nervous stimulation followed by depression. The effect observed depends on dosage and rate of administration. With steadily increasing doses, restlessness proceeds to tremor and agitation, followed by convulsions and then central nervous system depression with death from respiratory failure. Cocaine appears to exert a particularly powerful stimulant effect on the cortex compared with other local anaesthetics (Ritchie and Greene 1981).

In small doses, cocaine has potent hedonic effects (described above). Addicts describe a euphoria similar to that obtained from amphetamine, consisting of mood elevation, increased energy and alertness, loss of fatigue, a feeling of enhanced physical and mental capacity, and loss of desire for food. In laboratory situations, addicts cannot initially distinguish between the subjective effects of 8–10 mg cocaine or 10 mg dexamphetamine given intravenously. However, the effects of cocaine only last a few minutes after intravenous administration, while those of some amphetamines (e.g. methamphetamine) endure for hours. Other local anaesthetics are also rewarding: subjects cannot distinguish between the euphoric effects of cocaine or lignocaine taken intranasally, and animals will self-administer both procaine and cocaine (Jaffe 1980).

The effects of small doses of cocaine on behaviour are also similar to those of amphetamine: at first the subject is garrulous, excited, and insomniac, but with increasing doses tremor, agitation and anxiety are prominent. Some individuals experience dysphoria even with small doses. Further dose increases may cause vomiting, from stimulation of medullary vomiting centres, and convulsions before the depressant effects supervene. Acute intoxication with cocaine (or amphetamine) produces a state of extreme agitation and a toxic psychosis, with the physical accompaniments of tachycardia, hypertension, cardiac arrhythmias, sweating, hyperpyrexia, and convulsions. Without treatment, death may occur from cardiovascular and respiratory collapse or from convulsions. Drugs treatment includes chlorpromazine, which antagonizes the psychotic effects, hypertension and hyperpyrexia, and diazepam as an anticonvulsant.

Chronic effects.   Repeated use of large doses of cocaine produces a psychosis similar to that produced by large doses of amphetamine. The syndrome may be clinically indistinguishable from some forms of schizophrenia and typically includes paranoid ideation, thought disturbance, stereotyped movements, and hallucinations which may be visual, auditory, or tactile. Formication is a characteristic feature: a feeling of pricking or crawling under the skin which may lead to picking and excoriation and delusions of parasitosis (Jaffe 1980; Brecher 1972).

Mechanisms of action

The central stimulant effects of cocaine and other local anaesthetics have been ascribed to depression of inhibitory pathways due to the local anaesthetic effects on neuronal membranes, i.e. they result from disinhibition rather than stimulation of neurones (Rogers *et al.* 1981; Ritchie and Greene 1980). However, cocaine and other local anaesthetics produce many stimulant actions which are indistinguishable from those of amphetamine, and there is cross-tolerance between at least some of the actions of cocaine, amphetamine, and other sympathomimetic agents (Leith and Barrett 1981). Amphetamine (Chapter 4) is known to act largely by releasing catecholamines from nerve endings, although it also has some direct stimulant action on noradrenergic receptors, catecholamine reuptake blocking activity, and monoamine oxidase inhibitory action. The close similarities between local anaesthetics and indirectly acting sympathomimetic amines suggests that they have some mechanisms of action in common.

The euphoric effects of both cocaine and amphetamine are probably due to enhancement of dopaminergic activity in the brain. The reinforcing effects of both drugs in animals are blocked by dopamine receptor antagonists, and destruction of dopamine neurones in the nucleus accumbens attenuates cocaine self-administration in rats (Pettit *et al.* 1984). Cocaine, like amphetamine, increases dopaminergic tone in the mesolimbic system and potentiates the actions of dopamine on dopamine receptors in several brain areas including the nucleus accumbens, which is probably a key site for its rewarding actions (Galloway 1988; Lakosi and Cunningham 1988; Uchimura and North 1990; Lacey *et al.* 1990). Furthermore, cocaine and dopamine produce similar responses in 'hedonistic neurons' in brain reward areas (Stein and Belluzzi 1989; Chapter 5). Thus cocaine may produce central effects by a mechanism separate from its local anaesthetic actions.

Tolerance, abuse, dependence

Acute tolerance to cocaine appears to occur in man, since the euphoric effects following intranasal use decay more quickly than plasma concentrations (Jaffe 1980). To maintain a euphoric state, cocaine addicts tend to take the drug every 30–40 min. Chronic tolerance to the convulsant and cardiorespiratory effects has been reported in man, but increased sensitivity to the sympathetic effects may also occur, and is attributed to catecholamine reuptake block (Ritchie and Greene 1980). Crosstolerance between cocaine and amphetamine has been reported for the anorectic effects (Jaffe 1980) and for the enhancement of intracranial self-stimulation in animals (Leith and Barrett 1981).

Although the chewing of coca leaves, as practised by people living high in the Andes, does not give rise to signs of tolerance or dependence, the taking of cocaine in higher doses by 'snorting', smoking, or intravenous injection not only produces an intense 'high', but can also give rise to compulsive drug-taking behaviour in some subjects. The pattern of drug use is similar for cocaine and amphetamine, and characteristically includes 'runs' of often repeated dosage for several days, followed by periods of abstinence. Animals self-administering these stimulants show similar cyclical patterns (Villarreal and Salazar 1981). Some individuals may use these drugs for months or years without developing a toxic psychosis, which may suddenly appear during the course of a single 'run'. Cocaine and amphetamine use is often combined with the taking of central nervous system depressant drugs, preferably opiates, which are used to combat the dysphoric and psychogenic effects of the stimulants. As with other drugs of abuse, intravenous administration of cocaine carries a risk of infections, including AIDS.

Sudden cessation of cocaine after a 'run' of high dosage is followed by a deep sleep lasting 12–18 h or more. Upon awaking, a withdrawal syndrome of craving, lethargy, hunger, sleep disturbance with rebound of REMS, and depression appears and may run a protracted course. The symptoms are immediately alleviated by a further dose of the drug, thus reinstating the pattern. The dopamine agonist bromocriptine (Dackis *et al*. 1989) and the anticonvulsant carbamazepine (Halikas *et al*. 1989) may alleviate cocaine craving and have been used in some treatment programmes. The withdrawal syndrome appears to be more marked with cocaine than with amphetamine, although it is clinically similar. Nevertheless, there is a population of cocaine users who only take an occasional 'snort' and not appear to become dependent, although they often abuse other drugs.

Phencyclidine

Phencyclidine was introduced as a general anaesthetic and is structurally related to the anaesthetic agent ketamine. It was discarded because patients experienced delirium, vivid dreams, and hallucinations on emerging from anaesthesia. However, it became popular as a recreational drug (under the names Angel Dust, PCP, Peace Pill, and others), and by the 1970s it was one of the most commonly abused drugs in the USA. Phencyclidine, and analogues with similar properties, is easy to synthesize and many such agents are sold illicitly as 'street drugs' in the USA. Ketamine abuse has also been reported. At present the recreational use of such drugs is only sporadic in the UK.

Pharmacokinetics

Phencyclidine is well absorbed from any route and may be sniffed, smoked, ingested, or injected. It is lipid soluble and widely distributed in the body, and enters the nervous system and cerebrospinal fluid. Hydroxylation occurs in the liver, and the metabolites are conjugated with glucuronic acid and excreted in the urine. There is considerable gastroenteric recirculation which prolongs the action of the drug. The elimination half-life is about 1–2 h after small doses, but up to 3 days after overdose (Jaffe 1980).

Actions

Central nervous system

Acute effects. Phencyclidine has anaesthetic, analgesic, central nervous system stimulant and depressant actions, and is one of the most powerful psychotomimetic agents known (Jaffe 1980; *British Medical Journal* 1980). In man, small doses produce a sense and appearance of drunkeness with staggering gait, slurred speech, nystagmus, and numbness or complete analgesia of the fingers and toes. At this stage subjects describe a 'high' consisting of euphoria, sense of intoxication, increased response to external stimuli, and general excitement. Sweating, catatonic muscular rigidity, disturbances of body image, disorganized thoughts, restlessness, and anxiety may accompany the 'high'. Bizarre and sometimes aggressive behaviour and a schizophreniform psychosis may occur. There may be amnesia for the episode of intoxication. The typical 'high' from a single dose lasts 4–6 h and is followed by an extended 'coming down' period.

With increasing dosage, analgesia becomes marked and anaesthesia, drowsiness, stupor or coma and convulsions may follow. Anaesthesia and profound analgesia can coexist with normal pharyngeal and laryngeal reflexes. In some anaesthetic doses, a type of sensory isolation may occur (dissociative anaesthesia) in which the subject's eyes are wide open but he appears unresponsive to the environment. However, sensory impulses may reach to the cortex and be experienced in distorted form sometimes simulating 'near death' experiences including a sense of separation from the body (Jansen 1989). Unlike most anaesthetics, phencyclidine stimulates respiratory and cardiovascular systems, and autonomic activity generally: tachycardia, hypertension, sweating, hypersalivation, fever, repetetive movements, and muscle rigidity on stimulation are described. The course of intoxication is prolonged, due to the slow elimination of the drug, and a schizophrenia-like psychosis can persist for several weeks after a single dose. 'Flashback' psychotic episodes may occur several weeks after cessation of phencyclidine use.

Complications of acute phencyclidine intoxication include adrenergic crises precipitating high output cardiac failure, cerebrovascular accidents, malignant hyperthermia, and status epilepticus. Acute rhabdomyolysis has been described, probably resulting from excessive isometric muscular contractions. However, the principal causes of death associated with phencyclidine are homicide or suicide. Death from respiratory arrest can occur when phencyclidine is taken with barbiturates.

The management of acute intoxication involves keeping the patient in quiet surroundings; external stimulation aggravates the already hyperexcited state. Fits and muscular rigidity respond to benzodiazepines and haloperidol is recommended for psychotic symptoms. Acidification of the urine and continuous gastric suction hastens elimination of the drug.

Chronic effects.   Phencyclidine is often abused chronically. About half the users claim to take the drug at least once a week. 'Runs' of drug-taking lasting 2–3 days are not uncommon and are followed by depression and disorientation upon wakening. Some take the drug regularly several times a day. It is sniffed (snorted), taken orally, or injected intravenously, but usually it is sprinkled on tobacco or cannabis and smoked as a cigarette. Polydrug abuse including phencyclidine is also common.

Chronic phencyclidine usage appears to produce an organic brain disorder with long-term neuropsychological damage. Chronic abusers become aggressive, suffer loss of recent memory, have dysphasic speech difficulties and difficulty in time estimation, develop personality disorders with anxiety and a psychosis indistinguishable from schizophrenia which can last 6 months to a year after stopping the drug. Drug tolerance and dependence can almost certainly develop with craving and compulsive use. Phencyclidine is reinforcing in animals and tolerance develops in some species.

Mechanisms of action

The mechanisms of action of phencyclidine remain unclear although they have been the subject of much recent research. Phencyclidine specifically interacts with at least two receptor sites in the brain (Manallack *et al.* 1986; Quirion *et al.* 1987): the receptor for the excitatory amino acid *N*-methyl-*D*-aspartate (NMDA receptor; Chapter 8, Fig. 8.3) and the opioid sigma receptor (Chapter 5). At the NMDA site, phencyclidine antagonizes the excitatory effects of NMDA by blocking a channel for several ions (Na^+, K^+, Ca^{2+} and possibly Mg^{2+}). This action may underlie the dissociative anaesthesia (MacDonald and Nowak 1990) but it is doubtful whether it can account for the psychotomimetic and hedonic effects.

Phencyclidine also binds, though with lesser affinity, to the sigma opioid receptor (Winger 1987), an action which it shares with some opioids (pentazocine; Chapter 7). This action may mediate the psychotomimetic effects (Herberg and Rose 1989; Sonders *et al.* 1988). Greenberg and Segal (1986) suggest that phencyclidine may also interact with mu- as well as with sigma-opioid receptors, since some of its behavioural effects (including ingestive behaviour) are similar to those of morphine-like opiates and are antagonized by low doses of naloxone. Other evidence (Piercy and Ray 1988; Piercy *et al.* 1988) suggests that the psychotomimetic and reinforcing effects of phencyclidine are at least partly due to stimulation of dopaminergic activity in limbic system pathways.

Organic solvents

The abuse of household and industrial organic solvents originated in the USA and Puerto Rico in the 1950s. It became widespread in the USA in the 1960s and in the UK in the 1970s, and the practice continues in the 1990s. Adolescents in relatively deprived social groups are mainly involved; boys somewhat outnumber girls, and glue sniffing has been reported in children as young as 8 years old (King *et al.* 1981). Some of the substances abused are shown in Table 7.2, they all have properties similar to those of alcohol and gaseous anaesthetics. Usually, the solvent vapour is inhaled by means of a variety of techniques designed to increase the available concentration (such as inhaling deeply from a bag or placing a plastic bag over the head), but occasionally they are ingested in liquid form of sprayed directly into the throat.

Pharmacokinetics

The pharmacokinetics of industrial solvents are described by Waldron (1981). They are readily absorbed though the lungs and reach variable concentrations in the blood, depending on the blood/air partition coefficient of individual substances. They are highly lipid soluble and widely distributed in the body, reaching highest concentrations in the nervous system and fat depots.

Actions

Central nervous system

Like general anaesthetics and alcohol, organic solvents produce a dose-dependent central nervous system depression. Mild intoxication occurs within minutes of inhalation, lasting up to 30 min. However, with judicious repeated sniffing this state can be maintained for up to 12 h (Black 1982). There is an initial euphoria with apparent excitatory effects, probably due to disinhibition, followed, as dosage is increased, by confusion, perceptual distortion, hallucinations, and delusions. At this stage there may be marked aggressive and risk-taking behaviour. As central nervous system depression increases, ataxia, nystagmus, and dysathria become pronounced, followed by drowsiness and coma, and sometimes convulsions. On recovery there may be complete amnesia

Table 7.2 Some products inhaled by abusers of volatile solvents

Product	Principal volatile components
Adhesives	
Balsa wood cement	Ethylacetate
Contact adhesive	Toluene
Cycle tyre repair cement	Toluene and xylenes
PVC cement	Trichlorethylene
Aerosols	
Air freshener	Halons 11/12/22 and butane
Deodorants, antiperspirants	Halons 11/12/22 and butane
Fly spray	Halons 11/12/22 and butane
Hair lacquer	Halons 11/12/22 and butane
Local analgesic spray	Halons 11/12/22
Paint	Halons 11/12/22 and esters
Anaesthetic agents	
Gaseous	Nitrous oxide
Liquid	Halothane, enflurane, isoflurane
Local	Halons 11/12/22, ethyl chloride
Cosmetics (non-aerosol)	
Nail varnish remover	Acetone and esters
Degreasing agents	1,1,1-Trichloroethane
	Trichlorethylene
	Tetrachloroethylene
Domestic spot removers and dry cleaners	1,1,1-Trichloroethane
	Tetrachloroethylene
	Trichloroethylene
Dry cleaning (commercial)	Tetrachloroethylene
Fire extinguishers	BCF, Halon
Fuel gases	
Cigarette lighter refills	*n*-Butane and iso-butane
Butane	*n*-Butane and iso-butane
Propane	Propane and butanes
Paint stripper	Dichloromethane
	Toluene
Petrol	Petroleum
Typewriter correcting fluid and thinners	1,1,1-Trichloroethane

Reference: Ramsay *et al.* 1989

for the episode. Vomiting may occur at any stage and there is a risk of inhalational asphyxia.

Chronic solvent abuse produces organic damage in the nervous system, and the changes may sometimes be irreversible. Peripheral neuropathy has been described, especially with toluene, trichlorethylene, petrol containing lead, n-hexane and methylbutylketone. The latter two substances are metabolized to 2,5-hexanedione which causes giant axonal neuropathy. Cerebral cortical atrophy may occur with toluene, petrol containing lead and probably others, and prolonged cerebellar dysfunction may occur with chronic toluene abuse. Optic atrophy has also been described (Black 1982; Waldron 1981; King et al. 1981) and delayed latencies of visual evoked potentials were noted by Cooper et al. (1985).

Psychological changes with chronic use include craving, apathy, impaired psychomotor performance, and possibly precipitation of schizophrenia. Drug dependence definitely occurs and withdrawal symptoms probably contribute to continued use. Chronic solvent abusers have a variety of somatic and psychological complaints including headaches, photophobia, anxiety, irritability, tremor, sleep disturbance, hallucinations, anorexia, nausea, vomiting, abdominal pain, fits, tinnitus, diplopia, and paraesthesiae (O'Connor 1984). These symptoms probably represent a mixture of toxic and withdrawal effects.

Other health hazards are reviewed in *Human Toxicology* (1989). They include damage to hepatic, renal, cardiovascular, respiratory and haematological systems. Since 1985 there have been 100 deaths each year from solvent abuse (Ramsay et al. 1989). Causes of death include accidents or suicide during intoxication, asphyxiation, cardiac arrhythmia, and hepatic and renal failure.

Dependence, tolerance, withdrawal syndrome

Many adolescents sniff organic solvents as part of a group activity and after a short period move on to some other activity. However, drug dependence can occur and is not uncommon in 'solitary sniffers' who use solvents as adults use alcohol (Herzberg and Wolkind 1983). Tolerance is evidenced by the observation that 'in the initial stages of inhalation, prior to habit formation, a few whiffs of the vapors will produce a "jag" . . . but chronic users often have to "take" the contents of as many as 5 tubes . . . of cement in order to experience the desired results' (Glaser and Massengale 1962, p. 90). O'Connor (1982) describes several chronic abusers taking regular inhalations at least 4 days a week for a minimum of 3 h a day, with a history of abuse of at least 6 months. In cases of this sort, abrupt cessation of organic solvents undoubtedly gives rise to a withdrawal syndrome. This appears to be similar to the alcohol abstinence syndrome, although usually milder, and incudes anxiety, tremor, hallucinations, sleep disturbances, and a variety of somatic and psychological symptoms.

The mechanisms of action on the brain and the central changes involved in tolerance and withdrawal have not been systematically studied for organic solvents. It seems likely, however, that they are fundamentally similar to those of alcohol. Methods of treatment and sociological factors in solvent abuse are discussed by O'Connor (1982, 1984); Lowenstein (1982), and Herzberg and Wolkind (1983).

Part III
Learning and memory

8. Learning and memory systems

Learning and memory can be viewed as a system for modifying behaviour as a result of experience. Both functionally and anatomically this system is inextricably bound up with the systems for arousal (Chapter 2), and for reward and punishment (Chapter 5). In the simplest terms, arousal supplies the necessary degree of alertness and attention while reward/punishment supplies motivation, and the degree of either attention or motivation affects the efficiency of learning and memory. The three systems operate in synchrony, utilizing the same neurotransmitters and modulators, and relaying in many of the same brain structures and pathways.

Each new experience to which an animal is exposed is interpreted in the light of previous memories. The brain does not merely act as a blank screen for recording facts; it translates and edits external or internal information on the basis of previously acquired information. Just as the brain exerts a control over its own sensory input, as described in Chapter 2, so it selects which experiences are laid down as a basis for future action and which are discarded or forgotten.

The process of learning involves physical as well as functional changes in the brain. Yet there is no separate structure for memory, which resides to some degree in every living cell. In the central nervous system, various structures make particular contributions to certain aspects of memory, and there is considerable localization of function for specialized forms of memory. Even so, multiple interconnections between many parts of the brain are involved, and the formation and retrieval of memories is probably possible through numerous alternative and simultaneously active pathways. There is no discrete location in the brain for any one memory; rather each memory is synthesized as a pattern of selective neural activity in many pathways and in many areas. Activity in these pathways is almost infinitely adaptable and learned behaviours can be altered or reversed by later experience. There is increasing evidence, discussed below, that the crucial neural alterations necessary for memory occur at synapses. The speed and efficiency of learning and memory and the capacity for information storage, linkage, and retrieval are closely allied to, and may even constitute, the quality described as intelligence.

The general organization of learning and memory systems and some of the mechanisms thought to be involved are outlined in this chapter. The localization and biochemistry of memory in man is further explored in Chapter 9 in relation to clinical memory disorders, while some drugs which affect memory functions are described in Chapter 10.

Stages of learning and memory

Learning and memory are conventionally described as a continuum of stages: (1) *acquisition* or registration of information, (2) *ultra-short-term memory* (immediate memory), a transient form of retention by means of which information of transitory significance, such as a series of digits, is retained for a matter of seconds, (3) *short-term memory* (intermediate memory), a temporary form of retention which may last for minutes, hours or days and may be prolonged by 'rehearsal' — mental repetition of the data, (4) *long-term memory* a form of retention in which information, initially in short-term memory, is transferred to a more permanent store (*consolidation*) which may endure for decades or even a life-time. Finally (5) *retrieval* (recall), is a process whereby stored information is selectively made accessible as required. Whether or not these hypothetical stages of memory are really separate (and particularly whether long-term memories are stored or encoded in a different form from shorter-term memories) is controversial.

During learning, all the stages operate simultaneously. For example, new information, after initial registration, enters immediate or short-term memory; on the second and subsequent presentations, the information is added to that already entered in short-term memory, which is recalled as the information becomes familiar. Meanwhile, data relevant to the new information is retrieved from long-term memory, and finally the newly learned information, interpreted and edited in the light of previous experience, is itself consolidated and stored in long-term memory. Since learning depends on information storage, all types of learning are based on memory, and learning and memory can be viewed as parts of the same process.

Types of learning

Several types of learning have been described (Kupferman 1978). More complex types of learning may be based on these elementary forms, but the many processes of 'higher' learning, especially those involving language, are not fully understood.

Habituation

Habituation is the decrease in a behavioural response following repetition of an initially novel stimulus, such as diminution of the startle response to a repeated sound. 'Habituation . . . is probably the most widespread of all forms of learning. Through habituation animals, including human beings, learn to ignore stimuli that have lost novelty or meaning . . . Habituation is thought to be the first learning process to emerge in human infants and is commonly used to study the development of intellectual processes such as attention, perception and memory' (Kandel 1979; p. 64).

Sensitization

Sensitization is a slightly more complex form of learning which consists of a prolonged enhancement of the response to a stimulus if it is preceded by a noxious or intense stimulus. 'Whereas habituation requires an animal to learn to ignore a particular stimulus because its consequences are trivial, sensitization requires the animal to learn to attend to a stimulus because it is accompanied by potentially painful or dangerous consequences' (Kandel 1979; p. 67). Clearly both types of learning are accompanied by changes in arousal. Sensitization has been described as a precursor form of classical Pavlovian conditioning; in both types of learning a response to one stimulus is enhanced as a result of activation by a different stimulus.

Operant conditioning

Operant conditioning, described by Thorndike (1911), represents a process of trial and error learning. For example, if a rat is placed in a cage containing a protruding lever it will, in its random activity, occasionally press the lever. If this action is rewarded by food or drink or punished by an electric footshock, the animal soon learns to associate the action with the outcome and to modify its behaviour accordingly. Thus, the frequency of lever pressing increases if the result is rewarding (reinforcement) and declines if the result is aversive (punishment). An interaction with reward and punishment systems is obviously necessary for this type of learning.

Classical conditioning

Classical conditioning was described by Pavlov (1927) who showed that if a neutral (conditional) stimulus, such as the sound of a bell, is repeatedly paired with a second (unconditional) stimulus, such as food on the tongue, the animal learns to associate the two stimuli and will respond to the first stimulus in anticipation of the second. Thus, the sound of the bell initially elicits little overt response although the presentation of the food evokes obvious responses including salivation. After conditioning, the bell alone evokes many of the responses, including salivation, originally elicited only by the food. A conditioned response also develops if the second stimulus is aversive.

In both operant and classical conditioning, the strength of the response is related to the probability of occurrence of reinforcement or punishment. If after conditioning the expected result no longer occurs, the response undergoes *extinction*, a form of relearning which terminates a response to a stimulus which is no longer relevant. However not every stimulus or response needs to be reinforced to maintain conditioning; the rate of extinction can be slowed by various systems of partial reinforcement. In operant conditioning, the highest rates of response are obtained when rewards only occur after a number of responses have been made. In both types of conditioning the time interval between the stimulus or operant response and the reinforcement is critical; in general the longer the delay the poorer the associative learning.

There is evidence (Siegel 1983, 1984) that operant and classical conditioning, both of which involve reward and punishment systems (Chapter 5), contribute to drug dependence and behavioural tolerance to drugs in man and animals (Chapter 6, 7).

Types of memory

The tremendous scope and complexity of memory defies classification. Some categories of memory which have been classified largely from clinical data in man and lesion experiments in animals are mentioned here. They do not, however, cover the full range and subtlety of memory or convey how a single word can conjure up a host of further associations – pictures, smells, events, emotions, and other phenomena – and also trigger off a variety of physical responses.

Short-term memory

Although there is no direct evidence, it has been widely accepted that immediate and short-term memory may depend on reverberatory neural circuits maintained by excitatory feedback connections, and that such memories are temporarily encoded in terms of the firing patterns of complex sets of neurones (Hebb 1949). Immediate memory has a limited capacity of five to ten items in man and is acoustically rather than semantically coded (Warrington 1981). At some stage more permanent changes (perhaps synaptic) are thought to occur, with the result that a selection of the information is preserved in a more lasting form.

Long-term memory

There is evidence that long-term memory involves several functionally and anatomically separate systems, which can be selectively impaired by localized damage to the brain (Warrington 1981; Oakley 1981; Ojemann 1983). This hierarchy of different types of memory has developed with the expansion of the brain and of more sophisticated forms of environmental adaptation in the course of evolution (Oakley 1981). In practice, however, the different types of memory function interdependently.

Association memory

Association memory is the form of memory involved in learning by operant or classical conditioning. It requires the formation of an association between two events. This type of memory appears primarily to involve subcortical structures. It survives total removal of the neocortex in mammals; it can still be demonstrated after removal of all brain tissue rostral to the thalamus in the rat; and is still present after severe reductions in neural mass in man (Oakley 1981). The major locus for the associative mechanism is thought to be in the brainstem reticular formation.

Event memory or representational memory

A second type of memory has been termed event memory (Warrington 1981) or representational memory (Oakley 1981). This type of memory forms a record of the individual's experiences. A major difference from association memory is that event memory includes the ability to retain a representation or image of a prior event in the absence of the original stimulus. In addition, event memory involves not only the storage of single events, but also their organization into a spatio-temporal map or template which allows an orientation of each event in relation to space and time. The existence of such a template also confers predictive ability; future events can be compared or matched with past events, allowing appropriate action to be taken in familiar or unfamiliar circumstances.

The capacity of event memory is very large; indeed for practical purposes it is almost infinite (Warrington 1981). However, it is relatively unstable and appears to undergo continuous modification, possibly as a result of interaction with previous and subsequent learning and memories (Piaget and Inhelder 1969; Kupferman 1978). For example, subjects asked to repeat a previously learned story tend to shorten and reconstruct it, making alterations from the original and emphasizing the most important points. Apparent forgetting may therefore be due to reinterpretation as well as to failure to register, store or retrieve information. The neurological substrates for event memory consist of diencephalic and temporal lobe structures, including the hippocampus, mammillary bodies, certain thalamic nuclei, and the frontal neocortex. In man, event memory may be selectively impaired in the amnesic syndrome (Chapter 9) in which there is damage to these structures. Memory for recent events is more vulnerable to disturbance than that for remote events.

Semantic memory or abstract memory

Semantic memory (Warrington 1981) or abstract memory (Oakley 1981) is memory for words, facts, and concepts, including numerical concepts. It represents a general store of information composed of facts abstracted from several specific instances. The items in the memory are context free and lacking in spatiotemporal identity, and the meaning of objects and events are preserved separately from memories of the specific incidents in which they occurred. Such memories appear to represent abstracts of a prototype for each item as a result of the entry of similar examples into storage (Oakley 1981). Semantic memory has a very large, but probably limited capacity; it is extremely durable and relatively accessible. Thus, normal individuals have a large though limited vocabulary, and their visual and auditory memory of words and the meaning of words is immediate, almost permanent, and relatively unchanged by use. Semantic memory is associated primarily with the neocortex, particularly the occipital, parietal and temporal regions. Specialized cortical areas are involved in memory for language and are discussed further below and in Chapter 9.

Recognition memory

The ability to recognize places, people, objects, or events may involve semantic, event, and association memory systems. Conscious recognition of the *meaning* of sensory stimuli depends on semantic memory, and cortical lesions may result in 'psychic blindness' or agnosia. For example, destruction of the temporal cortex in the Rhesus monkey or man leads to inability to differentiate edible from inedible objects and loss of fear reactions to previously frightening visual stimuli (Oakley 1981). Agnosia may be limited to one sensory modality: in visual agnosia an object is not recognized by sight but may be recognized by touch, while the opposite is true of tactile agnosia. In prosopagnosia in man (discussed by Damasio 1985, 1990), there is inability to recognize by sight previously familiar faces, although faces as a category are recognized, and the familiar person may be recognized by voice. This agnosia results from bilateral lesions of occipitotemporal cortex. Prosopagnosia does not occur with unilateral lesions and it appears that each hemisphere can recognize faces via different strategies.

Despite the lack of conscious recognition, there is evidence that familiar faces are recognized at subcortical levels, since the faces of the subject himself, relatives, or friends generate greater autonomic responses than unfamiliar faces. This observation suggests that one level of recognition involves association memory. The lack of conscious recognition appears to be due to a failure of visual stimuli to activate other memories pertinent to the familiar face and suggests the existence of a template system for the individual recognition of faces. Such a template system or visuospatial map is an attribute of event memory, involving subcortical temporal lobe structures including the hippocampus. Failure of recognition of previously (and often) experienced faces, places, pictures, etc., occurs in the amnesic syndrome, associated with damage to these structures. Such stimuli never become familiar, however often they are repeated. Possibly such experiences are normally processed through event memory at each repetition, before being abstracted into semantic memory. The various aspects of recognition memory demonstrate the interdependence of the several categories of memory.

Motor memory

Motor memory is the ability to store and recall motor movements in temporal and spatial sequence. It appears to be subserved by a system located in the cerebellum (Marr 1969; Young 1979; Iversen 1977; Anderson 1982).

Neural mechanisms of learning and memory

In the widest sense learning and memory are incorporated in every body cell. The coding of information in DNA constitutes a type of genetic memory which interacts with the environment to determine which of a range of possible characteristics are selected for expression. In the nervous system too, the basis of learning and memory appears to be a process of selection between a range of genetically possible patterns of neural activity, followed by amplification of the selected paths and shutting down of alternative paths (Young 1979; Mark 1978; Marr 1969; Eccles 1977; Changeux and Danchin 1976; Edelman 1978). It seems likely that many of the underlying changes occur at the synaptic level and involve most of the brain as well as the spinal cord and probably much of the peripheral nervous system. However, different parts of the brain make specific contributions to various aspects of learning and memory. The major advantage of learning and memory in the nervous system is that it is far more plastic and rapidly adaptable than genetic memory and can alter behaviour in response to short-term or unpredictable changes in the environment.

Synaptic plasticity

Several recent studies have shown that synapses are capable of undergoing both structural and functional modification in response to environmental alterations. These modifications result in changes of synaptic efficiency and may increase or decrease the likelihood of transmission of impulses, with consequent modulation of behaviour. In some cases such synaptic plasticity appears to be directly linked to learning and memory.

Learning in invertebrates

Habituation. Some mechanisms of learning and memory have been elucidated for the sea hare *Aplysia californica* (Kandel 1978, 1979; Kandel and Schwartz 1982). This mollusc has a reflex for withdrawing its gill in response to stimulation of mechanoreceptors in the skin. The reflex involves monosynaptic connections between skin sensory neurones and gill motoneurones, and exhibits habituation, sensitization, and a form of classical conditioning. Short-term habituation, lasting a few hours, can be induced rapidly in a single training session of 10–15 tactile stimuli. It has been shown to be due to a progressive decline in amplitude of the synaptic potentials generated by the sensory terminals as the innocuous stimulus is repeated. The diminution of synaptic transmission is at least partly due to shutting down of calcium channels at the sensory nerve terminals with a consequent reduction of the amount of neurotransmitter released at the sensory-motor synapse. Eventually, insufficient transmitter is released to evoke an action potential in the motoneurones, and no withdrawal response is elicited.

Long-term habituation, lasting for weeks, can be induced over four training sessions of 10 stimuli each. In this case, similar but more profound changes in synaptic efficiency occur with disruption of the functional connections of many previously effective synapses. These results show that short-term and long-term habituation involve the same neuronal loci, and suggest that short-term and long-term memory share a common locus, the synapse, and differ only in the degree of functional change induced by learning.

Sensitization.   Sensitization of the gill withdrawal reflex can be elicited by a strong stimulus to the head of the animal. As with habituation, sensitization can last for hours or weeks, depending on the amount of training. In short-term sensitization, Kandel (1979) showed that noxious stimuli activate facilitatory interneurones which liberate an excitatory neurotransmitter at the terminals of the sensory neurones from the mechanoreceptors involved in the reflex. The excitatory neurotransmitter increases the amount of 3', 5 cyclic AMP in the presynaptic sensory terminals. Through a series of steps, this increase leads to opening of calcium channels and an increased release of transmitter at the sensory-motor synapse. Consequently there is increased spike-propagation at the post-synaptic motoneurone and a greater reflex response occurs. The facilitatory neurotransmitter was originally thought to be serotonin (Kandel 1979) but later work (cited by Dudai 1989) suggests that an amino acid and/or small polypeptides may be involved.

In long-term sensitization following noxious stimuli repeated over a few days, there is enhancement of the connections made by the sensory neurones on both the facilitatory interneurone and the motoneurones, with even further release of transmitter. In addition, the response becomes generalized to include increased escape locomotion and other defensive reflexes.

Classical conditioning.   A form of classical conditioning can also be demonstrated in *Aplysia* (Kandel 1979). If an unconditional noxious stimulus producing sensitization is paired for a few days with a conditional stimulus (exposure to shrimp extract which normally produces no response), the animal learns to respond with all the signs of long-term sensitization to the conditional stimulus alone. The mechanism for this response has not been elucidated, but it is suggested that the unconditional stimulus increases the activity of the facilitatory interneurones. This type of associative learning also occurs in other invertebrates including the octopus (Young 1966) and the marine snail *Hermissenda crassincornis* (Alkon 1983; Crow and Alkon 1978; Lederhendler *et al.* 1986), and appears similar to the classical conditioning demonstrated in dogs by Pavlov (1927).

These simple forms of learning thus involve (presynaptic) modulation of the strength of previously existing synaptic connections. However, widespread networks of hundreds of neurones may contribute even to the simplest learning reflexes in invertebrates (Altman and Kien 1990) and many more in more complex forms of learning.

Collateral sprouting in vertebrates

There is evidence in vertebrates for the growth of new synapses, for the activation of previously 'silent' synapses, and for change in the efficacy of existing synapses in the brain. For example, if kittens or newborn macaque monkeys are monocularly deprived by surgical closure of one eye during a critical period of their development, plastic changes occur in the connections to the visual cortex (Wiesel and Hubel 1963; Hubel and Wiesel 1977; Pettigrew 1978). The cortical columns which receive input from the normal eye become enlarged at the expense of those receiving input from the deprived eye, so that most of the neurones are activated only by the eye which has been open, instead of most neurones being binocularly activated, as in normal animals. This alteration may be due to synaptic competition, the input from the open eye displacing the synapses of the deprived eye terminals. Such morphological and functional synaptic plasticity is not limited to the growing nervous system of immature animals, but also occurs in adults (Azmitia 1978; Tsukahara 1981) and can probably occur at all levels in the nervous system throughout life (Wall 1988a; Asanuma 1991).

Studies of structural plasticity in the brain of adult songbirds are reviewed by Bottjer and Arnold (1984). In the canary the size and weight of certain brain nuclei are directly related to the learning of song sequences: the greater the vocal virtuosity, the greater the volume of these song-control nuclei, demonstrating a correlation between the degree of learning and the amount of space devoted to it in the brain. The canary's song-control nuclei are influenced by testosterone and enlarge each spring in male birds, coincident with a rise in endogenous testosterone concentration and the onset of singing. Female birds do not normally sing and have small or absent song-related nuclei. However, these can be induced by treatment with testosterone in adults and with the development of song-control nuclei, female birds start to sing. Histological studies reveal that testosterone treatment in females increases the size of the dendritic field of the neurones in the song-related nuclei, presumably increasing the number of synaptic connections made. In addition, Paton and Nottebohm (1984) showed by radioactive labelling techniques that neurogenesis can occur in the song-control nuclei of adult canaries and that the newly generated neurones are incorporated into functional brain circuits.

Functional synaptic changes in vertebrates

More rapidly occurring functional synaptic changes, without collateral sprouting, are associated with learning by classical conditioning (Tsukahara 1981) and probably also with other types of learning.

Long-term potentiation.   One basis for such changes may be the phenomenon of long-term potentiation (Bliss 1979; Bliss and Gardner-
Medwin, 1973). Electrical stimulation of the perforant pathway to
the hippocampus produces an extracellular post-synaptic potential or
synaptic wave in the hippocampus. The amplitude of this synaptic
wave remains constant if test shocks are given at intervals of 2–3 s,
but if the test shocks are interrupted by brief trains of higher frequency
conditioning shocks (10 Hz or more), a large increase in the amplitude
of the synaptic wave develops (Fig. 8.1). The effect occurs within
minutes of one 50 s burst of conditioning shocks, and after three or
four such trains the synaptic wave can show a 300 per cent increase
in amplitude which can last for days or weeks. This phenomenon was
first shown in the hippocampus of rats and rabbits but occurs in other
parts of the brain (Artola and Singer 1987) including amygdala and
cortex in many species including primates, and in peripheral synapses
(Dolphin 1985). Possible links with memory and learning include the
observation that senescent rats are deficient in simple memory tasks,
and also in the ability to sustain long-term potentiation and that the
amplitude of the long-term potentiation is correlated with the speed of
complex maze learning. However it is difficult to envisage how long-
term potentiation could be the means of encoding detailed information. It may represent an extension of neural mechanisms, such as
facilitation, augmentation and post-tetanic potentiation (which last
for milliseconds, seconds or minutes respectively) leading to increased
synaptic efficiency (Dudai 1989). Thus it may contribute more to

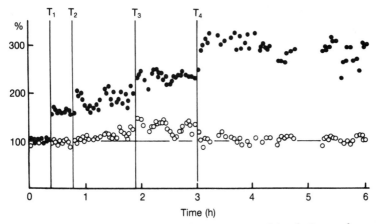

Fig. 8.1   Long-term potentiation in the hippocampus. Stimulating and recording
electrodes located bilaterally in the perforant path. Conditioning trains (15 Hz
for 10 s) delivered to one side at times T_{1-4}. Amplitude of synaptic wave evoked
by a contant test shock (ordinate) plotted against time (abscissa). Open circles,
control side; filled circles, conditioned side. (From Bliss 1979.)

general arousal and attention than to the learning of specific information. Long-term potentiation may underlie other processes in the body, including the generation of epileptiform discharges (Dingledine 1986), and the enhancement of nociceptive discharges (Dickenson 1990; Chapter 5).

Both pre- and post-synaptic mechanisms may be involved in the genesis and maintenance of long-term potentiation (Bliss and Dolphin 1982; Rawlins 1984). Post-synaptic effects are thought to be largely mediated by receptors for endogenous excitatory amino acids. Several types of such receptors have been identified (Fagg 1985; Fagg *et al.* 1986; Watkins *et al.* 1990) including two which respond to the exogenous specific agonists kainate (kainate receptors) and AMPA (AMPA receptors) and a third, the NMDA receptor, which is activated by *N*-methyl-D-aspartate (NMDA) (Table 8.1). All these receptors are activated by glutamate and all control ion channels for Na^+ and K^+; the NMDA receptor in addition controls a calcium ion channel and is also linked to the sigma opioid/phencyclidine receptor (Chapter 7). It appears that activation of NMDA receptors is required for the initiation of long-term potentiation and a mechanism has been proposed by Collingridge (1985) and Collingridge and Bliss (1987).

According to this model (Fig. 8.2), synaptic potentials evoked by glutamate released under conditions of low frequency stimulation are mediated by kainate and AMPA receptors, and the membrane depolarization produced is quickly reversed by GABA (or glycine-) mediated hyperpolarization (Chapter 4). Under these conditions, NMDA receptor-controlled channels are blocked by Mg^{2+} ions. However, after a train of high frequency stimulation, the Mg^{2+} block is reduced by the resulting increase in depolarization, allowing entry through the post-synaptic membrane of further monovalent cations and of Ca^{2+} ions. Calcium entry triggers a cascade of intracellular events (Dudai 1989) leading to a long-lasting increase in synaptic efficiency (the long-term potentiation) in response to further glutamate release. In support of this model are the observations that long-term potentiation is critically dependent on calcium and magnesium ion concentrations and that it can be blocked at some sites by NMDA receptor antagonists (which also impair learning) and by the dissociative anaesthetics (ketamine, phencyclidine) which act at the closely associated sigma opioid/phencyclidine sites (Collingridge 1985). There is some evidence for the existence of subtypes of NMDA receptors, possibly with different roles in long-term potentiation (Dudai 1989).

The maintenance, and probably also the initiation, of long-term potentiation involves simultaneous changes in pre-synpatic function (Gustafsson and Wigstrom 1988). There is evidence of an increased pre-synaptic release of glutamate (and to a lesser extent of aspartate)

Table 8.1 Excitatory amino acid receptors[1]

Receptors	NMDA	AMPA[2]	Kainate
Agonists	NMDA L-glutamate L-aspartate quisqualate	AMPA quisqualate L-glutamate L-aspartate	kainate domoate L-glutamate quisqualate
Antagonists	D-AP5 CPP	CNQX	CNQX
Channel blockers	MK-801 phencyclidine ketamine SKF10047 Mg^{2+}		
Effector pathways	$Na^+/K^+/Ca^{2+}$ channel activation	Na^+/K^+ channel activation	Na^+/K^+ channel activation
Localization	widespread in CNS, especially hippocampus, cortex	widespread in CNS, with NMDA receptors	specific CNS areas (e.g. stratum lucidum of hippocampus), dorsal root fibres

[1] Other excitatory amino acid receptors exist, including L-AP4 and metabotrophic receptors.
[2] Previous name: quisqualate receptor. AMPA: D, L-α-amino-3-hydroxy-5-methyl-4-isoxalone proprionic acid.
CPP: ($\pm$)-2-carboxypiperazine-4-yl)propyl-1-phosphonic acid.
CNQX: 6-cyano-7-nitroquinoxaline-2,3,-dione
DAP 5: D-amino-5-phosphonopentanoate.
References: Fagg (1985); Fagg *et al.* (1986); Watkins *et al.* (1990); *Trends in Pharmacological Sciences* (1990, 1991).

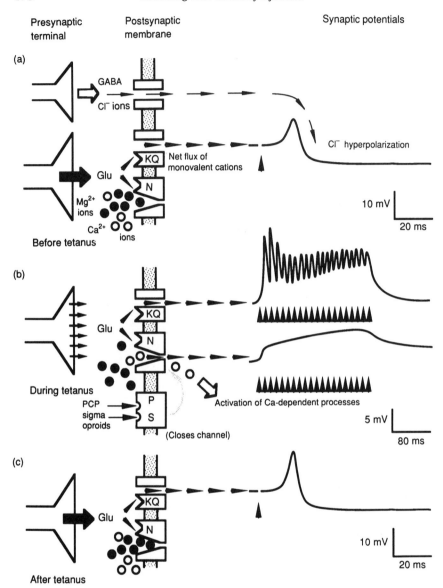

Presynaptic   Postsynaptic   Synaptic potentials
terminal   membrane

Fig. 8.2 Postulated mechanism for initiation of long-term potentiation in the
CA$_1$ region of the hippocampus. (a) L-glutamate released by low frequency
stimulation acts on kainate and/or quisqualate (KQ) receptors and on NMDA(N)
receptors, but the N channels are largely blocked by extracellular Mg^{2+} ions
(filled circles). The excitatory response is therefore mediated predominantly
by monovalent cations (arrow heads) permeating the KQ channel, but the
associated depolarization is curtailed rapidly by GABA-mediated hyperpolarization. (b) During high frequency stimulation (tetanus), the Mg^{2+} block of N

associated with the development of long-term potentiation (Bliss *et al.* 1986; Lynch *et al.* 1985). This release is calcium dependent and may be effected by stimulation of pre-synaptic NMDA receptors. Other neuromodulators such as noradrenaline, which facilitates long-term potentiation, and polypeptides may also be involved (Dudai 1989).

Dendritic spines.   Several authors (cited by Crick 1982; Bliss 1979) have drawn attention to the possible importance of dendritic spines in long-term potentiation and in synaptic plasticity. Denritic spines are small projections from the dendrites of certain types of neurones (pyramidal cells and stellate cells; Peters *et al.* 1976; Fig. 8.3). Spiny cells are numerous in the cerebral and cerebellar cortex, accounting for about 90 per cent of neurones in the cerebral cortex, and each may have from 300 to 30 000 spines. The spines are synaptic sites and most of them are believed to be excitatory, accounting for the great majority of excitatory synapses in the cerebral cortex. In most neurones the dendritic spines are post-synaptic, and vesicles of neurotransmitter can be seen on the pre-synaptic terminals with which they make contact.

The function of dendritic spines is not known, but it has been suggested that alterations in their width or conformation might account for some types of synaptic plasticity (Crick 1982; Koch and Poggio 1983). Contraction of a spine would increase the width of its neck, reducing its electrical resistance and increasing the amplitude of a synaptic current being conducted into a dendrite and reaching the impulse-generating site of the nerve cell. Converse changes in electrical resistance would occur if the neck of the spine elongated and became narrower. Large variations in the size and shape of spines, seen on the same dendrite, have been observed (Peters *et al.* 1976; Fig. 8.3) and increases in the diameter of dendritic spines have been reported in the hippocampus after high frequency stimulation of the perforant pathway under conditions that give rise to long-term potentiation (Bliss 1979).

Matus *et al.* (1982), and Fifkova and Delay (1982) have demonstrated the presence of the contractile protein actin in dendritic spines in the

---

channels is reduced by the increased depolarisation, allowing monovalent cations to permeate the N channels and contribute to the synaptic potential. The N receptor component is seen as a slow excitatory synaptic potential. Ca^{2+} ions (open circles) also permeate N channels and activate biochemical mechanisms involved in the plastic change. Drugs such as phencyclidine (PCP) and sigma opioids activate the phencyclidine/sigma opioid receptor (PS), closing the ion channel controlled by the N receptor. These drugs prevent long-term potentiation. (c) Following high frequency stimulation, N channels are again blocked by Mg^{2+}. The enhanced post-synaptic potential is due, at least in part, to increased release of glutamate. (Reproduced with permission from Collingridge and Bliss (1987); Collingridge (1985).)

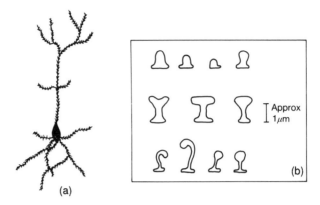

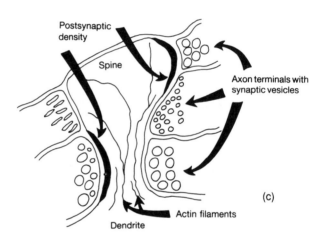

Fig. 8.3 Dendritic spines. (a) Pyramidal cell showing dendritic spines. (b) Observed variations in shape and form of dendritic spines. (c) Dendritic spine bearing synapses with axon terminals containing large, small, and elongated synaptic vesicles. (References: Crick 1982; Peters *et al*. 1976.)

rat cortex and hippocampus. They suggest that the actin is triggered to contract by the influx of calcium ions. This contraction may expose 'hidden' NMDA receptors, increasing their post-synaptic density (Lynch and Baudrey 1984; Siman *et al*. 1985). Horn *et al*. (1985) and McCabe and Horn (1988) found that imprinting in domestic chicks is accompanied by an increase in the size of the post-synaptic density of dendritic spine synapses in specific regions of the anterior forebrain and an increase in the density of NMDA receptors. Further related changes may include activation of the protein tubulin and the formation of an organized network of microtubules which may facilitate the transport of ions from the spines to the dendritic core (Hendrickson 1983*a, b*). Disruption of microtubule assembly occurs in Alzheimer's disease (Chapter 9) and may be one of the factors causing memory impairment.

Very rapid changes in synaptic efficiency produced by muscle contraction might occur during short-term memory, while longer-lasting conductance changes produced by repeated synaptic activity could facilitate learning and consolidation of memory by ensuring preferential selection of the pathways involved on future repetitions of the same stimuli, at the expense of other possible pathways. In certain areas of the brain, patterns of activity unique to each event could be envisaged to be built up over time. Portions or segments of these patterns might gradually be strengthened by events, while portions would tend to fade through under-use as the dendritic spines slowly reverted to their uncontracted state. In this way, the patterns for each memory would constantly be edited and changed over the years.

Formation of new synapses.   In addition to increased efficiency in individual synapses, there is considerable evidence for the formation of new synapses during learning. Greenhough (1984) has shown that synaptic density is more than doubled after long-term potentiation in rat hippocampal slices. The increase involved synapses onto axonal shafts and a specific type of dendritic spine synapse (sessile spines). Increases in synaptic density and in the frequency of dendritic spines were also observed in the occipital cortex of rats reared in complex, 'enriched' environments compared with litter mates reared singly or in groups in standard laboratory cages. The relationship of such changes to learning was demonstrated by experiments in which rats were exposed to maze training after total transection of the corpus callosum and eye occlusion arranged to direct visual input to one hemisphere. In these rats, increases in synaptic numbers were found in occipital cortical pyramidal neurones only in the hemisphere exposed to visual stimulation during maze training. The relation of memory to 'intelligence' is discussed by Hendrickson (1983*a, b*) and current theories on the biological basis of intelligence are brought together by Eysenck (1983).

Localization of learning and memory functions

Reward and punishment systems

Although in cellular terms learning and memory are widely represented in the brain, different parts appear to be organized to contribute in different and specific ways. Young (1966, 1979) has described in the octopus brain separate pairs of lobes that signal reinforcement or punishment for vision and touch. The output from these lobes allows the animal to select either approach/attack or avoidance behaviour for the object seen or touched, and it can be conditioned to avoid objects if their presence is paired with a painful electrical shock. Removal of the lobe signalling punishment deprives the octopus of the ability to learn *not* to approach objects even when such behaviour results in painful shocks.

Reinforcement and punishment pathways in vertebrates (Chapter 5) are intimately concerned with learning and the selection or approach of avoidance behaviour. Rolls *et al.* (1981), in microelectrode recordings from single cells in the monkey hypothalamus, found certain neurones which responded only when a visual discrimination stimulus presented to the animal was associated with a food reward, not to stimuli associated with saline. The activity of such neurones was suggested to underlie stimulus-reinforcement associations. Routtenberg (1978) found that continuous electrical stimulation of some rewarding areas (median forebrain bundle, substantia nigra, frontal cortex) during learning in the rat disrupts subsequent recall, but if the animals are allowed to self-stimulate for reward after learning, their retention is improved. He suggests that 'when something is learned, activity in the brain-reward pathways facilitates the formation of memory' (Routtenberg 1978; p. 129).

In the reward/punishment system, a specific role for the amygdala in learning and memory has been suggested by several authors. For example, Kapp and Gallagher (1979) noted that tests associated with painful stimuli were readily remembered and in many species the possibility of receiving a repeat stimulus evoked a fear reaction leading to avoidance. The site of this memory system may be based in the amygdala and may involve an opioid mediation since retention of aversive stimuli in rats is influenced by opioid agonists and antagonists, injected into the amygdala. The authors suggested that an amygdaloid opioid system is involved in generating an emotional component to painful experiences, and may interact with the noradrenergic system of the locus coeruleus with which it has anatomical connections. Kesner and Hardy (1983) and Mishkin and Appenzeller (1987) suggest that the amygdala encodes, stores, and retrieves the hedonic qualities — rewarding or aversive — of all sensory stimuli. In this function it interacts with the hippocampus, which at the same time encodes the environmental context of the same specific memory.

Arousal systems

The locus coeruleus (Mason 1979, 1980) and the amygdala (Douglas and Pribram 1966) may also be important in selective attention which, along with optimal activation of arousal systems, appears to be necessary for efficient learning and memory. In particular, lesions of the locus coeruleus in animals cause perseveration of inappropriate behaviour, increased distractibility and overinclusiveness of attention. Involvement of the locus coeruleus in arousal, anxiety, and reward systems is mentioned in Chapters 2, 3, and 5, respectively.

The hippocampus

Both the locus coeruleus and the amygdala have anatomical connections with the hippocampus which is widely believed to play a specific though complex role in memory functions, particularly in relation to event memory. Clinical studies, described in Chapter 9, have shown that bilateral surgical lesions of the temporal lobes and hippocampus in man cause a characteristic amnesic syndrome with loss of memory for recent events but preservation of immediate memory and of remote memories (Scoville and Milner 1957). As a result of such observations, it has been suggested that a function of the hippocampus may be the transfer of short-term memories into a permanently encoded or long-term store. However, in such patients the amnesia is not complete and apparently forgotten recent events can be recalled if suitable clues are provided (Weiskrantz 1977). Thus the hippocampus may also be involved in retrieval of memory.

Another function ascribed to the hippocampus is that of acting as a cognitive map (both spatial and temporal) of the environment. Patients with hippocampal bilateral lesions are sometimes permanently lost even in their everyday surroundings, if these are different from their surroundings prior to the lesion, and animal studies show that certain hippocampal neurones discharge only when the animal is in a particular place in relation to the environment. The hippocampus of the dominant hemisphere appears to be concerned with visual environment features, and that of the non-dominant hemisphere with spatial features in man (Norton 1981). In this capacity the hippocampus may act as a type of match/mismatch or error evaluation system which compares present environmental stimuli with those previously experienced and allows alteration of response in accordance with environmental changes (O'Keefe and Nadel 1978). Douglas (1967, 1975), and Douglas and Pribram (1966) stressed the inhibitory nature of the hippocampus which, in animals at least, appears to allow suppression of incorrect responses and hence selection of responses more appropriate to the circumstances. The importance of the postulated hippocampal behavioural inhibition system (Gray 1982) in anxiety is discussed in Chapter 3. Rawlins (1984) attempts to reconcile the many postulated functions of the hippocampus by suggesting that it acts as a high capacity memory for all types of information which is then retained (by long-term potentiation) for a considerable time. This retention allows the association of items occurring at widely separated times and also allows comparison and evaluation of presently occurring events with a spatiotemporal representation of previous events.

Diencephalic structures

Memory defects similar to those produced by temporal lobe and hippocampal lesions also occur after damage to diencephalic structures, including the inner portions of the dorsomedial, anteroventral and pulvinar nuclei of the thalamus and the mammillary bodies (Brierley 1977; Mair *et al*. 1979). These structures are connected to the hippocampus via the fornix and other tracts and there is some evidence that they are directly involved in certain memory functions. Microelectrode recordings of the activity in single neurones in the brain of the Rhesus monkey have shown that certain thalamic cells respond to familiar but not to unfamiliar visual stimuli (Rolls *et al*. 1981). Such cells might form the basis of recognition memory. In man, some lateral thalamic nuclei also seem to play an important part in modulating cortical language and spatial memory functions (Ojemann 1983).

The cerebral cortex

The cerebral cortex is not essential for some types of learning. Oakley (1979) has shown that associative learning, including classical and operant conditioning, can occur, and may even be shown more clearly, after removal of the whole neocortex in rats and rabbits, indicating that such forms of learning must involve subcortical structures. Indeed, learning of a sort can occur at all levels of the nervous system including the isolated spinal cord preparation which can show associative conditioning.

Lateralization

However, in humans the cerebral cortex is essential for the more complex forms of learning and memory involving abstract thought and language (Oakley 1981). It has long been known that there is considerable lateralization of function in the cortex. In the majority of individuals, the left hemisphere is specialized for language, logical analysis and deduction, the programming of refined manual movements, abstract and symbolic reasoning, and possibly an appreciation of temporal causality. The right hemisphere, on the other hand, is dominant and superior in spatial visualization, memory for and recognition of faces and other complex stimuli which are resistant to verbal description, musical appreciation, and possibly appreciation of physical principles and spatial organization. The left hemisphere is superior to the right in memory for temporal rhythm and pattern, while the right is superior in memory for non-verbalizable spatial patterns. In particular, the right hemisphere is able to represent the rich qualities of sensory and emotional experience and complex spatial relationships which defy description in terms of language (Sperry 1973, 1974, 1976; Levy 1979; Ross 1984; Cook 1986).

The advantages of such deduplication of cerebral function are discussed by Levy (1979) who concludes that the lateralization of function found in the human brain reflects a trend towards the optimally efficient use of neural space. The potential information capacity of the human brain is greatly increased by reduction in redundancy and the coexistence of mutually exclusive, but equally important mechanisms for understanding the environment. The lateralization of language function appears to be present soon after birth in humans (Woods 1983), and neuroanatomical asymmetries are present in human and non-human species (Geschwind and Levitsky, 1968; Sherman *et al.* 1982; LeMay 1982). The two hemispheres are normally in close communication through the cerebral commissures and subcortical connections (Sergent 1990).

Language functions

Early information concerning cortical language functions came from clinical studies relating various defects of speech and memory to brain lesions at particular sites. From such studies, the critical sites in the dominant hemisphere for the comprehension and production of written and spoken language have been classically held to include (Fig. 8.4): Broca's area, Wernicke's area, the connection between these two areas through the arcuate fasciculus, the interconnections between these areas and various parts of the cortex, and parts of the visual and auditory cortex. Damage to different sites in these systems is thought to account for various types of aphasia and alexia described in Chapter 9. However, it is always difficult in clinical studies to relate specific defects to particular areas of damage, and the traditional view may require revision.

More recently, brain electrical stimulation techniques in conscious subjects have allowed more detailed mapping of cortical language and memory functions (Ojemann 1983). Stimulation at certain discrete sites during a naming task evokes repeated errors, while at closely adjacent sites (0.5 cm or less) similar stimulation evokes no errors. Regions in which repeated naming errors occur on stimulation are

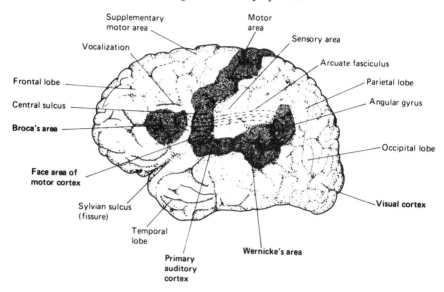

Fig. 8.4 Cortical areas classically associated with language functions. Areas concerned with language functions include Broca's area, Wernicke's area, their connections through the arcuate fasciculus, and parts of the visual and auditory cortex. (Reference: Kandel and Schwartz 1982.)

often well outside the traditional Broca and Wernicke zones, and in many patients naming changes do not occur when the classical areas are stimulated. Yet areas where errors are evoked seem to be essential for language function, since cortical resections encroaching on these areas produce aphasia. Sites where naming errors were evoked by electrical stimulation in one subject are shown in Fig. 8.5. The location of these areas varies somewhat between individual subjects and between males and females, and is related to verbal ability.

Examination of other language functions by this technique revealed that stimulation at different sites produced errors of different types including naming, reading, short-term verbal memory, and phoneme (single speech sound) identification. Not only different language functions, but the same function in different languages appears to be separately represented; thus, in the subject in Fig. 8.5, the naming of objects in English and in Greek was disrupted by stimulation at different sites. It is possible that the localization of these sites exhibits a degree of plasticity since they may change position after injury (Ojemann 1983).

From the results obtained with these techniques in several subjects, Ojemann (1983) concludes that language functions in the human cortex are organized in a mosaic of small areas subserving separate aspects: some sites are concerned with orofacial movements and identification

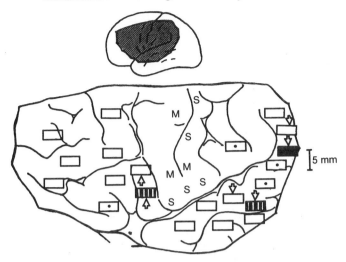

Fig. 8.5 Cortical sites in language-dominant hemisphere of one subject at which repeated naming errors were evoked by electrical stimulation. Open rectangles—no errors evoked; filled and striped rectangles, repeated errors; Single dot, single errors in multiple trials. Arrows identify adjacent sites separated by 5 mm or less. M, S, sites of evoked motor movements or sensations. Stimulation by trains of 60 Hz stimuli of 2.5 s duration, biphasic pulses at 8 mA, delivered through bipolar electrodes 5 mm apart. (From Ojemann 1983.)

of speech sounds; others relate only to syntactical aspects of language or only to word naming; yet other sites appear to subserve a short-term verbal memory system in which storage and retrieval of verbal memory can be separately interrupted by localized stimulation.

The cortical verbal memory system appears to be closely linked to a common memory and language system in the dominant lateral thalamus. From experiments in which thalamic sites were stimulated, Ojemann (1983) suggested that thalamo-cortical activating circuits select the cortical mosaics appropriate to the language task. A similar mechanism, modulating memory for spatial information processed in the opposite hemisphere, may be present in the non-dominant thalamus. The basal ganglia appear also to be involved in the processing of language. Lesions in this area may cause language disturbances which include not only articulatory difficulty but also fluent aphasia and impairment of auditory comprehension (Damasio 1983). It is becoming increasingly clear that language is by no means a monopoly of the cerebral cortex.

The cerebellum

The cerebral cortex, hippocampus and locus coeruleus all send impulses to the cerebellum which is possibly the seat of motor learning in vertebrates (Marr 1969; Changeux and Danchin 1976; Young 1979; Anderson 1982). The cerebellar Purkinje cells normally exert an inhibitory influence on muscle fibres, but this inhibition is opposed by afferents to the Purkinje cells from proprioceptors in the muscles. The learning of motor skills has been shown to be associated with selective changes in the firing of Purkinje cells, and it is suggested that proprioceptor activity from the particular muscle groups required for a motor task leads to adaptive changes in their cerebellar synapses (possibly in dendritic spines) which lessen the inhibitory discharge of the Purkinje cells and so increase the activity of the selected muscles. Due to the synaptic changes, the particular sequence of contractions will occur 'automatically' in the future (once initiated by cortical 'commands'). Motor learning usually involves a complex sequence of movements and the cerebellum may also function as a timing device by which the required strength and sequence of muscular contractions are learned. The cerebellum has also been implicated as a site of associative learning involving motor responses (Gellman and Miles 1985; Stein 1985).

Diffuse distribution of memory

In a sense, as many have claimed since Lashley's classic description ('In search of the engram', Lashley 1950) which revealed that memory could not be localized anywhere in the brain, learning and memory may be diffusely distributed throughout the nervous system. Nevertheless, it appears that a co-operative effort between closely interconnected structures is also involved, with critical changes occurring perhaps in different localities for different facets of the process. A perceived object or experience generates a multiplicity of central representations and can be recalled by activation of any one of these representations. Thus, for example, a person's identity can be recognized from his face, his voice, his gait or his posture (Damasio 1990), or any number of single attributes, each of which is normally capable of triggering a full picture not only of the individual but also of associated temporal, spatial and emotional contexts. Small lesions may reduce the accuracy of such memories but do not destroy them. O'Keefe and Speakman suggest from *in vivo* single unit recording experiments that 'any small area of the hippocampus contains enough information to identify (an) animal's location in an environment, albeit with coarse grain . . . . As larger numbers of units are added, the representation gets finer' (O'Keefe and Speakman 1987, p. 24). Such multiple representations are probably a general property of the brain (Cook 1986), although for very specialized functions, such as language, the importance of localized structures increases. Exactly how appropriate representations are made available when required is not clear; the process of recall remains the least understood and yet the most fundamental of all memory processes. The importance of the cytoarchitecture of the cortex in mammals and its organization into horizontally integrated columnar modules which act as processing and distributing units is discussed by Mountcastle (1978) and Gilbert (1985).

Pharmacology of learning and memory

Many drugs and physical agents affect learning and memory. Such treatments can be administered at different times in relation to the time of initial learning and their effects on various stages of the memory process can sometimes be distinguished (Mondadori 1981; Mathies 1980; Zornetzer 1978). If a substance is administered before a learning trial (*pre-trial*), any subsequent changes in memory may be due to a direct effect on memory processing, but may also be due to indirect effects on other functions such as perception, vigilance, and motivation. If a treatment is administered soon after the learning trial (*post-trial*) it cannot affect the initial learning, and any effects in later retention tests are traditionally ascribed to an action on memory processing. However, the memory is only susceptible to modulation for a short period after the learning, and this time depends on species, task, and type of treatment. Furthermore it is not usually clear whether memory defects are due to specific interference with some encoding process, consolidation, or retrieval. When treatment is deferred until before the test for retention (*pre-retest*), its effects may be limited to the retrieval processes, but these may also be indirectly affected by effects of the drug on other systems.

Thus, the study of drug effects on memory presents methodological problems and poses difficulties of interpretation. Other variables include the dose and route of administration of the drug and the type of memory test employed. There is also the problem of 'state-dependent learning'. Differences in performance may arise if learning and retention are not tested in same drug state (Mondadori 1981). Furthermore, changes in the functional condition of any single transmitter system in the brain almost certainly affects the function of other transmitter systems, and almost any functional change in the brain is likely to have consequences for learning and memory. In spite of these shortcomings, drug studies have provided some insights into the pharmacological aspects of memory.

Brain protein synthesis

The part played by brain protein synthesis in learning and memory has been the subject of a large number of animal studies (reviewed by Agranoff *et al.* 1978; Dunn 1980; Squire and Davis 1981; Mayes 1983). Learning-associated changes in RNA and various proteins, glycoproteins, and phosphoproteins have been demonstrated in several brain regions, including the hippocampus and forebrain. However, the results are difficult to interpret and have not always been reproducible. Memory is impaired by drugs which inhibit brain protein synthesis if these agents are administered just before or immediately after training. Similar effects are produced by drug or electrically induced convulsions or cerebral anoxia. However, the amnesia induced by these agents can be reversed by stimulant drugs and behavioural manipulations which do not affect the changes in protein synthesis. Hence it seems unlikely that brain protein synthesis *per se* is required for the encoding or storage of memory.

Nevertheless, there is little doubt that protein synthesis is generally involved in the establishment of synaptic changes related to memory. The cascade of intracellular events triggered by stimulation of NMDA and other membrane receptors includes the activation of protein kinases (Dudai 1989; Byrne 1985; Mishkin and Appenzeller 1987) which, with other second messenger systems, take part in a number of post-synaptic modifications. These include the synthesis of enzymes such as calpain (Lynch and Baudry 1984), proteins such as actin (Crick 1982), and modification of tubulin and microfilaments (Aoki and Siekovitz 1988) in dendritic spines, other plastic neuronal changes (Mayes 1983), and the activation or expression of genes (Dudai 1989; Comb *et al.* 1987). The importance of genetic factors for some types of learning and memory has been demonstrated in the fruit fly *Drosophila melanogaster* by Dudai (1989). In these insects, mutations which impair memory specifically involve genes which affect second messenger cascades by controlling the synthesis of enzymes such as phosphodiesterase, adenylate cyclase, protein kinases and of phosphoproteins.

Acetylcholine

Several authors (Deutsch 1971; Drachman 1978; Squire and Davis 1981) suggested that it is in cholinergic synapses that specific alterations related to memory occur. Animal work (Deutsch 1971) showed that drugs which affect cholinergic synaptic transmission can impair, facilitate or have no effect on retention, depending on the age of the memory at the time of treatment. For example, the same dose of an anticholinesterase injected intracerebrally in rats had no effect on performance if administered 1–4 days after learning a task, impaired performance if given 7 days after learning, and improved memory if injected 21 days after learning, at a time when untreated animals exhibited forgetting. Opposite, time-related effects occurred with anticholinergic drugs such as scopolamine.

These results were interpreted to mean that memory storage involves changes in the efficiency of transmission which develop over time at certain cholinergic synapses. Deutsch (1971) suggested that, in the appetitive and aversive tasks which he studied in rats, there was a gradual increase in efficacy of cholinergic transmission which continued for several days after learning until it reached an optimal level at about 2 weeks, and thereafter a gradual decline in efficacy during the course of forgetting. During the initial period, when cholinergic activity was rising, anticholinesterases were assumed to raise the synaptic concentration of acetylcholine above the optimal level and cause synaptic blockade, thus impairing performance. During the period of forgetting, however, when cholinergic activity was declining, the effect of anticholinesterases would be to improve synaptic efficacy and thus enhance memory.

Animal findings are supported by some observations on human subjects. In normal young subjects, a series of studies (cited by Squire and Davis 1981) showed that cholinergic drugs in suitable doses can improve word recall, while larger doses of physostigmine can impair cognitive function. Drachman (1978) found that central cholinergic blockade with scopolamine did not affect immediate memory (digit span) but seriously affected the ability to store new information (serial order of digits and free recall of words) and also impaired retrieval of old information as well as lowering general cognitive performance. The impairment induced by scopolamine was reversed by physostigmine, in doses which had no effect on memory or cognitive function when given alone, but not by the general stimulant amphetamine.

The memory and cognitive deficits produced by scopolamine closely resemble those which develop in normal elderly subjects, suggesting that the cognitive disorders or normal ageing may result from a relatively specific dysfunction of cholinergic transmission. This raises the possibility that cholinergic drugs might improve cognitive function in the aged, and Drachman (1978) noted a trend toward improvement in memory storage and IQ function in 13 normal elderly patients following a small subcutaneous dose of physostigmine. Memory loss in the early stages of Alzheimer's dementia is thought to result from relatively selective loss of cholinergic neurones (Chapter 10).

Anatomical sites in which cholinergic pathways are likely to be involved in memory and other cognitive functions include the cortex and the limbic system, particularly the septal-hippocampal structures and pathways. However, cholinergic systems, whether they are specific sites of memory or not, undoubtedly interact crucially with other systems, such as those involving monoamines.

Monoamines (noradrenaline, dopamine, serotonin)

Pharmacological studies in animals and man suggest that monoamines play some role in learning and memory. In general, agonists of mono-aminergic systems improve while antagonists interfere with learning and memory. Many authors (cited by Squire and Davis 1981; Mayes 1983) have studied the effects of altering central monoaminergic activity in animals. Post-trial intraventricular and localized intracerebral injections of noradrenaline improve retention and partially reverse memory deficits induced by various adrenergic antagonists in rats, while β-adrenergic and dopaminergic receptor antagonists impair acquisition and retention. In humans, systemically administered (pre-trial) amphetamine and methylphenidate can improve learning and memory in normal subjects, especially in boring or fatiguing tasks, and in learning-disabled children, healthy aged subjects and depressed patients (Squire and Davis 1981). However, in other studies, acute manipulation of brain monoamines had no effect on learning and memory in a range of tasks. For example lesions of the locus coeruleus, which reduce cortical and hippocampal noradrenaline concentration by 60–80 per cent, and lesions of the substantia nigra, reducing striatal dopamine concentrations by 95 per cent, do not appear to affect retention in several studies cited by Squire and Davies (1981).

Information concerning the part played by serotonin in memory is confusing (Mondadori 1981). Post-trial injection of serotonin into the hippocampus inhibits the retention of some learning tasks, and the administration of serotonin precursors depresses performance in active avoidance responses. However, serotonin reuptake inhibitors administered 24 h after training facilitate memory retention of an inhibitory avoidance task in mice (Altman *et al.* 1984). Serotonin depletion appears to facilitate learning and memory in some tests but to inhibit them in others. Raphe lesions which lower the serotonin content of the forebrain may facilitate memory. Serotonin may play an indirect role in learning and memory by modulating acetylcholine release. In vitro studies in the rat cortex (Barnes *et al.* 1989) showed that activation of 5-HT_3 receptors can reduce the release of acetylcholine from the cortex while 5-HT_3 receptor antagonists facilitate acetylcholine release.

On the whole, the evidence at present points to a general permissive rather than a specific role for monoamines in learning and memory, possibly by effects on arousal systems and interactions with polypeptide hormones and neuromodulators.

Amino acid neurotransmitters

The importance of excitatory amino acid neurotransmitters such as glutamate and aspartate has been discussed above in relation to long-term potentiation. Although the significance of this phenomenon in relation to learning and memory is not clear, there is evidence that antagonists of NMDA receptors which disrupt long-term potentiation also impair memory formation in rats and mice (Wozniak *et al.* 1990; Venables and Kelly 1990). Memory retention and retrieval are not affected and the effects may be due to indirect actions on arousal and attention. Diminished glutamate function is one of the biochemical abnormalities found in Alzheimer's disease and Huntingdon's chorea (Cross *et al.* 1986; Maragos *et al.* 1987; Chapter 9) and may partly account for the associated memory impairment.

Excitatory amino acid synapses are ubiquitous in the central nervous system (Headley and Grillner 1990) but it is not clear how they interact with other neurotransmitter systems. By actions on different receptor subtypes (Table 8.1), excitatory amino acids are able to mediate both fast and slow synaptic potentials (Fig. 8.2) and thus are likely to influence the effects both of relatively specific (cholinergic) and general (monoaminergic and peptidergic) influences on memory.

There is little information concerning the role of GABA in learning and memory, although it would be expected to exert at least an indirect influence through its effects on arousal (Chapter 2) and its opposing effects on glutamate neuronal depolarization (Fig. 8.2). Conflicting results have been reported (Mondadori 1981). Thus, pre-trial injection of GABA into the lateral ventricle exerts a dose-related, time-dependent facilitating effect on the learning of a dark-light discrimination task in rats. Pre-trial blockade of GABA by picrotoxin has been reported to improve learning in some studies but to impair memory in others. Benzodiazepines have amnesic effects which are thought to be due to enhancement of GABA activity (Chapter 4).

Neuropeptides

Some evidence points to the involvement of pituitary hormones and polypeptide neuromodulators in learning and memory. Of the 20 or more biologically active peptides present in the mammalian nervous system, ACTH, ACTH fragments, oxytocin, vasopressin, and opioid peptides have been most studied in this respect.

ACTH

Removal of the anterior lobe of the pituitary interferes with the acquisition of conditioned avoidance behaviour in rats (Rigter and van

Riezen 1978). This behaviour can be restored by ACTH and by various ACTH fragments (de Wied 1974; de Wied and Gispen 1977). The action is presumably due to a central effect, since ACTH fragments are devoid of adrenocorticotrophic properties. In intact rats, ACTH and ACTH 4-10 can stimulate acquisition in certain learning situations and, when given just prior to testing, can also delay the extinction of some learned behaviours (Dunn 1980). Furthermore, ACTH and ACTH fragments, when administered immediately before retention testing, can reverse the effects of amnesic agents including carbon dioxide, electroconvulsion, and drugs (Meyer and Beattie 1977). However, ACTH does not appear to be indispensable for memory since total hypophysectomy does not prevent an animal from learning new responses (Rigter and van Riezen 1978).

In humans, the effects of ACTH on memory appear to be small, though perhaps subtle. In normal subjects, intravenous infusion of ACTH fragments have been reported to delay habituation, improve performance in some memory tests (Benton Visual Retention Test, Wechsler Memory Test) and to enhance selective attention (Rigter and van Riezen 1978).

Vasopressin

Removal of the posterior lobe of the pituitary does not impair the acquisition of conditioned avoidance behaviour in rats; instead, it causes premature extinction of avoidance behaviour, suggesting a defect in consolidation or retrieval of memory. This abnormality can be reversed by lysine vasopressin and also by the fragment desglycinamide lysine vasopressin (desmopressin), which is devoid of endocrine and autonomic activity (Rigter and van Riezen 1978; Crabbe and Rigter 1980). Several authors have argued that vasopressin exerts a direct effect on memory in the rat (Bohus et al. 1973; Kovacs et al. 1982; de Wied 1984a, b; Muhlethaler et al. 1982). However other evidence suggests that the effects are secondary to increased arousal or possibly autonomic actions (Gash and Thomas 1983, 1984; Sahgal 1984; Hamburger et al. 1985). In man vasopressin and desmopressin have been found by some authors (Weingartner et al. 1981; Legros et al. 1978; Gold et al. 1979b; Snel et al. 1987), but not all (Sahgal et al. 1986), to improve concentration and mood, but there is no evidence for a specific involvement in memory.

Oxytocin

The other posterior pituitary neuropeptide, oxytocin, appears to have effects which are opposite to those of vasopressin. Oxytocin facilitates rather than delays extinction of active avoidance behaviour and attenuates rather than enhances passive avoidance behaviour in rats (Kovacs *et al.* 1982). Bohus *et al.* (1978) suggest that oxytocin might be a naturally occurring amnesic polypeptide. Ferrier *et al.* (1980) reported that oxytocin nasal spray reduced memory recall in a small number of normal human subjects.

Opioid peptides

The opioid peptides may also participate in a neurohumoral system which induces forgetting rather than remembering. Such an effect might be inferred from the fact that opioids inhibit the release of acetylcholine and other excitatory neurotransmitters (Izquierdo 1990*a*). The evidence for such a function has mostly been obtained from investigations in rats (Izquierdo 1982*a*). The intraperitoneal or intraventricular injection immediately after training of small doses of beta-endorphin causes a naloxone reversible retrograde amnesia for avoidance tasks and for habituation learning. The effective dose of beta-endorphin is extremely small, much smaller than that required to produce analgesia and similar to the amount released endogenously from the brain during training (5–25 ng per rat). Beta-endorphin does not, however, affect acquisition of avoidance or habituation learning even in doses that produce full amnesia. Subanalgesic does of morphine also produce naloxone-reversible retrograde amnesia.

Naloxone administered immediately post-training by contrast causes retrograde memory facilitation for a wide variety of tasks. This facilitation is independent of the response required and of the presence or absence of pain associated with training. It is prevented by β-adrenergic or dopaminergic receptor antagonists and potentiated by concurrent administration of nicotine or *d*-amphetamine. In addition low doses of naloxone and noradrenaline, which are ineffective when given alone, enhance retention of various memory tasks when administered together (Introini-Collison and McGaugh 1987). Izquierdo, (1982*a, b*; 1990*b*) suggested that naloxone acts by releasing central β-adrenergic, dopaminergic, and cholinergic systems from inhibition by endogenous opioids. Naloxone also completely blocks the amnesia induced by post-training electroconvulsive shock, a procedure which is accompanied by a massive release of beta-endorphin and methionine enkephalin from the hypothalamus and amygdala of the rat brain. Presumably, the amnesia results, at least partly, from the release of opioid peptides, the actions of which can be prevented by naloxone (Izquierdo 1982*a*). From a study of the relative potency of memory enhancement of various opioid antagonists, it appears that mu-opioid receptors are preferentially involved in opioid memory systems (Izquierdo 1983).

The fact that opioid agonists and antagonists affect memory when administered post-training confirms the view that the memory of an event continues to be modified after learning; perhaps the consequences of an event determine whether it, or which part of it, is remembered and which forgotten (Gold and McGaugh 1975). The presence of a polypeptide-mediated amnesic system in the brain might improve learning efficiency by allowing useless or obsolete information, or responses that have become inappropriate, to be economically discarded. Under many conditions this system would be independent of pain.

In man, narcotic analgesics (Chapter 7) induce forgetfulness, but this effect may be related to their sedative action. However, it seems possible from human experience that there might be a connection between opiate or opioid analgesia and the quick forgetting of pain. It is said that the pain of childbirth or of torture is rapidly forgotten. Those who have suffered pain 'may remember very vividly all the circumstances surrounding, or pertaining to, their painful experience, but can never actually revive the pain itself' (Izquierdo 1982a, p. 457).

In summary, pharmacological studies suggest the presence of multiple overlapping systems controlling learning and memory, similar to those described for pain modulation (Chapter 5). These systems probably involve both peripheral and central functions, both generalized and localized processes, and both specific and modulatory neurotransmitters which simultaneously co-ordinate memory, arousal, and reinforcement systems. The detailed mechanisms of how memory is stored or recalled remain obscure but at present some fundamental requirements in vertebrates appear to be a mechanism for synaptic plasticity, possibly provided by dendritic spines, the presence of synapses for certain neurotransmitters, probably including acetylcholine and excitatory amino acids, and, for higher functions such as language, a considerable degree of specialization in localized cortical-subcortical structures. It seems likely that memories are 'ultimately stored in neuronal circuits (or networks), not in molecules' and that 'the individuality and *content* of memories . . . are not reducible to molecular cascades' (Dudai 1989, p. 138).

Clinical findings in patients with memory disorders, described in the next chapter, in general support these conclusions and give further information on how memory systems might work.

9. Disorders of memory

Clinically occurring memory disorders are difficult to classify on the basis of the hypothetical stages of memory discussed in Chapter 8. Since memory functions are widely distributed in the brain, memory disturbance forms part of the clinical picture in many pathological states. These include acute conditions associated with alterations in consciousness and chronic conditions secondary to vascular, infective, neoplastic, traumatic, metabolic and other causes. Such memory disturbances are usually non-specific, involving several stages of memory, and are overshadowed by other clinical features. Much less commonly, relatively selective memory loss occurs and memory disturbance forms the major clinical symptom. These clinical disorders provide a window through which to study the organization of memory in man.

Impairment of immediate memory

Warrington (1981) described a rare syndrome characterized by a relatively selective loss of immediate memory. One such patient had a digit and letter span of only one to two items (normal: five to nine items), although he had no aphasia and could converse without difficulty. He could remember stimulus items normally if they were presented visually rather than acoustically. Other patients have been described with similar immediate memory defects, and it appears that the critical site for a lesion to produce this type of impairment is in the left inferior parietal lobe of the brain.

Impairment of semantic memory

Occasionally cerebral lesions lead to selective impairment of semantic memory: some forms of aphasia and alexia may be regarded as disorders of semantic memory, an amnesia for words or their meanings. The critical sites in the dominant hemisphere for the comprehension and production of written and spoken language have been described in Chapter 8 (Fig. 8.4). Different types of aphasia may result from damage at several of these sites, but since lesions are rarely discretely localized, most clinically occurring aphasias are mixed. They are usually classified functionally (Walton 1977; Geschwind 1975).

Nominal aphasia (*anomic or amnesic aphasia*) results from lesions in or near the angular gyrus of the dominant hemisphere interrupting the connection between Wernicke's area and the rest of the brain, and may occur with lesions at other sites (Ojemann 1983). The dominant feature is an inability to name objects, although comprehension is not greatly affected and the patient can usually describe objects by paraphrasing. Articulation of words is unimpaired and patients can repeat names supplied by the examiner, only to forget them rapidly. Reading and writing are similarly impaired and acalculia (difficulty in carrying out calculations) may be present. Limited forms of nominal aphasia may be encountered rarely. Warrington (1981) described two patients in whom the semantic deficit was category-specific: in one, comprehension of concrete words (blacksmith, macaroni) was much more impaired than that of abstract words (soul, opinion), while in the other the reverse was true. These patients showed no apparent general intellectual deficit, no amnesia for events, and were not disorientated in time or place. Studies of further patients with similar disorders suggest that the critical lesion for this type of semantic defect is in the temporo-occipital region of the brain and that memories for concrete and abstract word meanings are represented in structurally separate pathways.

Other forms of aphasia are not conventionally considered as memory disorders but are included here since they involve semantic memory systems (Ojemann 1983). In *Broca's aphasia* (*expressive or motor aphasia*), usually ascribed to damage to Broca's area, comprehension of speech and writing is normal but the patient is unable to translate speech into articulate sounds (non-fluent aphasia), or to write normally. The brain damage involves the dominant hemisphere and there is nearly always a crossed hemiplegia. In *Wernicke's aphasia* (*sensory or receptive aphasia*), ascribed to lesions involving Wernicke's area, comprehension of spoken and written language is impaired, but the patient can articulate words normally, although his conversation makes little sense (fluent aphasia). There is usually no hemiplegia. Occasionally cortical insufficiency or anoxia gives rise to the *syndrome of isolated speech area*, in which a lesion is thought to occupy a C-shaped configuration which spares Broca's area, Wernicke's area, and their interconnections, but destroys the cortex and underlying white matter which surround the region. The most striking clinical feature is an almost total lack of comprehension but normal repetition and no dysarthia. *Conduction aphasia* (*syntactical aphasia, central aphasia of Goldstein*) is usually ascribed to lesions which disrupt the connection between Broca's and Wernicke's areas, just above the Sylvian fissure. Comprehension of spoken and written language is intact, but speech and writing, though fluent, are severely impaired. *Global or total aphasia*, with impairment of both comprehension and production of speech and writing, results from damage to the dominant frontal and temporal lobes.

Impairment of recognition memory

Various agnosias, inability to recognize complex stimuli although perception is intact, appear to represent disorders of recognition memory. Such disorders may be associated with aphasias or with global amnesia, but occasionally occur as isolated defects, and may be limited to one sensory modality. The commonest form is *visual agnosia* in which faces or objects, or pictures of them, are not recognized by sight. Damasio (1985, 1990; Chapter 8) reviews recent findings in prosopagnosia, impaired recognition of previously familiar faces. Such patients also have difficulty in differentiating specific objects within a class, such as recognizing their own car, clothes, dog, or specific foods. The lesions in this case are bilateral and involve the mesial occipitotemporal region. The physiological basis of the defect appears to be a failure of visual stimuli to activate the host of memories pertinent to those stimuli. A similar type of dysfunction appears to underlie *auditory agnosia* (amusia), failure to recognize musical tunes, caused by temporo-sphenoidal lobe lesions, and *tactile agnosia*, inability to recognize an object placed in the hand, resulting from parietal lobe lesions.

Impairment of motor memory

Apraxia, the inability to perform a learned act or purposive movement in the absence of motor paralysis, sensory loss or ataxia, is sometimes clinically associated with aphasia. Some forms of apraxia may represent an amnesia for motor learning. Dressing apraxia may reflect a defect of spatial understanding and can occur after lesions of the non-dominant hemisphere. Right hemisphere lesions can also cause anosognosia, a tendency to neglect the left side of the body (Chapter 2). Left and right dissociation occurs after lesions of the corpus callosum.

However, most aspects of motor learning and memory appear to be functionally and anatomically separate from both semantic and event memory. Thus, motor learning is often preserved in patients with semantic memory defects and in the amnesic syndrome described below. It seems likely that the neural substrates for motor learning lie outside the brain sites damaged in these cases, possibly in the cerebellum (Marr 1969; Young 1979).

Impairment of event memory

Selective impairment of event memory can result from diverse pathological causes discussed below. The anatomical feature common to
all these disorders is damage within the diencephalon involving the
mammillary bodies and certain thalamic nuclei or in the interconnected
temporal lobes involving the hippocampal formation (Brierley 1977).
The importance of these structures in the organization of memory
has been discussed in Chapter 8. Their dysfunction may give rise to
the amnesic syndrome first described by Korsakoff in 1887 (cited in
Zangwill 1977).

Memory loss in the amnesic syndrome has been intensively studied
(Milner 1970; Scoville and Milner 1957; Mair *et al.* 1979; Iversen 1977;
Zangwill 1977; Warrington 1981). The impairment is most marked for
recent events, both verbal and non-verbal, and typically patients forget
new names, new faces, and new places, although they retain memories
of distant events. In new surroundings, they cannot remember the
geography for long enough to find their way around. In a sense, such
patients exist in a timeless void, permanently lost among strangers.
Occasionally, if the lesion is focal or unilateral, impairment of recent
memory may be limited to one sensory modality, one half of the body,
or to the function of one cerebral hemisphere (Ross 1982).

Despite the severe restriction of event memory, in the purest form
of the amnesic syndrome, attention, immediate recall, language (semantic memory), perception, performance in various types of intelligence
tests and motor learning and memory are all normal, as illustrated by
the noted patient H.M. who had undergone bilateral surgical removal
of the medial temporal cortex, amygdala, hippocampus and associated
connections (Milner 1970; Iversen 1977).

Much investigation, reviewed by Piercy (1977), has been directed to
the question of which stage or stages of memory are impaired in the
amnesic syndrome. Immediate memory appears to be intact, although
unduly sensitive to interference. Several possibilities have been suggested to explain the impairment of event memory: (a) a defect of
consolidation, (b) inadequate encoding of information at the time
it is entered into store, and (c) failure of retrieval of information.
Careful testing reveals that the amnesia is not as absolute as it appears.
Warrington and Weiskrantz (1970) and Warrington (1981) showed
that word fragments, initial letters of a word, and category information
can be used as clues by amnesic patients, suggesting that they can
encode and consolidate information, both pictorial and verbal, and
that their difficulty is one of access to the stored material.

Investigation of the various causes of disturbance of event memory, and particularly correlations of the memory defects with the localization of the associated lesions, has shed some light on the way memory systems are organized in the brain.

Thiamine deficiency

Of the original patients on whom Korsokoff based his description of the amnesic syndrome, a number were alcoholics, and the Korsakoff syndrome is still most commonly seen in chronic alcoholics (Whitty *et al.* 1977). The amnesia probably results from brain damage caused by the associated dietary thiamine deficiency; a similar syndrome is sometimes seen in other thiamine-deficient states (Handler and Perkin 1983) and can be induced in animals by thiamine deficient diets (Brierley 1977). The psychological abnormalities are not limited to memory defects, although loss of recent memory is prominent and retrograde amnesia is usual. A striking feature is a facile and expansive confabulation, a tendency to fill in memory gaps with improvized and often implausible explanations, and a marked lack of insight into the disability, both intellectual and physical.

Studies which have attempted to correlate the psychological features with neurological damage in chronic thiamine deficiency have been reviewed by Brierley (1977) and by Mair *et al.* (1979). The presence of amnesia appears to be related to bilateral damage to diencephalic structures, and the important foci of such lesions appear to include the inner portions of the dorsomedial, anteroventral, and pulvinar nuclei of the thalamus, the mammillary bodies, and the terminal portions of the fornix. Damage to the hippocampus, septal region, cortex, brainstem or cerebellum does not appear to be a constant feature, although changes here may account for associated cognitive and physical symptoms seen in individual cases. Confabulation seems to occur when acute frontal lobe damage accompanies the amnesic syndrome. The pathological processes include demyelinization and neuronal loss in some areas, and proliferation of microglia and fibrous astrocytes. There may be abnormalities in central monoaminergic function, but cholinergic pathways appear to be relatively intact (McEntee and Mair 1990). The mechanism by which thiamine deficiency induces the changes is not known.

Brain surgery

Neurosurgical procedures have been used for the removal of tumours and for the relief of epilepsy, Parkinson's disease, and chronic psychiatric states. Patients undergoing such operations have pre-existing brain damage or dysfunction, but some have developed postoperatively particular memory deficits clearly related to the surgical intervention and not to the original disease. The induction of memory disorders by removal or section of known brain structures has provided strong evidence for the critical participation of temporal lobe sites in certain memory functions in man.

Scoville and Milner (1957) reported the appearance of the typical amnesic syndrome in patients following bilateral removal of the anterior two-thirds of the hippocampus and hippocampal gyrus along with the uncus and amygdala. The memory defect was permanent and was confined to loss of memory for recent events with some retrograde amnesia, but no deterioration in personality, intelligence, or previously learned motor skills. The severity of the ensuing memory defect is related to the amount of hippocampal tissue removed at operation. Severe defects of recent memory probably result only from bilateral temporal lobe damage. However, unilateral temporal lobe damage is not entirely without effects on memory. Patients with left temporal lobectomies show disruption of performance in verbal-auditory recent memory tasks, while in patients with right temporal lobectomies visual-spatial and non-verbal auditory recent memory tasks is impaired (Ross 1982).

Less consistent memory defects follow operations on other brain areas. Operations on the frontal lobes rarely produce permanent memory deficits, although defects in retention and marked distractibility occur in the immediate post-operative period, along with a patchy retrograde amnesia. Transient difficulty in remembering the temporal sequence of events has been observed after limited ablations of the anterior cingulate cortex. Operations on the thalamus produce various memory disorders depending on the site affected, but interference with the anterior thalamic nuclei may cause gross and permanent defects of recent memory. Surgical interference with the fornix has produced variable results; it seems likely that bilateral section of the fornix does not produce memory loss unless there is coincident damage to periventricular structures (Whitty et al. 1977; Brierley 1977). Various subtle cognitive disorders have been described in 'split brain' patients (Sperry 1973, 1974, 1976; Cook 1986), but commisurotomy (including section of the corpus callosum and of the anterior hippocampal and habenular commisures), or even hemispherectomy, does not seem to be associated with general or specific memory impairment, except under particular experimental conditions (Sergent 1990).

Cerebral tumours

Cerebral tumours usually cause generalized effects, including a rise of intracranial pressure and interference with blood supply, and memory changes form only part of a widespread disturbance of consciousness.

Occasionally, however, a characteristic and florid confabulatory amnesic syndrome occurs with localized tumours, in the absence of generalized mental disturbance or evidence of pre-existing alcoholism. Whitty *et al.* (1977) and Brierley (1977) have reviewed the evidence suggesting that localized damage to particular brain structures is the cause of amnesia in these cases. The tumours usually involve deep midline diencephalic structures in the region of the hypothalamus and third ventricle either by neoplastic changes or by compression. Craniopharyngiomas are commonly associated with memory loss and removal of the tumour or removal of fluid from it can restore normal memory, suggesting that the amnesia is due to pressure on structures on the floor of the third ventricle. The amnesic syndrome has been described in patients with secondary neoplastic deposits confined to the mammillary bodies. Temporal lobe tumours are sometimes associated with selective memory impairment, depending on whether the tumour is situated on the dominant or non-dominant side.

Frontal lobe tumours have also been reported to cause amnesia, especially if they are bilateral and involve the corpus callosum. However, in these cases there is also a defect of motivation and attention which seriously interferes with memory testing. Tumours of the cerebral hemisphere may produce different types of impairment depending on their location, including a variety of aphasias when certain areas of the dominant hemisphere are affected and loss of memory for motor skills when the right parietal area is involved.

Intracranial infections

In herpes encephalitis, tissue necrosis and haemorrhage, with intranuclear inclusion bodies in nerve cells and glia, chiefly affect limbic structures: the uncus, amygdaloid nucleus, hippocampus, hippocampal and cingulate gyri, post-orbital regions, and sometimes the fornices and mammillary bodies (Whitty *et al.* 1977; Brierley 1977). The pathological changes are so discrete that the term 'limbic encephalitis' has been applied to this condition. A marked impairment of recent memory with the features of the amnesic syndrome including confabulation is found in such cases. The syndrome is not common as a major defect in other forms of encephalitis, in which the pathological changes in the brain are more widespread.

Vascular disorders and hypoxia

Transient disturbance of recent memory can occur in migraine, hypertensive encephalopathy, thromboangitis obliterans, and systemic lupus erythematosus. It has been suggested that in this case the amnesia is due to vertebral-basilar artery spasm with consequent ischaemia in the brainstem reticular formation, mammillary bodies, and hippocampal formation (Whitty *et al.* 1977).

More permanent amnesia may follow cerebral haemorrhage or thrombosis affecting the blood supply to the temporal lobes. Localized vascular lesions may give rise to fractional disorders of recent memory; Ross (1982) described two patients with posterior cerebral artery lesions causing infarction in the inferior occipital lobes and inferior-posterior, but not medial temporal lobes, bilaterally. These patients had recent memory disorders limited to the visual system. Progressive cerebral atherosclerosis may produce a clinical picture similar to other dementias of old age, in which impairment of recent memory is an early and at first isolated sign, followed gradually by general intellectual deterioration. *Post mortem* examination reveals multiple small cerebral infarcts.

Head injury

The typical results of a moderate to severe closed head injury are: a period of loss of consciousness, a period of behavioural confusion, a post-traumatic anterograde amnesia extending forwards in time from the first two events, and a retrograde amnesia extending backwards in time from the loss of consciousness (Whitty and Zangwill 1977). The duration of the post-traumatic amnesia correlates well with the severity of the injury. During this period the patient may behave apparently normally yet later have no recollection of events. Sometimes confabulation, delusions, or automatism occur during post-traumatic amnesia. Usually the retrograde amnesia shrinks as recovery occurs, but the return of memory is often patchy and does not necessarily occur in chronological order. A residual memory defect of some degree is probably common in spite of otherwise full recovery, although it may be difficult to detect. There may be some degree of impairment of recent memory and also 'islands of amnesia' well outside the period of retrograde amnesia. The anatomical basis of post-concussional amnesia is usually difficult to establish but in the common injury to the front of the head, the frontal and temporal lobes as well as the brainstem are especially liable to damage. The amnesic syndrome may also follow penetrating injuries of the temporal lobes, and bilateral diencephalic or hippocampal injuries.

Epilepsy

Transient or short-lasting amnesia occurs in tonic-clonic and absence seizures, associated with alteration in consciousness. Disturbance of memory is a characteristic feature of temporal lobe epilepsy. The aura preceding the attack may include feelings of intensified familiarity with the surroundings or situation (déjà vu) or feelings of strangeness and unfamiliarity, sometimes associated with fear and anxiety as in a panic attack (Chapter 3). There may also be confusion, with difficulty in recalling words, and a variety of epigastric gustatory, or olfactory sensations accompanied by salivation and lip-smacking. Manifestations of the subsequent seizure are variable and may consist only of a dazed look, confused behaviour, automatic repetition of an inappropriate motor sequence, a period of aggressiveness, or a prolonged fugue. Amnesia for the period of the seizure is the rule, and the amnesia typically has an abrupt onset and ending.

Study of temporal lobe epilepsy has been of particular value in localizing some of the sites involved in memory. Much evidence (reviewed by Brierley 1977) has shown that the attacks result from epileptic discharges originating in the medial temporal lobe. EEG recordings during attacks have shown spontaneous epileptic discharges in the medial and inferior temporal regions in most cases. Furthermore, electrical stimulation of these areas, especially around the amygdala and deep in the uncus, can reproduce both the automatism and the amnesia. Electrical stimulation of the medial aspect of the temporal lobe in unanaesthetized subjects can also reproduce the premonitory auras of epileptic attacks. Stimulation of the lateral aspects of the temporal lobes in cases where these are already the site of epileptic discharge can give rise to false recollections or 'experimental hallucinations'. These memories are often the same as those which occur in the spontaneous epileptic attacks (Penfield and Perot 1963). Similar 'stereotyped memories' have been induced by stimulation through implanted electrodes and the same memories can be evoked on several occasions by repeated stimulation (Bickford *et al.* 1958). Thus both amnesia and memories can be evoked by localized electrical stimulation in discrete temporal lobe areas.

Electroconvulsive therapy

A reversible memory deficit invariably follows electroconvulsive therapy; the impairment is similar to that following a closed head injury or an epileptic convulsion. The clinical features, reviewed by Williams (1977), consist of a retrograde amnesia, a confused phase following the convulsion, and a period of anterograde amnesia. The retrograde amnesia usually shrinks rapidly until it occupies only a few seconds, although there may be patches of amnesia which extend further back in time. During the anterograde amnesia, the main impairment is memory for recent events and is similar to the amnesic syndrome from other causes; this phase typically lasts about 4–6 h. There may be some residual memory defect persisting for some weeks.

In general, the memory defects appear to be proportional to the strength and duration of electrical stimulation and to the duration of the seizure. They can, however, be considerably modified if unilateral rather than bilateral electroconvulsive therapy is employed (Williams 1977; Iversen 1977; Ross 1982). Unilateral electroconvulsive therapy applied to the dominant hemisphere produces a limited memory defect, mainly affecting performance in verbal recent memory tests. When the shock is applied only to the non-dominant hemisphere, the resulting memory impairment is even less marked and affects performance predominantly in non-verbal recent memory tests.

The amnesic effect of electroconvulsive therapy is probably due to disruption of temporal lobe activity: the electrodes are normally applied over the temporal lobe; they cause local electrical charges as well as generalized activity; and the hippocampus has a very low threshold for electrically induced convulsions. Furthermore, electrical stimulation of the temporal lobe in conscious patients, when followed by an epileptic after-discharge, seriously impairs memory for recent events (Iverson 1977). Electroconvulsive therapy given through electrodes placed over the frontal lobes appears to cause less memory impairment.

Senile and presenile dementias

Alzheimer-type dementia

Progressive deterioration of intellectual activity leading to dementia is common with advancing years but not inevitable (Davison 1982). Its occurrence is a major problem in modern societies with ageing populations and has stimulated much recent research into age-related dementias. Historically, the term Alzheimer's disease was applied to a type of progressive dementia starting between the ages of 45 and 65, while the term senile dementia was used for a similar condition commencing at the age of 65 and over. Because of the close clinical and pathological similarities, however, Alzheimer's disease (or Alzheimer-type dementia) is now used by many authors to describe both the senile and presenile forms (Gottfries 1980; Corkin 1981; Rossor 1982). Alzheimer's disease is the commonest of the presenile dementias and it accounts for over 50 per cent of elderly patients diagnosed clinically as demented. Several millions of people in Britain and the USA are affected. Other dementias in old age include those caused by vascular disease, mixed forms, Lewy body dementia (Perry et al. 1989), and some rarer disorders (Besson 1983).

Clinical features. Alzheimer's disease, which is more prevalent among women than men, begins insidiously and is characterized by marked deficits in many cognitive functions, including memory, language, and complex sensorimotor and perceptual capacities. Typically the first symptom is loss of memory for recent events, and often there is especial difficulty in recalling names and words, a disability soon merging into an amnesic dysphasia, although memory for remote events may be relatively unimpaired. Ultimately generalized intellectual impairment and disorientation develops, social behaviour degenerates, and there may be associated psychological and neurological disorders.

Morphological changes.   Since memory disruption is prominent, and Alzheimer's disease is more common than most other causes of the amnesic syndrome, the histological and neurochemical changes found in the brain post-mortem are of particular interest as a source of information on the neural substrates of memory. Morphological changes consist of diffuse neocortical degeneration which is most marked in the temporal, parietal, and occipital lobes, but also involves the posterior cingulate gyrus, amygdala, hippocampus, hypothalamus, some midbrain and brainstem structures (Corkin 1981), and olfactory nucleus (Averback 1983). Ball *et al.* (1985), and de Leon *et al.* (1989) stress the importance of degenerative changes in the hippocampus as a factor in the memory defects. There is also marked neuronal loss (up to 76 per cent; Tagliavini and Pilleri 1983) in the basal nucleus of Meynert (Whitehouse *et al.* 1982), and in the nucleus of the diagonal band of Broca, the medial septal nucleus, and the locus coeruleus (Davison 1982). However, the anterior cingulate gyrus, caudate nucleus, thalamus, and mammillary bodies are only minimally affected.

Several distinctive pathological changes have been described (Fig. 9.1): (1) senile (neuritic) plaques, in which deposits of extracellular amyloid-like material are surrounded by abnormal unmyelinated neuronal processes; (2) neurofibrillary tangles, consisting of intracellular bundles of filaments in the cytoplasm surrounding cell nuclei; (3) progressive deterioration of the dendrites and dendritic spines of pyramidal cells in the cortex and hippocampus and of dentate granule cells; (4) vacuoles in the cytoplasm of hippocampal pyramidal cells, especially in areas CA1-3 (Wiesnieski and Iqbal 1980); (5) intraneuronal accumulation of the pigment lipofuscin in the parietal cortex and especially in the inferior olivary nucleus (Dowson 1982). These changes occur bilaterally but are not necessarily symmetrical. Inclusion bodies have also been found in adrenal medullary cells (Averback 1983).

Biochemical changes.   Accompanying these morphological changes, distinct neurochemical abnormalities have been found in post-mortem specimens. Compared with age-matched non-demented control subjects, there is significant impairment of cholinergic function in the brain in Alzheimer's disease, as indicated by a 50 per cent or more decrease in

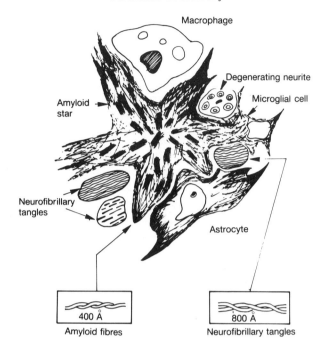

Fig. 9.1 Diagram of pathological features in the brain in Alzheimer-type dementia. Diagram shows various elements of a neuritic (senile) plaque, consisting of a central amyloid star containing paired helical fibres of amyloid-like material, surrounded by degenerating neurites with neurofibrillary tangles containing intracellular bundles of paired helical filaments, and by macrophages, fibrous astrocytes, and microglial cells. (Adapted from Wiesnieski and Iqbal 1980.)

the activity of the enzyme choline acetyltransferase (CAT), which is involved in the synthesis of acetylcholine and is a specific marker for cholinergic neurones. In addition, acetylcholinesterase activity and acetylcholine synthesis are reduced significantly in biopsy samples *in vitro*. These changes have been confirmed in many studies reviewed by Deakin (1983), Besson (1983), Rossor (1982), Coyle *et al*. (1983*a*, *b*), Bowen and Davison (1984), Corkin, (1981) and Gottfries (1980).

The cerebral cortex contains few intrinsic cholinergic neurones, and the CAT deficit reflects degeneration of ascending cholinergic projections which mainly arise from the basal nucleus of Meynert, the medial septal nucleus, and the diagonal band of Broca (Fig. 9.2). The neuronal loss is accompanied by a deficit in several subtypes of cholinergic receptors (Quirion *et al*. 1989). The density of nicotinic receptors in the cortex and hippocampus is markedly decreased. These receptors are thought to be located on cortical and hippocampal nerve terminals

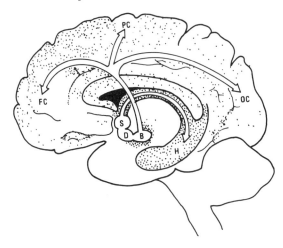

Fig. 9.2 Diagram of brain showing origin of ascending cholinergic projections from the basal nucleus of Meynert, the diagonal band of Broca, and the medial septal nucleus. B, basal nucleus of Meynert; D, diagonal band of Broca; S, medial septal nucleus; FC, frontal cortex; PC, parietal cortex; OC, occipital cortex; H, hippocampal formation. (Adapted from Coyle *et al.* 1983*b*.)

and to function normally as 'positive' autoreceptors ensuring the maintenance of constant basal synaptic concentrations of acetylcholine. There is a modest loss of post-synaptic muscarinic receptors (M_1 receptors) in the hippocampus, and remaining M_1 receptors may be partially uncoupled from their effector systems (Edwardson and Candy 1987; Fowler *et al.* 1990). There is also evidence of considerable reduction in the density of muscarinic M_2 receptors in the hippocampus and various cortical areas (Quirion *et al.* 1989). A similar loss of nicotinic and muscarinic receptors occurs in Parkinson's disease associated with dementia. A population of muscarinic M_2 receptors is thought to be located pre-synaptically on cholinergic nerve terminals where they act as negative autoreceptors, decreasing acetylcholine release. Antagonists of these autoreceptors facilitate acetylcholine release and improve learning in rats. In patients with Alzheimer's disease there is a close correlation between the decrease in CAT activity, the deficits in nicotinic and muscarinic (M_2) receptors found post-mortem and the degree of intellectual impairment during life. This correlation strengthens the suggestion that cholinergic systems are important for memory (Chapter 8) and offers a faint hope that mental function in Alzheimer's disease might be improved by cholinergic agents (Corkin 1981; Quirion *et al.* 1989; Chapter 10).

Monoaminergic systems may also be affected. There are decreases in brain concentrations of the enzymes tyrosine hydroxylase and

dopamine decarboxylase and of the neurotransmitters dopamine, noradrenaline, and serotonin and their metabolites, and an increase in
monoamine oxidase activity. These changes are seen in normal ageing but
the sum of damage in the different systems seems to be greater in Alzheimer's disease (Gottfries 1980). Nevertheless, the locus coeruleus has an
important population of noradrenergic neurones which send projections
to the cortex, and Bondareff et al. (1981) found cell numbers in this
nucleus to be reduced by nearly 80 per cent in some patients with severe
and early Alzheimer's disease. Reduction in cell numbers may also occur
in the raphe nuclei (serotonergic) and substantia nigra and ventral
tegmentum (dopaminergic) (Besson 1983). Recent work indicates in
addition that there are marked reductions in the concentration of the
polypeptides somatostatin in the temporal cortex, and of corticotrophin
releasing factor and perhaps other polypeptides (Zeisel et al. 1981;
Selkoe 1982; Whalley 1987). Reduced concentrations of GABA have
been noted in cortical areas, hippocampus and amygdala (Deakin 1983;

Table 9.1 Some biochemical changes in Alzheimer's disease

Neurotransmitters	Areas of cell loss	Loss of synaptic uptake in cortical terminal field (%)
Acetylcholine	nucleus basalis diagonal band medial septal nucleus	60
Noradrenaline	locus coeruleus	45
Serotonin	raphe nuclei	65
Dopamine	ventral tegmentum substantia nigra	?
Glutamate	pyramidal neurones cortex and hippocampus	60
Polypeptides		
somatostatin	cortex	decreased
corticotropin releasing factor	cortex	decreased
beta-endorphin	(cerebrospinal fluid)	decreased
Enzymes		
choline acetyltransferase		decreased
acetylcholinesterase		decreased
tyrosine hydroxylase		decreased
dopamine decarboxylase		decreased
monoamine oxidase		increased

References: Hardy and Cowburn (1987); Maragos et al. (1987); Whalley (1987).

Rossor 1982; Rossor *et al.* 1984). Glutamate concentration is also decreased (Hardy and Cowburn 1987), and Maragos *et al.* (1987) and Greenamyre *et al.* (1985, 1987) reported a profound loss of glutamate receptors, especially NMDA receptors, in the cortex and hippocampus. Bridges *et al.* (1988) found that such changes only occur when there is severe neuronal loss. However, disruption of glutamate function in these areas might account for much of the learning and memory deficit seen in Alzheimer's disease. Harrison (1986) suggests that pathological changes initially affect corticocortical and corticofugal pathways selectively, and that the disease process extends retrogradely, involving the many transmitters utilized in the pathways involved. Some of the biochemical changes found in Alzheimer's disease are summarized in Table 9.1.

It is probable that the cognitive impairments seen in Alzheimer's disease result from defects in many transmitters and modulator systems; the degree of mental deterioration correlates with decrease of CAT activity, decrease in cerebrospinal fluid glutamate concentration (Maragos *et al.* 1987) and the number of neuritic plaques and neurofibrillary tangles. Total cerebral blood flow is reduced and there are marked regional variations which may correlate with clinically observed mental impairment (Ingvar 1982). Positron emission tomography (PET) studies have shown that there is decreased cortical blood flow and glucose utilization which is confined, in the early stages of the disease, to posterior temporal and parietal regions (areas of association cortex), spreading later to the frontal cortex (Friedland *et al.* 1985; Katzman 1986; Frackowiak 1987; Geaney *et al.* 1990).

Relationship to age and to normal ageing.   The relation of Alzheimer's disease to normal ageing has also been debated (Bondareff 1983; Rossor *et al.* 1984; Wilcock and Esiri 1983). Most of the morphological and neurochemical changes that have been described in Alzheimer's disease also occur in non-demented elderly subjects (Selkoe 1982; Perry and Perry 1985; Gottfries 1980; Corkin 1981). There is progressive loss of neurones, particularly in the cortex, from adulthood onwards, and even in normal individuals a steady accumulation of neuritic plaques, neurofibrillary tangles, and lipofuscin deposits begins in about the fifth decade. At the same time there is a fall in cholinergic and monoaminergic activity, and a substantial neuronal loss in the locus coeruleus. All these changes in normal ageing occur without gross loss of cognitive function or memory, although most people past middle age admit to some deterioration of learning ability and memory, and the elderly are more susceptible to mental disruption from central depressant drugs (Chapter 4).

Thus the distinction between normal human brain ageing and

Alzheimer's disease seems to be essentially quantitative, Alzheimer's disease being characterized by a greater severity and wider distribution of a continuum of degenerative changes associated with ageing (Brayne and Calloway 1988).

Molecular pathogenesis.   Much interest has focused on the molecular structure of neuritic plaques, neurofibrillary tangles and amyloid and lipofuscin deposits (Selkoe 1982; Wiesnieski and Iqbal 1980; Edwardson and Candy 1987; Miller *et al.* 1986; Price *et al.* 1986). Plaques (Fig. 9.1) consist of dystrophic neuritic processes and glial elements surrounding a central core. This core has a fibrillary ultrastructure and contains two main consistuents: an amyloid protein and a deposit of alumino-silicates (Candy *et al.* 1984, 1985, 1986; Perry and Perry 1985). Neuro-fibrillary tangles are made up of paired helical filaments composed of relatively insoluble, abnormally phosphorylated tau protein which is involved in microtubule assembly. The tangles also contain an amyloid substance, which may not be the same as that found in plaques (Anderton and Miller 1986), and aluminosilicates which form rigid, self-replicating crystals. Lipofuscin granules may be derived from mito-chondria, lysosymes, or both by a process of autophagocytosis. They include lipoids, proteins, cations, and acid hydrolysis-resistant residues. The lipid moiety contains oxidized polymers of polyunsaturated fatty acids, and it is possible that the production of these results in the for-mation of lipid/free radical molecules which can, through a series of reactions, disrupt lipoidal structures, and also cross-link and damage proteins or nucleic acids. Thus, the development of tangles, plaques, and lipofuscin in the brain may lead to an accumulation of rigid, insolu-ble intra- and extracellular deposits and could be the cause, rather than the result of progressive neuronal degeneration and death (Selkoe 1982).

Aetiology.   What initiates the molecular changes is still conjectural. Faulty assembly of normal brain constituents due to an accumulation of errors with increasing age (Wiesnieski and Iqbal 1980; Hayflick 1979), or impaired ability to repair neuronal damage due to deficient synthesis or action of nerve growth factor (Deary and Walley 1988) have been suggested. Neurotoxic effects of excitatory amino acids resulting from a defect in glutamate metabolism is postulated by Maragos *et al.* (1987) and Meldrum and Gärthwaite (1990).

Such changes may be induced by genetic or environmental factors. A genetic link is suggested by observations that the incidence of Alzheimer's disease is increased among the first-degree relatives of patients (Heston and Mastri 1977) and that most patients with Down's syndrome who survive to the age of 40 develop dementia with histological changes resembling those of Alzheimer's disease (Selkoe 1982; Rossor 1982; Besson 1983). A defective gene on chromosome 21 (and possibly chromosome 19) has been linked to familial Alzheimer's disease, but most cases of Alzheimer's disease are sporadic and do not display this abnormality (Deary and Wally 1988; Hardy 1988). Other diseases in which an amyloid protein is produced in the brain (scrapie in sheep and goats, bovine spongiform encephalopathy, and kuru and Creutzfeld-Jakob disease in man) are associated with mutations on chromosome 20 (Brown *et al.* 1991). These diseases, unlike Alzheimer's disease, can be transmitted to other animals by innoculation or ingestion of affected tissue. However, there may be other, probably multiple genetic alterations which combine with environmental factors to increase susceptibility to Alzheimer's disease.

Among environmental toxins, exogenous (dietary) excitatory amino acids may account for some neurodegenerative diseases (Meldrum and Garthwaite 1990) but have not been identified for Alzheimer's disease. However, a potential role of aluminium in Alzheimer's disease, suggested by Crapper *et al.* (1976), has been a subject of renewed interest. Aluminium silicates are concentrated in the centre of senile plaques and neurofibrillary tangles (Candy *et al.* 1985) and serum aluminium concentrations have been shown in at least one study to be raised in Alzheimer's disease (Kellett *et al.* 1986). Sustained administration of the chelating agent desferrioxamine appears to slow the progression of the dementia, possibly by preventing accumulation of aluminium in the brain (McLachlan *et al.* 1991).

There is a geographical relationship between the prevalence of Alzheimer's disease and the concentration of aluminium in drinking water in the UK and in Norway (Martyn *et al.* 1989). Drinking water accounts for only a small proportion of aluminium intake, most of which is derived from foodstuffs and food additives (Lancet 1989). However, the presence of fluoride ions greatly increases the leaching of aluminium from cooking utensils (Tennakone and Wickramanayake 1987); in the UK aluminium cooking utensils were widely used until recently and drinking water in some areas contains relatively high concentrations of fluoride. In addition, calcium deficiency may lead to increased permeability of the blood-brain barrier to aluminium (Banks and Kastin 1983; Candy *et al.* 1984, 1985; Garruto *et al.* 1984) and there is some evidence suggesting that calcium metabolism may be altered in Alzheimer's disease (Katzman 1986).

Aluminium is transported into cells by the iron-carrying protein transferrin. In the brain, it is concentrated in areas with the highest concentration of transferrin receptors including the hippocampus and cortex (Edwardson and Candy 1987). Once in the cells, aluminium could cause toxic effects by a number of mechanisms including the disruption of phosphatidylinositol second messenger systems, causing neuronal malfunction and eventually cell death (Birchall and Chappell

1988) and interference with microtubule assembly, leading to neuro-fibrillary tangles (Deary and Hendrickson 1986). Silicon, a normal tissue constituent, combines with aluminium to form the aluminosilicates found in plaques and tangles. Some aluminosilicates are chemically reactive and may lead to spreading cellular damage around the plaque core (Edwardson and Candy 1987).

Other suggested aetiologies include an autoimmune response (Davison 1982) and trauma. Pearce (1984*a, b*) noted excessive senile plaques and neurofibrillary tangles in the cortex of subjects who had been boxers, and attributed this change to repeated brain trauma during life. It seems likely that Alzheimer's disease can result from any one or a combination of several causes in which genetic and environmental factors interact (Hardy and Allsop 1991).

Other neurodegenerative dementias

Probably the second commonest dementia of old age after Alzheimer's disease is cortical Lewy body disease (Perry *et al.* 1989; Burns *et al.* 1990), which has clinical similarities but presents more acutely and runs a fluctuating course, often with hallucinations and aggression. Neocortical senile plaques are present, but there are relatively few neurofibrillary tangles. Lewy bodies, occlusion bodies containing abnormally phosphorylated neurofilaments, are diffusely distributed in the cortex. There is neuronal loss in subcortical nuclei, a decrease in CAT activity and in cholinergic (M_2 and nicotinic) receptor density (Quirion *et al.* 1989), and decreased concentrations of serotonin, dopamine and their metabolites. Some of the changes in the brain are similar to those found in Alzheimer's dementia; others are also found in Parkinson's disease in which dementia develops in perhaps 20 per cent of patients (Small and Jarvik 1982; Lees 1985). The mesolimbic dopaminergic system, the serotonergic system and the noradrenergic projection from the locus coeruleus may all be affected. The neuropathological changes suggest a degree of overlap between Alzheimer's disease, Lewy body dementia, and Parkinson's disease.

Other neurodegenerative dementias, including Pick's disease, Creutzfeld–Jacob disease, and Huntington's chorea are reviewed by Gottfries (1980), Small and Jarvik (1982), Rossor (1982), Cross *et al.* (1986) and Albin *et al.* (1990).

Application of clinical studies to memory mechanisms in man

The theoretical basis of learning and memory (Chapter 8) is largely derived from experimental work on associative memory in animals, and it is generally agreed from this work that many basic memory functions are widely distributed in the brain. In man, memory functions are vastly more complex because of their close association with language, both verbal and numerate, and with the human capability for abstract thought. A study of clinically occurring memory disorders might thus be expected to provide an opportunity for testing the applicability of animal work to human memory. Clinical studies have indeed allowed some tentative conclusions to be drawn with regard to the organization of memory in man, but in general the information is limited to *where* memory occurs rather than *how* it occurs.

Clinical investigations clearly confirm the considerable degree of localization of memory functions in the human brain. Thus, the neo-cortex is the main neural substrate for semantic memory; temporal lobe structures including the hippocampus are the main substrates for event memory; subcortical as well as cortical structures are concerned in association memory, and the cerebellum probably subserves motor memory. For this reason, gross defects in event memory, for example, are compatible with apparently normal semantic memory, and vice versa. Localization of memory function also appears to exist within the main structures, and discrete lesions can lead to very discrete memory defects. Conversely, the same memory can be evoked repeatedly by stimulation of the same brain area. Thus, the localization of established memories appears to be both relatively discrete and relatively fixed.

These observations may seem to suggest that different types of memory are 'stored' in particular places in the brain. However, the fact that a certain type of memory is lost after a localized lesion or can be evoked by localized stimulation does not necessarily mean that the memory itself was housed at this site. It seems more likely that such lesions interrupt (or stimulate) pathways that are critical either for the forma-tion or recall of the memory. Each particular subjective memory, may, like each emotion, be conjured temporarily into existence as a three-dimensional pattern of neural activity involving many synapses, which are often congruent with those activated by other memories. (It is doubtful whether a memory exists as an entity at all, except during the times of learning or recall when the particular pattern is actually being used). Certain synapses may be crucial for the establishment or recall of specific components of memory, and dysfunction at these synapses could result in different types of amnesia. For example, the neural activity stimulated by an event may need to be referred through circuits in the temporal lobes in order to activate patterns which include an association with geographical or time location. If these circuits are lacking due to a lesion, the full memory pattern cannot be formed, and the patient will be lost in time and space.

Each memory pattern is envisaged to be honed into shape by synaptic modulations occurring during learning, so that once activity is triggered by a familiar stimulus it will tend to follow preferential pathways. The patterns initiated by a single memory would tend to spread like ripples in a pond as associated memory patterns are in turn sparked into activity. Thus a subject with nominal aphasia can still describe the attributes of an object even if he or she cannot name it. The ability to use memories, especially once they are well established, and to alter behaviour because of them, undoubtedly involves widespread inter-connections between many brain areas, and it is likely that many different possible pathways can be utilized both in the process of learning and in the execution of a learned behaviour. Because of this redundancy, selective memory loss is compatible with normal performance in many tests of intelligence. Yet the total capacity of the brain to store or recall information, with all its associated nuances, must be reduced by memory loss. Hence intelligence in the widest sense — global intelligence or maximal intellectual performance — must be correspondingly impaired.

With regard to the biochemical basis of human memory, clinical studies have so far yielded limited information. Investigations of patients with Alzheimer's disease conform with other evidence indicating that cholinergic and glutaminergic connections are of importance, at least in event memory. However, they do not rule out the possibility that other neurotransmitters are involved, since the post-mortem changes are diffuse, and patients do not usually die when the intellectual disability is limited to the amnesic syndrome. As to the nature of the synaptic changes postulated to underlie memory, degeneration of both dendritic spines and microtubular structures occurs in Alzheimer's disease, but other major pathological changes, including large-scale neuronal loss, occur in addition. Thus, it has not been possible to pinpoint the cellular mechanisms of memory loss. Pharmacological treatments aimed at restoring deficient neurotransmitters or stimulating neuronal meta-bolism in the central nervous system are considered in the next chapter.

10. Drugs and memory

Increasing interest has focused recently on the possibility of pharmacological treatment for memory disorders. Drugs, of course, cannot be expected to replace degenerated neurones, but they might theoretically improve the function of surviving neurones in chronic diseases, hasten neuronal recovery in acute conditions, and perhaps prevent further neuronal damage in both. Such measures are unlikely to have specific effects on memory, but may produce general improvement in mental efficiency. In other circumstances it is advantageous to facilitate forgetting. For example, the use of amnesic drugs as preoperative medication may not only calm the patient but also forestall the laying down of unpleasant memories.

Drugs for improving memory

Central nervous system stimulants

Central nervous system stimulants such as amphetamine and caffeine can improve performance of normal subjects in certain tasks, particularly in the presence of fatigue or boredom. In general these drugs may influence memory by improving arousal and attention, but it is doubtful whether they can contribute much to the treatment of memory disorders.

Methyl-phenidate over a range of doses has been reported to impair performance in memory tasks by disrupting attention during learning (Squire and Davis 1981), but to facilitate the learning of a pictorial paired-associate task in hyperactive children (Shea 1982). Facilitation of word-list recall has been observed after d-amphetamine in depressed patients and in normal children (Squire and Davis 1981). Pemoline and other central nervous system stimulants reviewed by Judd et al. (1987) have also been claimed to increase general performance, although not specifically memory, in fatigued or elderly subjects, and to reverse the sedative effects of central nervous system depressants.

Cholinergic agents

The demonstration of central cholinergic degeneration in Alzheimer's disease suggested a therapeutic potential for cholinergic agents. Drachman (1978; Chapter 8) showed that the memory defects produced by anticholinergic agents were similar to those which develop in old age and could be reversed by physostigmine. A parallel between dopamine replacement in Parkinson's disease and acetylcholine replacement in Alzheimer's disease was immediately suggested. However, early hopes (Corkin 1981) have been somewhat dashed by later findings of considerable deficits in cholinergic receptors in Alzheimer's disease, as well as deficits in many other neurotransmitter systems and widespread neuronal degeneration (Chapter 9; Fibiger 1991). Treatment with cholinergic agents, if it is to be effective, must probably be started early in the disease and continued for long periods, perhaps for life. Coyle *et al.* (1983*b*) point out that functional deficits caused by degeneration of the cholinergic system, which is normally phasically active, with rapid neuronal discharge rates conveying spatially and temporally coded information (Chapter 8), may not be amenable to pharmacological correction.

Trials with several cholinergic agents including acetylcholine precursors, anticholinesterases and cholinergic agonists have been reported, although there have been few well-designed, large-scale, long-term studies (Squire and Davis 1981; Zeisel *et al.* 1981; Kendall 1987). The results available suggest only limited therapeutic benefit. Dietary supplements of choline and lecithin increase the synthesis and concentration of acetylcholine in the rat brain, and possibly in humans. Corkin (1981) reviewed 11 studies in which choline was administered for periods of 2 weeks to 3 months to patients with Alzheimer dementia. No overall changes were seen although individual patients showed improvement in some memory tests. Levy *et al.* (1983) reported the preliminary results of a double blind trial of a preparation containing 90 per cent phosphatydyl choline in 52 patients with early Alzheimer dementia. A significant improvement in a test of general cognitive function and in a paired associate learning test was found in patients taking the drugs for 6 months. Pomara and Stanley (1982) raise the possibility that long-term treatment with cholinergic precursors might lead to receptor desensitization and eventually produce the opposite effect from that intended.

Of the anticholinesterases, physostigmine has been used in a number of studies reviewed by Mohs and Davis (1987). Significant improvement in some aspects of memory was found in a few subjects, but the utility of this drug is limited by adverse effects and the fact that it has a short half-life and a narrow effective dose range which needs individual titration (Castleden 1984). Intravenous infusion of physostigmine was shown to increase cerebral blood flow in the posterior parietal region, especially in the left hemisphere, in patients with Alzheimer's disease (Geaney *et al.* 1990). Oral tetrahydroaminoacridine (THA, tacrine), a potent centrally acting anticholinergic agent, has been used in some trials, either alone (Summers *et al.* 1986) or combined with lecithin (Kaye *et al.* 1982; Chatellier and Lacamblez 1990; Eagger *et al.* 1991). Early reports seemed encouraging in a few patients but the results were modest overall. Tacrine has other effects, including a central stimulant action and can also produce adverse effects (Byrne and Arie 1989).

Cholinergic receptor agonists have been investigated. The results, reviewed by Gray *et al*. (1989), in general show a clinically relevant response only in a minority of patients. Nicotine by various routes has been advocated (e.g. Sahakian *et al*. 1988) but there is no evidence that cigarette smoking, the most effective method of nicotine administration (Chapter 7), has therapeutic or prophylactic effects in Alzheimer's disease. Some authors (Quirion *et al*. 1989; Gray *et al*. 1989) suggest that centrally acting selective antagonists of muscarinic (M_2) autoreceptors or specific muscarinic (M_1) receptor agonists, might have a therapeutic potential, and some such drugs are under trial.

An alternative approach is the use of agents which increase acetylcholine release. Sarter *et al*. (1988, 1990) point out that acetylcholine release and choline uptake are largely under the control of $GABA_A$ receptors, and cite evidence that residual cholinergic neurones in Alzheimer's disease are subject to increased GABA inhibition. These observations suggest a therapeutic potential for drugs which inhibit $GABA_A$ receptors. Some beta-carbolines, such as ZK 93 426, combine antagonist and inverse agonist actions at $GABA_A$ receptors (Chapter 4). This drug has indirect cholinomimetic effects and has been shown to increase vigilance and information processing in normal subjects (Sarter *et al*. 1990). As yet data on the use of such drugs in Alzheimer patients is lacking, and adverse effects such as anxiogenesis (Dorow *et al*. 1983; Chapter 3) may prove a limiting factor. Acetylcholine release in the cortex also appears to be under serotonergic control, via $5\text{-}HT_3$ receptors (Table 3.1), and it has been suggested that antagonists of these receptors (such as ondansetron) may be of value in states of impaired cortical cholinergic function (Barnes *et al*. 1989).

Drugs which increase cerebral blood flow or enhance cellular metabolism in the brain

In cerebral arteriosclerosis, which occurs to some degree in about 30 per cent of patients with senile dementia, cerebral blood flow is reduced and areas of brain tissue are hypoxic. Several drugs have been tested for their ability to relieve cerebral hypoxia in animals. It was found, however, that many of the drugs, although vasodilators, also stimulated cerebral metabolism. This action is probably more important than vasodilatation since cerebral vascular tone depends largely on local factors and sclerotic blood vessels in anoxic areas are likely to be already maximally dilated. Recent efforts have therefore been directed towards developing drugs which increase neuronal oxidative activity, in the hope of improving neural function both in cerebrovascular disease and Alzheimer's disease.

Papaverine, procaine, cyclandelate

Papaverine produces vasodilatation by a direct action on arterial smooth muscle. It may also have some dopamine receptor blocking activity and may inhibit phosphodiesterase, resulting in raised tissue concentrations of cyclic AMP, which may stimulate neuronal metabolism (Scott 1979). Papaverine reduces the symptoms of cerebral ischaemia due to arterial spasm. Its effects in arteriosclerotic dementia or other dementias of old age are controversial although some trials have reported favourable results (Branconnier and Cole 1977). Beneficial effects when they occur are modest and are not restricted to memory functions. Similarly, procaine may have beneficial effects on mood and general performance in senile dementia (Ban 1978).

Dihydrogenated ergot alkaloids

Co-dergocrine mesylate (Hydergine) is a mixture of dihydrogenated derivatives of the constitutent alkaloids of ergotoxine. These substances block adrenergic receptors and act as partial agonists/antagonists at dopaminergic and serotonergic sites (Castleden 1984). They may increase the microcirculation in the brain but their major action appears to be on neurone metabolism. Co-dergocrine is reported to inhibit the action of Na/K ATPase, adenylate cyclase, and phosphodiesterase in brain cells, thus decreasing the breakdown of ATP and cyclic AMP, improving the energy balance of the cell, and enhancing cyclic AMP-mediated effects (Meier-Ruge *et al.* 1975). These changes are thought to account for an 'activating' effect on the EEG observed in hypoxic rats and elderly patients. Cerebral oxygen consumption is also reported to be increased by hydergine in patients with cerebrovascular disease (Sandoz 1977). Several placebo controlled double blind with dihydrogenated ergot alkaloids studies reviewed by Castleden (1984) have shown significant but limited improvement in general and cognitive functioning in geriatric patients.

Naftidrofuryl and other vasodilators

Naftidrofuryl is a vasodilator with sympatholytic and local anaesthetic properties; it is also said to stimulate brain metabolism (Scott 1979). It has been used in a number of small studies in patients with mixed dementias and may be modestly effective in improving cognitive performance in some patients (Castleden 1984).

Other vasodilator drugs which also stimulate cell metabolism include isoxsuprine, vinca alkaloids, nicergoline, and cinnarizine. Some studies have suggested that they are of therapeutic value and these are reviewed by Nicholson 1990.

Piracetam and other nootropic drugs

The term nootropic was applied to the compound piracetam, a cyclic derivative of GABA, which was claimed to be the first of a new class of drugs which enhance learning and memory by a selective effect on brain integrative mechanisms in the telencephalon (Giurgea 1976). Several more effective congeners, reviewed by Nicholson (1990) have since been developed. These drugs are reported to have rather dramatic effects on learning and memory in rodents. They facilitate information acquisition and enhance memory retrieval (Sara et al. 1979) in normal animals and in animals with impaired cognitive function induced by hypoxia, hypercapnia, scopolamine and cycloheximide. In addition, they enhance long-term potentiation, facilitate interhemispheric transfer of information (Bureseva and Bures 1976), and protect the brain from various physical and chemical injuries. Their mode of action is not known, but they are thought to increase the release of dopamine (Rago et al. 1981) and possibly of acetylcholine (Nicholson 1990).

Despite their promising pharmacological profile in animals, there is little evidence that nootropic drugs are therapeutically effective in dementia in man. Piracetam has been investigated in a number of clinical trials in patients with impaired mental function of mixed aetiology (Barnas et al. 1990). It has been reported to produce variable degrees of improvement in general mental function in cerebrovascular disease, post-concussional syndrome, senile and presenile dementia, chronic and acute alcoholism, and alcohol withdrawal syndromes, to shorten the duration of coma following drug intoxication, and to hasten recovery after neurosurgery. As a treatment for senile dementia, piracetam has received little support, eight out of 13 studies reviewed by McDonald (1982) showing no difference between drug and placebo. However, trials with a combination of piracetam and choline in Alzheimer's dementia may be worth pursuing (Castleden 1984).

Vasopressin

In spite of the demonstrable effects of vasopressin on memory in animals and the suggestion that it may be involved in human memory (Chapter 8), the use of vasopressin or its synthetic analogues for treatment of memory disorders in man has met with variable success. Vasopressin is usually administered by nasal catheter or as a nasal spray and treatment must usually be continued daily for some weeks before a measurable response occurs. Occasional reports have noted improvement after vasopressin in learning ability in the alcoholic amnesic syndrome (Le Boeuf *et al.* 1978) and partial reversal of retrograde amnesia due to head injury (Oliveros *et al.* 1978) or electroconvulsive therapy (Weingartner *et al.* 1981). Vasopressin has also been reported to improve learning and memory in patients with primary affective disorders (Gold *et al.* 1979*b*; Weingartner *et al.* 1981). Kovacs *et al.* (1982) claim that memory defects occurring in diabetes insipidus, in which there is a lack of endogenous posterior pituitary hormones, can be reversed with vasopressin or its derivatives.

Opioid antagonists

Considering the probable importance of opioid peptides in a physio-logical amnesic system and the proven effects of naloxone on memory in animals (Chapter 8), it is perhaps surprising that there is little published data on the effects of opioid antagonists on memory in man. Naloxone does not appear to improve memory in normal subjects but Reisberg *et al.* (1983) conducted a double blind, placebo controlled, multiple dose trial of naloxone in seven patients with Alzheimer's dementia. They noted significant improvement in tests of digit span and recall as well as in general cognitive function. In isolated cases, naloxone has been reported to reverse neurological defects associated with cerebral ischaemic attacks (Bousigue *et al.* 1982; Baskin and Hosobuchi 1981).

NMDA receptor antagonists

The importance of NMDA receptors in learning and memory has been mentioned in Chapter 8. Although agonists of these receptors can enhance learning and memory in animals (Collingridge and Bliss 1987), these substances are neurotoxic (Rothman and Olney 1987), and do not appear to offer a viable approach to the treatment of dementia. However, it has been suggested that excessive NMDA receptor activation may be a causative factor in neurodegenerative diseases including Alzheimer's disease (Maragos *et al.* 1987). Thus NMDA receptor antagonists could possibly retard the progression of such conditions (Nicholson 1990). Several non-competitive NMDA receptor antagonists are under investi-gation. These agents have anxiolytic and other benzodiazepine-like actions (Stephens *et al.* 1986; Moreau *et al.* 1989) which might be helpful in early Alzheimer's disease in which anxiety as well as deterioration of memory is often prominent, but their utility may be limited since they also impair memory (Venables and Kelly 1990; Wozniack *et al.* 1990) and are likely to produce psychotomimetic effects by interaction with phencyclidine/sigma opioid receptors (Sonders *et al.* 1988; Herberg and Rose 1989; Piercy *et al.* 1988).

A more promising approach might be the use of calcium entry blockers

(Wauquier 1984; Izquierdo 1990*b*), since the neurotoxic effect of NMDA receptor activation is thought to be due to excessive intracellular Ca^{2+} concentrations (Choi 1988). Other measures which may delay the onset or progression of neural degeneration include aluminium chelators (Cowburn and Blair 1989), free radical trapping agents (Calne *et al.* 1986) and calcium supplements (Deary and Hendrickson 1986).

Drugs for forgetting

The amnesic effects of certain drugs can sometimes be put to clinical use as preoperative medication or during minor surgical procedures.

Benzodiazepines

The amnesic effects of intravenous diazepam, flunitrazepam and lorazepam (4 mg) given preoperatively to healthy females undergoing minor gynaecological operations were assessed against a saline control by George and Dundee (1977). All the drugs produced an anterograde amnesia as tested by recognition of cards shown to the patients at various times after drug administration. There was no retrograde amnesia. The amnesia was accompanied by sedation, although the patients were rousable, and the sedation far outlasted the amnesic effects. Many other studies (reviewed by Curran 1986) have confirmed these findings and benzodiazepines are now routinely used as preoperative medication and for minor surgical procedures (Dundee *et al.* 1984). Of the benzodiazepines, midazolam appears to produce optimal amnesia (Hennessy *et al.* 1991). The sedative effects of benzodiazepines can be reversed by the antagonist flumazenil (Chapter 4) but there is much less effect on the amnesia, suggesting that these two actions of benzodiazepines are separate (Curran and Birch 1991).

Studies of benzodiazepine effects on memory in healthy subjects suggest that they exert dose-related effects on various stages (acquisition, retention, recall), and that acquisition is impaired at lower doses than retrieval (Liljequist *et al.* 1978; Ghoneim *et al.* 1981). In some subjects with high state anxiety single doses of oral diazepam may actually improve memory (Desai *et al.* 1983). This result is not surprising in view of the known interactions of psychotropic drugs with starting state and personality.

Anticholinergic drugs

Atropine and scopolamine primarily block the actions of acetylcholine at muscarinic receptors, although at high doses they may also have some

nicotinic receptor blocking action. Both muscarinic and nicotinic receptors appear to be involved in cholinergic transmission at cortical and subcortical levels in the brain. While the depressant effects of atropine and
scopolamine are usually ascribed to central muscarinic blockade, stimulant effects may result from other actions. The drugs cause an increase
in acetylcholine turnover which may result in the activation of nicotinic
receptors in the brain (Weiner 1980a). The mixed stimulant/depressant
effects of these drugs depend on dose and on individual susceptibility.
Since cholinergic systems are involved both in arousal (Chapter 2) and
memory (Chapter 8), amnesic effects of anticholinergic drugs could
result from disruption of either or both of these systems.

In the clinical setting, therapeutic doses of scopolamine (0.6 mg)
usually produce drowsiness, euphoria, amnesia, fatigue, and dreamless
sleep with decreased REM activity (Weiner 1980a). This action is useful
when scopolamine is employed for preanaesthetic medication or as an
adjunct to anaesthetic agents. However, some patients respond to the
same doses with excitement, restlessness, hallucinations, and delirium.
The excitatory effects are most common in patients with severe pain,
occur regularly with high doses, and are also seen with high doses of
atropine.

Several investigators have compared the effects of scopolamine
(0.8 mg IM, 1 mg SC), methscopalamine, a peripherally acting muscarinic blocker (0.5 mg IM, 1 mg SC), and normal saline on the performance
of normal subjects in multiple memory tests (Caine et al. 1981; Drachman
1978). From both studies, it appeared that the effects of scopolamine on
memory were not global and not due simply to non-specific central nervous system depression, although the subjects were drowsy. Scopolamine
impaired initial memory acquisition and retrieval, but even at these doses
there was no decrement in immediate memory and no decrease of attention or initial signal detection in an auditory vigilance task. Caine et al.
(1981) suggest that the amnesic effect of scopolamine was on definable
neuropsychological processes, especially encoding of new information
and retrieval of well-learned old information. The effect of scopolamine
was presumed to be mediated via cholinergic mechanisms since it was
reversed by physostigmine, but not by amphetamine.

Future prospects

While the use of drugs for forgetting has reached a considerable degree
of sophistication, the use of drugs to improve memory remains pro-
blematic. Despite intense interest in the pharmacology of memory over
the past few years (Chapters 8 and 9), and considerable advances in
understanding, it appears that the subject has hardly reached the stage
of direct clinical application to memory disorders. From experience to

date, it seems unlikely that drugs which influence neurotransmitter or modulator function will have major effects in clinical conditions — although possibly the development of drugs with specific sites of action in the brain is worth striving for. Drugs which improve cerebral oxygenation and stimulate neuronal metabolism and possibly calcium channel antagonists may be of more value in dementias and other amnesic syndromes if used early enough, but again specificity in site of action is so far lacking. The greatest hope for the future would seem to lie in drugs which stimulate neuronal plasticity, and such drugs are still in their infancy. However, information on nerve growth factor and other polypeptide growth factors is increasing (Greene 1984; Levi-Montalcini and Calissano 1986; Thoenen 1991). Since adult neurones are capable of increasing their dendritic aborizations (Chapter 8), it might be possible with such substances to encourage surviving neurones to take over the function of degenerated neurones in human dementias. Finally there remains the distant prospect of brain implantation with living embyronic or cultured neurones (Katzman 1986; Gage *et al.* 1984).

The possibility of using drugs to improve cognitive function in normal subjects opens another uncharted field, but there is a growing 'recreational' use of vasopressin, piracetam and ondansetron for this purpose.

Part IV
Depression and mania

11. Depression and mania: clinical features and brain mechanisms

In previous chapters, brain systems for arousal and sleep, reward and punishment, and learning and memory have been considered. It is clear, from the clinical manifestations and observed physiological changes, that all of these systems are involved in depression and mania, but the central feature is an alteration of mood. Similar mood changes may occur in organic brain disease, and it is possible that neuropathological changes underlie major affective disorders (Jeste *et al.* 1988). However, in many cases these conditions appear to result from a largely reversible, though recurrent, functional disorder of brain systems controlling emotional tone. Present evidence, discussed in this chapter, points to a dysfunction of the limbic system, particularly in pathways subserving reward and punishment. Depression and mania can thus be viewed as disorders of reward and punishment systems, with features in common with drug dependence and chronic pain syndromes (Chapter 6). Because of the integrated nature of brain systems, such disorders have secondary effects on arousal and sleep and on cognitive, autonomic and endocrine function.

Clinical features of depression and mania

Classification

A great deal of energy has been used in attempts to classify affective disorders, and the problems are still 'sufficient to keep armies of psychiatrists disputing happily for years' (Paykel 1983; p. 155S). Classification is difficult because these disorders are heterogeneous and the symptoms may merge with those of anxiety, schizophrenia, personality disorders, and even with normality. For clinical purposes, a division of depressive states into endogenous (psychotic) and neurotic (reactive) disorders has been widely used, although such distinctions may relate more to severity than to any clear categorical difference (Ashton *et al.* 1988), and both types respond to the same antidepressant drugs (Chapter 12). Other classifications differentiate between major depression and dysthymia, although again these differ only in severity and duration (DSM-III-R 1987). Mood disorders are further subdivided into bipolar disorder, in which there are episodes of mania, and unipolar disorder, in which only depressive episodes occur.

Symptoms and signs of depression

Psychological symptoms

The symptoms of depression encompass a whole gamut of emotional states, of which sadness and misery as normally experienced form only a part, and stand somewhere in the middle of the range. At one extreme there may be a feeling of hopelessness and despair, inability to experience pleasure or to envisage it in the future, and an attitude of apathy. At another extreme there may be intense anxiety, fear, agitation, and irritability. Yet another dimension of depression is characterized by feelings of guilt and unworthiness, feelings of deserved punishment, delusions, hallucinations of accusatory voices, obsessional ruminations, and hypochondriasis. There is considerable overlap in the clinical presentation of these symptoms and almost any combination or degree of severity may exist in individual patients.

The behaviour of the depressed patient varies according to the symptoms. Apathetic patients show psychomotor retardation: they walk and react slowly and take little interest in their surroundings. Thoughts are slowed and response to speech is noticeably delayed. On the other hand, agitated patients cannot remain still: they may be continually wringing their hands, pacing up and down, and repetitively expressing their fears.

A wide range of somatic symptoms may be present. Complaints of disturbed sleep are common: early morning waking is characteristic, but frequent awakenings during the night and delay in falling asleep may also occur. Typically, depressed mood is worst in the morning, coinciding with early waking, and mood may improve during the day. However, patients with anxiety may feel worst at the end of the day, coinciding with difficulty in falling asleep. Other patients sleep excessively, but still wake feeling unrefreshed and pessimistic. Loss of appetite and weight are common and are associated with poor sleep; in patients with excessive sleep, however, there may be increased eating and weight gain. Constipation, loss of libido, amenorrhoea, lethargy, impaired memory and concentration, and generalized or localized pain are all frequent symptoms. Sometimes the presenting symptoms are purely physical, and in such masked depression alteration of mood may not be apparent.

Symptoms and signs of mania

The symptoms and signs of mania are characterized by elevation of mood, hyperactivity, and self-important ideas. The mood may be predominantly one of euphoria or elation, but is typically labile and interspersed with irritability, episodes of anger, and brief periods of depression. Expansive ideas are common but insight and judgement are impaired so that extravagant and impractical projects are recklessly undertaken. Grandiose or sometimes persecutory delusions, and hallucinations, may occur. The behaviour reflects the changes in mood. The patient is hyperactive; he starts many activities, but often leaves them unfinished. He may become exhausted and present a dishevelled appearance. He sleeps little and may talk incessantly. Speech is rapid and may become incoherent, reflecting flight of ideas. Appetite and libido are increased, and social behaviour may be uninhibited.

Incidence and clinical course

Depressive symptoms are reported by 13–20 per cent of the population, but are not necessarily part of a depressive disorder. Using strict diagnostic criteria (Gelder *et al.* 1983), the prevalence of bipolar depressive disorder is less than 1 per cent, with a mean age of onset of about 30 years. Females outnumber males by 1.3:1 to 2:1. Unipolar depressive syndromes are more common, with a prevalence of about 3 per cent in males and 5–9 per cent in females. The peak age of onset in females is between 35–40 years, while in males the prevalence increases with increasing age. There appears to be a seasonal variation in the incidence of depressive episodes with peak occurrence in spring and autumn. In a subgroup (seasonal affective disorder) depression occurs only in the winter months (*Drug and Therapeutics Bulletin* 1991).

Most unipolar and bipolar depressions follow a self-limiting, but recurrent course. Manic episodes, if untreated, usually last several months, sometimes years. Eventual recovery nearly always occurs, but recurrence of manic and depressive episodes is frequent. The course of unipolar depressive illness is variable: the usual duration of individual episodes is 6–12 months but they may last from a few days to a few years. Most patients recover from a first episode but there is a tendency to relapse. Even with antidepressant drugs, follow-up studies after 15–20 years show the long-term outcome for patients with depressive illness is poor (Lee and Murray 1988; Kiloh *et al.* 1988). In these patients the mortality risk was doubled overall compared with the standard rate and was increased sevenfold for women under 40 when first admitted to hospital. There was a high incidence of unnatural deaths (suicides and accidents) and of carcinoma and autoimmune disease. The incidence of other psychiatric disorders (schizoaffective, alcoholism and schizophrenia) was also high. The outlook was worse for patients presenting with psychotic symptoms than for those with more neurotic symptoms. Less than 20 per cent of survivors remained well; 12 per cent remained incapacitated by their illness and the readmission rate was about 50 per cent. This poor prognosis may reflect the presence of organic brain changes in depressive illness.

Genetic factors

The prevalence of affective disorders is greater in the relatives of depressed patients than in the general population. Parents, siblings and children of affected patients have a morbid risk of 10–15 per cent, several times greater than the general population. Twin studies have shown high rates of concordance (nearly 70 per cent) for bipolar disorders in monozygotic twins, whether reared together or apart, and for dizygotic twins (23 per cent). Bipolar disorders appear to be more common in the relatives of bipolar probands, but both bipolar and unipolar disorders occur in the families of unipolar probands. There is also some evidence of a greater than normal incidence of other psychiatric disorders, including schizophrenia, alcoholism, and personality disorders, in the families of patients with depressive syndromes. In addition, the families of probands with schizophrenia have an increased incidence of affective disorders.

It is clear that genetic factors are important in determining the incidence of affective disorders. Linkage studies have suggested that at least three genes (in different families) may predispose to bipolar depression (Owen and Murray 1988; McGuffin 1988; Owen and Mullan 1990). Genetic factors may partially explain the greater prevalence in females, but for unipolar depression, genetic transmission is probably polygenic and interacts with environmental factors. Most genetic studies have been concerned only with patients with severe disorders. The frequency of depressive symptoms (as opposed to frank illness) and of depressive personality traits in patients who later develop depressive illness or in their families is not known. It has been suggested that certain personality types may be more prone to mood disorders, but there is no clear evidence from prospective studies.

Factors causing depressive and manic symptoms

For purposes of clinical classification, psychiatrists have usually taken pains to separate the symptom of depression, which may occur in many conditions, from the syndrome of depressive disorder, in which depression of mood is usually a central feature. However, in attempts to understand the aetiology of depressive syndromes, it seems important to inquire into any factors which can give rise to the symptom of depression. It seems that there is nothing unique about either the quality or the degree of depression experienced as part of a depressive disorder. The mechanisms by which this emotion is generated, although perhaps triggered in different ways, are likely to be the same wherever it is found. The same considerations apply to the symptom of elation and the syndrome of manic states.

Organic disease

Organic brain damage can give rise to disorders of affect. Jeste *et al.* (1988) reviewed 22 large-scale studies of affective disorders following trauma, neoplastic disease, cardiovascular disease and temporal lobe epilepsy. These disorders were most frequently associated with lesions of the temporal and frontal lobes: depression was prominent in temporal lobe lesions while euphoria was more common in frontal lobe lesions. These same areas have been implicated in the pathophysiology of schizophrenia (Chapter 13). Depression is also common in dementia, Parkinson's disease and alcoholism. Viral infections, particularly infectious mononucleosis, viral hepatitis, AIDS and influenza, and some chronic bacterial infections such as brucellosis can give rise to chronic depression. Brain imaging studies (reviewed by Jeste *et al.* 1988) suggest that there may also be neuronal damage in so-called primary depression.

Several computerized tomography (CT) investigations show that a proportion (10–30 per cent) of patients with unipolar or bipolar depression have abnormally large cerebral ventricles compared with controls. This proportion is similar to that found in schizophrenia (Chapter 13). Other CT indices (cortical or cerebellar atrophy) are also different from controls and similar to schizophrenic patients. Positron emission tomography (PET) scanning reveals a reduction in cerebral metabolism especially in fronto-temporal regions, and some but not all studies of cerebral blood flow using ^{133}Xenon inhalation show decreased blood flow especially in frontal regions (Mathew *et al.* 1980). Magnetic resonance imaging (MRI) has shown changes in density in the temporal lobes in some bipolar patients. Further work is needed to evaluate all these findings but at present they definitely suggest that structural abnormalities and quantitative neuronal loss in the brain, particularly in frontal and temporal regions, may be associated with major affective disorders.

Various endocrine diseases are associated with change in mood. Cushing's disease may be accompanied by either depression or by periods of elation, while Addison's disease, hyperparathyroidism, acromegaly, and hypopituitarism are associated with depression. Some endocrine abnormalities occurring in the affective disorders are discussed below.

Drugs

Several classes of drugs can cause depression. Many of these decrease the activity of monoaminergic systems in the brain. For example, reserpine, which depletes nerve terminals of monoamines, can cause severe depression. Other antihypertensive drugs which interfere with neuronal release or storage of monoamines, such as guanethidine, debrisoquine, methyl-dopa and clonidine, can also cause depression. Depression may also result from chronic use of central nervous system depressants, including alcohol, barbiturates, and benzodiazepines, all of which decrease central catecholaminergic activity, and from withdrawal of drugs with central nervous system stimulant effects, such as amphetamines, cocaine, and nicotine. Other drugs causing depression are reviewed by McClelland (1986).

Other drugs can produce elation, euphoria, and in high doses manic states. Many of these drugs have central nervous system stimulant actions and increase activity in catecholaminergic systems in the brain. Thus, amphetamines, cocaine, L-dopa, tricyclic antidepressants, and mono-amine oxidase inhibitors in high doses can all produce manic reactions. Euphoric reactions also sometimes occur after small, disinhibiting, doses of alcohol, benzodiazepines, barbiturates, phencyclidine, and organic solvents. Manic states with hallucinations and delirium can occur as part of the withdrawal reactions from central nervous system depressants, probably reflecting central catecholaminergic overactivity due to drug tolerance.

The observed effects of many of the above drugs, which can induce mania or depression in normal subjects, and relieve or aggravate clini-cally occurring mania or depression, have formed the cornerstone of the various monoaminergic theories of affective disorders discussed below.

Environmental factors

Life events.   Depressive disorders often follow distressing life events. Of these, maternal deprivation in childhood has been suggested to be a pre-disposing factor to affective illness in later life. Death or departure of a parent, however, appears also to be non-specifically related to psycho-neurosis, antisocial personality, and alcoholism (Paykel 1974). An excess of stressful or threatening life events, including loss or separation by death, has been shown in several studies to have occurred in the months before the onset of a depressive or manic disorder or a suicide attempt. Mills (1977), among others, has argued that depressive disorders may represent the breakdown of 'coping mechanisms' after periods of pro-longed stress or repeated adverse events, the final event acting as the 'last straw' which precipitates the illness. However, it has been noted that the relatives of depressed patients also report an excess of adverse life events (McGuffin *et al.* 1988), and the possibility has been raised that some families have a propensity to be involved in adversity (Owen and Murray 1988). A similar excess of events may precede the onset of neurosis, schizophrenia, cancer, and psychosomatic disorders, and only 10 per cent of people who experience loss develop a depressive syndrome (Paykel

1974). Thus, stress and bereavement appear to be non-specific factors in the aetiology of depression.

Animal separation studies.   There have been a number of studies of the affective responses to separation in monkeys and apes (Hinde 1977; Everitt and Keverne 1979). In some species, separation of an infant from its mother may cause a syndrome of despair which bears some resemblance to human depression. An initial stage of agitated activity is followed by depressed locomotor and play activity, and a generally depressed demeanour. In some primate societies, loss of social rank is sometimes associated with behaviour patterns seen in human depression. These include decreased locomotor activity, isolation from the group, endocrine changes, suspension of sexual activity, cessation of eating, and death from inanition or infection. Similar profiles are sometimes seen in human depression and human symptoms such as loss of self-esteem and feelings of rejection may be reminiscent of the role of a socially subordinate monkey. The relevance of such animal studies to human depression is clearly limited (Willner 1984), but irreparable loss of important bonds, either social or connected with activities of personal importance (work, art, religion, etc.) may be important though non-specific factors.

Learned helplessness.   If dogs are placed in a situation in which pain and stress are inescapable, for instance by being harnessed and subjected to electric shocks, a reaction termed 'learned helplessness' develops (Seligman 1975). During the stress, an initial period of hyperactivity and struggling is replaced by a state of immobility during which the animal apparently gives up all attempts to cope. If the animal is later exposed to an avoidable stress, it no longer tries to escape, exhibiting instead a severe deficit in escape avoidance behaviour. The phenomenon has been observed in several animal species, and such animals display a behaviour bearing some resemblance to human depression, including reduced voluntary activity, decreased food intake, and an opioid-mediated analgesia (Chapter 5). It was suggested that depression is a similar learned behaviour which develops when reward or punishment is perceived as no longer being contingent on the actions or responses of the animal. In relation to the human condition, Roth (1988, p. 29) quotes Charles Darwin: 'If we expect to suffer, we are anxious; if we have no hope of relief, we despair'.

However, Anisman *et al.* (1981) argued that learned helplessness behaviour depends not so much on cognitive functions involving learning and memory as on the biochemical responses to severe stress. Severe, prolonged stress causes central depletion of monoamines in animals, and learned helplessness behaviour is accentuated by pharmacological manipulations which further deplete central monoamines or block monoamine receptors, and attenuated by drugs which prevent amine depletion or increase monoaminergic activity including a variety of antidepressant drugs (Kametani *et al.* 1983). Thus, the failure of coping is held to reflect an inability to sustain adequate concentrations of central monoamines, either because the stress is uncontrollable and severe or because of some deficiency in the adaptive process to stress. This model seems to have some relevance to human depression, since drugs which deplete central monoamines or block their receptors induce depression in humans, while most drugs which act as antidepressants increase central monoaminergic activity. In addition some depressed patients (though not all) appear to have reduced brain concentrations of certain monoamines.

Cognitive factors

Gloomy and pessimistic thoughts (depressive cognitions) are character-istic of depressive disorders. Patients lose confidence and self-esteem and evaluate themselves as failures. They feel guilty, blame themselves unrea-sonably, and may dwell on unhappy past events. For the future, they see no hope, and there seems little point in continuing to live. By contrast, the thoughts in manic disorders are full of optimism with high hopes for the future and an exaggerated sense of self-confidence.

It has been questioned whether the thoughts are secondary to a primary disorder of mood, or whether a disorder of cognition is the primary, or at least an aggravating or perpetuating, factor. Beck (1967) suggested that people who habitually adopt certain ways of thinking are vulnerable to depression when faced with minor problems. To some extent, cogni-tive factors are also involved in psychoanalytic theories: some forms of depression are viewed as resulting from loss of a loved object, combined with inwardly turned hostility expressed as self-reproach (Gelder *et al.* 1983).

All these theories imply that depression could be alleviated by edu-cating patients to develop more successful cognitive strategies. In ani-mals, pre-training has been shown to arrest the development of learned helplessness behaviour, but in humans educational, psychoanalytic, and psychotherapeutic approaches, although sometimes helpful, are far from uniformly successful (Gelder 1990). Nor is there any evidence that par-ticular cognitive strategies are present before the onset of depression or that they are more frequent in those that develop depression than in those who do not (Gelder *et al.* 1983). The rapid, rationally uninfluenced, switches between mania and depression, accompanied (and sometimes preceded) by demonstrable somatic and biochemical changes, seen in bipolar affective disorders provide strong evidence for the primacy of emotional rather than cognitive factors. Nevertheless, depression (or elation) as a symptom can undoubtedly be perpetuated or inhibited by cortical activity. An interesting view of the interplay between prevailing mood and rational evaluation is presented by Pollitt (1982).

Brain mechanisms in affective disorders

Adaptive value of depression

Since systems in the brain are capable of producing depression in man and behaviours resembling depression in animals, it may be pertinent to consider the adaptive role, if any, of depression in animal behaviour. Emotions such as anxiety, fear, excitement, rage, or aggression are clearly protective, and useful for escape and for defence of self, territory, or food supply. Pleasure of all kinds, love, affection, and hope, and certain displeasures including disappointment, disgust, and hate, are all important for positive or negative reinforcement and for motivation towards actions promoting individual or group survival. However, severe depression, with its associated inactivity, lack of motivation, and failure of coping seems maladaptive.

Nevertheless, under certain adverse circumstances a depressive reaction might be an economic strategy for an individual or his or her closely related group. In a situation in which extreme adversity is inescapable and irremediable, or in which an important loss is apparently irreplaceable, a shut-down of brain motivation systems and a state of inactivity may conserve energy until conditions improve. If there is no abatement, continuance of such behaviour may lead to death, yet this event not only protects the individual from further suffering, but also conserves food supplies and social energies of the group to which he or she belongs. It is possible that depressive disorders in humans represent an echo of such self-destructive behaviour in animals. Thus the clinical syndrome of depression, like that of anxiety (Chapter 4), may represent an extreme range of activity in normally adaptive systems, and the psychophysiological differences between normal depression and depressive disorders are probably quantitative rather than qualitative. Psychoevolutionary aspects of depression are discussed by Gilbert (1984).

Brain systems in affective disorders

Reward and punishment systems

The salient feature of depression is unhappiness, or absence of pleasure; that of mania, at least in its early stages, is elation and increased drive or motivation. Therefore, the brain systems most likely to be primarily involved in both the symptoms and the syndromes of affective disorder are those for pleasure (reward) and punishment. As discussed in Chapter 5, evidence for the existence of such systems rests largely upon intracranial self-stimulation experiments in animals, but rewarding and aversive brain sites appear also to be present in man. These systems are thought to be important in generating both the behavioural and

emotional aspects of motivation, reinforcement or avoidance, and gratification. They are located in various interconnected limbic structures,
have many interconnections with the cerebral cortex, and with endocrine
and autonomic centres, and themselves form part of the limbic and reticular formation arousal systems. It is generally agreed that these systems
are responsible for mood, although the details of how the infinitely
graded nuances of normal mood are achieved remain obscure. Primary
dysfunction in reward and/or punishment systems could theoretically
account for most of the changes found in affective disorders. Involvement of any particular limbic structure or pathway has not been convincingly demonstrated in such disorders although brain imaging studies
suggest hypofunction in fronto-temporal regions.

The clinical picture of depression suggests underactivity in reward
systems and/or overactivity in punishment systems. It is relevant in this
context that treatments which decrease central monoaminergic activity
disrupt intracranial self-stimulation in animals, implying that these
treatments decrease the reinforcing value of stimulation. Conversely,
drugs which raise the central availability of catecholamines reverse these
effects and enhance self-stimulation, implying that they increase its
reinforcement value. Among the latter drugs are the clinically used antidepressants, tricyclic agents, and monoamine oxidase inhibitors, especially if used with amphetamine, which releases catecholamines. The
inference of these findings is that depression is accompanied by a fall
in catecholaminergic activity in reward systems, with perhaps relative
overactivity in antagonistic punishment systems. Mania would be a
reflection of the reverse process. This hypothesis is consistent with the
catecholamine theory of depression, discussed below.

Arousal systems

The fact that sleep disturbance almost always occurs in affective disorders suggests that arousal systems are closely involved. Characteristically, patients with depression show reduction in Stage 4 sleep,
fragmentation of the sleep pattern, multiple awakenings, and decreased
total sleep time (Gillin and Borbely 1985). A fairly consistent feature is
a shortened latency to the first REMS episode and increased REMS density. Some longitudinal studies indicate that REMS correlates inversely
with the severity of depressive symptoms, the greatest amount of REMS
and the shortest REMS latency occurring when the symptoms are worst
(Schulz et al. 1978). These changes indicate an abnormality of sleep/
wakening behaviour and it has been suggested (Mellerup and Rafaelson
1979) that there is a shift of the normal sleep/wake pattern, along with
a general disruption of circadian rhythms. However, hypersomnia can
also occur in depression, and cortical evoked potentials in the waking
state are usually, though not always, decreased (Shagass et al. 1985;

Timsit-Berthier *et al.* 1987; Ashton *et al.* 1988). The lack of a consistent pattern of activity in arousal systems in depression suggests that changes in arousal are largely secondary to the emotional state.

Cognitive systems

It has been claimed that depression is primarily a cognitive disorder which may develop as a result of learning (Seligman 1975) or of particular ways of thinking (Beck 1967). Certainly, cognitive dysfunction may occur in many patients with depression, as evidenced by the presence of delusions, hallucinations, rumination on pessimistic thoughts, and difficulty in learning and memory. However, the brain systems for rational thought, learning, and memory appear to have developed to evaluate rather than to generate emotions, and ablation or stimulation of large parts of the cortex is not associated with particular changes in mood. In fact, changes in mood are much more likely to occur when subcortical structures are involved. Hence, it seems likely that the cognitive changes seen in depression are secondary to emotional changes resulting from limbic dysfunction.

Nevertheless, because of the close anatomical and functional connections between the cortex and the limbic system, cognitive factors may well play a part in maintaining or aggravating depression. The connections between the frontal, especially prefrontal, cortical regions and subcortical circuits in the limbic system have for many years been believed to be particularly implicated, and this belief has formed the basis for psychosurgery aimed at disconnecting these brain regions.

Neurotransmitters in affective disorders

Catecholamines

The idea that specific alterations in central neurotransmitter activity might cause depression or mania was stimulated by the discovery of antidepressant drugs and the finding that they exerted profound effects on the function of certain transmitter systems. Early ideas were centred around the catecholamines, and the catecholamine hypothesis of affective disorders (Schildkraut 1965; Bunney and Davis 1965) proposed that 'some, if not all depressions are associated with an absolute or relative deficiency of catecholamines, particularly norepinephrine, at functionally important adrenergic sites in the brain, whereas manias might be associated with excess of catecholamines' (Schildkraut 1978, p. 1223). The original hypothesis proposed that an absolute or relative deficiency of noradrenaline at receptors could result from a number of different mechanisms, including decreased synthesis, impairment of binding or storage, increased release and deamination, or decreased receptor sensitivity. It was not claimed that such changes occurred in all types of depression, which was recognized to be heterogeneous group of disorders.

The theory was consistent with what was then known about the actions of several types of drugs. For example, many antidepressant drugs increase the availability of catecholamines at receptor sites. Acute effects of the tricyclic and related antidepressants include blockade of pre-synaptic reuptake of catecholamines, while monoamine oxidase inhibi-tors decrease their deamination with the result that increased amounts are available for release (Chapter 12). Drugs such as amphetamine, which release catecholamines, have a temporary antidepressant effect and also cause euphoria in normal subjects. Amphetamine, antidepressant drugs, and dopaminergic agents aggravate mania. Conversely, drugs which reduce central catecholaminergic activity by depletion, interference with release, synthesis, storage, or receptor blockade can cause or aggravate depression, and also alleviate mania. The ability of a drug to reverse the

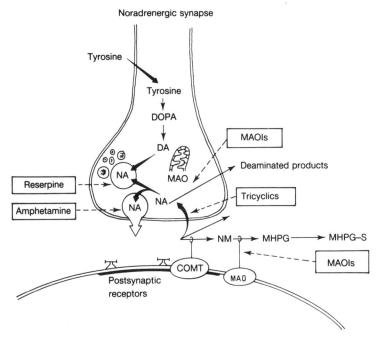

Fig. 11.1 Diagram of central noradrenergic synapse illustrating sites of action of antidepressant drugs. NA noradrenaline; MAO monoamine oxidase; COMT catechol-O-methyl-transferase; NM normetanephrine; MHPG 3-methoxy-4-hydroxyphenol-glycol. Tricyclic antidepressants inhibit the reuptake of released NA; monoamine oxidase inhibitors (MAOIs) inhibit the deamination of NA; amphetamine increases the release of NA. Reserpine (which can cause depression) depletes NA storage sites. For fuller explanation, see text. (Modified from Cooper *et al.* 1978, by kind permission of Oxford University Press, New York.)

effects resulting from monoamine depletion by reserpine in animals is a good predictor of antidepressant activity.

Thus, an impressive body of pharmacological evidence appeared to support the theory (Fig. 11.1). The theory is also consistent with results obtained from intracranial self-stimulation experiments which strongly suggest an important role of catecholamines in reinforcement and reward (Chapter 5). Clinical investigations (reviewed by Siever 1987) were therefore undertaken of catecholamine activity in patients with affective disorders.

Noradrenaline.   Concentrations of noradrenaline have been measured in plasma, cerebrospinal fluid and *post mortem* brain tissue in patients with depression. No consistent changes in the plasma concentration of noradrenaline or its precursor tyramine have been found although there appears to be a greater variability in depressed patients compared with normal controls. Higher concentrations have been noted in some patients with unipolar depression who fail to show normal cortical suppression by dexamethasone (see below). Cerebrospinal fluid concentrations of noradrenaline also show greater than normal variability among depressed patients. Increased concentrations may be associated with mania, while some patients with bipolar depression have decreased concentrations. No changes in brain concentration of noradrenaline or its metabolites have been found in *post mortem* studies of depressed patients and suicides (Bourne *et al.* 1968; Pare *et al.* 1969).

Investigations of the concentrations of the noradrenaline metabolite 3-methoxy-4-hydroxyphenylglycol (MHPG) in plasma and cerebrospinal fluid in general parallel the above results and support the idea that noradrenergic activity is altered in a subgroup of depressive disorders. In bipolar depression, high plasma and cerebrospinal fluid concentrations are found in mania and low concentrations in some patients with depression. No consistent changes have been found in monoamine oxidase activity in plasma and platelets.

Dopamine.   The relation of dopaminergic activity to depression is relatively unexplored. No consistent changes in brain dopamine concentrations have been found in post-mortem studies in depressive suicides. However, drugs which increase dopaminergic activity, such as amphetamine and L-dopa, can improve depression and produce euphoria or hypomania, and dopamine is an important neurotransmitter in reward systems (Chapter 5). It may be relevant that dyskinesia and other extrapyramidal symptoms suggesting dopaminergic underactivity occur in untreated depression, and that depressed patients have an increased vulnerability to tardive dyskinesia induced by neuroleptics with antagonistic actions at dopaminergic receptors (Jimerson 1987). The cerebrospinal fluid concentration of the dopamine metabolite, homovanillic acid (HVA) is reduced in some patients with unipolar or bipolar depression.

Serotonin

A sister hypothesis to the catecholamine theory of depression is the indoleamine theory which suggests that, in some types of depression at least, there is serotonergic underactivity and that the therapeutic actions of antidepressant treatments are due to reversal of this deficiency. Serotonin metabolism in affective disorders is reviewed by Van Praag (1980, 1982) and Meltzer and Lowy (1987). The results suggest that the metabolism of this amine is altered in some patients with depression.

Post-mortem studies

Several post-mortem studies have shown decreased concentrations of serotonin or its metabolic 5-hydroxy-indoleacetic acid (5-HIAA) in the hindbrain or raphe nuclei in depressed patients or suicides compared with controls (Bourne et al. 1968; Lloyd et al. 1974; Asberg et al. 1987). Asberg et al. (1976) found a bimodal distribution of 5-HIAA concentration in the lumbar cerebrospinal fluid of endogenously depressed patients, of whom 29 per cent had lower than control concentrations while the others had normal concentrations. There was little difference in the clinical features between the two groups, but it was suggested that low 5-HIAA concentrations are correlated with higher levels of anxiety, impulsive behaviour, aggression, and a greater risk of suicide (Banki 1977; Traskman et al. 1981; Goodwin and Post 1983). Later studies have in general confirmed the findings of low cerebrospinal concentrations of 5-HIAA in suicidal patients (Asberg et al. 1987). Westenberg and Verhoeven (1988) found a subgroup of depressed patients with low cerebrospinal fluid concentrations of both 5-HIAA and HVA, but there was no correlation with suicidal behaviour in this group. Low cerebrospinal fluid 5-HIAA concentrations appear to persist after clinical recovery in some depressed patients (Coppen 1972), a finding which may cast a doubt on the aetiological role of serotonin in depressed mood. In mania, normal or low rather than raised 5-HIAA values have been found in cerebrospinal fluid (Gelder et al. 1983).

The plasma concentration of free tryptophan (the precursor of serotonin) has been found to be lower than normal in a subgroup of depressed patients (Coppen and Wood 1978; Meltzer and Lowy 1987), and tryptophan appears to be of therapeutic value in some depressed patients and may potentiate the effects of electroconvulsive therapy and antidepressant drugs (Coppen et al. 1972; van Praag 1982; Byerley and Risch 1985). Furthermore, many antidepressant drugs increase the availability of serotonin (as well as catecholamines) at receptor sites. Selective serotonin reuptake blockers such as zimelidine and fluoxetine have been clearly shown to have antidepressant effects, although there are no significant differences in clinical efficacy between selective noradrenaline or serotonin reuptake blockers. It has been claimed that a low concentration of cerebrospinal fluid 5-HIAA is predictive of response to antidepressants with predominantly serotonergic effects (van Praag 1982; Goodwin *et al.* 1978), but other studies (for example, Montgomery 1982 and others reviewed by Meltzer and Lowy 1987) have found no difference in response to selective noradrenaline or serotonin reuptake blockers in patients with high or low cerebrospinal fluid concentrations of 5-HIAA. Thus studies with selective antidepressants have done little to clarify the role of serotonin in depression.

Present status of classical monoamine theories of affective disorders

On the whole, the vast amount of research devoted to investigating the various classical monoamine theories of affective disorders has so far yielded inconclusive and somewhat tentative results. It does appear that there are certain biochemically definable subgroups which show disordered central catecholamine metabolism or reduced brain serotonergic activity. Possibly the latter group carries a greater risk of suicide. However, no coherent picture of any biochemical changes underlying the whole range of affective disorders has emerged, and little new information on the part played by monoamines in the control of mood generally. Such a result is not necessarily surprising. If, as seems likely, moods reflect *patterns* of activity in different, but overlapping subcortical and cortical pathways, each utilizing several of a number of different transmitters, gross alterations of monoamines or metabolites in remote body compartments such as cerebrospinal fluid and urine would not be expected. Even where alterations in monoamine metabolism have been observed, it is not clear whether such changes are causative or whether they merely reflect the secondary consequences of some primary aetiological factor. Nor is there any evidence concerning which parts of the brain might be involved, since alterations in metabolite concentrations do not necessarily reflect transmitter activity at receptor sites.

Receptor sensitivity in affective disorders

The classical monoamine theories of depression were based largely on the observed acute biochemical effects of antidepressant drugs at monoaminergic synapses. A drawback of such theories has always been that drug effects at synapses develop rapidly, within hours or days, while the clinical effects take several weeks to develop (Iversen and Mackay 1979), a therapeutic time-lag which does not seem to be explicable on phar-macokinetic grounds (Peet and Coppen 1979). This and other discrepan-cies have led to the idea that the therapeutic effects of antidepressants are not due to acute changes in *transmitter concentration* but to changes in *receptor sensitivity* which occur secondarily over a longer time-course, in response to the chronic presence of the drugs in the body. As a corollary, alteration of receptor sensitivity might be an aetiological factor in depres-sion, a possibility which would account for the lack of alteration of trans-mitter or metabolite concentration in most patients. Recent technological advances have led to a much greater understanding of monoamine recep-tors and have added a new dimension to the investigation of the mono-amine hypothesis of affective disorders. In particular, two properties of receptors; their plasticity and their multiplicity have assumed increasing importance from such studies.

Receptor plasticity

As discussed in Chapter 6, receptors for neurotransmitters are dynamic structures which undergo adaptive changes in response to chronic alter-ations of agonist supply. Decreased neurotransmitter concentration results after a time in an increase in sensitivity of the specific receptors, while increased exposure to the neurotransmitter leads to a compensatory decrease in receptor sensitivity. A characteristic of these changes is that they tend to develop over a slow time course, of the order of weeks rather than hours or days. Since many antidepressants increase agonist supply at monoaminergic synapses, they might be expected to cause secondary changes in receptor sensitivity when chronically administered.

Receptor multiplicity

It has become clear that there are several different receptors for each neurotransmitter. In the case of adrenergic receptors, several different types of post-synaptic receptors (α_1, β_1, and β_2) have been recognized for some time (Ahlquist 1948; Lands *et al.* 1967). These receptors mediate the various responses to adrenergic stimulation. Their differing tissue distributions and pharmacological profiles are well known, and post-synaptic α- and β-agonists and antagonists are widely used in medicine. In addition, adrenergic autoreceptors modulate the release of neuro-transmitter (Langer 1980; Tepper *et al.* 1985). Pre-synaptic α_2-receptors appear to operate a local negative feedback system for noradrenaline release at the nerve terminal. They are stimulated by noradrenaline when the synaptic concentration reaches a certain threshold level, and the effect of stimulation is a decrease in noradrenaline release. Under physio-logical conditions the major local regulatory mechanism for noradre-naline release by nerve stimulation is probably mediated by α_2-receptors (Langer 1977).

α_2-receptors have a different pharmacological profile from α_1-receptors, and a variety of agonists and antagonists with differing degrees of specificity for the two types of receptor are known. Although α_2-receptors are situated presynaptically in the peripheral nervous system, they also exist at other sites. For example, they are present in platelets, and are located post-synaptically at some sites in the central nervous system. The α_2-receptors mediating cardiovascular depression in the medulla are postsynaptic, and α_2-somatodentritic autoreceptors mediate inhibition in the locus coeruleus. For example, clonidine is a relatively selective agonist of α_2 receptors, while noradrenaline and adrenaline have agonist actions at both α_1 and α_2 sites. In addition to the pre-synaptic noradrenergic autoreceptors through which noradrenaline modulates its own release, a whole mosaic of receptors for other substances appear to be present on pre-synaptic adrenergic nerve terminals, all of which can also modulate noradrenaline release (Langer 1977, 1980; Fig. 11.2).

Multiple receptor subtypes, both pre- and post-synaptic, also exist for other neurotransmitters (Langer 1980). Serotonin receptors have been described in Chapter 3; dopamine receptors are described in Chapter 13. The presence of multiple post-synaptic receptors which mediate different

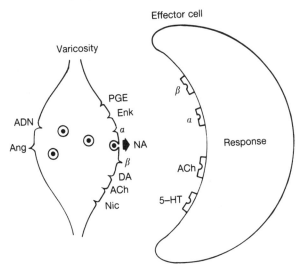

Fig. 11.2 Multiple pre-synaptic receptors on adrenergic nerve terminals. Schematic representation of pre-synaptic receptors at a noradrenergic synapse in the peripheral nervous system. Pre-synaptic receptors for PGE (prostaglandins of the E series), Enk (enkephalin), DA (dopamine), ACh (acetylcholine, muscarinic), ADN (adenosine) and α adrenergic receptors all inhibit NA (noradrenaline) release, while those for Nic (acetylcholine, nicotinic), Ang (angiotensin II) and β adrenergic receptors enhance NA release. (From Langer 1977)

tissue responses, and of autoreceptors, which modulate release, thus appears to be a generalized phenomenon applicable to most neurotransmitters. Most of these receptors have been demonstrated in the central nervous system. All types exhibit plasticity and chronic administration of several types of antidepressant drugs has been shown to cause changes in receptor sensitivity. Since such changes occur in both pre- and post-synaptic receptors, the effects of long-term dosage with antidepressant drugs are complex.

Receptor modulation by antidepressant drugs

Chronic administration of antidepressant drugs has been shown to cause secondary changes in adrenergic, serotonergic, and dopaminergic receptors.

α_2-*adrenergic receptors.*   Biochemical and physiological studies in animals and man (reviewed by Charney *et al.* 1981*b*; Langer *et al.* 1980) indicate that many antidepressant drugs, when administered chronically, cause down-regulation of central adrenergic α_2 receptors, resulting in a secondary increase in noradrenaline release on nerve stimulation. Such down-regulation has been shown after chronic administration of both tricyclic antidepressants and monoamine oxidase inhibitors (Sugrue 1980, 1981; Eriksson *et al.* 1982; Cohen *et al.* 1982; Smith *et al.* 1981; Svensson *et al.* 1981; Davis and Menkes 1982).

In man, Charney *et al.* (1981*b*) showed that long-term treatment with desipramine attenuated the effects of clonidine on MHPG excretion and blood pressure in depressed patients, indicating that α_2-receptors became subsensitive. Garcia-Sevilla *et al.* (1981) reported that chronic treatment of depressed patients with antidepressants produced a significant fall in the numbers of platelet α_2-receptors. In this study, platelet α_2-receptor density was significantly higher in depressed patients than in normal controls. Metz *et al.* (1983) also reported that platelet α_2-receptor density was higher in post-puerperal women developing symptoms of post-natal depression than in post-puerperal women without depression and normal controls. However, other studies on the sensitivity of α_2-receptors in depression have been conflicting (Heninger and Charney 1987).

These studies, although inconclusive, suggest not only that antidepressant drug effects might be mediated by the development of α_2-receptor subsensitivity, but also that α_2-receptor supersensitivity (increased α_2-density), perhaps induced by stress or other factors, might be a cause of depression. A critical site might be in central reward pathways such as the locus coeruleus (Kostowski 1985), but it is not yet clear whether platelet α_2-receptor density mirrors that in the central nervous system. In rats, Campbell and Durcan (1982) showed that strains which were genetically susceptible to 'learned helplessness' had a greater density of α_2-adrenoceptors in the brainstem (though not in the forebrain) than genetically more stable rats. Stress, caused by immobilization, significantly increased α_2-receptor density in the brainstem, and also increased β-receptor density, but decreased α_1-receptor density, in the vulnerable animals; no marked changes were seen in the stable group.

Post-synaptic (α_1) *adrenergic receptors.*   Evidence of adaptive changes in post-synaptic α_1-receptor sensitivity after chronic antidepressant treatment is conflicting. Binding studies have shown either no effect or a slight increase in α_1-receptor density after tricyclic drugs monoamine oxidase inhibitors or electroconvulsive treatment (Creese and Sibley 1981; Hu *et al.* 1981). Chronic treatment with the monoamine oxidase inhibitor clorgyline has been reported to cause a decrease in α_1-receptor binding (Cohen *et al.* 1982).

Beta adrenergic receptors.   A large number of studies have shown that chronic (but not acute) administration of a variety of antidepressant agents results in down-regulation of β-adrenergic receptors in the brain in animals. Such an effect has been demonstrated with monoamine reuptake blockers, atypical antidepressants, including iprindole and mianserin, monoamine oxidase inhibitors, and after repeated electroconvulsive therapy (Sulser 1981). These findings have led to the suggestion that the therapeutic actions of antidepressants are due to the delayed development of post-synaptic β-receptor subsensitivity and that depression might be caused by hypersensitivity of post-synaptic beta receptors. Such a suggestion would appear to be the opposite of that proposed in the original monoamine hypothesis of depression. However, there is little evidence of alteration in β-receptor sensitivity in patients with affective disorders (Heninger and Charney 1987), and β-receptor down-regulation does not appear to be a necessary component of antidepressant action (Meltzer and Lowy 1987). Nevertheless some authors have reported that β-adrenergic receptor agonists have antidepressant effects (Lerer *et al.* 1981; Lecrubier *et al.* 1980; Bouthillier *et al.* 1991). These are possibly due to secondary effects on serotonin receptors.

Synaptic stability.   The physiological significance of these varying effects of long-term antidepressant treatment on different adrenergic receptors is not clear. Many of the effects seem to be opposite: for example α_2-receptor subsensitivity would tend to increase noradrenergic transmission while postsynaptic β-receptor subsensitivity would decrease the effects of noradrenaline. However, several authours have suggested that antidepressant drugs may increase the stability of noradrenergic synaptic transmission by producing effects which tend to cancel out but which limit the capacity for maladaptive positive or negative alterations in transmission (Maas 1979; Svensson and Usdin 1978; Willner and Montgomery 1980). Such an action might explain not only the normalizing effects of the drugs over a wide range of symptoms in depressive disorders, but also their relative lack of effect in normal subjects (Harrison-Read 1981). This idea suggests that instability of synaptic control rather than primary changes in receptor or transmitter activity, determines the onset of affective disorders. Synaptic instability might also account for the recurrent nature of the illness and the sudden switches that can occur between depression and mania.

Dopamine receptors.   There is little information concerning the sensitivity of dopamine receptors in affective disorders. However, some antidepressant drugs have dopamine reuptake blocking actions, and neuroleptics which are effective in mania have dopamine receptor antagonist effects (Chapter 13).

Serotonin receptors.   Catecholaminergic systems normally interact closely with serotonergic systems in the central nervous system. Most antidepressant drugs affect both systems and there is evidence that both may be involved in affective disorders. For these reasons, much attention has recently been paid to serotonin receptor activity in depression. Serotonin receptors (Chapter 3; Table 3.1) include pre- and post-synaptic 5-HT_{1A} receptors and post-synaptic 5-HT_2 and 5-HT_3 receptors. In addition there is a neuronal uptake site for serotonin linked to the active transport of transmitter into the nerve endings. This site is selectively labelled by tritiated imipramine; it is not a receptor in the classical sense, but has similar properties in that it includes a serotonin recognition site, a coupling mechanism linked to the active transport of transmitter across the membrane, and it is inhibited by specific antagonists.

Langer (1980, 1984) and Langer and Briley (1981) have proposed that this neuronal serotonin uptake site (high affinity imipramine binding site) is the locus of action at which tricyclic antidepressant drugs exert their clinical effects and that it may be closely linked to the pathogenesis of depression. The site is asymmetrically distributed in the rat and human brain; the highest concentrations are found in the hypothalamus and amygdala, and the distribution parallels that of endogenous serotonin. It is also present in human platelets which are thought to represent a peripheral model for serotonergic neurones. Many tricyclic antidepressants bind with high affinity to this site and their affinity correlates significantly with clinically effective dosage. Some other monoamine uptake blockers also display moderate affinity, but the affinity of atypical antidepressants is low. Several authors have reported reduced platelet imipramine binding in patients with untreated reactive and endogenous depression (Langer and Briley 1981; Poirier *et al.* 1986), and Stanley *et al.* (1982) found a reduction in imipramine binding in the frontal cortex of suicide victims. It is not clear whether low platelet imipramine binding represents a trait or state marker for depression (Langer and Briley 1981; Marcusson and Ross 1990). Imipramine binding is not increased by 2–3 weeks treatment with tricyclic antidepressants or monoamine oxidase inhibitors, or 6–9 sessions of electroconvulsive therapy, despite clinical improvement of depression. However, chronic treatment with imipramine for 8–12 weeks increased platelet imipramine binding in depressed patients and the increase coincided with full clinical remission (Poirier *et al.* 1986).

Binding studies also suggest abnormalities in density of 5-HT$_2$ receptors in depression. Stanley and Mann (1983, 1984) found a 44 per cent increase in the density of these receptors in the brains of suicide victims compared with controls. The increase in 5-HT$_2$ receptor density was apparent in the frontal cortex and had a similar distribution to the (decreased) serotonin reuptake sites found previously in the same brains (Stanley *et al.* 1982). Similarly, Biegon *et al.* (1990*b*) found a 50% increase in platelet 5-HT$_2$ receptor binding in young drug-free suicides compared with controls. Platelet 5-HT$_2$ receptor binding was also high in patients with untreated major depression and treatment with antidepressant drugs (maprotiline, amitriptyline, trazodone) was associated with a fall in platelet 5-HT$_2$ receptor binding which correlated with clinical improvement (Biegon *et al.* 1990*a*). Thus, an increase in 5-HT$_2$ receptor binding appears to be a robust state marker for depressive illness. It may reflect a post-synaptic receptor supersensitivity resulting from decreased serotonin uptake and turnover in depression.

Investigations of 5-HT$_1$ receptors in binding studies have not shown consistent changes in man (Stanley and Mann 1984), although Cheetham *et al.* (1989) reported a reduction in the number of 5-HT$_1$ binding sites in the hippocampus in drug-free suicides. Yates and Ferrier (1990) found no difference in 5-HT$_{1A}$ receptor binding in the frontal cortex *post mortem* between patients with major depression and controls, and no consistent effects of antidepressant medication or mental state at death were observed. There is little information concerning 5-HT$_3$ receptors in depression. However, these receptors have been found in limbic and cortical areas and may be involved in the control of mood. Serotonin 5-HT$_3$ receptor antagonists may have antipsychotic properties (Chapter 14) and both 5-HT$_3$ and 5-HT$_2$ receptor antagonists appear to have anxiolytic and possibly antidepressant effects (Fozard 1987).

Receptor studies have thus revealed complex changes in monoamine receptors in depression and in response to chronic antidepressant drug treatment. With regard to noradrenergic mechanisms, it appears that there may be increased α_2-adrenoceptor sensitivity in depression, and that a_2 and β-adrenoceptor subsensitivity is induced over time by antidepressant drugs. In the case of serotonin, there appears to be a reduced capacity for serotonin uptake and an increase in 5-HT$_2$ receptor sensitivity in depression, changes which are reversed by chronic antidepressant drug treatment. It may well be that the several monoamine receptor changes are inseparable or closely interrelated, and that these changes, and their modification by antidepressant drugs, involve receptor-receptor interactions and comodulation by several monoamine neurotransmitters (Sulser *et al.* 1983; Barbaccia *et al.* 1983; Racagni and Brunello 1984; Goldstein *et al.* 1983). Thus it may be vain to search for an explanation of depression, or of the mechanism of action of antidepressant drugs, in terms of any single transmitter or its receptors. The delayed therapeutic effects of antidepressant drugs may result from the establishment, by a number of mechanisms, of greater overall stability at synapses for several monoamine transmitters, and/or an alteration of balance between them, resulting in greater efficiency in synaptic transmission through critical brain pathways (Ogren *et al.* 1983).

Endogenous opioids in affective disorders

Although considerable knowledge has accumulated concerning the role of endogenous peptide systems in pain modulation (Chapter 5), much less is known of their actions in modulating emotion. Endogenous opioids are distributed in limbic structures; they are important in reward systems, along with catecholamines (with which they are co-released), and one of their most prominent clinical effects is an action on behaviour and mood. Panksepp (1981) proposed a role of opioid systems in mediating social reward rather than reward in general. He drew attention to some similarities between narcotic dependence and social attachments or bonding, and between the narcotic withdrawal syndrome and the behaviour induced by separation or loss in animals, and suggested that the neurochemical underpinnings of the two conditions may be similar.

The similarity between the narcotic withdrawal syndrome and chronic pain syndromes has already been pointed out (Chapter 6), and the features of chronic pain syndromes described by Sternbach (1981; Table 6.2) are almost identical to those attributed to drug or social withdrawal by Panksepp (1981; Table 11.1). Chronic pain syndromes are in turn related to depression. The commonality between loss, pain, and depression were underlined by Panksepp who stated: 'From an evolutionary perspective, it is reasonable that social affect (panic, loneliness, comfort, and joy) might have arisen from brain systems which modulate pain. . . . The imprint of this evolutionary progression remains embedded within human and animal language. The semantics of social loss are the semantics of pain. It hurts to lose a loved one and we cry. Social separation makes young animals more sensitive to pain and they cry'. (Panksepp 1981, pp. 170–1).

Table 11.1 Similarities between narcotic addiction and social dependence

Narcotic addiction	Social dependence
Psychological dependence	Love
Tolerance	Estrangement
Withdrawal syndrome	Loss of a loved one
psychological distress	loneliness
lachrymation	crying
anorexia	loss of appetite
depression	despondency
insomnia	sleeplessness
aggressiveness	irritability

Reference: Panksepp 1981.

Stein (1978; Chapter 5) suggested that endogenous opioids in brain reward systems are important in signalling gratification on attaining an objective after goal-directed behaviour. Lack of a sense of gratification is a characteristic of some types of depression: activities which used to produce pleasure no longer do so. A similar incapacity may apparently be induced by giving naloxone to young animals, when they hurry to regain social contact but appear to gain little comfort from the contact (Bolles and Fanselow 1982). These and other observations reviewed by Benton (1988) suggest that human depressions may be characterized by underactivity of endogenous opioid systems in limbic reward pathways. However, the evidence for this suggestion is extremely limited.

Very few direct measurements have been made of endogenous opioids in depression or mania. Pickar *at al.* (1980) reported a single case study of a patient with bipolar depression in whom daily estimations of plasma opioid activity were made during repeated manic and depressive episodes. Plasma opioid activity was measured as β-endorphin-like radio-receptor activity assayed against β-endorphin on rat brain membranes. Significantly higher levels of such activity were observed during two manic phases than during two intervening depressive phases, and there was no overlap between mania and depression values. There was a highly significant inverse correlation between clinical ratings for severity of depression and plasma opioid activity. Lindstrom *et al.* (1978) also reported greater opioid activity in the cerebrospinal fluid of bipolar patients during mania than during depression. Apparently contradictory findings were reported by Terenius (1977) and von Knorring *et al.* (1978) who found low concentrations of endorphin-like activity in the cerebro-spinal fluid of manic patients and high levels in patients with depression.

There have been few trials of opioid agonists or antagonists in the treatment of affective disorders. Terenius (1977) reported inconclusive results with naloxone in depression, but pointed out that this drug is very short-acting. No evidence for a therapeutic effect of intravenous β-endorphin in depression has been found in double-blind studies (Clement-Jones and Besser 1983). In mania, some clinical studies have found beneficial effects of naloxone, but these effects were not confirmed in other studies. One double-blind study, but not others, have reported reduction of mania following intravenous injection of β-endorphin (Koob and Bloom 1983).

Information on the relation between endogenous opioid activity and mood in affective disorders, and on the possible therapeutic benefits of opioid agonists and antagonists is thus sparse. Investigations in the last decade, reviewed by Berger and Nemeroff (1987), have not clarified the picture.

Endocrine changes in affective disorders

A close relationship between depression and endocrine function is suggested by the fact that depression is a symptom of several endocrine disorders, and that patients with affective disorders often have evidence of endocrine dysfunction. Many endocrine disorders result from disturbance of hypothalmamic-pituitary function. The hypothalamus is part of the limbic system and is involved in mood control; furthermore, hypothalamic centres are partly controlled by monoamine systems postulated to be disturbed in affective disorders. In addition, the release of many anterior pituitary hormones is sleep-dependent and shows marked diurnal rhythmicity. Disorders of sleep and of circadian rhythm are prominent in depression (reviewed by Sack *et al.* 1987). These and other arguments have stimulated many investigations of endocrine function, particularly hypothalamic-pituitary relationships, in depression (see Stokes and Sikes 1987; Prange *et al.* 1987; Kalin and Dawson 1986 for reviews). Although various endocrine abnormalities have been found, it is still not known what part (if any) is played in the control of mood by the plethora of neuroendocrine chemicals secreted by the body.

Hypothalamic-pituitary-adrenal axis

Of the endocrine changes in affective disorders, those of the hypothalamic-pituitary axis have been most widely investigated. The systemic concentration of cortisol is determined by a complex control system (Fig. 11.3) and represents the final outcome of at least four processes: (1) the effects of monoaminergic and cholinergic influences on the hypothalamic release of corticotropin-releasing factor, (2) the effects of corticotropin-releasing factor on the anterior pituitary release of ACTH,

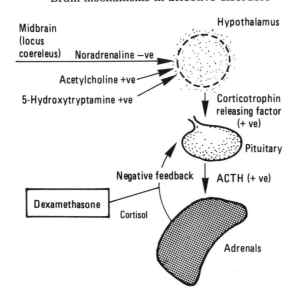

Fig. 11.3 The hypothalamic-pituitary-adrenal axis in the control of cortisol secretion. The systemic concentration of cortisol secretion is controlled by (1) monoaminergic and cholinergic influences on the hypothalamic release of corticotrophin releasing factor, (2) the effects of this factor on the anterior pituitary release of ACTH, (3) the effect of ACTH on adrenal release of cortisol, and (4) feedback effects of cortisol on pituitary ACTH release. The synthetic steroid dexamethasone normally suppresses release of ACTH and cortisol, but cortisol suppression is reduced in a proportion of patients with depression. (From Calloway 1982)

(3) the effects of ACTH on the release of cortisol by the adrenals, and (4) feedback affects of adrenal cortisol on pituitary ACTH release.

In about 50 per cent of patients with moderate to severe depression, the concentration of cortisol is raised above normal values in cerebrospinal fluid, plasma, and urine (Calloway 1982). In addition, there is a change in the diurnal pattern of cortisol secretion: in depression plasma cortisol concentration remains high in the afternoon and evening and during sleep, while in normal subjects there is a peak in cortisol concentration in the morning with declining concentrations later in the day and low levels at night. The raised cortisol secretion in depression is not thought to be the direct result of stress, which does not alter the diurnal pattern.

Dexamethasone suppression test. In addition, 20–40 per cent of depressed patients do not show the normal suppression of cortisol secretion induced by administration of the synthetic steroid dexamethasone given at night. This lack of response forms the basis of the dexamethasone suppression test (DST) (Carroll *et al.* 1981; Fig. 11.3). This test has been held to have some diagnostic and possibly prognostic utility in depression, but it is not specific since non-suppression of cortisol secretion also occurs in 5–10 per cent of normal subjects, abstaining alcoholics, and patients with neuroses and senile dementias. Mellsopp *et al.* (1985) suggest that the degree of non-suppression by dexamethasone reflects the degree of stress or distress experienced by the patient, a suggestion supported by the findings of a World Health Organisation collaborative study (Abou-Saleh *et al.* 1989). In most patients, the DST returns to normal on clinical recovery. A few patients continue to show dexamethasone resistance in spite of clinical recovery, and Goldberg (1980*a*, *b*) found in a small series that all of such patients relapsed on cessation of drug treatment.

It remains puzzling that plasma cortisol concentrations in some depressed patients are in the same range as those found in Cushing's disease, yet depressed patients show no signs of hypercortisolism. Brain cortisol concentrations may be paradoxically decreased in depressed suicide victims, suggesting perhaps a decrease in tissue cortisol binding in depression (Carroll 1978). According to this author: 'The evidence for a primary limbic-hypothalamic neuroendocrine disturbance in endo-·genous depression is compelling. It is strengthened by the observation that all of the neuroendocrine abnormalities in endogenous depression occur in diencephalic Cushing's disease, in which a high incidence of depression is noted also' (Carroll 1978; p. 494).

Thyroid hormones.   Depression is common in myxoedema and rare in thyrotoxicosis (Prange *et al.* 1987), an observation which suggests a disturbance of thyroid function in affective disorders. Circulating concentrations of thyroxine are normal in depression, but in about 40 per cent of depressed patients the anterior pituitary release of thyroid stimulating hormone (thyrotropin, TSH) in response to an intravenous injection of synthetic thryotropin releasing hormone (TRH) is depressed (Calloway *et al.* 1984). The release of TSH is under inhibitory dopaminergic control and release is increased by dopaminergic receptor blockers such as chlorpromazine. A blunted TSH response is not specific to depression: it occurs in 4 per cent of normal subjects, in alcoholism, and sometimes in mania (Prange *et al.* 1987). It is also seen in patients on chronic glucocorticoid treatment and in Cushing's disease, and it has been suggested that the TSH responses are related to the high cortisol concentration. However, there appears to be no relation in depressed patients between TSH response and plasma cortisol concentration or the presence or absence of non-suppression in the dexamethasone suppression test (Calloway 1982). The TSH response may be used to predict response to treatment. Kirkegaard (1981) found that patients whose TRH response tended to return to normal after treatment remained well for 6 months while those in whom the TRH response remained blunted relapsed within 4 months.

Growth hormone.   Basal fasting plasma growth hormone concentration is normal in patients with depression. However, the response to stimulation of growth hormone release by clonidine, L-dopa, amphetamine, and L-tryptophan is deficient in some patients (Siever 1987; Deakin *et al.* 1990). These processes involve suprapituitary mechanisms and a poor response in depressed patients suggests a limbic-hypothalamic dysfunction. The regulation of growth hormone release is complex, but there is evidence that stimulation of release involves α-adrenergic, dopaminergic, and serotonergic systems. The blunted growth hormone response may therefore reflect monoaminergic underactivity.

Prolactin.   There is some evidence that prolactin secretion is slightly increased in depressive disorders, although results are conflicting (Carroll 1978; Calloway 1982). Prolactin secretion undergoes diurnal rhythmic changes: it is released in a pulsatile fashion with a nocturnal rise which is dependent upon sleep. Morning concentrations of prolactin have been reported to be increased in patients with bipolar depression. Prolactin secretion, like that of TRH, is under inhibitory dopaminergic control and is suppressed by L-dopa and increased by dopamine receptor blockers. The suppression by L-dopa is more marked in bipolar depression, possibly implying dopaminergic dysfunction in these patients.

Sex hormones.   Many observations suggest a close relationship between sex hormones and affective disorders. Depression is twice as common in women as men, and women are most vulnerable between puberty and the age of 45 (*British Medical Journal* 1977). Affective disorders are associated with the puerperium, the menstrual cycle, the use of oral contraceptives, and perhaps with the menopause. Women with depression not uncommonly develop amenorrhoea, and in both sexes reduction of libido is a prominent symptom. In addition, the secretion of sex hormones exhibits pronounced circadian rhythmicity. Yet direct information relating sex hormone abnormalities to affective disorders is meagre. Plasma testosterone, oestrogen, and progesterone concentrations are within the normal range in most patients with depression (Calloway 1982).

Post-partum depression may be associated with the dramatic fall in circulating oestrogen levels that occurs at this time. This fall is normally accompanied by a decrease in peripheral α_2-receptor density (Metz *et al.* 1983). If these changes occur in the brain, central α_2-receptor hypersensitivity, with decreased noradrenaline release, may contribute to puerperal depression. Plasma concentrations of β-endorphin also fall rapidly after delivery and another suggestion is that 'maternity blues' may represent endogenous opioid withdrawal symptoms (Newnham *et al.* 1983).

In relation to puerperal mania, Cookson (1982) cited evidence from animal studies that chronic treatment with oestradiol leads to an increase in dopamine receptor density in the striatum, and suggested that puerperal mania might be due to supersensitivity of dopamine receptors exposed by the sudden fall in oestrogen secretion. In support of this idea, the condition responds to dopamine receptor antagonists.

Women with premenstrual tension syndromes have higher plasma prolactin concentrations than controls throughout the menstrual cycle. The cyclic decrease of oestrogen and progesterone concentrations, combined with high prolactin concentration, is thought to contribute to the affective symptoms (Carroll 1978). Cyclic changes in platelet α_2-receptor density also occurs, α_2-density being highest during the premenstruum (Grahame-Smith 1985), and this change may be more directly related to mood. Dalton (1964) found that the day of admission to hospital among women entering for depression was closely related to the menstrual cycle, 60 per cent being admitted on the 12 days of the month around ovulation, premenstruation, or during menstruation, and only 40 per cent on the other 16 days of the month. Suicide attempts in females appear to be similarly related to the menstrual cycle and are associated with low plasma oestradiol concentrations (Fourestie *et al.* 1986).

The use of oestrogen/progesterone oral contraceptives is sometimes associated with effects on mood, and the frequency of depression as an adverse effect attributed to such use has been estimated to be between 2 and 30 per cent (Madsen 1974). Grahame-Smith (1985) reports that platelet α_2 density increases during the cycle of 21 days that the combined contraceptive pill is taken but decreases during the 7 days when it is stopped. Oestrogen/progesterone combinations also decrease the secretion of both luteinizing and follicle-stimulating hormones. It is not known how these alterations are related to mood but Whalley *et al.* (1985) report that plasma luteinizing hormone was significantly increased in drug-free young men with mania compared with controls.

Appetite and weight.   Disturbances in appetite and weight are common in affective disorders. Anorexia and weight loss is often associated with depression, but overeating and weight gain can occur. These changes, combined with the endocrine abnormalities, are thought to result from the general disturbance of hypothalamic function. Somewhat similar changes are seen in anorexia nervosa in which there is also evidence of hypothalamic-pituitary malfunction.

The central control of appetite (reviewed by Blundell 1991) involves a cascade of overlapping regulatory systems located in hindbrain, hypo-thalamic and forebrain structures. These integrate information received from multiple sensory inputs describing the milieu interieur and main-tain nutritional homeostasis by activating or suppressing food-seeking and eating behaviour. The many neural connections involved include adrenergic, dopaminergic, serotonergic and opioid pathways which also form part of the reward and punishment systems (Chapter 5), and there is an undoubted relationship between food and mood. Several non-opioid peptides suppress eating behaviour in animals, including chole-cystokinin, calcitonin, bombesin, neurotensin, TRH, somatostatin and corticotrophin releasing factor among others, while some peptides (neuropeptide Y and others) increase food intake. Other neuronal mech-anisms involving acetylcholine and GABA are also implicated. Many of these complex interactions may be disturbed in affective disorders.

As well as those described above, other endocrine and metabolic changes, and disturbances of circadian and diurnal rhythms, including alterations in melatonin secretion in response to light (Wehr *et al.* 1986; Thompson *et al.* 1990), have been described in affective disorders. How-ever, as in the case of the monoamine neurotransmitters, no particular endocrine pattern seems to characterize all cases of depression or mania. It is likely that the changes in endocrine function and biological rhythms reflect instability of monoamine (and other) control mechanisms in the hypothalamus and more generally in the limbic system, rather than changes in the activity of any particular hormone.

12. Drugs used in depression and mania

The development of antidepressant drugs in the last 35 years has greatly altered the management and considerably improved the prognosis of affective disorders. However, drug treatment is neither fully effective nor curative. Perhaps 80–90 per cent of patients with depression respond to antidepressant drugs, but 30–50 per cent also respond to placebo. About 80 per cent of patients with mania respond to lithium carbonate, and manic episodes can be further controlled with antipsychotic drugs. Nevertheless, the relapse rate of affective disorders is still of the order of 20 per cent after 6 months and 30–50 per cent after 1 or 2 years, even with maintenance drug treatment.

In this chapter, the main drugs used in affective disorders are described. Many drugs produce euphoria in normal subjects (Chapter 7) and some of these, at least temporarily, lighten mood in depressed patients. However, a characteristic of antidepressant drugs is that they have little effect on mood in normal subjects, yet restore normal mood in patients with clinical depression. Similarly, some drugs which are effective in mania (lithium, carbamazepine) have little effect on mood in normal subjects. These drugs are thus essentially mood normalizers rather than euphoriants or mood-depressants. Most of them, even when effective, take some weeks to exert their full therapeutic actions and there remains a core of patients who appear to be refractory to drug treatment. For these reasons, alternative measures, such as electroconvulsive therapy for depression, remain important for the treatment of affective disorders when rapid action is required and for drug non-responders.

As discussed in Chapter 11, some evidence suggests that affective disorders are characterized by instability of synaptic control mechanisms in multiple neurotransmitter pathways in the limbic system. The clinical course of these syndromes indicates that such instability is, at least partly, reversible and has a tendency to right itself. The possibility is suggested in this chapter that an action common to the diverse treatments effective in affective disorders is the restoration of synaptic stability and efficiency, perhaps by alterations in receptor sensitivity, and a consequent hastening of the intrinsic tendency towards remission.

Tricyclic antidepressants

These compounds have generally similar biochemical and clinical effects (Table 12.1).

Pharmacokinetics

Tricyclic antidepressants are all well absorbed from the gut, widely distributed in the body, and concentrated in the brain, especially in limbic areas, basal ganglia, and cortex. They undergo extensive hepatic metabolism and some of the metabolites are pharmacologically active. Rates of metabolism are influenced by genetic and environmental factors and there are marked differences in steady state plasma concentrations between individuals on the same dose. In general there is little correlation between steady-state plasma concentration and clinical effect, despite evidence of a 'therapeutic window' for some tricyclic antidepressants (Asberg *et al.* 1971; Peet and Coppen 1979; Norman and Burrows 1983).

Biochemical actions

The biochemical actions of the tricyclic antidepressants are reviewed by Langer and Karobath (1980), and Iversen and Mackay (1979), among others.

Reuptake inhibition at monoaminergic synapses

An action common to all tricyclic antidepressants is inhibition of the high affinity, energy-dependent uptake of monoamines into cytoplasmic stores within the presynaptic membrane. Since this reuptake system normally terminates monoaminergic transmitter activity on synaptic neurones following nerve-stimulated release, the effect of its inhibition by tricyclic antidepressants is to prolong the actions of monoamines released at synapses, and to enhance their stimulation of pre- and post-synaptic receptors (Fig. 11.1). Among the tricyclic antidepressants, secondary amines have more potent effects on the uptake of noradrenaline, while tertiary amines are more potent in blocking the reuptake of serotonin. The reuptake of dopamine is much less affected by these drugs though all inhibit it to some degree.

Monoamine uptake block explains many of the pharmacological actions of the tricyclic antidepressants, and it has been widely accepted that it underlies their antidepressant effect. This possibility provided the main impetus for the monoamine hypothesis of affective disorders (Chapter 11). Both tricyclic antidepressants and monoamine oxidase in inhibitors (see below) increase the availability of active monoamines at

Table 12.1 Pharmacological properties of some antidepressant drugs

Antidepressant drugs	Plasma elimination half-life (h) [active metabolite]	Noradrenaline uptake inhibition	Serotonin uptake inhibition	Anticholinergic effects	Sedative effects
Tricyclic compounds					
imipramine	4–18[12–61][1]	++	+++	++	++
amitriptyline	10–25[13–93][2]	+	+++	+++	++
clomipramine	16–20	+	+++	++	+
nortriptyline	13–93	+++	+	++	0
desipramine	12–61	+++	0	+	0
protriptyline	54–198	+++	++	++	0
doxepin	8–25[31–81][3]	+	+	+++	++
dothiepin	14–40	+	+	++	++
lofepramine	5[12–61][1]	+++	+	0	0
Related compounds					
viloxazine	2–5	+++	0	0	0
maprotiline	27–58	+++	+	+	+
mianserin*	8–19	0	0	0	++
Newer compounds					
trazodone*	4	0	+	0	++
fluvoxamine	15	0	++	0	0
fluoxetine	2–3 days[7–9 days]	0	++	0	0
sertraline	26	0	++	0	0

Pharmacological activity: 0 = none; + = slight; ++ = moderate; +++ = marked.
1,metabolized to desipramine; 2,metabolized to nortriptyline; 3,metabolized to desmethyldoxepin.
* inhibits α_2-adrenoceptors.

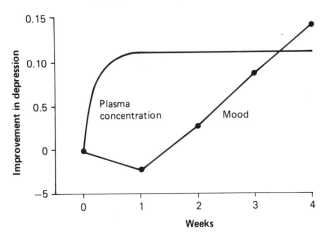

Fig. 12.1 Time course of therapeutic effect of tricyclic antidepressant drugs. Improvement in depression is considerably delayed compared with attainment of maximum plasma concentration (and biochemical effects). (From Oswald *et al.* 1972.)

receptor sites and reverse the biochemical, physiological, and behavioural effects of reserpine, a drug which depletes monoamine stores at nerve terminals, causes behavioural depression in animals, and can precipitate a depressive syndrome in man.

However, several of the newer, clinically effective, antidepressants are neither reuptake blockers nor monoamine oxidase inhibitors; thus, such an action does not appear to be a prerequisite for an antidepressant effect. In addition, inhibition of monoamine uptake can be demonstrated within minutes of the administration of tricyclic antidepressants while the clinical antidepressant effect takes weeks to develop (Fig. 12.1). It has recently become apparent that, with chronic administration, the initial reuptake blocking effect gives rise to a number of secondary effects, both on monoamine synthesis and turnover, and on receptor sensitivity. At present, the long-term effects on receptor sensitivity appear to have the most clinical relevance.

Other effects on monoamine systems

Animal studies indicate that the increased synaptic concentration of noradrenaline and serotonin, induced acutely by the tricyclic antidepressants, inhibits the synthesis of the respective monoamines through negative feedback mechanisms, resulting in decreased cerebral turnover of noradrenaline or serotonin. Thus, tertiary amines have been observed to depress the firing of serotonergic raphe neurones (Koe 1983) while secondary amines depress the firing of noradrenergic locus coeruleus neurones (Sulser and Mobley 1980). These actions may be relevant to their anxiolytic effects (Chapter 4).

Monoamine receptor modulation with chronic administration

Chronic administration of tricyclic antidepressants leads to changes in the sensitivity of a number of receptors for monoamines. These changes may represent, at least partially, a homeostatic response to the initial monoamine uptake blocking action of the drugs. Receptor adaptations to long-term antidepressant medication have been discussed (Chapter 11) and are reviewed by Heninger and Charney (1987). In general, it appears that tricyclic antidepressants, a number of non-tricyclic antidepressant drugs, and perhaps various other treatments for depression including lithium and electroconvulsive therapy, can produce some or all of the following changes in monoamine receptor activity in the brain:

(i) Down-regulation of α_2-adrenergic receptors (Chapter 11).

(ii) Down-regulation of β-adrenergic receptors (Chapter 11).

(iii) For post-synaptic α_1-receptors, the evidence is conflicting: increases, decreases, and no change after antidepressant treatment have all been reported.

(iv) Down-regulation of dopamine autoreceptors has been shown to occur in animals. There is little information in man and there have been few investigations of post-synaptic dopamine receptor density after antidepressants.

(v) Increase in density in human platelet imipramine binding sites; the importance of these binding sites in depression is still debatable (Marcusson and Ross 1990).

(vi) Down-regulation of 5-HT_2 receptors with inconsistent effects on 5-HT_1 receptors.

The effects of chronic antidepressant treatment on receptor sensitivity may vary in different parts of the brain, and adaptive receptor changes probably involve co-modulation by several different neurotransmitters. It seems likely that the therapeutic effects of chronic tricyclic antidepressant treatment stem from complex adaptive changes which ultimately result in greater synaptic efficiency and stability in several neurotransmitter systems.

Effects on other neurotransmitter systems

The tricyclic antidepressants are structurally related to the phenothiazines, and share with them both anticholinergic and antihistaminic effects. The anticholinergic effects do not correlate with antidepressant effects, and many of the newer antidepressants are almost devoid of anticholinergic activity. Antihistaminic effects are attributed to blockade of histamine receptors in the brain; there is no relationship between antihistaminic potency and antidepressant effect.

Long-term administration of many tricyclic antidepressants produces an up-regulation of $GABA_B$ binding sites in the rat frontal cortex and it has been suggested that an interaction with $GABA_B$ neurotransmission may be involved in the therapeutic effects of antidepressant treatments including tricyclic drugs, monoamine oxidase inhibitors, some benzodiazepines and electroconvulsive therapy (Heninger and Charney 1987).

Effects on mood and behaviour

In most normal subjects, tricyclic antidepressants have virtually no euphoriant or mood-elevating properties. Most of them induce at first a sense of fatigue and sleepiness, accompanied by anticholinergic symptoms. These effects are usually perceived as unpleasant. Continued administration for several days leads to impairment of cognition with difficulty in concentration and logical thought, and a decline in psychomotor performance (Baldessarini 1980).

By contrast, about 70 per cent of patients with depression respond to the tricyclic antidepressants, after a delay of some weeks, with elevation or normalization of mood and dulling of depressive ideation. Behaviour is correspondingly normalized with increased social interaction and cognitive and motor function. However, in patients with bipolar depression, the drugs may occasionally precipitate a sudden switch towards excitement, euphoria, and mania. Such a switch may also be precipitated by L-dopa, monoamine oxidase inhibitors, and sympathomimetic amines (Bunney 1978).

Tricyclic antidepressants are effective in anxiety states (Chapter 2). Some also have sedative actions (Table 12.1) but it is not clear whether anxiolytic, antidepressant, and sedative effects are really separable nor whether anxiety is separable from depression (Chapters 3, 11).

In animals, the behavioural effects of the tricyclic antidepressants are usually those of mild central nervous system depression. They exert little effect, when given alone, on intracranial self-stimulation behaviour, but potentiate the enhancing effect of amphetamine. They reverse the behavioural and physiological effect of reserpine and inhibit the development of 'depressive' behaviour in several animal models of depression, including behavioural despair in rodents, learned helplessness in dogs and rodents, separation distress in primates and abnormal behaviour in bulbectomized rats (Willner 1984).

Thus, tricyclic antidepressants exert effects on mood and behaviour only in special circumstances. In animals these circumstances are related to particular forms of stress. In man, the relationship to stress is less clear. The question of how the drugs influence thought patterns and ideation is obscure, even if it is accepted that they act by affecting synaptic transmission in the various ways discussed in previous sections. The question also arises of whether there is a critical point at which a previously normal person becomes depressed in the sense that he will respond to antidepressant drugs. Is it a matter of the severity of depression, or is there a phase shift when limbic synaptic control mechanisms become unstable so that certain thought processes are no longer constrained or readily reversible? Yet the process is often potentially reversible: a considerable proportion of patients with depression respond to placebo and most eventually remit without treatment. The antidepressant drugs appear to trigger or catalyse whatever processes are required for spontaneous remission.

Therapeutic efficacy of tricyclic antidepressants

Tricyclic antidepressants undoubtedly improve the prognosis in depression, but the degree to which they do this has been difficult to estimate. The drugs terminate attacks of depression in 60–80 per cent depending on the selection criteria for treatment (Amsterdam *et al.* 1980; Asberg and Sjoquist 1981), and most placebo-controlled trials show that tricyclic antidepressants are more effective than placebo. No particular tricyclic drug appears to have greater overall therapeutic efficacy, although the incidence and severity of adverse effects varies between drugs. Tricyclic agents have become the standard drugs against which new antidepressant drugs are compared for efficacy.

Continued administration of tricyclic antidepressants also reduces the likelihood of recurrence of depressive episodes. About 30–50 per cent of depressed patients relapse in 6 months after treatment with electroconvulsive therapy alone, while the relapse rate after 6 months of drug treatment is 10–20 per cent (Rogers *et al.* 1981). Three large collaborative studies cited by Berger (1977) have confirmed the finding that continued (6 months) tricyclic depressants treatment reduces the relapse rate compared with short-term treatment (6 weeks).

Reasons for failure of therapeutic response are discussed by Amsterdam *et al.* (1980). They include non-compliance, inappropriate dosage, and selective response to a particular tricyclic drug. There remains a core of depressed patients who do not respond to tricyclic antidepressants. These non-responders are clinically heterogeneous and there is no indication that their depression reflects a different aetiology from that of responders.

Effects on sleep and EEG

Tricyclic antidepressants have pronounced effects on sleep (Kay *et al.* 1976; Hartmann 1976). In depressive illness, Stage 4 sleep is decreased, REMS is increased, and there are frequent awakenings. This pattern is reversed by tricyclic antidepressant drugs which increase Stage 4 sleep,

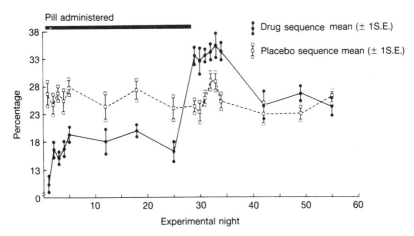

Fig. 12.2 Effect of amitriptyline of REMS percentage. Open symbols and dotted line, placebo; filled symbols and solid line, amitriptyline. n = 10. (From Hartmann 1976, by kind permission of John Wiley & Sons Inc., New York.)

markedly decrease REMS, and decrease the number of nocturnal awakenings (Fig. 12.2). The effects on sleep commence soon after the start of drug therapy and there is no temporal relationship with clinical recovery. The same effects on sleep are exerted by the drugs in normal subjects. A rebound of REMS occurs on cessation of antidepressant drug therapy.

These effects presumably result from actions on central monoaminergic activity; normalisation of the sleep pattern in depression occurs even with tricyclic antidepressants which do not have additional sedative effects. The drugs may also tend to restore diurnal rhythms and endocrine secretion patterns during sleep which are disturbed in depression.

The effects of tricyclic antidepressants on the waking EEG are reviewed by Itil and Soldatos (1980). Quantitative analysis using digital computer methods has shown that the drugs produce a characteristic EEG profile which is common to many antidepressants, regardless of their chemical structure or supposed mechanism of action. The ability to induce this profile is a predictor of antidepressant activity in newly developed drugs prior to clinical trial. The typical EEG changes after acute administration of a tricyclic antidepressant consist of an increase both in very slow and in fast activity, with a decrease in alpha activity. The effects on cortical evoked potentials are variable, but in some cases the amplitude of the late components of evoked potentials are increased in treated depressed patients when clinical improvement occurs (Ashton *et al.* 1988; Timsit-Berthier 1981).

Adverse effects

Many tricyclic antidepressants have anticholinergic effects (Table 12.1). Cardiovascular effects include hypo- or hypertension, tachycardia, and cardiac arrhythmias which are probably due to peripheral monoamine reuptake blockade. Direct cardiac depressant effects may cause cardiac failure in some elderly subjects. In acute overdose a combination of central nervous system and cardiovascular toxic effects, due to both anticholinergic actions and increased adrenergic activity, are seen. Self-poisoning with antidepressant drugs is common and may be fatal. The relative toxicity of antidepressant drugs is reviewed by Henry and Martin (1987) and Pinder (1988).

Some of the tricyclic agents have sedative effects (Table 12.1) while others have stimulant effects and may cause restlessness or insomnia. Occasionally the drugs may precipitate mania in bipolar disorders, acute psychosis in schizophrenia or toxic confusional states in the elderly. Paradoxical worsening of depression has been reported (Damluji and Ferguson 1988) and it is debatable whether suicide may be promoted in some patients (Montgomery and Pinder 1987). Increased appetite with carbohydrate craving occurs in some patients and may lead to considerable weight gain; amenorrhoea and menstrual irregularities may also occur.

Several drugs interact with tricyclic antidepressants at their sites of action. Monoamine oxidase inhibitors potentiate the increase of monoaminergic activity at synapses and the use of the two types of drugs together can precipitate excitement and hyperpyrexia. Rarely, this combination can also cause convulsions and coma, and the use of tricyclic antidepressants with monoamine oxidase inhibitors is generally contraindicated. Sympathomimetic amines may produce similar potentiation and give rise to a hypertensive reaction. On the other hand, the effects of certain antihypertensive drugs may be reversed. Drugs with anticholinergic effects may potentiate the central and peripheral anticholinergic effects of tricyclic antidepressants and at toxic concentrations produce a syndrome of hyperpyrexia, agitation and convulsions. Sedative/hypnotic drugs, including alcohol, have additive effects with sedative tricyclic antidepressants.

Withdrawal syndrome

Tolerance develops to the anticholinergic effects of the tricyclic antidepressants and a number of adaptive changes result from the monoamine uptake inhibition, as discussed above. No doubt as a result of these changes, a variety of withdrawal effects can occur when the drugs are discontinued after chronic use. Signs of cholinergic hyperactivity after withdrawal include malaise, chills, coryza, muscular aches, nausea and vomiting, and occasionally movement disorders (Dilsaver 1989; Dilsaver *et al.* 1987*a, b*). Signs of monoaminergic overactivity include anxiety, panic, irritability, restlessness, insomnia, nightmares and occasionally mania (Dilsaver *et al.* 1987*a, b*; Tyrer 1984; Bialos *et al.* 1982; Charney *et al.* 1982). In some cases (Tyrer 1984), the syndrome is similar to the benzodiazepine withdrawal syndrome (Chapter 4) and may be related to the anxiolytic effects of the drugs. Withdrawal symptoms emerge during the first two weeks after drug withdrawal and subside during the next two weeks (Ayd 1986). The symptoms are relieved if the drug is resumed. The incidence of the withdrawal syndrome appears to be about 30 per cent in patients with neurotic depression and phobic neuroses (Tyrer 1984). Similar withdrawal symptoms may occur in neonates whose mothers received antidepressants during pregnancy (Webster 1973).

New generation antidepressants

Following the apparent therapeutic success of the classical tricyclic antidepressants, a new generation of drugs was developed with the hope of finding agents with increased antidepressant potency, a more rapid onset of action, and fewer adverse effects. In spite of their diverse chemical structures, most of these new drugs have very similar therapeutic effects to the original tricyclics, including a delayed onset of action. On the other hand many have fewer adverse effects and are safer in overdose.

Newer antidepressants are reviewed by Enna and Eison (1987). *Maprotiline* is a bridged tricyclic and is a relatively selective inhibitor of noradrenaline reuptake. It has sedative properties and its adverse and toxic effects are similar to those of the tricyclics. *Mianserin* has a tetracyclic structure. It appears to have a different biochemical action from the tricyclic antidepressants since it has no effect on monoamine reuptake, no sympathomimetic activity, and no significant anticholinergic effects. There is some evidence that it blocks α_2-receptors, thus increasing noradrenaline release. It also has anxiolytic, sedative and antihistamine effects. Adverse effects are uncommon although it can produce blood dyscrasias especially in the elderly. The virtual lack of cardiotoxic and anticholinergic effects make this drug relatively safe in overdose.

Trazodone is a triazolopyridine derivative with a structure unrelated to other antidepressants. It inhibits neuronal serotonin reuptake but blocks central serotonin receptors. It also blocks α_2 adrenoceptors, having six times the affinity of mianserin for these receptors. There are no antichlolinergic effects and little cardiotoxicity.

Fluvoxamine, fluoxetine paroxetine, and *sertraline* are specific serotonin reuptake blockers with little anticholinergic activity, cardiotoxicity
or sedative effects. They do not cause weight gain but can cause nausea
and vomiting.

Monoamine oxidase inhibitors

The monoamine oxidase inhibitors were introduced as antidepressants in
the 1950s at about the same time as the tricyclic compounds, but they
were soon superseded by the tricyclics which had a wider therapeutic
range and less severe adverse effects. Monoamine oxidase inhibitors are
as effective as tricyclic antidepressants for most types of depression
including some which do not respond to tricyclics (Tyrer 1989). They are
also effective in depression accompanied by anxiety, and in phobic states.
The drugs most often used clinically are the hydrazine derivatives *phenelzine* and *isocarboxazid* and the non-hydrazine *tranylcypromine*. These
drugs are reviewed by Tyrer (1982) and Murphy *et al.* (1987). A shorter-
acting derivative, *moclobemide* has recently been introduced.

Pharmacokinetics

The monoamine oxidase inhibitors are rapidly absorbed after oral
administration and widely distributed in body tissues including the brain.
The metabolism of these drugs is poorly understood because it has been
difficult to isolate the various metabolites. They are extensively metabolized in the liver into inactive compounds, by routes which probably
include acetylation, oxidation, and oxidative deamination. The part
played by acetylation in the inactivation of these drugs has been much
discussed because it varies widely between individuals and may be related
to the therapeutic and toxic effects. Paykel *et al.* (1982) followed the
effect of phenelzine over 6 weeks in a double-blind controlled study. It
was found that slow acetylators showed significantly more improvement
with phenelzine than with placebo after 2 weeks, but fast acetylators
showed a similar level of improvement after 6 weeks. The importance of
acetylator status in the response to monoamine oxidase inhibitors is still
debated.

Biochemical actions

Monoamine oxidase inhibition

As their name implies, the monoamine oxidase inhibitors inhibit the
enzyme monoamine oxidase in brain and peripheral tissues. The hydrazines produce irreversible inhibition while that produced by non-

hydrazines is slowly reversible; with moclobemide, enzyme activity recovers completely in 24 h after stopping the drug (Warrington *et al.* 1991). Monoamine oxidase exists in at least two forms in the body, MAO-A and MAO-B. These forms have different substrate specificities. The preferred substrate for MAO-A is serotonin, but it also deaminates noradrenaline and dopamine. The preferred substrate for MAO-B is benzylamine. Tyramine and tryptamine are substrates for both types. MAO-A is thought to be more relevant to the activity of antidepressant drugs.

At monoaminergic nerve terminals, MAO-A appears to control the amount of transmitter which is held in synaptic storage vesicles. A stabilizing system seems to exist whereby the quantity of transmitter stored at these sites is kept roughly constant, any excess being deaminated by the enzyme and returned to the metabolic pool. Thus, the activity of monoamine oxidase determines the quantity of monoamine released into the synaptic cleft by a nerve impulse and the consequence of monoamine oxidase inhibition is an increase in the concentration of monoamine transmitter available to act on synaptic receptors following nerve stimulation (Fig. 11.1). This effect leads to enhancement of activity of serotonin, noradrenaline and dopamine, both centrally and peripherally. The effect persists for some weeks after the elimination of the drug from the body, because of the irreversible or only slowly reversible nature of the enzyme inhibition.

Monoamine oxidase inhibitors also have some catecholamine uptake blocking activity which adds to their effect (Kline and Cooper 1980). The non-hydrazine derivatives are similar in structure to amphetamine and have additional amphetamine-like effects including dopamine release.

In animal tests, monoamine oxidase inhibitors, like many other antidepressants, reverse the behavioural and physiological effects of reserpine, increase brain concentrations of monoamines, enhance intracranial self-stimulation, inhibit the development of learned helplessness and behavioural despair, and normalize the behaviour of bulbectomized rats.

Receptor modulation

On chronic administration, the monoamine oxidase inhibitors produce alterations in receptor sensitivity similar to those which have been observed with many of the tricyclic antidepressants, including down-regulation of α_2- and β-adrenergic receptors and of serotonergic 5-HT$_2$ receptors, although serotonin reuptake sites are not affected (Sulser 1981; Sulser *et al.* 1983; Sugrue 1981; Charney *et al.* 1981a). Similar adaptive receptor changes occur with pargyline which in clinical trials has little if any antidepressant effect (Tyrer 1982).

Relationship of biochemical effects to antidepressant action

It is not clear how much of the antidepressant effects of these drugs is related to secondary changes in receptor sensitivity and how much to inhibition of monoamine oxidase activity itself. The onset of antidepressant action is often delayed, but this may be partly due to pharmacokinetic factors. The offset of antidepressant activity on discontinuation occurs after a period of weeks and coincides with resynthesis of monoamine oxidase. Some monoamine oxidase inhibitors (particularly nonhydrazine derivatives) have additional amphetamine-like actions with a rapid onset of mood elevation. Like amphetamine, the drugs can precipitate mania or a schizophreniform psychosis and can aggravate symptoms in schizophrenia. As with tricyclic antidepressants, the crucial change produced by monoamine oxidase inhibitors may be an increase in stability in interacting central monoaminergic synapses. The drugs are particularly effective in disorders characterized by anxiety, rapid changes in mood in response to external events, diurnal mood swings, and phobic symptoms, and Tyrer (1982) notes from clinical observations that response to monoamine oxidase inhibitors, when it occurs, does not typically consist of a gradual improvement of symptoms, but of a sudden dramatic change which occurs over 24 h. 'It seems that a "switch mechanism" in the brain must be operating to produce such a qualitative change in such a short time' (Tyrer 1982, pp. 259–60).

Effects on sleep and EEG

The effects of monoamine oxidase inhibitors on sleep are reviewed by Kay *et al*. (1976). Many studies have shown that they cause marked reduction in REMS, and even complete suppression. Dunleavy and Oswald (1973) remarked upon the dramatic onset of REMS suppression caused by these drugs, which could occur over 24 hours and coincided with a sudden improvement of mood in the patients. In most studies drug effects on SWS have been much less marked, but patients frequently complain of insomnia. These effects of monoamine oxidase inhibitors on sleep are similar to those of amphetamine, although there is a lesser general stimulant effect. The effects on the waking EEG are also similar but less marked (Itil and Soldatos 1980). There is an increase in alpha- and slow beta-activity with a decrease in both slower and faster frequencies.

Effects on mood

There is little information on the effects of monoamine oxidase inhibitors in psychiatrically normal subjects although an early representative, iproniazid, was noted to cause euphoria in tuberculous patients, and the drugs were originally described as 'psychic energizers'. The general effect in patients with depressive and anxiety disorders is a delayed but fairly sudden normalization of mood with amelioration of depressive ideation, and a feeling of increased energy, confidence and self-esteem. The effect is reminiscent of similar sensations produced by amphetamine in normal subjects (Chapter 4) and Tyrer (1982) has described these drugs as 'delayed psychostimulants'.

Adverse effects

Anticholinergic effects are common, although a degree of tolerance develops with continued treatment. Hypo- or hypertension may result from central and peripheral monoamine oxidase inhibition. Insomnia occurs frequently, although paradoxical drowsiness is occasionally reported. Some patients develop agitation, tremor and hyperreflexia. The effects of acute overdose include agitation, hallucinations, hyperpyrexia, convulsions proceeding to coma, and hypo- or hypertension, occurring after a latent period of 6–12 h.

Drug interactions

Indirectly acting sympathomimetic amines, including those contained in certain foods (Stewart 1976), can give rise to a serious interaction with monoamine oxidase inhibitors, due to increased release of catecholamines. The reaction consists of severe hypertension and hyperthermia and may terminate in fatal subarachnoid haemorrhage. The risk of these interactions appears to be much less with moclobemide (Warrington *et al.* 1991). Hypertensive reactions have been reported with intravenous adrenaline and noradrenaline presumably because of additive effects at catecholaminergic receptors. The combination of monoamine oxidase inhibitors with tricyclic, and related tetracyclic antidepressants can interact to produce cerebral excitement which may be followed by coma and severe hyperthermia, and sometimes a hypertensive reaction. Reserpine, methyldopa and L-dopa can also precipitate hypertension.

The inactivation of some drugs which are normally metabolized by oxidizing enzymes is inhibited by monoamine oxidase inhibitors, with the result that the effects of these drugs are potentiated and prolonged. Such drugs include narcotic analgesics, barbiturates, and to a lesser extent other hypnotics and sedatives. The effects of general anaesthetics, suxamethonium, anticholinergic drugs, and caffeine may also be potentiated.

Drug dependence

Drug dependence can occur with monoamine oxidase inhibitors, especially those with amphetamine-like structure. Tolerance develops and some patients take large doses in order to maintain the stimulant and occasionally euphoric effects. A severe withdrawal reaction similar to that of amphetamine and cocaine withdrawal (Chapter 7) can occur on sudden cessation of these drugs. In addition, anxiety reactions with sudden onset of panic, shaking, sweating, headache, paraesthesiae and perceptual disturbances have been described (*Drug and Therapeutics Bulletin* 1986). A rebound of REMS with sleep disturbance and severe nightmares have also been noted. The incidence of withdrawal symptoms after chronic use is greater with monoamine oxidase inhibitors than with tricyclics (Tyrer 1984).

Other drugs used in affective disorders

Monoamine precursors

Monoamine precursors have been tried in depression on the basis that they might have therapeutic effects by increasing the (hypothetically) low monoamine activity in the brain (Chapter 11). On the whole, the results have been far from dramatic. However, tryptophan may potentiate therapeutic effects of antidepressant drugs (Byerley and Risch 1985; Baldessarini 1984). Barker *et al.* (1987) reported successful treatment of previously non-responsive severe depression with L-tryptophan, phenelzine and lithium. Some of these patients relapsed when L-tryptophan was stopped (Ferrier *et al.* 1990).

Flupenthixol

Flupenthixol is a thioxanthine derivative with acknowledged antipsychotic properties, and is widely used in the treatment of schizophrenia (Chapter 14). A number of reports have suggested that, when given in small doses, it may be effective in some forms of depression (Mindham 1979; Young *et al*, 1976). Other antipsychotic drugs including thioridazine and sulpiride have also been reported to be useful in depression, and as discussed below they are also effective in the treatment of mania.

Benzodiazepines

Benzodiazepines (Chapter 4) are not in general recommended for use in depression. Long-term benzodiazepine use may even aggravate depression and precipitate suicide (Baldessarini 1985). However, some benzodiazepines (alprazolam, bromazepam) have been claimed to have antidepressant actions separate from the anxiolytic effects (Feighner 1982). Their place in the treatment of depression is not established and they are not suitable for long-term use since tolerance and dependence develop readily.

Carbamazepine

Carbamazepine is an interesting drug which may have a therapeutic potential in manic-depressive disorders. It has a wide spectrum of activity with uses in paroxysmal pain syndromes, some types of epilepsy, and diabetes insipidus. It is structurally related to the tricyclic antidepressants and has a similar spatial molecular configuration to the anticonvulsant phenytoin.

Pharmacokinetics

Carbamazepine is slowly but well absorbed although plasma concentrations fluctuate during absorption. It has a plasma elimination half-life of 25–60 h after single dosage, falling to 10 h on chronic administration, possibly due to enzyme induction. It is metabolized to an epoxide derivative which has anti-epileptic activity but a half-life of only 2 h.

Biochemical effects

The biochemical actions of carbamazepine are complex and not well understood; they are reviewed by Post and Uhde (1983) and Post (1978). Carbamazepine is a weak noradrenaline reuptake blocker and also blocks stimulation-induced noradrenaline release in peripheral animal tissues. It increases the firing of the locus coeruleus, in action which may be relevant to its antidepressant effects. Carbamazepine also increases plasma concentrations of total and free tryptophan in humans, another action which may possibly be relevant to antidepressant effects. Despite its antimanic actions, carbamazepine does not block dopamine receptors like neuroleptics (Chapter 14). Effects on GABA mechanisms, adenosine, glutamate and calcium and sodium channels appear to relate to anticonvulsant effects.

Carbamazepine has several effects on endocrine activity. It decreases circulating concentrations of tri- and tetraiodothyronine, but does not alter concentrations of thyroid stimulating hormone. It may act as a direct vasopressin agonist and has antidiuretic effects which have been used in the treatment of diabetes insipidus. In addition, it induces escape from dexamethasone suppression of cortisol (Chapter 11). This effect may be partly due to enzyme induction which enhances the metabolism of dexamethasone, but it also alters the circadian rhythm of urinary cortiosteroid excretion and increases the 24-h excretion of cortisol in normal subjects and depressed patients. A possible effect on endogenous opioid systems is suggested by the observation that carbamazepine facilitates opiate and enkephalin-induced motor activity in the mouse, and it has also been observed to decrease cerebrospinal somatostatin concentration in patients with affective disorders.

Behavioural and neurophysiological effects in animals

Carbamazepine has a distinctive profile of effects on animal behaviour: it is active in some antidepressant tests but does not reverse the effects of reserpine. It is also active on some anxiolytic tests, showing a positive action in conflict procedures (Chapter 3). It has little or no dopamine or acetylcholine antagonist activity, but is active in inhibiting aggressive behaviour. Electrophysiological studies show that carbamazepine has marked effects on the limbic system. It inhibits after-discharges elicited by electrical stimulation from a variety of limbic areas. It is the most effective anticonvulsant in stabilizing limbic electrical activity, followed by valproic acid, phenobarbitone, and the benzodiazepines and succinimides.

Clinical effects

Anticonvulsant activity.   Carbamazepine is one of the treatments of choice for temporal lobe epilepsy (Chapter 9) and is also effective in tonic-clonic seizures although it has no effect in absence seizures. The effect is thought to be due to its actions on the limbic system where it possibly enhances GABA activity. It may be relevant that it is often beneficial for the mood and behavioural disturbances associated with complex partial seizures, even if the seizures are not fully controlled.

Paroxysomal pain disorders.   Carbamazepine is of value in trigeminal and other neuralgias. This effect may be partly due to its anticonvulsant activity or to a facilitating effect on endogenous opioid systems. The effect in these chronic pain syndromes is interesting in the light of their relationship to depressive disorders (Chapter 6).

Diabetes insipidus.   Carbamazepine has an antidiuretic effect possibly due to vasopressin agonist activity and has been used in diabetes insipidus.

Affective disorders.   The use of carbamazepine in affective disorders is discussed by Post and Uhde (1983), and Post *et al.* (1985). Carbamazepine is now recognized as an alternative or adjunctive treatment for several types of affective disorder. Antimanic effects have been demonstrated in placebo-controlled trials; carbamazepine is probably as effective as neuroleptics (Chapter 14) and has fewer adverse effects. The onset of action occurs within a few days, and it may be effective in lithium resistant disorders. In addition, carbamazepine appears to be effective as a prophylactic agent in both bipolar and unipolar depression including lithium-resistant cases. It may also have acute antidepressant properties.

Other anticonvulsants, including sodium valproate, clonazepam, phenytoin and acetazolamide are under evaluation for antimanic effects and prophylactic activity in affective disorders.

Adverse effects.   Adverse effects are common with carbamazepine and depend on dosage. They include dizziness and ataxia, clumsiness, drowsiness, slurred speech and diplopia. Less commonly skin rashes, aching or weakness in the limbs, paraesthesiae, water retention and cardiac arrhythmias occur. Teratogenic effects (retardation of fetal head growth) is a risk during pregnancy (Jones *et al.* 1989).

Lithium

Lithium is usually administered as lithium carbonate, and has been shown to have therapeutic actions in mania and depression and in the prophylaxis of affective disorders (reviewed by Tyrer and Shaw 1982, and Bunney and Garland-Bunney 1987).

Pharmacokinetics

Lithium carbonate is almost completely absorbed after oral administration. The lithium ion is initially distributed in the extracellular fluid and then more gradually enters most tissues. The serum elimination half-life varies between 18–20 h in young adults and 36–42 h in the elderly. Elimination of lithium is almost entirely renal. It readily passes into the glomerular filtrate and 70–80 per cent is reabsorbed in the proximal tubules. This reabsorption is competitive with that of sodium, and sodium deficiency or sodium diuresis can increase lithium retention: for this reason diuretics may enhance the toxicity of lithium.

Because of the low therapeutic index of lithium, (therapeutic: toxic serum concentration $= 1:2.5$) it is necessary to monitor serum concentrations to ensure that they are kept within the therapeutic range of approximately 0.6–1.2 mmol/l. There is considerable variation between individuals in both the dosage required and the serum concentration which produces either therapeutic or toxic effects.

Pharmacological actions

The mechanisms of action of lithium are not known. It is a monovalent alkaline metal and its ion competes with sodium, potassium, magnesium, and calcium ions in biological tissues. It can also interact with ammonium groups, including those of the biogenic amines. There have been many investigations of its actions on monoamine and other neurotransmitter systems, but the results are confusing.

Effects on noradrenaline

In isolated tissues, lithium decreases the release of exogenously administered ^{3}H-noradrenaline in response to electrical stimulation. This effect can be prevented by raising the concentration of calcium in the perfusing fluid, suggesting that lithium may interfere with the action of calcium in the stimulation-mediated release of noradrenaline. In man, chronic lithium treatment produces little overall change in the excretion of noradrenaline metabolites, but there is some evidence that it causes down-regulation of α_2-adrenergic receptors, an effect similar to that induced by chronic treatment with tricyclic antidepressants. The mechanisms for these effects of lithium are not known but lithium may compete with calcium and magnesium in various catecholamine transport and release systems. The net effect of lithium administration appears to be a decrease in the amount of noradrenaline available to receptors. Such an effect might possibly be a basis for its actions, at least in mania, while effects on α_2 receptors may be involved in the antidepressant actions.

Effects on dopamine

The effects of lithium on dopaminergic systems are not clear, but inhibition of dopamine synthesis has been demonstrated in rats treated with lithium for 2 weeks. The electrically stimulated, calcium dependent, release of dopamine from nerve terminals is inhibited by lithium. The development of Parkinsonian symptoms in patients maintained on lithium also suggests dopaminergic underactivity (Tyrer 1982) and lithium also appears to prevent the development of dopamine receptor supersensitivity in patients treated with haloperidol (Chapter 14) and may block the euphoriant effects of amphetamine and cocaine. Decreased dopaminergic activity may be relevant to the therapeutic action in mania.

Effects on serotonin

Short-term (1–5 days) administration of lithium to rats increases the high affinity uptake of tryptophan into forebrain synaptosomes. There is an associated increase in serotonin synthesis and turnover. The concentration of 5-HIAA in the forebrain in response to electrical stimulation of the raphe nuclei is increased. The effect of chronic treatment on concentrations of serotonin varies between different parts of the brain: decreased serotonin concentrations have been reported in hypothalamus and brainstem, but increased concentrations and turnover with increased release on electrical stimulation, in the forebrain. Bunney and Garland-Bunney (1987), and Price *et al.* (1990) conclude from a review of human and animal studies that chronic lithium treatment probably enhances serotonergic activity and that this may be important in its antidepressant action. The effect on serotonergic receptors is not clear: animal studies suggest a down-regulation of 5-HT$_2$ receptors in the frontal cortex and of 5-HT$_1$ receptors in the hippocampus.

Effects on other systems

The effects of lithium on other neurotransmitters are not clear. It may decrease the synthesis and release of acetylcholine in the cortex (Friedman 1973), and it appears to increase GABA concentrations in several brain areas. In addition, it appears to inhibit cyclic AMP and phosphoinositol second messenger systems in the brain in both animals and man (Bunney and Garland-Bunney 1987; Drummond 1987), an action which may account for some of its endocrine effects and possibly its antimanic action.

Effects on EEG

In man acute administration of lithium produces a tendency towards synchronization of the EEG. There is slowing of the dominant alpha-frequency with a general increase in amplitude, and an increase in theta, delta, and beta activity. The pattern is similar to that produced by neuroleptics. On chronic administration of lithium to patients with affective disorders, these changes persist. In addition there is an accentuation of any pre-existing paroxysmal abnormalities. Patients with abnormal EEG records prior to treatment are liable to develop neurological and neurotoxic problems during lithium administration (Tyrer and Shopsin 1980).

Effects on sleep

The effects of lithium on sleep are reviewed by Tyrer and Shopsin (1980). In patients with mania or depression, lithium reverses the abnormal sleep pattern. It produces a decrease in REMS, an increase in REM latency, an increase in SWS, and an increase in total sleep. These effects are observed with 24 h of lithium administration and appear to reverse promptly, even after chronic treatment, with no evidence of rebound.

Clinical effects

Lithium in clinically used doses produces no discernible psychotropic effects in normal subjects. However, it has potent effects in a variety of affective disorders reviewed by Tyrer and Shaw (1982) and Bunney and Garland-Bunney (1987).

Effects in mania

Lithium is effective in 60 per cent of patients with acute mania, although the onset of therapeutic effects may be delayed for up to 2 weeks. Several controlled trials have compared lithium with neuroleptics, usually chlorpromazine (Prien *et al*. 1972; Johnson *et al*. 1971). The general conclusion has been that neuroleptics are superior: the symptoms are controlled more rapidly, within days as opposed to 2 weeks, and the adverse effects are less dangerous. However, both neuroleptics and lithium terminate manic episodes within 3 weeks in patients who continue treatment.

Although the neuroleptics are clearly more practical drugs to use initially in the management of acute mania because of their more rapid onset of action, there are some interesting qualitative differences in the response to neuroleptics and lithium (Gerbino *et al*. 1978). The neuroleptics produce an early decrease in motor activity but this effect is accompanied by considerable central nervous system depression. There is no clear early break in the mania, and euphoria and excitement may still be apparent despite the drug effects which, initially at least, appear to allow the patient to be 'quietly manic'. In contrast, the mood change with lithium appears to be much sharper and more specific. Hyperactivity and affect return to normal without sedation, and once normality is achieved it is virtually complete with no accompanying central nervous system depression. These qualitative differences, which are difficult to rate objectively, have suggested that lithium affects some underlying neuronal dysfunction fundamental to mania, while neuroleptics merely override some of the symptoms, chiefly the overactivity.

Effects in depression

Lithium has been investigated as a treatment for depression in several trials in which it has been compared with tricyclic antidepressants or placebo. In mixed groups of depressed patients, it was found to be as effective as imipramine, with a therapeutic effect appearing in the second or third week of treatment. Later studies suggest that lithium is of particular value in patients with bipolar disorders, and when used in combination with other antidepressant drugs.

Prevention of recurrence

Several prolonged placebo controlled trials continued over several months to years have shown that long-term lithium treatment has a significant prophylactic effect in preventing, in attenuating the length or severity, or in reducing the frequency of relapses of affective illness. This effect appears to apply almost equally to recurrences of mania or depression, and to unipolar and bipolar depression. Nevertheless, the relapse rate of affective disorders, even with maintenance drug treatment, is of the order of 30 per cent and debate continues concerning the long-term value of lithium prophylaxis (Coppen *et al.* 1990; Cowen 1988; *Lancet* 1987*a*; Maj *et al.* 1989). There is no clear way of predicting response to the prophylactic effect of lithium and the high incidence of adverse effects limits the use of lithium in some patients.

Other disorders of affect

Lithium has been used in a number of other disorders associated with changes of affect, discussed by Tyrer and Shaw (1982). In milder cases of schizoaffective disorder lithium has a possible therapeutic effect, but it is less effective than neuroleptics in more severe cases. Anti-aggressive actions of lithium have been demonstrated in impulsively aggressive male prisoners, and possibly in aggressive epileptics and mentally subnormal individuals. It has also been used in character disorders with emotional instability, hyperactive children, affective disorders associated with alcoholism, amphetamine abuse, prementrual tension, Kleine–Levin syndrome, and cluster headaches.

Adverse effects

Lithium is a toxic drug and serious adverse effects can occur if serum concentrations are excessive, and may also occasionally result from long-term therapy. Unwanted effects occurring during the first few days of treatment include fine tremor of the hands, gastrointestinal symptoms, thirst, and polyuria. These symptoms can be minimized by starting with small doses which are then gradually increased until therapeutic serum concentrations are attained. Muscle weakness, fatigue, ataxia, and sometimes emotional blunting may also be seen in the first few weeks of treatment. Development of coarse tremor, confusion, spasticity, convulsions, and dehydration are indications of overdose and necessitate withdrawal of drug or adjustment of dosage. Toxic signs usually appear at a concentration of about 1.3 mmol/l. Concentrations of 3–5 mmol/l may be lethal. After 6 weeks or more, further symptoms may appear, including oedema, weight gain due to increased eating or drinking, alteration in taste, and less commonly, signs of hypothyroidism or impaired renal function. The incidence of unwanted effects in patients on long-term treatment is high: in a survey of 237 such patients (Vestergaard *et al.* 1980) only one-tenth had no symptoms attributed to the drug.

Other undesirable effects (Tyrer and Shaw 1982) include toxic effects on the kidney, thyroid and heart, adverse effects in pregnancy and interactions with other drugs.

Electroconvulsive therapy

Electroconvulsive therapy is mentioned briefly here since it remains an important treatment for patients in whom a rapid response is required because of the severity of the depression or the risk of suicide, and for those who have not responded adequately to drugs. It is effective in depressive disorders, as shown by numerous trials in which it has been compared with sham electroconvulsive therapy and antidepressant drugs. It is more effective than drugs in terminating attacks of depression and has a much quicker onset of action, although repeated treatments may be necessary. It is less effective in preventing recurrent episodes but the treatment can be combined with drugs which may potentiate its effects.

The mode of action of electroconvulsive therapy is not clear, but it appears to increase post-synaptic responsiveness to noradrenaline, serotonin and dopamine, possibly by increasing receptor sensitivity. The treatment is sometimes followed by a dramatic switch from a grossly abnormal to an apparently normal clinical state, and Lerer (1987, p. 585) remarks: 'the fact that a series of electrically induced seizures may so effectively alleviate the most severely disturbed mood states is one of the most intriguing phenomena in biological psychiatry'. Possibly such treatment acts like antidepressant drugs to restore a degree of stability at central monoaminergic synapses.

Part V
Schizophrenia

13. Schizophrenia: clinical features and brain mechanisms

Schizophrenia is to many the most fascinating and elusive of medical disorders. The strangeness of its psychiatric manifestations, particularly the thought distortion and the flatness or inappropriateness of affect, seems to set them apart from common experience. Yet, like the affective syndromes (Chapter 11), schizophrenia merges with the normal condition and with other psychiatric states. As in depression and mania, the seat of dysfunction is probably the limbic system and involves many brain systems. The aetiology is probably multiple, but in spite of a plethora of theories, the cellular mechanism remains obscure. However, there is growing evidence that schizophrenia is an organic psychosis associated with structural pathology in the brain.

Clinical features of schizophrenia

Symptoms

'Schizophrenia can only be defined in terms of its symptomatology' (Fairburn 1981, p. 1115). The diagnosis is made on clinical grounds, and depends largely on the presence of some of a variable collection of symptoms and the exclusion of others. Various diagnostic criteria are available (for example DSM-III-R, *American Psychiatric Association* 1980), but the exclusion of organic disease from the diagnosis of schizophrenia has probably hindered the search for common mechanisms underlying the symptomatology.

The symptoms of schizophrenia are vividly described in psychiatric textbooks (for example Mayer-Gross *et al.* 1954; Gelder *et al.* 1983). They are conveniently divided into positive symptoms, which are characteristic of the acute schizophrenic syndrome, and negative symptoms, seen mainly in chronic schizophrenic states, although many patients show a mixed picture.

Positive symptoms

Hallucinations. Auditory hallucinations are among the most common symptoms, occurring in nearly 75 per cent of patients with acute schizo-phrenia (*World Health Organisation* 1979). Of particular importance for diagnosis are hallucinations of voices giving commands, speaking the patient's thoughts out loud, giving a running commentary on his or her actions, or discussing the patient in the third person. Similar auditory hallucinations without insight may occur in temporal lobe epilepsy (Trimble 1981) and this observation suggests temporal lobe involvement in schizophrenia. Visual, tactile, olfactory, gustatory, and somatic hallucinations are less common and also occur in temporal lobe epilepsy. Complex visual hallucinations are a feature of delirious states and can be provoked by psychotomimetic drugs (Chapter 14).

Delusions.   Delusions are characteristic of schizophrenia, particularly delusions concerning the possession of thoughts and delusions of outside control. Delusions of persecution and of grandeur occur in schizophrenia and are also seen in affective disorders and in organic brain disease.

Thought disorder.   Impairment or loss of the normal logical structure of thought is characteristic of schizophrenia, but also may be seen to some degree in affective disorders and dementia. The disorder of logical thought, difficulty in abstract conception, and distortion of language suggests cortical dysfunction particularly affecting the dominant hemisphere.

Disorders of affect.   Several abnormalities of mood are seen in schizophrenia. Flattening and incongruity of affect are characteristic, and lead to social withdrawal. However, considerable intensity of emo-tion which appears to be out of context may sometimes be displayed. Sustained abnormalities of mood, including anxiety, irritability, depres-sion, or elation, also occur. As mentioned in Chapter 11, schizophrenia may merge with depressive and manic syndromes. Disorders of mood in schizophrenia, as in anxiety and the affective disorders, point to dysfunction of limbic arousal and reward/punishment systems controll-ing affect.

Negative symptoms

Chronic schizophrenia is sometimes referred to as the schizophrenic defect state. Patients display no drive or initiative, little emotion, poverty of thought and speech, and are slow in all their actions. There is evidence of cognitive impairment and loss of insight and the patient does not recognize that his symptoms are due to illness (Crow and Johnstone 1980). These symptoms suggest cortical and limbic degenerative changes.

Motor disturbances

Various disorders of motor activity, occur rarely in schizophrenia. These include a catatonic stupor in which the patient is immobile, mute, and unresponsive although fully conscious, but may suddenly undergo a change to uncontrollable motor activity and excitement. Disorders of muscle tone may occur, such as muscle rigidity or flexibilitas cerea, in which the patient can passively be placed into awkward postures which he then maintains for long periods. Stereotyped movements, complex behavioural mannerisms, automatic obedience, and various other complex disorders of movement are occasionally seen. The catatonic syndrome may also occur in a number of other conditions reviewed by Gelenberg (1976): affective disorders; neurological disorders involving the basal ganglia, limbic system, temporal lobes, diencephalon, and frontal lobes; metabolic conditions; and certain drugs (psychotomimetic drugs, amphetamine, phencyclidine, antipsychotic drugs, and others). A common factor appears to be dysfunction in striato-limbic pathways.

Incidence and clinical course

Schizophrenia is less common than the affective disorders. Surveys from 12 countries, using strict diagnostic criteria, show a prevalence of 0.2–0.4 per cent. The peak age of onset is 20–39 years; the age of onset is younger and the frequency slightly greater in males than females. Certain discrete populations have a higher or lower prevalence of schizophrenia than the general average.

The clinical course is variable. Schizophrenia usually presents as an acute syndrome with the sudden emergence of predominantly positive symptoms. Most patients respond to therapy but are liable to relapses of acute illness, even with antipsychotic drug treatment. In one study reported by Crow (1978a), over 70 per cent of schizophrenics treated with placebo relapsed within 12 months and 80 per cent by 2 years. The corresponding figures for antipsychotic drug-treated patients were approximately 33 per cent and 48 per cent.

Some patients with acute schizophrenia progress to a chronic state and develop negative symptoms or disabling degrees of anxiety or depression. Occasionally, negative symptoms appear insidiously without a preceding acute phase. Various follow-up studies reviewed by Gelder et al., (1981) and Tsuang (1982) have shown that about 20 per cent of patients have complete remissions and 30 per cent make a good social readjustment, but the outcome for the remainder is poor. About 25 per cent remain severely disturbed, while up to 10 per cent of schizophrenic patients die by suicide.

Aetiological factors

Genetic factors

There is little doubt that there is a strong genetic basis in schizophrenia although the mode of inheritance is unknown (Murray *et al*. 1985; Kendler 1987). The risk of developing schizophrenia is greatly increased in the relatives of schizophrenics. While the lifetime risk for the general population is less than 1 per cent, the risk for second degree relatives of schizophrenics is 3 per cent, for first degree relatives 10 per cent, and for children with both parents affected 40 per cent. Twin studies show concordance rates of 12–14 per cent for dizygous twins and 45 per cent for monozygous twins, regardless of whether they are reared together or apart. The heritability of schizophrenia is estimated as 60–70 per cent, but the transmitted factor (or factors) appears to be a liability towards certain personality traits or to psychosis (including affective disorders) rather than a specific liability to typical schizophrenia.

Personality

The spectrum concept of schizophrenia (Kretschmer 1936; Reich 1975) proposed that there is continuum between normal personality, a range of personality disorders (schizoid personality, borderline personality, borderline schizophrenia) and schizophrenia itself. These views were developed by Schulsinger (1985) who suggested that the genetically transmitted abnormality is a borderline personality state which carries vulnerability to stress. There has been considerable difficulty in defining borderline states, although analysis of questionnaire data (Spitzer *et al*. 1979) suggested that schizoid personality might be related to schizophrenia. Individuals with this type of personality are lacking in emotional warmth, detached, and may be cold, callous, reclusive, and friendless. However, only a minority of those with schizoid personalities become schizophrenic. Another personality dimension, psychoticism, is related to psychosis and other behavioural abnormalities, and to certain physiological variables also seen in schizophrenia (Eysenck and Eysenck 1976; Venables 1980; 1981).

Psychosocial stresses

Several psychosocial theories of schizophrenia have suggested that the disease arises as a reaction to abnormal relationships within the family, particularly the relationship with the mother. However, it is not clear whether such factors, when they exist, are the cause or result of schizophrenic behaviour. Life stresses may precipitate schizophrenia and the rate of stressful life events is increased in the three months before a schizophrenic breakdown (Brown and Birley 1968); however, this is also true for depressive and anxiety disorders.

Social and environmental factors appear to influence the outcome of schizophrenia. Too little or too much social stimulation can aggravate symptoms in schizophrenics and relapse rates are higher in schizophrenics returning to families with high emotional involvement in the patient's illness than to less emotionally involved families. Stressful life events can also precipitate relapses. The evidence in general indicates that psychosocial factors, although important in schizophrenia, are not specific (Leff 1978; Hirsch 1983).

Neurological diseases

Converging lines of evidence from many sources indicate the presence of structural brain damage of schizophrenia. Typical schizophrenic features are seen in several neurological diseases, particularly of the temporal lobe and diencephalon, such as temporal lobe epilepsy, Huntingdon's chorea, Wilson's disease, brain tumours, head injury, and encephalitis. In addition, as many as two-thirds of schizophrenics without obvious neurological disease show neurological abnormalities, such as defects in stereognosis, balance and proprioception, suggesting impaired integration of proprioceptive and other sensory information (Cox and Ludwig 1979). Similar signs are found in subjects with schizoid personality characteristics (Quitkin *et al.* 1976).

Cerebral atrophy

Early reports of ventricular enlargement (Haug 1962) in schizophrenia have been confirmed by many investigations using computerized tomography (CT) (Johnstone *et al.* 1976; Weinberger *et al.* 1979; Revely *et al.* 1983; Marsden 1976; Crow *et al.* 1980). These and other studies reviewed by Shelton and Weinberger (1987) demonstrate cortical atrophy, with enlarged lateral and third ventricles, widening of cerebral sulci, and cerebellar atrophy in a high proportion (probably over 50 per cent) of schizophrenics. These changes are not due to age, drug treatment or dementia but may be related to negative symptoms, intellectual deterioration and poor response to antipsychotic drugs. The changes may not be specific to schizophrenia: similar though less marked cortical atrophy has been observed in depression (Chapter 11) and could account for an overlap between schizophrenia and affective disorders.

Crow (1980, 1982) suggested that there might be two types of schizophrenia: Type I with positive symptoms, little cognitive impairment, and normal ventricular size; and Type II with negative symptoms and structural brain damage. However, ventricular enlargement may predate the onset of clinical illness; enlarged ventricles have been found in teenage patients during the first episode of acute schizophrenia with positive symptoms (Schulz *et al.* 1983). It seems likely (Roberts 1990) that all schizophrenics have some degree of structural brain abnormality and that the symptoms reflect the degree rather than the kind of lesions. CT studies in patients followed for 5–8 years suggest that the process is static rather than progressive.

Post-mortem examination of the brains of schizophrenic patients confirm the CT findings and show ventricular enlargement, decreased brain weight, and cortical thinning, particularly affecting periventricular, limbic, and diencephalic structures including hippocampus and prefrontal association cortex. Histological changes include neuronal degeneration, cellular disarray and ultrastructural abnormalities. There is little gliosis and no evidence of an active degenerative or inflammatory process or of haemorrhage or infarction. The changes appear to be static and could be the result of a developmental anomaly (Roberts 1990). Roberts and Crow (1987) propose that the brain pathology of schizophrenia is caused by a foetal injury (perinatal, toxic, viral or genetic), occurring in the last trimester before birth during the development of the limbic system, and impairing the development of this system.

The finding of structural brain damage in schizophrenia is clearly of great importance and has led to the exploration factors which might interact with genetic susceptibility to produce a neurodevelopmental disorder, or trigger the onset of psychosis many years later.

Birth injury

One factor which might cause cerebral atrophy and eventually precipitate schizophrenia in predisposed individuals is injury to the brain during birth. There is some evidence that schizophrenics are more likely than controls to have a history of obstetric complications (Schulsinger 1985; Lewis and Murray 1987; Eagles *et al.* 1990) and it is possible that such complications may increase the risk of schizophrenia (Lewis and Murray 1987). The hippocampus is sensitive to anoxia and part of the genetic predisposition to schizophrenia could be a pattern of neuronal migration into the hippocampus which is particularly vulnerable to hypoxic-ischaemic damage (Murray and Lewis 1988). The same pattern may predispose to a schizoid personality, in the absence of perinatal injury. However, not all schizophrenics have a history of birth complications, and such a history, as well as large cerebral ventricles, occurs in non-schizophrenic subjects (Revely *et al.* 1983). Furthermore, Roberts (1990) reports that there is little evidence in the brains of schizophrenics for the type of injury (intra-ventricular haemorrhages and infarcts) which would be expected to arise from birth difficulties. Nevertheless, there appears to have been a reduction in the number of new cases of schizophrenia over the past 20 years, possibly attributable to improvement in perinatal care (Nutt 1990*a*).

Viral infection

Another environmental factor which might cause or precipitate schizophrenia is infection with a virus or virus-like agent. Such agents, including cytomegalovirus (Kaufman *et al.* 1983) and the HIV virus (Thomas 1987) can cause cerebral atrophy and psychotic symptoms, although no virus specifically linked with schizophrenia has yet been identified. Viral infection or expression of latent viral pathogenicity might possibly explain the curious seasonal distribution of schizophrenia: the illness presents most commonly in the early summer and patients who develop schizophrenia are more likely to have been born in the winter than at other times of the year (Crow 1986, 1987). Episodes of mania show a similar seasonal variation.

Crow (1985, 1986, 1987*a*, *b*) has raised some interesting speculations which link a possible virus infection, genetic factors and the evidence (discussed below) that schizophrenia is related to dysfunction of the dominant hemisphere. He suggests that schizophrenia may result from the expression of a retrovirus, retrotransposon, or 'virogene' which has become incorporated in the genome, possibly a gene that determines cerebral dominance. Activation of the agent, which may depend on environmental factors, results in an asymmetric disturbance of cerebral function, especially in the left temporal lobe. A similar aetiology, expressed predominantly in the right temporal lobe, might account for affective disorders and Crow (1986, 1987) further suggests that psychotic illnesses form a genetically-related continuum including unipolar and bipolar affective illness, schizoaffective disorder and the various forms of schizophrenia. Such a continuum could explain the clinical overlap between the psychoses, the occurrence of both affective and schizophrenic disorders in the families of patients with either psychosis, and recent findings of organic pathology in the brain in both schizophrenia and affective disorders. These ideas remain hypothetical but may helpfully direct research towards the genetic and neuropathological features of the psychoses and away from further attempts to circumscribe their symptomatology. Molecular genetic techniques may soon allow the hypothesis to be tested (Gurling 1988; Byerley *et al.* 1988).

Another possibility suggested by Knight (1982) is that schizophrenia is an autoimmune disease in which the positive symptoms are due to the presence of dopamine receptor stimulating autoantibodies and the negative symptoms represent an autoimmune encephalitis-like syndrome in which a viral infection triggers a destructive autoimmune response against certain dopaminergic pathways in the limbic system.

Hemispheric dysfunction

As described in Chapter 8, the normal human brain is functionally asymmetric. The dominant hemisphere, usually the left, is specialized for verbal-linguistic and analytic processing and the non-dominant (right) hemisphere for visuospatial functions and for emotional perception and expression. All these functions are disturbed in schizophrenia, but some evidence (reviewed by Crow 1986 and Robertson and Taylor 1987) suggests that the normal asymmetry is both structurally and functionally disturbed in schizophrenia, and that the dominant hemisphere is predominantly affected.

Structural and neurochemical changes. *Post-mortem* studies of the brains of schizophrenics have shown that ventricular enlargement and cortical atrophy tends to be most marked on the left side (Brown *et al.* 1986). CT studies reveal apparent decreased density of brain tissue in the left hemisphere in schizophrenic patients but not in controls (Largen *et al.* 1983; Revely and Trimble 1987). When schizophrenia occurs in neurological disorders such as temporal lobe epilepsy and brain tumours, the lesion is usually in the left hemisphere (Trimble 1981; Flor-Henry 1976). Furthermore, Reynolds (1983) found that the concentration of dopamine in the left amygdala was greatly increased at necropsy in the brains of schizophrenics compared with controls. Dopamine concentration in the right amygdala was normal, and dopamine and noradrenaline concentrations in the caudate nucleus were normal and symmetrical. This finding is of particular interest in view of the dopamine theory of schizophrenia discussed below. Abnormal distribution of glutamate receptor subtypes (Chapter 8) has also been reported in the brains of schizophrenics, with a decrease in kainate receptor density in the left hippocampus (Kerwin *et al.* 1988).

Blood flow and cerebral metabolism.   Investigations of cerebral blood flow and metabolism suggest regional abnormalities in schizophrenia. Ingvar (1982), using xenon inhalation techniques, reported decreased blood flow in frontal regions in chronic schizophrenics, and this 'hypofrontality' of brain blood flow and metabolism has been confirmed in later studies using positron emission tomography (PET) (Buchsbaum 1987). Reviewing the evidence, Revely and Trimble (1987) conclude that 30–40 per cent of schizophrenics show a hypofrontal pattern of brain activity, which may correlate with the presence of negative symptoms. This finding is of interest in relation to the observations that many of the intellectual and emotional deficits of schizophrenia suggest frontal lobe dysfunction (Posner and Presti 1987), and Weinberger (1988) points out that structural damage in the temporal lobes could disrupt function in the prefrontal cortex. PET studies in schizophrenia also show decreased metabolism in the basal ganglia which is reversed by neuroleptic drugs (Buchsbaum 1987).

Evidence of lateral asymmetry is more variable. Increased blood flow in the left hemisphere has been shown in some studies while others have shown no change or increased activity in the right hemisphere (Revely and Trimble 1987). Gur *et al.* (1983) attempted to correlate regional blood flow changes with different types of cognitive activity and concluded that the normal lateralized patterns of activation for verbal and spatial tasks were disturbed in schizophrenic patients.

Cognitive performance. Gur (1978, 1979*a, b*) and Wexler and Heninger (1979) discussed evidence derived from many psychometric tests that cognitive performance in schizophrenia reflects left hemispheric dysfunction, particularly in the initial processing of verbal information. However, later investigations reported by Robertson and Taylor (1987) indicate that cognitive impairment in schizophrenia is often general and bilateral and largely reflects frontal-temporal dysfunction.

There is also evidence of defective interhemispheric transfer of information in schizophrenics. Green (1978) and Butler (1979) described the results of various tests designed to assess this function. In one such test, the subject learns a tactile discrimination task with one hand and is then required to perform the task with the other hand, necessitating transfer of the information to the opposite hemisphere. Schizophrenics perform poorly on such tasks and manifest impaired ability to transfer information both from right to left and left to right hemispheres. Their performance is similar to that of 'split-brain' (divided hemisphere) monkeys. Green (1978) suggests that some schizophrenic symptoms, both cognitive and emotional may be related to defective interhemispheric communication.

Electroencephalographic studies. EEG changes in schizophrenia are reviewed by Shagass *et al.* (1985), Saletu (1980), Roth (1987), and Gruzelier and Liddiard (1989). On the whole, investigations show generalized abnormalities with some evidence of disturbed lateralization. Recordings from deep electrodes have revealed abnormal spikes and high voltage paroxysmal activity in the septal region, hippocampus, amygdala and fronto-orbital area in some schizophrenics, coinciding with psychiatric episodes and disappearing on remission (Heath and Walker 1985). Surface recordings show increased fast activity, especially in posterior and left parietal regions and there appears to be less intra- and interhemispheric coherence of frequency in schizophrenia than in normal subjects. Patients with negative symptoms who respond poorly to antipsychotic drugs (Type II schizophrenia) show a 'hypofrontal' pattern with increased alpha activity in frontal areas. Cortical evoked potentials are often decreased in magnitude over temporoparietal regions and the P_{300} potential is characteristically decreased or absent. There is some evidence of increased left hemispheric activity in patients with positive symptoms and a predominance of right hemispheric activity in patients with negative symptoms. These changes may reflect alterations both in arousal activity and in central processing mechanisms.

Sleep EEG studies in schizophrenia show reduced total sleeping time and reduced amounts of Stages 2, 3 and 4 sleep. REM sleep is approximately normal in amount, but its distribution may be somewhat altered. There is a disturbance of the normal rhythmicity of the 90-min cycles of REMS, frequent changes of sleep stage, and different sleep patterns from night to night. In general sleep studies indicate instability and increased arousal in schizophrenics. The sleep pattern reverts towards normal in patients who respond to antipsychotics.

Autonomic responses.   Autonomic variables have been assiduously studied in schizophrenia and are reviewed by Venables (1980, 1981). Electrodermal responses have perhaps given the most informative results. These responses are of interest because they appear to be under the major control of influences from the reticular formation and limbic system. In normal subjects, the electrodermal response to an external stimulus, such as a tone, is a momentary increase in skin electrical conductance due to a phasic increase in sweat gland activity. On successive repetitions of the tone, the response becomes smaller, a phenomenon attributed to habituation. This response is altered in schizophrenics: there is a bimodal distribution consisting of 50 per cent of patients who show no skin conductance responsivity and 50 per cent who show hyper-responsivity and a remarkable lack of habituation.

Limbic lesions in monkeys cause similar changes in electrodermal responses. Lesions of the amygdala can cause electrodermal non-responsivity, hypo-responsivity or hyper-responsivity, and bilateral removal of the hippocampus results in failure of habituation. Alterations of electrodermal response in schizophrenia have therefore been interpreted as reflecting involvement of limbic arousal control systems.

Motor laterality.   If schizophrenia reflects altered hemispheric function, it might be associated with alterations in motor laterality (handedness). This proposition appears to be true, although in a complex manner. Flor-Henry (1979) reviewed many studies related to sinistrality and dextrality in schizophrenia. Investigations involving large (over 1200) numbers of schizophrenic patients show an excess of sinistrality compared with controls. Schizophrenics also have a high representation of intermediate states with left/right confusion. Estimates of the incidence of left handedness in schizophrenia vary, but overall about 40–60 per cent of schizophrenics are left-handed compared with 20 per cent of control subjects.

These studies of handedness in schizophrenia are consistent with the other evidence indicating a disturbance of cerebral laterality. However, they give no evidence of whether the excess in sinistrality is a cause or effect of schizophrenia. It is possible that early injury to or maldevelopment of the left side of the brain is one cause of both schizophrenia and sinistrality; equally, there may be a genetic link between handedness and vulnerability to schizophrenia (Crow 1987). It is not clear whether cerebral dominance for other functions shifts with motor laterality in normal subjects. Many normal left-handers have left sided speech representation similar to dextral subjects, while some have a less clear lateralization of speech, with both hemispheres contributing to language processing. The latter condition appears to be the case in some schizophrenics.

Brain mechanisms in schizophrenia

Brain systems in schizophrenia

It is clear from the clinical and physiological evidence described above that brain systems regulating arousal, affect, and cognition are all disturbed in schizophrenia. Perception of external stimuli, central processing of information, motivation, affective state, muscle tone, tonic and phasic central and autonomic arousal, and other diverse functions may all be distorted simultaneously and to varying degrees. Thus, it is not possible to classify the syndrome as a primary disorder of any one functional system. Probably no clinical condition demonstrates more clearly that the various systems modulating behaviour cannot be operationally isolated. Indeed, the salient feature of schizophrenia appears to be a fault in the interrelationships between different functional systems; it seems to reflect a breakdown of communications both within the brain, and between the brain and the outside world.

There is abundant evidence incriminating the limbic system and its prefrontal connections, especially in the left hemisphere as the primary site of dysfunction. It is in this intercourse of phylogenetically ancient and modern neural pathways that the main functional systems determining behaviour — arousal, reward and punishment, learning, memory and cognition — are normally integrated to produce meaningful and goal-directed responses, and it is here too, it seems, that there is a failure of integration in schizophrenia.

Within the limbic system, it is not at present possible to delineate precisely the pathways concerned, and in any case these may not be identical in all schizophrenics. Pharmacological evidence, discussed below, suggests the prime importance of dysfunction in dopaminergic mesolimbic, mesocortical, and corticostriatal pathways but other neurotransmitter systems are also involved. As to the nature and direction of the limbic perturbation in schizophrenia, the answers are even less clear. It seems likely that the condition reflects a whole spectrum of neural states ranging from markedly increased to markedly reduced activity in the affected pathways. Symptoms such as hallucinations and certain types of thought disorder suggest an excess of uncontrolled cerebral activity, while symptoms such as anhedonia, loss of drive, poverty of thought and speech suggest loss of function in some systems. Neuropathological examination shows widespread, sometimes asymmetric but usually bilateral structural damage. Thus both structure and function are disorganized and the clinical picture presumably depends on the degree and distribution of neuronal loss.

Neurotransmitters in schizophrenia

Dopamine

Of the various biochemical theories of schizophrenia, those involving dopamine are supported by the most abundant evidence. The 'classical' dopamine theory, which suggested that schizophrenia results from absolute or relative dopaminergic overactivity at critical brain sites, has a history similar to that of the various monoamine theories of depression (Chapter 11). It stemmed from the observation that antipsychotic drugs, which are effective in controlling some schizophrenic symptoms, have in common a dopamine receptor blocking action, and that dopamine receptor agonists and drugs which release dopamine can precipitate schizoid psychotic reactions, and greatly aggravate the symptoms of existing schizophrenia. Subsequent advances in the understanding of the distribution and physiology of dopamine receptors have, if anything, strengthened the idea that dopaminergic dysfunction may account for at least some of the clinical features of schizophrenia.

Antipsychotic drugs. Antipsychotic drugs (Chapter 14) do not cure schizophrenia, but can greatly improve many of the symptoms and it is generally accepted they affect fundamental features including thought disorder. These drugs are chemically heterogeneous and have actions on many neurotransmitter systems, but their antagonist actions at certain dopamine receptors (Table 13.1) correlate with their clinical potency. Furthermore, in the case of flupenthixol and butaclamol, which exist in two isomeric forms, only one isomer (alpha-flupenthixol and (+)-butaclamol) has antipsychotic potency and only this isomer has dopamine blocking activity. Hence, it seems that the antipsychotic effects result from dopamine receptor blockade and this in turn suggests the possibility of dopaminergic overactivity in schizophrenia.

Dopaminergic drugs. Amphetamine, which releases dopamine and noradrenaline from monoaminergic nerve terminals, and probably also has some receptor agonist activity, can in normal subjects precipitate a psychotic state which is indistinguishable from acute paranoid schizophrenia (Chapter 4). In schizophrenics, low doses of amphetamine

Table 13.1 Dopamine receptors in the brain

Receptors*	D_1	D_2
Agonists	SKF 38393 (s) bromocriptine (m) dopamine (m)	quinpirole (s) bromocriptine (n) apomorphine (n)
Antagonists	SCH 23390 (s) bromocriptine (partial) phenothiazines	sulpiride (s) clozapine phenothiazines butyrophenones
Location	post-synaptic striatum, frontal cortex, amygdala nucleus accumbens	pre- and post-synaptic striatum limbic areas pituitary, retina
Effector pathways	cAMP ↑	cAMP ↓ or O open K^+ channels close Ca^{2+} channels

*Subtypes of both D_1 and D_2 receptors with different pharmacological profiles may exist, and a D_3 receptor and a D_4 receptor have recently been indentified (see text, p. 294).
(s), selective agonist/antagonist; (m), micromolar concentrations; (n), nanomolar concentrations.
SCH 23390: 7-chloro-2,3,4,5-tetrahydro-3-methyl-5-phenyl-1H-3-benzapine-7-d
SKF 38393: 2,3,4,5-tetrahydro-7,8-dihydroxy-1-phenyl-1H-3-benzapine HCl
References: *Trends in Pharmacological Sciences* (1991); Andersen *et al.* (1990); Creese (1987); Kebabian and Calne (1979); Offermeier and Van Rooyen (1982); Sokoloff *et al.* (1990).

can exacerbate schizophrenic symptoms, and the degree to which this effect occurs correlates with the degree of the patient's response to antipsychotic drugs. L-dopa, which increases dopamine synthesis, and bromocriptine, a dopamine receptor agonist, can similarly precipitate psychotic reactions and aggravate schizophrenic symptoms. The effects are reversed by small doses of neuroleptics. These observations indicate that schizophrenic symptoms can be caused by activation of dopamine receptors.

Dopamine release. There is no evidence of increased dopamine release or turnover in schizophrenia. Concentrations of dopamine metabolites in cerebrospinal fluid and in post-mortem brain tissue are normal or decreased, and prolactin secretion, which is under inhibitory dopaminergic control, is also normal. However, Reynolds (1983) found increased concentrations of dopamine in the left amygdala but not elsewhere in post-mortem brains of schizophrenic patients. Such a localized and asymmetric increase seems unlikely to be due to medication and its significance is unclear. Meanwhile attention has been directed to the possibility that the sensitivity of dopamine receptors is altered in schizophrenia.

Dopamine receptors. Dopamine receptors, however, like those for other neurotransmitters, are heterogenous, and there has been much discussion over which of them might be involved in schizophrenia. The characterization of dopamine receptors is far from complete; their classification and properties continue to be discussed by many authors (for example, Beart 1982; Creese 1987; Andersen *et al.* 1990; Sokoloff *et al.* 1990).

At present it seems likely that there are two main types of central dopamine receptors, D_1 and D_2 (Table 13.1), although there are probably distinct subtypes of each (Andersen *et al.* 1990). D_1 receptors are situated post-synaptically in the striatum, frontal cortex, amygdala and nucleus accumbens. Some of them are linked to the enzyme adenylate cyclase. Their actions are not clear but appear to include inhibition of cell firing in the nucleus accumbens (Creese 1987). D_2 receptors are situated both pre- and post-synaptically in the striatum, limbic areas, pituitary and retina. Some inhibit adenylate cyclase activity while others are not linked to this enzyme. Pre-synaptic D_2 receptors appear to act as autoreceptors which inhibit dopamine synthesis and release. A third type of dopamine receptor, the D_3 receptor, has recently been identified (Sokoloff *et al.* 1990). This has some pharmacological similarities with the D_2 receptor and binds to most antipsychotic drugs, but appears to be localized in limbic and cortical areas of the brain. There may also be a D_4 receptor, but its functions are even less clear. The various dopamine receptors are probably functionally interactive (Creese 1987; Clarke and White 1988; Waddington 1986, 1989) and may also be co-operatively linked with serotonergic and noradrenergic receptors (Cools 1982). Together, dopamine receptors are involved in a diversity of functions, including motor control, hypothalamic and pituitary secretion, emesis, motivation and reward (Chapter 5) and probably other psychological activities. The question of whether there are alterations in dopamine receptors in schizophrenia is discussed below.

Dopaminergic pathways. Dopaminergic pathways have a widespread distribution and can be divided into four separate systems (Fig. 13.1). The *nigrostriatal system* arises from cell bodies in the substantia nigra (cell groups $A_{8,9}$) and projects to the corpus striatum. The fact that degeneration of these dopaminergic cell bodies occurs in Parkinson's disease indicates that this system is concerned with the control of muscle tone and movement. In addition, some dopaminergic cells from cell group A_9 project to the cingulate cortex. Exactly how the receptor subtypes are involved in motor control is not known. Parkinsonism occurs as an adverse effect of neuroleptic drugs which antagonize both D_1 and D_2 receptors (phenothiazines) and also with those which are relatively selective D_2 receptor antagonists (butyrophenones). However, there is

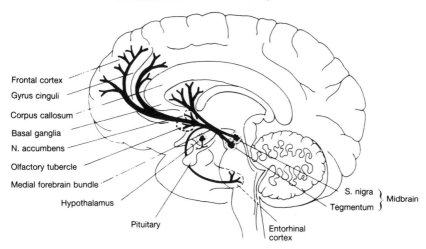

Fig. 13.1   Dopaminergic pathways in the brain.

Frontal cortex
Gyrus cinguli
Corpus callosum
Basal ganglia
N. accumbens
Olfactory tubercle
Medial forebrain bundle
Hypothalamus
Pituitary
S. nigra } Midbrain
Tegmentum }
Entorhinal cortex

no correlation between the propensity of neuroleptic drugs to cause Parkinsonism and their antipsychotic action.

The *tuberoinfundibular* pathway arises from cells in the median eminence which project within the hypothalamus. This system exerts an inhibitory control on the pituitary release of prolactin and other hormones (Chapter 11). The receptors involved are D_2 receptors, but their activity in this area does not appear to be related to psychiatric symptoms.

The *chemoreceptor trigger* zone of the medullary vomiting centre is under dopaminergic control. The receptors involved are probably D_2 receptors since agonists (apomorphine and bromocriptine) cause vomiting while D_2 antagonists including neuroleptics have antiemetic effects. The actions of neuroleptic drugs at this site have no relation to their antipsychotic efficacy.

The *mesolimbic pathway* arises from cell group A_{10} in the ventral tegmental area and projects via the median forebrain bundle to many limbic structures including the nucleus accumbens, amygdala, and in the *mesocortical pathways* to the frontal entorhinal cortex. There are many reasons for suspecting that this system is the seat of dysfunction in schizophrenia. As already discussed, evidence from physiological and clinical studies points towards dysfunction of the limbic system and its frontal lobe connections. Limbic structures and prefrontal cortex contain both D_1 and D_2 receptors. The clinical potency of several different types of antipsychotic drugs was shown to correlate very closely with their D_2 receptor blocking activity, suggesting that D_2 receptor sensitivity might be increased in schizophrenia. Accordingly, there has been much interest in investigating brain dopamine receptor density in this condition.

Dopamine receptor density in schizophrenia.   There have been many post-mortem studies of receptor binding in the brains of schizophrenics (Owen *et al.* 1981; Lee and Seeman 1980; MacKay *et al.* 1980; Cross *et al.* 1981; Reynolds *et al.* 1980). All agree that there is no abnormality in the density of D_1 receptors, but most have shown an increase in D_2 receptor density compared with controls. However, it is likely that much of this increase is the result of antipsychotic medication. As discussed in Chapter 6, chronic exposure to receptor antagonists leads to increases in the density of the antagonised receptors, and the D_2 antagonist activity of many antipsychotic drugs (Chapter 14) is followed by increased D_2 receptor density.

More recently dopamine receptors in schizophrenic patients have been studied by brain imaging techniques. A positron emission tomography (PET) study reported by Owen and Crow (1987) showed a small but significant increase of D_2 receptor binding in the striatum of neuroleptic-free schizophrenic patients. These authors thought that such a modest increase could not be the primary disturbance in schizophrenia. In a later PET scan study Sedvall (1990) showed no consistent alterations in D_2 receptor density or affinity in the basal ganglia of drug-naïve schizophrenic patients. However, they clearly showed that a variety of chemically different antipsychotic drugs all occupied D_2 receptors. This occupancy appeared earlier than the antipsychotic effect and was also present in patients who did not respond to treatment. Other PET studies are reported by Sedvall (1990); although the question is still not definitely resolved, it seems unlikely that increased D_2 receptor density or sensitivity is a universal feature of schizophrenia.

Drawbacks of dopamine theory.   Thus the once promising dopamine theory of schizophrenia seems to slip through the fingers. Despite the fact that some of the symptoms respond to dopamine receptor antagonists (Chapter 14), there is no convincing evidence of dopaminergic overactivity or receptor hypersensitivity in schizophrenia. There are also other drawbacks of the theory. One of these is that antipsychotic drugs do not alleviate all schizophrenic symptoms. Significant drug effects are apparent only for positive symptoms, such as hallucinations, delusions, and thought disorder; there is less effect on negative symptoms (Johnstone *et al.* 1978 although these are not always irreversible (Angst *et al.* 1989)). Even in patients who respond to drugs, the response is often only partial, and in many instances the drugs appear to control rather than to normalize the psychiatric state. These findings indicate that increased dopamine receptor activation, if present in schizophrenia, is responsible only for some symptoms seen most commonly in the acute forms of the condition. In chronic schizophrenia, dopaminergic overactivity may not be involved at all. Indeed, it has been suggested that negative symptoms may result from dopaminergic underactivity and that they may respond to dopaminergic agonists (Alpert and Friedhof 1980; Chouinard and Jones 1978). Yet positive and negative symptoms may co-exist in both acute and chronic schizophrenia. It is clear that the dopamine hypothesis cannot explain all the phenomena of schizophrenia. A further drawback of the classical dopamine theory is that, like the antidepressants (Chapter 11), the antipsychotic drugs are associated with a therapeutic time-lag. Although some symptoms may respond in a few days (Angst *et al.* 1989), the full antipsychotic effects do not become manifest for some weeks, although the D_2 receptor antagonism occurs quickly. The discrepancy does not appear to be due to pharmacokinetic factors and suggests that immediate D_2 receptor antagonism is not directly responsible for antipsychotic effects, which may result from some secondary process with a longer time course. Two such possibilities have been considered: the slow induction of depolarization block of dopamine neurones by neuroleptics, and homeostatic receptor changes involving dopamine autoreceptors.

Depolarization block.   Electrophysiological studies in animals (Bunney 1984) indicate that in the neurones of cell group A_{10} (the origin of the mesolimbic pathway) antipsychotic drugs produce a slowly developing depolarization block which has a much greater effect in reducing dopaminergic transmission than the initial dopamine receptor antagonism. The development of this state requires chronic drug administration and occurs over approximately the same time course as the therapeutic delay. Bunney (1984) suggests that the therapeutic effects coincide with this delayed and potent blocking action which affects both pre-synaptic and post-synaptic neuronal sites. It is of interest that with antipsychotic drugs which produce fewer extrapyramidal effects (clozapine, sulpiride, Chapter 14), this depolarization block is limited to A_{10} cells, while the other neuroleptics produce depolarization block of A_9 cells in addition.

Dopamine autoreceptors.   The release of dopamine at synapses (and also its synthesis and release) appears to be partly controlled by complex feedback loops involving acetylcholine, GABA and glutamate (described below) and partly by dopamine autoreceptors. The latter are located on neuronal cell bodies, dendrites, and nerve terminals and are present in the nigrostriatal and mesolimbic pathways. Dopamine autoreceptors are more sensitive than postsynaptic receptors to dopaminergic agonists, and their stimulation decreases synaptic dopamine release and hence dopaminergic activity. Meltzer (1980) reported that low doses of dopamine agonists (apomorphine and bromocriptine) had 'paradoxical' sedative actions in normal subjects and also transiently improved psychotic symptoms in schizophrenia. Some but not all studies reviewed by Losonczy et al. (1987) have confirmed their observations, but it is difficult to obtain a dose of apomorphine which stimulates dopamine autoreceptors without also stimulating post-synaptic receptors. Nevertheless these findings raise the possibility that specific dopamine autoreceptor agonists might have a therapeutic potential in schizophrenia. Such substances are under investigation (Chapter 14).

It is possible that the delayed therapeutic effects of antipsychotic agents are due to the development of autoreceptor hypersensitivity following chronic administration. There is evidence that neuroleptics have antagonist actions at autoreceptors, although these are less marked than at post-synaptic sites, but it is not clear whether autoreceptor blocking correlates with antipsychotic potency, nor to what degree autoreceptor hypersensitivity develops. However, as has been proposed for affective disorders (Chapter 11), some schizophrenic symptoms could reflect instability of synaptic control mechanisms. Dopamine autoreceptors are normally most active in inhibiting dopamine release when impulse traffic is high (Meltzer 1980), and presumably their activity under these conditions prevents excessive stimulation of post-synaptic dopamine receptors. Neuronal damage causing subsensitivity of autoreceptors might render the subject more vulnerable to extremes of dopaminergic hyperactivity. However, dopamine release at synapses is also influenced by other neurotransmitter systems, any of which could be involved in schizophrenia.

GABA, acetylcholine and glutamate

The release of dopamine from nerve terminals in some parts of the brain is also modulated through a complex of neuronal circuits involving GABA, acetylcholine and glutamate. The exact connections involved in this interplay are not known but are outlined diagrammatically in Fig. 13.2. Such feedback loops are thought to exert a major inhibitory influence on the firing rate of dopaminergic neurones in the ventral tegmentum and substantia nigra, and it has been suggested that hypofunction in one or more of these systems might be important in schizophrenia.

Investigations of GABA activity in schizophrenia have shown no consistent abnormalities, and treatment with $GABA_A$ and $GABA_B$ agonists has on the whole been unsuccessful (Losonczy et al. 1987; Van Kammen and Gelernter 1987b). Similarly, cholinergic dysfunction does not appear to be primarily involved in schizophrenia. Although many neuroleptics have anticholinergic effects, there is no relation between these and antipsychotic potency. However, there are some indications that glutamate

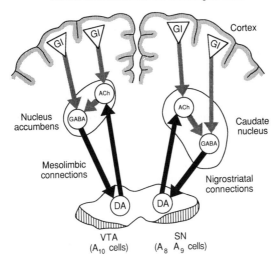

Fig. 13.2 Diagram of some central feedback mechanisms controlling dopamine (DA) release in limbic and striatal areas. Ach, acetylcholine; Gl, glutamate; VTA, ventral tegmental area; SN, substantia nigra; dark arrows, inhibitory pathways; stippled arrows, excitatory pathways. A deficit of acetylcholine, GABA or glutamate would tend to increase dopaminergic tone. (However, the neuronal circuitry may differ between striatal and limbic areas; for example, anti-cholinergic drugs decrease the acute extrapyramidal effects of neuroleptic drugs without apparently diminishing their antipsychotic effects.) References: Stevens (1979); Carlsson and Carlsson (1990); Watchel and Turski (1990).

transmission might be deficient in schizophrenia. Alterations in glutamate receptor binding have been found *post mortem* in the frontal cortex, hippocampus and putamen in brains of schizophrenic patients (Kerwin *et al.* 1988, and others cited by Carlsson and Carlsson 1990). These abnormalities may be secondary to cortical atrophy but may nevertheless reflect a critical disturbance in brain function since the major glutamatergic pathways originate in the cerebral cortex (Carlsson and Carlsson 1990). Secondly, the drugs phencyclidine and ketamine (Chapter 7) are potent psychotomimetics which can produce both positive and negative schizophrenic symptoms. These drugs antagonize glutamate NMDA receptors via an interaction with phencyclidine/sigma opioid receptors (Fig. 8.2). A synthetic NMDA receptor antagonist, MK-801, has amphetamine-like actions in animals and stimulates catecholamine neurones. It is not clear whether the psychotomimetic effects of these drugs are due to NMDA receptor antagonism, but if so there might be a therapeutic role for glutamate agonist drugs in schizophrenia (Watchel and Turski 1990).

Noradrenaline

Noradrenergic activity in schizophrenia has been vigorously investigated. Stein *et al.* (1977) and Hartman (1976) proposed that noradrenergic underactivity might account for anhedonia and other features of chronic schizophrenia, while others (for example Lake *et al.* 1980) produced evidence suggesting increased activity. Drugs with anti-adrenergic effects (propranolol and clonidine) have been tried with mixed success. It now seems likely that noradrenergic systems can be over- or underactive in schizophrenia and that the disturbances reflect different subgroups or states but are not specific for schizophrenia (van Kammen and Gelernter 1987*a*).

Serotonin

The possible involvement of serotonin in schizophrenia has also attracted attention. Alterations in serotonin metabolism and receptor binding have been reported (van Kammen and Gelertner 1987*b*). The direction of changes bears some relation to clinical type and to degree of cortical atrophy but does not appear to reflect a fundamental aspect of schizophrenia. Theories that a metabolic defect in schizophrenia might lead to the formation of endogenous psychotomimetic substances related to serotonin and other monoamines (Smythies 1984) have not been generally substantiated. However, increased understanding of serotonergic receptor subtypes (Chapter 3, Table 3.1) has rekindled interest in this area, and present evidence suggests that increased serotonergic activity may at least contribute to some schizophrenic symptoms.

Serotonergic systems are widely distributed in cortical and limbic brain areas including the amygdala and nucleus accumbens (Fig. 2.7) and are involved in sensory perception and many aspects of behaviour. Many hallucinogenic drugs, including both indoleamines such as LSD (Chapter 14) and phenylethylamines, are agonists at $5\text{-}HT_2$ receptors, and this action is thought to be the basis of their psychotomimetic effects (Aghajanian *et al.* 1987; Chapter 14). Antagonists at $5\text{-}HT_2$ receptors (for example ritanserin) have antipsychotic properties and antipsychotic drugs of several types bind preferentially at serotonergic binding sites in the human auditory cortex (Andorn *et al.* 1989). These authors suggest that serotonergic activity is involved in the generation of auditory hallucinations. Serotonin $5\text{-}HT_3$ receptors appear to interact with dopaminergic systems, and $5\text{-}HT_3$ receptor antagonists (for example ondansetron) inhibit the excitatory effects in animals of amphetamine and dopamine infusion into the nucleus accumbens and amygdala (Tricklebank 1989). These drugs also have antipsychotic effects. Thus it seems possible that a disturbance in serotonin systems may contribute to the effects of generalized neurotransmitter disruption in causing schizophrenic symptoms. The observations that 5-HT$_2$ and 5-HT$_3$ receptor antagonists have antipsychotic properties opens new therapeutic prospects.

Opioids and other endogenous polypeptides

There are many reasons for suspecting that endogenous opioids are somehow involved in schizophrenia. Enkephalins and other opioids and non-opioid peptides coexist in monoaminergic neurones and are co-released with dopamine and noradrenaline in limbic areas, including the ventral tegmental area and the locus coeruleus (Lundberg and Hokfelt 1983). Opioid receptors are present on dopaminergic nerve terminals in the corpus striatum and mesolimbic regions (Reisine *et al.* 1980). Endogenous opioids have been shown to stimulate dopaminergic activity in the mesolimbic system (Koob and Bloom 1983). Such opioid-dopamine interactions provide a possible interface by which opioid systems could affect activity in pathways which appear to be involved in schizophrenia.

Large doses of opiate narcotics administered systematically, and intracisternally injected enkephalin and β-endorphin, produce in animals a naloxone reversible state of immobilization and generalized muscular rigidity. This state is accompanied by seizure discharges in the limbic system (Smith and Copolov 1979) and bears a certain resemblance to the catatonic syndrome seen in some forms of schizophrenia, an observation which led to the suggestion that schizophrenia might be associated with excessive endogenous opioid activity in the brain. However, the postural rigidity also has a similarity to a cataleptic state induced by high doses of neuroleptics; this interpretation led to the suggestion that schizophrenia might be associated with a deficiency of endogenous opioids.

Opioids. The evidence relating to these theories is discussed by Nemeroff *et al.* (1987). Information is sparse, although there is a suggestion that opioid activity may be increased in acute but decreased in chronic schizophrenia. However, neither opioid antagonists (naloxone, naltrexone) nor opioid agonists (morphine, methadone, β-endorphin, synthetic enkephalin analogues) have proved to be generally effective in schizophrenia.

Non-opioid peptides. Although neither opioid excess nor deficiency has been convincingly demonstrated in schizophrenia, some data has emerged concerning the possible involvement of a number of non-opioid peptides (Nemeroff *et al.* 1987; Owen and Crow 1987). Many of these peptides are co-secreted by dopaminergic neurones and some inhibit dopamine release. Reduced concentrations of cholecystokinin, somatostatin, substance P, thyrotrophin-releasing hormone, and neurotensin, and in some studies alterations in vasoactive intestinal peptide, have been found *post mortem* in limbic areas of the brains of schizophrenics. Clinical trials of the various peptides have, however, been inconclusive.

Other biochemical theories

Many other hypotheses of schizophrenia have been advanced. The condition has been linked *inter alia* with zinc deficiency, folate deficiency, gluten sensitivity, hyperallergy, and pineal gland dysfunction. Some of these ideas have been synthesized by Horrobin (1979) who proposed an underlying metabolic error leading to a deficiency of prostaglandins of the I series. At present no strong evidence for any of these theories has appeared and the numerous theories no doubt reflect the presence of many non-specific factors in schizophrenia and the probable heterogeneity of its causes. If schizophrenia is a neurodevelopmental abnormality, the factors which trigger the onset and progression of the clinical condition remain obscure. At present the strongest biochemical and pharmacological evidence suggests a critical involvement of dopaminergic mesocortical pathways. However, a chaotic disruption of many interacting pathways, involving multiple neurotransmitters and modulators, may mirror the structural disarray noted in histopathological studies. An initial functionally hyperactive phase, partially responding to antipsychotic medication, may be followed by a phase of permanent deficit which is relatively resistant to pharmacological manipulation. The actions of antipsychotic and psychotomimetic drugs, discussed in the next chapter, provide further evidence on this question.

14. Antipsychotic and psychotomimetic drugs

Antipsychotic drugs

The antipsychotic drugs are a chemically heterogenous group with the property of controlling certain psychotic symptoms in man. The earlier drugs, reserpine and chlorpromazine, were described by Delay and Deniker (1952) as neuroleptics, a term which differentiated their effects from those of classical central nervous system depressants. The neuroleptic syndrome consisted of suppression of spontaneous movements, disinterest in the environment, lack of emotional response, but little change in the level of consciousness. At the same time, neurological effects resembling Parkinsonism were described in the early reports, and for a while it was thought that these effects were inevitably connected with the antipsychotic effects. Some of the newer drugs, however, are relatively free of extrapyramidal effects and the term antipsychotic applies better than the term neuroleptic to the whole range of drugs.

Classification

The pharmacological profiles of the antipsychotic agents have many similarities which, as discussed below, depend on their ability to antagonize dopamine receptors in the brain. There are, however, considerable differences in chemical structure, potency and liability to produce extrapyramidal and other effects (Table 14.1). The 'classical' antipsychotics include most of the phenothiazines, butyrophenones and thioxanthines. Thioridazine (a phenothiazine), sulpiride and clozapine are less likely to produce extrapyramidal effects and are sometimes classed as atypical antipsychotic agents.

Pharmacokinetics

The pharmacokinetics of the antipsychotic drugs have not been fully worked out because of difficulties in measurement and the multiplicity of metabolites. In general, the drugs tend to be erratically absorbed, are highly lipid soluble, and are concentrated in the brain. In blood, they are highly protein bound and have long elimination half-lives. They are extensively metabolized in the liver to form several metabolites, some of

Table 14.1   Some antipsychotic drugs

Drugs and chemical groups	Incidence of effects at antipsychotic dosage[1]			
	Extrapyramidal effects	Antiemetic effects	Sedative effects	Hypotensive effects
Phenothiazines				
Aliphatic side-chain (e.g. chlorpromazine)	+ +	+ +	+ + +	+ +
Piperidine side-chain (e.g. thioridazine)	+	+	+ +	+ +
Piperazine side-chain (e.g. perphenazine)	+ + +	+ + +	+ +	+
Butyrophenones (e.g. haloperidol)	+ + +	+ + +	+ +	+
Thioxanthines (e.g. flupenthixol)	+ +	+ +	+ +	+ +
Diphenylbutylpiperazines (e.g. pimozide)	+ +	+	+	+
Dibenzodiazepine (e.g. clozapine)	+	+	+ +	+
Substituted benzamide (e.g. sulpiride)	+	+	+	0

[1] Incidence of effects: +, low; + +, moderate; + + +, high.
References: Rogers *et al.* (1981); Baldessarini (1985).

which may be pharmacologically active. Steady state plasma concentration varies at least ten-fold between individuals on the same dose.

Steady-state plasma concentration and therapeutic effect

The problems of relating steady state plasma concentration of antipsychotic drugs to their therapeutic effects in schizophrenia have been discussed by Grahame-Smith and Orr (1978). One of the problems is the heterogeneity of the schizophrenic syndrome. Some patients will not respond to drugs whatever the plasma concentration; others may improve irrespective of medication. There may nevertheless be a group of patients in whom clinical response is related to plasma drug concentrations and pharmacodynamic drug effects. Yet within the group, some symptoms may respond to drugs but not others, and the improvement may be related to the formation of active metabolites rather than to the effects of the parent drug. In general it appears that the best response to antipsychotic drugs occurs in patients with acute schizophrenic episodes and positive symptoms. In these patients there is probably an optimal therapeutic range of antipsychotic drug concentration.

Depot preparations

Compliance with oral medication is particularly low in schizophrenia; the absorption of most oral preparations is erratic; and in many cases the requirement for medication is indefinite. For these reasons, depot preparations offer considerable advantages for maintenance therapy. These preparations consist of fatty acid esters of the drugs in an oily solution. When injected intramuscularly the duration of action is 2–4 weeks. Long acting depot neuroleptics have proved successful in preventing relapses of schizophrenia in many trials reviewed by Kane and Lieberman (1987). They can also be used in acutely disturbed patients, but are unsuitable for initiation of therapy.

Biochemical actions

Dopamine receptor antagonism

The antipsychotic drugs exert a wide range of pharmacological effects which differ between drug groups (Fig. 14.1), but an action common to them all is antagonism of dopamine receptors in the brain. It is this action which appears to be related to their therapeutic effects in schizophrenia.

Acute effects. The drugs selectively increase the rate of release and turnover of dopamine in the animal brain, and increase concentrations of dopamine metabolites have also been demonstrated in the cerebrospinal fluid. This increase in dopamine turnover has been interpreted as the consequence of increased firing rates of dopaminergic neurones responding homeostatically to receptor blockade through cholinergic and GABAergic feedback loops (Fig. 13.2). Direct neurophysiological recordings of the activity of dopaminergic neurones in cell groups A_9 and A_{10} have shown an increase in firing rate after acute administration of drugs which have antipsychotic effects but not after administration of chemical analogues without antipsychotic potency (Bunney 1984).

Secondly, antipsychotic drugs antagonize the physiological and behavioural effects of drugs which directly or indirectly stimulate dopamine receptors (amphetamine, apomorphine), an effect of predictive value in screening for new antischizophrenic drugs. The increased release of prolactin and the extrapyramidal effects exerted by most antipsychotic drugs have likewise been shown to be due to dopamine receptor antagonism.

Biochemical studies in isolated tissues also demonstrate antagonism of central dopamine receptors. Some antipsychotic agents inhibit the dopamine-stimulated formation of cyclic AMP in homogenates of dopamine-rich brain areas. This effect is due to antagonism of

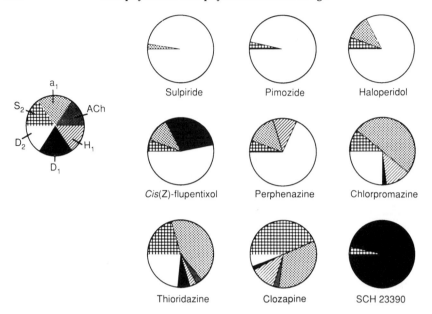

Fig. 14.1 Receptor affinity profiles for various antipsychotic drugs. Receptors: D_1, D_2, dopamine; S_2, serotonin, 5-HT_2; a_1, α-adrenergic; ACh, cholinergic; H_1 histamine. Adapted with permission from Tamminga and Gerlach (1987).

dopamine (D_1) receptors which are coupled to adenylate cyclase (Chapter 13). For many phenothiazines and thioxanthines the potency of this effect correlates with clinical potency in schizophrenia. Of particular importance was the finding that only the alpha isomer of flupenthixol and only the ($+$) isomer of butaclamol have dopamine antagonist activity, and only these isomers have antipsychotic effects. Some drugs with antipsychotic pharmacological profiles in animals, such as the compound SCH 23390, are highly selective D_1 antagonists (Fig. 14.1). Some of the drugs may also bind to a D_1 receptor subtype which is not linked to adenylate cyclase (Lundberg *et al.* 1989).

However, the butyrophenones and benzamides, which are clinically potent, have only weak D_1 receptor antagonist activity. These drugs, as well as other antipsychotics (including those with D_1 antagonist properties) also antagonize D_2 receptors, and the rank order of potency of most antipsychotic drugs in antagonizing D_2 receptors correlates very closely with their clinical potency in schizophrenia. In particular, the clinically effective agents pimozide and sulpiride almost exclusively antagonize D_2 receptors (Taminga and Gerlach 1987). As discussed in Chapter 13, these findings suggested that antipsychotic action depends on D_2 receptor antagonism and originally raised the possibility that schizophrenia is associated with increased D_2 receptor sensitivity.

This idea seemed to be supported by later positron emission tomography (PET) studies which showed that treatment of schizophrenic patients with 10 chemically distinct classical antipsychotics resulted in a 65–89 per cent occupancy of brain D_2 receptors, while no D_1 receptor occupancy was found with sulpiride and perphenazine (Farde *et al.* 1989).

However, the question of whether D_1 or D_2 receptor blockade is more important in the control of schizophrenia is still under discussion (Waddington 1986, 1989; Clark and White 1988); there is evidence that both sites are important for the atypical agent clozapine. As mentioned in Chapter 13, D_1 and D_2 receptors may be interactive, and antipsychotic drugs also affect D_3 receptors (Sokoloff *et al.* 1990), and other receptors discussed below, all of which modulate dopaminergic function. Since many neurotransmitter systems are probably involved in schizophrenia (Chapter 13), the fact that effective antipsychotic drugs have multiple sites of action is perhaps not surprising.

A feature of most of the drugs is that they are non-selective in their sites of action, antagonizing dopamine receptors in all the dopaminergic pathways (Chapter 13). This widespread effect gives the drugs their characteristic profile of pharmacological effects, both adverse and therapeutic. Dopamine receptor antagonism in the nigrostriatal pathway may be related to the development of Parkinsonism and other extrapyramidal effects. Antagonism in the tuberoinfundibular pathway results in neuroendocrine effects including a rise in prolactin secretion. Dopamine receptor antagonism at the chemoreceptor trigger zone confers on many antipsychotic drugs their antiemetic property. Finally, antagonistic effects on dopamine receptors in the mesolimbic and mesocortical pathways appears to be associated with antipsychotic effects. An advantage of the atypical antipsychotics is that they have relatively selective actions in this pathway. For example, clozapine and thioridazine, which rarely cause extrapyramidal effects, appear to have selective actions on the firing rate of A_{10} cells in the ventral tegmental area with minimal effects on A_9 cells in the substantia nigra. Clozapine also appears to interact with receptors in the frontal cortex, a site apparently not affected by other antipsychotic drugs (Lundberg *et al.* 1989). These frontal cortical binding sites may be D_3 receptors, and this area is an important locus of dysfunction in schizophrenia.

Chronic effects. Dopamine receptor antagonism in the mesolimbic pathway does not, however, by itself explain the therapeutic effects of antipsychotic drugs in schizophrenia. There is often a delay of some weeks before therapeutic effects are apparent, although dopamine receptor blockade occurs immediately. The Parkinsonian effects of antipsychotic drugs are also slow to develop and tend to coincide with the onset of antipsychotic activity, while tardive dyskinesia (described below) takes even longer to appear.

Two mechanisms have been proposed to account for the delayed therapeutic and adverse effects of antipsychotic drugs.

(i) Adaptive receptor changes. The subject of receptor modulation by drugs has been discussed in general in Chapter 6 and in relation to antidepressant drugs in Chapter 11. There is little doubt that chronic administration of antipsychotic agents also leads to receptor changes. Increased D_2 receptor density in striatal and limbic brain areas following chronic treatment with a variety of antipsychotic drugs has been shown in animals and man (Creese and Snyder 1980; Reynolds *et al.* 1981; Sedvall 1990). If this effect is exerted mainly on presynaptic D_2 receptors (autoreceptors) it is possible that it could account for the antipsychotic and Parkinsonian effects of the drugs, since increased autoreceptor activity would decrease dopamine release. However, increased postsynaptic D_2 receptor density would be expected to augment dopaminergic activity, thereby aggravating schizophrenic symptoms and preventing rather than precipitating Parkinsonism. Understanding of the receptor changes induced by chronic administration of antipsychotic drugs requires elucidation of the effects mediated by the various dopaminergic receptors. Meanwhile, the effects of chronic administration of these drugs on D_3 receptors have not been fully investigated.

Thus, the question remains unresolved at present. However, it is probable that both pre- and post-synaptic receptor hypersensitivity is a normal adaptive response to chronic treatment with antipsychotic drugs and to dopamine receptor antagonists in general. The situation may be similar to the effects of antidepressant drugs at noradrenergic synapses (Chapter 11). The opposing receptor adaptations would tend to cancel out in terms of overall dopaminergic transmission, but it is possible that together they would confer a greater stability at dopaminergic synapses. This effect may be of therapeutic value for some schizophrenic symptoms, but it does not convincingly account for all the delayed actions of the antipsychotic drugs.

(ii) Depolarization blockade. Another explanation for the time dependent effects of these drugs is provided by electrophysiological recordings of dopaminergic neurone activity in the substantia nigra (A_9 cells) and ventral tegmentum (A_{10} cells; Bunney 1984; White and Wang 1983; Creese 1983). The acute effect of antipsychotic drugs is an increase in firing rate of dopaminergic neurones, as a consequence of pre- and post-synaptic receptor antagonism. Chronic treatment, however, is followed by an almost complete silencing of these neurones. This electrical silence was shown to be due to depolarization blockade, since activity could be reinstated by hyperpolarizing agents such as GABA, but not by depolarizing agents such as glutamate. Direct intracellular recording confirmed the presence of tonic depolarization, and the cells could be induced to fire by the injection of a hyperpolarizing current. Lesioning studies show that the depolarization block is not due to a local effect on neurone cell bodies but depends on the presence of innervated pathways. It is presumed that the block develops as a result of post-synaptic and possibly presynaptic dopamine receptor antagonism.

Examination of the brain sites involved in depolarization block showed that all the antipsychotic drugs studied produced depolarization in cells of the A_{10} area, the origin of the mesolimbic and mesocortical pathways. Classical antipsychotic drugs also silenced cells of the A_9 area, but the firing of these cells was not affected by atypical antipsychotic agents (thioridazine, sulpiride) which have a low liability to produce Parkinsonism. Drugs without antipsychotic activity (metoclopramide, promethazine) did not affect the firing of A_{10} cells, although metoclopramide, which can produce extrapyramidal effects, did decrease the firing of A_9 cells. Thus there was a relationship between the pharmacological profiles of the drugs and their blocking affects on A_{10} and A_9 cells. The tonic depolarization began to develop after a week of treatment and was observed to be still maintained at 8 weeks.

The mechanism whereby depolarization block is produced by the drugs is not known. However, the electrophysiological findings strengthen the evidence from other sources that the therapeutic effects of the antipsychotic drugs are, eventually, due to dopamine receptor blockade in mesolimbic pathways, nevertheless, these drugs also have effects in many other neurotransmitter systems which, as discussed in Chapter 13, may be involved in schizophrenia.

Effects on cholinergic activity

As mentioned in Chapter 13 (see also Fig. 13.2), there are reciprocal feedback connections between dopaminergic, cholinergic, and GABAergic neurones in many parts of the brain. Activity in these circuits is influenced in a complex manner by the actions of antipsychotic drugs. In the corpus striatum, some cholinergic interneurones appear to be under a tonic inhibitory influence from dopaminergic neurones. Dopamine receptor blockade by antipsychotic agents releases these neurones from inhibitory control and results in an increase in striatal turnover of acetylcholine (Bartholini and Lloyd 1980). The production of Parkinsonian symptoms such as rigidity and tremor by antipsychotic drugs is probably the consequence of striatal cholinergic hyperactivity secondary to the dopamine receptor blockade. These drug-induced symptoms are markedly alleviated by anticholinergic drugs.

In addition to these indirect effects on cholinergic transmission, many antipsychotic drugs, especially phenothiazines, have direct cholinergic (muscarinic) receptor antagonistic activity. In general the likelihood of production of extrapyramidal effects is inversely related to potency of anticholinergic action. The lack of Parkinsonian effects of atypical antipsychotic agents such as clozapine and thioridazine may be partially due to their anticholinergic effects, as well as to their relative lack of striatal activity as discussed above.

Effects on GABAergic activity

Both limbic and striatal dopaminergic neurones receive an inhibitory GABA-ergic input (Fig. 13.2). This influence may be affected by antipsychotic drugs, although it is not clear whether the drugs act directly on GABA receptors or indirectly via their actions on dopaminergic activity. It is noteworthy that some antipsychotic drugs (the butyrophenones) contain the GABA moiety in their molecular structure. Antipsychotic drugs of diverse structures cause increases in central GABA turnover and alterations in GABA receptor binding (Bartholini and Lloyd 1980). However, GABA systems do not appear to be directly involved in schizophrenic symptoms (Chapter 13) or in the therapeutic effects of antipsychotic drugs.

Effects on serotonin receptors

The interaction between dopamine and serotonin receptors and the possible involvement of serotonergic systems in schizophrenia has been mentioned in Chapter 13. Several antipsychotic drugs bind to 5-HT_2 receptors (Fig. 14.1). Although the degree of binding to these receptors does not correlate with antipsychotic potency over the range of drugs, it is possible that 5-HT_2 antagonism contributes to the antipsychotic actions, particularly antihallucinatory effects (Andorn *et al.* 1989) in some cases.

Effects on noradrenaline and histamine receptors

Some antipsychotic drugs have significant central and peripheral alpha- and beta-adrenoceptor antagonistic activity. They stimulate the synthesis and turnover of noradrenaline in the brain, presumably by a receptor-mediated feedback mechanism, and can block or reverse the pressor effects of noradrenaline. Adrenergic blocking actions produce postural hypotension and may contribute to the sedative and possibly to the antipsychotic effects of some of these drugs. Some of the agents have fairly potent antagonistic actions at H_1 and H_2 receptors. It does not seem likely that this is important for the antischizophrenic actions but it may contribute to sedative effects.

Effects on endogenous opioids

Chronic administration of several antipsychotics (haloperidol, pimozide, chlorpromazine, sulpiride) produces changes in opioid concentrations and receptor binding in the striatum, nucleus accumbens and cortex of rats (Giardino *et al.* 1990). The effects are probably secondary to dopamine receptor blockade, but their importance in relation to the antipsychotic actions of the drugs is not clear.

Atypical antipsychotics

These drugs are mentioned separately since they display interesting differences from the classical antipsychotics and may represent an advance in the treatment of schizophrenia. Their salient feature is a relative selectivity for mesolimbic pathways. This selectivity is displayed by the phenothiazine thioridazine and also by some more recently developed drugs.

Clozapine. Clozapine has been particularly well studied and many of the findings are reviewed in a symposium (*Psychopharmacology* 1989, *99* Suppl.). Its use is now restricted to closely monitored hospital inpatients because of a 1–2 per cent incidence of agranulocytosis. However, its unusual profile has stimulated a search for similar less toxic congeners (Tamminga and Gerlach, 1987).

Clozapine has antagonistic actions at both D_1 and D_2 receptors and also binds to several other receptors (Fig. 14.1). Binding to D_2 receptors is short-lived due to a high dissociation rate; possibly for this reason it causes only a transient elevation of serum prolactin concentration. Binding to D_1 receptors, which is more prolonged, is considered important for its antipsychotic actions. Chronic administration of clozapine does not appear to increase D_2 receptor density (perhaps because of the high dissociation rate) but may increase D_1 receptor density (Tamminga and Gerlach 1987). Chronic administration causes a depolarisation blockade which is limited to the mesolimbic A_{10} cells, sparing most A_9 cells (White and Wang 1983). Preferential binding to dopamine receptors in mesolimbic pathways probably accounts for the low propensity of clozapine to induce extrapyramidal effects including Parkinsonism and tardive dyskinesia.

Clozapine is also a potent antagonist of 5-HT_2 receptors and increases serotonin release. Meltzer (1989) proposes that the combined effect of this drug on dopamine and 5-HT_2 receptors could be the final common pathway for its ability to ameliorate both positive and negative symptoms in schizophrenia. Like the classical antipsychotics, clozapine also has anticholinergic actions and considerable antagonist effects at α-adrenergic and histamine (H_1) receptors as well as indirect effects on GABA-ergic systems.

Clinically, clozapine has an unusual ability to improve both positive and negative schizophrenic symptoms while carrying a minimal risk of inducing extrapyramidal effects (Meltzer 1989). In addition it can produce clinical improvement in neuroleptic-resistant schizophrenia and may improve some cases of tardive dyskinesia caused by classical neuroleptics (Lieberman *et al.* 1989).

Sulpiride. In contrast to clozapine, this drug is a relatively specific antagonist of D_2 receptor with little D_1 antagonist effects although it also has a high affinity for mesolimbic sites (Bunney 1984). It does not appear to increase D_2 receptor density on chronic administration (Tamminga and Gerlach 1987) and has minimal effects on other neurotransmitter receptors apart from a mild α-adrenergic blocking effect. Sulpiride has antipsychotic effects similar to those of the classical antipsychotics and its chief clinical advantage is an apparently low propensity to cause extrapyramidal symptoms and tardive dyskinesia. Other specific D_2 antagonists such as raclopride and remoxipride are under investigation.

Dopamine autoreceptor agonists. These drugs selectively stimulate dopamine autoreceptors, thus decreasing dopamine release. A prototype of this class is 3-PPP (3-(3-hydroxyphenyl-*N*-*n*-propylpiperidine) (Nilsson and Carlson 1982), but clinically useful successors are so far unforthcoming.

Effects on mood and behaviour

Normal subjects

In psychiatrically normal subjects, antipsychotic drugs typically produce an ataractic state, characterized by diminution in emotional responsiveness, indifference to environmental stimuli, and reduction in initiative and spontaneous activity. Although tiredness and sedation may be present, the subject remains rousable and intellectual performance is little impaired. Normal individuals treated with high doses of antipsychotic agents become more tractable, compliant, and suggestible: these effects led to the misuse of the drugs on political dissidents in the USSR. Patients with acute schizophrenia require much larger doses than normal subjects to produce the ataractic state.

Acute psychotic states

In excited or agitated psychotic states, such as acute episodes of schizophrenia, mania, and organic or drug-induced delirium, the drugs have an immediate calming effect, and reduce aggressive and impulsive behaviour. This effect is exerted without pronounced sedation, so that the patient remains accessible and becomes more amenable and easier to handle. More gradually, psychotic symptoms of hallucinations, delusions, and thought disorder diminish and finally disappear. These effects are not confined to subjects with schizophrenia as defined by strict diagnostic criteria, but occur in any disorder in which positive schizophreniform symptoms, excitement, agitation, or delirium are prominent. The use of antipsychotic drugs in manic episodes of bipolar affective disorders is described in Chapter 12. The psychosis induced by amphetamine or LSD responds rapidly to antipsychotic drugs, usually within hours.

Anxiety and depression

Patients with acute severe anxiety states and panic reactions who have failed to respond to sedative/anxiolytic drugs may respond to antipsychotic agents, especially those with sedative effects such as chlorpromazine and haloperidol (Chapter 4). Some depressed patients respond to flupenthixol, thioridazine, or sulpiride in low doses (Chapter 12).

Therapeutic efficacy in schizophrenia

Antipsychotic drugs do not cure schizophrenia. Some patients do not respond at all; few among those who do respond revert to complete or permanent normality, and even the best drug responders tend to relapse when treatment is stopped. Nevertheless, it is generally agreed after carefully controlled trials involving thousands of patients that the drugs have unique and relatively specific effects on certain schizophrenic symptoms. Improvement is seen mainly in certain symptoms including thought insertion, thought broadcasting, thought block, delusions, feelings of passivity, and auditory hallucinations.

Most authors report little effect on negative symptoms in patients with chronic (Stage II) schizophrenia (Johnstone *et al.* 1978; Angrist *et al.* 1980). However, negative symptoms can occur in the early stages of schizophrenia and often coexist with positive symptoms. Klein and Davies (1969) reported that phenothiazines improved blunted affect, withdrawal and autistic behaviour, and Angst *et al.* (1989) suggest that antipsychotic drugs ameliorate both positive and negative symptoms in both acute and chronic schizophrenics, but over a different time course. Insomnia and psychomotor agitation may respond first, delusions and hallucinations second, depression third, and negative symptoms fourth. These authors query the reality of a therapeutic time lag with antipsychotic drugs and point out that the positive effect of drugs often starts in the first few days. It is possible that drug effects on different neurotransmitter systems differentially improve different symptom clusters.

Maintenance of improvement requires long-term treatment, perhaps for life, since if drug therapy is stopped 25 per cent of patients relapse within a week and 75–95 per cent within a year. Even on continued drug treatment the relapse rate is over 25 per cent within 1 year. Patients maintained on long-term antipsychotic therapy may complain of lack of emotional responsivity: although better able of cope socially they feel cut off from emotional experiences, either pleasurable or painful.

Effects on arousal

The effects of antipsychotic drugs on arousal are of interest in view of the evidence that some schizophrenic patients appear to be hyperaroused. For example, in schizophrenia sleep is disturbed; EEG frequency is increased; the sedation threshold is raised, higher doses of central nervous system depressants being required to produce a given degree of sedation in schizophrenics than in normal subjects; and skin conductance responses may be exaggerated with poor habituation. It has been suggested that the social withdrawal of schizophrenia may be a defence against a feeling of being bombarded with sensory stimuli, a state similar to that produced by psychotomimetic drugs such as LSD.

Bradley and Key (1958) found in animals that phenothiazines inhibit arousal responses in the electrocorticogram, decrease spontaneous electrical activity of neurones in the brainstem reticular formation, and decrease the response of these neurones to stimulation via peripheral sensory pathways. Phenothiazines were also shown to block the increase in reticular formation activity provoked by amphetamine and LSD. These experiments provided electrophysiological evidence that antipsychotic drugs dampen the central arousing effects of afferent and pharmacological stimulation. In addition, Killam and Killam (1956) showed that the arousal threshold of neurones in the limbic system to electrical stimulation of the reticular formation was raised by phenothiazines. This finding is consistent with the behavioural evidence that emotional responses to external stimuli are reduced with little alteration in consciousness or decrement of cognitive performance. This action is probably of prime importance in determining the therapeutic benefit of antipsychotic drugs in schizophrenia. These early studies fit in well with the later work (described above) showing that antipsychotic drugs decrease the firing rates of A_{10} cells in the ventral tegmental area due to dopamine receptor anatagonistic activity.

At the opposite extreme, chronic schizophrenics show evidence of underarousal, such as non-responsiveness of electrodermal activity (Chapter 13). As would be expected from the electrophysiological evidence, antipsychotic drugs are of little benefit in these cases.

Effects on sleep.   Antipsychotic drugs tend to normalize the disturbed sleep pattern (Chapter 13) in psychotic patients. Chlorpromazine increases SWS and REMS initially, in both normal and schizophrenic subjects. The increased SWS persists with chronic use, but tolerance apparently develops to the effect on REMS (Kay *et al.* 1976).

Effects on EEG.   Antipsychotic drugs produce characteristic effects on the EEG which are of predictive value in screening for new drugs with antipsychotic potency (Itil and Soldatos 1980; Saletu 1989). These effects are reviewed by Roubicek (1980). Typically the drugs produce EEG slowing and increased synchronization; there is an increase in delta and theta activity and a decrease in fast beta activity. The amplitude of EEG waves is increased and variability of rhythm reduced. Arousal reactions, such as alpha-blocking on external stimulation, are decreased.

Effects on perception and cognitive performance

The effects of single small doses of antipsychotic drugs on perception, cognitive function, and psychomotor performance in normal subjects are reviewed by Janke (1980). There is no evidence of a specific effect on perception. Performance in IQ tests may be improved in schizophrenics, but is not altered in normal subjects. Learning and memory are not affected in doses below 100 mg chlorpromazine.

Adverse effects

The acute toxicity of antipsychotic drugs is very low and even large doses rarely produce coma (Baldessarini 1985). Nevertheless, the incidence of adverse effects is high and (Table 14.1) gives rise to considerable morbidity.

Extrapyramidal effects

Several types of movement disorders reviewed by Marsden *et al.* (1986) can be caused by antipsychotic drugs. These all result directly or indirectly from perturbations in dopaminergic function in the corpus striatum. Extrapyramidal effects are produced by drugs with prominent dopamine receptor antagonist activity at A_9 cells, and are less likely to occur with the atypical drugs, with have a more selective action on A_{10} cells (Table 14.2). Some extrapyramidal effects occur at the start of drug treatment, others may be delayed for weeks or months, while some may not appear for months or years, or may even emerge when treatment is stopped. At present there is no explanation for the fact that only some patients develop these syndromes.

Acute dystonic reactions.   Acute dystonic reactions can affect any muscle group but commonly take the form of spasms of the tongue, neck or back muscles, or oculogyric crises. The greatest period of risk is the first 5 days of treatment. Dystonic reactions are more common at higher drug dosage but there is a large interindividual variation in susceptibility and they may sometimes be precipitated by small or even single doses.

The exact mechanism by which the drugs cause localized spasm in particular muscle groups is unknown, but the symptoms respond dramatically to parenteral administration of anticholinergic drugs and are presumably largely due to striatal cholinergic overactivity secondary to dopamine receptor blockade.

Akathisia.   Akathisia, an uncontrollable motor restlessness which can be very distressing, may occur between 5 and 60 days from the start of treatment. The response to anticholinergic of antihistamine agents is only partial and a reduction in dosage is usually necessary.

Parkinsonism.   A Parkinsonism syndrome, which may be indistinguishable from idiopathic Parkinsonism, develops in some patients. Its onset is usually delayed for two weeks or more and its appearance often coincides with signs of clinical improvement in schizophrenia. The syndrome probably results from blockade of dopaminergic A_9 neurones in the substantia nigra, resulting in relative cholinergic and possibly GABA-ergic hyperactivity (Richelson 1981). It responds to treatment with anticholinergic drugs. A certain degree of tolerance seems to develop to the Parkinsonian effects of antipsychotic drugs. The symptoms may disappear or improve after some weeks or months of continued treatment, or they may merge with or be replaced by the quite different syndrome of tardive dyskinesia.

Tardive dyskinesia.   Tardive dyskinesia is a delayed adverse effect which appears months or sometimes several years after the start of antipsychotic drug treatment. The clinical features (described by McClelland 1985; Berger and Dunn 1985) consist of bizarre movements involving oral, lingual, buccal, facial, trunk, or limb muscles. The incidence has been variously estimated but is about 10–20 per cent in patients receiving antipsychotic drugs for over a year (Teoh 1988). Elderly patients and those with brain damage appear to be most at risk. The condition is not confined to schizophrenics but may occur in psychiatrically normal subjects taking antipsychotic drugs: a proportion of schizophrenics and patients with affective disorder show signs of dyskinesia on first presentation (before drug treatment), possibly as a reflection of brain damage. Tardive dyskinesia has been associated with all the classical antipsychotic drugs but so far the risk with atypical antipsychotic agents appears to be lower. The syndrome may be caused by non-antipsychotic agents with D_2 receptor antagonistic actions (metoclopramide). There is only a weak correlation between the incidence of tardive dyskinesia and length of drug exposure or drug dose, and the presence of or treatment for Parkinsonism does not appear to be related (Teoh 1988). In most cases cessation of medication is followed by substantial improvement in the condition, but this may take months or up to 2 years and there is often an initial exacerbation. In a significant number of patients the disorder appears to be irreversible (Creese 1983).

The underlying mechanism of tardive dyskinesia is not clear. One factor may be the development of D_2 receptor supersensitivity in the corpus striatum. However, Waddington (1985) found no differences in D_2 receptor density (^{3}H-spiperone binding) in post-mortem brains between schizophrenic patients with or without tardive dyskinesia during life. Nevertheless, the condition is temporarily ameliorated by increasing receptor blockade and aggravated by decreasing dopamine receptor blockade and by dopamine receptor agonists. Fibiger and Lloyd (1984) suggest that GABA underactivity is also involved.

Treatment of tardive dyskinesia is unsatisfactory. Increasing the dose of antipsychotic drugs provides only temporary relief; results with cholinergic agents are not impressive and anticholinergic drugs aggravate the condition; GABA-enhancing drugs provide only partial benefit. Reserpine and tetrabenazine may be helpful but can aggravate depression; L-dopa may produce a transient deterioration followed by long-term benefit (Teoh 1988). Calcium channel blockers and vitamin E are under trial.

Stopping the antipsychotic drug is a possible solution once the condition has developed, but for patients in whom the psychosis is thereby aggravated it may be necessary to continue treatment despite the presence of tardive dyskinesia. Substitution of more selective atypical antipsychotic drugs which spare the nigrostriatal system may be a practical alternative (Casey *et al.* 1979), and the use of these drugs may perhaps prevent the occurrence of tardive dyskinesia in patients requiring long-term treatment.

Neuroleptic malignant syndrome. The neuroleptic malignant syndrome (Baldessarini 1985) is a rare idiosyncratic response which has been observed after treatment with antipsychotic drugs and sometimes after withdrawal of L-dopa or bromocriptine in Parkinson's disease (Koehler and Mirandolle 1988). It carries a 10 per cent mortality and is characterized by akinesia, muscle rigidity, hyperthermia, autonomic instability, and altered consciousness. The cause of the syndrome is unknown, but it is thought to be related to dopamine receptor blockade in the basal ganglia.

Neuroendocrine effects

Many antipsychotic drugs exert a wide range of neuroendocrine effects, reviewed by Nathan and van Kammen (1985). The effects stem from dopamine receptor antagonist actions in the tuberoinfundibular system (Chapter 13) resulting in alterations in the secretion of hypothalamic releasing factors which are normally under inhibitory or excitatory dopaminergic control. Consequently, the release of several anterior pituitary hormones is either increased or decreased. Some of the effects may also result from drug actions on dopamine receptors localized to cells in the anterior pituitary.

The most studied effects are those on prolactin (Meltzer and Fang 1976). Serum concentrations of prolactin are increased after administration of most of the commonly used antipsychotic agents. The effect is almost immediate and provides a measure of the drug's D_2 receptor blocking potency, since there are no D_1 receptors in this region. Although the effects on prolactin secretion and the antischizophrenic effects do not appear at the same time, there is a good correlation between the rise in prolactin secretion and clinical potency in schizophrenia for many of the antipsychotic drugs. The effect on prolactin, however, is not necessary for an antischizophrenic action, since some agents (pimozide, clozapine) do not affect prolactin secretion. Raised prolactin secretion is responsible for adverse effects including breast engorgement and galactarrhoea which may occur in male and female patients.

Other effects on pituitary hormones include a decrease in gonodotropin release, which may cause amenorrhoea and testicular atropy; a decrease in growth hormone release; and a decrease in corticotropin secretion, which may reduce the adrenal corticosteroid response to stress. Hypothalamic dysfunction may explain the increase in appetite and weight gain which is sometimes caused by phenothiazines.

Effects on other systems

Some antipsychotic drugs (Table 14.1) cause postural hypotension due to α-adrenoceptor blockade. This is combined with reflex tachycardia and peripheral vasodilatation which can lead to hypothermia. Many of the drugs also have cholinergic and sedative effects. Long term administration of high doses of phenothiazines may give rise to pigmentary changes in the skin and eyes (oculodermal melanosis). Pigmentary retinopathy which may cause visual impairment only occurs after high doses (1 g daily) of thioridazine.

Drug interactions

Antipsychotic drugs with sedative effects potentiate the effects of other central nervous system depressants including alcohol, hypnotics, narcotic analgesics, and general anaesthetics. The analgesic actions of opiates may be potentiated by an additive effect in dampening the emotional reaction to pain. The antiemetic effect of antipsychotic drugs is useful for countering narcotic-induced nausea and vomiting and a combination of phenothiazines and opiates is often used in terminal care.

Tolerance and dependence

Tolerance develops to the sedative, hypotensive, and even the Parkinsonian actions of antipsychotic drugs, although tolerance to the antipsychotic effects seems to be much less. A degree of physical dependence is produced and dosage reduction or sudden cessation of these drugs may cause withdrawal dyskinesias, usually of the tardive dyskinesia type with choreo-athetosis. Acute withdrawal may also be followed by anxiety, insomnia, agitation and gastrointestinal symptoms, probably due to cholinergic overactivity (*Drug and Therapeutics Bulletin* 1987).

Other drugs used in schizophrenia

The incomplete effect of antipsychotic agents in schizophrenia has prompted trials with other drugs. Some of these may benefit individual patients, but none so far represent a pharmacological breakthrough. At present it seems doubtful if cure, as opposed to symptomatic control, of schizophrenia will ever be attainable by pharmacological means, since drugs cannot reverse long-standing structural damage. Nevertheless, the pursuit of drugs which can improve control of symptoms while exerting lesser adverse effects than present antipsychotic agents is a worthwhile objective.

Drugs which have been tested in controlled trials include benzodiazepines and other GABA agonists, opioid antagonists and other polypeptides, and propranolol in high doses, but none of these have been found to be generally efficacious (Tamminga and Gerlach 1987). Dopamine agonists may be helpful when negative symptoms are prominent and glutamate agonists have yet to be explored. Present interest is focused on drugs which interact with serotonergic systems. Many of the classical and atypical antipsychotic drugs bind to serotonin receptors (Fig. 14.1) and may exert some of their therapeutic effects through this action (Andorn *et al.* 1989; Meltzer 1989). The serotonin 5-HT$_2$ antagonist ritanserin is reported to reduce negative symptoms in schizophrenia (Reyntjens *et al.* 1988) and has been found to activate midbrain dopaminergic neurones (Ugedo *et al.* 1989). Several 5-HT$_3$ antagonists (ondansetron, zacopride) may have antidopaminergic activity in the limbic system and are under investigation for schizophrenia (Tricklebank 1989).

Psychotomimetic drugs

Classification

The psychotomimetic drugs (sometimes described as hallucinogenic or

Table 14.2   Some psychotomimetic drugs

Agents	Plant source
Substances related to serotonin	
mescaline	peyote cactus (*Lopophora williamsii*)
psilocybin, psilocin	'magic mushrooms' (*Psilocybe mexicana, Stropharia cubensis*)
d-lysergic acid diethylamide (LSD)	ergot (*Claviceps purpura*)
dimethyltryptamine	alkaloid in New World snuff
harmaline	beta-carboline (*Banisteriopsis*)
Sympathomimetic amines	
amphetamine derivatives	
MDMA ('Ecstasy', 3,4-methylenedioxymethylamphetamine)	
Cannabis preparations	marijuana, hashish (*Cannabis sativa*)
Anticholinergic drugs	
atropine	*Atropa belladonna*
hyoscine	*Hyoscyamus niger*
strammonium	*Datura strammonium*
Organic solvents	

psychodelic agents) are a miscellaneous group of substances, often of plant origin, which can produce effects sometimes resembling psychiatric states in man. Many of these substances exist in nature and some are widely used for recreational and religious purposes in various parts of the world. They have few therapeutic uses, but have generated considerable interest as possible models for schizophrenia. Examples of the main groups of psychotomimetic agents are shown in Table 14.2. Some of these drugs have already been described (amphetamine: Chapter 4; phencyclidine and organic solvents: Chapter 7; anticholinergic drugs: Chapter 10). There is no sharp distinction between drugs classed as psychotomimetic and other centrally acting drugs: for example amphetamine, bromides, ACTH, opioids, alcohol, and many drugs classified under diverse headings can, in suitable doses, produce psychotomimetic effects. In this chapter, the properties of d-lysergic acid diethylamide (LSD) and of cannabis are considered. Other hallucinogens are reviewed by Glennon (1987).

d-Lysergic acid diethylamide (LSD)

LSD is one of the most potent of known drugs; an oral dose of 25 μg can produce central nervous system effects in man. The drug enjoyed a temporary vogue as a recreational agent, and in 1977 approximately 20 per cent of people aged 18–25 in the United States had sampled it (Jaffe 1980). Its popularity has now declined although it is still available illicitly. Mescaline, psylocin, and other drugs in this group produce similar effects, but are less potent.

Pharmacokinetics

LSD is rapidly absorbed after oral or parenteral administration, and rapidly distributed in the body. Only very small amounts reach the brain, where it has been shown in the monkey to be selectively concentrated in the visual and limbic areas, and also in the pineal gland. The brain and plasma elimination half-life is about 3–4 h in man but is dose-dependent, high doses having longer half-lives. The onset, severity, and duration of clinical effects correlate with brain and plasma concentrations, although symptoms may considerably outlast the half-life of the drug. LSD is metabolized in the body and subsequently eliminated by the kidney. No active metabolites are formed.

Clinical effects

LSD produces three characteristic types of symptoms in man: somatic, perceptual, and psychological (Hollister 1982; Jaffe 1980). The somatic symptoms, which appear within a few minutes, include dizziness, weakness, tremor, nausea, drowsiness, paraesthesiae, and blurred vision. They are accompanied by few somatic alterations, although pupillary dilatation, increased reflexes, incoordination, and ataxia may occur and there may be signs of sympathetic and parasympathetic stimulation.

Perceptual and mood effects appear within an hour and last for several hours. Perceptual symptoms include complex, changeable alterations in shapes and colours, difficulty in focusing, heightened perception of hearing and of visual detail, distortion of space with macropsia and micropsia, and sometimes a running together of sensory modalities (synaesthesia). There is a distortion of body image and of time, perceived time being much faster than clock time. These sensory distortions undergo wave-like recurrences, and the environment is perceived in a novel way. Changes in mood depend on personality and setting. Euphoria, elation, anxiety, fear, irritability or depression may predominate. Often several of these feelings coexist or rapidly change from one to another, accompanied by alternate laughing or crying. The subject may appear hypervigilant or withdrawn and may display irritability on interruption. Not uncommonly there is a fear of fragmentation and of loss of control of perceptions, thoughts, and memories.

After about 4 h, major disturbances in cognition are apparent. Initially, thought patterns are altered and thoughts become difficult to express, accompanied by deterioration in performance tests involving reasoning and memory. Later, feelings of depersonalization, unreality, and dreamlike sensations are prominent. Subjects may feel that their thoughts are of great clarity and meaningfulness. Metaphysical preoccupations dominate, and there may be a feeling of disembodiment and oneness with the world or the cosmos. Hallucinations (visual or auditory) may occur, but these may represent sensory illusions or distortions. A feeling of omnipotence may supervene with irrational beliefs, such as a belief in the ability to fly. During this time, the subject may be in a trance-like state which gradually clears over the next few hours. The entire syndrome may last 12–24 h. This variegated syndrome was well described by Hofmann (quoted in Brecher 1972, pp. 346–7), who supplied the first personal report of the effects of 0.25 mg of LSD taken by mouth.

Biochemical actions

LSD is an indolamine structurally related to serotonin and many of its effects result from effects on serotonergic activity. LSD decreases the release, turnover, synthesis and utilization of serotonin, an effect which lasts several hours or days (Freedman and Boggan 1982). It has agonist properties at 5-HT_1 and 5-HT_2 receptors (Chapter 3; Fig. 3.1). It inhibits activity in the dorsal raphe nuclei and hippocampus by its action on 5-HT_{1A} receptors (Aghajanian et al. 1987). However, the behavioural and psychological effects of LSD and related hallucinogens are probably due to potent agonist actions on 5-HT_2 receptors located in the temporal and prefrontal cortex (Aghajanian et al. 1987; Sadzot et al. 1989). It is noteworthy that the nucleus accumbens, a mesolimbic site thought to be involved in schizophrenia, also contains 5-HT_2 receptors, stimulation of which depolarizes the neurones (Henderson 1990). These effects are all reversed by specific 5-HT_2 receptor antagonists such as ritanserin, suggesting that such drugs might have a therapeutic potential in schizophrenia. Stimulation of 5-HT_2 receptors indirectly facilitates activity in the locus coeruleus and may increase transmission through afferent collaterals to the reticular activating system (Bradley 1961; Fig. 2.3) resulting in enhanced excitatory effects of sensory stimulation, a mechanism which may be involved in producing the positive symptoms of schizophrenia.

LSD also has both agonist and antagonist activity at dopamine and noradrenergic receptors and binds to dopamine, alpha- and beta-adrenergic and histamine H_2 receptors in the brain (Freedman and Boggan 1982). The role of these actions in the psychomimetic effects is not clear, but the synthetic drug MDMA (3,4-methylenedioxymethamphetamine, 'Ecstasy') combines dopamine and serotonin stimulating actions and has properties similar to both amphetamine and LSD (Gold et al. 1989).

Adverse effects

The acute toxicity of LSD is low and deaths attributable to direct effects of the drug have not been reported in man (Jaffe 1980). However, acute dysphoric reactions ('bad trips') occur in about 20 per cent of drug exposures. These usually consist of panic attacks and feelings of loss of control or of going insane. They are influenced by the prevailing mood and personality of the subject and by the environmental setting, but sometimes occur in users who have previously experienced 'good trips'. Acute delusional or paranoid states, hallucinations, suicide, self-injury, or fatal accidents may occur in these subjects. 'Flashbacks', consisting of recurrence of drug effects without repeated drug dosage, occur occasionally. These unpredictable episodes, weeks or months after drug exposure, are unexplained. In a few individuals who are presumably constitutionally susceptible, LSD and related drugs may precipitate prolonged psychotic states for weeks or months. The clinical picture may resemble dementia, depression, or schizophrenia. In schizophrenic subjects the drugs aggravate the symptoms, suggesting that a disturbance of serotonergic mechanisms may be one of the factors contributing to schizophrenic symptoms. Homicide has been reported on several occasions during psychotic states precipitated by LSD (Hollister 1982). MDMA is more toxic and can cause death (Campkin and Davies 1992).

Tolerance and dependence

Tolerance to the behavioural and biochemical effects of LSD occurs extremely rapidly in man and animals and can be seen after three or four daily doses. Cross-tolerance to psilocin and other related drugs occurs but not to central stimulants such as amphetamine. LSD does not support intracranial self-stimulation and is not self-administered by animals, nor does it appear to produce a withdrawal syndrome on abrupt cessation after chronic administration. Its dependence-producing potential in man appears to be low. The pattern of drug use in man is usually one of a small number of exposures (often only a single exposure) over a brief timespan, followed by complete or nearly complete abstinence. The occasional chronic user typically takes the drug once or twice a week and eventually discontinues it on his or her own volition (Jaffe 1980).

Cannabis

The use of cannabis preparations has been increasing in the western world since the 1960s and has reached massive proportions. In the USA, one in 20 high school seniors are reported to smoke it daily (Mendelson 1987); in the UK the practice is less common but still considerable among students (Golding et al. 1983). In the UK and USA, cannabis preparations are usually smoked in cigarettes which deliver, in relatively small, but variable quantities, several psychoactive cannabinoids, as well as substances which both enhance and inhibit their actions (Fairburn and Pickens 1979, 1980). The most potent psychotropic agent is delta-9-tetrahydrocannabinol (delta-9-THC). This substance can be obtained pure and has been used in much experimental work. In North Africa, Greece, the Middle East, and the Far East, much larger quantitites of cannabinoids are smoked or ingested.

Much research has been devoted to the chemistry and pharmacology of cannabinoids over the past decades (reviewed by Paton and Crown 1972, Nahas and Paton 1979, Coper 1982 and Jaffe 1980). The recent discovery and cloning of cannabinoid receptors (Matsuda *et al.* 1990) has finally suggested a mechanism of action.

Pharmacokinetics

Cannabinoids are highly fat soluble and are quickly and completely absorbed after oral administration or inhalation, although they are rapidly metabolised in the liver and lungs so that their bioavailability is low. On reaching the blood, cannabinoids are gradually taken up by fat depots and the brain, from which they are only slowly released. Metabolism of cannabinoids is largely by hydroxylation and some of the metabolites, are pharmacologically active. The elimination half-life of delta-9-THC is 56 h. Traces of this compound and its metabolites persist in the plasma for several days and can be detected in the fat and brain of animals for days after a single administration. Metabolites have been found in the human urine weeks after administration. Because of this extremely slow elimination, repeated use of cannabis can lead to cumulation of cannabinoids in the body.

The distribution of delta-9-THC and the 7-hydroxy metabolite within the brain has been studied in the monkey by McIsaac *et al.* (1971) (Table 14.3). Over the time course corresponding with the behavioural effects, the drug was concentrated in the frontal cortex and limbic areas, including hippocampus and amygdala, and in areas concerned with auditory and visual perception, the geniculate bodies, and superior and inferior colliculi. Accumulation of the drug in these areas might account for some of the psychotropic effects. The drug was also found in the pons where it may exert cardiovascular effects, and in the cerebellum and caudate nucleus, which may account for the ataxia and inco-ordination.

Clinical effects

Pharmacologically-active cannabinoids have a marked sedative effect which contrasts with the arousing effect of LSD. Apart from this difference, the effects of cannabis are similar to, though usually less intense than, those produced by LSD. They follow a similar temporal sequence:

Table 14.3 Distribution of ³H-delta-9-tetrahydrocannabinol in the monkey brain after intravenous administration*

Neocortical areas, especially frontal cortex
Limbic areas, especially hippocampus and amygdala
Sensory areas, including geniculate nuclei, superior and inferior colliculi, visual and parietal cortex
Motor areas, caudate nucleus, putamen, cerebellum
Pons
Highest concentrations occur at 15 min and coincide with maximal behavioural effects

* ³H-delta-9-tetrahydrocannabinol and its 7-hydroxy metabolite detected by autoradiography and liquid scintillation.
Reference: McIsaac *et al.* 1971.

the initial symptoms are mainly somatic, appearing within minutes of the start of smoking. Then follows a 'high' characterized by changes in perception and mood, which reaches a peak in about 30 min and may continue for some hours. Finally, with higher doses a variety of psychotic states may be produced. All these effects are influenced by dosage, personality characteristics, starting state, surroundings, and expectation. Some of the complex interactions between these variables are described by Ashton *et al.* (1981).

The most consistent somatic effects are on the cardiovascular system. There is a dose-related increase in heart rate, sometimes accompanied by hypo- or hypertension and often followed by reddening of the conjuctiva due to vasodilatation. Dry mouth, decreased sweating, and symptoms of gastrointestinal and bronchial irritation may occur, especially in unaccustomed smokers.

Perceptual changes affect all sensory modalities. There may be heightened perception of colour and subjects may see patches or patterns of colours, dimming, brightening, and flowing. Sounds seem more vivid and musical appreciation is increased. General bodily sensations include feelings of floating, weightlessness, heaviness or swelling, hot and cold sensations, numbness, and tingling. Spatial perception is distorted: objects can seem abnormally small or large, distances immense or minute, and the surroundings may appear to advance and recede. The perception of time is disturbed, so that felt or reported time is greater than clock time. Feelings of timelessness, of time standing still, and blurring of past, present, and future may come and go. As with LSD, all these symptoms characteristically wax and wane in fluctuating surges.

Mood alterations accompany the perceptual changes. A dose-related euphoria is common; this may vary from contentment and a sense of well-being to exhilaration and ecstasy. When, as commonly practised, small doses are taken at social gatherings, a pleasant euphoria and loquaciousness may be the only symptoms experienced: these effects are very similar to those produced by social doses of alcohol. Fatuous giggling commonly occurs with social doses and paroxysmal attacks similar to some types of 'laughing epilepsy' have been described. The euphoric effect depends to a large degree on the surroundings: it is less common in naïve subjects and is most likely to occur when the drug is taken in company. Dysphoria is also common and includes feelings of anxiety and panic, unpleasant somatic sensations and paranoid feelings. Euphoria and dysphoria, laughing and crying, may alternate with each other.

Thought processes are initially characterized by a feeling of increased speed of thought, rapid and racing thoughts, flight of ideas, crowding of perceptions, and flooding with thoughts. Thoughts may get out of control, become fragmented, and lead to mental confusion. There are corresponding difficulties in concentrating and impairment of performance in complex tasks occurs even after very small doses. Performance is affected by a combination of increased distractibility, impairment of selective attention and difficulty in shifting from one focus of attention to another. Memory, especially short-term memory, is impaired.

Accompanying the changes in perception, mood, and cognition is an initial state of excitement and increased motor activity. This is followed by a dose-related central nervous system depression, leading to drowsiness and sleep. Initially, the EEG shows a combination of increased fast activity and hypersynchronization. The effect on the sleeping EEG is similar to that of other hypnotics, including a suppression of REMS. Motor changes induced by cannabis include a state of physical inertia with inco-ordination, ataxia, and dysarthria, which accompanies the sedative effects.

With higher doses, cannabis can produce frank psychotic changes. Visual and auditory hallucinations may occur. Feelings of unreality and depersonalization are common. The subject may feel disembodied, or feel that he or she is divided into two individuals, one watching the other. Feelings of great insight and significance may occur, and may alternate with sensations of utter meaninglessness. Anxiety, mounting to panic, severe depression, paranoid delusions, and schizophreniform and psychotic states have been described.

Cannabinoids also exert considerable analgesic, anti-nausea, anticonvulsant, and other effects which suggest a therapeutic potential (Ashton 1987a).

Mechanism of action

The mechanism of action of cannabis was completely unknown until recently, although the presence of cannabinoid receptors in the brain was suggested by Paton (1979). Using potent synthetic cannabinoids, Matsuka *et al.* (1990) succeeded in identifying and cloning such stereoselective receptor sites. These sites have now been demonstrated in human and animal brain and are unevenly distributed, reaching greatest density in the basal ganglia, hippocampus, cerebellum and cerebral cortex, sites which correspond to the earlier autoradiographic findings of McIsaac *et al.* (1971; Table 14.3). It is suggested that the psychotropic effects of cannabis are mediated by cannabinoid receptors in the hippocampus and cortex (Howlett *et al.* 1990). Stimulation of these receptors inhibits adenylate cyclase via a G protein and decreases CAMP production.

The mechanism for the hedonic effects of cannabis appears to be the same as for other drugs of dependence (Chapter 7). Delta-9-tetrahydrocannabinol increases electrical intracranial self-stimulation in the medial forebrain bundle in animals and at the same time increases the efflux of dopamine in the nucleus accumbens (Chen *et al.* 1990). An opioid link may be involved in this action since the dopamine efflux is blocked by naloxone. Several cannabinoid receptor subtypes may mediate the various other actions (antinauseant, anticon-vulsant, analgesic) of cannabinoids (Synder 1990). The analgesic effects may involve cannabinoid receptors in the substantia gelatinosa in the dorsal horns of the spinal cord, possibly interacting with opioid receptors (Howlett *et al.* 1990). The normal function of cannabinoid receptors is not known: as yet there is no evidence of an endogenous ligand.

Adverse effects

The acute toxicity of cannabis preparations is low and deaths from overdose almost never occur (Paton *et al.* 1973). 'Bad trips' with acute panic reactions occur in some subjects and 'flashbacks' of psychological symptoms despite periods of abstinence have been reported. Acute psychotic reactions can occur with high doses. Cannabis aggravates the symptoms of schizophrenia. Many cases have been reported in which the use of cannabis caused a recurrence of acute psychotic symptoms in patients well controlled with antipsychotic drugs. Several cases have also been described in which the taking of cannabis appeared to initiate schizophrenia in apparently normal subjects.

Long-term chronic cannabis use has been said to cause an amotiva-tional syndrome which includes apathy, dullness, impairment of concen-tration and memory, and general unwillingness to undertake complex tasks or to make long-term plans. Others have claimed permanent intellectual impairment and personality change but studies of EEG (Fink 1976), cerebral blood flow (Tunving 1985) and computerized tomography (Hannerz and Hindmarsh 1983) have shown no evidence of cerebral atrophy. However, the very slow elimination of cannabinoids and extended half-life of psychoactive principles, as well as possible cumulative effects of repeated cannabis use are likely to lead to considerable impairment of performance in regular users. Other health risks are reviewed by Ashton (1987a).

Tolerance and dependence

There is little doubt that a marked degree of tolerance of cannabis occurs both in animals and man (Coper 1982). This applies to the autonomic, sedative, and psychological effects. Cross-tolerance with alcohol and some other central nervous system depressants occurs, but there is no cross-tolerance to LSD or other psychotomimetic agents. The so-called 'reverse tolerance' in which experienced users obtain psychological effects from smaller doses than previously necessary may be due to learning, placebo effects, saturation of lipid binding sites, increased formation of active metabolites, or practice at inhaling the drug.

Delta-9-THC is rewarding in animals who can be trained to self-administer it and it facilitates electrical intracranial self-stimulation (Chapter 4). In man, a degree of dependence can occur although its dependence-producing potential appears to be relatively low. Abrupt withdrawal of cannabis after chronic high dose usage leads to a syndrome of irritability, restlessness, anxiety, anorexia, weight loss, insomnia, tremor, and hyperpyrexia. There is a rebound in REMS which is suppressed by cannabis (Jaffe 1980). Occasional social doses, however, do not seem to lead to severe drug-dependence in the vast majority of individuals.

Relationship to schizophrenia

The relationship of cannabis actions to schizophrenia has been discussed by Paton *et al.* (1973) and by Ashton (1982). As with LSD, there are certain similarities between the clinical symptoms of the psychosis and the psychotic symptoms produced by large doses of cannabis. It is well documented that cannabis, like LSD and amphetamines, can aggravate the symptoms of established schizophrenia and may possibly precipitate the condition in predisposed subjects. However, it appears that any agent, pharmacological or non-pharmacological, which disrupts limbic integrative functions may produce similar symptoms. Psychotomimetic drugs may act primarily on serotonergic (LSD), dopaminergic or noradrenergic (amphetamine, cocaine), opioid (phencyclidine, alcohol, narcotics), or other pathways. The clinical picture produced may depend on the anatomical site and the functional state of the pathways affected.

To understand why some individuals develop depression or mania, some anxiety states, some schizophrenia, and some intermediate states when exposed to similar circumstances requires a greater knowledge of the way limbic functions are organized than is at present available.

References

Abouh-Saleh, M. T., Gastpar, M., and Coppen, A. (1989). The dexamethasone suppression test in depression: WHO collaborative study. *J. Psychopharmac.,* **3**, 19P.

Adam, K. and Oswald, I. (1977). Sleep is for tissue restoration. *J. Roy. Coll. Physns.,* **11**, 376–88.

Adam, K., Adamson, L., Brezinova, V., Hunter, W. M. and Oswald, I. (1976). Nitrazepam: lastingly effective but trouble on withdrawal. *Br. Med. J.,* **1**, 1558–62.

Adam, K. and Oswald, I. (1987). Effects of ritanserin on middle-aged poor sleepers. *Psychopharmacology,* **99**, 219–21.

Agarwal, D. P., Harada, S., Goedde, H. W., and Schrappe, O. (1983). Cytosolic aldehyde dehydrogenase and alcoholism. *Lancet,* **1**, 68.

Aghajanian, G. K., and Rogawski, M. A. (1983). The physiological role of alpha-adrenoceptors in the CNS: new concepts from single cell studies. *Trends in Pharmac. Sci.,* **4**, 315–17.

Aghajanian, G. K., Sprouse, J. S., and Rasmussen, K. (1987). Physiology of the midbrain serotonin system. In *Psychopharmacology: the third generation of progress* (ed. H. Y. Meltzer), pp. 141–9. Raven Press, New York.

Agnew, H., Webb, W. B., and Williams, R. L. (1967). Comparison of stage 4 and 1-REM sleep deprivation. *Perceptual Motor Skills,* **24**, 851–8.

Agranoff, B. W., Burrell, H. R., Dokas, L. A., and Springer, A. D. (1978). Progress in Biochemical approaches to learning and memory. In *Psychopharmacology: a generation of progress* (ed. M. A. Lipton, A. DiMascio, and K. F. Killam), pp. 623–35. Raven Press, New York.

Ahlquist, R. P. (1948). A study of the adrenotropic receptors. *Am. J. Physiol.,* **153**, 586–600.

Akil, H., Richardson, D. E., Barchas, J. D., and Li, C. H. (1978a). Appearance of beta-endorphin-like immunoreactivity in human ventricular cerebrospinal fluid upon analgesic electrical stimulation. *Proc. Natl. Acad. Sci.,* **75**, 5170–2.

Akil, H., Richardson, D. E., Hughes, J., and Barchas, D. (1978b). Enkephalin-like material in ventricular cerebrospinal fluid of pain patients after analgesic focal stimulation. *Science,* **201**, 463–5.

Albin, R. L., Young, A. B., Penney, J. B., Handelin, B., Balfour, R., Anderson, K. D., Markel, D. S., Tourtelotte, W. W., and Reiner, A. (1990). Abnormalities of striatal projection neurons and *N*-methyl-D-aspartate receptors in presymptomatic Huntington's disease. *New Eng. J. Med.,* **322**, 1293–8.

Aldrich, M. S. (1991). The neurobiology of narcolepsy. *Trends Neurosci.,* **14**, 235–9.

Alexander, B. K. and Hadaway, P. F. (1982). Opiate addiction: the case for an adaptive orientation. *Psychol. Bull.,* **92**, 367–81.

Alkon, D. L. (1983). Learning in a marine snail. *Scientific American,* **249,** 64–74.

Almay, B. G. L., Johansson, F., von Knorring, L., Sedvall, G., and Terenius, L. (1980). Relationships between CSF levels of endorphins and monoamine metabolites in chronic pain patients. *Psychopharmacology,* **62,** 139–42.

Almay, B. G. L., Johansson, F., von Knorring, L., Le Greres, P., and Terenius, L. (1988). Substance P in CSF of patients with chronic pain syndrome. *Pain,* **33,** 3–9.

Alpern, H. P. and Jackson, S. J. (1978). Stimulants and depressants: drug effects on memory. In *Psychopharmacology: a generation of progress* (ed. M. A. Lipton, A. DiMascio, and K. F. Killam), pp. 663–75. Raven Press, New York.

Alpert, M. and Friedhoff, A. J. (1980). An un-dopamine hypothesis of schizophrenia. *Schizophrenia Bull.* **6,** 387–90.

Altman, J. S. and Kien, J. (1990). Highlighting aplysia's networks. *Trends in Neuroscience,* **13,** 81–2.

Altman, H. J., Nordy, D. A., and Ogren, S. O. (1984). Role of serotonin in memory: facilitation by alaprocate and zimeldine. *Psyhopharmacology,* **84,** 496–502.

American Psychiatric Association (1987). *Diagnostic and statistical manual of mental disorders* (3rd edn, revised) (DSM-III-R). Washington DC.

Amsterdam, J., Brunswick, D., and Mendels, J. (1980). The clinical application of tricyclic antiderressant pharmacokinetics and plasma levels. *Am. J. Psychiat.,* **137,** 653–62.

Andersen, P. H., Gingrich, J. A., Bates, M. D., Dearry, A., Falardeau, P., Senogles, S. E. and Caron, M. G. (1990). Dopamine receptor subtypes: beyond the D_1/D_2 classification. *Trends in Pharmac. Sci.,* **11,** 231–6.

Anderson, P. (1982). Cerebellar synaptic plasticity—putting theories to the test. *Trends Neurosci.,* **5,** 324–5.

Andersson, K. (1975). Effects of cigarette smoking on learning and retention. *Psychopharmacologia, (Berl.),* **41,** 1–5.

Andersson, K. and Hockey, G. R. J. (1977). Effects of cigarette smoking on incidental memory. *Psychopharmacology,* **52,** 223–6.

Anderton, B. and Miller, C. (1986). Proteins in a twist: are neurofibrillary tangles and amyloid in Alzheimer's disease composed of the same protein? *Trends in Neurosci.,* **9,** 337–8.

Ando, K. and Yanagita, T. (1981). Cigarette smoking in rhesus monkey. *Psychopharmacology,* **72,** 117–27.

Andorn, A. C., Vittorio, J. A., and Bellflower, J. (1989). ³H-Spiroperidol binding in temporal cortex (Brodmann areas 41–42) occurs at multiple high affinity states with serotonergic selectivity. *Psychopharmacology,* **99,** 520–5.

Anggard, T. (1988). Ethanol, phosphoinositides, and transmembrane signalling-towards a unifying mechanism of action. In *The psychopharmacology of addiction* (ed. M. Lader), pp. 50–9. Oxford University Press.

Angrist, B., Rotrosen, J., and Gershon, S. (1980). Differential effects of amphetamine and neuroleptics on negative vs. positive symptoms in schizophrenia. *Psychopharmacology,* **72,** 17–19.

Angst, J., Stassen, H. H., and Woggon, B. (1989). Effects of neuroleptics on positive and negative symptoms and the deficit state. *Psychopharmacology,* **99,** (Suppl.) S41–6.

Anisman, H., Kokkinidis, L., and Sklar, L.S. (1981). Contribution of neuro-chemical change to stress-induced behavioural deficits. In *Theory in psychopharmacology*, Vol. I. (ed. S. J. Cooper), pp. 65–102. Academic Press, London.

Annear, W.C. and Vogel-Sprott, M. (1985). Mental rehearsal and classical conditioning contribute to ethanol tolerance in humans. *Psychopharmacology*, **87**, 90–3.

Aoki, C. and Siekevitz, P. (1988). Plasticity in brain development. *Scientific American*, **259**, 34–40.

Armitage, A.K., Hall, G.H., and Morrison, C. (1968). Pharmacological basis for the tobacco smoking habit. *Nature*, **217**, 331–4.

Armitage, A.K., Hall, G.H., and Sellers, C.M. (1969). Effects of nicotine on electrical activity and acetylcholine release from the cat cerebral cortex. *Br. J. Pharmac.*, **35**, 152–60.

Artola, A. and Singer, W. (1987). Long-term potentiation and NMDA receptors in rat visual cortex. *Nature*, **330**, 649–52.

Asanuma, C. (1991). Mapping movements within a moving motor map. *Trends Neurosci.*, **14**, 217–19.

Asberg, M., and Sjoqvist, F. (1981). Therapeutic monitoring of tricyclic anti-depressants: clinical aspects. In *Therapeutic drug monitoring*. (ed. A. Richens and V. Marks), pp. 224–38. Churchill Livingstone, Edinburgh.

Asberg, M., Cronholm, B., Sjoqvist, F., and Tuck, D. (1971). Relationship between plasma level and therapeutic effect of nortriptyline. *Br. Med J.*, **3**, 331–4.

Asberg, M., Thoren, P., Trasken, L., Bertilsson, L., and Ringberger, V. (1976). 'Serotonin depression' a biochemical subgroup within the affective disorders? *Science*, **191**, 478–80.

Asberg, M., Schalling, D., Traskman-Benz, L., and Wagner, A. (1987). Psychobiology of suicide, impulsivity and related phenomena. In *Psychopharmacology: the third generation of progress* (ed. H. Y. Meltzer), pp. 655–68. Raven Press, New York.

Aserinsky, E. and Kleitman, N. (1953). Regularly occurring periods of eye motility and concomitant phenomena during sleep. *Science*, **118**, 273–4.

Ashton, H. (1982). Actions of cannabis: do they shed light on schizophrenia? In *Biological aspects of schizophrenia and addiction* (ed. G. Hemmings), pp. 225–41. Wiley, London.

Ashton, H. (1984). Benzodiazepine withdrawal: an unfinished story. *Br. Med. J.*, **288**, 1135–40.

Ashton, H. (1985). Benzodiazepine overdose: are specific antagonists useful? *Br. Med J.*, **290**, 805–6.

Ashton, H. (1986). Adverse effects of prolonged benzodiazepine use. *Adverse Drug Reaction Bull.*, **118**, 440–3.

Ashton, H. (1987a). Cannabis: dangers and possible uses. *Br. Med. J.*, **294**, 141–2.

Ashton, C.H. (1987b). Caffeine and health. *Br. Med. J.*, **295**, 1293–4.

Ashton, H. (1987c). Benzodiazepine withdrawal: outcome in 50 patients. *Br. J. Addict.*, **82**, 665–71.

Ashton, H. (1989). Risks of dependence on benzodiazepine drugs: a major problem of long-term treatment. *Br. Med. J.*, **298**, 103–4.

Ashton, H. (1991*a*). Protracted withdrawal syndromes from benzodiazepines. *J. Subst. Abuse Treatment,* **8** 19–28.

Ashton, H. (1991*b*). Adverse effects of nicotine. *Adverse Drug React. Bull.* **149**, 560–3.

Ashton, H. and Golding, J. F. (1989*a*). Tranquillisers: prevalence, predictors and possible consequences. Data from a large United Kingdom Survey. *Br. J. Addict.,* **84**, 541–6.

Ashton, H. and Golding, J. F. (1989*b*). Smoking: motivation and models. In *Smoking and human behaviour* (ed. T. Ney and A. Gale), pp. 21–56. John Wiley, Chichester.

Ashton, H. and Stepney, R. (1982). *Smoking: psychology and pharmacology.* Tavistock Publications, London.

Ashton, H. and Watson, D. W. (1970). Puffing frequency and nicotine intake in cigarette smokers. *Br. Med. J.,* **3**, 679–81.

Ashton, H., Millman, J. E., Telford, R., and Thompson, J. W. (1974). The effect of caffeine, nitrazepam and cigarette smoking on the contingent negative variation in man. *Electroenceph. clin. Neurophysiol.,* **37**, 59–71.

Ashton, H., Millman, J. E., Telford, R., and Thompson, J. W. (1976). A comparison of some physiological and psychological effects of propranolol and diazepam in normal subjects. *Br. J. clin. Pharmac.,* **3**, 551–9.

Ashton, H., Marsh, V. R., Millman, J. E., Rawlins, M. D., Telford, R., and Thompson, J. W. (1980). Biphasic dose-related responses of the CNV (contingent negative variation) to IV nicotine in man. *Br. J. Clin. Pharmac.,* **10**, 579–89.

Ashton, H., Golding, J. F., Marsh, V. R., Millman, J. E., and Thompson, J. W. (1981). The seed and the soil: effects of dosage, personality and starting state on the response to delta^9 tetrahydrocannabinol in man. *Br. J. Pharmac.,* **12**, 705–20.

Ashton, H., Golding, J. F., Marsh, V. R., Thompson, J. W., Hassanyeh, F., and Tyrer, S. P. (1988). Cortical evoked potentials and clinical rating scales as measures of depressive illness. *Psychological Medicine.,* **18**, 305–17.

Ashton, H., Teoh, R., and Davies, D. M. (1989). Drug-induced stupor and coma: some physical signs and their pharmacological basis. *Adverse Drug Reaction and Acute Poisoning Rev.,* **7**, 1–59.

Ashton, C. H., Rawlins, M. D., and Tyrer, S. P. (1990). A double blind placebo controlled trial of buspirone in diazepam withdrawal in chronic benzodiazepine users. *Br. J. Psychiat.,* **157**, 232–8.

Ashworth, B. (1989). Intracranial bumps in the night. *Br. Med. J.,* **299**, 1117.

Atweh, S. F. and Kuhar, M. J. (1983). Distribution and function of opioid receptors. *Br. Med. Bull.,* **39**, 47–52.

Averback, P. (1983). Two new lesions in Alzheimer's disease. *Lancet,* ii, 1203.

Ayd, F. J. (1986). Five to fifteen years' maintenance doxepin therapy. *Int. Clin. Psychopharmacol.,* **1**, 53–65.

Azmitia, E. (1978). Reorganisation of the 5-HT projections to the hippocampus. *Trends Neurosci.,* **1**, 45–8.

Baber, N. S., Dourish, C. T., and Hill, D. R. (1989) The role of CCK, caerulein, and CCK antagonists in nociception. *Pain,* **39**, 307–28.

Badawy, A. A-B. and Evans, M. (1981). The mechanism of the antagonism by naloxone of acute alcohol intoxication. *Br. J. Pharmac.*, **74**, 514-6.

Baldessarini, R. J. (1984). Treatment of depression by altering monoamine metabolism. *Psychopharmacol. Bull.*, **20**, 224-30.

Baldessarini, R. J. (1985). Drugs and the treatment of psychiatric disorders. In *The pharmacological basis of therapeutics* (ed. A. G. Gilman, L. S. Goodman, T. W. Rall, and F. Murad), pp. 387-445. Macmillan, New York.

Ball, M. J., Fisman, M. Hachinski, V., Blume, W., Fox, A., Kral, V. A., Kirshen, A. J., Fox, H., and Merskey, H. (1985). A new definition of Alzheimer's disease: a hippocampal dementia. *Lancet*, **1**, 14-16.

Balter, M. H., Manheimer, D. I., Melinger, G. D., and Uhlenhuth, E. H. (1984). A cross-national comparison of antianxiety/sedative drug use. *Curr. Med. Res. Opinion*, **8**, 5-20.

Ban, T. A. (1978). Vasodilators, stimulants, and anabolic agents in the treatment of geropsychiatric patients. In *Psychopharmacology: a generation of progress* (ed. M. A. Lipton, A. DiMascio, and K. F. Killam), pp. 1525-33. Raven Press, New York.

Banki, C. M. (1977). Correlation of anxiety and related symptoms with cerebrospinal fluid 5-hydroxyindolacetic acid in depressed women. *J. Neurol. Transm.*, **41**, 135-43.

Banks, W. A., and Kastin, A. J. (1983). Aluminium increases permeability of the blood-brain barrier to labelled D.S.I.P. and beta-endorphin: possible implications for senile and dialysis dementia. *Lancet*, **ii**, 1227-9.

Barbaccia, M. L., Reggiani, A., Spano, P. F., and Trabucchi, M. (1981). Ethanol-induced changes of dopaminergic function in three strains of mice characterised by a different population of opiate receptors. *Psychopharmacology*, **74**, 260-2.

Barbaccia, M. L., Chuang, D-M., Gandolfi, O., and Costa, E. (1983). Trans-synaptic mechanisms in the actions of imipramine. In *Frontiers in neuropsychiatric research*. (ed. E. Usdin, M. Goldstein, A. J. Friedhoff, and A. Georgatas), pp. 19-31. Macmillan, London.

Barker, W. A., Scott, J. S., and Eccleston, D. (1987). The Newcastle chronic depression study: results of a treatment regime. *Int. Clin. Psychopharmacol.*, **2**, 261-72.

Barnard, E. A., and Demoliou-Mason, C. (1983). Molecular properties of opioid receptors. *Br. Med. Bull.*, **39**, 37-46.

Barnas, C., Miller, C., Ehrman, D. I., Schett, P., Gunther, V., and Fleischhacker, W. W. (1990). High versus low-dose piracetam in alcoholic organic mental disorder: a placebo controlled study. *Psychopharmacology*, **100**, 361-5.

Barnes, P. J. (1981). Radioligand binding studies of adrenergic receptors and their clinical relevance. *Br. Med. J.*, **282**, 1207-10.

Barnes, J. M., Barnes, N. M., Costall, B., Naylor, R. J., and Tyers, M. B. (1989). 5-HT$_3$ receptors mediate inhibition of acetylcholine release in cortical tissue. *Nature*, **338**, 762-3.

Bartholini, G., and Lloyd, K. G. (1980). Biochemical effects of neuroleptic drugs. In *Psychotropic agents part I: antipsychotics and antidepressants* (ed. F. Hoffmeister and G. Stille), pp. 193-212. Springer-Verlag, Berlin.

Baskin, D.S., and Hosobuchi, Y. (1981). Naloxone reversal of ischaemic neurological deficits in man. *Lancet*, **ii**, 272-5.

Bassenge, E. (1988). Cardiovascular actions of nicotine. In *The pharmacology of nicotine* (ed. M.R. Rand and K. Thurau), pp. 117-37. IRL Press, Oxford.

Batini, C., Moruzzi, G., Palestrini, M., Rossi, G.R., and Zanchetti, A. (1959). Effects of complete pontine transection on the sleep-wakefulness rhythm: The mid-pontine pretrigeminal section. *Arch. Ital. Biol.*, **97**, 1-12.

Beart, P.M. (1982). Multiple dopamine receptors-new vistas. In *More about receptors*. (ed. J.W. Lamble), pp. 87-92. Elsevier Biomedical Press, Amsterdam.

Beary, M.D., Lacey, J.H., and Bhat, A.V. (1983). The neuroendocrine impact of 3-hydroxy-diazepam (temazepam) in women. *Psychopharmacology*, **79**, 295-7.

Beaumont, G. (1988). Buspirone: clinical studies in general practice. In *Buspirone: a new introduction to the treatment of anxiety* (ed. M. Lader), pp. 51-7. Royal Society of Medicine Services, London, New York.

Beck, A.T. (1967). *Depression: clinical experimental and theoretical aspects*. Harper and Row, New York.

Beeley, L. (1978). Drugs in early pregnancy. *J. Pharmacother.*, **1**, 189.

Beersma, D.G.M., Dijk, D.J., Blok, C.G.H., and Everhardus, I. (1990). REM sleep deprivation during 5 hours leads to an immediate REM sleep rebound and to suppression of non-REM sleep intensity. *Electroenceph. clin. Neurophysiol.*, **76**, 114-22.

Behar, M., Magora, F., Olshwang, D., and Davidson, J.T. (1979). Epidural morphine in treatment of pain. *Lancet*, **i**, 527-8.

Behdehami, M.M., Jiang, M., Chanella, S.D., and Ennis, M. (1990). The effect of GABA and its antagonists on midbrain periaqueductal grey neurones in the rat. *Pain*, **40**, 195-204.

Bejerot, N. (1980). Addiction to pleasure: a biological and social-psychological theory of addiction. In *Theories on drug abuse* (ed. D.J. Lettieri, M. Sayers, and H.W. Pearson), pp. 246-55. Dept. of Health and Human Services, National Institute of Drug Abuse, Rockville, Maryland.

Benedittis, G. de, and Gonda, F. de, (1985). Hemispheric specialisation and the perception of pain: a task-related EEG power spectrum analysis in chronic pain patients. *Pain*, **22**, 375-84.

Benowitz, N.L. (1988). Pharmacokinetics and pharmacodynamics of nicotine. In *The pharmacology of nicotine* (ed. M.R. Rand and K. Thurau), pp. 3-18. IRL Press, Oxford.

Benton, D. (1988). The role of opiate mechanisms in social relationships. In *The psychopharmacology of addiction* (ed. M. Lader), pp. 115-40. Oxford University Press.

Berger, P.A. and Barchas, J.D. (1977). Biochemical hypotheses of affective disorders. In *Psychopharmacology: from theory to practice* (ed. J.D. Barchas, P.A. Berger, R.D. Ciaranello, and G.R. Elliott), pp. 151-73. Oxford University Press, New York.

Berger, P.A. and Dunn, M.J. (1985). Tardive dyskinesia: the major problem with antipsychotic maintenance therapy. In *Drugs in psychiatry*. (ed. G.D. Burrows, T.R. Norman, and B. Davies), Vol. 3, pp. 185-212. Elsevier, Amsterdam.

Berger, P. A. and Nemeroff, C. B. (1987). Opioid peptides in affective disorder. In *Psychopharmacology: the third generation of progress* (ed. H. Y. Meltzer), pp. 637–54. Raven Press, New York.

Berntson, G. G., Beattie, M. S., and Walker, J. M. (1976). Effects of nicotine and muscarinic compounds in biting attack in the cat. *Pharmacol. Biochem. and Behav.*, **5**, 235–9.

Berridge, M. J. (1981). Receptors and calcium signalling. In *Towards understanding receptors* (ed. J. W. Lamble), pp. 122–31. Elsevier/North Holland, Amsterdam.

Besson, J. (1983). Dementia: biological solution still a long way off. *Br. Med. J.*, **287**, 926–7.

Betts, T. A., and Birtle, J. (1982). Effects of two hypnotic drugs on actual driving performance next morning. *Br. Med J.*, **285**, 852.

Bevan, P., Bradshaw, C. M., and Szabadi, E. (1977). The pharmacology of adrenergic neuronal responses in the cerebral cortex: evidence for excitatory alpha and inhibitory beta receptors. *Br. J. Pharmac.*, **59**, 635–41.

Bialos, D., Giller, E., Jatlow, P., Docherty, J., and Harkness, M. S. W. (1982). Recurrence of depression after long-term amitriptyline treatment. *Am. J. Psychiat.*, **139**, 325–7.

Bickford, R. G., Mulder, D. W., Dodge, H. W., Svien, H. J., and Rome, P. R. (1958). Changes in memory function produced by electrical stimulation of the temporal lobe in man. *Res. Publ. Ass. Res. Nerv. Ment. Dis.*, **36**, 227.

Biegon, A., and Samuel, D. (1980). Interaction of tricyclic antidepressants and opiate receptors. *Biochem. Pharmacol.*, **29**, 460–2.

Biegon, A., Essar, N., Israeli, M., Elizur, A., Bruch, S., and Bar-Nathan, A. A. (1990*a*). Serotonin 5-HT$_2$ receptor binding on blood platelets as a state dependent marker in major affective disorder. *Psychopharmacology*, **100**, 73–5.

Biegon, A., Gruispoon, A., Blumenfeld, B., Bleich, A., Apter, A., and Merter, R. (1990*b*). Increased serotonin 5-HT$_2$ receptor binding on blood platelets of suicidal men. *Psychopharmacology*, **100**, 165–7.

Bierness, D., and Vogel-Sprott, M. (1984). Alcohol tolerance in social drinkers: operant and classical conditioning effects. *Psychopharmacology*, **84**, 393–7.

Birchall, J. D., and Chappell, J. S. (1988). Aluminium, chemical physiology, and Alzheimer's disease. *Lancet*, **ii**, 1008–10.

Bird, K. D., Chesher, G. B., Perl, J., and Starmer, G. A. (1982). Naloxone has no effect on ethanol-induced impairment of psychomotor performance in man. *Psychopharmacology*, **76**, 193–7.

Black, D. (1982). Misuse of solvents. *Health Trends.*, **14**, 27–8.

Blackburn, J. R., Phillips, A. C., Jakubovic, A., and Fibiger, H. C. (1989). Dopamine and preparatory behaviour: II a neurochemical analysis. *Behav. Neurosci.*, **103**, 15–23.

Bliss, T. V. P. (1979). Synaptic plasticity in the hippocampus. *Trends Neurosci.*, **2**, 42–5.

Bliss, T. V. P. and Dolphin, A. C. (1982). What is the mechanism of long-term potentiation in the hippocampus? *Trends Neurosci.*, **5**, 289–90.

Bliss, T. V. P. and Gardner-Medwin, A. R. (1973). Long-lasting potentiation of synaptic transmission in the dentate area of the unanaesthetised rabbit following stimulation of the perforant path. *J. Physiol. Lond.,* **232**, 357–74.

Bliss, T.V.P., Douglas, R.M., Errington, M.L., and Lynch, M.A. (1986). Correlation between long-term potentiation and release of endogenous amino acids from dentate gyrus of anaesthetised rats. *J. Physiol.,* **377**, 394–408.

Bloch, V. and Bonvallet, M. (1960). Le controle inhibiteur bulbaire des responses electrodermales. *C. R. Soc. Biol.,* **154**, 42–5.

Bloom, F.E. (1985). Neurotransmitter diversity and its functional significance. *J. Roy. Soc. Med.* **78**, 189–92.

Blum, K., Hamilton, M.G., Hirst, M., and Wallace, J.E. (1978). Putative role of isoquinoline alkaloids in alcoholism: a link to opiates. *Alcoholism: clinical and Exp. Res.* **2**, 113–20.

Blum, K., Noble, E.P., Sheridan, P.J., Montgomery, A., Ritchie, T., Jagadesswaran, P., Nogami, H., Briggs, A.H., and Cohn, J.B. (1990). Allelic association of human dopamine D_2 receptor gene in alcoholism. *J. Am. Med. Ass.,* **263**, 2055–60.

Blundell, J. (1991). Pharmacological approaches to appetite suppression. *Trends Pharmac. Sci.,* **12**, 147–57.

Bobker, D.H. and Williams, J.T. (1990). Ion conductance affected by 5-HT receptor subtypes in mammalian neurons. *Trends in Neurosci.,* **13**, 169–73.

Bohus, B., Gispen, W.H., and Wied, D. de, (1973). Effect of lysine vasopressin and ACTH 4–10 on conditional avoidance behaviour of hypophysectomised rats. *Neuroendocrinology,* **11**, 137–43.

Bohus, B., Kovacs, G.L., and Wied, D. de, (1978). Oxytocin, vasopressin and memory: opposite effects on consolidation and retrieval processes. *Brain Research,* **157**, 414–17.

Bolles, R.C. and Fanselow, M.S. (1982). Endorphins and behaviour. *Ann. Rev. Psychol.,* **33**, 87–101.

Bond, M.R. (1979). *Pain its nature, analysis and treatment.* Churchill Livingstone, Edinburgh.

Bond, M.R. (1980). Personality and Pain. In *Persistent Pain: modern methods of treatment* (ed. S. Lipton), Vol. 2, pp. 1–26. Academic Press, London and Grune and Stratton, New York.

Bond, A. and Lader, M. (1981). After-effects of sleeping drugs. In *Psychopharmacology of sleep* (ed. D. Wheatley), pp. 177–97. Raven Press, New York.

Bond, A. and Lader, M. (1988). Differential effects of oxazepam and lorazepam on aggressive responding. *Psychopharmacology,* **95**, 369–73.

Bondareff, W. (1983). Age and Alzheimer disease. *Lancet,* **i**, 1447.

Bondareff, W., Mountjoy, C.Q., and Roth, M. (1981). Selective loss of neurones of origin of adrenergic projection to cerebral cortex (nucleus locus coeruleus) in senile dementia. *Lancet,* **i**, 783–4.

Bottjer, S.W. and Arnold, A.P. (1984). Hormones and structural plasticity in the adult brain. *Trends Neurosci.,* **7**, 168–71.

Boulenger, J-P., Uhde, T.W., Wolff, E.A., and Post, R.M. (1984). Increased sensitivity to caffeine in patients with panic disorders. *Arch. Gen. Psychiat.,* **41**, 1067–71.

Bourne, H.R., Bunney, W.E., Colburn, R.W., Davis, J.M., Davis, J.N., Shaw, D.M., and Coppen, A.J. (1968). Noradrenaline, 5-hydroxytryptamine, and 5-hydroxyindolacetic acid in hind brains of suicidal patients. *Lancet,* **ii,** 805–8.

Bousigue, Y. X., Girand, L., Fournie, D., and Tremoulet, M. (1982). Naloxone reversal of neurological deficit. *Lancet,* **ii,** 618–19.

Bouthillier, A., Blier, P., and Montigny C. de (1991). Flerobuterol, a beta-adrenoceptor agonist, enhances serotonergic neurotransmission: an electro-physiological study in the rat brain. *Psychopharmacology,* **103,** 357–65.

Bowen, D. M. and Davison, A. N. (1984). Dementia in the elderly: biochemical aspects. *J. Roy. Coll. Physicians,* **18,** 25–7.

Bowman, W. C., Rand, M. J., and West. G. B. (1968). *Textbook of pharmacology.* Blackwell Scientific Publications, Oxford.

Bowsher, D. (1978*a*). Pain pathways and mechanisms. *Anaesthesia,* **33,** 935–44.

Bowsher, D. (1978*b*). *Mechanisms of nervous disorder: an introduction.* Blackwell Scientific Publications, Oxford.

Bradley, P. B. (1961). The pathophysiology of consciousness. In *Bewussteinsstorung.* (ed. H. Staub and H. Tholen), pp. 14–22. Symposium von 10 January. St. Moritz, Switzerland Georg Thieme Verlag, Stuttgart.

Bradley, P. B. and Key, B. J. (1958). The effect of drugs on arousal responses produced by electrical stimulation of the reticular formation of the brain. *Electroenceph. Clin. Neurophysiol.,* **10,** 97–110.

Bradley, P. B., Engel, G., Feniuk, W., Fozard, J. R., Humphrey, P. B. A., Middlemiss, D. N., Mylecharane, E. J., Richardson, B. P., and Saxena, P. R. (1986). Proposals for the classification and nomenclature of functional receptors for 5-hydroxytryptamine. *Neuropharmacol.,* **25,** 563–75.

Braestrup, C. and Nielsen, M. (1980). Benzodiazepine receptors. *Arzneimittelforschung,* **30,** 852–7.

Braestrup, C., Nielsen, M., Jenson, L. H., Honore, T., and Petersen, E. N. (1983). Benzodiazepine receptor ligands with positive and negative efficacy. *Neuropharmacol.,* **22,** 1451–8.

Branconnier, R. J. and Cole, J. O. (1977). Effects of chronic papaverine administration on mild senile Organic Brain Syndrome. *J. Am. Geriatr. Soc.,* **25,** 458–62.

Brayne, C. and Calloway, P. (1988). Normal ageing, impaired cognitive function and senile dementia of the Alzheimer's type: a continuum? *Lancet,* **ii,** 1265–6.

Brecher, E. M. (1972). *Licit and illicit drugs.* Consumers Union, Mount Vernon, New York.

Bremer, F. (1935). Cerveau isolé et physiologie du sommeil. *C. R. Soc. Biol. (Paris),* **118,** 1235–42.

Bremer, F. (1970). Preoptic hypnogenic focus and mesencephalic reticular formation. *Brain Res.,* **21,** 132–4.

Bridges, R. J., Gedder, J. W., Monaghan, D. T., and Cotman, C. W. (1988). Excitatory amino acid receptors in Alzheimer's disease. In *Excitatory amino acids in health and disease* (ed. D. Lodge), pp. 321–35. Wiley, Chichester.

Brierley, J. B. (1977). Neuropathology of amnesic states. In *Amnesia.* (ed. C. W. M. Whitty and O. L. Zangwill), pp. 199–23. Butterworth, London, Boston.

British Medical Bulletin (1983). *Opioid peptides.* (ed. J. Hughes), **39,** 1–100.

British Medical Journal (1968). Sleep disorder. *Br. Med. J.,* **2,** 450.

British Medical Journal (1971). Terrors of sleep. *Br. Med. J.,* **2**, 507-8.

British Medical Journal (1977). Depression in men and women. *Br. Med. J.,* **2**, 849-50.

British Medical Journal (1980). Phencyclidine: the new American street drug. *Br. Med. J.,* **281**, 1511-12.

British Medical Journal (1981). Minor brain damage and alcoholism. *Br. Med. J.,* **282**, 455-6.

Broughton, R. and Gastaut, H. (1973). Memory and sleep. In *Sleep: physiology, biochemistry, psychology, pharmacology, clinical implications* (ed. W. P. Koella and P. Levin), pp. 53-8. S. Karger, Basel.

Brown, G. M. and Birley, J. L. T. (1968). Crises and life changes at the onset of schizophrenia. *J. Health and Soc. Behav.,* **9**, 203-24.

Brown, R., Colter, N., and Corsellis, J. A. N. (1986). Post-mortem evidence of structural; brain changes in schizophrenia. Differences in brain weight, temporal horn area, and parahippocampal gyrus compared with affective disorder. *Arch. Gen. Psychiat.,* **43**, 36-42.

Brown, P., Goldfarb, L. G., and Gajdusek, D. C. (1991) The new biology of spongiform encephalopathy: infectious amyloidoses with a genetic twist. *Lancet,* **337**, 1019-22.

Buchsbaum, M. S. (1987). Positron emission tomography in schizophrenia. In *Psychopharmacology: the third generation of progress* (ed. H. Y. Meltzer), pp. 783-91. Raven Press, New York.

Buchsbaum, M. S., Mendelson, B., Duncan, W. C., Coppola, R., Kelsoe, J., and Gillin, J. C. (1982). Topographical cortical mapping of EEG sleep stages during daytime naps in normal subjects. *Sleep,* **5**, 248-55.

Buchsbaum, M. S., Davis, G. C., Naber, D., and Pickar, D. (1983). Pain enhances naloxone-induced hyperalgesia in humans as assessed by somatosensory evoked potentials. *Psychopharmacology,* **79**, 99-103.

Buchsbaum, M. S., Wu, J., Haier, R., Hazlett, T., Ball, R., Katz, M., Sokolski, K., Lagunas-Solar, M., and Langer, D. (1987). Positron emission tomography assessment of effects of benzodiazepines on regional glucose metabolic rate in patients with anxiety disorder. *Life Sciences,* **40**, 2393-400.

Bunney, W. E. (1978). Psychopharmacology of the switch process in affective illness. In *Psychopharmacology: a generation of progress* (ed. M. A. Lipton, A. DiMascio, and K. F. Killam), pp. 1249-59. Raven Press, New York.

Bunney, B. S. (1984). Antipsychotic drug effects on the electrical activity of dopaminergic neurones. *Trends Neurosci.,* **7**, 212-15.

Bunney, W. E. and Davis, J. M. (1965). Norepinephrine in depressive reactions. *Arch. Gen. Psychiat.,* **13**, 483.

Bunney, W. E. and Garland-Bunney, B. L. (1987). Mechanisms of action of lithium in affective illness: basic and clinical implications. In *Psychopharmacology: the third generation of progress* (ed. H. Y. Meltzer), pp. 553-65. Raven Press, New York.

Bureseva, O. and Bures, J. (1976). Piracetam-induced facilitation of interhemispheric transfer of visual information in rats. *Psychopharmacologia,* **46**, 93-102.

Burns, A., Luthest, P., Levy, R., Jacoby, R., and Lentos (1990). Accuracy of clinical diagnosis of Alzheimer's disease. *Br. Med. J.,* **301**, 1026.

Burrows, G. D. and Davies, B. (1984). Recognition and management of anxiety. In *Antianxiety agents* (ed. G. D. Burrows, T. R. Norman, and B. Davies), pp. 1–11. Elsevier, Amsterdam.

Butler, S. (1979). Interhemispheric relations in schizophrenia. In *Hemisphere asymmetries of function in psychopathology* (ed. J. Gruzelier and P. Flor-Henry), pp. 47–59. Elsevier/North Holland, Amsterdam.

Butler, S. H., Colpitts, Y. H., Gagliardi, G. J., Chen, A. C. N., and Chapman, C. R. (1983). Opiate analgesia and its antagonism in dental event-related potentials: evidence for placebo antagonism. *Psychopharmacology,* **79**, 325–8.

Byerley, W., Mellor, C., O'Connell, P., Lalouel, J-M, Nakamura, Y., Leppert, M., and White, R. (1988). Mapping genes for manic-depression and schizophrenia with DNA markers. *Trends Neurosci.,* **12**, 46–8.

Byerly, W. F. and Risch, S. C. (1985). Depression and serotonin metabolism: rationale for neurotransmitter precursor treatment. *J. Clin. Psychopharmacol.,* **5**, 191–206.

Byrne, J. H. (1985). Neural and molecular mechanisms underlying information storage in *Aplysia:* implications for learning and memory. *Trends in Neurosci.,* **8**, 478–82.

Byrne, J. and Arie, T. (1989). Tetrahydroaminoacridine (THA) in Alzheimer's disease. *Br. Med. J.,* **298**, 845–6.

Caine, E. D., Weingartner, H., Ludlow, C. L., Cudahy, E. A., and Wehry, S. (1981). Qualitative analysis of scopolamine-induced amnesia. *Psychopharmacology,* **74**, 74–80.

Calloway, S. P. (1982). Endocrine changes in depression. *Hospital Update,* **8**, 1345–50.

Colloway, S. P., Dolan, R. J., Fonagy, P., Souza, V. F. A. de, and Wakeling, A. (1984). Endocrine changes and clinical profiles in depression: II. The thyrotropin-releasing hormone test. *Psychol. Med.,* **14**, 759–65.

Calne, D. B., Eisen, A., McGear, E., and Spencer, P. (1986). Alzheimer's disease, Parkinson's disease and motoneurone disease: a biotropic interaction between ageing and environment? *Lancet,* **ii**, 1067–70.

Campbell, I. C. and Durcan, M. J. (1982). Genetic variation in response of central adrenoceptors to stress.? *Br. J. Clin. Pharmac.* **75**, 32P.

Campkin, N. T. A., and Davies, U. M. (1992). Another death from Ecstasy. *J. Roy. Soc. Med.,* **85**, 61.

Candy, J. M. and Key, B. J. (1977). A presynaptic site of action within the mesencephalic reticular formation for (+)-amphetamine-induced electro-cortical desynchronisation. *Br. J. Pharmac.,* **61**, 331–8.

Candy, J. M., Oakley, A. E., Atak, J., Perry, R. H., Perry, E. K., and Edwardson, J. A. (1984). New observations on the nature of senile plaque cores. In *Regulation of transmitter function. Proc. 5th Meeting Eur. Soc. Neurochem. Budapest.* (ed. E. S. Vizi and K. Magyar). Academic Press, New York.

Candy, J. M., Edwardson, J. A., Klinowski, J., Oakley, A. E., Perry, E. K., and Perry, R. H. (1985). Co-localisation of aluminium and silicon in senile plaques: implications for the neurochemical pathology of Alzheimer's disease. In *Ageing of the brain* (ed. W. H. Crispen and J. Traber). Springer-Verlag, Berlin.

Candy, J.M., Klinowski, J., Perry, R.H., Perry, E.K., Fairbrain, A., Oakley, A.E., Carpenter, T.A., Atack, J.R., Blessed, G., and Edwardson, J.A. (1986). Aluminosilicates and senile plaque formation in Alzheimer's disease. *Lancet,* i, 354-7.

Canon, W.B. (1936). *Bodily changes in pain, hunger, fear and rage.* (2nd ed). Appleton-Century-Crofts, New York.

Capell, P.J. (1978). Trends in cigarette smoking in the U.K. *Health Trends,* **10**, 49-54.

Carlsson, M. and Carlsson, A. (1990). Interactions between glutaminergic and monoaminergic systems within the basal ganglia — implications for schizophrenia and Parkinson's disease. *Trends Neurosci.,* **13**, 272-6.

Carlton, P.L. and Wolgin, D.C. (1971). Contingent tolerance to the anorexigenic effect of amphetamine. *Physiol. Behav.,* **7**, 331-3.

Carmichael, F.J. and Israel, Y. (1975). Effects of ethanol on neurotransmitter release by rat brain cortical slices. *J. Pharmac. Exp. Therap.,* **193**, 824-34.

Carr, G.D. and White, N.M. (1986). Anatomical dissociation of amphetamine's rewarding and aversive sites: an intracranial microinjection study. *Psychopharmacology,* **89**, 340-6.

Carroll, B.J. (1978). Neuroendocrtine function in psychiatric disorders. In *Psychopharmacology: a generation of progress* (ed. M.A. Lipton, A. DiMascio, and K.F. Killam), pp. 487-97. Raven Press, New York.

Carroll, B.J., Feinberg, M., and Greden, J.F. (1981). A specific laboratory test for the diagnosis of melancholia. *Arch. Gen. Psychiat.,* **38**, 15-24.

Castleden, C.M. (1984). Therapeutic possibilities in patients with senile dementia. *J. Roy. Coll. Physicians.,* **18**, 28-31.

Castleden, C.M., George, C.F., Marcer, D., and Hallett, C. (1977). Increased sensitivity to nitrazepam in old age. *Br. Med. J.,* i, 1067-70.

Catley, D.M., Lehane, J.R., and Jones, J.G. (1981). Failure of naloxone to reverse alcohol intoxication. *Lancet,* i, 1263.

Changeux, J-P. (1985). *Neuronal man: the biology of mind,* Oxford University Press.

Changeux, J-P. and Danchin, A. (1976). Selective stabilisation of developing synapses as a mechanism for the specification of neuronal networks. *Nature,* **264**, 705-12.

Chapman, C.R. and Bonica, J.J. (1985). Chronic pain. *Current Concepts.* Scope publication, Upjohn Company.

Charney, D.S., Heninger, G.R., Sternberg, D.E., Redmond, D.E., Leckman, J.F., Maas, J.W., and Roth, R.H. (1981a). Presynaptic adrenergic receptor sensitivity in depression. *Arch. Gen. Psychiat.,* **38**, 1334-40.

Charney, D.S., Menkes, D.B., and Heninger, G.R. (1981b). Receptor sensitivity and the mechanism of action of antidepressant treatment. *Arch. Gen. Psychiat.,* **38**, 1160-80.

Charney, D.S., Heninger, G.R., Sternberg, D.E., and Landis, H. (1982). Abrupt discontinuation of tricyclic antidepressant drugs: evidence for noradenergic hyperactivity. *Br. J. Psychiat.,* **141**, 377-86.

Chase, M.H. and Morales, F.R. (1984). Supraspinal control of spinal cord motoneurone membrane potential during active sleep. In *Modulation of sensorimotor activity during alterations in behavioural states* (ed. R. Bandler), pp. 167-78. Alan R. Liss, New York.

Chatellier, G. and Lacamblez, L. (1990). On behalf of Groupe Francais d'Etude de la Tetrahydroaminoacridine Tacrine (tetrahydroaminoacrinidine; THA) and lecithin in senile dementia of the Alzheimer type: a multicentre trial. *Br. Med. J.*, **300**, 495-9.

Cheetham, S. C., Crompton, M. R., Katona, C. L. E. and Horton, R. W. (1989). 5-HT$_1$ and 5-HT$_{1A}$ binding sites in brains of depressed suicides. *J. Psychopharmac.*, **3**, 23P.

Chen, J., Paredes, W., Li, J., Smith, D., Lowinson, J., and Gardner, E. L. (1990). Δ^9-tetrahydrocannabinol produces naloxone-blockade enhancement of presynaptic dopamine efflux in nucleus accumbens of conscious, freely moving rats as measured by intracerebral microdialysis. *Psychopharmacology*, **102**, 156-62.

Choi, D. (1988). Calcium-mediated neurotoxicity: relationship to specific channel types and role in ischaemic damage. *Trends Neurosci.*, **10**, 465-9.

Chopin, P. and Briley, M. (1987). Animal models of anxiety: the effect of compounds that modify 5-HT transmission. *Trends Pharmac. Sci.*, **8**, 303-8.

Chouinard, G. and Jones, B. D. (1978). Schizophrenia as a dopamine deficiency disease. *Lancet*, **ii**, 99-100.

Church, R. E. (1989). Smoking and the human EEG. In *Smoking and human behaviour* (ed. T. Ney and A. Gale), pp. 115-40 Wiley, Chichester.

Cicero, T. J. (1978). Tolerance to and physical dependence on alcohol: behavioural and neurobiological mechanisms. In *Brain and pituitary peptides*, Ferring Symposium, Munich, 1979, pp. 1603-17 Karger, Basel.

Clark, D. and White, F. J. (1988). D$_1$ dopamine receptor − the search for a function: a critical evaluation of the D$_1$/D$_2$ dopamine receptor classification and its functional implications. *Synapse*, **1**, 347-88.

Clark, C. R., Geffen, L. B., and Geffen, G. M. (1984). Monoamines in the control of state-dependent cortical functions: evidence from studies of selective attention in animals and humans. In *Modulation of sensorimotor activity during alterations in behavioural states* (ed. R. Bandler), pp. 487-502. Alan R. Liss, New York.

Clement-Jones, V. and Besser, G. M. (1983). Clinical perspectives in opioid peptides. *Br. Med. Bull.*, **39**, 95-100.

Clement-Jones, V., McLoughlin, L., Lowry, P. J., Besser, G. M., Rees, L. H., and Wen, L. H. (1979). Acupuncture in heroin addicts: changes in met-enkephalin and beta endorphin in blood and cerebrospinal fluid. *Lancet*, **ii**, 380-2.

Cloninger, C. R. (1987). Recent advances in the genetics of anxiety and somatoform disorders. In *Psychopharmacology: the third generation of progress* (ed. H. Y. Meltzer), pp. 955-65. Raven Press, New York.

Clough, C. (1989). Non-migrainous headaches. *Br. Med. J.*, **299**, 70-2.

Cohen, S. I. (1989). Risks of dependence on benzodiazepine drugs. *Br. Med. J.*., **298**, 456-7.

Cohen, M. R., Cohen, R. M., Pickar, D., Weingartner, H., Murphy, D. L., and Bunney, W. E. (1981). Behavioural effects after high dose naloxone administration to normal volunteers. *Lancet*, **ii**, 1110.

Cohen, R. M., Campbell, I. C., Dauphin, M., Tallman, J. F., and Murphy, D. L. (1982). Changes in alpha and beta receptor densities in rat brain as a result of treatment with monoamine oxidase inhibiting antidepressants. *Neuropharmacology*, **21**, 293-8.

Collingridge, G. L. (1985). Long-term potentiation in the hippocampus: mechanisms of initiation and modulation by neurotransmitters. *Trends Pharmac. Sci.*, **6**, 407-11.

Collingridge, G. L. and Bliss, T. V. P. (1987). NMDA receptors: their role in long-term potentiation. *Trends Neurosci.*, **10**, 288-93.

Collins, M. A. (1982). A possible neurochemical mechanism for brain and nerve damage associated with chronic alcoholism. *Trends Pharmac. Sci.*, **3**, 373-5.

Collins, M. A., Nijm, W. F., Borge, G. F., Teas, G., and Golfarb, C. (1979). Dopamine-related tetrahydroisoquinolines: significant urinary excretion by alcoholics after alcohol consumption. *Science*, **206**, 1184-6.

Comb, M., Hyman, S. E., and Goodman, H. M. (1987). Mechanisms of trans-synaptic regulation of gene expression. *Trends Neurosci.*, **10**, 473-78.

Committee on Safety of Medicines (1990). *Current Problems*, **30**.

Cook, P. (1979). How drug activity is altered in the elderly. *Geriatric Medicine*, **9**, 45-6.

Cook, N. D. (1986). *The brain code*. Methuen, London.

Cookson, J. C. (1982). Post-partum mania, dopamine and oestrogens. *Lancet*, **ii**, 672.

Cools, A. R. (1982). The puzzling 'cascade' of multiple receptors for dopamine: an appraisal of the current situation. In *More about receptors* (ed. J. W. Lamble), pp. 76-86. Elsevier Amsterdam.

Cooper, S. J. (1984). Neural substrates for opiate-produced reward: solving the dependency puzzle. *Trends Pharmac. Sci.*, **5**, 49-50.

Cooper, S. J. (1985). Possible endogenous basis for anxiety. *Trends Pharmac. Sci.*, **6**, 312.

Cooper, J. R., Bloom, F. E., and Roth, R. H. (1978). *The biochemical basis of pharmacology*. Oxford University Press, New York.

Cooper, R., Newton, P., and Reed, M. (1985). Neurophysiological signs of brain damage due to glue sniffing. *Electroenceph. clin. Neurophysiol.*, **60**, 23-6.

Cooper, R., Osselton, J. W., and Shaw J. C. (1980). *EEG technology* (3rd edn). Butterworth, London.

Cooper, S. J., Kirkham, T. C., and Estall, L. B. (1987). Pyrazoloquinolones: second generation benzodiazepine receptor ligands have heterogeneous effects. *Trends Pharmac. Sci.*, **8**, 180-4.

Coper, H. (1982). Pharmacology and toxicology of cannabis. In *Psychotropic agents part III* (ed. F. Hoffmeister and S. Stille), pp. 135-58. Springer-Verlag, Heidelberg.

Coppen, A. and Wood, K. (1978). Tryptophan and depressive illness. *Psychol. Med.*, **8**, 49-57.

Coppen, A., Whybrow, P. C., Noguera, R., Maggs, R., and Prange, A. J. (1972). The comparative antidepressant value of L-tryptophan and imipramine with and without attempted potentiation by liothyronine. *Arch. Gen. Psychiat.*, **26**, 234-7.

Coppen, A., Standish-Barry, H., Bailey, J., Honston, G., Silcocks, P., and Hermon, C. (1990). Long-term lithium therapy and mortality. *Lancet*, **335**, 1347.

Corcoran, D. W. J. (1965). Personality and the inverted-U relation. *Br. J. Psychol.*, **56**, 267-73.

Corkin, S. (1981). Acetylcholine, ageing and Alzheimer's disease: implications for treatment. *Trends Neurosci.*, **4**, 287-90.

Costa, E. (1981). Receptor plasicity: biochemical correlates of pharmacological significance. In *Long-term effects of neuroleptics*, Adv. Biochem. Psychopharmacol, Vol. 24 (ed. F. Cattabeni) pp. 363-77. Raven Press, New York.

Costa, E., Corda, M. G., and Guidotti, A. (1983). On a brain polypeptide functioning as a putative effector for the recognition sites of benzodiazepine and beta-carboline derivatives. *Neuropharmacol.*, **22**, 1481-92.

Cousins, M. J., Mather, L. E., Glynn, C. J., Wilson, P. R., and Graham, J. R. (1979). Selective spinal analgesia. *Lancet*, **i**, 1141.

Cowburn, J. D. and Blair, J. A. (1989). Aluminium chelator (transferrin) reverses biochemical deficiency in Alzheimer brain preparations. *Lancet*, **i**, 99.

Cowen, P. J. (1987). Psychotropic drugs and human 5-HT neuroendocrinology. *Trends Pharmac. Sci.*, **8**, 105-8.

Cowen, P. J. (1988). Depression resistant to tricyclic antidepressants. *Br. Med. J.*, **297**, 435.

Cowen, P. J. and Nutt, D. J. (1982). Abstinence symptoms after withdrawal from tranquillising drugs: is there a common neurochemical mechanism? *Lancet*, **ii**, 360-2.

Cox, S. M. and Ludwig, A. M. (1979). Neurological soft signs and psychopathology. I. Findings in Schizophrenia. *J. Nerv. Ment. Dis.*, **167**, 161-5.

Coyle, J. T., Price, D., and Long, M. de (1983*a*). Anatomy of cholinergic projections to cerebral cortex: implications for the pathophysiology of senile dementia of the Alzheimer's type. *Trends Pharmac. Sci.*, Suppl. 90-3.

Coyle, J. T., Price, D. L., and Long, M. R. de (1983*b*). Alzheimer's disease: a disorder of cortical cholinergic innervation. *Science*, **219**, 1184-90.

Crabbe, J. C. and Rigter, H. (1980). Learning and the development of alcohol tolerance and dependence. The role of vasopressin-like peptides. *Trends Neurosci.*, **3**, 20-3.

Crapper, D. R., Krishman, S. S., and Quittket, S. (1976). Aluminium, neurofibrillary degeneration and Alzheimer's disease. *Brain*, **99**, 67-80.

Creese, I. (1983). Classical and atypical antipsychotic drugs: new insights. *Trends Neurosci.*, **6**, 479-81.

Creese, I. (1987). Biochemical properties of CNS dopamine receptors. In *Psychopharmacology: the third generation of progress* (ed. H. Y. Meltzer), pp. 257-64. Raven Press, New York.

Creese, I. and Sibley, D. R. (1981). Receptor adaptations to centrally acting drugs. *Ann. Rev. Pharmacol. Toxicol.*, **21**, 357-91.

Creese, I. and Snyder, S. H. (1980). Chronic neuroleptic treatment and dopamine receptor regulation. In *Long-term effects of neuroleptics*, Adv. Biochem. Psychopharmacol., Vol. 24. (ed. F. Cattabeni), pp. 89-94. Raven Press, New York.

Crick, F. (1982). Do dendritic spines twitch? *Trends Neurosci.*, **5**, 44–6.

Crick, F. and Mitchison, G. (1983). The function of dream sleep. *Nature*, **304**, 111–4.

Crisp, A.H., Matthews, B.M., Oakey, M., and Crutchfield, M. (1990). Sleep-walking, night terrors and consciousness. *Br. Med. J.*, **300**, 360–2.

Criswell, H.E. and Levitt, R.A. (1975). Cholinergic drugs. In *Psychophar-macology: a biological approach* (ed. R.A. Levitt), pp. 91–117. Hemisphere Publishing Corporation, Washington DC.

Cross, A.J., Crow, T.J., and Owen, F. (1981). ^{3}H-flupenthixol binding in post-mortem brains of schizophrenics: evidence for a selective increase in dopamine D 2 receptors. *Psychopharmacology*, **74, B** 122–4.

Cross, A.J., Slater, P., and Reynolds, G.P. (1986). Reduced high-affinity glutamate uptake sites in the brains of patients with Huntington's disease. *Neurosci. Lett.*, **67**, 198–202.

Cross, A.J., Stirling, J.M., Robinson, T.N., Bowen, D.M., Francis, P.T., and Green, R. (1989). The modulation by chlormethiazole of the $GABA_A$-receptor complex in rat brain. *Br. J. Pharmac.*, **98**, 284–90.

Crow, T.J. (1978). Rational drug treatment in schizophrenia. In *Biological basis of schizophrenia*. (ed. G. Hemmings and W.A. Hemmings), pp. 113–16. MTP Press, Lancaster.

Crow, T.J. (1980). Molecular pathology of schizophrenia: more than one disease process? *Br. Med. J.*, **1**, 66–8.

Crow, T.J. (1982). Two syndromes in schizophrenia? *Trends Neurosci.*, **5**, 351–4.

Crow, T.J. (1985). Integrated viral genes as the cause of schizophrenia: a hypothesis. In *Psychopharmacology; recent advances and future prospects* (ed. S.D. Iverson), pp. 228–42. Oxford University Press.

Crow, T.J. (1986*a*). Left brain, retrotransposons, and schizophrenia. *Br. Med. J.*, **293**, 3–4.

Crow, T.J. (1986*b*). The continuum of psychosis and its implication for the structure of the gene. *Br. J. Psychiat.*, **149**, 419–29.

Crow, T.J. (1987). Psychosis as a continuum and the virogene concept. *Br. Med. Bull.*, **43**, 754–67.

Crow, T.J. and Alkon, D.L. (1978). Retention of an associative behavioural change in *Hermissenda*. *Science*, **201**, 1239–41.

Crow, T.J. Frith, C.D., Johnstone, E.C., and Owen, D.G.C. (1980). Schizophrenia and cerebral atrophy. *Lancet*, **i**, 1129–30.

Crow, T.J. and Johnstone, E.C. (1980). Dementia praecox and schizophrenia: was Bleuler wrong? *J. Roy. Coll. Phys.*, **14**, 238–40.

Cuello, A.C. (1983). Central distribution of opioid peptides. *Br. Med. Bull.*, **39**, 11–6.

Cuello, A.C. and Sofroniew, M.V. (1984). The anatomy of the CNS cholinergic neurons. *Trends Neurosci.*, **7**, 74–8.

Curran, H.V. (1986). Tranquillising memories: a review of the effects of benzodiazepines on human memory. *Biol. Psychol.*, **23**, 179–213.

Curran, H.V. and Birch, B. (1991). Differentiating the sedative, psycho-motor and amnesic effects of benzodiazepines: a study with midazolam and the benzodiazepine antagonist, flumazenil. *Psychopharmacology*, **103**, 519–23.

Dackis, C. A., Gold, M. S., and Sweeney, D. R. (1989). Physiology of cocaine craving and 'crashing'. *Arch. Gen. Psychiatry*, **44**, 298-9.

Dalton, K. (1964). *The premenstrual syndrome*. Heinemann, London.

Damasio, A. R. (1983). Language and the basal ganglia. *Trends Neurosci.*, **6**, 442-4.

Damasio, A. R. (1985). Prosopagnosia. *Trends Neurosci.*, **8**, 132-5.

Damasio, A. R. (1990). Category-related recognition defects as a clue to the neural substrates of knowledge. *Trends Neurosci.*, **13**, 95-8.

Damluji, N. F. and Ferguson, J. M. (1988). Paradoxical worsening of depressive symptomatology caused by antidepressants. *J. Clin. Psychopharmac.*, **8**, 347-9.

Darragh, A., Lambe, R., Kenny, M., Brick, I., Taaffe, W., and O'Boyle, C. (1982). RO 15-1788 antagonises the central effects of diazepam in men without altering diazepam bioavailability. *Br. J. Clin. Pharmac.*, **14**, 677-82.

Darragh, A., Lambe, R., O'Boyle, C., Kenny, M., and Brick, I. (1983). Absence of central effects in man of the benzodiazepine antagonist RO 15-1788. *Psychopharmacology*, **80**, 192-5.

Davis, M. (1989). The role of the amygdala and its efferent projections in fear and anxiety. In *Psychopharmacology of anxiety*, pp. 52-79. Oxford University Press.

Davis, M. and Menkes, D. B. (1982). Tricyclic antidepressants vary in decreasing alpha$_2$-adrenoceptor sensitivity with chronic treatment: assessment of clonidine inhibition of acoustic startle. *Br. J. Pharmac.*, **77**, 217-22.

Davis, M., Cassella, J. V., and Kehne, J. H. (1988). Serotonin does not mediate anxiolytic effects of buspirone in the fear-potentiated startle paradigm: comparison with 8-OH-DPAT and ipsapisone. *Psychopharmacology*, **94**, 14-20.

Davison, A. N. (1982). Ageing research matures. *Trends Neurosci.*, **5**, 217-18.

Deakin, J. F. W. (1983). Alzheimer's disease: recent advances and future prospects. *Br. Med. J.*, **287**, 1323-4.

Deakin, J. F. W., Pennell, I., Upadhyaya, A. J., and Lofthouse, R. (1990). A neuroendocrine study of 5HT function in depression: evidence for biological mechanisms of endogeneous and psychosocial causation. *Psychopharmacology*, **101**, 85-92.

Deary, I. J. and Hendrickson, A. E. (1986). Calcium and Alzheimer's disease. *Lancet*, **i**, 1219.

Deary, I. J. and Tait, R. (1987). Effects of sleep disruption on cognitive performance and mood in medical house officers. *Br. Med. J.*, **295**, 1513-16.

Deary, I. J. and Whalley, L. J. (1988). Recent research on the causes of Alzheimer's disease. *Br. Med. J.*, **297**, 807-10.

De Freitas, B. and Schwartz, G. (1979). Effects of caffeine in chronic psychiatric patients. *Am. J. Psychiat.*, **136**, 1337-8.

Dehen, H., Willer, J. C., Boureau, F., and Cambier, J. (1977). Congenital insensitivity to pain, and endogenous morphine-like substances. *Lancet*, **ii**, 293-4.

Delay, J. and Deniker, P. (1952). Trente-hiut cas de psychoses traitees par la cure prolongee et continue de 456ORP. *Le Congres des Al. et Neurol. de Langue Fr. Compte rendu de Congres*. Masson et Cie, Paris.

De Leon, M. J., George, A. E., Stylopoulos, L. S., Smith, G., and Miller, D. C. (1989). Early marker for Alzheimer's disease: the atrophic hippocampus. *Lancet*, **ii**, 672-3.

Delgado, J. M. R., Roberts, W. W., and Miller, N. (1954). Learning motivated by electrical stimulation of the brain. *Am. J. Physiol.*, **179**, 587-9.

Demellweek, C. and Goudie, A. J. (1983). Behavioural tolerance to amphetamine and other psychostimulants: the case for considering behavioural mechanisms. *Psychopharmacology*, **80**, 287-307.

Dement, W. and Kleitman, N. (1957). Cyclic variations in EEG during sleep and their relation to eye movements, body motility, and dreaming. *Electroenceph. clin. Neurophysiol.*, **9**, 673-90.

Deneau, G. and Inoki, C. (1967). Nicotine self-administration in monkeys. *Ann. N. Y. Acad. Sci.*, **142**, 277-9.

Deneau, G., Yanagita, T., and Seevers, M. H. (1969). Self-administration of psychoactive substances by the monkey. *Psychopharmacologia, (Berl.)*, **16**, 30-48.

Desai, N., Taylor-Davies, A., and Barnett, D. B. (1983). The effects of diazepam and oxprenolol on short term memory in individuals of high and low state anxiety. *Br. J. clin. Pharmac.*, **15**, 197-202.

Deutsch, J. A. (1971). The cholinergic synapse and the site of memory. *Science*, **174**, 788-94.

Di Chiari, G. and Imperato, A. (1988). Drugs abused by humans preferentially increase synaptic dopamine concentrations in the mesolimbic system of freely moving rats. *Proc. Natl. Acad. Sci., U.S.A.*, **85**, 5274-8.

Dickinsen, A. H. (1990). A cure for wind-up; NMDA receptor antagonists as potential analgesics. *Trends Pharmac. Sci.*, **11**, 307-9.

Dilsaver, S. C. (1989). Antidepressant withdrawal syndrome: phenomenology and pathophysiology. *Acta. Psychiat. Scand.*, **79**, 113-17.

Dilsaver, S. C., Snider, R. M., and Alessi, N. E. (1987a). Amitriptyline supersensitises a central cholinergic mechanism. *Biol. Psychiat.*, **22**, 495-507.

Dilsaver, S. C., Greden, J. F., and Snider, R. M. (1987b). Antidepressant withdrawal syndromes: phenomenology and pathophysiology. *Int. Clin. Psychopharmac.*, **2**, 1-19.

Dingledine, R. (1986). NMDA receptors: what do they do? *Trends Neurosci.*, **9**, 47-9.

Dolphin, A. C. (1985). Long-term potentiation at peripheral synapses. *Trends Neurosci.*, **8**, 376-8.

Domino, E. F. (1979). Behavioural, electrophysiological, endocrine and skeletal muscle actions of nicotine and tobacco smoking. In *Electrophysiological effects of nicotine* (ed. A. Remond and C. Izard), pp. 136-46. Elsevier/North Holland, Amsterdam.

Dongier, M., Dubrovsky, B., and Engelsmann, L. (1977). Event-related slow potentials in psychiatry. In *Psychopathology and brain dysfunction* (ed. C. Shagass, S. Gershon, and A. J. Friedhoff), pp. 291-352. Raven Press, New York.

Dorian, P., Sellers, E. M., Kaplan, H., and Hamilton, C. (1983). Evaluation of zopiclone physical dependence liability in normal volunteers. *Pharmacology*, **27**, (Suppl. 2), 228-34.

Dorow, R., Horowski, R., Paschelke, G., Amin, M., and Braestrup, C. (1983). Severe anxiety induced by FG 7142, a beta-carboline ligand for benzodiazepine receptors. *Lancet*, **ii**, 98–9.

Douglas, R. J. (1967). The hippocampus and behaviour. *Psychol Bull.*, **67**, 416–42.

Douglas, R. J. (1975). The development of hippocampal function; implications for theory and for therapy. In *The hippocampus* (ed. R. L. Isaacson and K. H. Pribram), pp. 327–57. Plenum Press, New York.

Douglas, R. J. and Pribram, K. H. (1966). Learning and limbic lesions. *Neuropsychologia*, **4**, 197–220.

Dourish, C. T., Hutson, P. H., and Curzon, G. (1986). Putative anxiolytics 8-OH-DPAT, buspirone and TVX Q 7821 are agonists at 5-HT autoreceptors in the raphe nuclei. *Trends Pharmac. Sci.*, **7**, 212–15.

Dowson, J. H. (1982). Neuronal lipofucsin accumulation in ageing and Alzheimer dementia: a pathogenic mechanism? *Br. J. Psychiat.*, **140**, 142–8.

Drachman, D. A. (1978). Central cholinergic system and memory. In *Psychopharmacology a generation of progress* (ed. M. A. Lipton, A. DiMascio, and K. F. Killam), pp. 651–62. Raven Press, New York.

Drubach, D. A. and Kelly, M. P. (1989). Panic disorder associated with a right paralimbic lesion. *Neuropsychiatry, Neuropsychology and Behavioural Neurology*, **2**, 282–9.

Drucker-Colin, R. (1981). Endogeneous sleep peptides. In *Psychopharmacology of sleep* (ed. D. Wheatly), pp. 53–71. Raven Press, New York.

Drug and Therapeutics Bulletin (1979). Triazolam (Halcion) psychological disturbances. *Drug. Therap. Bull.*, **17**, 76.

Drug and Therapeutics Bulletin (1980). The CRM on benzodiazepines. *Drug Therap. Bull.*, **18**, 97–8.

Drug and Therapeutics Bulletin (1986). Problems when withdrawing anti-depressives. *Drug and Therap. Bull.*, **24**, 29–30.

Drug and Therapeutics Bulletin (1987). Stopping drug treatment in schizophrenia. *Drug Therap. Bull.*, **25**, 31–2.

Drug and Therapeutics Bulletin (1991). Shedding light on seasonal affective disorders. *Drug and Therap. Bull.*, **29**, 33–4.

Drummond, A. H. (1987). Lithium and inositol lipid-linked signal mechanisms. *Trends. Pharmac. Sci.*, **8**, 129–33.

Dudai, Y. (1989). *The Neurobiology of Memory*. Oxford University Press.

Duggan, A. W. (1983). Electrophysiology of opioid peptides and sensory systems. *Br. Med. Bull.*, **39**, 65–70.

Duggan, A. W. and Foong, F. W. (1985). Bicuculline and spinal inhibitors produced by dorsal column stimulation in the cat. *Pain*, **22**, 249–59.

Duggan, A. W., Hall, J. G., and Headley, P. M. (1977a). Suppression of transmission of nociceptive impulses by morphine: selective effects of morphine administered in the region of the substantia gelatinosa. *Br. J. Pharmac.*, **61**, 65–76.

Duggan, A. W., Hall, J. G., and Headley, P. M. (1977b). Enkephalins and dorsal horn neurones of the cat: effects on responses to noxious and innocuous skin stimuli. *Br. J. Pharmac.*, **61**, 399–408.

Dugovic, C., Wauquier, A., Leysen, J.E., Marrannes, R., and Janssen, P.A.J. (1989). Functional role of 5-HT$_2$ receptors in the regulation of sleep and wakefulness in the rat. *Psychopharmacology*, **97**, 436–42.

Drug and Therapeutics Bulletin (1987). Stopping drug treatment in schizophrenia. *Drug Therap. Bull.* **25**, 31–2.

Drug and Therapeutics Bulletin (1991). Shedding light on seasonal affective disorders. *Drug and Therap. Bull.* **29**, 33–4.

Dundeee, J.W., Halliday, N.J., Harper, K.W. and Brogden, R.N. (1984). Midazolam: a review. *Drugs*, **28**, 519–43.

Dunleavy, D.L.F., and Oswald, J. (1973). Phenelzine, mood response and sleep. *Arch. Gen. Psychiat.*, **28**, 353–56.

Dunn, W.L. (1978). Smoking as a possible inhibitor of arousal. In *Behavioural effects of nicotine* (ed. K. Battig). S. Karger, Basel.

Dunn, A. (1980). Neurochemistry of learning and memory: an evaluation of recent data. *Ann. Rev. Psychol.*, **31**, 343–90.

Eagger, S.A., Levy, R. and Sahakian, B.J. (1991). Tacrine in Alzheimer's disease. *Lancet*, **337**, 989–92.

Eagles, J.M., Gibson, I., Bramner, M.H., Clunie, F., Ebmeier, K.P., and Smith, N. (1990). Obstetric complications in DSM-III schizophrenics and their siblings. *Lancet*, **335**, 1139–41.

Eccles, J.C. (1977). An instruction-selection theory of learning in the cerebellar cortex. *Brain Res.*, **127**, 327–52.

Edelman, G.M. (1978). Group selection and phasic reentrant signalling: a theory of higher brain function. In *The mindful brain* (ed. G.M. Edelman and V.B. Mountcastle), pp. 51–100. MIT Press, Massachusetts.

Edwardson, J.A. and Candy, J.M. (1987). Neurochemical pathology of Alzheimer's disease. In *Alzheimer's disease: current approaches* (ed. J.C. Malkin and M.N. Rossor), pp. 27–35. Duphar Laboratories Ltd., Southampton.

Eison, M.S. and Eison, A.S. (1984). Buspirone as a midbrain modulator: anxiolysis correlated to traditional benzodiazepine mechanisms. *Drug Develop. Res.*, **4**, 109–19.

Eison, A.S., Eison, M.S., Stanley, M., and Riblet, L.A. (1986). Serotonergic mechanisms in the behavioural effects of buspirone and gepirone. *Pharmac. Biochem. & Behavior*, **24**, 701–7.

Ekstrand, B.R., Barrett, T.R., West, J.N., and Maier, W. (1977). The effect of sleep on human long term memory. In *Neurobiology of sleep and memory* (ed. R. Drucker-Colin and J.L. McGough), pp. 419–39. Academic Press, New York.

Elde, R., Hokfelt, T., Johansson, O., and Terenius, L. (1976). Immunohistological studies using antibodies to leucine enkephalin: initial observations on the nervous system of the rat. *Neuroscience*, **1**, 349–52.

Ellingboe, J. (1978). Effects of alcohol on neurochemical processes. In *Psychopharmacology: a generation of progress* (ed. M.A. Lipton, A. DiMascio, and K.F. Killam), pp. 1653–64. Raven Press, New York.

Emery, F.E., Hilgendorf, E.L., and Irving, B.L. (1968). The psychological dynamics of smoking. *Tobacco Research Council*. Research Paper, 10. London.

Enna, S.J. and Eison, M.S. (1987). Second generation antidepressants. In *Handbook of Psychopharmacology*, Vol. 19 (ed. L.L. Iversen, S.D. Iversen, and S.H. Snyder), pp. 609–26. Plenum Press, New York.

Erickson, C.K. and Graham, D.T. (1973). Alteration of cortical and reticular acetylcholine release by ethanol *in vivo. J. Pharmacol. Exp. Therap.*, **185**, 583–93.

Eriksson, E., Eden, S., and Modigh, K. (1982). Up- and down-regulation of central postsynaptic alpha$_2$ receptors reflected in the growth hormone response to clonidine in reserpine-pretreated rats. *Psychopharmacology*, **77**, 327–31.

Evans, J.I., Lewis, S.A., Gibb, I.A.M., and Cheetham, M. (1968). Sleep and barbiturates: some experiments and observations. *Br. Med. J.*, **4**, 291–3.

Everitt, B.J. and Keverne, E.B. (1979). Models of depression based on behavioural observations of experimental animals. In *Psychopharmacology of affective disorders* (ed. E.S. Paykel and A. Coppen), pp. 41–59. Oxford University Press.

Ewusi-Mensah, F., Saunders, J.B., Wodak, A.D., Murray, R.M., and Williams, R. (1983). Psychiatric morbidity in patients with alcoholic liver disease. *Br. Med. J.*, **287**, 1417–19.

Exton-Smith, A.N. and McLean, A.E.M. (1979). Uses and abuses of chlormethiazole. *Lancet*, **i**, 1093.

Eysenck, H.J. (1967). *The biological basis of personality.* C.C. Thomas, Springfield, Illinois.

Eysenck, H.J. (ed.) (1981). *A model for personality.* Springer-Verlag, Berlin.

Eysenck, H.J. (ed.) (1983). *A model for intelligence.* Springer-Verlag, Berlin.

Eysenck, H.J. and Eaves, L.J. (1980). *The causes and effects of smoking.* Maurice Temple Smith, London.

Eysenck, H.J. and Eysenck, S.B.G. (1975). *Eysenck Personality Questionnaire.* Hodder and Stoughton, Essex.

Eysenck, H.J. and Eysenck, S.B.G. (1976). *Psychoticism as a dimension of personality.* Hodder and Stoughton, London.

Fagg, G.E. (1985). L-glutamate, excitatory amino acid receptors and brain function. *Trends Neurosci.*, **8**, 207–10.

Fagg, G.E., Foster, A.C., and Ganong, A.H. (1986). Excitatory amino acid synaptic mechanisms and neurological function. *Trends Pharmac. Sci.*, **7**, 357–63.

Fairbairn, J.W. and Pickens, J.T. (1979). The oral activity of delta^1-tetrahydrocannabinol and its dependence on prostaglandin E$_2$. *Br. J. Pharmacol.*, **67**, 379–85.

Fairburn, C.G. (1981). Schizophrenia. *Hospital Update*, **7**, 1115–27.

Farde, L., Wiesel, F-A., Nordstrom, A-L and Sedvall, G. (1989) D1- and D2-dopamine receptor occupancy during treatment with conventional and atypical neuroleptics. *Psychopharmacology*, **99**, (Suppl.), S28.

Feighner, J.P. (1982). Benzodiazepines as antidepressants. In *Modern problems of pharmacopsychiatry* (ed. T.A. Ban), pp. 196–212. S. Karger, Basel.

Feinmann, C., Harris, M., and Cawley, R. (1984). Psychogenic facial pain: presentation and treatment. *Br. Med. J.*, **288**, 436–8.

Fenton, G.W. (1984). The electroencephalogram in psychiatry: clinical and research applications. *Psychiatric Developments*, **2**, 53–75.

Ferrier, B. M., Kennett, D. J., and Devlin, M. C. (1980). Influence of oxytocin on human memory processes. *Life Sci.*, **27**, 2311-17.

Ferrier, I. N., Eccleston, D., Moore, P. B., and Wood, K. A. (1990). Relapse in chronic depression on withdrawal of L-tryptophan. *Lancet*, **336**, 380-1.

Feyerabend, C. and Russell, M. A. H. (1978). Effect of urinary pH and nicotine excretion on plasma nicotine during cigarette smoking and chewing nicotine gum. *Br. J. clin. Pharmac.*, **5**, 293-7.

Fibiger, H. C. and Lloyd, K. G. (1984). Neurobiological substrates of tardive dyskinesia: the GABA hypothesis. *Trends Neurosci.*, **7**, 462-4.

Fibiger, J. (1991). Cholinergic mechanisms in learning, memory and dementia: a review of recent evidence. *Trends Neurosci.,* **14**, 220-3.

Fields, H. L. (1987). *Pain.* McGraw Hill, New York.

Fields, H. L. (1988). Sources of variability in the sensation of pain. *Pain*, **33**, 195-200.

Fields, H. L. and Levine J. D. (1984). Placebo analgesia — a role for endorphins? *Trends Neurosci.*, **7**, 271-3.

Fifkova, E. and Delay, R. J. (1982). Cytoplasmic action in neuronal processes as a possible mediator of synaptic plasticity. *J. Cell. Biol.*, **95**, 345-50.

File, S. and Baldwin, H. A. (1987). Flumazenil: a possible treatment for benzodiazepine withdrawal anxiety. *Lancet*, **ii**, 106-7.

File, S. and Baldwin, H. A. (1989). Changes in anxiety in rats tolerant to, and withdrawn from, benzodiazepines: behavioural and biochemical studies. In *The psychopharmacology of anxiety* (ed. P. Tyrer), pp. 28-51. Oxford University Press.

File, S. E. and Hitchcott, P. K. (1990). A theory of benzodiazepine dependence that can explain whether flumazenil will enhance or reverse the phenomena. *Psychopharmacology*, **101**, 525-32.

File, S. E. and Pellow, S. (1983). RO 5-4864, a ligand for benzodiazepine micromolar and peripheral binding sites: antagonism and enhancement of behavioural effects. *Psychopharmacology*, **80**, 166-70.

File, S. E. and Silverstone, T. (1981). Naloxone changes self-ratings but not performance in normal subjects. *Psychopharmacology*, **74**, 353-4.

Fink, M. (1976). Effects of acute and chronic inhalation of hashish, marijuana and Δ^9tetrahydrocannabinol on brain electrical activity in man: evidence for tissue tolerance. *Ann. N.Y. Acad. Sci.*, **282**, 387-98.

Fink, M. (1978). Psychoactive drugs and the waking EEG. In *Psychopharmacology: a generation of progress* (ed. M. A. Lipton, A. DiMascio, and K. F. Killam), pp. 691-8. Raven Press, New York.

Fischman, M. W. (1987). Cocaine and the amphetamines. In *Psychopharmacology: the third generation of progress* (ed. H. Y. Meltzer), pp. 1543-53. Raven Press, New York.

Fitzgerald, M. (1986). Monoamines and descending control of nociception. *Trends Pharmac. Sci.*, **91**, 51-2.

Fitzgerald, M. (1990). c-Fos and the changing face of pain. *Trends Neurosci.*, **13**, 439-40.

Flood, J. F., Bennett, E. L., Orme, A. E., Rosenzweig, M. P., and Jarvik, M. E. (1978). Memory: modification of anisomycin-induced amnesia by stimulants and depressants. *Science*, **199**, 324-6.

Flor-Henry, P. (1976). Lateralised temporo-limbic dysfunction and psycho-pathology. *Ann. N.Y. Acad. Sci.*, **280**, 777–97.

Flor-Henry, P. (1979). Laterality, shifts of cerebral dominance, sinistrality and psychosis. In *Hemisphere asymmetries of function in psychopathology*. (ed. J. Gruzelier and P. Flor-Henry), pp. 3–19. Elsevier/North Hollan, Amsterdam.

Fourestie, V., Ligmeres, B. de, Roudot-Thoroval, F., Fulli-Lemaire, I., Cremniter, D., Nahoul, K., Fournier, S., and Lejone, J.-L. (1986). Suicide attempts in hypo-oestrogenic phases of the menstrual cycle. *Lancet*, **ii**, 1357–9.

Fowler, C.J., O'Neill, C., Garlind, A., and Cowburn, R. (1990). Alzheimer's disease: is there a problem beyond recognition? *Trends Pharmac. Sci.*, **11**, 183–4.

Fozard, J.R. (1987). 5-HT: the enigma variations. *Trends Pharmac. Sci.*, **8**, 501–6.

Fozard, J.R. and Gray, J.W. (1989). 5-HT$_{1C}$ receptor activation: a key step in the initiation of migraine? *Trends Pharmac. Sci.*, **10**, 307–9.

Frackowiak, R.S.J. (1987). Imaging and function. In *Alzheimer's disease: current approaches* (ed. J.C. Malkin and M.N. Rossor), pp. 41–50. Duphar Laboratories Ltd., Southampton.

Franks, N.P. and Lieb, W.R. (1982). Molecular mechanisms of general anaesthesia. *Nature*, **300**, 487–93.

Freedman, D.X. and Boggan, W.O. (1982). Biochemical pharmacology of psychotomimetics. In *Psychotropic agents part III*. (ed. F. Hoffmeister and S. Stille), pp. 57–88. Springer-Verlag, Heidelberg.

Freemon, F.R. (1972). *Sleep research: a critical series*. Charles C. Thomas, Springfield, Illinois.

Frenk, H., Cannon, J.T., Lewis, J.W., and Liebeskind, J.C. (1988). Neural and neurochemical mechanisms of pain inhibition. In *The psychology of pain* (ed. R.A. Sternbach), pp. 25–47. Raven Press, New York.

Frid, M. and Singer, G. (1979). Hypnotic analgesia in conditions of stress is partially reversed by naloxone. *Psychopharmacology*, **63**, 211–15.

Friedland, R.P., Brun, A., and Budinger, T.F. (1985). Pathological and positron emission tomographic correlations in Alzheimer's disease. *Lancet*, **i**, 228.

Gadea-Ciria, M., Stadler, H., Lloyd, K.G., and Bartholini, G. (1973). Acetylcholine release within the cat striatum during sleep-wakefulness cycles. *Nature*, **243**, 518–19.

Gage, F.H., Bjorklund, A., Steveni, V., Dunnet, S.B. and Kelly, P.A.T. (1984). Intrahippocampal septal grafts ameliorate learning impairment in aged rats. *Science*, **225**, 553–6.

Galloway, M.P. (1988). Neurochemical interactions of cocaine with dopaminergic systems. *Trends Pharmac. Sci.*, **9**, 451–4.

Garcia-Arraras, J.E. (1981). Effects of sleep-promoting factor from human urine on sleep cycle of cats. *Am. J. Physiol.*, **24**, 269–74.

Garcia-Sevilla, J.A., Zis, A.P., Hollingsworth, P.J., Greden, J.F., and Smith, C.B. (1981). Platelet alpha$_2$-adrenergic receptors in major depressive disorder. *Arch. Gen. Psychiat.*, **38**, 1327–33.

Garruto, R.M., Fukatsu, R., Yanagihava, R., Gajdusek, D.C., Hook, G., and Fiori, C.E. (1984). Imaging of calcium and aluminium in neurofibrillary tangle bearing neurons in Parkinsonian-dementia of Guam. *Proc. Natl. Acad. Sci.*, **81**, 1875-9.

Gash, D. M. and Thomas, G. J. (1983). What is the importance of vasopressin in memory processes? *Trends Neurosci.*, **6**, 197-8.

Gash, D. M. and Thomas, G. J. (1984). The importance of vasopressin in memory. *Trends Neurosci.*, **7**, 64-6.

Gath, D. and Iles, S. (1990). Depression and the menopause. *Br. Med. J.*, **300**, 1287-8.

Geaney, D. P., Soper, N., Shepstone, B. J., and Cowen, P. J. (1990). Effect of cholinergic stimulation on regional cerebral blood flow in Alzheimer's disease. *Lancet*, **335**, 1484-7.

Gelder, M. G. (1990). Psychological treatment for depressive disorder. *Br. Med. J.*, **300**, 1087-8.

Gelder, M., Gath, D., and Mayou, R. (1983). *Oxford textbook of psychiatry*. Oxford University Press.

Gelenberg, A. J. (1976). The catatonic syndrome. *Lancet*, **i**, 1339-41.

Gellman, R. S. and Miles, F. A. (1985). A new role for the cerebellum in conditioning? *Trends Neurosci.*, **8**, 181-2.

George, K. A. and Dundee, J. W. (1977). Relative amnestic actions of diazepam, flunitrazepam and lorazepam in man. *Br. J. clin. Pharmac.*, **4**, 45-50.

George, F. R. and Goldberg, S. R. (1989). Genetic approaches to the analysis of addiction processes. *Trends Pharmac. Sci.*, **10**, 78-83.

George, R., Haslett, W. L., and Jenden, D. J. (1964). A cholinergic mechanism in the brainstem reticular formation: induction of paradoxical sleep. *Int. J. Neuropharmacol.*, **3**, 541-52.

Gerbino, L., Oleshansky, M., and Gersham, S. (1978). Clinical use and mode of action of lithium. In *Psychopharmacology: a generation of progress* (ed. M. A. Lipton, A. DiMascio, and K. F. Killam), pp. 1261-75. Raven Press, New York.

German, D. C., and Bowden, D. M. (1974). Catecholamine systems as the neural substrate for intracranial self-stimulation: a hypothesis. *Brain Res.*, **73**, 381-419.

Geschwind, N. (1975). Focal disturbances of higher nervous function. In *Textbook of medicine* (ed. P. B. Beeson and W. McDermott), p. 557. W. B. Saunders Company, Philadelphia.

Geschwind, N. (1983). Biological foundations of cerebral dominance. *Trends Neurosci.*, **6**, 354-6.

Geschwind, N. and Levitsky, W. (1968). Human brain: left-right asymmetries in temporal speech region. *Science (Wash. DC)*, **161**, 186-7.

Ghoneim, M. M., Mewaldt, S. P., Berie, J. L., and Hinruchs, J. V. (1981). Memory and performance effects of single and 3-week administration of diazepam. *Psychopharmacology*, **73**, 147-51.

Giardino, L., Colza, L., Piazza, P. V., Zanni, M., Sorbera, F., and Amato, G. (1990). Opiate receptor modifications in the rat brain after chronic treatment with haloperidol and sulpiride. *J. Psychopharmacology*, **4**, 7-12.

Gilbert, P. (1984). *Depression: from psychology to brain state*. Lawrence Erlbaum Associates, Hillsdale, New Jersey.

Gilbert, C. D. (1985). Horizontal integration in the neocortex. *Trends Neurosci.* **8**, 160-5.

Gillin, J. C. and Borbely, A. A. (1985). Sleep: a neurobiological window on affective disorders. *Trends Neurosci.*, **8**, 537–42.

Gilmartin, J. J., Corris, P. A., Stone, T. N., Veal, D., and Gibson, G. J. (1988). Effects of diazepam and chlormethiazole on ventilatory control in normal subjects. *Br. J. clin. Pharmac.*, **25**, 766–70.

Giurgea, C. (1976). Piracetam: nootropic pharmacology of neurointegrative activity. In *Current developments in psychopharmacology*. (ed. W. B. Essman and L. Valzelli), Vol. 3, pp. 223–73. Spectrum Publications, New York.

Glaser, H. H., Massengale, O. H. (1962) Glue sniffing in children: deliberate inhalation of vaporized plastic cement. *JAMA*, **181**, 300–3.

Glatt, M. A. (ed.) (1977). *Drug dependence: current problems and issues*. MTP Press, Lancaster.

Glennon, R. A. (1987). Psychoactive phenylisopropylamines. In *Psychopharmacology: the third generation of progress* (ed. H. Y. Meltzer), pp. 1627–34. Raven Press, New York.

Glover, V. and Sandler, M. (1989). Can the vascular and neurogenic theories of migraine finally be reconciled? *Trends Pharmac. Sci.*, **10**, 1–3.

Goadsby, P. J., Lambert, G. A., and Lance, J. W. (1982). Differential effects on the external circulation of the monkey evoked by locus coeruleus stimulation. *Brain Research*, **249**, 247–54.

Godschalk, M., Dzoljic, M. R., and Bonta, I. L. (1977). The role of dopaminergic systems in gamma-hydroxybutyrate-induced electrocorticogram hypersynchronisation in the rat. *J. Pharm. Pharmac.*, **29**, 605–8.

Gold, P. E. and McGaugh, J. L. (1975). A single-trace, two-process view of memory storage processes. In *Short-term memory* (ed. D. Deutsch and J. A. Deutsch), pp. 355–78. Academic Press, New York.

Gold, M. S., Redmond, D. E., and Kleber, H. D. (1978). Clonidine blocks acute opiate-withdrawal symptoms. *Lancet*, **ii**, 599–601.

Gold, M. S., Redmond, D. E., and Kleber, H. D. (1979a). Noradrenergic hyperactivity in opiate withdrawal supported by clonidine reversal of opiate withdrawal. *Am. J. Psychiat.*, **136**, 100–2.

Gold, P. W., Weingartner, H., Ballenger, J. C., Goodwin, F. K., and Post, R. M. (1979b). Effects of 1-desamo-8-D-arginine vasopressin on behaviour and cognition in primary affective disorder. *Lancet*, **ii**, 992–4.

Gold, L. H., Hubner, C. B., and Koob, G. F. (1989). A role for the mesolimbic dopamine system in the psychostimulant actions of MDMA. Psychopharmacology, **99**, 40–7.

Goldberg, I. K. (1980). L-tyrosine in depression. *Lancet*, **ii**, 364.

Golding, J. F. and Cornish, A. M. (1987). Personality and life style in medical students: psychopharmacological aspects. *Psychology and Health*, **1**, 287–301.

Golding, J. F., Harpur, T., and Brent-Smith, H. (1983). Personality and drug taking correlates of cigarette smoking. *Person. Individ, Diff.*, **4**, 703–6.

Goldstein, A., Fischli, W., Lowney, L. I., Hunkapiller, M., and Hood, L. (1981). Porcine pituitary dynorphin, complete amino and sequence of the biologically active heptadecapeptide. *Proc. Natl. Acad. Sci. USA*, **78**, 7219–23.

Golstein, M., Engel, J., Regev, I., and Mino, S. (1983). The possible role of central epinephrine alpha$_2$-adrenoceptors and presynaptic dopamine receptors in affective disorders. In *Frontiers in neuropsychiatric research* (ed. E. Usdin, M. Goldstein, A.J. Friedhoff, and A. Georgatas), pp. 55–64. Macmillan, London.

Gonzales, R.A. and Hoffman, P.L. (1991) Receptor gated channels may be selective CNS targets for ethanol. *Trends in Pharmac. Sci.*, **12**, 1–3.

Goodwin, F.K. and Post, R.M. (1983). 5-Hydroxytryptamine and depression: a model for the interaction of normal variance with pathology. *Br. J. Clin. Pharmac.*, **15**, 393S–405S.

Goodwin, F.K., Cowdry, R.W., and Webster, M.H. (1978). Predictors of drug response in the affective disorders: towards an integrated approach. In *Psychopharmacology: a generation of progress* (ed. M.A. Lipton, A. DiMascio, and K.F. Killam), pp. 1277–88. Raven Press, New York.

Gorman, J.M., Fyer, M.R., Liebowitz, M.R., and Klein, D.F. (1987). Pharmacological provocation of panic attacks. In *Psychopharmacology: the third generation of progress* (ed. H.Y. Meltzer), pp. 985–93. Raven Press, New York.

Gorman. J.M., Liebowitz, M.R. Fyer, A.J., and Stein, J. (1989). A neuroanatomical hypothesis for panic disorder. *Am.J. Psychiat.*, **146**, 148–61.

Gottfries, C.G. (1980). Biochemistry of dementia and normal ageing. *Trends Neurosci.*, **23**, 55–7.

Goudie, A.J. and Griffiths, J.W. (1986). Behavioural factors in drug tolerance. *Trends Pharmac. Sci.*, **7**, 192–6.

Grahame-Smith, D.G. (1985). Pharmacological adaptive responses occurring during drug therapy and in disease. *Trends Pharmac. Sci.*, **6**, 38–41.

Grahame-Smith, D.G. and Orr, M.W. (1978). Clinical psychopharmacology. In *Recent advances in clinical pharmacology* (ed. P. Turner and D.G. Shand), pp. 163–87. Churchill Livingstone, Edinburgh.

Gray, J.A. (1977). Drug effects on fear and frustration: possible limbic site of action of major tranquillisers. In *Handbook of psychopharmacology* (ed. L.L. Iverson, S.D. Iverson, and S.H. Snyder), Vol. 8, pp. 433–529. Plenum Press, New York.

Gray, J.A. (1981*a*). Anxiety as a paradigm case of emotion. *Br. Med. Bull.* **37**, 193–7.

Gray, J.A. (1981*b*). A critique of Eysenck's theory of personality. In *A Model for Personality* (ed. H.J. Eysenck), pp. 246–76. Springer-Verlag, Berlin.

Gray, J.A. (1982). *The neuropsychology of anxiety*. Clarendon Press, Oxford and Oxford University Press, New York.

Gray, J.A. (1985). A whole and its parts: behaviour, the brain, cognition and emotion. *Bull. Br. Psychol. Soc.*, **38**, 99–112.

Gray, J.A. (1987*a*). The neuropsychology of emotion and personality. In *Cognitive neurochemistry* (ed. S.M. Stahl, S.D. Iversen, and E.C. Goodman), pp. 171–90. Oxford University Press.

Gray J.A. (1987*b*). Interactions between drugs and behaviour therapy. In *Theoretical foundations of behaviour therapy* (ed. H.J. Eysenck and I. Martin), pp, 433–47. Plenum Press, New York and London.

Gray, J.A., Enz, A., and Spiegel, R. (1989). Muscarinic agonists for senile dementia: past experience and future trends. *Trends Pharmac. Sci.*, (Suppl) 85–8.

Greden, J. F. (1974). Anxiety or caffeinism: a diagnostic dilemma. *Am. J. Psychiat.*, **131**, 1089-92.

Greden, J. F., Fontaine, P., Lubetsky, M., and Chamberlain, K. (1978). Anxiety and depression associated with caffeinism among psychiatric in-patients. *Am. J. Psychiat.*, **135**, 963-6.

Green, P. (1978). Defective interhemispheric transfer in schizophrenia. *J. Abnormal Psychol.*, **87**, 472-80.

Greenamyre, J. T., Penney, J. B., Young, A. B., D'Amato, C. J., Hicks, S. P., and Shorlson, I. (1985). Alterations in L-glutamate binding in Alzheimer's and Huntingdon's disease. *Science,* **227**, 1496-8.

Greenamyre, J. T., Penney, J. B., D'Amato, C. J., and Young, A. B. (1987). Dementia of the Alzheimer's type: changes in hippocampal L-^{3}H-glutamate binding. *J. Neurochem.*, **48**, 543-9.

Greenblatt, D. J., Shader, R. I., Divoll, M., and Harmatz, J. S. (1981). Benzodiazepines; a summary of pharmacokinetic properties. *Br. J. Clin. Pharmac.*, **11**, 11-16S.

Greenblatt, D. J., Divoll, M., Abernethy, D. R., Ochs, H. R., and Shader, R. (1983). Clinical pharmacokinetics of the newer benzodiazepines. *Clin. Pharmacokinet.*, **8**, 233-52.

Greenberg, B. D. and Segal, D. S. (1986). Evidence for multiple opiate receptor involvement in different phencyclidine-induced unconditioned behaviours in rats. *Psychopharmacology,* **88**, 44-53.

Greene, L. A. (1984). The importance of both early and delayed responses to the biological actions of nerve growth factor. *Trends Neurosci.*, **7**, 91-4.

Greenhough, W. T. (1984). Structural correlates of information storage in the mammalian brain: a review and hypothesis. *Trends Neurosci.*, **7**, 229-35.

Griffiths, R. R. and Sannerud, C. A. (1987). Abuse of and dependence on benzodiazepines and other anxiolytic/sedative drugs. In *Psychopharmacology: the third generation of progress* (ed. H. Y. Meltzer), pp. 1535-41. Raven Press, New York.

Griffiths, R. R. and Woodson, P. P. (1988). Caffeine dependence and reinforcement in humans and laboratory animals. In *The psychopharmacology of addiction* (ed. M. Lader), pp. 141-56. Oxford University Press.

Griffiths, R. R., Bigelow, G. E., Stitzer, M. L., and McLeod, D. R. (1983). Behavioural effects of drugs of abuse. In *Applications of behavioural pharmacology in toxicology.* (ed. G. Zbinden, V. Cuomo, G. Racagini, and B. Weiss), pp. 367-82. Raven Press, New York.

Griffiths, R. R., McLeod, D. R., Bigelow, G. E., Liebson, I. A., and Roache, J. D. (1984). Relative abuse liability of diazepam and oxazepam: behavioural and subjective dose effects. *Psychopharmacology,* **84**, 141-54.

Griffiths, R. R., Bigelow, G. E., Liebson, I. A., O'Keefe, M., O'Leary, D., and Russ, N. (1986). Human coffee drinking: manipulation of concentration and caffeine dose. *J. Exp. Anal. Behav.*, **45**, 133-48.

Gruzelier, J. and Liddiard, D. (1989). The neuropsychology of schizophrenia in the context of topographical mapping of electrocortical activity. In *Topographical brain mapping of EEG and evoked potentials* (ed. K. Maurer), pp. 421-37. Springer-Verlag, Berlin.

Guilleminault, C. and Tilkian, A. (1976). The sleep apnoea syndrome. *Ann. Rev. Med.,* **27**, 465-83.

Guilleminault, C., Eldridge, F., and Dement, W. (1973). Insomnia with sleep apnoea: a new syndrome. *Science,* **181**, 856-85.

Guilleminault, C. Winkle, R., Connolly, S., Melvin, K., and Tilkian, A. (1984). Cyclical variation of the heart rate in sleep apnoea syndrome. *Lancet,* **i**, 126-31.

Guilleminault, C., Mignot, E., and Grumet, F.C. (1989). Familial patterns of narcolepsy. *Lancet,* **334**, 1376-9.

Gur, R.E. (1978). Left hemisphere dysfunction and left hemisphere over-activation in schizophrenia. *J. Abn. Psychol.,* **87**, 226-38.

Gur, R.E. (1979*a*). Cognitive concomitants of hemispheric dysfunction in schizophrenia. *Arch. Gen. Psychiat.,* **36**, 269-74.

Gur, R. (1979*b*). Hemispheric overactivation in schizophrenia. In *Hemisphere Asymmetries of Function in Psychopathology* (ed. G. Gruzelier and P. Flor-Henry), pp. 113-23. Elsevier/North Holland, Amsterdam.

Gur, R.E., Skolnick, B.E., and Gur, R.C. (1983). Brain function in psychiatric disorders. *Arch. Gen. Psychiat.,* **40**, 1250-4.

Gurling, H.M.D. (1988). Testing the retrovirus hypothesis of manic depression and schizophrenia with molecular genetic techniques. *J. Roy. Soc. Med.,* **81**, 332-4.

Gustafsson, B., and Wigstrom, H. (1988). Physiological mechanisms underlying long-term potentiation. *Trends Neurosci.,* **11**, 156-62.

Haefely, W. (1978). Behavioural and neuropharmacolgical aspects of drugs used in anxiety and related states. In *Psychopharmacology: a generation of progress* (ed. M.A. Lipton, A. DiMascio, and K.F. Killam) pp. 1359-74. Raven Press, New York.

Haefely, W. (1989). Neurochemistry of benzodiazepines, barbiturates and alcohol. Paper given at Second Maudsley Conference on New Developments in Psychiatry, Waldorf Hotel, London, July 11-14 1989.

Haefely, W. (1990). Benzodiazepine receptor and ligands: structural and functional differences. In *Benzodiazepinmes: current concepts* (ed. I. Hindmarch, G. Beaumont, S. Brandon, and B.E. Leonard) pp. 1-18. John Wiley and Sons, Chichester.

Haefely, W., Pieri, L., Pole, P., and Schaffer, R. (1981). General pharmacology and neuropharmacology of benzodiazepine derivatives. In *Handbook of experimental pharmacology.* Vol. 55, II (ed. H. Hoffmeister and G. Stille), pp. 13-62. Springer-Verlag, Berlin.

Haider, I. and Oswald, I. (1970). Late brain recovery after drug overdose. *Br. Med. J.,* **2**, 318-22.

Haigh, J.R. and Feeley, M. (1988) RO 16-6028, a benzodiazepine receptor partial agonist, does not exhibit anticonvulsant tolerance in mice. *Eur. J. Pharmacol.,* **147**, 283-5.

Halikas, J., Kemp, K., Kuhn, K., Carlson, G., and Crea, F. (1989). Carbamazepine for cocaine addition? *Lancet,* **i**, 623-4.

Hall, G.H. (1970). Effects of nicotine and tobacco smoke on the electrical activity of the cerebral cortex and olfactory bulb. *Br. J. Pharmac.,* **38**, 271-86.

Hall, G. H. and Morrison, C. F. (1973). New evidence for a relationship between tobacco smoking, nicotine dependence and stress. *Nature,* **243**, 199-201.

Hall, G. H. and Turner, D. M. (1972). Effects of nicotine on the release of ³H-noradrenaline from the hypothalamus. *Biochem. Pharmacol.* **21**, 1829-38.

Hamburger, R., Sela, A., and Belamker, R. H. (1985). Differences in learning and extinction in response to vasopressin in six inbred mouse strains. *Psychopharmacology,* **87**, 124-5.

Han, J. S. and Terenius, L. (1982). Neurochemical basis of acupuncture analgesia. *Ann. Rev. Pharmacol. Toxicol.,* **22**, 193-220.

Handler, C. E. and Perkin, G. D. (1983). Wernicke's encephalopathy. *J. Roy. Soc. Med.,* **76**, 339-41.

Hardy, J. (1988). Molecular biology and Alzheimer's disease: more questions than answers. *Trends Neurosci.,* **11**, 293-4.

Hardy, J., and Allsopp, D. (1991). Amyloid deposition is the central event in the aetiology of Alzheimer's disease. *Trends Pharmac. Sci.,* **12**, 383-91.

Hardy, J. and Cowburn, R. (1987). Glutamate toxicity and Alzheimer's disease. *Trends Neurosci.,* **10**, 406.

Harper, C. G., Kril, J. J., and Holloway, R. L. (1985). Brain shrinkage in chronic alcoholics: a pathological study. *Br. Med. J.,* **290**, 501-4.

Harper, C., Kril, J., and Daly, J. (1987). Are we drinking our neurones away? *Br. Med. J.,* **294**, 534-6.

Harris, R. A., and Hood, W. F. (1980). Inhibition of synaptosomal calcium uptake by ethanol. *J. Pharmac. Exper. Therap.,* **213**, 562-8.

Harrison, P. J. (1986) Pathogenesis of Alzheimer's disease — beyond the cholinergic hypothesis: discussion paper. *J. Roy. Soc. Med.,* **79**, 347-52.

Harrison, N. L. and Simmonds, M. A. (1983). Two distinct interactions of barbiturates and chlormethiazole with the GABA A receptor complex in rat cuneate nucleus in vitro. *Br. J. Pharmac.,* **80**, 387-94.

Harrison-Read, P. E. (1981). Synaptic and behavioural actions of antidepressant drugs. *Trends Pharmac. Sci.,* **4**, 28-34.

Hartmann, E. (1976). Long term administration of psychotropic drugs: effects on human sleep. In *Pharmacology of sleep.* (ed. R. L. Williams and I. Karacan), pp. 211-24. Wiley, New York.

Hartmann, E. L. (1979). L-tryptophan and sleep. In *Pharmacology of the states of alertness* (ed. P. Passouant and I. Oswald), pp. 75-84. Pergamon Press Ltd., Oxford.

Hartmann, E. L. (1980). Sleep and the sleep disorders. In *Handbook of biological psychiatry, part II. Brain mechanisms and abnormal behaviour — psychopharmacology.* (ed. H. M. van Praag), pp. 331-57. Marcel Dekker, New York.

Hartvig, P., Gillberg, P.R., Gordh, T., and Post, C. (1989). Cholinergic mechanisms in pain and analgesia. *Trends Pharmac. Sci. Suppl.,* 75-9.

Harvey, S. C. (1985). Hypnotics and sedatives. In *The pharmacological basis of therapeutics* (ed. A. G. Gilman, L. S. Goodman, T. W. Rall, and F. Murad), pp. 339-71. Macmillan, New York.

Hatsukami, D. K., Hughes, J. R., Pickens, R. W., and Srikis, D. (1984). Tobacco withdrawal symptoms: an experimental analysis. *Psychopharmacology,* **84**, 231-6.

Haug, J. O. (1962). Pneumoencephalographic studies in mental disease. *Acta Psychiatrica Scand.*, Suppl. **165**, 1–114.

Hayflick, L. (1979). Cell ageing. In *Physiology and cell biology of age*, Vol. 8 (ed. A. Cherkin, C. E. Finch, N. Kharasch, T. Makindon, and F. L. Scott), pp. 3–9. Raven Press, New York.

Hayward, M. (1977). Headache and pain in the head and neck. In *Persistent pain: modern methods of treatment,* Vol. 1 (ed. S. Lipton), pp. 35–60. Academic Press, London and Grune and Stratton, New York.

Headley, P. M. and Grillner, S. (1990). Excitatory amino acids and synaptic transmission: the evidence for a physiological function. *Trends Pharmac. Sci.,* **11**, 205–11.

Heath, R. G. (1964). Pleasure responses of human subjects to direct stimulation of the brain: physiological and psychodynamic considerations. In *The role of pleasure in behaviour* (ed. R. G. Heath) Harper and Row, New York.

Heath, R. G. and Walker, C. F. (1985). Correlation of deep and surface electroencephalographs with psychosis and hallucinations in schizophrenics: a report of two cases. *Biol. Psychiat.,* **20**, 669–74.

Hebb, D. O. (1949). *The organisation of behaviour.* Wiley, New York.

Heimstra, N. W. (1973). The effects of smoking on mood change. In *Smoking behaviour: motives and incentives* (ed. W. L. Dunn), pp. 197–207. Winston, Washington.

Heiss, W. D., Pawlick, G., Herholz, K., Wagner, R., and Weinhard, K. (1985). Regional cerebral glucose metabolism in man during wakefulness, sleep and dreaming. *Brain Research,* **327**, 362–6.

Henderson, G. (1983). Electrophysiological analysis of opioid action. *Br. Med. Bull.,* **39**, 59–64.

Henderson, G. (1990). Complexity of 5-HT pharmacology compounded by electrophysiological data. *Trends Pharmac. Sci.* **11**, 265–6.

Hendrickson, A. E (1983*a*). The biological basis of intelligence. Part I: theory. In *A model for intelligence* (ed. H. J. Eysenck), pp. 151–96. Springer-Verlag, Berlin.

Hendrickson, D. E. (1983*b*). The biological basis of intelligence. Part II: measurement. In *A model for intelligence* (ed. H. J. Eysenck), pp. 197–230 Springer-Verlag, Berlin.

Heninger, G. R. and Charney, D. S. (1987). Mechanisms of antidepressant treatments: implications for the etiology and treatment of depressive disorders. In *Psychopharmacology: the third generation of progress* (ed. H. Y. Meltzer), pp. 535–44. Raven Press, New York.

Hennessy, M. J., Kirkby, K. C., and Montgomery, I. M. (1991). Comparison of the amnesic effects of midazolam and diazepam. *Psychopharmacology,* **103**, 545–50.

Henry, J. A. and Martin, A. J. (1987). The risk-benefit assessment of antidepressant drugs. *Med. Toxicol.,* **2**, 445–62.

Herberg, L. J., and Rose, I. C. (1989). The effect of MK-801 and other antagonists of NMDA-type glutamate receptors on brain-stimulation reward. *Psychopharmacology,* **99**, 87–90.

Herman, J. B., Brotman, A. W., and Rosenbaum, J. F. (1987). Rebound anxiety in panic disorder patients treated with shorter-acting benzodiazepines. *J. clin. Psychiat.*, **48**, (Suppl. 10), 22–6.

Herz, A. (1981). Role of endorphins in addiction. *Mod. Probl. Pharmacopsychiat.*, **17**, 175–80.

Herz, A. and Hollt, V. (1982). On the role of endorphins in addiction. In *Advances in pharmacology and therapeutics II. Vol. 1. CNS pharmacology – neuropeptides* (ed. H. Yoshida, Y. Hagihara, and S. Ebashi), pp. 67–76. Pergamon Press, Oxford.

Herz, A., Hollt, V., and Przewlocki, R. (1980a). Endogenous opioids and addiction. In *Brain and pituitary peptides,* Ferring Symposium, Munich, 1979, pp. 183–9. Karger, Basel.

Herz, A., Schulz, R., and Wuster, M. (1980b). Some aspects of opiate receptors. In *Receptors for Neurotransmitters and Peptide Hormones.* (ed. G. Pepeu, M. J. Kuhar, and S. J. Enna), pp. 329–37. Raven Press, New York.

Herzberg, J. L. and Wolkind, S. N. (1983). Solvent sniffing in perspective. *Br. J. Hosp. Med.*, **29**, 72–6.

Heston, L. L. and Mastri, A. R. (1977). The genetics of Alzheimer's disease. *Arch. Gen. Psychiat.*, **34**, 976–81.

Hillyard, S. A. (1985) Electrophysiology of human selective attention. *Trends Neurosci.*, **8**, 400–5.

Hinde, R. A. (1977). Mother-infant separation and the nature of inter-individual relationships; experiments with rhesus monkeys. *Proc. Roy. Soc. Lond. (Ser. B),* **196**, 29–50.

Hirsch, S. R. (1983). Psychosocial factors in the cause and prevention of schizophrenia. *Br. Med. J.,* **286**, 1600–1.

Hoffman, B. B. and Lefkowitz, R. J. (1980). Radioligand binding studies of adrenergic receptors: new insights into molecular and physiological regulations. *Ann. Rev. Pharmacol. Toxicol.,* **20**, 581–608.

Hoffman, D., Adams, J. D., LaVoie, E. J., and Hecht, S. S. (1988). Biochemistry, pharmacokinetics and carcinogenicity of nicotine-derived nitrosamines. In *The pharmacology of nicotine* (ed. M. R. Rand and K. Thurau), pp. 43–60. IRL Press, Oxford.

Hoke, M., Lehnhertz, B., Lutkenhoner, B., and Pantec, V. (1989). Cortical auditory evoked magnetic fields: mapping of time and frequency domain aspects. In *Topographic brain mapping of EEG and evoked potentials* (ed. K. Maurer), pp. 537–64. Springer-Verlag, Berlin.

Holaday, J. W. and Faden, A. I. (1982). Endorphins and thyrotropin releasing hormone in shock and trauma. In *CNS pharmacology of neuropeptides* (ed. H. Yoshida, Y. Hagihara, and S. Ebashi), pp. 45–56. Pergamon Press, Oxford.

Hollister, L. E. (1982). Pharmacology and toxicology of psychotomimetics. In *Psychotropic agents part III. Alcohol and psychotomimetics, psychotropic effects of central acting drugs* (ed. F. Hoffmeister and G. Stille), pp. 321–44. Springer-Verlag, Berlin.

Holmes, S. W. and Sugden, D. (1982). Effects of melanotonin on sleep and neurochemistry in the rat. *Br. J. Pharmac.,* **76**, 95–101.

Hore, B. D. and Ritson, E. B. (1982). *Alcohol and health.* Medical Council on Alcoholism, London.

Horn, G., Bradley, P., and McCabe, B.J. (1985). Changes in the structure of synapses associated with learning. *J. Neurosci.*, **5**, 3161-8.

Horne, J.A. (1976). Hail slow wave sleep: goodbye REM. *Bull. Br. Psychiat. Soc.*, **29**, 74-9.

Horne, J.A. (1979). Restitution and human sleep: a critical review. *Physiol. Psychol.*, **7**, 115-25.

Horne, J. (1988). *Why we sleep.* Oxford University Press.

Horne, J.A. and Wilkinson, S. (1985). Chronic sleep reduction: daytime vigilance, performance and EEG measures of sleepiness, with particular reference to 'practice' effects. *Psychophysiology*, **22**, 69-78.

Horrobin, D.F. (1979). Schizophrenia: reconciliation of the dopamine, prostaglandin, and opioid concepts and the role of the pineal. *Lancet,* **i**, 529-31.

Houde, R.W. (1979). Systemic analgesics and related drugs: narcotic analgesics. In *Advances in pain research and therapy* (ed. J.J. Bonica and V. Ventafridda), Vol. 2, pp. 263-73. Raven Press, New York.

Howlett, A.C., Bidant-Russell, M., Devane, W.A., Melvin, L.S., Johnson. M.R., and Herkenham, M. (1990). The cannabinoid receptor: biochemical, anatomical and behavioral characterization. *Trends Neurosci.*, **13**, 420-3.

Hu, H-Y.Y., Davis, J.M., and Pandey, G.N. (1981). Characterisation of alpha-adrenergic receptors in guinea pig cerebral cortex: effect of chronic antidepressant treatments. *Psychopharmacology*, **74**, 201-3.

Hubel, D.H. and Wiesel, T.N. (1977). Ferrier Lecture: Functional architecture of macaque monkey visual cortex. *Proc. Roy. Soc. Ser. B.,* **198**, 1-59.

Hughes, J. (1983). Biogenesis, release and inactivation of enkephalins and dynorphins. *Br. Med. Bull.,* **39**, 17-24.

Hughes, J. and Kosterlitz, H.W. (1983). Introduction. *Br. Med. Bull.,* **39**, 1-3.

Human Toxicology (1989), **8**, 255-334. (Special issue on volatile substance abuse).

Hunkeler, W., Mohler, H., Pieri, L., Pole, P., Bonetti, E.P., Cumin, R., Schaffner, R., and Haefely, W. (1981). Selective antagonists of benzodiazepines. *Nature,* **290**, 514-6.

Hutchison, R.R. and Emley, G.S. (1973). Effects of nicotine on avoidance, conditioned suppression and aggression response measures in animals and man. In *Smoking behaviour: motives and incentives.* (ed. W.L. Dunn), pp. 171-96. Winston, Washington.

Idzikowski, C., Mills, F.J., and Glennard, R. (1986). 5-Hydroxytryptamine-2 antagonist increases human slow wave sleep. *Brain Research,* **378**, 164-86.

Idzikowski, C., Cowen, P.J., Nutt, D., and Mills, F.J. (1987). The effects of chronic ritanserin treatment on sleep and the neuroendocrine response to L-tryptophan. *Psychopharmacology,* **93**, 416-20.

Illis, L.S. (1990). Central pain: much can be offered from a methodological approach. *Br. Med. J.,* **300**, 1284-6.

Ingvar, D.H. (1979). Cerebral circulation and metabolism in sleep. In *Sleep research* (ed. R.G. Priest, A. Pletscher, and J. Ward), pp. 13-18. MTP Press Ltd., Lancaster.

Ingvar, D.H. (1982). Mental illness and regional brain metabolism. *Trends Neurosci.,* **5**, 199-203.

Inque, S., Uchizono, K., and Nagasaki, H. (1982). Endogenous sleep-promoting factors. *Trends Neurosci.,* **5**, 218–20.

International Association for the Study of Pain: Subcommittee on Taxonomy (1986). Classification of chronic pain. *Pain,* Suppl. **3**, S1–S225.

Introini-Collison, I.B., and McGaugh, J.L. (1987). Naloxone and β-endorphin alter the effects of post-training epinephrine on memory. *Psychopharmacology,* **92**, 229–35.

Isaacson, R.L. (1974). *The limbic system.* Plenum Press, New York.

Isaacson, R.L. (1982). *The limbic system* (2nd edn). Plenum Press, New York.

Itil, T.M. and Soldatos, C. (1980). Clinical neurophysiological properties of antidepressants. In *Psychotropic agents part I: antipsychotics and antidepressants* (ed. F. Hoffmeister, and G. Stille), pp. 437–69. Springer-Verlag, Berlin.

Itil, T.M., Shapiro, D.M., Eralp, E., Akman, A., Itil, K.Z., and Garbizu, C. (1985). A new brain function diagnostic unit, including the dynamic brain mapping of computer analysed EEG, evoked potential and sleep (a new hardware/software system and its application in psychiatry and psychopharmacology). *New Trends in Experimental and Clinical Psychiatry,* **1**, 107–77.

Iversen, S.D. (1977). Temporal lobe amnesia. In *Amnesia* (ed. C.W.M. Whitty and O.L. Zangwill), pp. 136–82. Butterworth, London and Boston.

Iversen, S.D. and Iversen, L.L. (1981). *Behavioural pharmacology.* Oxford University Press, New York.

Iversen, L.L. and McKay, A.V.P. (1979). Pharmacodynamics of antidepressants and antimanic drugs. In *Psychopharmacology of affective disorders* (ed. E.S. Paykel and A. Coppen), pp. 60–90. Oxford University Press.

Izquierdo, I. (1982*a*). Beta-endorphin and forgetting. *Trends Pharmac. Sci.,* **3**, 455–547.

Izquierdo, I. (1982*b*). Memory modulation, the sympathoadrenal system and the effect of drugs. *Trends Pharmac. Sci.,* **3**, 352–3.

Izquierdo, I. (1983). Naloxone facilitation of memory. *Trends Pharmac. Sci.,* **4**, 410.

Izquierdo, I. (1990*a*). Acetylcholine release is modulated by different opioid receptor types in different brain regions and species. *Trends Pharmac. Sci.,* **11**, 179–80.

Izquierdo, I. (1990*b*). Nimodipine and the recovery of memory. *Trends Pharmac. Sci.,* **11** 309–10.

Jacobs, B.L. (1984). Single unit activity of brain monoaminergic neurones in freely moving animals: a brief review. In *Modulation of sensorimotor activity during alterations in behavioural states* (ed. R. Bandler), pp. 99–120. Alan R. Liss, New York.

Jaffe, J.H. (1980). Drug addiction and drug abuse. In *The pharmacological basis of therapeutics* (ed. A.G. Gilman, L.S. Goodman, and A. Gilman), pp. 535–607. Macmillan, New York.

Jaffe, J.H. and Martin, W.R. (1980). Opioid analgesics and antagonists. In *The pharmacological basis of therapeutics* (ed. A.G. Gilman, L.S. Goodman, and A. Gilman), pp. 494–534. Macmillan, New York.

James, I.M., Griffith, D.N.W., Pearson, R.M., and Newberry, P. (1977). Effect of oxprenolol on stage-fright in musicians. *Lancet,* **ii**, 952–4.

Janig, W. (1985). Causalgia and reflex sympathetic dystrophy: in which way is the sympathetic nervous system involved? *Trends Neurosci.* **8**, 471-7.

Janke, W. (1980). Psychometric and psychophysiological actions of antipsychotics in man. In *Psychotropic agents. Part I: antipsychotics and antidepressants* (ed. F. Hoffmeister and G. Stille), pp. 305-36. Springer-Verlag, Berlin.

Jansen, K. (1989). Near death experience and the NMDA receptor. *Br. Med. J.,* **298**, 1708.

Jarvik, M.E. (1967). Tobacco smoking in monkeys. *Ann. N.Y. Acad. Sci.,* **142**, 280-94.

Jasinski, D.R., Johnson, R.E., and Henningfield, J.E. (1984). Abuse liability assessment in human subjects. *Trends Pharmac. Sci.,* **5**, 196-200.

Jasper, H.H. and Tessier, J. (1971). Acetylcholine liberation from cerebral cortex during paradoxical (REM) sleep. *Science,* **172**, 601-2.

Jasper, H.H., Khan, R.T., and Elliott, K.A.C. (1965). Amino acids released from cerebral cortex in relation to its state of activation. *Science,* **147**, 1448-51.

Jeffcoate, W.J., Herbert, M., Cullen, M.H., Hastings, A.G., and Walder, C.P. (1979). Prevention of effects of alcohol intoxication by naloxone. *Lancet,* **i**, 1157-9.

Jeffreys, D.B., Flanagan, R.J., and Volans, G.N. (1980). Reversal of ethanol-induced coma with naloxone. *Lancet,* **i**, 308-9.

Jenkins, W.J., Cakebread, K., and Palmer, K.R. (1982). Hepatic aldehyde dehydrogenase and alcoholism. *Lancet,* **ii**, 1275.

Jensen, H.H., Hutchings, B., and Poulsen, J.C. (1989). Conditioned emotional responding under diazepam: a psychophysiological study of state dependent learning. *Psychopharmacology,* **98**, 392-7.

Jeste, D.V., Lohr, J.B., and Goodwin, F.K. (1988). Neuroanatomical studies of major affective disorders: a review and suggestions for further research. *Br. J. Psychiat.,* **153**, 444-59.

Jhamandas, K. and Sutak, M. (1976). Morphine-naloxone interaction in the central cholinergic system: the influence of subcortical lesioning and electrical stimulation. *Br. J. Pharmac.,* **58**, 101-7.

Jimerson, D.C. (1987). Role of dopaminergic mechanisms in the affective disorders. In *Psychopharmacology: the third generation of progress* (ed. H.Y. Meltzer), pp. 505-11.

Johansson, F. and Knorring, L. von (1979). A double blind controlled study of a serotonin uptake inhibitor (zimelidine) versus placebo in chronic pain. *Pain,* **7**, 69-78.

Johnson, L.C., Naitoh, P., Moses, J.M., and Lubin, A. (1974). Interaction of REM deprivation and stage 4 deprivation with total sleep loss. *Psychophysiology,* **11**, 147-59.

Johnstone, E.C., Crow, T.J., Frith, C.D., Husband, J., and Kreel, L. (1976). Cerebral ventricular size and cognitive impairment in chronic schizophrenia. *Lancet,* **ii**, 924-6.

Johnstone, E.C., Crow, T.J., Frith, C.D., Carney, M.W.P., and Price, J.S. (1978). Mechanism of the antipsychotic effect in the treatment of acute schizophrenia. *Lancet,* **i**, 848-51.

Jonas, J.M. and Gold, M.S. (1986). Cocaine abuse and eating disorders. *Lancet,* **i**, 390-1.

Jones, B.J. (1988). 5-HT₃ receptor antagonists in anxiety and schizophrenia. In *Serotonin explored,* paper presented at conference 27th/28th June, 1988, London Marriott Hotel, London W 1. IBC Technical Services Ltd.

Jones, H.S. and Oswald, I. (1968). Two cases of healthy insomnia. *Electroenceph. Clin. Neurophysiol.,* **24**, 378-80.

Jones, K.L., Lacro, R.V., Johnson, K.A., and Adams, J. (1989). Pattern of malformations in the children of women treated with carbamazepine during pregnancy. *New Eng. J. Med.,* **320**, 1661-6.

Jones, K.L., Smith, D.W., and Myrianthopoulos, N.C. (1974). Outcome of offspring of chronic alcoholic women. *Lancet,* **i**, 1076-8.

Jouvet, M. (1967). Neurophysiology of states of sleep. *Physiol. Rev.,* **47**, 117-77.

Jouvet, M. (1969). Biogenic amines and the states of sleep. *Science,* **163**, 32-41.

Jouvet, M. (1972). The role of monoamines and acetylcholine containing neurons on the regulation of the sleep-waking cycle. *Ergebrisse der Physiologie.,* **64**, 166-307.

Jouvet, M. (1973). Telencephalic and rhombencephalic sleep in the cat. In *Sleep: an active process; research and commentary* (ed. W.B. Webb), pp. 12-32. Scott Foresman, Glenview, Illinois.

Jouvet, M. (1977). Neuropharmacology of the sleep-waking cycle. In *Handbook of psychopharmacology Vol. 8 Drugs, neurotransmitters and behaviour.* (ed. L.L. Iverson, S.D. Iverson, and S.H. Snyder), pp. 233-93. Plenum Press, New York.

Joyce, E.M., Moodley, P., Keshaven, M.S., and Lader, M.H. (1990). Failure of clonidine treatment in benzodiazepine withdrawal. *J. Psychopharmacology,* **4**, 42-5.

Judd, L.L., Squire, L.R., Butters, N., Salmon, D.P., and Paller, K.A. (1987). Effects of psychotropic drugs on cognition and memory in normal humans and animals. In *Psychopharmacology: the third generation of progress* (ed. H.Y. Meltzer), pp. 1467-75. Raven Press, New York.

Kahn, R.S., Wetzler, S., Asnis, G.M., Kling, M.A., Suckow, R.F., and van Praag, H.M. (1990). Effects of m-chlorophenylpiperazine in normal subjects: a dose-response study. *Psychopharmacology,* **100**, 339-44.

Kales, A., Tan, T., Kollar, E.J., Naitoh, P., Preston, T., and Malstrom, E.J. (1970). Sleep patterns following 205 hours of sleep deprivation. *Psychosom. Med.,* **32**, 189-200.

Kales, A., Scharf, M.B., and Kales, J.D. (1978). Rebound insomnia: a new clinical syndrome. *Science,* **201**, 1039-41.

Kalin, N.H., and Dawson, G. (1986). Neuroendocrine dysfunction in depression: hypothalamic-anterior pituitary systems. *Trends Neurosci.,* **9**, 261-6.

Kametani, H., Nomura, S., and Shimizu, J. (1983). The reversal effect of antidepressants on the escape deficit induced by inescapable shock in rats. *Psychopharmacology,* **80**, 206-8.

Kandel, E.R. (1978). Environmental determinants of brain architecture and of behaviour: early experience and learning. In *Principles of neural sciences.* (ed. E.R. Kandel and J.H. Schwartz), pp. 620-32. Edward Arnold, London.

Kandel, E.R. (1979). Small systems of neurones. *Scientific Am.,* **241**, 61-70.

Kandel, E.R., and Schwartz, H. (1982). Molecular biology of an elementary form of learning: modulation of transmitter release. *Science*, **218**, 433-43.

Kane, J.M. and Lieberman, J.A. (1987). Maintenance pharmacotherapy in schizophrenia. In *Psychopharmacology: the third generation of progress* (ed. H.Y. Meltzer), pp. 1103-9. Raven Press, New York.

Kanno, O. and Clarenbach, P. (1985). Effect of clonidine and yohimbine on sleep in man: polygraphic study and EEG analysis by normalised slope descriptors. *Electroenceph. Clin. Neurophysiol.*, **60**, 478-84.

Kapp, B.S., and Gallagher, M. (1979). Opiates and memory. *Trends Neurosci.*, **2**, 172-80.

Karli, P. (1984). Complex dynamic interrelations between sensorimotor activities and so-called behavioural states. In *Modulation of sensorimotor activity during alterations in behavioural states*. (ed. R. Bandler), pp. 1-21. Alan R. Liss, New York.

Karras, A. and Kane, J.M. (1980). Naloxone reduces cigarette consumption. *Life Science*, **27**, 1541-5.

Katz, R.J. (1980). Behavioural effects of dynorphin — a novel opioid neuropeptide. *Neuropharmacol.*, **19**, 801-3.

Katzman, R. (1986). Alzheimer's disease. *Trends Neurosci.*, **9**, 522-5.

Kaufmann, C.A., Weinberger, D.R., Yolken, R.N., Torrey, E.F., and Potkin, S.G. (1983). Viruses and schizophrenia. *Lancet*, **ii**, 1136-7.

Kay, D.C., Blackburn, A.B., Buckingham, J.A., and Karacan, J. (1976). Human pharmacology of sleep. In *Pharmacology of sleep*. (ed. R.L. Williams and I. Karacan), pp. 83-210., New York.

Kaye, W.H., Siturnam, N., and Weingartner, H. (1982). Modest facilitation of memory in dementia with combined lecithin and anticholinesterase treatment. *Biol. Psychiat.*, **17**, 275-80.

Kaymakcalan, S. (1979). Pharmacological similarities and interactions between cannabis and opioids. In *Marihuana: biological effects*. (ed. G.G. Nahas and W.D.M. Paton), pp. 591-605. Pergamon Press, Oxford.

Kebabian, J.W. and Calne, D.F. (1979). Multiple receptors for dopamine. *Nature*, **277**, 93-6.

Kellett, J.M., Taylor, A., and Oram, J.J. (1986). Aluminosilicates and Alzheimer's disease. *Lancet*, **i**, 682.

Kemperman, C.J.F. (1982). Salsolinol in the brain. *Lancet*, **i**, 927.

Kemperman, C.J.F. (1983). Beta-carbolines, alcohol and depression. *Lancet*, **i**, 124-5.

Kendall, MS. (1987). Review of treatment in Alzheimer's disease. In *Alzheimer's disease: current approaches* (ed. J.C. Malkin and MN. Rossor), pp. 65-74. Duphar Laboratories Ltd., Southampton.

Kendler, K.S. (1987) The genetics of schizophrenia: a current perspective. In *Psychopharmacology: the third generation of progress* (ed. H.Y. Meltzer), pp. 705-13. Raven Press, New York.

Kerwin, R.W., Patel, S., Meldrum, B.S., Czudek, C., and Reynolds, G.P. (1988). Asymmetrical loss of glutamate receptor subtypes in left hippocampus in schizophrenia. *Lancet*, **i**, 583-4.

Keshavan, M.S. and Crammer, J.L. (1985). Clonidine in benzodiazepine withdrawal. *Lancet*, **i**, 1325-6.

Kesner, R.P. and Hardy, J.D. (1983). Long-term memory for contextual attributes: dissociation of amygdala and hippocampus. *Behav. Brain Res.*, **8**, 139–42.

Khachaturian, H., Lewis, M.E., Schafer, M.K-H., and Watson, S.J. (1985). Anatomy of the CNS opioid systems. *Trends Neurosci.*, **8**, 111–9.

Kiianmaa, K., Hoffman, P.L., and Tabakoff, B. (1983). Antagonism of the behavioural effects of ethanol by naltrexone in BALB/C, C57BL/6 and DBA/2 mice. *Psychopharmacology*, **79**, 291–4.

Killam, E.K. and Killam, K.F. (1956). A comparison of the effects of reserpine and chlorpromazine to those of barbiturates on central afferent systems in the cat. *J. Pharmacol. Exp. Therap.*, **116**, 35–41.

Kiloh, L.G., Andrews, G., and Neilson, M. (1988). The long-term outcome of depressive illness. *Br. J. Psychiat.*, **153**, 752–7.

King, M.D., Day, R.E., Oliver, J.S., Lush, M., and Watson, J.M. (1981). Solvent encephalopathy. *Br. Med. J.*, **283**, 663–5.

Kirkegaard, C. (1981). The thyrotropin response to TRH in endogenous depression. *Psychopharmacology*, **6**, 189–212.

Klein, D.F. and Davis, J.M. (1969). *Diagnosis and drug treatment of psychiatric disorder*. Williams and Williams, Baltimore.

Kline, N.S. and Cooper, T.B. (1980). Monmoamine oxidase inhibitors as antidepressants. In *Psychotropic agents part I: antipsychotics and antidepressants* (ed. F. Hoffmeister and G. Stille), pp. 369–97. Springer-Verlag, Berlin.

Klockgether, T., Turski, L., and Sontag, K-H. (1987). Towards an understanding of the physiological role of *N*-methyl-D-aspartate receptors: a more expansive interpretation. *Trends Pharmac. Sci.*, **8**, 20.

Knight, J.G. (1982). Dopamine receptor-stimulating autoantibodies; a possible cause of schizophrenia. *Lancet*, **ii**, 1073–6.

Knorring, L. von., Almay, B.G.L., Johansson, F., and Terenius, L. (1978). Pain perception and endorphin levels in cerebrospinal fluid. *Pain*, **5**, 359–65.

Knott, V.J. (1989). Brain event-related potentials (ERPs) in smoking performance research. In *Smoking and human behaviour* (ed. T. Ney and A. Gale), pp. 93–114. Wiley, Chichester.

Knott, V.J. and Venables, P.H. (1977). EEG alpha correlates of non-smokers, smokers, smoking and smoking deprivation. *Psychophysiology*, **14**, 150–6.

Koch, C. and Poggio, T. (1983). Electrical properties of dendritic spines. *Trends Neurosci.*, **6**, 80–3.

Koe, B.K. (1983). A common mechanism of action for antidepressant drugs? *Trends Pharmac. Sci.*, **6**, 110.

Koehler, P.J. and Mirandolle, J.F. (1988). Neuroleptic malignant-like syndrome and lithium. *Lancet*, **ii**, 1499–500.

Koella, W.P. (1981). Neurotransmitters and sleep. In *Psychopharmacology of sleep* (ed. D. Wheatley), pp. 19–51. Raven Press, New York.

Koella, W.P. (1983). Polypeptides and sleep. *Trends Pharmac. Sci.*, **4**, 210–11.

Koob, G.F. and Bloom, F.E. (1983). Behavioural effects of opioid peptides. *Br. Med. Bull.*, **39**, 89–94.

Kornetsky, C., Esposito, R.U., McLean, S., and Jacobson, O. (1979). Intracranial self-stimulation threshold. *Arch. Gen. Psychiat.*, **36**, 289–92.

Koslow, S.H. (1974). 5-Methoxytryptamine: a possible central nervous system transmitter. In *Serotonin—new vistas*. Adv. Biochem. Psychopharmacol, Vol. II (ed. E. Costa, G.L. Gessa, and M. Sandler), pp. 95-101. Raven Press, New York.

Kosten, T.A. and Kosten, T.R. (1989). Cocaine abuse and opioid withdrawal. *Lancet*, **ii**, 165-6.

Kosterlitz, H. (1979). Endogenous peptides and the control of pain. *Psych. Med.*, **9**, 1-4.

Kostowski, W. (1975) Brain serotonergic and catecholaminergic system: facts and hypothesis. In *Current developments in psychopharmacology*, Vol. I (ed. W.B. Essman and L. Valzelli), pp. 39-64. Spectrum Publications Inc., New York.

Kostowski, W. (1985). Desipramine—correlation of receptor changes with function. *Trends Pharmac. Sci.*, **6**, 393-4.

Kovacs, G.L., Bohus, B.E., Versteeg, D.H.G., Telegdy, G., and Weid, D. de (1982). Neurohypophyseal hormones and memory. In *Advances in pharmacology and therapeutics II, Vol. I, CNS pharmacology-neuropeptides* (ed. H. Yoshida, Y. Hagihara, and S. Ebashi), pp. 175-87. Pergamon Press, Oxford.

Krause, D.N. and Dubocovich, M.L. (1990). Regulatory sites in the melatonin system of mammals. *Trends Neurosci.*, **13**, 464-70.

Kreek, M.J. (1987). Multiple drug abuse patterns and medical consequences. In *Psychopharmacology: the third generation of progress* (ed. H.Y. Meltzer), pp. 1597-604. Raven Press, New York.

Kretschmer, E. (1936). *Physique and character* (2nd edn) (trans. W.J.H. Sproff and K.P. Trench). Trubner, New York.

Krueger, J., Walter, J., and Levin, C. (1985). Factor S and related somnogens: an immune theory for slow wave sleep. In *Brain mechanisms of sleep* (ed. D.J. McGinty, R. Drucker-Colin, A. Morrison, and P-L. Parmeggiani), pp. 253-69. Raven Press, New York.

Kruk, Z.L. and Pycock, C.J. (1979). *Neurotransmitters and drugs*. Croom Helm, London.

Kuhar, M.J. (1986). Neuroanatomical substrates of anxiety: a brief survey. *Trends Neurosci.*, **97**, 307-11.

Kupferman, I. (1978). Learning. In *Principles of neural science*. (ed. E.R. Kandel and J.H. Schwartz), pp. 570-9. Edward Arnold, London.

Kutas, M. and Hillyard, S.A. (1984). Brain potentials during reading reflect work expectancy and semantic association. *Nature*, **307**, 161-3.

Lacey, M.G., Mercuri, N.B., and North, R.A. (1990). Actions of cocaine on rat dopaminergic neurones *in vitro*. *Br. J. Pharmacol.*, **99**, 731-5.

Lader, M. (1978). Current psychophysiological theories of anxiety. In *Psychopharmacology: a generation of progress* (ed. M.A. Lipton, A. DiMascio, and K.F. Killam), pp. 1375-80. Raven Press, New York.

Lader, M. (1980). The psychophysiology of anxiety. In *Handbook of biological psychiatry* (ed. H.M. van Praag), Part II, pp. 225-47. Marcel Dekker, New York.

Lader, M.H. (1987). Long-term benzodiazepine use and psychological functioning. In *The benzodiazepines in current clinical practice* (ed. H. Freeman and Y. Rue), pp. 55-69. Royal Society of Medicine Services Ltd., London.

Lader, M.H. (1989). Newer anti-anxiety drugs. In *Psychopharmacology of anxiety* (ed. P. Tyrer), pp. 243-54. Oxford University Press.

Lader, M.H. and Bruce, M. (1986). States of anxiety and their induction by drugs. *Br. J. Clin. Pharmac.*, **22**, 251-61.

Lader, M.H. and Morton, S. (1991) Benzodiazepine withdrawal syndrome. *Br. J. Psychiat.*, **158**, 435.

Lader, M. and Olajide, D. (1987). A comparison of buspirone and placebo in relieving benzodiazepine withdrawal symptoms. *J. Clin. Psychopharmac.*, **7**, 11-15.

Lader, M. H. and Petursson, H. (1981). Benzodiazepine derivatives-side effects and dangers. *Biol. Psychiatry.*, **16**, 1195-212.

Lader, M.H., Ron, M., and Petursson, H. (1984). Computed axial brain tomography in long-term benzodiazepine users. *Psychol. Med.,* **14**, 203-6.

Laegreid, L., Olegard, R., Wahlstrom, J., and Conradi, N. (1987). Abnormalities in children exposed to benzodiazepines in utero. *Lancet*, **i**, 108-9.

Lake, C.R., Sternberg, D.E., Kammen, D.P. van., Ballenger, J.C., Ziegler, M.G., Post, R.M., Kopin, I.J., and Bunney, W.E. (1980). Schizophrenia: elevated cerebrospinal fluid norepinephrine. *Science*, **207**, 331-3.

Lakosi, J.M. and Cunningham, K.A. (1988). Cocaine interaction with central monoamine systems: electrophysiological approaches. *Trends Pharmac. Sci.*, **9**, 177-80.

Lal, H. and Fielding, S. (1983). Clonidine in the treatment of narcotic addiction. *Trends Pharmac. Sci.*, **4**, 70-1.

Lambiase, M. and Serra, C. (1957). Fume a sistema nervoso. I. modificazioni dell' attivita elettrica corticale da fumo. *Acta Neurologica (Napoli).*, **12**, 475-93.

Lance, J.W. and McLeod, J.G. (1981). *A physiological approach to clinical neurology*. Butterworth, London.

Lancet (1979). Sleep apnoea syndromes. *Lancet*, **i**, 25-6.

Lancet (1980). Treatment of opiate-withdrawal symptoms. *Lancet*, **i**, 349-50.

Lancet (1981). If at first you do succeed. *Lancet*, **337**, 650-1.

Lancet (1984*a*). Management of trigeminal neuralgia. *Lancet*, **i**, 662-3.

Lancet (1984*b*). The challenge of addiction. *Lancet*, **ii**, 1019-20.

Lancet (1985). Beta-blockers in situational anxiety. *Lancet*, **ii**, 193.

Lancet (1987*a*). Doubts about the value of maintenance lithium. *Lancet*, **i**, 424.

Lancet (1987*b*). Crack. *Lancet*, **ii**, 1061-2.

Lancet (1989). Aluminium and Alzheimer's disease. *Lancet*, **i**, 82-3.

Lancet (1990*a*). Vasodilatation and migraine. *Lancet*, **335**, 822-3.

Lancet (1990*b*). Magnetoencephalography. *Lancet*, **335**, 576-7.

Lancet (1990*c*) Zopiclone: another carriage on the tranquilliser train. *Lancet*, **335**, 507-8.

Lands, A.M., Arnold, A., McAucliff, J.P., Luduena, F.P., and Brown, T.G. (1967). Differentiation of receptor systems activated by sympathomimetic amines. *Nature*, **214**, 597-8.

Lang, P.J., Rice, D.G., and Sternbach, R.A. (1972). The psychophysiology of emotion. In *Handbook of psychophysiology*. (ed. N.S. Greenfield and R.S. Sternbach), pp. 623-63. Holt, Rinehart and Winston, New York.

Langer, G. and Karobath, M. (1980). Biochemical effects of antidepressants in man. In *Psychotropic agents part I: antipsychotics and antidepressants.* (ed. F. Hoffmeister and G. Stille), pp. 491-504. Springer-Verlag, Berlin.

Langer, S. Z. (1977). Presynaptic receptors and their role in the regulation of transmitter release. *Br. J. Pharmac.*, **60**, 481-97.

Langer, S. Z. (1980). Presynaptic receptors and modulation of neurotransmission: pharmacological implications and therapeutic relevance. *Trends Neurosci.* **3**, 110-12.

Langer, S. Z. (1984). [^{3}H]Imipramine and [^{3}H]desipramine binding: nonspecific displaceable sites or physiologically relevant sites associated with the uptake of serotonin and noradrenaline? *Trends Pharmac. Sci.*, **5**, 51.

Langer, S. Z. and Arbilla, S. (1984). The amphetamine paradox in dopaminergic transmission. *Trends Pharmac. Sci.*, **5**, 387-90.

Langer, S. Z. and Briley, M. (1981). High-affinity ^{3}H-imipramine binding: a new biological tool for studies in depression. *Trends Neurosci.*, **4**, 28-31.

Langer, S. Z., Briley, M. S., and Raisman, M. (1980). Regulation of neurotransmission through presynaptic receptors and other mechanisms: possible clinical relevance and therapeutic potential. In *Receptors for neurotransmitters and Peptides* (ed. G. Pepeu, and M. J. Kuhar), pp. 203-12. Raven Press, New York.

Largen, J. W., Calderon, M., and Smith, R. C. (1983). Asymmetries in the densities of white and grey matter in the brains of schizophrenic patients. *Am. J. Psychiat.*, **140**, 1060-2.

Larson, P. S. and Silvette, H. (1975). *Tobacco: experimental and clinical studies*, Suppl. III. Williams and Wilkins, Baltimore.

Lashley, K. S. (1950). In search of the engram. *Symp. Soc. Exp. Biol.*, **4**, 454-82.

Lauritzen, M. (1987). Cortical spreading depression as a putative migraine mechanism. *Trends Neurosci.*, **10**, 8-13.

LeBoeuf, A., Lodge, J., and Eames, P. G. (1978). Vasopressin and memory in Korsakoff's Syndrome. *Lancet*, **ii**, 1370.

Lecrubier, Y., Puech, A. J., Jouvent, R., Simon, P., and Widlocher, D. (1980). A beta adrenergic stimulant (salbutamol) versus clomipramine in depression: a controlled study. *Br. J. Psychiat.*, **136**, 354-8.

Lederhendler, I. I., Gart, S., and Alkon, D. L. (1986). Classical conditioning of *Hermissenda*: origin of a new response. *J. Neurosci.*, **6**, 1325-31.

Lee, A. S. and Murray, R. M. (1988). The long-term outcome of Maudsley depressives. *Br. J. Psychiat.*, **153**, 741-51.

Lee, T. and Seeman, P. (1980). Elevation of brain neuroleptic/dopamine receptors in schizophrenia. *Am. J. Psychiat.*, **137**, 191-7.

Lee, K., Moller, L., Hardt, F., Haubek, A., and Jenson, E. (1979). Alcohol-induced brain damage and liver damage in young males. *Lancet*, **ii**, 759-61.

Lee, M. A., Cameron, O. G., and Greden, J. F. (1985). Anxiety and caffeine consumption in people with anxiety disorders. *Psychiat. Res.*, **15**, 211-17.

Lees, A. J. (1985). Parkinson's disease and dementia. *Lancet*, **i**, 43-4.

Leff, J. P. (1978). Social and psychological causes of the acute attack. In *Schizophrenia: towards a new synthesis.* (ed. J. K. Wing), Academic Press, London.

Legros, J. J., Gilot, P., Seron, X., Claessens, J., Adam, A., Moeglin, J. M., Audibert, A., and Berchier, P. (1978). Influence of vasopressin on learning and memory. *Lancet*, **i**, 41-2.

Leith, N.J. and Barrett, R.J. (1981). Self-stimulation and amphetamine: tolerance to *d* and *l* isomers and cross tolerance to cocaine and methylphenidate. *Psychopharmacology*, **74**, 23–8.

LeMay, M. (1982). Morphological aspects of human brain asymmetry: an evolutionary perspective. *Trends Neurosci.*, **5**, 273–5.

Lenard, H.G. and Schulte, F.J. (1972). Polygraphic sleep study in craniophagus twins (where is the sleep transmitter?). *J. Neurol. Neurosurg. Psychiat.*, **35**, 756–62.

Leonard, B.E. (1985). New antidepressants and the biology of depression. *Stress Medicine*, **1**, 9–16.

Lerer, B. (1987). Neurochemical and other neurobiological consequences of ECT: implications for the pathogenesis and treatment of affective disorders. In *Psychopharmacology: the third generation of progress* (ed. H.Y. Meltzer), pp. 577–88. Raven Press, New York.

Lerer, B., Ebstein, R.P., and Belmaker, R.H. (1981). Subsensitivity of human beta-adrenergic adenylate cyclase after salbutamol treatment of depression. *Psychopharmacology*, **75**, 169–72.

Levi-Montalcini, R. and Calissano, P. (1986). Nerve growth factor as a paradigm for other polypeptide growth factors. *Trends Neurosci.*, **9**, 473–6.

Levine, S. (1988). Buspirone: clinical studies in psychiatry. In *Buspirone: a new introduction to the treatment of anxiety* (ed. M. Lader), pp. 43–9. Royal Society of Medicine Services, London.

Levine, J.P., Gordon, N.O., and Fields, H.L. (1978). The mechanisms of placebo analgesia. *Lancet*, **ii**, 654–7.

Levine, J.D., Gordon, N.C., Jones, R.T., and Fields, H.L. (1978). The narcotic antagonist naloxone enhances clinical pain. *Nature*, **272**, 826–7.

Levison, P.K. (1981). An analysis of commonalities in substance abuse and habitual behaviour. In *Behavioural pharmacology of human drug dependence*. (ed. T. Thompson and C.E. Johansson), N.I.D.A. Research Monograph 37. National Institute of Drug Abuse, Rockville, Maryland.

Levy, J. (1979). Human cognition and lateralisation of cerebral function. *Trends Neurosci.*, **2**, 222–5.

Levy, R., Little, A., Chuaqui, P., and Reith, M. (1983). Early results from double blind, placebo controlled trial of high doses phosphatidylcholine in Alzheimer's Disease. *Lancet*, **i**, 987–8.

Lewis, J.W. and Liebeskind, J.C. (1983). Pain suppressive systems of the brain. *Trends Pharmac. Sci.*, **4**, 73–5.

Lewis, S.W. and Murray, R.M. (1987). Obstetric complications, neurodevelopmental deviance and risk of schizophrenia. *J. Psychiat. Res.*, **21**, 413–21.

Lewis, S.A., Oswald, I., and Dunleavy, D.L.F. (1971). Chronic fenfluramine administration: some cerebral effects. *Br. Med. J.*, **2**, 67–70.

Lieberman, J., Johns, C., Cooper, T., Pollack, S., and Kane, J. (1989). Clozapine pharmacology and tardive dyskinesia. *Psychopharmacoloy*, **99**, (Suppl.), S54–9.

Liljequist, R., Linnoila, M., and Mattila, M.J. (1978). Effect of diazepam and chlorpromazine on memory functions in man. *Eur. J. Clin. Pharmac.* **13**, 339–43.

Lindstrom, L.H., Widerlov, E., and Gunne, L. (1978). Endorphins in human cerebrospinal fluid: clinical correlations to some psychotic states. *Acta Psychiat. Scand.*, **57**, 153–64.

Lipman, J.L., Miller, B.E., Mays, K.S., Miller, M.N., North, W.C., and Byrne, W.L. (1990). Peak β endorphin concentration in cerebrospinal fluid: reduced in chronic pain patients and increased during the placebo response. *Psychopharmacology*, **102**, 112–16.

Littleton, J., Harper, J., Hudspith, M., Pagonis, C., Dolin, S., and Little, H. (1988). Adaptation in neuronal Ca^{2+}-channels may cause alcohol physical dependence. In *The psychopharmacology of addiction* (ed. M. Lader), pp. 60–72. Oxford University Press.

Llinas, R. (1987). 'Mindness' as a functional state of the brain. In *Mindwaves* (ed. C. Blakemore and S. Greenfield), pp. 339–60. Basil Blackwell, Oxford.

Lloyd, K.J., Farley, I.J., Deck, J.H.N., and Hornykiewicz, O. (1974). Serotonin and 5-hydroxy-indoleacetic acid in discrete areas of the brainstem of suicide victims and control patients. *Adv. Biochem. Psychopharmacol.*, **11**, 387–97.

Lorens, S.A. (1976). Comparison of the effects of morphine on hypothalamic and medial frontal cortex self-stimulation in the rat. *Psychopharmacology*, **48**, 217–24.

Lorig, T.S. and Schwartz, G.E. (1989). Factor analysis of the EEG indicates inconsistencies in traditional frequency bands. *J. Psychophysiol.*, **3**, 369–75.

Losonczy, M.F., Davidson, M., and Davis, K.L. (1987). The dopamine hypothesis of schizophrenia. In *Psychopharmacology: the third generation of progress* (ed. H.Y. Meltzer) pp. 715–26. Raven Press, New York.

Lovick, T.A. (1987). Tonic GABAergic and cholinergic influences on pain control and cardiovascular control neurones in nucleus paragigantocellularis lateralis in the rat. *Pain*, **31**, 401–9.

Lowenstein, L.F. (1982). Glue sniffing: background features and treatment by aversion methods and group therapy. *Practitioner*, **226**, 1113–16.

Lukin, P.R. and Ray, A.B. (1982). Personality correlates of pain perception and tolerance. *J. Clin. Psychol.*, **38**, 317–20.

Lundberg, J.M. and Hokfelt, T. (1983). Coexistence of peptides and classical neurotransmitters. *Trends Neurosci.*, **6**, 325–33.

Lundberg, T., Lindstrom, L.H., Hartig, P., Eckernas, S-A, Ekblom, B., Lundqvist, H. Fasth, K.J., Gullbery, P., and Langstrom, B. (1989). Striatal and frontal cortex binding of 11-C-labelled clozapine visualised by positron emission tomography (PET) in drug-free schizophrenics and healthy volunteers. *Psychopharmacology*, **99**, 8–12.

Luttinger, D., Burgess, S.K., Nemeroff, C.B., and Prange, A.J. (1983). The effects of chronic morphine treatment on neurotensin-induced antinociception. *Psychopharmacology*, **81**, 10–3.

Lynch, G. and Baudry, M. (1984). The biochemistry of memory: a new and specific hypothesis. *Science*, **224**, 1057–63.

Lynch, M., Errington, M.L., and Bliss, T.V.P. (1985). Long-term potentiation of synaptic transmission in the dentate gyrus: increased release of [^{14}C] glutamate without increase in receptor binding. *Neurosci. Lett.*, **62**, 123–9.

Lyon, L. J. and Anthony, J. (1982). Reversal of alcoholic coma by naloxone. *Ann. Int. Med.*, **96**, 464-5.

Maas, J. W. (1979). Neurotransmitters in depression: too much, too little or too unstable? *Trends Neurosci.*, **2**, 306-8.

MacDonald, J. F., and Nowak, L. M. (1990). Mechanism of blockade of excitatory amino acid receptor channels. *Trends Pharmac. Sci.*, **11**, 167-71.

MacKay, A. V. P., Bird, E. D., Spokes, E. G., Rossor, M., Iversen, L. L., Creese, I., and Snyder, S. H. (1980). Dopamine receptors and schizophrenia: drug effect or illness? *Lancet*, **ii**, 915-16.

MacKenzie, A. I. (1979). Naloxone in alcohol intoxication. *Lancet*, **i**, 733-4.

MacLean, P. D. (1949). Psychosomatic disease and the 'visual brain'. *Psychosomatic Med.*, **11**, 338-53.

MacLean, P. D. (1969). The hypothalamus and emotional behaviour. In *The hypothalamus* (ed. E. Anderson and W. J. H. Nauta). pp. 659-72. Charles C. Thomas, Springfield, Illinois.

MacLennan, J. A., Drugan, R. C., and Maier, S. F. (1983). Long-term stress analgesia blocked by scopolamine. *Psychopharmacology*, **80**, 267-8.

Madden, J. S. (1979). *Alcohol and drug dependence*. Wright, Bristol.

Madsen, J. A. (1974). Depressive illness and oral contraceptives. A study of urinary 5-hydroxyindoleactetic acid excretion. In *Serotonin — new vistas*, Adv. Biochem. Psychopharmacol. Vol. II. (ed. E. Costa, G. L. Gessa, and M. Sandler), pp. 249-53. Raven Press, New York.

Magni, G. (1987). On the relationship between chronic pain and depression where there is no organic lesion. *Pain*, **31**, 1-21.

Mair, W. G. P., Warrington, E. K., and Weiskrantz, L. (1979). Memory disorder in Korsakoff's psychosis. *Brain*, **102**, 749-83.

Maj, M., Pirozzi, R., and Kemali, D. (1989). Long-term outcome of lithium prophylaxis in patients initially classified as complete responders. *Psychopharmacology*, **98**, 535-8.

Manallack, D. T., Beart, P. M., and Gundlach, A. L. (1986). Psychotomimetic sigma-opiates and PCP. *Trends Pharmac. Sci.*, **7**, 448-51.

Mangan, G. L. and Golding, J. F. (1978). An 'enhancement' model of smoking maintenance. In *Smoking behaviour: physiological and psychological influences* (ed. R. E. Thornton), pp. 87-114. Churchill Livingstone, Edinburgh.

Mangan, G. L. and Golding, J. F. (1983). The effects of smoking on memory consolidation. *J. Psychol.*, **115**, 65-77.

Mansour, A., Khachaturian, H., Lewis, M. E., Akil, H., and Watson, S. J. (1988). Anatomy of CNS opioid receptors. *Trends Neurosci.*, **11**, 308-14.

Maragos, W. F., Greenamyre, J. T., Penney, J. B., and Young, A. B. (1987). Glutamate dysfunction in Alzheimer's disease: an hypothesis. *Trends Neurosci.*, **10**, 65-8.

Marcusson, J. O. and Ross, S. B. (1990). Binding of some antidepressants to the 5-hydroxytryptamine transporter in brain and platelets. *Psychopharmacology*, **102**, 145-55.

Mark, R. F. (1978). The developmental view of memory. In *Studies in neurophysiology* (ed. R. Porter), pp. 301-8. Cambridge University Press.

Marks, J. (1978). The benzodiazepines: use, overuse, misuse, abuse. MTP Press, Lancaster.

Marks, J. (1988). Techniques of benzodiazepine withdrawal in clinical practice. *Medical Toxicology*, **3**, 324–33.

Marks, J. and Nicholson, A. N. (1984). Drugs and insomnia. *Br. Med. J.*, **288**, 261.

Marr, D. (1969). A theory of cerebellar cortex. *J. Physiol. (Lond.)*, **202**, 437–70.

Marsden, C. D. (1976). Cerebral atrophy and cognitive impairment in chronic schizophrenia. *Lancet*, **ii**, 1079.

Marsden, C. D., Mindham, R. H. S., and Mackay, A. V. P. (1986). Extrapyramidal movement disorders produced by antipsychotic drugs. In *The psychopharmacology and treatment of schizophrenia* (ed. P. B. Bradley and S. R. Hirsch), pp. 340–402. Oxford University Press.

Marshall, B. E. and Wollman, H. (1980). General Anaesthetics. In *The pharmacological basis of therapeutics*. (ed. A. G. Gilman, L. S. Goodman, and G. Gilman). pp. 276–98. Macmillan Co., New York.

Martyn, C. N., Barker, D. J. P., Osmond, C., Harris, E. C., Edwardson, J. A., and Lacey, R. F. (1989). Geographical relation between Alzheimer's disease and aluminium in drinking water. *Lancet*, **i**, 59–62.

Mason, J. W. (1972). Organisation of psychoendocrine mechanisms. In *Handbook of psychophysiology* (ed. N. S. Greenfield, and R. S. Sternbach), pp. 3–91. Holt, Rinehart and Winston, New York.

Mason, S. T. (1979). Noradrenaline and behaviour. *Trends Neurosci.*, **2**, 82–4.

Mason, S. T. (1980). Noradrenaline and selective attention: a review of the model and the evidence. *Life Sci.*, **27**, 617–31.

Mason, S. T. and Fibiger, H. C. (1979). Possible behavioural function for noradrenaline-acetycholine interaction in brain. *Nature*, **277**, 396–97.

Mathew, R. J., Meyer, J. S., Semchuk, K. M., Francis, D. M., Mortel, K., and Claghorn, J. L. (1980). Cerebral blood flow in depression. *Lancet*, **i**, 1308.

Mathies, H. (1980). Pharmacology of learning and memory. *Trends Pharmac. Sci.*, **1**, 333–6.

Matsuda, L. A., Lolait, S. J., Brownstein, M. J., Young, A. C., and Bonner, T. I. (1990). Structure of a cannabinoid receptor and functional expression of the cloned cDNA. *Nature*, **346**, 561–4.

Matus, A., Ackerman, M., Pehling, G., Byers, H. R., and Fujiwara, K. (1982). High actin concentrations in brain dendritic spines and postsynaptic densities. *Proc. Natl. Acad. Sci., USA*, **79**, 7590–4.

Maurier, K., Dierks, T., Ihl, R. and Laux, G. (1989). Mapping of evoked potentials in normals and patients with psychiatric diseases. In *Topographic brain mapping of EEG and evoked potentials* (ed. K. Maurier), pp. 458–73. Springer-Verlag, Berlin.

Mayer-Gross, W., Slater, E., and Roth, M. (1954). *Clinical Psychiatry*, Cassell and Co. Ltd., London.

Mayes, A. (1983). The development and course of long-term memory. In *Memory in Animals and Humans* (ed. A. Mayes), pp. 133–76. Van Nostrand Reinhold (UK) Co. Ltd.

McCabe, B. J. and Horn, G. (1988). Learning and memory: regional changes in N-methyl-D-Aspartate receptors in the chick brain after imprinting. *Proc. Natl. Acad. Sci. USA*, **85**, 2849–53.

McClelland, H. (1985). Psychiatric disorders. In *Textbook of adverse drug reactions* (ed. D. M. Davies), pp. 549–77. Oxford University Press.

McClelland, H. A. (1986). Psychiatric reactions to psychotropic drugs. *Adv. Reaction Bull.*, **119**, 444–7.

McDonald, R. J. (1982). Drug treatment of senile dementia. In *Psychopharmacology of old age* (ed. D. Wheatley), pp. 113–38. Oxford University Press.

McEntee, W. J. and Mair, R. G. (1990). The Korsakoff syndrome: a neurochemical perspective. *Trends Pharmac. Sci.*, **13**, 340–4.

McGuffin, P. (1988). Major genes for major affective disorder? *Br. J. Psychiat.*, **153**, 591–6.

McGuffin, P., Katz, R., and Bebbington, P. (1988). The Camberwell Collaborative Study III: depression and adversity in the relatives of depressed probands. *Br. J. Psychiat.*, **152**, 775–82.

McIsaac, W. M., Fritchie, G. E., Idanpaan-Heikkila, J. E., Ho, B. T., and Englert, L. F. (1971). Distribution of marihuana in monkey brain and concomitant behavioural effects. *Nature*, **230**, 593–5.

McLachlan, D. C. R., Dalton, A. J., Kruck, T. P. A., Bell, M. Y., Smith, W. L., Kalow, W., and Andrews, D. F. (1991). Intramuscular desferrioxamine in patients with Alzheimer's disease. *Lancet*, **337**, 1304–8.

Meier-Ruge, W., Enz, A., Gygax, P., Hunziker, O., Iwangoff, P., and Reichlmeier, K. (1975). Genesis and treatment of psychologic disorders in the elderly. In *Ageing* (ed. S. Gershon and A. Rashin), pp. 55–126. Raven Press, New York.

Meldrum, B. and Garthwaite, J. (1990). Excitatory amino acids and neurodegenerative disease. *Trends Pharmac. Sci.*, **11**, 379–87.

Mellerup, E. T. and Rafaelson, O. J. (1979). Circadian rhythms in manic-melancholic disorders. In *Current developments in psychopharmacology* (ed. W. B. Essman and W. B. Valzelli), Vol. 5., pp. 51–66. Spectrum Publications, New York.

Mello, N. K. (1987). Alcohol abuse and alcoholism: 1978–1987. In *Psychopharmacology: the third generation of progress* (ed. H. Y. Meltzer), pp. 1515–20. Raven Press, New York.

Mello, N. K. and Griffiths, R. R. (1987). Alcoholism and drug abuse: an overview. In *Psychopharmacology: the third generation of progress* (ed. H. Y. Meltzer), pp. 1511–14. Raven Press, New York.

Mellsop, G. W., Hutton, J. D., and Delahunt, J. W. (1985). Dexamethasone suppression test as a simple measure of stress? *Br. Med. J.*, **290**, 1804–6.

Meltzer, H. Y. (1980). Relevance of dopamine autoreceptors for psychiatry: preclinical and clinical studies. *Schizophrenia Bull.*, **6**, 456–74.

Meltzer, H. Y. (1989). Clinical studies in the mechanism of action of clozapine: the dopamine-serotonin hypothesis of schizophrenia. *Psychopharmacology*, **99** (Suppl.), S18–27.

Meltzer, H. Y. and Fang, V. S. (1976). Serum prolactin levels in schizophrenia — effect of antipsychotic drugs: a preliminary report. In *Hormones, behaviour and psychopathology* (ed. E. J. Sachar), pp. 178–91. Raven Press, New York.

Meltzer, H. Y. and Lowy, M. T. (1987). The serotonin hypothesis of depression. In *Psychopharmacology: the third generation of progress* (ed. H. Y. Meltzer), pp. 513–33. Raven Press, New York.

Melzack, R. (1986). Neurophysiological foundations of pain. In *The psychology of pain* (ed. R.A. Sternbach), pp. 1–24. Raven Press, New York.

Melzack, R. (1990). Phantom limbs and the concept of a neuromatrix. *Trends Neurosci.*, **13**, 88–92.

Melzack, R. and Wall, P.D. (1965). Pain mechanisms: a new theory. *Science, N.Y.*, **150**, 971–80.

Melzack, R. and Wall, P. (1988). *The challenge of pain* Penguin Books, London.

Mendelson, J.H. (1987). Marijuana. In *Psychopharmacology: the third generation of progress* (ed. H.Y. Meltzer), pp. 1565–71. Raven Press, New York.

Menon, P., Evans, R., and Madden, J.S. (1986). Methadone withdrawal regime for heroin misusers: short-term outcome and effect of parental involvement. *Br. J. Addiction*, **81**, 123–6.

Merskey, H. (1986). Psychiatry and pain. In *The psychology of pain* (ed. R.A. Sternbach), pp. 97–120. Raven Press, New York.

Mesulam, M-M. (1983). The functional anatomy and hemispheric specialisation for directed attention: the role of the parietal lobe and its connections. *Trends Neurosci.*, **6**, 384–7.

Metz, A., Stump, K., Cowen, P.J., Elliott, J.M., Gelder, M.G., and Grahame-Smith, D.G. (1983). Changes in platelet alpha$_2$-adrenoceptor binding post-partum: possible relation to maternity blues. *Lancet*, **i**, 495–8.

Meyer, D.R. and Beattie, M.S. (1977). Some properties of substrates of memory. In *Neuropeptide influences on the brain and behaviour* (ed. L.H. Miller, C.A. Sandman, and A.J. Kastin), pp. 145–62. Raven Press, New York.

Mikkelson, E.J. (1978). Caffeine and schizophrenia. *J. Clin. Psychiat.*, **39**, 732–6.

Miles, J. (1977). Surgery for the relief of pain. In *Persistent pain* (ed. S. Lipton), Vol. 1, pp. 129–48. Academic Press, London, and Grune and Stratton, New York.

Miller, J.G. (1989). Phenylpropanolamine: a controversy unresolved. *J. Clin. Psychopharm.*, **9**, 1–2.

Miller, C., Haugh, M., Kahn, J., and Anderton, B. (1986). The cytoskeleton and neurofibrillary tangles in Alzheimer's disease. *Trends Neurosci.*, **9**, 76–81.

Mills, I.H. (1977). Noradrenaline and the coping process in the brain. In *Depression — the biochemical and physiological role of ludiomil* (ed. A. Jukes), pp. 53–8. Ciba Laboratories, Horsham.

Milner, B. (1970). Memory and the medial temporal lobes of the brain. In *Biology of memory* (ed. K.H. Pribram and D.E. Broadbent), pp. 29–50 Academic Press, New York.

Mindham, R.H.S. (1979). Tricyclic antidepressants and amine precursors. In *Psychopharmacology of affective disorders* (ed. E.S. Paykel and A. Coppen), pp. 123–58. Oxford University Press.

Mishkin, M. and Appenzeller, T. (1987). The anatomy of memory. *Scientific American*, **256**, 62–71.

Mogenson, G.L. (1984). Limbic-motor integration — with emphasis on initiation of exploratory and goal-directed locomotion. In *Modulation of sensorimotor activity during alterations in behavioural states* (ed. R. Bandler), pp. 121–37. Alan R. Liss, New York.

Mohler, H. and Okada, T. (1977). Benzodiazepine receptor: demonstration in the central nervous system. *Science*, **198**, 849–51.

Mohler, H. and Okada, T. (1978). The benzodiazepine receptor in normal and pathological human brain. *Br. J. Psychiat.*, **133**, 261–8.

Mohs, R. C. and Davis, K. L. (1987) Experimental pharmacology of Alzheimer's disease and related dementias. In *Psychopharmacology: the third generation of progress* (ed. H. Y. Meltzer), pp. 921–8. Raven Press, New York.

Moiseeva, N. I. (1979). Sleep as a regulator of brain electrical activity. *Human Physiology*, **4**, 283–8.

Moldofsky, H. (1982). Rheumatic pain modulation syndrome: the interrelationships between sleep, central nervous system serotonin, and pain. *Adv. Neurol.*, **33**, 51–7.

Mondadori, C. (1981). Pharmacological modulation of memory: trends and problems. *Acta Neurol. Scand.*, Suppl. 89, **64**, 129–40.

Monnier, M. and Gaillard, J. M. (1981). Biochemical regulation of sleep. *Experimentia*, **36**, 21–4.

Monro, J., Carini, C., and Brostoff, J. (1984). Migraine as a food-allergic disease. *Lancet*, **ii**, 719–21.

Montgomery, S. A. (1982). The non-selective effect of selective antidepressants. *Adv. Biochem. Psychopharmacol.*, **31**, 49–56.

Montgomery, S. A., and Pinder, R. H. (1987). Do some antidepressants promote suicide? *Psychopharmacology*, **92**, 265–6.

Moreau, J-L., Pieri, L., and Prud'hon, B. (1989). Convulsions induced by centrally administered NMDA in mice: effects of NMDA antagonists, benzodiazepines, minor tranquillisers and anticonvulsants. *Br. J. Pharmacol.*, **98**, 1050–4.

Morley, J. S. (1983). Chemistry of opioid peptides. *Br. Med. Bull.*, **39**, 5–10.

Morrison, C. F. and Armitage, A. K. (1967). Effects of nicotine upon the free operant behaviour of rats and spontaneous motor activity of mice. *Ann. N. Y. Acad. Sci.*, **142**, 268–76.

Moruzzi, G. and Magoun, H. W. (1949). Brain stem reticular formation and evolution of the EEG. *Electroenceph. Clin. Neurophysiol.* **1**, 455–73.

Mountcastle, V. B. (1974). Sleep wakefulness and the conscious state: intrinsic regulatory mechanisms of the brain. In *Medical physiology* (ed. V. B. Mountcastle), pp. 254–81. The C. V. Mosby Company, Saint Louis.

Mountcastle, V. B. (1978). An organising principle for cerebral function: the unit module and the distributed system. In *The mindful brain, cortical organisation and the group-selective theory of higher brain function* (ed. G. M. Edelman and V. B. Mountcastle), pp. 7–50. MIT Press, Cambridge, Massachusetts.

Muhlethaler, M., Dreifuss, J. J., and Gohwiler, B. H. (1982). Vasopressin excites hippocampal neurones. *Nature*, **296**, 749–51.

Mullaney, D. J., Kripke, D. F., Fleck, P. A., and Johnson, L. C. (1983). Sleep loss and nap effects on sustained continuous performance. *Psychphysiol.*, **20**, 643–51.

Mullen, A. and Wilson, C. W. M. (1974). Fenfluramine and dreaming. *Lancet*, **ii**, 594.

Mullin, M. J. and Ferko, A. P. (1983). Alterations in dopaminergic function after subacute ethanol administration. *J. Pharmac. Exp. Therap.*, **225**, 694–98.

Murphree, H. B., Pfeiffer, C. C., and Price, L. M. (1967). Electroencephalographic changes in man following smoking. *Ann. N. Y. Acad. Sci.*, **142**, 245–60.

Murphy, S. M., Owen, R. T., and Tyrer, P. J. (1984). Withdrawal symptoms after six week's treatment with diazepam. *Lancet*, **ii**, 1389.

Murphy, D. L., Aulakh, C. S., Garrick, N. A., and Sunderland, T. (1987) Monoamine oxidase inhibitors as antidepressants: Implications for the mechanism of action of antidepressants and the psychobiology of the affective disorders and some related disorders. In *Psychopharmacology: the third generation of progress* (ed. H. Y. Meltzer), pp. 545–52. Raven Press, New York.

Murphy, S. M., Owen, R., and Tyrer, P. (1989). Comparative assessment of efficacy and withdrawal symptoms after six and twelve weeks treatment with diazepam or buspirone. *Br. J. Psychiat.*, **154**, 529–34.

Murray, S. M. and Lewis, S. W. (1988). Is schizophrenia a neurodevelopmental disorder? *Br. Med. J.*, **296**, 63.

Murray, R. M., Lewis, S. W., and Reveley, A. M. (1985). Towards an aetiological classification of schizophrenia. *Lancet*, **i**, 1023–6.

Myers, R. D. (1978). Psychopharmacology of alcohol. *Ann. Rev. Pharmac. Toxicol.*, **18**, 125–44.

Nahas, G. G. and Paton, W. D. M. (1979). *Marihuana: biological effects*. Pergamon Press, Oxford.

Nathan, R. S. and Kammon, D. P. van (1985). Neuroendocrine effects of antipsychotic drugs. In *Drugs in psychiatry*, Vol. 3, antipsychotics (ed. G. D. Burrows, T. R. Norman, and B. Davies), pp. 11–26. Elsevier, Amsterdam.

Navaratnam, V. and Foong, K. (1990). Opiate dependence — the role of benzodiazepines. *Current Medical Research and Opinion*, **11**, 620–30.

Nelsen, J. M. (1978). Psychological consequences of chronic nicotinisation: a focus on arousal. In *Behavioural effects of nicotine* (ed. K. Battig), pp. 1–17. S. Karger, Basel.

Nelson, W. T., Steiner, S. S., Brutus, M., Farrell, R., and Ellman, S. J. (1981). Brain site variation in effects of morphine on electrical self-stimulation. *Psychopharmacology*, **74**, 58–65.

Nemeroff, C. B. Berger, P. A., and Bissette, G. (1987). Peptides in schizophrenia. In *Psychopharmacology: the third generation of progress* (ed. H. Y. Meltzer) pp. 727–43. Raven Press, New York.

Nestoros, J. N. (1980). Ethanol selectively potentiates GABA-mediated inhibition of single feline cortical neurons. *Life Sci.*, **26**, 519–23.

Neville, H. J. (1985). Brain potentials reflect meaning in language. *Trends Neurosci.*, **8**, 91–2.

Newlin, D. B. (1986). Conditional compensatory response to alcohol placebo in humans. *Psychopharmacology*, **88**, 247–51.

Newnham, J. P., Tomlin, S., Ratter, S. J., Bourne, G. L., and Rees, L. H. (1983). Endogenous opioids in pregnancy. *Br. J. Obstet. Gynaecol.*, **90**, 535–8.

Ney, T. N., Gale, A., and Morris, H. (1989). A critical evaluation of laboratory studies of the effects of smoking on learning and memory. In *Smoking and human behaviour* (ed. T. Ney and A. Gale), pp. 239–59. Wiley, Chichester.

Nicholson, A. N. (1980*a*). Hypnotics: rebound insomnia and residual sequelae. *Br. J. Clin. Pharmac.*, **9**, 223–5.

Nicholson, A. N. (1980*b*). The use of short and long-acting hypnotics in clinical medicine. *Br. J. Clin. Pharmac.*, **11**, Suppl. 1, 61S–9S.

Nicholson, A. N. (1987). New antihistamines free of sedative side effects. *Trends Pharmac. Sci.*, **8**, 247–8.

Nicholson, C. D. (1990). Pharmacology of nootropics and metabolically active compounds in relation to their use in dementia. *Psychopharmacology*, **101**, 147–59.

Nielsen, M., Braestrup, C., and Squires, R. F. (1978). Evidence for a late evolutionary appearance of brain-specific benzodiazepine receptors: an investigation of 18 vertebrate and 5 invertebrate species. *Brain Res.*, **141**, 342–6.

Nilsson, J. L. and Carlsson, A. (1982). Dopamine-receptor agonist with apparent selectivity for autoreceptors: a new principle for antipsychotic action? *Trends Pharmac. Sci.*, **3**, 322–5.

Norman, T. R. and Burrows, G. D. (1983). Plasma concentrations of antidepressant drugs and clinical responses. In *Antidepressants* (ed. G. D. Burrows, T. R. Norman, and R. Davies), pp. 111–20. Elsevier, Amsterdam.

North, R. A. and Williams, J. T. (1983). How do opiates inhibit neurotransmitter release? *Trends Neurosci.*, **6**, 337–9.

Norton, A. (1981). Old men forget. *Br. Med. J.*, **283**, 1201–2.

Nuotto, E., Palva, E. S., and Lahdenranta, U. (1983). Naloxone fails to counteract heavy alcohol intoxication. *Lancet*, **ii**, 167.

Nutt, D. (1990*a*). Specific anatomy, non-specific drugs: the present state of schizophrenia. 5th Biennial Winter Workshop on Schizophrenia. *J. Psychopharmacol.*, **4**, 171–5.

Nutt, D. J. (1990*b*). Benzodiazepine dependence: new insights from basic research. In *Benzodiazepines: current concepts*, (ed. I. Hindmarch, G. Beaumont, S. Brandon, and B. E. Leonard), pp. 19–35. John Wiley & Sons, Chichester.

Nutt, D. J. and Cowen, P. J. (1987). Benzodiazepine-serotonin interactions in man. *Psychopharmacol. Ser.*, **3**, 72–6.

Oakley, D. A. (1979). Neocortex and learning. *Trends Neurosci.*, **2**, 149–52.

Oakley, D. A. (1981). Brain mechanisms of mammalian memory. *Br. Med. Bull.*, **37**, 175–80.

O'Boyle, C. A., Harris, D., Barry, H., and Cullen, J. H. (1986). Differential effects of benzodiazepine sedation in high and low anxious patients in 'real life' stress setting. *Psychopharmacology*, **88**, 266–9.

O'Connor, D. (1982). The use of suggestion techniques with adolescents in the treatment of glue sniffing and solvent abuse. *Human Toxicol.*, **1**, 313–20.

O'Connor, D. (1984). *Glue Sniffing and Volatile Substance Abuse*. Gower, Aldershot.

Oehme, P. and Krivoy, W. A. (1983). Substance P: a peptide with unusual features. *Trends Pharmac. Sci.*, **4**, 521–3.

Offermeier, J. and Rooyen, J. H. van. (1982). Is it possible to integrate dopamine receptor terminology? In *More about receptors* (ed. J. W. Lamble), pp. 93–7. Elsevier, Amsterdam.

Ogren, S-O., Fuxe, K., Berge, O.G., and Agnati, L.F. (1983). Effects of chronic administration of antidepressant drugs on central serotonergic receptor mechanisms. In *Frontiers in Neuropsychiatric Research* (ed. E. Usdin, M. Goldstein, A.J. Friedhoff, and A. Georgatas), pp. 93-108. Macmillan, London.

Ogunremi, O.O., Adamson, L., Brezinova, V., Hunter, W.M., Maclean, A.W., Oswald, I., and Percy-Robb, I.W. (1973). Two antianxiety drugs: a psychoendocrine study. *Br. Med. J.*, **2**, 202-7.

Ojemann, G.A. (1983). The intrahemispheric organisation of human language, derived with electrical stimulation techniques. *Trends Neurosci.*, **6**, 184-9.

Okamoto, M. (1978). Barbiturates and alcohol: Comparative overviews on neurophysiology and neurochemistry. In *Psychopharmacology: a generation of progress* (ed. M.A. Lipton, A. DiMascio, and K.F. Killam), pp. 1575-90. Raven Press, New York.

O'Keefe, J. and Nadel, L. (1978). *The hippocampus as a cognitive map.* Clarendon Press, Oxford.

O'Keefe, J. and Speakman, A. (1987). Single unit activity in the rat hippocampus during a spatial memory task. *Exp. Brain Res.*, **68**, 1-27.

Olds, J. (1956). Pleasure centres in the brain. *Scientific Am.*, **195**, 105-17.

Olds, J. (1977). *Drives and reinforcements: behavioural studies of hypothalamic functions.* Raven Press, New York.

Olds, J. and Milner, P. (1954). Positive reinforcement produced by electrical stimulation of septal area and other regions of rat brain. *J. Comp. Physiol. Psychol.*, **47**, 419-27.

Olds, J. and Travis, R.P. (1960). Effects of chlorpromazine, meprobamate, pentobarbital and morphine on self-stimulation. *J. Pharmac. Exp. Therap.*, **128**, 397-404.

Olds, M.E. and Olds, J. (1963). Approach avoidance analysis of the rat diencephalon. *J. Comp. Neurol.*, **120**, 259-62.

Oliveros, J.C., Jandali, M.K., Timsit-Berthier, M., Remy, R., Benghezal, A., Audibert, P., and Moeglen, P. (1978). Vasopressin in amnesia. *Lancet*, **i**, 42.

Orton, D.I. and Gruzelier, J.H. (1989). Adverse changes in mood and cognitive performance of house officers after night duty. *Br. Med. J.*, **298**, 21-3.

Oswald, I. (1976). The function of sleep. *Postgrad. Med. J.*, **52**, 15-18.

Oswald, I. (1980). *Sleep.* Penguin Books, Middlesex.

Oswald, I. (1989). Risks of dependence on benzodiazepine drugs. *Br. Med. J.*, **298**, 456.

Oswald, I., Lewis, S.A., Dunleavy, D.L.F., Brezinova, V., and Briggs, M. (1971). Drugs of dependence though not of abuse: fenfluramine and imipramine. *Br. Med. J.*, **2** 70-3.

Oswald, I., Brezinova, V., and Dunleavy, D.L.F. (1972). On the slowness of action of tricyclic antidepressant drugs. *Br. J. Psychiat.*, **120**, 673-7.

Oswald, I., French, C., Adam, K., and Gilham, J. (1982). Benzodiazepine hypnotics remain effective for 24 weeks. *Br. Med. J.*, **284**, 860-3.

Otero Losada, M.E. (1988). Changes in central GABAergic function following acute and repeated stress. *Br. J. Pharmacol.*, **93**, 483-90.

Otero Losada, M.E. (1989). Acute stress and GABAergic function in the rat brain. *Br. J. Pharmacol.*, **96**, 507-12.

Otsuka, M. and Yanagisawa, M. (1987). Does substance P act as a pain transmitter? *Trends Pharmac. Sci.*, **8**, 506–10.

Owen, F. and Crow, T.J. (1987). Neurotransmitters and psychosis. *Br. Med. Bull.*, **43**, 651–71.

Owen, F., Cross, A.J., Crow, T.J., Lofthouse, R., and Poulter, M. (1981). Neurotransmitter receptors in brain in schizophrenia. *Acta. Psychial. Scand.*, **63**, Suppl. 289, 20–6.

Owen, M.J. and Mullan, M.J. (1990). Molecular genetic studies of manic-depression and schizophrenia. *Trends Neurosci.*, **13**, 29–31.

Owen, M.J. and Murray, R.M. (1988). Blue genes: three genes linked to bipolar affective disorder. *Br. Med. J.*, **297**, 871–2.

Owen, R.T. and Tyrer, P. (1983). Benzodiazepine dependence: a review of the evidence. *Drugs*, **25**, 385–98.

Oyama, T., Jin, T., Yamaya, R., Ling, N., and Guillemin, R. (1980) Profound analgesic effects of beta-endorphin in man. *Lancet*, **i**, 122–4.

Oyama, T., Jin, T., Yamaya, R., Matsuki, A., Ling, N., and Guillemin, R. (1982). Intrathecal use of beta-endorphin as a powerful analgesic agent in man. In *Advances in pharmacology and therapeutics II. Vol. 1. CNS pharmacology — neuropeptides* (ed. H. Yoshida, Y. Hagihara, and S. Ebashi), pp. 39–43. Pergamon Press, Oxford.

Paiva, T., Arnaga, F., Nauguier, A., Lara, E., Largo, R., and Leitao, J.N. (1988). Effects of ritanserin on sleep disturbance of dysthymic patients. *Psychopharmacology*, **96**, 395–9.

Panksepp, J. (1981). Brain opioids — a neurochemical substrate for narcotic and social dependence. In *Theory in psychopharmacology Vol. 1* (ed. S.J. Cooper), pp. 149–76. Academic Press, London.

Papez, J. (1937). A proposed mechanism of emotion. *Arch. Neurol. Psychiat.*, **38**, 725–43.

Pappenheimer, J.R., Miller, T.B., and Goodrich, C.A. (1967). Sleep-promoting effects of cerebrospinal fluid from sleep-deprived goats. *Proc. Natl. Acad. Sci.*, **58**, 513–17.

Pare, C.M., Yeung, D.P., Price, K., and Stacey, R.S. (1969). 5-hydroxytryptophan, noradrenaline, and dopamine in brainstem, hypothalamus and caudate nucleus of controls and of patients committing suicide by gas poisoning. *Lancet*, **ii**, 133–5.

Parkes, J.D. (1981). Day-time drowsiness. *Lancet*, **ii**, 1213–7.

Parkes, J.D. (1986). The parasomnias. *Lancet*, **ii**, 1021–4.

Parkes, J.D., Langdon, N., and Lock, C. (1986). Narcolepsy and immunity. *Br. Med. J.*, **292**, 359–60.

Parrott, A.C. and Davies, S. (1983). Effects of a 1-5 benzodiazepine derivative upon performance in an experimental stress situation. *Psychopharmacology*, **79**, 367–9.

Parrott, A.C. and Kentridge, R. (1982). Personal constructs of anxiety under the 1, 5 benzodiazepine derivative clobazam related to trait-anxiety levels of the personality. *Psychopharmacology*, **75**, 353–7.

Pasternak, G.N. (1987). Opioid receptors. In *Psychopharmacology: the third generation of progress* (ed. H.Y. Meltzer), pp. 281–8. Raven Press, New York.

Paton, A. (1985). The politics of alcohol. *Br. Med. J.*, **290**, 1-2.

Paton, J.A. and Nottebohm, F.N. (1984). Neurons generated in the adult brain are recruited into functional circuits. *Science*, **225**, 1046-8.

Paton, W.D.M. (1979). Concluding summary. In *Marihuana: biological effects* (ed. G.G. Nahas and W.D.M. Paton), pp. 735-8. Pergamon Press, Oxford.

Paton, W.D.M. and Crown J. (ed.) (1972). *Cannabis and its derivatives. Pharmacology and experimental psychology.* Oxford University Press.

Paton W.D.M., Pertwee, R.G., and Tylden, E. (1973). Clinical aspects of cannabis action. In *Marihuana.* (ed. R. Mechoulam), pp. 335-65. Pergamon Press, Oxford.

Pavlov, I.P. (1927). *Conditioned reflexes: an investigation of the physiological activity of the cerebral cortex.* Oxford University Press.

Paykel, E.S. (1974). Recent life events and clinical depression. In: *Life stress and illness.* (ed. E.G. Gunderson and R.H. Rahe), pp. 134-63. Thomas Springfield, Illinois.

Paykel, E.S. (1983). The classification of depression. *Br. J. Clin. Pharmac.*, **15**, 155-9.

Paykel, E.S., West, P.S., Rowan, P.R., and Parker, R.R. (1982). Influence of acetylator phenotype on antidepressant effects of phenelzine. *Br. J. Psychiat.*, **141**, 243-8.

Pearce, J.M.S. (1984*a*). Migraine: a cerebral disorder. *Lancet*, **ii**, 86-9.

Pearce, J.M.S. (1984*b*). Boxer's brains. *Br. Med. J.*, **288**, 933-4.

Pearce, J.M.S. (1985). Is migraine explained by Leao's spreading depression? *Lancet*, **ii**, 763-6.

Pearce, J.M.S. (1988). Exploding head syndrome. *Lancet*, **ii**, 270-1.

Peet, M. and Coppen, A. (1979). The pharmacokinetics of antidepressant drugs: relevance to their therapeutic effect. In *Psychopharmacology of affective disorders* (ed. E.S. Paykel and A. Coppen), pp. 9-107. Oxford University Press.

Pellow, S. and File, S.E. (1984). Multiple sites of action for anxiogenic drugs. *Psychopharmacology*, **83**, 304-15.

Pellow, S. and File, S. (1986). Anxiolytic and anxiogenic drug effects in exploratory activity in an elevated plus-maze: a novel test of anxiety in the rat. *Pharmacol. Biochem. and Behaviour*, **24**, 525-9.

Penfield, W. and Perot, P. (1963). The brain's record of auditory and visual experience. *Brain*, **86**, 595-9.

Perera, K.M.H., Powell, T. and Jenner, F.A. (1987). Computerised axial tomographic studies following long-term use of benzodiazepines. *Psycholog. Med.*, **17**, 775-7.

Perkins, J.P. (1982). Catecholamine-induced modification of the functional state of beta-adrenergic receptors. In *More about receptors.* (ed. J.W. Lamble), pp. 48-53. Elsevier, Amsterdam.

Peroutka, S.J. (1988). 5-Hydroxytryptamine receptor subtypes: molecular, biochemical and physiological characterisation. *Trends Neurosci.*, **11**, 496-500.

Perry, E.K. and Perry, R.H. (1985). New insights into the nature of senile (Alzheimer-type) plaques. *Trends Neurosci.*, **8**, 301-3.

Perry, R. H., Irving, D., Blessed, G., Perry, E. K., and Fairbairn, A. F. (1989). Clinically and neuropathologically distinct form of dementia in the elderly. *Lancet*, **i**, 166.

Peters, T. J. (1983). Aldehyde dehydrogenase and alcoholism. *Lancet*, **i**, 364.

Peters, A., Palay, S. L., and Webster, H. deF. (1976). *The Fine Structure of the Nervous System*. W. B. Saunders Company, Philadelphia.

Petrie, A. (1967). *Individuality in pain and suffering*, University of Chicago Press.

Petrie, K., Conaglen, J. V., Thompson, L., and Chamberlain, K. (1989). Effect of melatonin on jet lag after long haul flights. *Br. Med. J.*, **298**, 705–7.

Pettigrew, J. D. (1978). The locus coeruleus and cortical plasticity. *Trends Neurosci.*, **1**, 73–4.

Pettit, H-O., Ettenberg, A., Bloom, F. E., and Koob, G. F. (1984). Destruction of dopamine in the nucleus accumbens selectively attenuates cocaine but not heroin self-administration in rats. *Psychopharmacology*, **84**, 167–73.

Petursson, H. and Lader, M. H. (1981*a*). Withdrawal from long-term benzodiazepine treatment. *Br. Med. J.*, **283**, 643–5.

Petursson, H. and Lader, M. H. (1981*b*). Benzodiazepine dependence. *Br. J. Addiction*, **76**, 133–45.

Petursson, H. and Lader, M. H. (1984). *Dependence on tranquillisers*. Oxford University Press.

Petursson, H., Shur, E., Checkley, S., Slade, A., and Lader, M. H. (1981). A neuroendocrine approach to benzodiazepine tolerance and dependence. *Br. J. clin. Pharmac.*, **11**, 526–8.

Phillips, A. G., Blaha, C. D., and Fibiger, H. C. (1989). Neurochemical correlates of brain-stimulation reward measured by ex-vivo and in-vivo analyses. *Neurosci. and Biobehav. Rev.*, **13**, 99–104.

Phillips, A. G. and Fibiger, H. C. (1989). Neuroanatomical bases of intracranial self-stimulation: untangling the Gordian Knot. In *The neuropharmacologic basis of reward* (ed. J. M. Lieberman and S. J. Cooper), pp. 66–105. Clarendon Press, Oxford.

Phillis, J. W. and Jhamandas, K. (1971). The effects of chlorpromazine and ethanol on in vivo release of acteylcholine from the cerebral cortex. *Comp. Gen. Pharmac.*, **2**, 306–10.

Piaget, J. and Inhelder, B. (1969). *The psychology of the child*. Basic Books, New York.

Pickar, D., Culter, N. R., Naber, D., Post, R. M., Pert, C. B., and Bunney, W. E. (1980). Plasma opioid activity in manic-depressive illness. *Lancet*, **i**, 937.

Piercy, M. F. (1977). Experimental studies of the organic amnesic syndrome. In *Amnesia* (ed. C. W. M. Whitty and O. L. Zangwill), pp. 1–51. Butterworth, London.

Piercy, M. F. and Ray, C. A. (1988). Dramatic limbic and cortical effects mediated by high affinity PCP receptors. *Life Sci.*, **43**, 379–85.

Piercy, M. F., Hoffman, W. E., and Kaczkofsky, P. (1988). Functional evidence for PCP-like effects of the anti-stroke candidate MK-801. *Trends Pharmac. Sci.*, **9**, 153–4.

Pinder, R.M. (1988). The benefits and risks of antidepressant drugs. *Human Psychopharmac.* **3**, 73–86.

Poirier, M-F., Benkelfat, C., Loo, H., Sechter, D., Zarifian, E., Galzin, A-M., and Langer, S.Z. (1986). Reduced B_{max} of [^{3}H]-imipramine binding to platelets of depressed patients free of previous medication with 5HT uptake inhibitors. *Psychopharmacology*, **89**, 456–61.

Pollard, H. and Schwartz, J-C. (1987). Histamine pathways and their functions. *Trends Neurosci.*, **10**, 86–9.

Pollitt, J. (1982). Moodiness: a heavenly problem? *J. Roy. Soc. Med.*, **75**, 7–16.

Pomara, N. and Stanley, M. (1982). Cholinergic precursors in Alzheimer's disease. *Lancet*, **ii**, 1049.

Pomerleau, O.F., and Pomerleau, C.S. (ed.) (1988). *Nicotine replacement: a clinical evaluation.* Alan R. Liss, New York.

Pomerleau, O.F. and Pomerleau, C.S. (1989). A biobehavioural perspective on smoking. In *Smoking and human behaviour* (ed. T. Ney and A. Gale), pp. 69–90. Wiley, Chichester.

Pomerleau, O.F., Fertig, J.B., Seyler, L.E., and Jaffe, J. (1983). Neuroendocrine reactivity to nicotine in smokers. *Psychopharmacology*, **81**, 61–7.

Pomerleau, O.F., Turk, D.C., and Fertig, J.B. (1984). The effects of smoking on pain and anxiety. *Addictive Behaviours*, **9**, 265–71.

Posner, M.I. and Prestie, D.E. (1987). Selective attention and cognitive control. *Trends Neurosci.*, **10**, 13–16.

Post, R.M. (1978). Frontiers in affective disorder research: new pharmacological agents and new methodologies. In *Psychopharmacology: a generation of progress* (ed. M.A. Lipton, A. DiMascio, and K.F. Killam), pp. 1323–36. Raven Press, New York.

Post, R.M. and Uhde, T.W. (1983). Biochemical and physiological mechanisms of action of carbamazepine in affective illness. In *Frontiers in neuropsychiatric research* (ed. E. Usdin, M. Goldstein, A.J. Friedhoff, and A. Georgatas), pp. 175–91. Macmillan, London.

Post, R.M., Rubinow, D.R., Uhde, T.W., Ballenger, J.C., Lake, C.R., Linnoila, M. Jimerson, D.C., and Reus, V. (1985). Effects of carbamazepine on noradrenergic mechanisms in affectively ill patients. *Psychopharmacology*, **87**, 59–63.

Praag, H.M. van. (1980). Central monoamine metabolism in depression. I Serotonin and related compounds. *Comp. Psychiat.*, **21**, 30–43.

Praag, H.M. van. (1982). Neurotransmitters and CNS disease. *Lancet*, **ii**, 1259–63.

Prange, A.J., Garbutt, J.C., and Loosen, P.T. (1987). The hypothalamic-pituitary-thyroid axis in affective disorders. In *Psychopharmacology: the third generation of progress* (ed. H.Y. Meltzer), pp. 629–38. Raven Press, New York.

Price, D.L., Whitehouse, P.J., and Struble, R.G. (1986). Cellular pathology in Alzheimer's and Parkinson's diseases. *Trends Neurosci.*, **9**, 29–33.

Price, L.H., Charney, D.S., Delgado, P.L., and Heninger, G.R. (1990). Lithium and serotonin function: implications for the serotonin hypothesis of depression. *Psychopharmacology*, **100**, 3–12.

Proudfoot, A. (1982). *Diagnosis and management of acute poisoning*. Blackwell Scientific Publications, Oxford.

Prunell, M., Boada, M., Feria, M., and Benitez, M. A. (1987). Antagonism of the stimulant and depressant effects of ethanol in rats by naloxone. *Psychopharmacology*, **92**, 215-18.

Psychopharmacology. (1989). Clozapine (Leponex[R]/Clozaril[R]). Scientific update meeting, Montreux, Switzerland, 1988. *Psychopharmacology*, **99** (Suppl.).

Quirion, R., Aubert, I., Lapchak, A., Schaum, R. P., Teolis, S., Gauthier, S., and Araujo, D. M. (1989). Muscarinic receptor subtypes in human neurodegenerative disorders: focus on Alzheimer's disease. *Trends Pharmac. Sci.*, December Suppl., 80-4.

Quirion, R., Chicheportiche, P. C., Conteras, K. M., Johnson, D. L., Tam, S. W., Woods, J. H., and Zukin, S. P. (1987). Classification and nomenclature of phencyclidine and sigma receptor sites. *Trends Neurosci.*, **11**, 444-6.

Quitkin, F., Rifkin, A., and Klein, D. F. (1976). Neurologic soft signs in schizophrenia and character disorders. *Arch. Gen. Psychiat.*, **33**, 845-53.

Racagni, G., and Brunello, N. (1984). Transynaptic mechanisms in the action of antidepressant drugs. *Trends Pharmac. Sci.*, **5**, 527-31.

Rago, L. K., Allikonets, L. H., and Zarkovsky, A. M. (1981). Effects of piracetam on the central dopaminergic transmission. *Naunyn-Schmiedeberg's Arch. Pharmacol.*, **318**, 36-7.

Rall, T. W. (1980). Central nervous system stimulants. In *The pharmacological basis of therapeutics*. (ed. A. G. Gilman, L. S. Goodman, and A. Gilman), pp. 592-607. Macmillan, New York.

Rall, T. W. and Schleifer, S. (1980). Drugs effective in the therapy of the epilepsies. In *The pharmacological basis of therapeutics*. (ed. A. G. Gilman, L. S. Goodman, and A. Gilman), pp. 448-74. Macmillan, New York.

Ramsay, J., Anderson, H. R., Bloor, K., and Flanegan, R. J. (1989). An introduction to the practice, prevalence and chemical toxicology of volatile substance abuse. *Hum. Toxicol.*, **8**, 261-9.

Rance, M. J. (1983). The antagonist analgesics: actions at multiple opiate receptors. In *Persistent pain* (ed. S. Lipton and J. Miles), Vol. 4, pp. 21-40. Grune and Stratton, London.

Ravard, S. and Dourish, C. T. (1990). Cholecystokinin and anxiety. *Trends Pharmac. Sci.*, **11**, 271-3.

Rawlins, J. N. P. (1984). Some neurophysiological properties of the septo-hippocampal system. In *Psychopharmacology of the limbic system* (ed. M. R. Trimble and E. Zarifian), pp. 17-50. Oxford University Press.

Reavill, C. (1990). Actions of nicotine on dopaminergic pathways and implications for Parkinson's disease. In *Nicotine pharmacology: molecular, cellular and behavioural aspects* (ed. S. Wonacott, M. A. H. Russell, and I. P. Stolerman), pp. 307-40. Oxford University Press.

Redgrave, P. and Dean, P. (1981). Intracranial self-stimulation. *Br. Med. Bull.*, **37**, 141-6.

Redmond, D. E. (1987). Studies of the nucleus locus coeruleus in monkeys and hypotheses for neuropharmacology. In *Psychopharmacology: the third generation of progress* (ed. H. Y. Meltzer), pp. 967–75. Raven Press, New York.

Reich, W. (1975). The spectrum concept of schizophrenia; problems for diagnostic practice. *Arch. Gen. Psychiat.*, **32**, 489–98.

Reiman, E. M. (1987). The study of panic disorder using positron emission tomography. *Psychiatric Developments*, **1**, 63–78.

Reiman, E. M., Fusselman, M. J., Fox, P. T., and Raichle, M. E. (1989*a*). Neuroanatomical correlates of anticipatory anxiety. *Science*, **243**, 1071–4.

Reiman, E. M., Raichle, M. E., Robins, E., Mintun, M. A., Fusselman, M. J., Fox, P. R., Price, J. L., and Hackman, K. A. (1989*b*). Neuroanatomical correlates of a lactate-induced anxiety attack. *Arch. Gen. Psychiat.*, **46**, 493–500.

Reisberg, B., Ferris, S. H., Anand, R., Mir, P., Geibel, V., DeLeon, M. J., and Roberts, E. (1983). Effects of naloxone in senile dementia: a double blind trial. *New Engl. J. Med.*, **308**, 721–2.

Revely, A. M., Revely, M. A., and Murray, R. M. (1983). Enlargement of cerebral ventricles in schizophrenics is confined to those without genetic prodisposition. *Lancet*, **ii**, 525.

Reveley, M. A. and Trimble, M. R. (1987). Application of imaging techniques. *Br. Med. Bull.*, **43**, 616–33.

Reynolds, G. P. (1983). Increased concentrations and lateral asymmetry of amygdala dopamine in schizophrenia. *Nature*, **305**, 527–9.

Reynolds, G. P., Reynolds, L. M., Reiderer, P., Jellinger, K., and Gabriel, E. (1980). Dopamine receptors and schizophrenia; drug effect or illness? *Lancet*, **ii**, 1251.

Reynolds, G. P., Riederer, P., Jellinger, K., and Gabriel, E. (1981). Dopamine receptors and schizophrenia: the neuroleptic drug problem. *Neuropharmacol.*, **20**, 1319–20.

Reyntjens, A., Gelders, Y. G., Hoppenbrouwers, M-L. J. A., and Bussche, G. (1988). Thymostenic effects of ritanserin (R55667), a centrally acting serotonin-S$_2$ receptor blocker. *Drug Dev. Res.*, **8**, 205–11.

Richardson, B. P. and Engel, G. (1986). The pharmacology of 5-HT$_3$ receptors. *Trends Neurosci.*, **9**, 424–8.

Richelson, E. (1981). Pharmacology and clinical considerations of the neuroleptics. In *Neuropharmacology of central nervous system and behavioural disorders* (ed. G. C. Palmer), pp. 125–46. Academic Press, New York.

Rifkin, A. and Siris, S. (1984). Sodium lactate response as a model for panic disorders. *Trends Neurosci.*, **7**, 188–9.

Rigter, H. and Riezen, H. van. (1978). Hormones and Memory. In *Psychopharmacology: a generation of progress* (ed. M. A. Lipton, A. DiMascio, and K. F. Killam), pp. 677–89. Raven Press, New York.

Ritchie, J. M. (1980). The aliphatic alcohols. In *The pharmacological basis of therapeutics* (ed. A. G. Gilman, L. S. Goodman, and A. Gilman), pp. 376–90. Macmillan, New York.

Ritchie, J. M., and Greene, N. B. (1980). Local anaesthetics. In *The pharmacological basis of therapeutics* (ed. A. G. Gilman, L. S. Goodman, and A. Gilman), pp. 300–20. Macmillan, New York.

Roberts, G. W. (1990). Schizophrenia: the cellular biology of a functional psychosis. *Trends Neurosci.*, **13**, 207–11.

Roberts, G. W. and Crow, T. J. (1987). The neuropathology of schizophrenia – a progress report. *Br. Med. Bull.*, **43**, 599–615.

Robertson, G. and Taylor, P. J. (1987). Laterality and psychosis: neuropsychological evidence. *Br. Med. Bull.*, **43**, 634–50.

Robertson, D., Frohlich, J. C., and Carr, R. K. (1978). Effects of caffeine on plasma renin activity, catecholamines and blood pressure. *N. Eng. J. Med.*, **298**, 181–6.

Robinson, J. H. and Wang, S. C. (1979). Unit activity of limbic system neurones: effects of morphine, diazepam and neuroleptic agents. *Brain Res.*, **166**, 149–59.

Rogers, H. J., Spector, R. G., and Trounce, J. R. (1981). *A textbook of clinical pharmacology*. Hodder and Stoughton, Kent.

Roland, P. (1991). Cortical representation of pain. *Trends Neurosci.,* **15**, 3–5.

Rolls, T., Caan, A. W., Perrett, D. I., and Wilson, F. A. W. (1981). Neuronal activity related to long term memory. *Acta neurol. Scand.* Suppl. 89, **64**, 121–4.

Roper, P. (1989). Bulimia while sleepwalking, a rebuttal for sane automatism? *Lancet*, **334**, 769.

Ross, E. D. (1982). Disorders of recent memory in humans. *Trends Neurosci.*, **5**, 170–3.

Ross, E. D. (1984). Right hemisphere's role in language, affective behaviour and emotion. *Trends Neurosci.*, **7**, 342–6.

Rossor, M. N. (1982). Neurotransmitters and CNS disease: dementia. *Lancet*, **ii**, 1200–4.

Rossor, M. N., Iversen, L. L., Reynolds, G. P., Mountjoy, C. Q., and Roth, M. (1984). Neurochemical characteristics of early and late onset types of Alzheimer's disease. *Br. Med. J.*, **288**, 961–4.

Roth, M. (1984). Agoraphobia, panic disorder and generalised anxiety disorder: some implications of recent advances. *Psychiat. Devel.*, **2**, 31–52.

Roth, M. (1988). The relationship between anxiety and depression. In *Emotion and emotional disorders*, Reports on First Maudsley Conference on New Developments in Psychiatry (ed. B. Beakon), pp. 29–30. Hoffman-La Roche, Basle.

Roth, W. T. (1987). Electrical brain activity in psychiatric disorders. In *Psychopharmacology: the third generation of progress* (ed. H. Y. Meltzer), pp. 793–801. Raven Press, New York.

Rothman, S. J., and Olney, J. W. (1987) Excitotoxicity and the NMDA receptor. *Trends Neurosci.*, **10**, 299–302.

Routtenberg, A. (1968). The two arousal hypothesis: reticular formation and limbic system. *Psychol. Rev.*, **75**, 51–80.

Routtenberg, A. (1978). Reward systems of the brain. *Scientific Am.*, **239**, 125–31.

Routtenberg, A. and Santos-Anderson, R. (1977). The role of prefrontal cortex in intracranial self-stimulation. In *Handbook of psychopharmacology* (ed. L. L. Iverson, S. D. Iverson, and S. H. Snyder), pp. 1–24. Plenum Press, New York.

Royall, D. R. and Klemm, W. R. (1981). Dopaminergic mediation of reward: evidence gained using a natural reinforcer in a behavioural contrast paradigm. *Neurosci. Lett.*, **21**, 223–9.

Russell, M. A. H. (1978*a*). Cigarette smoking: a dependence on high nicotine boli. *Drug Metabolism Reviews.*, **8**, 29–57.

Russell, M. A. H., Raw, M., and Jarvis, M. J. (1980). Clinical use of nicotine chewing gum. *Br. Med. J.*, **280**, 1599.

Sack, D. A., Rosenthal, N. E., Parry, B. L., and Wehr, T. A. (1987). Biological rhythms in psychiatry. In *Psychopharmacology: the third generation of progress* (ed. H. Y. Meltzer), pp. 669–85. Raven Press, New York.

Sadzot, B., Baraban, J. M., Glennon, R. A., Lyon, R. A., Leonhardt, S., Jan, C-R., and Titeler, M. (1989). Hallucinogenic drug interactions at human brain 5-HT$_2$ receptors: implications for treating LSD-induced hallucinogenesis. *Psychopharmacology*, **98**, 495–9.

Sahakian, B., Jones, G., Levy, R., Gray, J., and Warburton, P. (1988). The effects of nicotine on attention, information processing, and short-term memory in patients with dementia of the Alzheimer type. *Br. J. Psychiat.*, **154**, 797–800.

Sahgal, A. (1984). A critique of the vasopressin-memory hypothesis. *Psychopharmacology*, **83**, 215–28.

Sahgal, A., Wright, C., and Ferrier, I. N. (1986). Desamino-D-arg^8-vasopressin (DDAVP), unlike ethanol, has no effect on a boring vigilance task in humans. *Psychopharmacology*, **90**, 58–63.

Salamy, J. G. (1976). Sleep: some concepts and constructs. In *Pharmacology of sleep* (ed. R. L. Williams and I. Karacan), pp. 53–82., New York.

Saletu, B. (1980). Central measures in schizophrenia. In *Biological psychiatry part II. Brain mechanisms and abnormal behaviour—psychophysiology* (ed. M. H. van Praag, M. H. Lader, O. J. Rafaelson, and E. J. Sachar), pp. 97–144. Marcel Dekker, New York.

Saletu, B. (1989). EEG imaging of brain activity in clinical psychopharmacology. In *Topographic brain mapping of EEG and evoked potentials* (ed. K. Maurer), pp. 482–506. Springer-Verlag, Berlin.

Sandler, M. (1982). The emergence of tribulin. *Trends Neurosci.*, **5**, 471–2.

Sandoz (1977). *Hydergine.* Sandoz Information Service, Sandoz Products Ltd., Middlesex.

Saper, C. B. (1987). Function of the locus coeruleus. *Trends Neurosci.*, **10**, 343–4.

Sara, S. J., David-Remacle, M., Weyers, M., and Giurgea, C. (1979). Piracetam facilitates retrieval but does not impair extinction of bar-pressing in rats. *Psychopharmacology*, **61**, 71–5.

Sarter, M., Bruno, J. P., and Dudchenko, P. (1990). Activating damaged basal forebrain cholinergic system: tonic stimulation versus signal amplification. *Psychopharmacology*, **101**, 1–17.

Sarter, M., Schneider, H. H., and Stephens, D. N. (1988). Treatment strategies for senile dementia: antagonist B-carbolines. *Trends Neurosci.*, **11**, 13–16.

Saunders, J. B. (1982). Alcoholic liver disease. *Hospital Update*, **8**, 905–14.

Schachter, S. (1971). *Emotion, obesity and crime.* Academic Press, New York.

Schachter, S., Silverstein, B., Kozlowski, L. T., Herman, C. P., and Liebling, B. (1977). Effects of stress on cigarette smoking and urinary pH. *J. Exp. Psychol: Gen.,* **106**, 24–30.

Schaefer, G. J. and Michael, R. P. (1990). Interactions of naloxone with morphine, amphetamine and phencyclidine on fixed interval responding for intracranial self-stimulation in rats. *Psychopharmacology,* **102**, 263–8.

Schildkraut, J. J. (1965). The catecholamine hypothesis of affective disorders: a review of supporting evidence. *Am. J. Psychiat.,* **122**, 509–22.

Schildkraut, J. J. (1978). Current status of the catecholamine hypothesis of affective disorders. In *Psychopharmacology: a generation of progress* (ed. M. A. Lipton, A. DiMascio, and K. F. Killam), pp. 1223–34. Raven Press, New York.

Schmiterlow, C. G., Hansson, E., Andersson, G., Applegren, L. E., and Hoffman, P. C. (1967). Distribution of nicotine in the central nervous system. *An. N. Y. Acad. Sci.,* **142**, 2–14.

Schmitt, P., Di Scala, G., Jenck, F., and Sander, G. (1984). Periventricular structures, elaboration of aversive effects and processing of sensory information. In *Modulation of sensorimotor activity during alterations in behavioural states* (ed. R. Bandler), pp. 393–414. Alan R. Liss, New York.

Schuckit, M. A. (1987). The natural history of opiate addiction. In *Psychopharmacology: the third generation of progress* (ed. H. Y. Meltzer), pp. 1527–33. Raven Press, New York.

Schulsinger, F. (1985). Schizophrenia: genetics and environment. In *Psychopharmacology. Recent advances and future prospects.* (ed. S. D. Iverson), pp. 185–95. Oxford University Press.

Schultz, H., Lund, R., and Doerr, P. (1978). The measurement of change in sleep during depression and remission. *Arch. Psychiat. Nervenkr.,* **225**, 233–41.

Schultz, R., Wuster, M., Duka, T., and Herz, A. (1980). Acute and chronic ethanol treatment changes endorphin levels in brain and pituitary. *Psychopharmacology,* **68**, 221–7.

Schulz, S. C., Koller, M. M., Kishore, P. R., Hamer, R. M., Gehl, J. J., and Friedel, R. O. (1983). Ventricular enlargement in teenage patients with schizophrenic spectrum disorder. *Am. J. Psychiat.,* **140**, 1592–5.

Schulz, H., Geisber, P., Pollmaecher, T., Andreas-Zietz, A., Keller, E., Scholz, S., and Albert, E. D. (1986). HLA-DRZ correlates with rapid-eye-movement sleep latency in normal human subjects. *Lancet,* **ii**, 803.

Schwartz, J. C., Arrang, J. M., and Garbarg, M. (1986). Three classes of histamine receptors in brain. *Trends Pharmac. Sci.,* **7**, 24–8.

Scott, D. F. (1981). Other sleep disorders and their treatments. In *Psychopharmacology of sleep.* (ed. D. Wheatley), pp. 214–31. Raven Press, New York.

Scott, F. L. (1979). A review of some current drugs used in the pharmacotherapy of organic brain syndromes. In *Physiology of cell biology of ageing,* Ageing vol. 8 (ed. A. Cherkin, C. E. Finch, N. Kharasch, T. Makinodam, F. L. Scott, and B. Strehler), pp. 151–84. Raven Press, New York.

Scoville, W. B. and Milner, B. (1957). Loss of recent memory after bilateral hippocampal lesions. *J. Neurol. Neurosurg. Psychiat.,* **20**, 11–21.

Sedvall, G. (1990). PET imaging of dopamine receptors in human basal ganglia: relevance to mental illness. *Trends Neurosci.,* **13**, 302–8.

Seligman, M. E. P. (1975). *Helplessness: on depression, development and death.* Freeman, San Francisco.

Selkoe, D. J. (1982). Molecular pathology of the aging human brain. *Trends Neurosci.*, **5**, 332-6.

Selye, H. (1956). *The stress of life.* McGraw Hill, New York.

Sepinwall, J. and Cook, L. (1979). Mechanism of action of the benzodiazepines: behavioural aspects. *Fed. Proc.*, **39**, 3024-31.

Sergent, J. (1990). Furtive incursions into bicameral mind: integrative and co-ordinating role of subcortical structures. *Brain*, **113**, 537-68.

Shader, R. I., Goodman, M., and Gever, J. (1982). Panic disorders: current perspectives. *J. Clin. Psychopharmacol.*, **2**, Suppl. 6, 2-10.

Shagass, C. (1977). Twisted thoughts, twisted brainwaves? In *Psychopathology and brain dysfunction* (ed. C. Shagass, S. Gershon, and A. J. Friedhoff), pp. 353-78. Raven Press, New York.

Shagass, C. and Straumenis, J. J. (1978). Drugs and human sensory evoked potentials. In: *Psychopharmacology: A Generation of Progress.* (eds M. A. Lipton, A. DiMascio, and K. F. Killam), pp, . 699-709. Raven Press, New York.

Shagass, C., Ornitz, E. M., Sutton, S., and Tueting, P. (1978). Event related potentials and psychopathology. In *event-related brain potentials in man* (ed. E. Callaway, P. Tueting, and S. H. Koslow), pp. 443-95. Academic Press, New York.

Shagass, C., Roemer, R. A., Straumenis, J. J., and Josiassen, R. C. (1985). Combinations of evoked potential amplitude measurements in relation to psychiatric diagnosis. *Biol. Psychiat.*, **20**, 701-22.

Shapiro, A. P. and Nathan, P. E. (1986). Human tolerance to alcohol: the role of Pavlovian conditioning processes. *Psychopharmcology*, **88**, 90-5.

Sharav, Y., Singer, E., Schmidt, E., Dionne, R. A., and Dubner, R. (1987). The analgesic effect of amitriptyline on chronic facial pain. *Pain*, **31**, 199-209.

Sharpless, S. K. (1970). Hypnotics and sedatives. I. The barbiturates. In: *The Pharmacological Basis of Therapeutics.* (ed. L. S. Goodman, and A. Gilman), pp. 98-120. Macmillan, London.

Shea, V. T. (1982). State-dependent learning in children receiving methyl phenidate. *Psychopharmacology*, **78**, 266-70.

Shelton, R. C. and Weinberger, D. R. (1987). Brain morphology in schizophrenia. In *Psychopharmacology: the third generation of progress* (ed. H Y. Meltzer) pp. 773-81. Raven Press, New York.

Sherlock, S. (ed.) (1982). Alcohol and disease. *Br. Med. Bull.*, **38**.

Sherman, G. F., Galaburda, A. M., and Geschwind, N. (1982). Neuroanatomical asymmetries in non-human species. *Trends Neurosci.*, **5**, 429-31.

Shinoto, H., Iyo, M., Yamada, T., Inone, O., Suzaki, K., Itoh, T., Fukuda, H., Yamasaki, T., Tateno, Y., and Hirayama, K. (1989). Detection of benzodiazepine receptor occupancy in the human brain by positron emission tomography. *Psychopharmacology*, **99**, 202-7.

Sicuteri, F. (1981). Persistent non-organic central pain: headache and central panalgesia. In *Persistent pain.* (ed. S. Lipton and J. Miles), Vol. 3, pp. 119-40. Academic Press, London, and Grune and Stratton, New York.

Siegel, S. (1983). Classical conditioning, drug tolerance and drug dependence. In *Research advances in alcohol and drug problems* (ed. Y. Israel, F. B. Glaser, H. Kalant, R. E. Popham, W. Schmidt, and R. G. Smart), Vol. 7, pp. 207–46. Plenum Press, New York.

Siegel, A. (1984). Anatomical and functional differentiation within the amygdala-behavioural state modulation. In *Modulation of sensorimotor activity during alterations in behavioural states* (ed. R. Bandler), pp. 299–303. Alan R. Liss, New York.

Siegel, S. (1988). Drug anticipation and drug tolerance. In *Psychopharmacology of addiction*. (ed. M. Lader), pp. 73–96. Oxford University Press.

Sieghart, W. (1989). Multiplicity of $GABA_A$-benzodiazepine receptors. *Trends Pharmac. Sci.*, **10**, 407–11.

Siever, L. J. (1987). Role of noradrenergic mechanisms in the etiology of the affective disorders. In *Psychopharmacology: the third generation of progress* (ed. H. Y. Meltzer), pp. 493–504. Raven Press, New York.

Siman, R., Baudry, M., and Lynch, G. (1985). Regulation of glutamate receptor binding by the cytoskeletal protein fodrin. *Nature*, **313**, 225–8.

Singh, S. M., George, C. F. P., Kryger, M. H., and Jung, J. H. (1990). Genetic heterogeneity in narcolepsy. *Lancet*, **335**, 726–7.

Singh, S. and Mirkin, B. L. (1973). Drug effects on the foetus. *New Ethicals.*, **10**, 150–66.

Sjoquist, B., Eriksson, A., and Winblad, B. (1982). Brain salsolinol levels in alcoholism. *Lancet*, **i**, 675–6.

Skegg, D. C. G., Richards, S. M., and Doll, R. (1979). Minor tranquillisers and road accidents. *Br. Med. J.*, **1**, 917–9.

Skjelbred, P. and Lokken, P. (1983). Effects of naloxone on post-operative pain and steroid-induced analgesia. *Br. J. Clin. Pharmac.*, **15**, 221–6.

Small, G. and Jarvik, L. F. (1982). The dementia syndrome. *Lancet*, **ii**, 1443–5.

Smith, C. B., Garcia-Savilla, J. A., and Hollingworth, P. J. (1981). $Alpha_2$-Adrenoceptors in rat brain are decreased after long-term tricycline antidepressant drug treatment. *Brain Res.*, **210**, 413–18.

Smith, G. C. and Copolov, D. (1979). Brain amines and peptides — their relevance to psychiatry. *Aust. N. Z. J. Psychiat.*, **13**, 283–91.

Smith, M. E., Holgren, E., Sokolik, M., Baudena, P., Musolino, A., and Liegeois-Chauvel, P. (1990). The intracranial topography of the P_3 event-related potential elicited during auditory oddball. *Electroenceph. Clin. Neurophysiol.* **76**, 233–48.

Smith, S. E. and Rawlins, M. D. (1973). *Variability in human drug response*. Butterworth, London.

Smythies, J. R. (1984). The transmethylation hypotheses of schizophrenia re-evaluated. *Trends Neurosci.*, **7**, 45–7.

Snel, J., Taylor, J., and Wegman, M. (1987). Does DGAVP influence memory, attention and mood in young healthy men? *Psychopharmacology*, **92**, 224–8.

Snyder, S. H. (1981). Adenosine receptors and the actions of methylxanthines. *Trends Neurosci.*, **4**, 242–4.

Snyder, S. H. (1990). Planning for serendipity. *Nature*, **346**, 508.

Sokoloff, P., Giros, B., Martres, M.P., Bouthenet, M.L., and Schwartz, J.C. (1990). Molecular cloning of a novel dopamine receptor (D_3) as a target for neuroleptics. *Nature*, **347**, 146-51.

Sonders. M.S., Keana, F.W., and Webber, E. (1988). Phencyclidine and psychomimetic sigma opiates: recent insights into their biochemical and physiological sites of action. *Trends Neurosci.*, **11**, 37-40.

Sovner, R. and DiMascio, A. (1978). Extrapyramidal syndromes and other neurological side effects of psychotropic drugs. In *Psychopharmacology: a generation of progress.* (ed. M. a. Lipton, A. DiMascio, and K.F. Killam), pp. 1021-32. Raven Press, New York.

Spealman, R.D. and Goldberg, S.R. (1982). Maintenance of schedule-controlled behaviour by intravenous injection of nicotine in squirrel monkeys. *J. Pharm. Exp. Therap.*, **223**, 402-8.

Sperry, R.W. (1973). Lateral specialisation of cerebral function in the surgically separated hemispheres. In *The psychophysiology of thinking* (ed. F.J. McGuigan and R.A. Schoonover). Academic Press, New York.

Sperry, R.W. (1974). Lateral specialisation in surgically separated hemispheres. In *The neurosciences; third study program* (ed. F.O. Schmitt and F.G. Worden). MIT Press, Cambridge, Mass.

Sperry, R.W. (1976). Mental phenomenona as causal determinants in brain function. In *Consciousness and the brain: a scientific and philosophic enquiry* (ed. G.G. Globus, G. Maxwell, and I. Savodnik). Plenum Press, New York.

Speth, R.C., Guidotti, A., and Yamamura, H. (1980). The pharmacology of the benzodiazepines. In *Neuropharmacology of central nervous system and behavioural disorders* (ed. G.C. Palmer), pp. 243-83. Academic Press, New York.

Spitzer, R.L., Endicott, J., and Gibbon, M. (1979). Crossing the border into borderline personality and borderline schizophrenia; the development criteria. *Arch. Gen. Psychiat.*, **39**, 17-24.

Squire, L.R. and Davis, H.P. (1981). The pharmacology of memory: a neurobiological perspective. *Ann. Rev. Pharmac. Toxicol.*, **21**, 323-56.

Squires, R.F. and Braestrup, C. (1977). Benzodiazepine receptors in the rat brain. *Nature*, **266**, 732-4.

Standing Medical Advisory Committe, The (1989). Drinking problems. HMSO.

Stanley, M. and Mann, J.J. (1983). Increased serotonin-2 binding sites in frontal cortex of suicide victims. *Lancet*, **i**, 214-16.

Stanley, M. and Mann, J.J. (1984). Suicide and serotonin receptors. *Lancet*, **i**, 349.

Stanley, M., Virgilio, J., and Gershon, S. (1982). Tritiated imipramine binding sites are decreased in the frontal cortex of suicide victims. *Science*, **216**, 1337-9.

Stein, J.F. (1982). *An introduction to neurophysiology* Blackwell Scientific Publications, Oxford.

Stein, J.F. (1985). The control of movement. In *The functions of the brain* (ed. C.W. Coen) pp. 67-97. Clarendon Press, Oxford.

Stein, L. (1968). Chemistry of reward and punishment. In *Psychopharmacology—a review of progress 1957-1967.* (ed. D.H. Efron), Publ. No. 1836, pp. 105-23. US Government Printing Office, Washington DC.

Stein, L. (1971). Neurochemistry of reward and punishment. Some implications for the etiology of schizophrenia. *J. Psychiat. Res.*, **8**, 345–61.

Stein, L. (1978). Reward transmitters: catecholamines and opioid peptides. In *Psychopharmacology: a generation of progress*. (ed. M.A. Lipton, A. DiMascio, and K.F. Killam), pp. 569–81. Raven Press, New York.

Stein, L. (1989). Neurochemistry of opiates and stimulants. (Abstract) *Drug Dependence: clinical phenomena and basic mechanisms*, Second Maudsley Conference on New Developments in Psychiatry, Waldorf Hotel, London, July 11–14, 1989.

Stein, L. and Belluzi, J.D. (1987). Reward transmitters and drugs of abuse. In *Brain reward systems and abuse* (ed. J. Engel and L. Oreland), pp. 19–33. Raven Press, New York.

Stein, L. and Belluzi, J.D. (1988). Operant conditioning of individual neurons. In *Quantitative analysis of behavior, Vol. 7, Biological determinants of reinforcement and memory* (ed. M.L. Commons, R.M. Church, J.R. Stellar, and A.R. Wagner), pp. 249–64. Lawrence Erlbaum Associates, Hillsdale, New Jersey.

Stein, L. and Belluzi, J.D. (1989). Cellular investigations of behavioural reinforcement. *Neurosci. and Biobehav. Rev.*, **13**, 69–80.

Stein, L. and Wise, C.D. (1969). Release of norepinephrine from hypothalamus and amygdala by rewarding median forebrain bundle stimulation and amphetamine. *J. Comp. Physiol. Psychol.*, **67**, 189–98.

Stein, L. and Wise, C.D. (1974). Serotonin and behavioural inhibition. *Adv. Biochem. Psychopharmacol.*, **11**, 281–91.

Stein, L., Wise, C.D., and Belluzzi, J.D. (1977). Neuropharmacology of reward and punishment. In *Handbook of psychopharmacology*, 8 (ed. L.L. Iverson, S.D. Iverson and S.H. Snyder), pp. 23–53. Plenum Press, New York.

Stephens, D.N., Meldrum, B.S., Weidmann, R., Schneider, C., and Grutzner, M. (1986). Does the excitatory amino acid receptor antagonist 2-APH exhibit anxiolytic activity? *Psychopharmacology*, **90**, 166–9.

Stephenson, F.A. (1987a). Benzodiazepines in the brain. *Trends Neurosci.*, **10**, 185–6.

Stephenson, F.A. (1987b). Understanding the $GABA_A$ receptor: a chemically gated ion channel. *Biochem. J.*, **249**, 21–32.

Stern, W.C. and Morgane, P.J. (1977). Sleep and memory: effects of growth hormone on sleep, brain neurochemistry and behaviour. In *Neurobiology of sleep and memory* (ed. R.R. Drucker-Colin, and J.L. McGaugh), pp. 373–401. Academic Press, New York.

Sternbach, R.A. (1981). Chronic pain as a disease entity. *Triangle (Sandoz).*, **20**, 27–32.

Stevens, J.R. (1979). Schizophrenia and dopamine regulation in the mesolimbic system. *Trends Neurosci.*, **2**, 102–5.

Stinus, L., Kelley, A.E., and Winnock, M. (1984). Neuropeptides and limbic system function. In *Psychopharmacology of the limbic system* (ed. M.R. Trimble and E. Zarifian), pp. 209–25. Oxford University Press.

Stirrat, G.M. and Beard, R.W. (1973). Drugs to be avoided or given with caution in the second and third trimesters of pregnancy. *Prescrib. J.*, **13**, 135–9.

Stokes, P. E. and Sikes, C. R. (1987). Hypothalamic-pituitary-adrenal axis in affective disorders. In *Psychopharmacology: the third generation of progress* (ed. H. Y. Meltzer), pp. 589–608. Raven Press, New York.

Strang, J. and Edwards, G. (1989). Cocaine and Crack. *Br. Med. J.*, **299**, 337–8.

Strange, P. O. (1988). The structure and mechanism of neurotransmitter receptors. *Biochem. J.*, **249**, 309–18.

Stutzman, J-M., Cintrat, P., Laduron, P. M., and Blanchard, J-C (1989). Riluzole antagonises the anxiogenic properties of the beta-carboline FG 7142 in rats. *Psychopharmacology*, **99**, 515–19.

Sugrue, M. F. (1980). Effects of acutely and chronically administered anti-depressants on the clonidine-induced decrease in rat brain of 3-methoxy-4-hydroxy phenethyleneglycol sulphate. *Life Sci.*, **28**, 377–84.

Sugrue, M. F. (1981). Effect of chronic antidepressant administration on rat frontal cortex alpha$_2$ and beta-adrenoceptor binding *Br. J. Pharmac.*, **74**, 760P.

Sulser, F. (1981). Perspectives on the mode of action of antidepressant drugs. In *Towards understanding receptors* (ed. J. W. Lamble), pp. 99–104. Elsevier/North Holland, Amsterdam.

Sulser, F., and Mobley, P. L. (1980). Biochemical effects of antidepressants in animals. In *Psychotropic agents part I: antipsychotics and antidepressants* (ed. E. Hoffmeister and G. Stille), pp. 471–90. Springer-Verlag, Berlin.

Sulser, S., Okada, F., Manier, D. H., Gillespie, D. D., Janowsky, A., and Mishra, R. (1983). Noradrenergic signal transfer as a target of anti-depressant therapy. In *Frontiers in neuropsychiatric research* (ed. E. Usdin, M. Goldstein, A. J. Friedhoff, and A. Georgatas), pp. 3–17. Macmillan, London.

Summers, W. K., Majovski, L. V., Marsh, G. M., Tachiki, K., and Kling, A. (1986). Oral tetra-hydroaminoacridine in long-term treatment of senile dementia. *New Engl. J. Med.*, **315**, 124, 111–5.

Svensson, T. H. and Usdin, T. (1978). Feedback inhibition of brain noradrena-line neurones by tricyclics: alpha-receptor mediation after acute and chronic treatment. *Science*, **202**, 1081–91.

Svensson, T. H., Dahlhof, C., Engberg. G., and Hallberg, H. (1981). Central pre- and postsynaptic monoamine receptors in antidepressant therapy. *Acta. Psychiat. Scand.*, **63**, Suppl. 289, pp 67–78.

Tabakoff, B. and Hoffman, P L. (1987). Biochemical pharmacology of alcohol. In *Psychopharmacology: the third generation of progress* (ed. H. Y. Meltzer), pp. 1521–6. Raven Press, New York.

Taggart, P., Carruthers, M., and Somerville, W. (1973). Electrocardiogram, plasma catecholamines and lipids, and their modification by oxprenolol when speaking before an audience. *Lancet*, **ii**, 341–5.

Tagliavini, F. and Pilleri, G. (1983). Neuronal counts in basal nucleus of Meynert in Alzheimer Disease and in simple senile dementia. *Lancet*, **i**, 469–70

Taha, A. and Ball, K. (1980). Smoking and Africa; the coming epidemic. *Br. Med. J.*, **280**, 991–3.

Tamminga, C. A., and Gerlach, J. (1987). New neuroleptics and experimental antipsychotics in schizophrenia. In *Psychopharmacology: the third generation of progress* (ed. H. Y. Meltzer), pp. 1129–40. Raven Press, New York.

Taylor, P. (1980). Ganglion stimulating and blocking agents. In *The Pharmacological basis of therapeutics* (ed. A.G. Gilman, L.S. Goodman, and A. Gilman), pp. 211-19. Macmillan, New York.

Taylor, D. (1987). Current usage of benzodiazepines in Britain. In *The benzodiazepines in current clinical practice* (ed. H. Freeman, and Y. Rue), pp. 13-17. Royal Society of Medicine Services Ltd., London.

Tecce, J.J., Savingnano-Bowman, J., and Cole, J.O. (1978). Drug effects on contingent negative variation and eyeblinks: the distraction-arousal hypothesis. In *Psychopharmacology: a generation of progress* (ed. M.A. Lipton, A. DiMascio, and K.F. Killam), pp. 745-58. Raven Press, New York.

Tennakone, K. and Wickramanayake, S. (1987). Aluminium leaching from cooking utensils. *Nature*, 325, 202.

Teoh, R. (1988). Tardive dyskinesia. *Adv. Drug Reaction Bull.*, 132, 496-9.

Tepper, J.M., Groves, P.M., and Young, S.J. (1985). The neuropharmacology of the autoinhibition of monoamine release. *Trends Pharmac. Sc.*, 6, 251-6.

Terenius, L. (1977). *Physiological and clinical relevance of endorphins*. Communication to symposium on Centrally Acting Peptides. Biological Council, April 4/5 1977, Middlesex Hospital Medical School, London.

Terenius, L. (1981). Biochemical mediators of pain. *Triangle (Sandoz)*, 20, 19-26.

Terenius, L. (1982). Endorhphins — clinical relevance in neurology. In *Advances in pharmacology and therapeutics II Vol. 1. CNS pharmacology — neuropeptides* (ed. H. Yoshida, Y. Hagihara, and S. Ebashi), pp 57-65. Pergamon Press, Oxford.

Thoenen, H. (1991). The changing scene of neurotrophic factors. *Trends Neurosci.*, 14, 165-70.

Thomas, C.B. (1973). The relationship of smoking and habits of nervous tension. In *Smoking behaviour: motives and incentives.* (ed. W.L. Dunn), pp. 157-70. Winston and Sons, Washington DC.

Thomas, C.S. (1987). HIV and schizophrenia. *Lancet*, ii, 101.

Thomas, M., Halsall, S., and Peters, T.J. (1982). Role of hepatic aldehyde dehydrogenase in alcoholism: demonstration of persistent reduction of cytosolic activity in abstaining patients. *Lancet*, ii, 1057-9.

Thompson, C., Stinson, D., and Smith, A. (1990) Seasonal affective disorder and season-dependent abnormalities of melatonin suppression by light. *Lancet*, 336, 703-6.

Thompson, J.W. (1984a). Pain: mechanisms and principles of management. In *Advanced geriatric medicine* (ed. J. Grimley Evans and F.I. Caird), Vol. 4, pp. 3-16 Pitman Publishing Ltd.

Thompson, J.W. (1984b). Opioid peptides. *Br. Med. J.*, 288 259-61.

Thorndike, E.L. (1911). *Animal Intelligence*. Macmillan, New York.

Ticku, M.K. (1983). Benzodiazepine-GABA receptor-ionophore complex: current concepts. Neuropharmacol., 22, 1459-70.

Timsit-Berthier, M. (1981). A propos de l'interpretation de la variation contingente negative en psychiatrie. *Rev. EEG Neurophysiol.*, 11, 236-44.

Timsit-Berthier, M., Mantanus, H., Ansseau, M., Devoitille, J-M., Mas, A.D., and Legras, J-J. (1987). Contingent negative variation in major depressive disorders. In *Current trends in event-related research (EEG Suppl. 40)* (ed. R. Johnson J. W. Rohrbangh and R. Parasuraman), pp. 762–71. Elsevier, Amsterdam.

Traber, J., and Glaser, J. (1987). 5-HT$_{1A}$ receptor-related anxiolytics. *Trends Pharmac. Sci.*, **8**, 432–7.

Tranel, D. T. (1983). The effects of monetary incentive and frustrative non-reward on heart rate and electrodermal activity. *Psychophysiology*, **20**, 652–7.

Traskman, L., Asberg, M., Bartilsson, L., and Sjostrand, L. (1981). Monoamine metabolites in CSF and suicidal behaviour. *Arch. Gen. Psychiat.*, **38**, 631–6.

Trends in Pharmacological Sciences (1990). Receptor nomenclature supplement. *Trends Pharmac. Sci.*, **11** (Suppl.), 1–29.

Trends in Pharmacological Sciences (1991). Receptor nomenclature supplement. *Trends Pharmac. Sci.*, **12** (Suppl.), 1–35.

Tricklebank, M. D. (1989). Interactions between dopamine and 5-HT$_3$ receptors suggest new treatments for psychosis and drug addiction. *Trends Pharmacol. Sci.*, **10**, 127–8.

Triggle, D. J. (1981). Desensitization. In *Towards understanding receptors* (ed. J. W. Lamble), pp. 28–33. Elsevier/North Holland, Amsterdam.

Trimble, M. R. (1981). Visual and auditory hallucinations. *Trends Neurosci.*, **4**, I–IV.

Trullas, R., Havoundjian, H., Zamir, N., Paul, S., and Skolnick, P. (1987). Environmentally-induced modification of the benzodiazepine GABA receptor coupled chloride ionophore. *Psychopharmacology*, **91**, 384–90.

Tsuang, M. T. (1982). Long-term outcome in schizophrenia. *Trends Neurosci.*, **5**, 203–5.

Tsuchiya, T. and Kitagawa, S. (1976). Effects of benzodiazepines and pentobarbital on the evoked potentials in the cat brain. *Japan. J. Pharmacol.*, **26**, 411–18.

Tsukahara, N. (1981). Sprouting and the neuronal basis of learning. *Trends Neurosci.*, **4**, 234–7.

Tucker, D. M., Antes, J. R., Stenslie, C. E., and Barnhardt, T. M. (1978). Anxiety and lateral cerebral function. *J. Abn. Psychol.*, **87**, 380–3.

Tucker, D. M., Roth, R. S., Arneson, B. A., and Buckingham, V. (1977). Right hemisphere activation during stress. *Neuropsychologia*, **15**, 697–700.

Turner, P. (1976). Beta-adrenoceptor blockade in hyperthyroidism and anxiety. *Proc. Roy. Soc. Med.*, **69**, 375–7.

Twycross, R. G. and Lack, S. A. (1983). *Symptom control in far advanced cancer: pain relief*. Pitman Publishing Ltd., London.

Tyrer, P. J. (1982). Monoamine oxidase inhibitors and amine precursors. In *Drugs in psychiatric practice* (ed. P. J. Tyrer), pp. 249–79. Butterworth, London.

Tyrer, P. J. (1984). Clinical effects of abrupt withdrawal from tricyclic antidepressants and monoamine oxidase inhibitors after long-term treatment. *J. Affect. Dis.*, **6**, 1–7.

Tyrer, P. J. (1985). Neurosis divisible? *Lancet*, **i**, 685–8.

Tyrer, S. P. (1986). Learned pain behaviour. *Br. Med. J.*, **292**, 1.

Tyrer, P. (1989). Choice of treatment in anxiety. In *Psychopharmacology of anxiety* (ed. P. Tyrer), pp. 255–82. Oxford University Press.

Tyrer, P.J. and Lader, M.H. (1974). Response to propranolol and diazepam in somatic and psychic anxiety. *Br. Med. J.*, **2**, 14–16.

Tyrer, P., Owen, R., and Dawling, S. (1983). Gradual withdrawal of diazepam after long-term therapy. *Lancet*, **i**, 1402–6.

Tyrer, S. and Shaw, D.M. (1982). Lithium carbonate. In *Drugs in psychiatric practice* (ed. P.J. Tyrer), pp. 280–312. Butterworth, London.

Tyrer, S. and Shopsin, B. (1980). Neural and Neuromuscular side-effects of lithium. In *Handbook of lithium therapy* (ed. F.N. Johnson), pp. 289–309. MTP Press, Lancaster.

Tyrer, S.P., Capon, M.N., Peterson, D.M., Charlton, J.E., and Thompson, J.W. (1989). The detection of psychiatric illness and psychological handicaps in a British pain clinic population. *Pain*, **36**, 63–74.

Uchimura, N., and North, A.R. (1990). Actions of cocaine on rat nucleus accumbens neurons *in vitro*. *Br. J. Pharmac.*, **99**, 736–40.

Ugedo, L., Grenhoff, J., and Svensson, T.H. (1989) Ritanserin, a 5-HT$_2$ receptor antagonist, activates midbrain dopamine neurons by blocking serotonergic inhibition. *Psychopharmacology*, **98**, 45–50.

Uhde, T.A., and Tancer, M.E. (1989) Chemical models of panic: a review and critique: In *Psychopharmacology of anxiety* (ed. P. Tyrer), pp. 108–31. Oxford University Press.

Uhlenuth, E.H., Balter, M.B., Mellinger, G.D., Cisin, I.H., and Clinthorne, J. (1983). Symptom checklist syndromes in the general population. *Arch Gen Psychiat.*, **40**, 1167–73.

Vanderwolf, C.H. and Robinson, T.E. (1981). Reticulo-cortical activity and behaviour: a critique of the arousal theory and a new synthesis. *Behav. Brain Sci.*, **4**, 459–514.

Van Kammen, D.P. and Gelernter, J. (1987*a*). Biochemical instability in schizophrenia I. The norepinephrine system. In *Psychopharmacology: the third generation of progress* (ed. H.Y. Meltzer) pp. 745–51. Raven Press, New York.

Van Kammen, D.P., and Gelernter, J. (1987*b*). Biochemical instability in schizophrenia II. the serotonin and aminobutyric acid systems. In *Psychopharmacology: the third generation of progress* (ed. H.Y. Meltzer), pp. 753–8. Raven Press, New York.

Venables, P.H. (1980). Peripheral measures of schizophrenia. In *Handbook of biological psychiatry part II. Brain mechanisms and abnormal behaviour — psychophysiology* (ed. H.M. van Praag, M.A. Lader, O.J. Rafaelson, and E.J. Sachar), pp. 79–96. Marcel Dekker, New York.

Venables, P.H. (1981). Psychophysiology of abnormal behaviour. *Br. Med. Bull.*, **37**, 199–203.

Venables, N and Kelly, P.H. (1990). Effects of NMDA receptor antagonists on passive avoidance learning and retrieval in rats and mice. *Psychopharmacology*, **100**, 215–21.

Vestergaard, P., Amdisen, A., and Schou, M. (1980). Clinically significant side effects of lithium treatment. A survey of 237 patients in long-term treatment. *Acta Psychiat. Scand.*, **62**, 193–200.

Villarreal, J.E. and Salazar, L.A. (1981). The dependence-producing properties of psychomotor stimulants. In *Psychotropic agents part II.* (ed. F. Hoffmeister and S. Stille), pp. 607–35. Springer-Verlag, Heidelberg.

Vogel, G. W. (1975). A review of REM sleep deprivation. *Arch. Gen. Psychiat.*, **32**, 749-61.

Vogel, G. W. (1978). An alternative view of the neurobiology of dreaming. *Am. J. Psychiat.*, **135**, 1531-5.

Volicer, L. and Biagioni, T. M. (1982). Effect of ethanol administration and withdrawal on benzodiazepine receptor binding in the rat brain. *Neuropharmacol.*, **21**, 283-6.

Waddington, J. L. (1986). Behavioural correlates of the actions of selective dopamine D-1 receptor agonists: impact of SCH 23390 and SKT 83566, and functionally interactive D-1: D-2 receptor systems. *Biochem. Pharmacol.*, **35**, 3611-67.

Waddington, J. L. (1989). Functional interactions between D-1 and D-2 dopamine receptor systems: their role in the regulation of psychomotor behaviour, putative mechanisms, and clinical relevance. *J. Psychopharmacol.*, **3**, 54-63.

Waldhauser, F., Saletu, B., and Trinchard-Lugan, J. (1990). Sleep laboratory investigations on hypnotic properties of melatonin. *Psychopharmacology*, **100**, 222-6.

Waldron, H. A. (1981). Effects of organic solvents. *Br. J. Hosp. Med.*, **26**, 645-9.

Wall, J. T. (1988*a*). Variable organisation in cortical maps of the skin as an indication of the lifelong adaptive capacities of circuits in the mammalian brain. *Trends Neurosci.*, **11**, 549-57.

Wall, P. D. (1988*b*). Stability and instability of central pain mechanisms. In *Proceedings of the Vth World Congress on Pain* (ed. R. Dubner, G. F. Gebart, and M. R. Bond), pp. 13-24. Elsevier Science Publishers, Amsterdam.

Wall, P. D. and McMahon, S. B. (1986). The relationship of perceived pain to afferent nerve impulses. *Trends Neurosci.*, **96**, 254-5.

Wall, R., Linford, S. M. J., and Akhter, M. (1980). Addiction to Distalgesic (dextropropoxyphene). *Br. Med. J.*, **280**, 1213-14.

Walter, W. G. (1964). Slow potential waves in the human brain associated with expectancy, attention and decision. *Arch. Psychiat. Nervenkr.*, **206**, 309-22.

Walton, J. M. (1977). *Brain's diseases of the nervous system* (8th edn, revised by J. M. Walton). Oxford University Press.

Warburton, D. M. and Walters, A. C. (1989). Attentional processing. In *Smoking and human behaviour* (ed. T. Ney and A. Gale), pp. 223-7. Wiley, Chichester.

Warrington, E. K. (1981). Neuropsychological evidence for multiple memory systems. *Acta Neurol. Scand.*, **64**, Suppl. 89, 13-19.

Warrington, E. K. and Weiskrantz, L. (1970). Amnesic syndrome: consolidation or retrieval? *Nature (Lond.)*, **228**, 628-30.

Warrington, S. J., Turner, P., Mant, T. G. K., Morrison, P., Haywood, G., Glover, V., Goodwin, B. L., Sandler, M., John-Smith, P. St., and McClelland, G. R. (1991). Clinical pharmacology of moclobemide, a new reversible monoamine oxidase inhibitor. *J. Psychopharmac.* **5**, 82-91.

Watchell, H. and Turski, L. (1990). Glutamate: a new target in schizophrenia? *Trends Pharmac. Sci.*, **11**, 219-20.

Watkins, J.C., Krogsgaard-Larson, P., and Honore, R. (1990). Structure-activity relationships in the development of excitatory amino acid receptor agonists and competitive antagonists. *Trends Pharmac. Sci.*, **11**, 25-33.

Wauquier, A. (1984). Effect of calcium entry blockers in models of brain hypoxia. *Developments in Cardiovascular Medicine*, **40**, 241-54.

Way, E.L. and Glasgow, C. (1978). Recent developments in morphine analgesia: tolerance and dependence. In *Psychopharmacology: a generation of progress* (ed. M.A. Lipton, A. DiMascio, and K.F. Killam), pp. 1535-56. Raven Press, New York.

Webster, K.E. (1978). The brainstem reticular formation. In *The biological basis of schizophrenia* (ed. G. Hemmings and W.A. Hemmings), pp. 3-27. MTP Press Ltd., Lancaster.

Webster, P.A.C. (1973). Withdrawal symptoms in neonates associated with maternal antidepressant therapy. *Lancet*, **ii**, 318.

Wehr, T.A., Jacobsen, F.M., and Sack, D.A. (1986). Timing of phototherapy and its effect on melatonin secretion do not appear to be critical for its antidepressant effect in seasonal affective disorder. *Arch. Gen. Psychiat.*, **43**, 870-5.

Weinberger, D.R. (1988). Schizophrenia and the frontal lobe. *Trends Neurosci.*, **11**, 367-70.

Weinberger, D.R., Torrey, E.F., Neophytides, A.N., and Wyatt, R.J. (1979). Lateral cerebral ventricular enlargement in chronic schizophrenia. *Arch. Gen. Psychiat.*, **36**, 735-9.

Weiner, N. (1980*a*). Atropine, scopolamine and related antimuscarinic drugs. In *The pharmacological basis of therapeutics* (ed. A.G. Gilman, L.S. Goodman, and A. Gilman), pp. 120-37. Macmillan, New York.

Weiner, N. (1980*b*). Norepinephrine, epinephrine and the sympathomimetic amines. In *The pharmacological basis of therapeutics* (ed. A.G. Gilman, L.S. Goodman, and A. Gilman), pp. 138-75. Macmillan, New York.

Weingartner, H., Gold, P., Ballenger, J.C., Smallberg, S.A., Summers, R., Rubinow, D.R., Post, R.M., and Goodwin, F.K. (1981). Effects of vasopressin on human memory functions. *Science*, **211**, 601-3.

Weiskrantz, L. (1977). Trying to bridge some neurophysiological gaps between monkey and man. *Br. J. Psychol.* **66**, 431-45.

Wen, H.L. and Cheung, S.Y.C. (1973). Treatment of drug addiction by acupuncture and electrical stimulation. *Asian J. Med.*, **9**, 138-41.

Wesnes, K. and Warburton, D.M. (1978). The effects of cigarette smoking and nicotine tablets upon human attention. In *Smoking behaviour: physiological and psychological influences* (ed. R.E. Thornton), pp. 131-47. Churchill Livingstone, Edinburgh.

Westenberg, H.G.M. and Verhoeven, W.M.A. (1988). CSF monoamine metabolites in patients and controls: support for a bimodal distribution in major affective disorders. *Acta psychiat. Scand.*, **78**, 541-9.

Wexler, B.E. (1980). Cerebral laterality and psychiatry: a review of the literature. *Am. J. Psychiat.*, **137**, 279-91.

Wexler, B.E. and Heminger, G.R. (1979). Alterations in cerebral laterality during acute psychotic illness. *Arch. Gen. Psychiat.*, **36**, 278-84.

Whalley, L.J. (1987). Causal models of Alzheimer's disease. In *Alzheimer's disease: current approaches* (ed. J.C. Malkin and M.N. Rossor), pp. 1-26. Duphar Laboratories Ltd., Southampton.

Whalley, L.J., Christie, J.E., Bennie, J., Dick, H., Blackburn, I.M., Blackwood, D., Sanchez Watts, G., and Fink, G. (1985). Selective increase in plasma luteinising hormone in drug free young men with mania. *Br. Med. J.*, **290**, 99-102.

Wheatley, D. (1981). Effects of drugs on sleep. In *Psychopharmacology of sleep* (ed. D. Wheatley), pp. 153-76. Raven Press, New York.

White, F.J. and Wang, R.Y. (1983). Differential effects of classical and atypical antipsychotic drugs on A_9 and A_{10} dopamine neurones. *Science*, **221**, 1054-7.

Whitehouse, P.J., Price, D.L., Struble, R.G., Clark, A.W., Coyle, J.T., and DeLong, M.R. (1982). Alzheimer's disease and senile dementia: loss of neurones in the basal forebrain, *Science*, **215**, 1237-9.

Whitehouse, A. (1987). Should sympathomimetics be available over the counter? *Br. Med. J.*, **295**, 1308.

Whitty, C.W.M., Stores, G., and Lishman, W.A. (1977). Amnesia in cerebral disease. In *Amnesia* (ed. C.W.M. Whitty and O.L. Zangwill), pp. 52-92. Butterworth, London.

Whitty, C.W.M. and Zangwill, O.L. (1977). Traumatic amnesia. In *Amnesia* (ed. C.W.M. Whitty and O.L. Zangwill), pp. 118-35. Butterworth, London.

Widerlov, E., Heilig, M., Ekman, R. and Wahlstedt, C. (1989). Neuropeptide Y — possible involvement in depression and anxiety. In *Neuropeptide-Y* (ed. V. Mutt, T. Hokfelt, K. Fuxe, and J. Lundberg), pp. 331-42. Raven Press, New York.

Wied, D. de. (1974). Pituitary-adrenal system hormones and behaviour. In *The neurosciences*. Third Study Program (ed. F.O. Schmitt, and F.G. Worden), pp. 653-66. MIT Press, Cambridge. Mass.

Wied, D. de. (1984*a*). The importance of vasopressin in memory. *Trends Neurosci.*, **7**, 63-4.

Wied, D. de. (984*b*). The importance of vasopressin in memory. *Trends Neurosci.*, **7**, 109.

Wied, D. de., and Gispen, W.H. (1977). Behavioural effects of peptides. In *Peptides in neurobiology*, (ed. H. Gainer), pp. 397-448. Plenum Press, New York.

Wiesel, T.N. and Hubel, D.H. (1963). Single cell response in striate cortex of kittens deprived of vision in one eye. *J. Neurophysiol.*, **26**, 1003-17.

Wiesnieski, H.M., and Iqbal, K. (1980). Ageing of the brain and dementia. *Trends Neurosci.*, **3**, 226-8.

Wilcock, G.K. and Esiri, M.M. (1983). Age and Alzheimer's disease. *Lancet*, **ii**, 346.

Wilkins, A.J., Jenkins, W.J., and Steiner, J.A. (1983). Efficacy of clonidine in treatment of alcohol withdrawal state. *Psychopharmacology*, **81**, 78-80.

Wilkinson, R.T. (1965). Sleep deprivation. In *The physiology of human survival* (ed. O.G. Edholm and A.L. Bacharach), pp. 399-430. Academic Press, London.

Williams, M. (1977). Memory disorders associated with electroconvulsive therapy. In *Amnesia* (ed. C. W. M. Whitty and O. L. Zangwill), pp. 183-98. Butterworth, London.

Williams, D. G. (1980). Effects of cigarette smoking on immediate memory and performance in different kinds of smoker. *Br. J. Psychol.*, **71**, 83-90.

Williams, M. (1984). Adenosine — a selective neuromodulator in mammalian CNS? *Trends Neurosci.*, **7**, 164-8.

Willner, P. (1984). The validity of animal models of depression. *Psychopharmacology*, **83**, 1-16.

Willner, P. and Montgomery, T. (1980). Neurotransmitters and depression: too much, too little, too unstable — or not unstable enough? *Trends Neurosci.*, **3**, 201.

Wilson, P. R. and Yaksh, T. L. (1980). Pharmacology of pain and analgesia. *Anaesth. Intens. Care.*, **8**, 248-56.

Winger, G. (1987). PCP-NMDA connection provides hope in cerebral ischemia but new direction for antipsychotics. *Trends Pharmac. Sci.*, **8**, 321-5.

Wise, R. A. (1980). The dopamine synapse and the notion of 'pleasure centres' in the brain. *Trends Neurosci.*, **3**, 91-5.

Wise, R. A. and Bozarth, M. A. (1987). A psychomotor stimulant theory of addiction. *Psychological Review*, **94**, 469-92.

Wodak, A. D., Saunders, J. B., Ewusi-Mensah, I., Davis, M., and Williams, R. (1983). Severity of alcohol dependence in patients with alcoholic liver disease. *Br. Med. J.*, **287**, 1420-2.

Wood, P. L. and Stotland, L. M. (1980). Actions of enkephalin, mu and partial agonist analgesics on acetylcholine turnover in the rat brain. *Neuropharmacol.*, **19**, 975-82.

Woods, B. T. (1983). Is the left hemisphere specialised for language at birth? *Trends Neurosci.*, **6**, 115-17.

Woods, J. H. (1978). Behavioural pharmacology of drug self-administration. In *Psychopharmacology: a generation of progress* (ed. M. A. Lipton, A. DiMascio, and K. F. Killam), pp. 595-607. Raven Press, New York.

Woods, J. H., Katz, J. L., and Winger, G. (1987). Abuse liability of benzodiazepines. *Pharmacol. Rev.*, **39**, 251-419.

World Health Organization (1979). *Schizophrenia: an international follow-up study*. Wiley, Chichester.

Wozniak, D. F., Olney, J. W., Kettinger, L., Price, M., and Miller, J. P. (1990). Behavioural effects of MK-801 in the rat. *Psychopharmacology*, **101**, 47-56.

Wyatt, R. J. and Gillin, J. C. (1976). Biochemistry and human sleep. In *Pharmacology of sleep* (ed. R. L. Williams, I. Karacan, and J. H. Masserman), pp. 239-74. Wiley, New York.

Yaksh, T. L. (1982). Opioid peptides and analgesics: sites of action. In *Advances in pharmacology and therapeutics II Vol. 1. CNS pharmacology — neuropeptides* (ed. H. Yoshida, Y. Hagihara, and S. Ebashi), pp. 29-38. Pergamon Press, Oxford.

Yaksh, T. L. and Hammond, D. L. (1982). Peripheral and central substrates involved in the rostral transmission of nociceptive information. *Pain*, **13**, 1-85.

Yaksh, T. L. and Rudy, T. A. (1978). Narcotic analgetics: CNS sites and mechanisms of action as revealed by intracerebral injection techniques. *Pain*, **4**, 299–359.

Yanagida, H. (1978). Congenital insensitivity and naloxone. *Lancet*, **ii**, 520–1.

Yanagita, T. (1981). Dependence-producing effects of anxiolytics. In *Handbook of experimental pharmacology* (ed. H. Hoffmeister and G. Stille), Vol. 55, pp. 395–408. Springer-Verlag, Berlin.

Yates, M. and Ferrier, I. N. (1990). 5-HT$_{1A}$ receptors in major depression. *J. Psychopharmacol.*, **4**, 69–74.

Young, J. P. R., Hughes, W. C., and Lader, M. H. (1976). a controlled comparison of flupenthixol and amitriptyline in depressed outpatients. *Br. Med. J.*, **1**, 1116–18.

Young, J. Z. (1966). *The memory system of the brain*. Oxford University. Oxford.

Young, J. Z. (1979). Learning as a process of selection and amplification. *J. Roy. Soc. Med.*, **72**, 801–14.

Young, W. S. and Kuhar, M. J. (1980) Radiohistochemical localisation of benzodiazepine receptors in rat brain. *J. Pharmacol. Exp. Ther.*, **212**, 337–46.

Zangwill, O. L. (1977). The Amnesic Syndrome. In *Amnesia* (ed. C. W. M. Whitty and O. L. Zangwill), pp. 104–35. Butterworth, London and Boston.

Zeisel, S. H., Reinstein, D. K., Wurtman, R. J., Corkin, S., and Growdon, J. H. (1981). Memory disorders associated with ageing. *Trends Neurosci.*, **4**, VIII–IX.

Zelsen, C., Lee, S. J., and Casalino, M. (1973). Comparative effects of maternal intake of heroin and methadone. *New Engl. J. Med.*, **289**, 1216–19.

Zimmerman, M. (1981). Physiological mechanisms of pain and pain therapy. *Triangle (Sandoz).*, **20**, 7–17.

Zornetzer, S. F. (1978). Neurotransmitter modulation and memory: a new neuropharmacological phrenology. In *Psychopharmacology: a generation of progress* (ed. M. A. Lipton, A. DiMascio, and K. F. Killam), pp. 637–49. Raven Press, New York.

Recommended further reading

Chapter 1

Blakemore, C. and Greenfield, S. (ed.) (1987). *Mindwaves*. Basil Blackwell, Oxford.

Bloom, F.E. (1985). Neurotransmitter diversity and its functional significance. *J. Roy. Soc. Med.*, **78**, 189–92.

Changeux, J.P. (1985). *Neuronal man: the biology of mind*. Oxford University Press.

Chapter 2

Horne, J. (1988). *Why we sleep*. Oxford University Press.

Isaacson, R.L. (1982). *The Limbic System* (2nd edn). Plenum Press, New York.

Vanderwolf, C.H. and Robinson, T.E. (1981). Reticulo-cortical activity and behaviour: a critique of the arousal theory and a new synthesis. *Behav. Brain Sci.*, **4**, 459–514.

Chapter 3

Gorman, J.M., Liebowitz, M.R., Fyer, A.J., and Stein, J. (1989). A neuro-anatomical hypothesis for panic disorder. *Am.J. Psychiat.*, **146**, 148–61.

Gray, J.A. (1982). *The neuropsychology of anxiety*. Clarendon Press, Oxford and Oxford University Press, New York.

Lader, M. (1980). The psychophysiology of anxiety. In *Handbook of biological psychiatry* (ed. H.M. van Praag), Part II, pp. 225–47. Marcel Dekker, New York.

Parkes, J.D. (1986). The parasomnias. *Lancet*, **ii**, 1021–4.

Chapter 4

Griffiths, R.R. and Woodson, P.P. (1988). Caffeine dependence and rein-forcement in humans and laboratory animals. In *The psychopharmacology of addiction* (ed. M. Lader), pp. 141–56. Oxford University Press.

Hindmarch, I., Beaumont, G., Brandon, S., and Leonard, B.E. (ed.) (1990). *Benzodiazepines: current concepts*. Wiley, Chichester.

Owen, R.T. and Tyrer, P. (1983). Benzodiazepine dependence: a review of the evidence. *Drugs*, **25**, 385–98.

Tyrer, P. (ed.) *Psychopharmacology of Anxiety*. Oxford University Press.

Chapter 5

Melzack, R. and Wall, P. (1988). *The challenge of pain*. Penguin Books, London.

Routtenberg, A. (1978). Reward systems of the brain. *Scientific Am.*, **239**, 125–31.

Wise, R.A. and Bozarth, M.A. (1987). A psychomotor stimulant theory of addiction. *Psychological Reviews*, **94**, 469–92.

Chapter 6

Lader, M. (ed.) (1988). *Psychopharmacology of addiction*. Oxford University Press.

Melzack, R. (1990). Phantom limbs and the concept of a neuromatrix. *Trends Neurosci.*, **13**, 88–92.

Stein, L. and Belluzi, J.D. (1987). Reward transmitters and drugs of abuse. In *Brain reward systems and abuse* (ed. J. Engel and L. Oreland), pp. 19–33. Raven Press, New York.

Chapter 7

Brecher, E.M. (1972). *Licit and illicit drugs*. Consumers Union, Mount Vernon, New York.

Miller, N.S. (ed.) (1991). *Comprehensive handbook of drug and alcohol addiction* Marcel Dekker, New York.

Ney, T. and Gale, A. (ed.) (1989) *Smoking and human behaviour*. Wiley, Chichester.

Schuckit, M.A. (1987). The natural history of opiate addiction. In *Psychopharmacology: the third generation of progress* (ed. H.Y. Meltzer), pp. 1527–33. Raven Press, New York.

Chapter 8

Dudai, Y. (1989). *The neurobiology of memory*. Oxford University Press.

Eysenck, H.J. (ed.) (1983). *A model for intelligence*. Springer-Verlag, Berlin.

O'Keefe, J. and Nadel, L. (1978). *The hippocampus as a cognitive map*. Clarendon Press, Oxford.

Young, J.Z. (1979). Learning as a process of selection and amplification. *J. Roy. Soc. Med.*, **72**, 801–14.

Chapter 9

Damasio, A. R. (1990). Category-related recognition defects as a clue to the neural substrates of knowledge. *Trends Neurosci.*, **13**, 95-8.

Malkin, J. C. and Rossor, M. N. (ed.) (1987) *Alzheimers disease: current concepts*. Duphar Laboratories, Southampton.

Warrington, E. K. (1981). Neuropsychological evidence for multiple memory systems. *Acta Neurol. Scand.*, **64**, Suppl. **89**, 13-9.

Chapter 10

Curran, H. V. (1986). Tranquillising memories: a review of the effects of benzodiazepines on human memory. *Biol. Psychol.*, **23**, 179-213.

Kendall, M. S. (1987). Review of treatment in Alzheimer's disease. In *Alzheimer's disease: current approaches* (ed. J. C. Malkin and M. N. Rossor), pp. 65-74. Duphar Laboratories Ltd., Southampton.

Nicholson, C. D. (1990). Pharmacology of nootropics and metabolically active compounds in relation to their use in dementia. *Psychopharmacology*, **101**, 147-59.

Chapter 11

Jeste, D. V., Lohr, J. B., and Goodwin, F. K. (1988). Neuroanatomical studies of major affective disorders: a review and suggestions for further research. *Br. J. Psychiat.*, **153**, 444-59.

Meltzer, H. Y. and Lowy, M. T. (1987). The serotonin hypothesis of depression. In *Psychopharmacology: the third generation of progress* (ed. H. Y. Meltzer), pp 513-33. Raven Press, New York.

Siever, L. J. (1987). Role of noradrenergic mechanisms in the etiology of the affective disorders. In *Psychopharmacology: the third generation of progress* (ed. H. Y. Meltzer), pp. 493-504. Raven Press, New York.

Willner, P. (1984). The validity of animal models of depression. *Psychopharmacology*, **83**, 1-16.

Chapter 12

Bunney, W. E. and Garland-Bunney, B. L. (1987). Mechanisms of action of lithium in affective illness: basic and clinical implications. In *Psychopharmacology: the third generation of progress* (ed. H. Y. Meltzer), pp. 553-65. Raven Press, New York.

Dilsaver, S. C. (1989). Antidepressant withdrawal syndrome: pharmacology and pathophysiology. *Acta. Psychiat. Scand.*, **79**, 113-7.

Heninger, G. R. and Charney, D. S. (1987). Mechanisms of antidepressant treatments: implications for the etiology and treatment of depressive disorders. In *Psychopharmacology: the third generation of progress* (ed. H. Y. Meltzer), pp. 535–44. Raven Press, New York.

Murphy, D. L., Aulakh, C. S., Garrick, N. A., and Sunderland, T. (1987). Monoamine oxidase inhibitors as antidepressants: implications for the mechanism of action of antidepressants and the psychobiology of the affective disorders and some related disorders. In *Psychopharmacology: the third generation of progress* (ed. H. Y. Meltzer), pp. 545–552. Raven Press, New York.

Chapter 13

Crow, T. J. (1987). Psychosis as a continuum and the virogene concept. *Br. Med. Bull.*, **43**, 754–67.

Kendler, K. S. (1987) The genetics of schizophrenia: a current perspective. In *Psychopharmacology: the third generation of progress* (ed. H. Y. Meltzer) pp. 705–13. Raven Press, New York.

Roberts, G. W. and Crow, T. J. (1987). The neurophathology of schizophrenia — a progress report. *Br. Med. Bull.*, **43**, 599–615.

Weinberger, D. R. (1988). Schizophrenia and the frontal lobe. *Trends Neurosci.*, **11**, 367–70.

Chapter 14

Angst, J., Stassen, H. H., and Woggon, B. (1989). Effects of neuroleptics on positive and negative symptoms and the deficit state. *Psychopharmacology*, **99**, (Suppl.), S41–6.

Tamminga, C. A. and Gerlach, J. (1987). New neuroleptics and experimental antipsychotics in schizophrenia. In *Psychopharmacology: the third generation of progress* (ed. H. Y. Meltzer), pp. 1129–40. Raven Press, New York.

Waddington, J. L. (1989). Functional interactions between D-1 and D-2 dopamine receptor systems: their role in the regulation of psychomotor behaviour, putative mechanisms, and clinical relevance. *J. Psychopharmacol.*, **3**, 54–63.

Index